P9-EGC-027

Houghton Mifflin

Reading

Unique for North Carolina

.....

Research Based

.....

Comprehensive Balanced Literacy

Everything you need to build the foundation for reading success

Unique for North Carolina

Flexible teaching options

- North Carolina Planning Guide for Balanced Literacy — streamlined plans to combine core instruction with Guided Reading

- North Carolina Teacher's Edition — comprehensive teaching support aligned to North Carolina Standard Course of Study

- Both plans provide complete coverage of North Carolina objectives

All the leveled books you need, developed by Irene Fountas

- Leveled Readers for Grades K–5 with On Level, Below Level, Above Level, and Language Support strands

- Nonfiction Vocabulary Readers to support key vocabulary development

- Additional nonfiction leveled books to support North Carolina social studies and science objectives

- Easy-to-use Guided Reading lessons to accompany student books

Hands-on classroom management support

- A wealth of independent activities to keep other students learning while you work with small groups

- Easy 3-step process for developing student independence

- Convenient Work Chart to help students schedule independent activities

- Includes activity cards, vocabulary cards, and manipulatives that students love

Support for high achievement on North Carolina End-of-Grade Tests

- End-of-Grade Test preparation in every North Carolina Pupil Edition

- Edusoft platform online scoring and reporting aligned to the North Carolina Standard Course of Study

- North Carolina EOG Aligned Assessments and Practice

Research Based

Houghton Mifflin Reading lays the foundation for reading success! Based on the most respected scientific research, this program delivers effective standards-based instruction in the five key areas of reading through a consistent lesson format.

Our Approach

Phonemic Awareness

- Skills sequenced by difficulty
- Daily, engaging activities
- Links to phonics

Phonics

- Systematic, explicit instruction
- Immediate application of new skills—in the Anthology and in decodable books
- Phonics/Decoding strand links to Spelling through grade 6!

Fluency

- Fluent reading modeled in teacher Read-Alouds, Audio CDs, and more!
- Lots of books for students to read and reread at their own level
- Support for assessing oral reading rates

Vocabulary

- Direct instruction of key vocabulary
- Development of vocabulary skills and strategies
- Scaffolded vocabulary instruction and related readings for application

Comprehension

- Comprehension strategies taught explicitly and consistently to develop
  — Monitoring
  — Questioning
  — Previewing
  — Summarizing
  — Evaluating
- Graphic Organizers that support comprehension with every selection

Look for this color coding system throughout our program.

| Phonemic Awareness |
| Phonics |
| Comprehension |
| Vocabulary |
| Fluency |

"Critical reading skills are essential for both social and economic success in our complex society as well as for the health and future of our society itself."

Senior Authors

J. David Cooper
Ball State University

Literacy instruction; intervention for struggling readers in grades 3–8

John J. Pikulski
University of Delaware

Reading acquisition, including the prevention of reading problems; the teaching and development of vocabulary

Authors

Consultants

Phyllis Hunter
University of Pittsburgh

David J. Chard
University of Oregon

Gilbert García
Area 10, Los Angeles, California

Claude Goldenberg
California State University, Long Beach

Linda H. Butler
District of Columbia Public Schools

MaryEllen Vogt
California State University, Long Beach

Sheila Valencia
University of Washington, Seattle

Shane Templeton
University of Nevada, Reno

Marjorie Y. Lipson
University of Vermont

Carla Ford
Baltimore City Public School System

Phonetics Consultant

Linnea C. Ehri   City University of New York

Comprehensive Balanced Literacy

Everything you need for **Student Success!**

The right balance of Guided Reading and core instruction.

- Student Anthology and North Carolina Teacher's Edition for Shared Reading and core instruction.

- Vocabulary Readers reinforce key vocabulary and develop oral language.

- Leveled Readers for Guided Reading apply core skills and strategies.

- Three levels of Theme Paperbacks extend each theme.

Outstanding literature engages and delights students.

- Delightful Leveled Readers by Irene Fountas.

- Culturally diverse selections provide a balance of fiction and nonfiction.

- Read Alouds, Big Books, and Audio CDs.

- Content-area Links extend learning across the curriculum.

Everything you need for **Teacher Success!**

North Carolina Teacher's Editions provide flexible teaching options.

- Consistent, comprehensive skill and strategy instruction provides scaffolded support to reach all learners.
- Cross-curricular centers and independent activities reinforce weekly lessons.
- Integrated Language Arts lessons link reading to writing, grammar, and spelling.

Management tools make planning easy.

- Classroom Management Kits provide simple routines and ready-made activities for managing flexible groups.
- Intervention Kits offer extra reading and ELL support.
- North Carolina Lesson Planner CD-ROM puts daily planning at your fingertips.

Assessment-based teaching ensures student success.

- Built-in diagnostic checks and rubrics help to monitor student progress daily, weekly, and by theme.
- End-of-theme skill review supports both fiction and nonfiction.
- Built-in test-prep strategies prepare students for state tests.
- North Carolina Technology resources help manage and record student progress.

Grade 5 Resources

Core Materials

Pupil's Edition

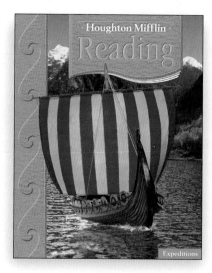

Six themes, featuring

- Award-winning, culturally diverse literature
- Four genre Focus sections
- Letters from noted authors to make theme connections
- Content-area Links
- Check Your Progress sections with test prep
- Get Set to Read background building
- Student writing models

Teacher's Editions

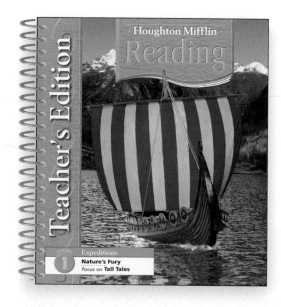

Separately bound themes, stored in a slipcase, featuring

- 5-day plans
- Support for all learners
- Monitoring Student Progress section
- Managing Flexible Groups charts
- Independent activities
- Teacher read-aloud selections
- Reading strategy models
- Reading-writing workshops

Vocabulary Readers

One nonfiction book for each week, featuring

- Support for key vocabulary and comprehension
- Accessible text for students who need extra support and English language learners
- Questions and activities to reinforce and expand vocabulary
- Audio CD and take-home book

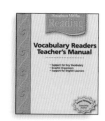

Vocabulary Readers Teacher's Manual

- Lesson support for small-group instruction and English language learners

Practice Book

- Abundant skill and test-taking practice!
- Two volumes per grade to lighten backpacks

Leveled Books for All Readers

Leveled Readers

Language Support, Below Level, On Level, Above Level

Irene Fountas, Consulting Author

- Four levels of independent reading to build fluency
- Lessons in the Teacher's Editions, plus leveled practice

Leveled Readers Teaching Resource Kits with support materials also available!

Leveled Theme Paperbacks

Below Level, On Level, Above Level

- Three levels of trade paperbacks
- Lessons in the Teacher's Editions

Classroom Bookshelf

- Theme-related Houghton Mifflin trade books

Classroom Management

Classroom Management Kit

Easy three-step system for classroom management, featuring

- Routine Cards and ready-made activities for student independence
- Work Chart to group, assign, and schedule daily independent work and small-group instruction
- Weekly envelopes to organize and store materials

Additional Ready-Made Manipulatives package also available!

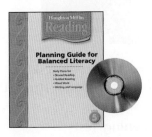

Planning Guide for Balanced Literacy

Guide for combining Houghton Mifflin's research-based instruction and small-group guided reading, featuring

- A concise five-day plan for each week
- Shared reading and skill instruction using the Anthology and Teacher's Editions
- Small-group instruction with leveled texts
- Options for differentiated instruction and assessment

For contents of the Classroom Management Kit, see the Program Components chart on pages xii–xiii.

Resources for Teachers

Teaching Resource Kit*

Used with the Teacher's Edition to provide timesaving support for planning, teaching, and more

Classroom Intervention Kit*

Coordinates with the core program to provide ongoing intervention for English language learners and students who need extra support

Assessment

Diagnose and Plan

Assess phonemic awareness, decoding skills, reading skills and levels, instructional strengths, and individual needs

- Phonics/Decoding Screening Test
- Baseline Group Tests
- Lexia Quick Phonics Assessment CD-ROM

Assess reading accuracy, rate, fluency, and comprehension— quickly, easily, accurately!

- Leveled Reading Passages Assessment Kit

Monitor Progress, Report, and Manage

Assess by week, by theme, and periodically

- Selection Tests
- Weekly Skills Tests
- Theme Skills Tests
- Integrated Theme Tests
- Benchmark Progress Tests

The power of information. The path to success.
A Houghton Mifflin Company

Online assessment—rapid scoring, reports, and support for grouping and differentiating instruction

- Edusoft assessment platform

Timesaving software for monitoring student progress

- Learner Profile™

x

*For contents of these kits, see the Program Components chart on pages xii–xiii.

Technology Resources

Internet Support and Extension

Education Place®

- Houghton Mifflin's FREE (and fun!) Internet resource for parents, teachers, and students
- Includes **WEEKLY WR READER** articles!

www.eduplace.com

Book Adventure

- Online quizzes about favorite books

www.bookadventure.org

 CDs for Your Class and You

Leveled Readers audio CDs available in Teaching Resource Kit!

For Students

- Anthology Audio CDs
- Vocabulary Readers Audio CDs

Plus these CD-ROMs:

- Get Set for Reading CD-ROM
- Wacky Web Tales®
- Spelling Spree®
- Accelerated Reader®

For Teachers

- Lesson Planner CD-ROM
- Planning Guide for Balanced Literacy CD-ROM
- Learner Profile™ CD-ROM
- Lexia Quick Phonics Assessment CD-ROM

Research-Based Intervention Programs

Soar to Success

- Proven effective!
- For grades 3–8

Phonics Intervention Kits

- Three levels of explicit instruction and practice

Lexia Phonics Intermediate Intervention CD-ROM

- Promotes phonemic awareness, sound-symbol correspondence, and word recognition

Program Components

Literature

	K	1	2	3	4	5	6
Student Anthology		●	●	●	●	●	●
Anthology Audio CDs		●	●	●	●	●	●
Vocabulary Readers	●	●	●	●	●	●	●
Vocabulary Readers Audio CDs	●	●	●	●	●	●	●
Leveled Readers	●	●	●	●	●	●	●
Leveled Theme Paperbacks		●	●	●	●	●	●
Houghton Mifflin Classroom Bookshelf	●	●	●	●	●	●	●
Big Books plus Content Links	●						
Big Books		●	●				
Big Book Audio CDs	●	●	●				
Little Big Books plus Content Links	●						
Little Big Books		●	●				
Read Aloud Books	●						
Phonics Library Books	●	●	●				
On My Way Practice Readers	●	●	●				
I Love Reading Books (Blackline Masters)		●	●				
Little Readers for Guided Reading	●	●	●				

Student Practice

	K	1	2	3	4	5	6
Practice Book	●	●	●	●	●	●	●
Kindergarten Phonics Center	●						
Word and Picture Books	●						
Phonics Library Books/ Take-Home Version	●	●	●				
Vocabulary Readers Take-Home Version	●	●	●	●	●	●	●
Kindergarten Leveled Readers Take-Home Version	●						
On My Way Practice Readers	●	●	●				
I Love Reading Books Take-Home Version		●	●				

Teacher Materials

	K	1	2	3	4	5	6
Teacher's Editions	●	●	●	●	●	●	●
Vocabulary Readers Teacher's Manual	●	●	●	●	●	●	●
Planning Guide for Balanced Literacy	●	●	●	●	●	●	●

Teacher Materials, cont.

	K	1	2	3	4	5	6
Read Aloud Books	●						
Alphafriends Package	●	●					
Theme Posters	●						
Instruction Charts/Strategy Posters		●	●				
Lesson Planner CD-ROM	●	●	●	●	●	●	●
Phonics Intervention Kits		●	●	●	●	●	●
Leveled Readers Teaching Resource Kits	●	●	●	●	●	●	●

Teaching Resource Kit

	K	1	2	3	4	5	6
Teacher's Resource Blackline Masters	●	●	●	●	●	●	●
Instruction Transparencies/Masters/ Strategy Posters		●	●	●	●	●	●
Instructional Activities for Challenge	●	●	●	●	●	●	●
Phonics Library Blackline Masters	●	●	●				
I Love Reading Blackline Masters		●	●				
Anthology Audio CDs		●	●	●	●	●	●
Vocabulary Readers Audio CDs	●	●	●	●	●	●	●
Word and Picture Books (Blackline Masters)	●						
Practice Book	●						
Practice Book Teacher's Annotated Edition		●	●	●	●	●	●
Letter, Word, and Picture Cards		●					
Blending Routines Cards	●	●	●				
Sound/Spelling Cards		●	●				
Vocabulary and Spelling Word Cards (Blackline Masters)	●	●	●	●	●	●	●
Handwriting disc		●	●				
Weekly Skill Tests Blackline Masters and Teacher's Manual	●	●	●	●	●	●	●
Integrated Theme Tests Blackline Masters and Teacher's Manual	●	●	●	●	●	●	●
Theme Skills Tests Blackline Masters and Teacher's Manual	●	●	●	●	●	●	●
Teacher's Assessment Handbook	●	●	●	●	●	●	●
Home/Community Connections	●	●	●	●	●	●	●

Classroom Management Kit

	K	1	2	3	4	5	6
Classroom Management Guide	●	●	●	●	●	●	●
Routine Cards	●	●	●	●	●	●	●
Weekly Envelopes	●	●	●	●	●	●	●
Work Chart	●	●	●	●	●	●	●
Vocabulary and Spelling Word Cards	●	●	●	●	●	●	●
Assignment Cards			●	●	●	●	●
Activity Cards			●	●	●	●	●
Activity Blackline Masters	●	●	●	●	●	●	●
Challenge Cards	●	●	●	●	●	●	●
Challenge Blackline Masters	●	●	●	●	●	●	●
Ready-Made Manipulatives Package	●	●	●	●	●	●	●

Classroom Intervention Kit

	K	1	2	3	4	5	6
Intervention Strategies for Extra Support	●	●	●	●	●	●	●
Instructional Strategies for English Language Learners	●	●	●	●	●	●	●
English Language Learners Transparencies	●	●	●	●	●	●	●
English Language Learners Student Practice	●	●	●	●	●	●	●
Picture/Word Cards	●	●	●	●	●	●	●
English Language Learners CD-ROM	●	●	●	●	●	●	●
Extra Support CD-ROM	●	●	●	●	●	●	●

Assessment

	K	1	2	3	4	5	6
Emerging Literacy Survey	●	●	●				
Leveled Reading Passages Assessment Kit	●	●	●	●	●	●	●
Integrated Theme Tests/TAE	●	●	●	●	●	●	●
Weekly Skills Tests/TAE	●	●	●	●	●	●	●
Theme Skills Tests/TAE	●	●	●	●	●	●	●
Baseline Group Test/TAE			●	●	●	●	●
Lexia Quick Phonics Assessment CD-ROM	●	●	●	●	●	●	●
Cumulative Evaluation Record Form	●	●	●	●	●	●	●
Phonics/Decoding Screening Test			●	●	●	●	●
Benchmark Progress Tests/TAE		●	●	●	●	●	●
Selection Tests			●	●	●	●	●

Assessment, cont.

	K	1	2	3	4	5	6
Teacher's Assessment Handbook	●	●	●	●	●	●	●
Learner Profile™ / Learner Profile™ To Go	●	●	●	●	●		
Edusoft Assessment Platform	●	●	●	●	●	●	●

Technology

	K	1	2	3	4	5	6
Big Book Audio CDs	●	●	●				
Anthology Audio CDs		●	●	●	●	●	●
Vocabulary Readers Audio CDs	●	●	●	●	●	●	●
Leveled Readers Audio CDs	●	●	●	●	●	●	●
Get Set for Reading CD-ROM		●	●	●			
Curious George® Learns Phonics CD-ROM	●	●	●				
Curious George® Learns to Spell CD-ROM	●	●					
Spelling Spree® CD-ROM				●	●	●	●
Wacky Web Tales®				●	●	●	●
Education Place® www.eduplace.com	●	●	●	●	●	●	●
Book Adventure™ www.bookadventure.org	●	●	●	●	●	●	●
Accelerated Reader®		●	●	●	●	●	●
Learner Profile™/ Learner Profile™ To Go	●	●	●	●	●	●	●
Edusoft Assessment Platform	●	●	●	●	●	●	●
Lesson Planner CD-ROM	●	●	●	●	●	●	●
Lexia Phonics Primary Intervention CD-ROM	●	●	●				
Lexia Phonics Intermediate Intervention CD-ROM				●	●	●	●
Lexia Quick Phonics Assessment CD-ROM	●	●	●	●	●	●	●

Research-Based Intervention Programs

	K	1	2	3	4	5	6
Phonics Intervention Kits		●	●	●	●	●	●
Reading Intervention for EARLY SUCCESS™		●	●				
Lexia Phonics Primary Intervention CD-ROM	●	●	●				
Lexia Phonics Intermediate Intervention CD-ROM				●	●	●	●
SOAR TO SUCCESS				●	●	●	●

Skills Across Grades K–6

READING	K	1	2	3	4	5	6
Phonemic Awareness							
Recognize and produce rhyming words	✔						
Count words in oral sentences							
Recognize and produce beginning sounds	✔						
Blend and segment onset and rime	✔						
Blend phonemes	✔						
Segment, count phonemes	✔						
Segment, count syllables in spoken words							
Phoneme substitution							
Manipulate phonemes							
Concepts of Print							
Understand that print conveys meaning	✔						
Understand how print is organized and read	✔						
Know directionality: left-to-right, top-to-bottom	✔						
Gain alphabet recognition	✔						
Distinguish letters, words, and sentences	✔						
Name and match all uppercase and lowercase letter forms	✔						
Note capital at the beginning of a sentence	✔						
Recognize use of all capital letters	✔						
Recognize end punctuation	✔						
Match spoken words to print	✔						
Phonics/Decoding Skills and Decoding Longer Words							
Initial consonants	✔	✔					
Final consonants; double consonants		✔					
Short vowels	✔	✔	✔				
Understand and apply the alphabetic principle	✔	✔	✔				
Apply the Phonics/Decoding Strategy							
Consonant clusters		✔	✔				
Consonant digraphs		✔	✔				
CVC, CVC*e*, other patterns		✔	✔				
Long vowels, vowel pairs		✔	✔				
r-controlled vowels		✔	✔				
Possessives				✔	✔	✔	✔

	K	1	2	3	4	5	6
Contractions		✔	✔	✔	✔	✔	✔
Compound words		✔	✔	✔	✔	✔	✔
Syllabication patterns				✔	✔	✔	✔
Affixes			✔	✔	✔	✔	✔
Stressed and unstressed syllables						✔	✔
Three-syllable words					✔	✔	✔
Word roots					✔	✔	✔
High-Frequency Words							
Recognize, read high-frequency words	✔	✔	✔				
Comprehension Skills							
Distinguish between fantasy/realism	✔	✔	✔	✔	✔		
Compare and contrast	✔	✔	✔	✔	✔	✔	✔
Predict outcomes	✔	✔	✔	✔	✔	✔	✔
Understand sequence of events	✔	✔	✔	✔	✔	✔	✔
Recognize story structure	✔	✔	✔	✔	✔	✔	✔
Determine cause and effect	✔	✔	✔	✔	✔	✔	✔
Determine text organization	✔	✔	✔	✔	✔	✔	✔
Draw conclusions	✔	✔	✔	✔	✔	✔	✔
Categorize and classify	✔	✔	✔	✔	✔	✔	✔
Note important details	✔	✔	✔	✔	✔	✔	✔
Recognize a main idea, topic, and supporting details	✔	✔	✔	✔	✔	✔	✔
Follow directions, oral and written			✔	✔	✔	✔	✔
Make inferences			✔	✔	✔	✔	✔
Make judgments			✔	✔	✔	✔	✔
Solve problems/make decisions		✔	✔	✔	✔	✔	✔
Make generalizations		✔	✔	✔	✔	✔	✔
Understand genres							
Recognize author's viewpoint			✔	✔	✔	✔	✔
Recognize fact and opinion			✔	✔	✔	✔	✔
Visualize							
Recognize persuasive devices and propaganda						✔	✔
Comprehension Strategies							
Predict/Infer		✔	✔	✔	✔	✔	✔
Summarize		✔	✔	✔	✔	✔	✔
Phonics/Decoding		✔	✔	✔	✔	✔	✔
Evaluate		✔	✔	✔	✔	✔	✔
Question		✔	✔	✔	✔	✔	✔
Monitor/Clarify		✔	✔	✔	✔	✔	✔
Reading Fluency							
Read fluently, at appropriate rate							

■ skills taught at grade level ✔ skills tested at grade level

Information and Study Skills	K	1	2	3	4	5	6
Use a dictionary/glossary		✔	✔	✔	✔	✔	✔
Use the library			✔	✔	✔	✔	✔
Use graphic organizers							
Use multimedia resources				✔		✔	
Interview							
Read/use graphic aids, including charts, tables, graphs, schedules, time lines, diagrams, maps, calendars			✔	✔	✔	✔	✔
Follow directions				✔	✔		✔
Locate/use parts of a book			✔	✔			✔
Use print references				✔	✔	✔	
Take notes				✔	✔	✔	
Use newspapers/magazines							
KWL/SQRR/SQP3R							
Skim/scan							
Use electronic resources				✔		✔	
Outline					✔		
Adjust reading rate					✔		
Paraphrase and synthesize						✔	✔
Select and evaluate sources						✔	✔
Use multiple sources							✔
Reading primary sources							
Categorize information							
Compare information						✔	✔
Complete applications and forms						✔	✔
Create and organize disk files							

Test-Taking Skills

	K	1	2	3	4	5	6
Answering phonics items							
Answering multiple-choice items							
Completing fill-in-the-blank items							
Writing an answer to a question							
Writing a personal response							
Answering vocabulary items							
Writing a personal narrative							
Writing a story							
Writing an opinion essay							
Writing a persuasive essay							

WORD WORK

Spelling

	K	1	2	3	4	5	6
Build words with short vowels							
Recognize sound and letter patterns		✔	✔	✔	✔	✔	✔

	K	1	2	3	4	5	6
Understand word structure		✔	✔	✔	✔	✔	✔
Spell words frequently misspelled		✔	✔	✔	✔	✔	
Use meaning relationships							

Vocabulary

	K	1	2	3	4	5	6
Recognize and read high-frequency words	✔	✔	✔				
Vocabulary expansion							
Content-area words							
Alphabetical order			✔	✔	✔	✔	✔
Antonyms			✔	✔	✔	✔	✔
Synonyms			✔	✔	✔	✔	✔
Homophones			✔	✔	✔	✔	✔
Multiple-meaning words			✔	✔	✔	✔	✔
Compound words			✔		✔	✔	✔
Dictionary, glossary, and thesaurus			✔	✔	✔	✔	✔
Word families			✔	✔	✔	✔	✔
Use context			✔	✔	✔	✔	✔
Make analogies				✔	✔	✔	✔
Word histories/connotations					✔	✔	✔
Understand idioms						✔	✔
Jargon, slang							

WRITING AND LANGUAGE

Grammar, Usage, and Mechanics

	K	1	2	3	4	5	6
Punctuation		✔	✔	✔	✔	✔	✔
Capitalization		✔	✔	✔	✔	✔	✔
Complete sentences		✔	✔	✔	✔	✔	✔
Types of sentences		✔	✔	✔	✔	✔	✔
Subjects and predicates		✔	✔	✔	✔	✔	✔
Nouns		✔	✔	✔	✔	✔	✔
Plurals		✔	✔	✔	✔	✔	✔
Possessives			✔	✔	✔	✔	✔
Verbs		✔	✔	✔	✔	✔	✔
Present, past and future tense		✔	✔	✔	✔	✔	✔
Subject-verb agreement		✔	✔	✔	✔	✔	✔
Irregular verbs		✔	✔	✔	✔	✔	✔
Adjectives		✔	✔	✔	✔	✔	✔
Comparisons		✔	✔	✔	✔	✔	
Pronouns		✔	✔	✔	✔	✔	✔
Adverbs				✔	✔	✔	✔
Prepositions/prepositional phrases					✔	✔	✔
Conjunctions						✔	✔
Interjections						✔	✔

Skills Across Grades K–6 continued

Writing Process	K	1	2	3	4	5	6
Writing Process							
Engage in modeled, shared, interactive writing							
Independent writing							
Use the five-step writing process							
Writing Skills							
Read as a writer							
Use technology							
Writer's Craft skills							
(See also the categories that follow.)							
Prewriting Skills							
Choose a topic							
Organize and plan							
Use graphic organizers							
Discuss							
Consider audience and purpose							
Take notes							
Drafting Skills							
Write a good beginning, middle, and end							
Organize ideas in logical order							
Use details, facts, examples							
State topic/purpose							
Find/evaluate information							
Use voice							
Revision Skills							
Tell more							
Elaborate/expand sentences with details					✔		✔
Use exact words			✔	✔	✔	✔	✔
Self-assessment							
Conference							
Perform sentence combining			✔		✔	✔	✔
Focus on purpose, audience, organization							
Delete							
Proofreading Skills							
Capitalize/punctuate		✔	✔	✔	✔	✔	✔
Use complete sentences		✔	✔	✔	✔	✔	✔
Spell accurately		✔	✔	✔	✔	✔	✔
Use correct grammar and usage		✔	✔	✔	✔	✔	✔
Modes of Writing*							
Write in a journal							
Write a letter		✔	✔				

	K	1	2	3	4	5	6
Write a story		✔	✔	✔	✔	✔	✔
Do descriptive writing		✔	✔	✔	✔	✔	✔
Write instructions/directions		✔	✔	✔			
Write in a variety of forms							
Write a personal narrative		✔	✔	✔	✔	✔	✔
Write a research report		✔	✔	✔	✔	✔	✔
Use persuasive writing				✔	✔	✔	✔
Expository writing		✔	✔	✔	✔	✔	✔
Write a personal essay					✔	✔	✔
Traits of Writing*							
Ideas							
Organization							
Word Choice				✔	✔	✔	✔
Conventions		✔	✔	✔	✔	✔	✔
Voice							
Sentence fluency			✔	✔	✔	✔	✔
Presentation							
Listening/Speaking/Viewing							
View environmental print							
Compare information							
Listen for comprehension							
Retell/summarize/report							
Listen for information							
Listen to/read aloud poetry							
Participate in group discussion/conversations							
Tell a story/retell a story							
Listen to a story							
Give and follow directions							
View illustrations							
View/evaluate media, information, and art							
Dramatize							
Visualize							
Use nonverbal cues							
Participate in reader's theater/choral reading							
Deliver a presentation/speech/report							
Resolve a conflict, problem							
Explain a process							
Hold a debate							
Plan a multimedia presentation							
Listen to take notes/summarize							

These writing skills are also evaluated through rubrics.   ▨ skills taught at grade level   ✔ skills tested at grade level

Houghton Mifflin
Reading
North Carolina

Teacher's Edition
Grade 5

Expeditions

Senior Authors J. David Cooper, John J. Pikulski

Authors David J. Chard, Gilbert G. Garcia, Claude N. Goldenberg,
Phyllis C. Hunter, Marjorie Y. Lipson, Shane Templeton,
Sheila W. Valencia, MaryEllen Vogt

Consultants Linda H. Butler, Linnea C. Ehri, Carla B. Ford

HOUGHTON MIFFLIN   BOSTON

NORTH CAROLINA REVIEWERS

Kathy Evans, Wake County Public Schools, North Carolina; **Sandy Francis-Smith,** Alamance-Burlington School System, North Carolina; **Rose Hayes,** Johnston County Public Schools, North Carolina; **Sue Johnson,** Clayton, North Carolina

LITERATURE REVIEWERS

Consultants: Dr. Adela Artola Allen, Associate Dean, Graduate College, Associate Vice President for Inter-American Relations, University of Arizona, Tucson, AZ; **Dr. Manley Begay,** Co-director of the Harvard Project on American Indian Economic Development, Director of the National Executive Education Program for Native Americans, Harvard University, John F. Kennedy School of Government, Cambridge, MA; **Dr. Nicholas Kannellos,** Director, Arte Publico Press, Director, Recovering the U.S. Hispanic Literacy Heritage Project, University of Houston, TX; **Mildred Lee,** author and former head of Library Services for Sonoma County, Santa Rosa, CA; **Dr. Barbara Moy,** Director of the Office of Communication Arts, Detroit Public Schools, MI; **Norma Naranjo,** Clark County School District, Las Vegas, NV; **Dr. Arlette Ingram Willis,** Associate Professor, Department of Curriculum and Instruction, Division of Language and Literacy, University of Illinois at Urbana-Champaign, IL

Teachers: Midge Anuson, Ridge Hall Lutheran School, Rodona Beach, CA; **Sue Hooks,** Lebanon Road Elementary School, Charlotte, NC; **Anatia Gayle Mills,** Cranberry-Prosperity School, Beckley, WV; **Tom Torres,** Elaine Wynn Elementary School, Las Vegas, NV; **Celeste Watts,** Meadow Hill Magnet Elementary School, Newburgh, NY

PROGRAM REVIEWERS

Linda Bayer, Jonesboro, GA; **Sheri Blair,** Warner Robins, GA; **Faye Blake,** Jacksonville, FL; **Suzi Boyett,** Sarasota, FL; **Carol Brockhouse,** Madison Schools, Wayne Westland Schools, MI; **Patti Brustad,** Sarasota, FL; **Jan Buckelew,** Venice, FL; **Marcia M. Clark,** Griffin, GA; **Kim S. Coady,** Covington, GA; **Eva Jean Conway,** Valley View School District, IL; **Carol Daley,** Sioux Falls, SD; **Jennifer Davison,** West Palm Beach, FL; **Lynne M. DiNardo,** Covington, GA; **Kathy Dover,** Lake City, GA; **Debbie Friedman,** Fort Lauderdale, FL; **Anne Gaitor,** Lakeland, GA; **Rebecca S. Gillette,** Saint Marys, GA; **Buffy C. Gray,** Peachtree City, GA; **Merry Guest,** Homestead, FL; **Jo Nan Holbrook,** Lakeland, GA; **Coleen Howard-Whals,** St. Petersburg, FL; **Beverly Hurst,** Jacksonville, FL; **Debra Jackson,** St. Petersburg, FL; **Vickie Jordan,** Centerville, GA; **Cheryl Kellogg,** Panama City, FL; **Karen Landers,** Talladega County, AL; **Barb LeFerrier,** Port Orchard, WA; **Ileana Masud,** Miami, FL; **David Miller,** Cooper City, FL; **Walsetta W. Miller,** Macon, GA; **Debbie Peale,** Miami, FL; **Loretta Piggee,** Gary, IN; **April Raiford,** Columbus, GA; **Cheryl Remash,** Manchester, NH; **Francis Rivera,** Orlando, FL; **Marina Rodriguez,** Hialeah, FL; **Marilynn Rose,** MI; **Kathy Scholtz,** Amesbury, MA; **Kimberly Moulton Schorr,** Columbus, GA; **Linda Schrum,** Orlando, FL; **Sharon Searcy,** Mandarin, FL; **Melba Sims,** Orlando, FL; **Judy Smith,** Titusville, FL; **Dottie Thompson,** Jefferson County, AL; **Dana Vassar,** Winston-Salem, NC; **Beverly Wakefield,** Tarpon Springs, FL; **Joy Walls,** Winston-Salem, NC; **Elaine Warwick,** Williamson County, TN; **Audrey N. Watkins,** Atlanta, GA; **Marti Watson,** Sarasota, FL

Supervisors: Judy Artz, Butler County, OH; **James Bennett,** Elkhart, IN; **Kay Buckner-Seal,** Wayne County, MI; **Charlotte Carr,** Seattle, WA; **Sister Marion Christi,** Archdiocese of Philadelphia, PA; **Alvina Crouse,** Denver, CO; **Peggy DeLapp,** Minneapolis, MN; **Carol Erlandson,** Wayne Township Schools, IN; **Brenda Feeney,** North Kansas City School District, MO; **Winnie Huebsch,** Sheboygan, WI; **Brenda Mickey,** Winston-Salem, NC; **Audrey Miller,** Camden, NJ; **JoAnne Piccolo,** Westminster, CO; **Sarah Rentz,** Baton Rouge, LA; **Kathy Sullivan,** Omaha, NE; **Rosie Washington,** Gary, IN; **Theresa Wishart,** Knox County Public Schools, TN

English Language Learners Reviewers: Maria Arevalos, Pomona, CA; **Lucy Blood,** NV; **Manuel Brenes,** Kalamazoo, MI; **Delight Diehn,** AZ; **Susan Dunlap,** Richmond, CA; **Tim Fornier,** Grand Rapids, MI; **Connie Jimenez,** Los Angeles, CA; **Diane Bonilla Lether,** Pasadena, CA; **Anna Lugo,** Chicago, IL; **Marcos Martel,** Hayward, CA; **Carolyn Mason,** Yakima, WA; **Jackie Pinson,** Moorpark, CA; **Jenaro Rivas,** NJ; **Jerilyn Smith,** Salinas, CA; **Noemi Velazquez,** Jersey City, NJ; **JoAnna Veloz,** NJ; **Dr. Santiago Veve,** Las Vegas, NV

CREDITS

Cover
Cover photography Nick Vedros, Vedros & Associates.

Photography
BTS1 © Kwame Zikomo/SuperStock. **BTS2** © PhotoDisc/Getty Images. **Theme Opener** © Byron Aughenbaugh/The Image Bank/Getty Images. **30** John Meyer/Morgan-Cain & Associates. **53T** Mark Epstein/DRK Photo. **59** © CORBIS. **62** Hemera Technologies, Inc. **81CC** Studio 212. **92** © Getty Images. **105** © CORBIS. **107K** © PhotoDisc/Getty Images.

Assignment Photography
i, ii, iii, iv, v © HMCo./Michael Indresano.

Illustration
BTS9–17 Nancy Carpenter.
All kid art by Morgan-Cain & Associates.

ACKNOWLEDGMENTS

Grateful acknowledgment is made for permission to reprint copyrighted material as follows:

Theme 1
"The Pumpkin Box," from *Maniac Monkeys on Magnolia Street,* by Angela Johnson. Text copyright © 1999 by Angela Johnson. Cover illustration copyright © 1999 by John Ward. Used by permission of Alfred A. Knopf, an imprint of Random House Children's Books, a division of Random House, Inc.

"Making Waves!," by Gail Skroback Hennessey from *Contact Kids* Magazine, October 1999 issue. Copyright © 1999 by Children's Television Workshop (New York, New York). All rights reserved. Reprinted by permission of Sesame Workshop.

"The Wreck of the E. S. Newman," by Ruth Ewers from *Cricket* Magazine, December 1995 issue, Vol. 23, No. 4. Copyright © 1995 by Ruth L. Ewers. Reprinted by permission of *Cricket* Magazine.

STUDENT WRITING MODEL FEATURE

Special thanks to the following teachers whose students' compositions appear as Student Writing Models: **Cindy Cheatwood,** Florida; **Diana Davis,** North Carolina; **Kathy Driscoll,** Massachusetts; **Linda Evers,** Florida; **Heidi Harrison,** Michigan; **Eileen Hoffman,** Massachusetts; **Julia Kraftsow,** Florida; **Bonnie Lewison,** Florida; **Kanetha McCord,** Michigan

Copyright © 2006 by Houghton Mifflin Company. All rights reserved.

No part of this work may be reproduced or transmitted in any form or by any means, electronic or mechanical, including photocopying or recording, or by any information storage or retrieval system without the prior written permission of the copyright owner unless such copying is expressly permitted by federal copyright law. With the exception of nonprofit transcription into Braille, Houghton Mifflin is not authorized to grant permission for further uses of this work. Permission must be obtained from the individual copyright owner as identified herein. Address requests for permission to make copies of Houghton Mifflin material to School Permissions, Houghton Mifflin Company, 222 Berkeley Street, Boston, MA 02116.

Printed in China

ISBN: 978-0-61862-917-6

2 3 4 5 6 7 8 9 10 L 12 11 10 09 08 07 06

Back to School

Use this section to get to know your students at the beginning of the school year and to get them off to a good start with reading strategies. Also use the overview of assessment tools to help you plan for student evaluation and differentiated instruction.

Getting to Know Your Students

Strategy Workshop

In the first few weeks of school, you will want to get acquainted with the unique individuals who make up your class. Back to School presents the first opportunity for informal screening of students in the Strategy Workshop. Use the workshop to—

- introduce the reading strategies students will use throughout the year,
- observe and evaluate skill development and instructional strengths and needs,
- evaluate students' understanding of reading strategies,
- evaluate how well they express their thoughts in writing.

Other Suggestions for Informal Evaluation

- Have a short conference with each student. Ask about interests and attitudes toward reading and writing.
- Review student portfolios from the previous year.
- To check for fluency, have each student read aloud.
- Ask each student for a writing sample on a topic of his or her choice.
- Observe students as they work together on a small-group activity.

For more information on instructional planning and placement, see the *Teacher's Assessment Handbook*.

Initial Screening

In addition to your own informal observation and evaluation, the *Baseline Group Test* will help you to estimate the amount of support students are likely to need with the level of reading materials you are using with them.

Use the *Baseline Group Test* for screening at the beginning of the year to assess your students' reading level, writing, and comprehension skills. Analysis of the test results will help you to evaluate your students' needs and to customize your teaching to help them achieve their full potential.

The following schematic shows the suggested sequence for evaluation, starting at the beginning of the school year with the Strategy Workshop.

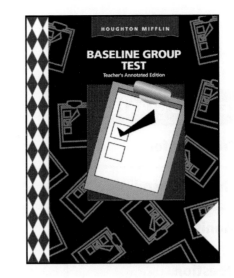

Evaluating Your Students

Strategy Workshop

Baseline Group Test

Phonics/Decoding Screening Test

For further evaluation, use the *Leveled Reading Passages Assessment Kit* and each theme's **Reading-Writing Workshop**.

To further evaluate students' skills, use the *Lexia Quick Phonics Assessment CD-ROM*.

Refer to pages BTS20–BTS22 at the end of Back to School for resources available for differentiating student instruction.

Getting Started with Reading Strategies

North Carolina Competency Goals for Back to School.

1.01, 2.01, 2.02a,b, 2.07, 3.01b,c,f,g

READING STRATEGIES

Predict/Infer

Phonics/Decoding

Monitor/Clarify

Question

Evaluate

Summarize

The reading strategies covered in the Strategy Workshop are the same ones students will work with throughout the year. Students will learn that they should usually apply *all* the reading strategies to *every* selection they read. However, for instructional purposes, starting with Theme 1, students will focus on an individual reading strategy with each selection of the Anthology. In this way, all the strategies are modeled and scaffolded in a systematic way through the year.

In the Strategy Workshop, a different strategy will be introduced and taught with each segment of the story *The Pumpkin Box*. This Read Aloud selection is intended to be read in six segments, with one segment and one strategy presented each day.

Strategy Workshop Steps

Use these steps with each reading strategy in the workshop to help students become successful readers.

1. **Introduce the Strategy.**

2. **Read Aloud.**

3. **Try It Out.**

4. **Discussion/Modeling**

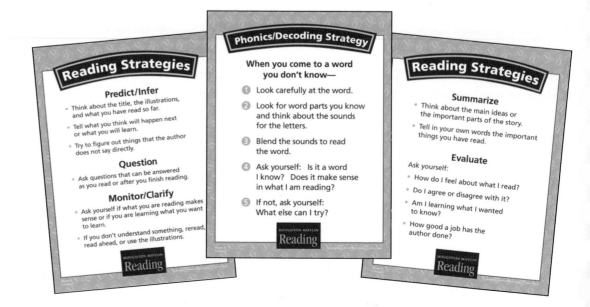

Reading Strategies

Predict/Infer
* Think about the title, the illustrations, and what you have read so far.
* Tell what you think will happen next or what you will learn.
* Try to figure out things that the author does not say directly.

Question
* Ask questions that can be answered as you read or after you finish reading.

Monitor/Clarify
* Ask yourself if what you are reading makes sense or if you are learning what you want to learn.
* If you don't understand something, reread, read ahead, or use the illustrations.

Phonics/Decoding Strategy

When you come to a word you don't know—
1. Look carefully at the word.
2. Look for word parts you know and think about the sounds for the letters.
3. Blend the sounds to read the word.
4. Ask yourself: Is it a word I know? Does it make sense in what I am reading?
5. If not, ask yourself: What else can I try?

Houghton Mifflin Reading

Reading Strategies

Summarize
* Think about the main ideas or the important parts of the story.
* Tell in your own words the important things you have read.

Evaluate
Ask yourself:
* How do I feel about what I read?
* Do I agree or disagree with it?
* Am I learning what I wanted to know?
* How good a job has the author done?

Houghton Mifflin Reading

Introducing the Strategy Workshop

Discuss with students what good readers do when they read. Talk about the following points:

- Good readers use strategies whenever they read.
- Different strategies are used before, during, and after reading.
- As readers learn to use strategies, they must think about how each strategy will help them.

Then display the strategies, using either the **Strategy Posters** or **Transparencies BTS–1** and **BTS–2**. Tell students that you will review with them each of the strategies that will help them be successful readers.

Explain that you will read aloud the story *The Pumpkin Box* and help students use a different strategy with each segment of the story. Students will respond in their **Practice Books** to each strategy. Then you will help them as needed to model use of this strategy and discuss how it is helpful. **Transparencies BTS–3** through **BTS–17** will enable you to display the appropriate passages of text for modeling. Students can refer to **Practice Book** page 1 throughout the workshop as a reminder of how the strategies will be of use to them.

Remind students that all of the reading strategies together are meant to be used when they read, but that in this workshop, they will study each strategy separately during the reading of the story. One or more strategies may be presented each day, depending on the needs of your students.

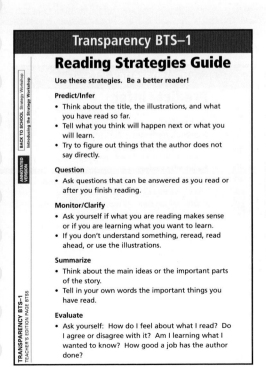

Transparency BTS–1
Reading Strategies Guide

Use these strategies. Be a better reader!

Predict/Infer
- Think about the title, the illustrations, and what you have read so far.
- Tell what you think will happen next or what you will learn.
- Try to figure out things that the author does not say directly.

Question
- Ask questions that can be answered as you read or after you finish reading.

Monitor/Clarify
- Ask yourself if what you are reading makes sense or if you are learning what you want to learn.
- If you don't understand something, reread, read ahead, or use the illustrations.

Summarize
- Think about the main ideas or the important parts of the story.
- Tell in your own words the important things you have read.

Evaluate
- Ask yourself: How do I feel about what I read? Do I agree or disagree with it? Am I learning what I wanted to know? How good a job has the author done?

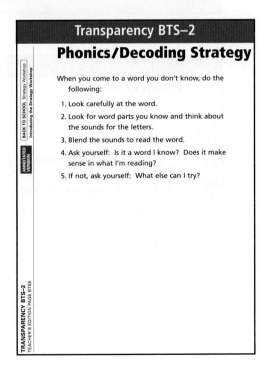

Transparency BTS–2
Phonics/Decoding Strategy

When you come to a word you don't know, do the following:

1. Look carefully at the word.
2. Look for word parts you know and think about the sounds for the letters.
3. Blend the sounds to read the word.
4. Ask yourself: Is it a word I know? Does it make sense in what I'm reading?
5. If not, ask yourself: What else can I try?

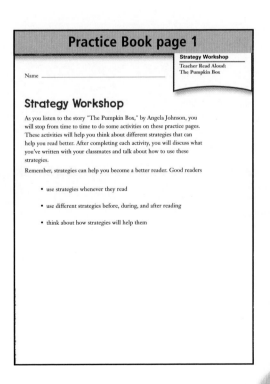

Practice Book page 1

Strategy Workshop
Teacher Read Aloud:
The Pumpkin Box

Name _____

Strategy Workshop

As you listen to the story "The Pumpkin Box," by Angela Johnson, you will stop from time to time to do some activities on these practice pages. These activities will help you think about different strategies that can help you read better. After completing each activity, you will discuss what you've written with your classmates and talk about how to use these strategies.

Remember, strategies can help you become a better reader. Good readers

- use strategies whenever they read
- use different strategies before, during, and after reading
- think about how strategies will help them

STRATEGY
Predict/Infer

1. **Introduce the Strategy** Use **Practice Book** page 2 and **Transparency BTS–4,** and together with students, read and discuss the steps of the Predict/Infer strategy.

2. **Read Aloud** Invite students to listen as you read aloud the title and the first three paragraphs of *The Pumpkin Box*. Continue reading Segment 1 after you have finished discussing the Predict/Infer strategy with students.

3. **Try It Out** Have students turn to **Practice Book** page 2 and write what they think the pumpkin box is.

Teacher Read Aloud

The Pumpkin Box
by Angela Johnson
SEGMENT 1

It all started because I'm a digger.

Digging is something that I can't help. I have done it since I was a little baby. Dad says I used to try to dig my way out of the playpen.

I don't talk about my digging too much 'cause every time I dig it usually gets me in trouble.

Billy understands about my digging. He says that he knows how hard it can be to break a habit like that. He has a nosy problem and that is pretty hard for him.

When we moved to Magnolia Street, one of the first things I noticed was a vacant lot that looked like the perfect place to dig.

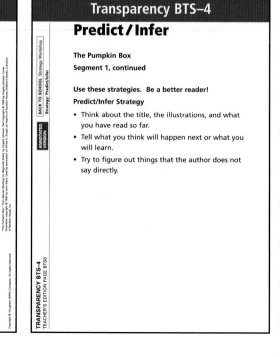

Transparency BTS–3
Predict / Infer

The Pumpkin Box
by Angela Johnson
Segment 1

It all started because I'm a digger.

Digging is something that I can't help. I have done it since I was a little baby. Dad says I used to try to dig my way out of the playpen.

I don't talk about my digging too much 'cause every time I dig it usually gets me in trouble.

Billy understands about my digging. He says that he knows how hard it can be to break a habit like that. He has a nosy problem and that is pretty hard for him.

When we moved to Magnolia Street, one of the first things I noticed was a vacant lot that looked like the perfect place to dig.

So —

I had been trying not to dig for a long time. But a few nights ago, I dreamed I was in a cave that had treasures and fossils. I woke up digging in my sleep. It was time to do something about this digging problem.

When I asked Billy what I should do about it, he blew a big bubble and spun around on his skates.

"Dig!"

So what was I going to do?

TRANSPARENCY BTS–3
TEACHER'S EDITION PAGE BTS6

ANNOTATED VERSION

BACK TO SCHOOL Strategy Workshop
Strategy: Predict/Infer

"The Pumpkin Box," from *Magnolia Blossoms on Magnolia Street*, by Angela Johnson. Text copyright © 1999 by Angela Johnson. Cover illustration copyright © 1999 by John Ward. Used by permission of Alfred A. Knopf, an imprint of Random House Children's Books, a division of Random House, Inc.

Transparency BTS–4
Predict / Infer

The Pumpkin Box
Segment 1, continued

Use these strategies. Be a better reader!
Predict/Infer Strategy

- Think about the title, the illustrations, and what you have read so far.
- Tell what you think will happen next or what you will learn.
- Try to figure out things that the author does not say directly.

TRANSPARENCY BTS–4
TEACHER'S EDITION PAGE BTS6

ANNOTATED VERSION

BACK TO SCHOOL Strategy Workshop
Strategy: Predict/Infer

So —

I had been trying not to dig for a long time. But a few nights ago, I dreamed I was in a cave that had treasures and fossils. I woke up digging in my sleep. It was time to do something about this digging problem.

When I asked Billy what I should do about it, he blew a big bubble and spun around on his skates.

"Dig!"

So what was I going to do?

STRATEGY
Predict/Infer

4. **Discussion/Modeling** Have students model how to use the Predict/Infer strategy. Have them discuss their predictions and whether or not their predictions are based on what you have read so far and on their own background information. If students need help with the strategy, use the Think Aloud.

Think Aloud *I can see from the title that this story will be about a pumpkin box. I wonder what a pumpkin box might be. The girl in the story says she's a digger. I bet it's something she buries or digs up. I'll start reading to see if I'm right.*

Practice Book page 2

Back to School
Practice Book Page 2

Name _____

Strategy 1: Predict/Infer

Use this strategy before and during reading to help make predictions about what happens next or what you're going to learn.

Here's how to use the Predict/Infer Strategy:
1. Think about the title, the illustrations, and what you have read so far.
2. Tell what you think will happen next—or what you will learn. Thinking about what you already know on the topic may help.
3. Try to figure out things the author does not say directly.

Listen as your teacher begins "The Pumpkin Box." When your teacher stops, complete the activity to show that you understand how to predict what the pumpkin box is.

Think about the story and respond to the question below.

What do you think the pumpkin box is?

_____
_____

As you continue listening to the story, think about whether your prediction was right. You might want to change your prediction or write a new one below.

_____
_____
_____

Monitoring Student Progress

If . . .	Then . . .
students have difficulty making reasonable predictions,	guide them in looking for clues in the title and in the beginning text. Tell them that thinking about what they have just read and about any background knowledge they have will help them think about what will happen next.

Strategy Workshop BTS7

STRATEGY

Phonics/Decoding

1. **Introduce the Strategy** Tell students that as they are reading, they will use the Phonics/Decoding Strategy to help them figure out new words. Use **Practice Book** page 3 and **Transparency BTS–6,** and together with students, read and discuss the steps of the Phonics/Decoding Strategy.

2. **Read Aloud** Continue reading the story, stopping at the word *munching*. Then print *munching* on the chalkboard.

3. **Try It Out** Now have students turn to **Practice Book** page 3 and write the words in the blanks to complete the steps of the Decoding Strategy. Discuss the decoding steps.

Teacher Read Aloud

The Pumpkin Box
SEGMENT 2

I'd been looking at the empty place across the street from my house for a long time. I decided to drag Billy away from his skating. I had to tell him I was pretty sure that there was a sabertooth tiger or something just waiting for us to dig up.

"Okay, Charlie, where is it?" Billy said, munching on an apple and looking real unhappy.

I had expected more from Billy, even though I know that everybody is not a digger. But I figured that Billy should have been a little happier that I was sharing with him.

"Billy?"

"What?"

"Guess what?"

"What, Charlie?"

"What are you going to do with your part of the sabertooth tiger bones you find?"

"Well, I guess I'll put them together with yours."

"Then you'll help me dig?"

Well, I can say this about Billy, and it's probably why we're friends, if you bug him enough, he'll join in sooner or later. He even looked like he might be getting excited about the sabertooth across the street.

Transparency BTS–5

Phonics/Decoding

The Pumpkin Box
Segment 2

I'd been looking at the empty place across the street from my house for a long time. I decided to drag Billy away from his skating. I had to tell him I was pretty sure that there was a sabertooth tiger or something just waiting for us to dig up.

"Okay, Charlie, where is it?" Billy said, munching on an apple and looking real unhappy.

I had expected more from Billy, even though I know that everybody is not a digger. But I figured that Billy should have been a little happier that I was sharing with him.

"Billy?"

"What?"

"Guess what?"

"What, Charlie?"

"What are you going to do with your part of the sabertooth tiger bones you find?"

"Well, I guess I'll put them together with yours."

"Then you'll help me dig?"

Well, I can say this about Billy, and it's probably why we're friends, if you bug him enough he'll join in sooner or later. He even looked like he might be getting excited about the sabertooth across the street.

Transparency BTS–6

Phonics/Decoding

The Pumpkin Box
Segment 2, continued

While we were both hanging upside down in Miss Marcia's apple tree, Billy asked, "What do we need to dig? You know we have to be careful. We don't want to break any sabertooth bones or anything."

I thought for a while.

"A shovel might be too much. Anyway, my mom won't let me use it after that flower-digging accident I had."

Billy swung by his legs faster.

"What flower-digging accident?"

Phonics/Decoding Strategy

When you come to a word you don't know:

1. Look carefully at the word.

2. Look for word parts you know and think about the sounds for the letters.

3. Blend the sounds to read the word.

4. Ask yourself: Is it a word I know? Does it make sense in what I'm reading?

5. If not, ask yourself: What else can I try?

While we were both hanging upside down in Miss Marcia's apple tree, Billy asked, "What do we need to dig? You know we have to be careful. We don't want to break any sabertooth bones or anything."

I thought for a while.

"A shovel might be too much. Anyway, my mom won't let me use it after that flower-digging accident I had."

Billy swung by his legs faster.

"What flower-digging accident?"

STRATEGY
Phonics/Decoding

4. **Discussion/Modeling** Have students model how to use the Phonics/Decoding Strategy. Have them discuss the steps they find most helpful as they read. If students need help, use the Think Aloud to model the strategy.

Think Aloud *First, I look carefully at the word; I want to see if there are any word parts I know. I see* munch, *which I think is a word that means "chew," but I'm not sure about that. I know the* m *sound, and* un *probably rhymes with* fun. *I know the* ch *sound is often /ch/ as in* change. *When I blend those together,* m-un-ch, *add the familiar* -ing *ending, and look at the word in the sentence, I see that Billy is munching on an apple. That makes sense.*

Practice Book page 3

Back to School
Practice Book Page 3

Name —————

Strategy 2: Phonics/Decoding

Use this strategy during reading when you come across a word you don't know.

Here's how to use the Phonics/Decoding Strategy:

1. Look carefully at the word.
2. Look for word parts you know and think about the sounds for the letters.
3. Blend the sounds to read the words.
4. Ask yourself: Is this a word I know? Does it make sense in what I am reading?
5. If not, ask yourself: What else can I try? Should I look in a dictionary?

Listen as your teacher continues the story. When your teacher stops, use the Phonics/Decoding Strategy.

Now write down the steps you used to decode the word *munching*.

———————
———————
———————
———————
———————
———————

Remember to use this strategy whenever you are reading and come across a word that you don't know.

Monitoring Student Progress

If . . .	Then . . .
students have difficulty using the Phonics/ Decoding Strategy in their reading,	review the steps with them. Remind them to use the letter sounds they know. Also point out that some words are made up of smaller words they know.

Strategy Workshop BTS9

Monitor/Clarify

1. **Introduce the Strategy** Remind students that good readers ask themselves if what they are reading makes sense. Tell them that when they are confused by what they are reading they can reread or read ahead. Use **Practice Book** page 4 and **Transparency BTS–9,** and together with students, read and discuss the Monitor/Clarify strategy.

2. **Read Aloud** Invite students to listen as you read aloud Segment 3 of *The Pumpkin Box.*

3. **Try It Out** Have students open their **Practice Books** to page 4 and answer the questions about the pumpkin box.

Teacher Read Aloud

The Pumpkin Box
SEGMENT 3

I closed my eyes, remembering all the dirt and flowers lying around the backyard. I only meant to move the different flowers around so all the colors would be lined up together. Well, I got kind of tired and there was this funny movie on television that Sid was watching.

Mom wasn't happy.

So I just said, "Nothing."

Billy jumped down from the tree.

"My dad has digging tools he uses for the garden out back. They're small, and I'm sure he won't miss them."

"Yeah, he probably won't miss them. I'll get some bags to keep the bones and other stuff we find."

Me and Billy were set.

The digging was hard in the beginning. An old house used to be there, but the only thing left from it was part of the chimney. You wouldn't believe the things we started to find underneath the dirt. I just knew that there had to be a sabertooth or something there.

The first thing we dug up was spoons.

Billy said, "We could clean these things up. They probably are gold!"

Billy put the gold spoons in the bag that was for everything else but bones.

After a while it started getting real hot. I could almost make believe that me and Billy were digging way off in a

Transparency BTS–7
Monitor/Clarify

The Pumpkin Box
Segment 3

I closed my eyes, remembering all the dirt and flowers lying around the backyard. I only meant to move the different flowers around so all the colors would be lined up together. Well, I got kind of tired and there was this funny movie on television that Sid was watching.

Mom wasn't happy.
So I just said, "Nothing."
Billy jumped down from the tree.
"My dad has digging tools he uses for the garden out back. They're small, and I'm sure he won't miss them."
"Yeah, he probably won't miss them. I'll get some bags to keep the bones and other stuff we find."
Me and Billy were set.
The digging was hard in the beginning. An old house used to be there, but the only thing left from it was part of the chimney. You wouldn't believe the things we started to find underneath the dirt. I just knew that there had to be a sabertooth or something there.
The first thing we dug up was spoons.

TRANSPARENCY BTS–7
TEACHER'S EDITION PAGE BTS10

BACK TO SCHOOL Strategy Workshop
Strategy: Monitor/Clarify

ANNOTATED VERSION

Copyright © Houghton Mifflin Company. All rights reserved.

Transparency BTS–8
Monitor/Clarify

The Pumpkin Box
Segment 3, continued

Billy said, "We could clean these things up. They probably are gold!"
Billy put the gold spoons in the bag that was for everything else but bones.
After a while it started getting real hot. I could almost make believe that me and Billy were digging way off in a desert somewhere. We were far away from home with only a little water. We were famous archaeologists.
I would find bones.
Billy would find gold spoons.
I would find fossils.
Billy would find gold spoons.
I would find a whole city buried way down underneath the desert.
And there, Billy would find more gold spoons.
Me and Billy didn't even talk to each other while we dug. We were too busy finding all kinds of treasures.

TRANSPARENCY BTS–8
TEACHER'S EDITION PAGE BTS10

BACK TO SCHOOL Strategy Workshop
Strategy: Monitor/Clarify

ANNOTATED VERSION

Copyright © Houghton Mifflin Company. All rights reserved.

desert somewhere. We were far away from home with only a little water. We were famous archaeologists.

I would find bones.

Billy would find gold spoons.

I would find fossils.

Billy would find gold spoons.

I would find a whole city buried way down underneath the desert.

And there, Billy would find more gold spoons.

Me and Billy didn't even talk to each other while we dug. We were too busy finding all kinds of treasures.

Billy found a cracked mirror.

I found a scrub brush.

Billy found a bottle with a metal top on it, and I found an old can.

The non-bone bag was filling up, and I noticed that Billy was smiling. Sometimes you just have to bring out the digger in some people.

Just as I was starting to get a little worried 'cause we hadn't run into any bones yet, I hit something with the little hand shovel I had. I took a while to dig it up 'cause I didn't want to wreck any of it.

I'd found something better than a sabertooth.

It was a pumpkin box.

It was metal and square, and somebody had pasted paper pumpkins all over it.

STRATEGY
Monitor/Clarify

4. **Discussion/Modeling** Have students model how to use the Monitor/Clarify strategy and discuss how it helps them understand what they are reading. Remind them that when they're confused by what they're reading, they can reread or read ahead. If students need help, use the Think Aloud to model the strategy.

Think Aloud *After I read the part about finding the pumpkin box, I was confused about how it got there and what it might be. What was a box doing under the ground? I reread the last few paragraphs to see if I had missed something. But I didn't find anything that told me why it was there. I have read other stories about buried treasure, or about people burying valuable things, so maybe it's something like that. I will now read ahead to see if there's something later that will tell me why the box was buried—and who buried it!*

Transparency BTS–9
Monitor/Clarify

The Pumpkin Box
Segment 3, continued

Billy found a cracked mirror.
I found a scrub brush.
Billy found a bottle with a metal top on it, and I found an old can.
The non-bone bag was filling up, and I noticed that Billy was smiling. Sometimes you just have to bring out the digger in some people.
Just as I was starting to get a little worried 'cause we hadn't run into any bones yet, I hit something with the little hand shovel I had. I took a while to dig it up 'cause I didn't want to wreck any of it.
I'd found something better than a sabertooth.
It was a pumpkin box.
It was metal and square, and somebody had pasted paper pumpkins all over it.

Monitor/Clarify Strategy

• Ask yourself if what you are reading makes sense or if you are learning what you want to learn.
• If you don't understand something, reread, read ahead, or use the illustrations.

TRANSPARENCY BTS–9
TEACHER'S EDITION PAGE BTS11

BACK TO SCHOOL Strategy Workshop
Strategy: Monitor/Clarify
ANNOTATED VERSION

Practice Book page 4

Name _____

Strategy 3: Monitor/Clarify
Use this strategy during reading whenever you're confused about what you are reading.

Here's how to use the Monitor/Clarify Strategy:
• Ask yourself if what you're reading makes sense—or if you are learning what you need to learn.
• If you don't understand something, reread, use the illustrations, or read ahead to see if that helps.

Listen as your teacher continues the story. When your teacher stops, complete the activity to show that you understand how to figure out how the pumpkin box got underground.

Think about the pumpkin box and respond below.

1. Describe the pumpkin box.

_____
_____

2. Can you tell from listening to the story how the pumpkin box got there? Why or why not?

_____
_____
_____

3. How can you find out why the pumpkin box was buried in the ground?

_____
_____
_____

Monitoring Student Progress

If . . .	Then . . .
students have difficulty monitoring as they read,	tell them to stop and think about the story as you continue reading. Tell them that thinking about how well they understand what they are reading will help them understand and enjoy the story more.

Strategy Workshop **BTS11**

STRATEGY
Question

1. **Introduce the Strategy** Remind students that good readers ask themselves questions about important ideas as they read. Tell them that by asking questions they will understand and enjoy the story more. Use **Practice Book** page 5 and **Transparency BTS–10,** and together with students, read and discuss the Question strategy.

2. **Read Aloud** Invite students to listen as you read aloud Segment 4 of *The Pumpkin Box.*

3. **Try It Out** Have students turn to **Practice Book** page 5 and write down a question they might ask themselves at this point.

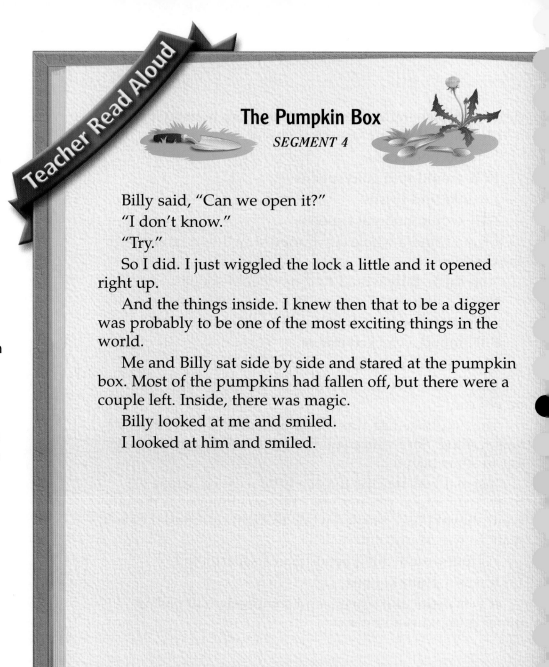

Teacher Read Aloud

The Pumpkin Box
SEGMENT 4

Billy said, "Can we open it?"

"I don't know."

"Try."

So I did. I just wiggled the lock a little and it opened right up.

And the things inside. I knew then that to be a digger was probably to be one of the most exciting things in the world.

Me and Billy sat side by side and stared at the pumpkin box. Most of the pumpkins had fallen off, but there were a couple left. Inside, there was magic.

Billy looked at me and smiled.

I looked at him and smiled.

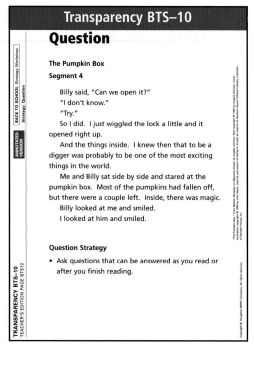

Transparency BTS–10

Question

The Pumpkin Box
Segment 4

Billy said, "Can we open it?"
"I don't know."
"Try."
So I did. I just wiggled the lock a little and it opened right up.
And the things inside. I knew then that to be a digger was probably to be one of the most exciting things in the world.
Me and Billy sat side by side and stared at the pumpkin box. Most of the pumpkins had fallen off, but there were a couple left. Inside, there was magic.
Billy looked at me and smiled.
I looked at him and smiled.

Question Strategy
• Ask questions that can be answered as you read or after you finish reading.

STRATEGY

Question

4. **Discussion/Modeling** Have students model how to use the Question strategy and discuss how asking about something they want to know more about will help them understand what they are reading. Have students discuss the questions they've written. If students need help, use the Think Aloud to model the strategy.

Think Aloud *In the story, the things inside the pumpkin box cause the narrator to feel that to be a digger is very exciting. I wonder why.*

Practice Book page 5

Back to School
Practice Book Page 5

Name _____

Strategy 4: Question

Use this strategy during and after reading to ask questions about important ideas in the story.

Here's how to use the Question Strategy:

• Ask yourself questions about important ideas in the story.
• Ask yourself if you can answer these questions.
• If you can't answer the questions, reread and look for answers in the text. Thinking about what you already know and what you've read in the story may help you.

Listen as your teacher continues the story. Then complete the activity to show that you understand how to ask yourself questions about important ideas in the story.

Think about the story and respond below.

Write a question you might ask yourself at this point in the story.

_____

_____

_____

_____

_____

_____

_____

_____

If you can't answer your question now, think about it while you listen to the rest of the story.

Monitoring Student Progress

If . . .	Then . . .
students have difficulty coming up with questions,	have them think about the story and discuss things that they want to know more about. Model for them how to formulate questions.

Strategy Workshop

Evaluate

1. **Introduce the Strategy** Remind students that good readers should always think about their reactions to what they are reading and why they are reacting that way.

   Tell students that they can evaluate a story in many different ways by thinking about

   - how well the author writes
   - what the story is about
   - their reaction to the story

   Use **Practice Book** page 6 and **Transparency BTS–12,** and together with students, read and discuss the Evaluate strategy.

2. **Read Aloud** Read aloud Segment 5 of *The Pumpkin Box.*

3. **Try It Out** Now have students turn to **Practice Book** page 6 and respond to one of the prompts on that page.
   1. Tell whether or not you think this story is interesting and why.
   2. Is the writing clear and easy to understand?
   3. This is a realistic fiction story. Did the author make the characters interesting and believable?

Teacher Read Aloud

The Pumpkin Box
SEGMENT 5

The first thing we found in the box was a yo-yo. It was red and wooden.

We laid it out beside the pumpkin box. We didn't want to put it in the non-bone bag.

Next we found three nickels tied up in a handkerchief. They had buffaloes on them.

After that, we found an old watch. It didn't run.

The only way you could tell we liked everything we found was when we'd say, "Wow." And we said that a lot.

Underneath that, we found a book. It had cowboys on the front of it. The pages were falling apart and we were afraid to open it too much, so we laid it down gently beside the other stuff.

The next thing we found was a note. It was wrapped in wax paper. Billy handed it to me to read, since I was the main digger. The note said:

> **Whoever finds this box must share it. It doesn't matter who you share it with. When you have shared the things in this box, you must put your own treasures in it and bury it again.**
>
> **Signed,**
> **Tracy and David**

Transparency BTS–11
Evaluate

The Pumpkin Box
Segment 5

The first thing we found in the box was a yo-yo. It was red and wooden.

We laid it out beside the pumpkin box. We didn't want to put it in the non-bone bag.

Next we found three nickels tied up in a handkerchief. They had buffaloes on them.

After that, we found an old watch. It didn't run.

The only way you could tell we liked everything we found was when we'd say, "Wow." And we said that a lot.

Underneath that, we found a book. It had cowboys on the front of it. The pages were falling apart and we were afraid to open it too much, so we laid it down gently beside the other stuff.

The next thing we found was a note. It was wrapped in wax paper. Billy handed it to me to read, since I was the main digger. The note said:

> Whoever finds this box must share it. It doesn't matter who you share it with. When you have shared the things in this box, you must put your own treasures in it and bury it again.
>
> Signed,
> Tracy and David

TRANSPARENCY BTS–11
TEACHER'S EDITION PAGE BTS14

ANNOTATED VERSION

BACK TO SCHOOL Strategy Workshop
Strategy: Evaluate

Transparency BTS–12
Evaluate

The Pumpkin Box
Segment 5, continued

The note was brown and falling apart.

And in the bottom of the box was a picture of two kids dressed in funny clothes. The picture was old and a little blurry, but you could still see the kids, and they were smiling.

Billy pointed at the picture, then pointed at my house across the street. Sure enough, there was my tree and house right there in the picture. There is nothing like digging . . .

Evaluate Strategy

- Ask yourself: How do I feel about what I read? Do I agree or disagree with it? Am I learning what I wanted to know? How good a job has the author done?

TRANSPARENCY BTS–12
TEACHER'S EDITION PAGE BTS14

ANNOTATED VERSION

BACK TO SCHOOL Strategy Workshop
Strategy: Evaluate

The note was brown and falling apart.

And in the bottom of the box was a picture of two kids dressed in funny clothes. The picture was old and a little blurry, but you could still see the kids, and they were smiling.

Billy pointed at the picture, then pointed at my house across the street. Sure enough, there was my tree and house right there in the picture. There is nothing like digging …

STRATEGY
Evaluate

4. **Discussion/Modeling** Have students model how to use the Evaluate strategy and discuss how following the steps can help them understand the story. If students need help, use the Think Aloud to model the Evaluate strategy.

Think Aloud *The author gets me interested in the story right from the beginning. I liked the way she tells the story from her own point of view. It made the story that much more interesting to me. It made me want to read it to see what happened to the characters.*

Practice Book page 6

Back to School
Practice Book Page 6

Name _____

Strategy 5: Evaluate
Use this strategy during and after reading to help you form an opinion about what you read.

Here's how to use the Evaluate Strategy:
• Tell whether or not you think this story is entertaining and why.
• Is the writing clear and easy to understand?
• This is a realistic fiction story. Did the author make the characters believable and interesting?

Listen as your teacher continues the story. When your teacher stops, complete the activity to show that you are thinking of how you feel about what you are reading and why you feel that way.

Think about the story and respond below.

1. Tell whether or not you think this story is entertaining and why.
_____
_____
_____

2. Is the writing clear and easy to understand?
_____
_____
_____

3. This is a realistic fiction story. Did the author make the characters interesting and believable?
_____
_____
_____

Monitoring Student Progress

If . . .	Then . . .
students have difficulty evaluating the story,	guide them with questions that require students to give opinions about the story. Explain that when giving opinions, they are evaluating the story.

Strategy Workshop **BTS15**

STRATEGY
Summarize

1. **Introduce the Strategy** Explain to students that summarizing means telling the most important parts of a story in a quick way. Remind students that thinking about the following story elements can help them summarize a story:
   - who the main character is
   - where the story takes place
   - what the problem is
   - what happens in the beginning, middle, and end

   Use **Practice Book** page 7 and **Transparency BTS–17,** and together with students, read and discuss the Summarize strategy.

2. **Read Aloud** Invite students to listen as you read aloud the last segment of *The Pumpkin Box* on pages BTS16 through BTS19.

3. **Try It Out** Now have students turn to **Practice Book** page 7 and respond to the three prompts on that page.
   1. Who is the main character?
   2. Where does the story take place?
   3. What is the problem and how is it resolved?

Teacher Read Aloud

The Pumpkin Box
SEGMENT 6

We put all the pumpkin box stuff back in the box and loaded up to go home.

Billy thought I should keep the pumpkin box and he should keep the spoons until we figured out what we should do with them.

I slept that night with the pumpkin box right beside my turtle night light.

I dreamed of Tracy and David. I dreamed that they liked the things that me and Billy liked and did the things that me and Billy did.

Maybe they were diggers too. One of them must have been, because the box was buried to be dug up. In my dreams, they ran alongside me and Billy. We ate ice cream at Mo's and played and raced around the block for hours. They also got separated a lot and had to go to porch time-out for the whole afternoon.

The next morning, Billy was at my door.

"So who have you been thinking about giving the pumpkin box stuff to?"

I stuffed a doughnut in my mouth and handed Billy one, too. We munched and thought.

It was going to take us a while to think.

We decided to walk around with the box and figure it out. We walked up and down Magnolia Street. We looked at

---

Transparency BTS–13
Summarize

The Pumpkin Box
Segment 6

We put all the pumpkin box stuff back in the box and loaded up to go home.

Billy thought I should keep the pumpkin box and he should keep the spoons until we figured out what we should do with them.

I slept that night with the pumpkin box right beside my turtle night light.

I dreamed of Tracy and David. I dreamed that they liked the things that me and Billy liked and did the things that me and Billy did.

Maybe they were diggers too. One of them must have been, because the box was buried to be dug up. In my dreams, they ran alongside me and Billy. We ate ice cream at Mo's and played and raced around the block for hours. They also got separated a lot and had to go to porch time-out for the whole afternoon.

The next morning, Billy was at my door.

"So who have you been thinking about giving the pumpkin box stuff to?"

I stuffed a doughnut in my mouth and handed Billy one too. We munched and thought.

It was going to take us a while to think.

Transparency BTS–14
Summarize

The Pumpkin Box
Segment 6, continued

We decided to walk around with the box and figure it out. We walked up and down Magnolia Street. We looked at the street like we never had before. Who would we give the pumpkin box treasures to? I said, "Magnolia Street must have been here a long time. My mom says that the picture in the box is probably sixty years old."

Billy said, "I don't think I know anybody that old. Do I?"

All of a sudden Billy got a big smile on his face, grabbed my hand, and started running toward Mr. Pinkton's. Mr. Pinkton was out in his yard with his roses.

Billy took the watch out of the pumpkin box and handed it to Mr. Pinkton.

"For you," Billy said, and then grabbed me by the hand and ran away. Then he stopped and called to Mr. Pinkton, "So you'll have more time with your fish."

When we got to Billy's yard, I smiled at him.

I dreamed of Tracy and David again that night, and when I woke up the next morning, I knew who we could give the yo-yo to.

the street like we never had before. Who would we give the pumpkin box treasures to?

I said, "Magnolia Street must have been here a long time. My mom says that the picture in the box is probably sixty years old."

Billy said, "I don't think I know anybody that old. Do I?"

All of a sudden Billy got a big smile on his face, grabbed my hand, and started running toward Mr. Pinkton's. Mr. Pinkton was out in his yard with his roses.

Billy took the watch out of the pumpkin box and handed it to Mr. Pinkton.

(SEGMENT 6 *continues on next page.*)

STRATEGY
Summarize

4. **Discussion/Modeling** Have students model how to use the Summarize strategy by telling the following in their own words:

- who the main character is
- what the problem is
- how the character's problem is solved

If students need help, use the Think Aloud to model the strategy.

Think Aloud *The main character in the story is Charlie, who is a digger. Charlie's problem is deciding what to do with the things she finds in the pumpkin box. She solves the problem by thinking of the right people to receive the items in the box.*

Transparency BTS–15

TRANSPARENCY BTS-15
TEACHER'S EDITION PAGE BTS17

ANNOTATED VERSION

BACK TO SCHOOL Strategy Workshop
Strategy: Summarize

Summarize

The Pumpkin Box
Segment 6, continued

The sun was shining real bright out back when Sid sprayed me with the hose. He laughed for a long time.

Mom called from the window, "Sid!"

Sid said, "I didn't do it," like he always does when he's been caught.

I made my mind up then. I went to the pumpkin box and handed the yo-yo to Sid. And the look on his face made me so happy. He was real surprised and said, "Why?"

I said, "'Cause I like you sometimes, and you're a yo-yo, too."

I skipped away to Billy's.

The pumpkin box was great.

When I got to Billy's house, his mom was on the phone.

Billy said, "Mom's calling the library. She says the book in the box is real old and the library may want it."

We smiled at each other.

The next night, Billy said he dreamed of Tracy and David too.

The Pumpkin Box, from *Mama's Monkeys on Magnolia Street,* by Angela Johnson. Text copyright © 1999 by Angela Johnson. Cover illustration copyright © 1999 by John Ward. Used by permission of Alfred A. Knopf, an imprint of Random House Children's Books, a division of Random House, Inc.

Copyright © Houghton Mifflin Company. All rights reserved.

Transparency BTS–16

TRANSPARENCY BTS-16
TEACHER'S EDITION PAGE BTS17

ANNOTATED VERSION

BACK TO SCHOOL Strategy Workshop
Strategy: Summarize

Summarize

The Pumpkin Box
Segment 6, continued

While Billy skated behind me, I rode my bike to Mo's. I walked up to the counter and handed Mo the nickels. The whole store smelled like cookies and French fries.

Mo looked confused when I said, "For you."

Mo said, "I used to collect these when I was your age."

He wiped his eyes, smiled, and said, "Thanks, kid."

Being a digger must be the best thing you could ever be in this world. You can find things that nobody ever thought could be found again.

Being a digger helps people remember gone things.

Me and Billy have decided to keep the picture of Tracy and David. He will keep it for a week, then I will have it for a week. We will always think about them running and playing on Magnolia Street like us.

We were swinging from the tree in my front yard, wondering what to put back into the pumpkin box.

Billy said, "Why do you think they put what they put in the pumpkin box, Charlie?"

"I don't know. Maybe it was stuff that they found. But it was probably stuff that made them happy."

The Pumpkin Box, from *Mama's Monkeys on Magnolia Street,* by Angela Johnson. Text copyright © 1999 by Angela Johnson. Cover illustration copyright © 1999 by John Ward. Used by permission of Alfred A. Knopf, an imprint of Random House Children's Books, a division of Random House, Inc.

Copyright © Houghton Mifflin Company. All rights reserved.

Monitoring Student Progress

If . . .	Then . . .
students have difficulty summarizing the story,	use a Story Map to chart where the story takes place, who the main characters are, what the problem is, and what happens in the beginning, middle, and end. Then have students use the information on the chart to summarize the story.

Strategy Workshop BTS17

The Pumpkin Box

SEGMENT 6 continued

"For you," Billy said, and then grabbed me by the hand and ran away. Then he stopped and called to Mr. Pinkton, "So you'll have more time with your fish."

When we got to Billy's yard, I smiled at him.

I dreamed of Tracy and David again that night, and when I woke up the next morning, I knew who we could give the yo-yo to.

The sun was shining real bright out back when Sid sprayed me with the hose. He laughed for a long time.

Mom called from the window, "Sid!"

Sid said, "I didn't do it," like he always does when he's been caught.

I made my mind up then. I went to the pumpkin box and handed the yo-yo to Sid. And the look on his face made me so happy. He was real surprised and said, "Why?"

I said, "'Cause I like you sometimes, and you're a yo-yo, too."

I skipped away to Billy's.

The pumpkin box was great.

When I got to Billy's house, his mom was on the phone.

Billy said, "Mom's calling the library. She says the book in the box is real old and the library may want it."

We smiled at each other.

Transparency BTS–17

Summarize

The Pumpkin Box

Segment 6, continued

Billy said, "I figure we can take a little time and think about the stuff that makes us happy before we put it in the pumpkin box."

And because a serious digger understands these things, I thought Billy was right.

Summarize Strategy

• Think about the main ideas or the important parts of the story. Tell in your own words the important things you have read.

"The Pumpkin Box," from *Mondays Mondays on Magnolia Street* by Angela Johnson. Text copyright © 1999 by Angela Johnson. Cover illustration copyright © 1999 by John Ward. Used by permission of Alfred A. Knopf, an imprint of Random House Children's Books, a division of Random House, Inc.

TRANSPARENCY BTS–17
TEACHER'S EDITION PAGE BTS18

BACK TO SCHOOL Strategy Workshop
Strategy: Summarize

ANNOTATED
VERSION

Copyright © Houghton Mifflin Company. All rights reserved.

Practice Book page 7

Back to School
Practice Book Page 7

Name _____

Strategy 6: Summarize

Use this strategy after reading to summarize what you read.

Here's how to use the Summarize Strategy:
• Think about the characters.
• Think about where the story takes place.
• Think about the problem in the story and how the characters solve it.
• Think about what happens in the beginning, middle, and end of the story.

Think about the story you just listened to. Complete the activity to show that you understand how to identify important story parts that will help you summarize the story.

Think about the story and respond to the questions below:

1. Who is the main character?

_____

_____

2. Where does the story take place?

_____

_____

3. What is the problem and how is it resolved?

_____

_____

_____

Now use this information to summarize the story for a partner.

The next night, Billy said he dreamed of Tracy and David, too.

While Billy skated behind me, I rode my bike to Mo's. I walked up to the counter and handed Mo the nickels. The whole store smelled like cookies and French fries.

Mo looked confused when I said, "For you."

Mo said, "I used to collect these when I was your age."

He wiped his eyes, smiled, and said, "Thanks, kid."

Being a digger must be the best thing you could ever be in this world. You can find things that nobody ever thought could be found again.

Being a digger helps people remember gone things.

Me and Billy have decided to keep the picture of Tracy and David. He will keep it for a week, then I will have it for a week. We will always think about them running and playing on Magnolia Street like us.

We were swinging from the tree in my front yard, wondering what to put back into the pumpkin box.

Billy said, "Why do you think they put what they put in the pumpkin box, Charlie?"

"I don't know. Maybe it was stuff that they found. But it was probably stuff that made them happy."

Billy said, "I figure we can take a little time and think about the stuff that makes us happy before we put it in the pumpkin box."

And because a serious digger understands these things, I thought Billy was right.

Comprehension: Story Response

1. What habit did the narrator have that caused the story events to happen? (She was a digger.)

2. What did the kids do with the things inside the pumpkin box? Why? (They gave them to people in the neighborhood because the note told them to.)

3. Why do you think that the people who buried the pumpkin box wanted the finders to put other treasures in it and bury it again? (Answers will vary.)

4. What do you think the kids will put in the pumpkin box? (Answers will vary.)

Evaluating Reading Strategies

Discuss with students the strategies that they have used in listening to this story. Have students respond to the following prompts:

1. What strategies were the most helpful to you in understanding this story?

2. What strategies do you use when you are reading? Why do you find them helpful?

Encourage students to be strategic readers as they begin reading this year. Discuss from time to time which strategies students are using and which strategies would be helpful to use. Remind students that the opening page of their **Practice Book** provides a quick reference to use of the strategies.

Learning More About Your Students

Now that you have had a chance to observe your class at work, you probably have an idea about which students will need extra support. In addition to ongoing informal assessment, you may wish to use one or more diagnostic instruments to assess certain students' strengths and needs. Your diagnosis can help in planning instruction and customizing your teaching to meet students' individual needs.

Test	Assesses
Baseline Group Test (Group Administration)	Comprehension Reading Level Writing
Leveled Reading Passages Assessment Kit (Individual Administration)	Reading Level Decoding Comprehension Strategies Oral Reading Fluency
Phonics/Decoding Screening Test (Individual Administration)	Phonics Structural Analysis
Lexia Quick Phonics Assessment CD-ROM (Individual Administration, with Computer)	Phonics

Diagnosing Needs

Once you have administered the *Baseline Group Test* for initial screening, you can use the *Leveled Reading Passages Assessment Kit* to take an Oral Reading Record. This individual assessment can give a more detailed diagnosis, providing information about the individual student's reading level, phonics and decoding skills, comprehension, use of strategies, and fluency. See the chart at left for additional assessment instruments that you can use.

Monitoring Student Progress

As students begin work in Theme 1, you may want to make some of the informal observations listed below. Additional suggestions for informal assessment are in Planning for Assessment at the start of each theme.

- Listen to students read aloud to observe fluency, decoding, and expression.

- To note students' comprehension of Anthology selections, check answers to Comprehension/Critical Thinking and Think About the Selection questions in the *Teacher's Edition,* or use the Selection Tests in the *Teacher's Resource Blackline Masters.*

- Use the suggestions in the Monitoring Student Progress boxes provided throughout the theme to evaluate student performance and to differentiate further instruction or practice.

- Observe students' writing in the Reading-Writing Workshop writing lessons or in Quick Writes, Practice Book pages, Journals, or other writing assignments.

- Note students' interest in and motivation for reading.

Planning for Instruction

Results of diagnostic assessment can be used to help plan appropriate instruction for each student. Instructional support to meet a variety of individual needs is included in this *Teacher's Edition* and in other components of *Houghton Mifflin Reading*. The chart below suggests the appropriate instructional emphasis and resources for students with different individual needs.

Differentiating Instruction

Student Performance Shows	Modifications to Consider
Difficulty with Decoding or Word Skills	• **Emphasis:** Word skills, phonics, reading for fluency; check for phonemic awareness • **Resources:** Teacher's Edition: *Phonics Review, Structural Analysis Reteaching lessons;* Leveled Readers; Lexia Phonics CD-ROM: Intermediate Intervention; Get Set for Reading CD-ROM
Difficulty with Oral Fluency	• **Emphasis:** Reading and rereading of independent level text; vocabulary development • **Resources:** Teacher's Edition: *Fluency Practice;* Leveled Readers; Theme Paperbacks; Reader's Library; Audio CD for main selections and Selection Summary Masters; Book Adventure® website
Difficulty with Comprehension	• **Emphasis:** Oral comprehension; strategy development; story comprehension; vocabulary development • **Resources:** Teacher's Edition: *Teacher Read Alouds, Strategies, Extra Support notes, Comprehension Reteaching lessons, Vocabulary Skills;* Leveled Readers; Get Set for Reading CD-ROM; Extra Support Handbook
Overall High Performance	• **Emphasis:** Independent reading and writing; vocabulary development; critical thinking • **Resources:** Teacher's Edition: *Think About the Selection questions, Challenge notes, Challenge/Extension Activities, Assignment Cards;* Leveled Readers; Theme Paperbacks; Book Adventure® website; Education Place® website; Challenge Handbook

Managing Instruction

Throughout *Houghton Mifflin Reading,* you will find support for differentiating and managing instruction in the following features and components:

Reaching All Learners

Monitoring Student Progress

students score 8 or below on **Practice Book** page 85,

have them focus on a few paragraphs at a time to identify key selection information.

Use these notes to help you evaluate student performance and to differentiate further instruction or practice.

Extra Support / Intervention

On Level   Challenge

Challenge

English Language Learners

Use the suggestions in these boxes to provide differentiated instruction for students at all levels of ability.

Classroom Management

Managing Flexible Groups

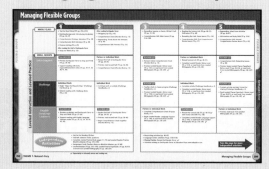

Plan your reading block with these suggested grouping options.

Classroom Management

Assign these independent cross-curricular activities while you work with small groups.

Classroom Management Kit

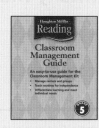

Use this kit to manage the individual needs of your students. The kit includes handbooks for differentiated instruction, independent activities, classroom management, and more.

Assessment Management and Reporting

Learner Profile® CD-ROM

Use this CD-ROM to plan lessons, track students' performance, and manage administrative duties.

Nature's Fury

Theme 1

OBJECTIVES

Reading Strategies predict/infer; question; monitor/clarify; phonics/decoding

Comprehension sequence of events; text organization; categorize and classify

Decoding Longer Words base words; syllabication; word roots *struct* and *rupt*; short vowels; long vowels /ā/, /ē/, /ī/; long vowels /ō/, /o͞o/, /yo͞o/

Vocabulary using a thesaurus; dictionary guide words; dictionary definitions

Spelling short vowels; /ā/, /ē/, /ī/; /ō/, /o͞o/, /yo͞o/

Grammar kinds of sentences; subjects and predicates; conjunctions; compound sentences; singular and plural nouns; more plural nouns

Writing news article; response to a prompt; paragraph of information; process writing: description

Listening/Speaking/Viewing panel discussion; literature discussion; discuss favorite photos

Information and Study Skills using print and electronic reference sources; using print and electronic card catalogs; using graphic aids: maps, globes, charts, tables, and graphs

Nature's Fury

C O N T E N T S

Vocabulary Reader

Nonfiction

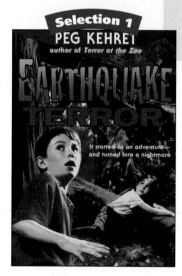

Selection 1
PEG KEHRET
author of *Terror at the Zoo*

Realistic Fiction

Below Level   **On Level**   **Above Level**   **Language Support**

Leveled Readers

Writing Process

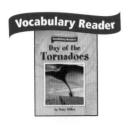

Vocabulary Reader
Day of the Tornadoes
by Gary Miller

Nonfiction

Selection 2
Eye of the Storm
STEPHEN KRAMER
photographs by
WARREN FAIDLEY

Nonfiction

Below Level   On Level   Above Level   Language Support

Leveled Readers

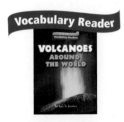

Vocabulary Reader
VOLCANOES
AROUND THE WORLD

Nonfiction

Selection 3

VOLCANOES
SEYMOUR SIMON

Nonfiction

Below Level   On Level   Above Level   Language Support

Leveled Readers

Theme 1

Realistic
Fiction

Nonfiction

Focus on Genre

TALL TALES

Vocabulary Reader

Nonfiction

Below Level   On Level   Above Level   Language Support

Leveled Readers

Leveled Theme Paperbacks

Leveled Bibliography

BOOKS FOR INDEPENDENT READING AND FLUENCY BUILDING

 To build vocabulary and fluency, choose books from this list for students to read outside class. Suggest that students read for at least thirty minutes a day, either independently or with an adult who provides modeling and guidance.

Key

 Science

 Social Studies

 Multicultural

 Music

 Math

 Classic

 Art

Career

Classroom Bookshelf

WELL BELOW LEVEL

Hurricane!
by Connie Demas Bliss
Cavendish 2000 (32p)
A family rides out the storm when Hurricane Bob strikes Cape Cod.

 The Blizzard's Robe
by Robert Sabuda
Atheneum 1999 (32p)
In this Arctic tale, a young girl makes a robe for Blizzard, who then creates the Northern Lights.

Aunt Minnie and the Twister
by Mary Skillings Prigger
Clarion 2002 (32p)
Aunt Minnie and the nine orphans she cares for emerge from the root cellar after a twister.

The Tornado Watches: An Ike and Mem Story
by Patrick Jenkins
Holiday 2002 (64p)
When a tornado alert is lifted, Ike worries another tornado may be coming and stays up night after night, causing him to fall asleep in school.

Birdie's Lighthouse
by Deborah Hopkinson
Atheneum 1997 (32p)
Young Birdie is the only one who can tend the lighthouse in the midst of a violent storm.

BELOW LEVEL

 Rain Player
by David Wisniewski
Clarion 1991 (32p)
Pik hopes to save the people of his Mayan village from a drought.

 **Rescue on the Outer Banks**
by Candice Ransom
Lerner 2002 (48p)
Ten-year-old Sam Deal becomes part of an African American lifesaving crew to rescue the victims of a ship-wreck off the coast of North Carolina.

Anna, Grandpa, and the Big Storm
by Carla Stevens
Puffin 1985 (64p) paper
Anna is determined to get to school, despite a major snowstorm.

 Wild Weather: Lightning
by Lorraine Hopping
Scholastic 1999 (48p)
The author explains the power of lightning and its positive and negative effects.

 Rocking and Rolling
by Philip Steele
Candlewick 1997 (24p)
Volcanologists and other scientists study volcanoes, tsunami, geysers, and glaciers.

 Tornadoes
by Seymour Simon
Morrow 1999 (32p)
Simon explains how tornadoes are formed and how we can protect ourselves from them.

ON LEVEL

 Trial by Ice
by K.M. Kostyal
Nat'l Geo 1999 (64p)
This photobiography of explorer Ernest Shackleton is introduced by his granddaughter.

The Volcano Disaster
by Peg Kehret
Minstrel 1998 (136p) also paper
Warren and Betsy get more than they expect when they research Mount St. Helens.

 Tracks in the Snow
by Lucy Jane Bledsoe
Holiday 1997 (96p)
Erin and Tiffany struggle to survive a snowstorm in the Sierras.

Earthquake at Dawn
by Kristiana Gregory
Harcourt 1992 (192p)
This story of the 1906 earthquake is based on an actual letter and on photographs.

Earthquake! A Story of Old San Francisco
by Kathleen Kudlinski
Puffin 1995 (64p)
Philip must save his horses during the San Francisco earthquake.

Castaways: Stories of Survival
by Gerald Hausman
Greenwillow 2003 (160p)
In these six stories, people battle severe weather, wild animals, hunger, and thirst in their efforts to survive.

Firestorm
by Jan Neubert Schultz
Carolrhoda 2002 (203p)
Young Maggie tells the story of the tragic 1894 forest fire that struck Hinckley, Minnesota.

Shock Waves Through Los Angeles

by Carole G. Vogel
Little 1996 (32p)

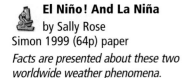

Causes of the 1994 earthquake, its devastation, and the heroic rescues it inspired are recounted here.

Escaping the Giant Wave
by Peg Kehret
Simon 2003 (160p)

On vacation in Oregon, Kyle and his sister BeeBee must save themselves from giant tsunami waves caused by an earthquake.

El Niño! And La Niña

by Sally Rose
Simon 1999 (64p) paper

Facts are presented about these two worldwide weather phenomena.

Night of the Twisters
by Ivy Ruckman
Harper 1986 (159p) paper

A boy and his family struggle to survive a series of devastating tornadoes.

Fire in Their Eyes
by Karen Magnuson Beil
Harcourt 1999 (64p)

The author explores the training and dangers faced by people who fight wildfires.

Missing in the Mountains
by T.S. Fields
Rising Moon 1999 (136p)

A brother and sister fight for their lives when they are caught in a sudden avalanche.

Blizzard: Estes Park, Colorado, 1886

by Kathleen Duey
Aladdin 1998 (64p)

Maggie must try to save her cousin who is lost in the sudden blizzard.

ABOVE LEVEL

Stolen by the Sea
by Anna Myers
Walker 2001 (132p)

Maggie must put aside her jealousy of Felipe when the two of them attempt to rescue people trapped by a flood in Galveston, Texas.

El Niño

by Caroline Arnold
Clarion 1999 (48p)

Learn more about the wild weather phenomenon that's been making headlines around the world.

BOOKS FOR TEACHER READ ALOUD

The Long Winter
by Laura Ingalls Wilder
Harper 1961 (334p)

After a blizzard, Almanzo must try to save the village from starvation.

I Am Lavina Cumming

by Susan Lowell
Milkweed 1993 (200p)

Lavina visits her grandmother and learns of her ordeal during the 1906 San Francisco earthquake.

Technology

Computer Software Resources

- ***Nature's Fury* Get Set for Reading CD-ROM**
  Provides background building, vocabulary support, and selection summaries in English and Spanish

- **Spelling Spree!® CD-ROM**
  Provides interactive spelling and proofreading practice

- **Wacky Web Tales® floppy disk**
  Helps students create humorous stories and review parts of speech

Video Cassettes

- **El Niño.** *Filmic Archives*
- **Can't Drown This Town.** *Nat'l Geo*
- **After the Hurricane.** *Nat'l Geo*
- **When the Earth Quakes.** *Nat'l Geo*
- **Volcano: Nature's Inferno.** *Nat'l Geo*
- **Eyewitness: Volcanos.** *Filmic Archives*
- **Eyewitness: Natural Disasters.** *Filmic Archives*
- **The Eruption of Mount St. Helens.** *Filmic Archives*

Audio

- **El Niño: Stormy Weather for People and Wildlife** *by Caroline Arnold. Recorded Books*
- **Keep the Lights Burning, Abbie** *by Peter and Connie Roop. Audio Bookshelf*
- **The Rain Player** *by David Wisniewski. Houghton Mifflin Company*
- **I Am Lavina Cumming** *by Susan Lowell. Recorded Books*
- **CD-ROM for *Nature's Fury*.** *Houghton Mifflin Company*

Technology Resources addresses are on page R31.

Education Place®

www.eduplace.com *Log on to Education Place for more activities relating to* Nature's Fury, *including vocabulary support—*
  e • **Glossary**
  e • **WordGame**

Book Adventure®

www.bookadventure.org *This Internet reading incentive program provides thousands of titles for students to read.*

Accelerated Reader® Universal CD-ROM

This popular CD-ROM provides practice quizzes for Anthology selections and for many popular children's books.

Theme Skills Overview

	Selection 1	Selection 2	Selection 3
Pacing Approximately 5–6 weeks	**Earthquake Terror** Realistic Fiction pp. 24A–51R 	**Eye of the Storm** Nonfiction pp. 53I–81R 	**Volcanoes** Nonfiction pp. 81S–105R 
Reading **Comprehension** **Information and Study Skills** **Vocabulary Readers** **Leveled Readers** • Fluency Practice • Independent Reading	**Guiding Comprehension** ⊙ **Sequence of Events** T 2.04b ⊙ **Predict/Infer** T 2.05, 3.01g **Science Link** How to Read a Science Article 1.05c, 2.01 Using Reference Sources T 3.06 **Vocabulary Reader** 1.02 **Leveled Readers** *Riding Out the Storm* *Earthquake: Alaska, 1964* *Clearing the Dust* *Alone in the Storm* 1.05a; 2.02d,f; 2.03a; 2.04b; 3.01a; 4.01 Lessons and Leveled Practice	**Guiding Comprehension** ⊙ **Text Organization** T 2.07 ⊙ **Question** 2.01, 2.02 **Career Link** How to Read a Sequence Chart 2.07 Using Library Catalogs 3.06 **Vocabulary Reader** 1.02 **Leveled Readers** *White Dragon: Anna Allen in the Face of Danger* *Hurricane Opal: Into the Storm* *Benjamin Franklin, A Scientist by Nature* 1.05a; 2.02d,f; 2.03a-b; 4.01 *Anna Allen Faces the White Dragon* Lessons and Leveled Practice	**Guiding Comprehension** ⊙ **Categorize and Classify** T 3.02 ⊙ **Monitor/Clarify** 2.01 **Folktale Link** How to Read a Folktale 2.03a Using Graphic Aids T 2.07 **Vocabulary Reader** 1.02 **Leveled Readers** *Floods* *Mexico's Smoking Mountains* *A Deep Blue Lake* *Dangerous Waters* 2.02d,f; 2.03b; 3.02; 4.01 Lessons and Leveled Practice
Word Work **Decoding** **Phonics** **Spelling** **Vocabulary**	⊙ **Base Words** T 1.01 **Short Vowels** T 5.05 ⊙ **Using a Thesaurus** T 1.04 Short Vowels T	⊙ **Syllabication** T 1.01 **Long Vowels: /ā/, /ē/, /ī/** 5.05 ⊙ **Dictionary Guide Words** T 1.04 /ā/, /ē/, and /ī/ T	⊙ **Word Roots *rupt* and *struct*** T 1.01 **Long Vowel Sounds /ō/, /o͞o/, and /yo͞o/** 5.05 ⊙ **Dictionary Definitions** T 1.04 /ō/, /o͞o/, and /yo͞o/ T
Writing and Oral Language **Writing** **Grammar** **Listening/Speaking/ Viewing**	✏️ **Writing a News Article** 4.04, 4.05, 4.06, 4.07, 4.08a, 5.06, 5.07 Adding Details Sentence Kinds and Parts T 5.01 Panel Discussion 4.02a-c	✏️ **Writing a Response to a Prompt** 4.04, 4.05, 4.06, 4.07, 4.08a, 4.09, 5.01 Capitalizing and Punctuating Sentences T 5.01, 5.07 Longer Sentences T 5.01, 5.03c Literature Discussion 1.03a, 2.06, 4.02a-c	✏️ **Writing a Paragraph of Information** 4.04, 4.05, 4.06, 4.07, 4.08c, 4.09, 5.01, 5.07 Correcting Sentence Fragments T Singular/Plural Nouns T 1.05j Discuss Favorite Photos 2.07, 4.02a-c
Cross-Curricular Activities	Responding: Health and Safety, Listening and Speaking, Internet 3.01f,g; 3.02; 4.07 Classroom Management Activities SC1.05, SC3.02a-e, SC3.03	Responding: Math, Viewing, Internet 3.01f,g; 3.02; 4.07 Classroom Management Activities SC4.01, SS1.03	Responding: Science, Social Studies, Internet 3.01f,g; 3.02; 4.07 Classroom Management Activities

T Skill tested on Weekly or Theme Skills Test and/or Integrated Theme Test

See also: North Carolina EOG Aligned Assessments and Practice

Target Skills

TARGET SKILL

Comprehension
Vocabulary
Phonics/Decoding
Fluency

Nonfiction

Monitoring Student Progress	Focus on Genre

Monitoring Student Progress

Check Your Progress

Night of the Twisters
Realistic Fiction

Blizzard!
Nonfiction
pp. M1–M45

Focus on Genre

Tall Tales
pp. 107A–129R

Guiding Comprehension

Theme Connections

🎯 **Comprehension Skills Review** T 3.01a,g; 3.02; 3.03

🎯 **Predict/Infer** T 3.01

Taking Tests: Cognition

Guiding Comprehension

Theme Connections

🎯 **Understanding Tall Tales** 3.01e

🎯 **Summarize** 3.06

Using an Atlas

Vocabulary Reader 1.02

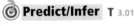
Connecting Leveled Readers

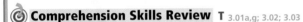

Leveled Readers

Apples for America
Grandpa's Rail Tales
Davy Crockett, Frontier Hero
The Unbelievable Johnny Appleseed
2.02d,f; 2.03a; 3.01e; 4.01

Lessons and Leveled Practice

🎯 **Structural Analysis Skills Review** T 1.01

🎯 **Vocabulary Skills Review** T 1.03c, 1.04

Spelling Skills Review

🎯 **Word Roots *vis* and *vid*** 1.01

The Vowel Pair *ea* 1.01

🎯 **Slang and Informal Language** 1.03b

Vowel Changes

✏️ **Writing Skills Review** 4.02a, 4.07, 4.09, 5.01, 5.04

Grammar Skills Review 5.03

✏️ **Writing a Tall Tale** 4.04, 4.05, 4.06, 4.07, 4.08a, 4.09, 5.06, 5.07

Using Exact Nouns

Varying Sentence Types; Appositives 5.01

Comparing Art Styles 2.07

Cross-Curricular Activities

Classroom Management Activities SC4.04, SS1.01, SS1.03

Responding: Internet 3.01f,g; 3.02

Classroom Management Activities

Combination Classroom

See the **Combination Classroom Planning Guide** for lesson planning and management support.

Writing Process ✏️

Reading-Writing Workshop: Description
• Student Writing Model
• Writing Process Instruction
• Writing Traits Focus

Additional Theme Resources

• Leveled Theme Paperbacks Lessons
• Reteaching Lessons
• Challenge/Extension Activities

Technology

Education Place
www.eduplace.com

Log on to Education Place for more activities relating to *Nature's Fury*.

Lesson Planner CD-ROM

Customize your planning for *Nature's Fury* with the Lesson Planner CD-ROM.

Cross-Curricular Activities

Independent Activities

Assign these activities at any time during the theme while you work with small groups.

Independent Activities

- Challenge/Extension Activities, Theme Resources, pp. R9, R11, R13, R15, R17, R19

- Theme 1 Assignment Cards 1–13, Teacher's Resource Blackline Masters, pp. 47–53

- Classroom Management Activities, pp. 25E–25F, 53Q–53R, 81AA–81BB, M6–M7, 107I–107J

- Language Center, 51M–51N, 81M–81N, 105M–105N, 129M–129N

- **Classroom Management Handbook,** Activity Masters CM1-1–CM1-12

- **Challenge Handbook,** Challenge Masters CH1-1–CH1-6

Look for more activities in the Classroom Management Kit.

Science

Storm Watch

👥 Pairs	🕐 45 minutes
Objective	Present a report on storm activity.
Materials	Internet, newspapers

How many storms—and what kinds—occur across the country or around the world in a typical week? Prepare a report telling about storm activity in the United States or around the globe.

- Use Internet weather sites and daily newspapers to research this week's weather.

- Write a report that summarizes the storm activity.

- Include a catchy headline.

Art

Show the Fury

👤 Singles	🕐 30 minutes
Objective	Illustrate a storm or other natural upheaval.
Materials	Markers, colored pencils, paints, brushes

What kind of powerful storm or natural upheaval do you find most visually fascinating? Choose a blizzard, thunderstorm, hurricane, tornado, earthquake, volcano, or tidal wave. Then bring it to life in an illustration.

- Choose art materials you like to work with, or that best fit your subject.

- Decide which elements of your subject you want to portray.

- Give your picture a caption or catchy title.

Consider copying and laminating these activities for use in centers.

Language Arts

Wordquake!

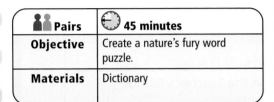 Pairs	⏱ 45 minutes
Objective	Create a nature's fury word puzzle.
Materials	Dictionary

What's a *rcianrheu*? Unscramble the letters, and you'll find the word *hurricane*. Create a word puzzle from the following list of words: *thunderstorm, earthquake, hurricane, typhoon, volcano, mudslide, tornado, sandstorm, blizzard*.

- Scramble each word, then write it in a column on a piece of paper.
- Use a dictionary to define each word.
- Write each definition in a second column. List them in mixed-up order.
- Challenge other students to unscramble the words and then match them with their definitions.

Math

Follow the Storm

🧍 Singles	🕐 30 minutes
Objective	Write math word problems.
Materials	United States map with a map scale, ruler

Write a math word problem to figure out the time it takes for a storm to travel between two U. S. cities.

1. Choose a storm from the chart below.
2. Choose two cities on a map of the United States. Use a ruler and the map scale to find the distance between them.
3. Divide the distance between cities by the speed of the storm to figure out the time. Round it off to the nearest hour.
4. Write the word problem.
5. Exchange word problems with a partner. Check your answers.

Type of Storm	How Fast It Travels
hurricane	200 miles per hour
tornado	300 miles per hour
blizzard	45 miles per hour

Social Studies

Web of Effects

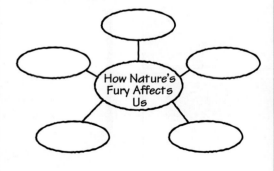 Pairs	🕐 20 minutes
Objective	Create a word web.
Materials	Writing materials

Nature can sometimes affect our communities and environment in violent ways. Make a concept web that details some of these effects.

- Draw a web like the one shown.
- Brainstorm how violent hurricanes, tornadoes, blizzards, volcanoes, and earthquakes can affect people.
- Samples might include: *power failure, destroyed bridges*.
- Write an effect in each circle.
- Compare word webs with other students.

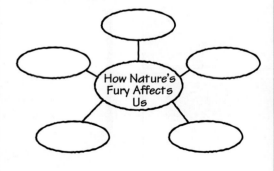

How Nature's Fury Affects Us

Planning for Assessment

During the first few weeks of school . . .

1 SCREENING

To obtain information about all students' instructional levels and to identify students in need of further diagnostic assessment, administer the **Baseline Group Test**.

If performance is	Then use these teaching resources:
■ **ABOVE LEVEL**	• Systematic instruction in the Teacher's Edition • Practice Book • Challenge Handbook • Leveled Readers and Leveled Practice
▲ **ON LEVEL**	• Systematic instruction in the Teacher's Edition • Classroom Management Handbook • Practice Book • Leveled Readers and Leveled Practice
● **BELOW LEVEL** If below level, further diagnose student needs.	• Systematic instruction in the Teacher's Edition • Practice Book • Extra Support Handbook • Vocabulary Readers • Leveled Readers and Leveled Practice

2 DIAGNOSIS

To determine individual students' specific instructional needs and to plan instruction, you may wish to administer the following tests:

- **Leveled Reading Passages Assessment Kit**
- **Phonics/Decoding Screening Test**
- **Lexia Quick Phonics Assessment CD-ROM**

Once you have begun your instructional plan . . .

3 MONITORING PROGRESS

To ensure that students are making adequate progress throughout this theme, use the following resources:

- **Monitoring Student Progress boxes**
- **Theme 1: Selection Tests**
- **End-of-Theme Monitoring Student Progress**
- **Assessing Student Progress**
- **Theme 1: North Carolina EOG Aligned Assessments, Weekly Skills Tests, Theme Skills Test**

4 MANAGING AND REPORTING

 **Technology**   To manage your assessment information, record each student's performance on the **Learner Profile® CD-ROM**.

North Carolina Test Correlation

GRADE-LEVEL COMPETENCIES AND OBJECTIVES

Receptive Literacy	Theme 1 Skill Instruction Pages	Houghton Mifflin Assessments	EOG Tests or Writing Assessment*
1.01 Expand and refine vocabulary.	129C	O	O
1.02 Select key vocabulary critical to the text.	27, 55, 81		
2.01 Use strategies to monitor comprehension.	110, 112, 124	O	O
2.02 Interact with the text before, during, and after by: **a.** making predictions **c.** supporting answers from textual information, previous experience, and/or other sources **f.** making connections	28, 32, 42, M10, 107K, 129A, 105H, M26	O	O
2.03 a., b. Read a variety of texts, including fiction; non-fiction	110–113, 107K, 129A, 48, 105H	O	O
2.04 a., d. Interpret elements of fiction: plot development; tone	37, 43, 39	O	O
2.07 Evaluate usefulness and quality of information.	105H	O	O
2.08 b., c. Explain and evaluate relationships that are: hierarchical; temporal	84, 97, 105A, M35, R12 51A, M34, R8	O	O
2.10 Identify strategies used by a speaker or writer.	81A, M34, R10	O	O
3.01 Respond to fiction, nonfiction, poetry, drama by: **a.** analyzing word choice and content **e.** evaluating the differences among genres **f.** examining relationships among characters **g.** making inferences	53C, 105J, 129G, 129L 107K, 129A 32, 37, 42, 43, 117 M10, M14, M20	O	O
Expressive Literacy			
4.02 Formulate hypotheses, evaluate information and ideas; **4.03** Make presentations to inform or persuade; **4.05** Plan and organize; **4.06** Compose a draft; **4.07** Compose fiction, nonfiction; **4.08** Focus revision; **4.09** Follow genre conventions; **5.03** Elaborate information.	51S–53H, 81I–K, 105K, M43, R22–R23, 129I–129J	O	O
5.01 Use correct capitalization and punctuation; **5.02** Demonstrate understanding in writing; **5.05** Spell accurately; **5.06** Proofread; **5.07** Edit; **5.08** Create readable documents.	51E, 51I, 53E, 53G, 81E, 105E, 105I, M40–M43, R20, R24, 129E	O	O

*Administered at Grades 4 and 7

Launching the Theme

Theme **1**

Nature's Fury

Now the house of wind is thundering.
Now the house of wind is thundering.
As I go roaring over the land,
the land is covered in thunder.

— from "Wind Song" (Pima)

20   21

Introducing the Theme: Discussion Options

Combination Classroom

See the **Combination Classroom Planning Guide** for lesson planning and management support.

Read aloud the theme title and lyrics on Anthology page 21. Ask:

1 What do you think is the meaning of the theme title *Nature's Fury*? (extremely large-scale, violent, or powerful acts of nature)

2 In what ways does the passage from "Wind Song" express nature's fury? (It describes powerful forces of nature, such as wind and thunder, and uses strong words such as *roaring* to describe them.)

3 Select one example of nature's fury and explain how people can protect themselves from it. (Sample answer: To protect themselves from a hurricane, people should stay indoors and stock plenty of bottled water and canned goods.)

Nature's Fury

with Warren Faidley

Are you ready to face nature at its most explosive? Start with a letter that just blew in from storm chaser Warren Faidley!

Dear Reader,

I chase storms — anywhere, anytime.

I pursue tornadoes, lightning, hurricanes and other natural disasters. I capture the events on film and video.

In this theme you'll get a taste of my adventures on the job. You'll also encounter other examples of nature's power, from earthquakes to blizzards.

One of the biggest storms I have chased was Hurricane Andrew in August of 1992. Andrew hit South Florida with winds of over 160 miles per hour.

It was both exciting and frightening to be in the middle of a "category 5" storm, the biggest of all hurricanes.

22

23

Building Theme Connections

Read Aloud Anthology page 22. Tell students that Warren Faidley took the storm photographs shown in *Eye of the Storm: Chasing Storms with Warren Faidley,* a selection that they will read later in this theme. (See Teacher's Edition page 56 for more information on Warren Faidley.)

Ask volunteers to read aloud the author's letter on Anthology pages 23–24. Use the following questions to prompt discussion.

1 Warren Faidley chases all forms of nature's fury. If you could chase one form, which would it be, and why?
(Sample answer: rain clouds, because they are very mysterious)

2 What areas of the world experience nature's fury severely?
(Sample answers: Many countries in the Pacific have active volcanoes. Areas with high elevations often have avalanches.)

3 What kind of equipment would you want to have with you if you were to join Warren Faidley in his storm chasing?
(Sample answers: waterproof clothing and shoes, bottled water, film)

Step Into the Storm

As a storm chaser, Warren Faidley *chooses* to go out into tornadoes and hurricanes. Have you ever been caught in a storm or in some other example of nature gone wild? Think about that experience as you read the selections in this theme, which are shown below. Try putting yourself into the different situations in the selections. Sometimes the storm you read about can be as exciting as the storm you were in!

I had to be very careful. The rain hit so hard it stung. Large trees were uprooted and debris flew through the air.

Huge waves crashed inland, bringing boats and wreckage toward me.

I had to use all of my experiences as a storm chaser to survive. I wore safety glasses to protect my eyes, and I kept my camera equipment in waterproof cases.

When the storm passed I was safe.

I was also a little tired and wet.

You won't have to worry about the wind and rain as you read the selections in this theme. Just enjoy the forces of nature on display!

Sincerely yours,

Warren Faidley

Internet

To learn about the authors in this theme, visit Education Place. **www.eduplace.com/kids**

24   25

Building Theme Connections, *continued*

Home Connection

Send home the theme letter for *Nature's Fury* to introduce the theme and suggest home activities. (See the **Teacher's Resource Blackline Masters**.)

For other suggestions relating to *Nature's Fury*, see **Home/ Community Connections**.

Read aloud the paragraph on Anthology page 25.

- Have students brainstorm ideas, images, and words they associate with the words *nature's fury*. Record their thoughts.
- Discuss how students' ideas compare with Warren Faidley's.

Have students finish reading Anthology page 25.

- Explain that the books in the photograph show the selections students will read in the theme *Nature's Fury*.
- Ask students to predict which forms of nature's fury will be included in the selections. Have the students explain their predictions. (Answers will vary.)
- Allow students time to look ahead at the selections and photographs. Have them revise their original predictions as necessary.

Making Selection Connections

Introduce Selection Connections in the Practice Book.

- Preview the **Graphic Organizers** on **Practice Book** pages 9 and 10. Read aloud the directions, column heads, and selection titles. Explain that when they finish reading each selection, students will add to the chart to deepen their understanding of the theme *Nature's Fury*.

Classroom Management

At any time during the theme, you can assign the independent cross-curricular activities on Teacher's Edition pages 23I–23J while you give differentiated instruction to small groups. For additional independent activities related to specific selections, see the Teacher's Edition pages listed below.

- Week 1: pages 25E–25F, 51M–51N
- Week 2: pages 53Q–53R, 81M–81N
- Week 3: pages 81AA–81BB, 105M–105N
- Week 4: pages M6–M7, M26–M27, M28–M29, M44–M45

Monitoring Student Progress

Monitoring Progress

Throughout the theme, monitor your students' progress by using the following program features in the Teacher's Edition:

- Guiding Comprehension questions
- Literature discussion groups
- Skill lesson applications
- Monitoring Student Progress boxes

Wrapping Up and Reviewing the Theme

Use the two selections and support material in **Monitoring Student Progress** on pages M1–M48 to review theme skills, connect and compare theme literature, and prepare students for the **North Carolina EOG Aligned Assessments** as well as for standardized tests measuring adequate yearly progress.

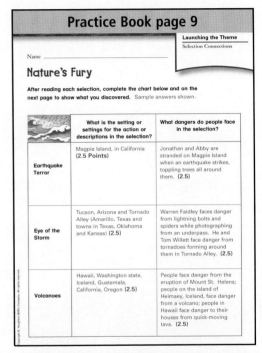

Practice Book page 9

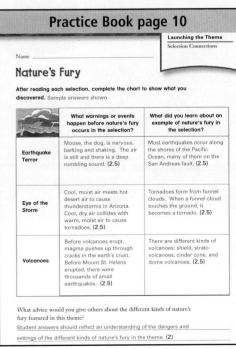

Practice Book page 10

Lesson Overview

Literature

PEG KEHRET
author of *Terror at the Zoo*

EARTHQUAKE TERROR

It started as an adventure—
and turned into a nightmare

Selection Summary

While on a camping trip in California, Jonathan confronts nature's fury as he struggles to save his sister and himself from a dangerous earthquake.

24A

Vocabulary Reader

1 Background and Vocabulary

Nonfiction

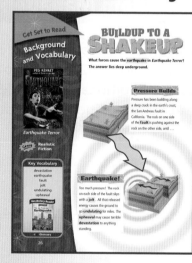

2 Main Selection

Earthquake Terror
Genre: Realistic Fiction

3 Science Link

Instructional Support

Planning and Practice

- Planning and classroom management
- Reading instruction
- Skill lessons
- Materials for reaching all learners

- Independent practice for skills

- Newsletters
- Selection Summaries
- Assignment Cards
- Observation Checklists
- Selection Tests

- Transparencies
- Strategy Posters
- Blackline Masters

Reaching All Learners

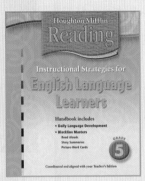

Coordinated lessons, activities, and projects for additional reading instruction

For
- Classroom Teacher
- Extended Day
- Pull Out
- Resource Teacher
- Reading Specialist

Technology

Audio Selection

Earthquake Terror

Get Set for Reading CD-ROM
- Background building
- Vocabulary support
- Selection Summary in English and Spanish

Accelerated Reader
- Practice quizzes for the selection

www.eduplace.com

Log on to Education Place for more activities related to the selection.

e•Glossary
e•WordGame

Leveled Books for Reaching All Learners

Leveled Readers and Leveled Practice

- Independent reading for building fluency
- Topic, comprehension strategy, and vocabulary linked to main selection
- Lessons in Teacher's Edition, pages 51O–51R
- Leveled practice for every book

Technology

Leveled Readers
Audio available

Book Adventure

- Practice quizzes for the Leveled Theme Paperbacks

www.eduplace.com

Log on to Education Place® for activities related to the Leveled Theme Paperbacks.

● **BELOW LEVEL**

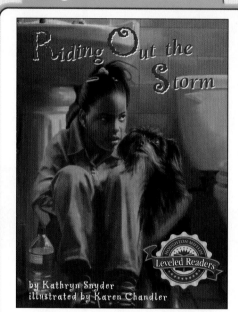

▲ **ON LEVEL**

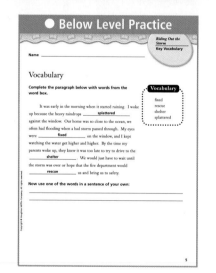

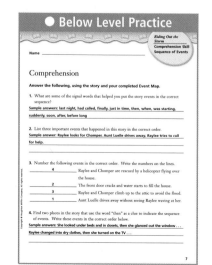

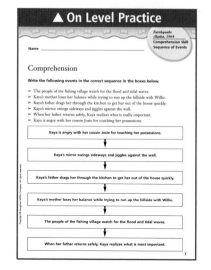

ABOVE LEVEL

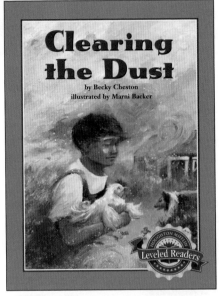

Clearing the Dust
by Becky Cheston
illustrated by Marni Backer

HOUGHTON MIFFLIN
Leveled Readers

◆ LANGUAGE SUPPORT

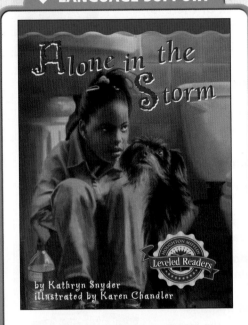

Alone in the Storm

HOUGHTON MIFFLIN
Leveled Readers

by Kathryn Snyder
illustrated by Karen Chandler

Leveled Theme Paperbacks

- Extended independent reading in theme-related trade books
- Lessons in Teacher's Edition, pages R2–R7

Below Level

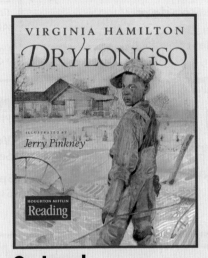

VIRGINIA HAMILTON
DRYLONGSO
ILLUSTRATED BY
Jerry Pinkney
HOUGHTON MIFFLIN
Reading

On Level

HURRICANES
EARTH'S MIGHTIEST STORMS ● PATRICIA LAUBER
HOUGHTON MIFFLIN
Reading

Challenge

■ Above Level Practice

Clearing the Dust
Key Vocabulary

Name _____

Vocabulary

The first pair of words or phrases in each exercise is related in some way. This is called an analogy. Choose a word from the box to show the same relationship between the second pair of words or phrases.

Vocabulary
abandoned
debris
galvanized
generations
hoisted
impact
languished
shuddered
terrified
warble

1. Lowered is to dropped as lifted is to __hoisted__
2. Well-tended is to flourished as neglected is to __languished__
3. Calmed is to quieted as shivered is to __shuddered__
4. Lulled is to soothed as energized is to __galvanized__
5. Litter is to rubbish as rubble is to __debris__
6. Bee is to buzz as bird is to __warble__
7. Hot is to sizzling as frightened is to __terrified__
8. Legal is to lawful as deserted is to __abandoned__
9. Child is to ancestors as family is to __generations__

5

◆ Language Support Practice

Alone in the Storm
Build Background

Name _____

Build Background

The sentences below are about hurricane safety. Read each sentence and write the word *before, during,* or *after* on the line after each sentence. Then write each sentence in the box where it belongs.

- Stay away from windows. __DURING__
- Buy batteries. __BEFORE__
- Call friends to see if they are safe. __AFTER__
- Listen to a radio that uses batteries. __DURING__
- Make sure the storm is over before you go outside. __AFTER__
- Get lots of bottled water. __BEFORE__

BEFORE
Buy batteries.
Get lots of bottled water.

DURING
Stay away from windows.
Listen to a radio that uses batteries.

AFTER
Call friends to see if they are safe.
Make sure the storm is over before you go outside.

5

■ Above Level Practice

Clearing the Dust
Comprehension Skill
Sequence of Events

Name _____

Comprehension

Answer the following, using *Clearing the Dust* and your completed Event Map.

1. Write some words or phrases from the story that help you identify the sequence of events.
Sample answers: ever since, but now, as they walked, then, after breakfast, suddenly, finally, the next morning.

2. Find a place in the story that uses the word "suddenly" as a clue to indicate the sequence of events. Write this example below.
Sample answers: Aaron's mother screamed from the porch; suddenly he saw Morgan, the mare, bolt for the open gate. Aaron walked with one hand extended, almost feeling his way forward; suddenly, he stumbled into his mother in the path.

3. Find a place in the story that uses the word "finally" as a clue to indicate the sequence of events. Write this example below.
Morgan bolted for the open gate. The collie nipped at her legs, so that Aaron could finally catch up with her.

4. List three events that you think might happen to Aaron and his family after they decide to stay on the farm. List these events in order.
Sample answers: Aaron helps his dad run the farm. The Soil Conservation Service gives Aaron's dad lessons in irrigation and soil protection. In a year, the farm is successful.

7

◆ Language Support Practice

Alone in the Storm
Key Vocabulary

Name _____

Vocabulary

Use the words from the box to complete the sentences below.

Vocabulary
attic
debris
frightened
hurricane
ride out the storm
shrieking

1. During a storm, the __attic__ can be a dangerous place.
2. We heard the strong winds make __shrieking__ sounds.
3. Animals are often __frightened__ by the loud noises of a storm.
4. It is best to find a safe place to __ride out the storm__
5. The winds of a __hurricane__ sometimes blow at 200 miles per hour.
6. After a storm, there is often __debris__ from trees on the streets.

6

Lesson Overview 24D

Daily Lesson Plans

Technology

Lesson Planner CD-ROM allows you to customize the chart below to develop your own lesson plans.

T Skill tested on Weekly or Theme Skills Test and/or Integrated Theme Test

 North Carolina Competency Goals indicated in blue.

	DAY 1 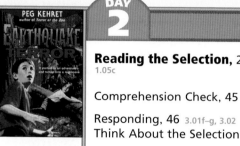	**DAY 2** 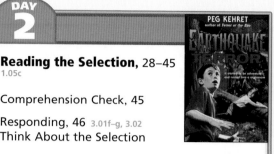
50–60 minutes 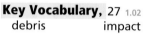		

Reading
Comprehension

Leveled Readers
- Fluency Practice
- Independent Reading

DAY 1

Teacher Read Aloud, 25G–25H
The Wreck of the E. S. Newman

Building Background, 26 1.05b, 2.02a, f, 2.03b

Key Vocabulary, 27 1.02

debris	impact	susceptible
devastation	jolt	undulating
earthquake	shuddered	upheaval
fault		

Vocabulary Reader 1.02

Reading the Selection, 28–45 1.05c

 **Comprehension Skill,** 28 2.04b
Sequence of Events **T**

Comprehension Strategy, 28 2.05, 3.01g
Predict/Infer **T**

....

Leveled Readers
Riding Out the Storm
Earthquake Alaska, 1964
Clearing the Dust
Alone in the Storm

Lessons and Leveled Practice, 51O–51R
1.05a, 2.02d, f, 2.03a, 2.04b, 3.01a, 4.01

DAY 2

Reading the Selection, 28–45 1.05c

Comprehension Check, 45

Responding, 46 3.01f–g, 3.02
Think About the Selection

Vocabulary Reader 1.02

Comprehension Skill Preview, 33 2.04b
Sequence of Events **T**

Leveled Readers
Riding Out the Storm
Earthquake Alaska, 1964
Clearing the Dust
Alone in the Storm

Lessons and Leveled Practice, 51O–51R
1.05a, 2.02d, f, 2.03a, 2.04b, 3.01a, 4.01

20–30 minutes

Word Work
Phonics/Decoding
Vocabulary
Spelling

DAY 1

Phonics/Decoding, 29
Phonics/Decoding Strategy

Vocabulary, 28–45 1.02
Selection Vocabulary

Spelling, 51E 5.05
Short Vowels **T**

DAY 2

Structural Analysis, 51C 1.01
Base Words **T**

Vocabulary, 28–45 1.02
Selection Vocabulary

Spelling, 51E 5.05
Short Vowels Review and Practice **T**

20–30 minutes

Writing and Oral Language
Writing
Grammar
Listening/Speaking/Viewing

DAY 1

Writing, 51K 4.05
Prewriting a News Article

Grammar, 51I 5.01
Kinds of Sentences **T**

Daily Language Practice 5.06
1. Did you tie the boat to the doct (dock?)
2. take a deep breeth before you begin. (Take; breath)

2.02e, f, 2.04b, 2.09c–e
Listening/Speaking/Viewing, 25G–25H, 35
Teacher Read Aloud, Stop and Think

DAY 2

Writing, 51K 4.06, 4.07
Drafting a News Article

Grammar, 51I 5.01
Kinds of Sentences Practice **T**

Daily Language Practice 5.06
3. The mayor will set up a fuhnd for the flood victims! (fund; victims.)
4. watch out for that dich! (Watch; ditch!)

Listening/Speaking/Viewing, 45, 46 4.02a, c
Wrapping Up, Responding

Target Skills of the Week

Comprehension	Predict/Infer; Sequence of Events
Vocabulary	Using a Thesaurus
Phonics/Decoding	Base Words
Fluency	Leveled Readers

DAY 3

Rereading the Selection
Rereading for Genre, 31 3.01e
Realistic Fiction
2.04b, 3.01a
Rereading for Writer's Craft, 39
Mood

Vocabulary Reader 1.02

Comprehension Skill, 51A–51B 2.04b
Sequence of Events **T**

Leveled Readers
Riding Out the Storm
Earthquake Alaska, 1964
Clearing the Dust
Alone in the Storm

Lessons and Leveled Practice, 51O–51R
1.05a, 2.02d, f, 2.03a, 2.04b, 3.01a, 4.01

Phonics Review, 51D
Short Vowels

Vocabulary, 51G 1.04
Using a Thesaurus **T**

Spelling, 51F 1.04, 5.05
Vocabulary: Definitions; Short Vowels
Practice **T**

Writing, 51L 4.08a
Revising a News Article
Adding Details

Grammar, 51J
Subjects and Predicates **T**

Daily Language Practice 5.06
5. The two boys sleept until noon? (slept; noon.)
6. Who swepped the leaves under the fence.
(swept; fence?)

DAY 4

Reading the Science Link,
48–51 1.05c, 2.03b
"El Niño"
Skill: How to Read a Science
Article 2.01

Rereading for Genre, 50 3.01e
Expository Nonfiction

Comprehension Skill Review, 37
Noting Details

Leveled Readers
Riding Out the Storm
Earthquake Alaska, 1964
Clearing the Dust
Alone in the Storm

Lessons and Leveled Practice, 51O–51R
1.05a, 2.02d, f, 2.03a, 2.04b, 3.01a, 4.01

Phonics/Decoding, 48–51
Apply Phonics/Decoding Strategy to Link

Vocabulary, 51M 1.03b
Language Center: Building Vocabulary

Spelling, 51F 5.06
Short Vowels Game, Proofreading **T**

Writing, 51L 5.06, 5.07
Proofreading a News Article

Grammar, 51J
Subjects and Predicates Practice **T**

Daily Language Practice 5.06
7. Be careful not to cresh your fingers in the car
door? (crush; (door.) or (door!))
8. Justin and amanda shared a buhch of bananas.
(Amanda; bunch)

Listening/Speaking/Viewing, 51 3.01g, 3.02
Discuss the Link

DAY 5

Rereading for Fluency, 41
4.01
3.01f–g, 3.02
Responding Activities, 46–47
Write an Adventure Story 4.07
Cross-Curricular Activities

Information and Study Skills, 51H 3.06
Using Reference Sources **T**

Comprehension Skill Review, 43 2.04a
Story Structure

Other Cross-Curricular Activities, 23I–23J and
25E–25F SC1.05, SC3.02a–e, SC3.03

Leveled Readers
Riding Out the Storm
Earthquake Alaska, 1964
Clearing the Dust
Alone in the Storm

Lessons and Leveled Practice, 51O–51R
1.05a, 2.02d, f, 2.03a, 2.04b, 3.01a, 4.01

Phonics, 51M 1.01
Language Center: Trading Bases

Vocabulary, 51M 1.03b
Language Center: Vocabulary Game

Spelling, 51F 5.05
Test: Short Vowels **T**

Writing, 51L 4.04
Publishing a News Article

Grammar, 51J, 51N 5.01
Sentence Combining
Language Center: Safety Sentences

Daily Language Practice 5.06
9. Did the staf tell you when your puppy could
come home (staff; home?)
10. is she fonde of chocolate chip cookies?
(Is; fond)

Listening/Speaking/Viewing, 51N 4.02a–c
Language Center: Panel Discussion
Other Cross-Curricular Activities, 23I–23J and
25E–25F SC1.05, SC3.02a–e, SC3.03

Managing Flexible Groups

	DAY 1	**DAY 2**
WHOLE CLASS	• Teacher Read Aloud (TE pp. 25G–25H) • Building Background, Introducing Vocabulary (TE pp. 26–27) • Comprehension Strategy: Introduce (TE p. 28) • Comprehension Skill: Introduce (TE p. 28) • Purpose Setting (TE p. 29) **After reading first half of *Earthquake Terror*** • Stop and Think (TE p. 35)	**After reading *Earthquake Terror*** • Wrapping Up (TE p. 45) • Comprehension Check (Practice Book p. 13) • Responding: Think About the Selection (TE p. 46) • Comprehension Skill: Preview (TE p. 33)

SMALL GROUPS

Leveled Instruction and Leveled Practice

	DAY 1	**DAY 2**
Extra Support	**TEACHER-LED** • Preview vocabulary; support reading with Vocabulary Reader. • Preview *Earthquake Terror* to Stop and Think (TE pp. 28–35). • Support reading with Extra Support/Intervention notes (TE pp. 29–31, 34, 38, 41, 44).	**Partner or Individual Work** • Reread first half of *Earthquake Terror* (TE pp. 28–35). • Preview, read second half (TE pp. 36–45). • Comprehension Check (Practice Book p. 13)
Challenge	**Individual Work** • Begin "Major Earthquake Map" (Challenge Handbook p. 2). • Extend reading with Challenge Note (TE p. 44).	**Individual Work** • Continue work on activity (Challenge Handbook p. 2).
English Language Learners	**TEACHER-LED** • Preview vocabulary; support reading with Vocabulary Reader. • Preview *Earthquake Terror* to Stop and Think (TE pp. 28–35). • Support reading with English Language Learners notes (TE pp. 26, 32, 34, 39, 40, 42, 45).	**TEACHER-LED** • Review first half of *Earthquake Terror* (TE pp. 28–35). ✔ • Preview, read second half (TE pp. 36–45). • Begin Comprehension Check together (Practice Book p. 13).

Independent Activities

• Get Set for Reading CD-Rom
• Journals: selection notes, questions
• Complete, review Practice Book pages (11–15) and Leveled Readers Practice Blackline Masters (TE pp. 51O–51R).
• Assignment Cards (Teachers Resource Blackline Masters, pp. 47–48)
• Leveled Readers (TE pp. 51O–51R), Leveled Theme Paperbacks (TE pp. R2–R7), or book from Leveled Bibliography (TE pp. 23E–23F)

✔ Opportunity to informally assess oral reading rate

DAY 3

- Rereading: Lessons on Genre, Writer's Craft (TE pp. 31, 39)
- Comprehension Skill: Main lesson (TE pp. 51A–51B)

TEACHER-LED

- Reread, review Comprehension Check (Practice Book p. 13).
- Preview Leveled Reader: Below Level (TE p. 51O), or read book from Leveled Bibliography (TE pp. 23E–23F). ✔

TEACHER-LED

- Teacher check-in: Assess progress (Challenge Handbook p. 2).
- Preview Leveled Reader: Above Level (TE p. 51Q), or read book from Leveled Bibliography (TE pp. 23E–23F). ✔

Partner or Individual Work

- Complete Comprehension Check (Practice Book p. 13).
- Begin Leveled Reader: Language Support (TE p. 51R), or read book from Leveled Bibliography (TE pp. 23E–23F).

DAY 4

- Reading the Science Link (TE pp. 48–51): Skill lesson (TE p. 48)
- Rereading the Link: Genre lesson (TE p. 50)
- Comprehension Skill: First Comprehension Review lesson (TE p. 37)

Partner or Individual Work

- Reread Science Link (TE pp. 48–51).
- Complete Leveled Reader: Below Level (TE p. 51O), or read book from Leveled Bibliography (TE pp. 23E–23F).

Individual Work

- Complete activity (Challenge Handbook p. 2).
- Complete Leveled Reader: Above Level (TE p. 51Q), or read book from Leveled Bibliography (TE pp. 23E–23F).

TEACHER-LED

- Reread the Science Link (TE pp. 48–51) ✔ and review Link Skill (TE p. 48).
- Complete Leveled Reader: Language Support (TE p. 51R), or read book from Leveled Bibliography (TE pp. 23E–23F). ✔

DAY 5

- Responding: Select from Activities (TE pp. 46–47)
- Information and Study Skills (TE p. 51H)
- Comprehension Skill: Second Comprehension Review lesson (TE p. 43)

TEACHER-LED

- Comprehension Skill: Reteaching lesson (TE p. R8)
- Preview, begin Leveled Theme Paperback: Below Level (TE pp. R2–R3), or read book from Leveled Bibliography (TE pp. 23E–23F). ✔

TEACHER-LED

- Evaluate activity and plan format for sharing (Challenge Handbook p. 2).
- Read Leveled Theme Paperback: Above Level (TE pp. R6–R7), or read book from Leveled Bibliography (TE pp. 23E–23F). ✔

Partner or Individual Work

- Preview, read book from Leveled Bibliography (TE pp. 23E–23F).

- Responding activities (pp. 46–47)
- Language Center activities (TE pp. 51M–51N)
- **Fluency Practice:** Reread *Earthquake Terror*. ✔
- Activities relating to *Earthquake Terror* at Education Place www.eduplace.com

Turn the page for more independent activities.

Classroom Management

Independent Activities

Assign these activities while you work with small groups.

Differentiated Instruction for Small Groups

- **Handbook for English Language Learners**, pp. 18–27

- **Extra Support Handbook**, pp. 14–23

Independent Activities

- Language Center, pp. 51M–51N

- Challenge/Extension Activities, Resources, pp. R9, R15

- **Classroom Management Handbook**, Activity Masters CM1-1–CM1-4

- **Challenge Handbook**, Challenge Masters CH1-1–CH1-2

Look for more activities in the Classroom Management Kit.

Technology

Earthquake Alert!

👥 Pairs	🕐 45 minutes
Objective	Research and report on earthquake technology.
Materials	Internet, encyclopedia, paper, pencils

Knowing when and where an earthquake will strike can help save lives. But how do scientists predict earthquakes? How do they know when or where an earthquake might strike? Write a brief report that answers these questions.

- Use Internet sites or encyclopedias to research the science of earthquake prediction.

- Write a brief report that summarizes what instruments scientists use to help them.

- If possible, include a diagram or other visual aid.

Social Studies

Location, Location, Location

👥 Pairs	🕐 30 minutes
Objective	Find out where earthquakes happen.
Materials	World map, almanac, paper, pencils

Jonathan remembers learning that earthquakes occur along the Pacific Ocean. Find out where else they occur.

- Use an almanac to find the names of places that have experienced major earthquakes.

- With a partner, make a list of cities and countries that have had earthquakes.

- Using a world map, locate the places on your list.

- Practice finding the cities and countries on the map as quickly as possible.

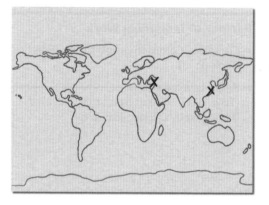

Consider copying and laminating these activities for use in centers.

Art

Name That Tree

Singles	⏲ 45 minutes
Objective	Learn about and draw trees.
Materials	Encyclopedia, paper, colored pencils, markers, paints

If you saw a redwood tree, would you recognize it? Use art to add to your knowledge about different kinds of trees.

- Use an encyclopedia to learn about types of trees, such as redwood, maple, birch, elm, or pine.
- Note different features of these trees, including their leaves, bark, height, and circumference.
- Make pictures of three trees that interest you. For each, include an inset of an enlarged leaf or needle.
- Label your pictures.

Writing

Extra!

👥 Pairs	⏲ 30 minutes
Objective	Write a fictional news article.
Materials	Anthology

Write a news article about what might have happened during the aftermath of the Magpie Island earthquake.

- Use story details and your imagination to describe events.
- Begin with a lead sentence that tells the most important information.
- Be sure your article answers the questions *Who?, What?, Where?, When?, Why?,* and *How?*
- Remember to write a catchy headline for your article.

Science

Dog Smarts

👥 Pairs	⏲ 30 minutes
Objective	Research canine senses.
Materials	Encyclopedia, paper, pencils

If the sky turns dark gray at noon and the air feels sticky, you can tell a storm is approaching. But a dog can sometimes sense storms or earthquakes before noticeable clues appear. Find out why!

- Use an encyclopedia or dog reference book to find out about dog senses.
- Note which senses are particularly strong in dogs.
- Write a brief report about how these senses can help dogs predict storms and earthquakes.

Listening Comprehension

OBJECTIVES

- Listen to identify the sequence of events.

Building Background

Tell students that you are going to read aloud an exciting true story about a very difficult rescue in stormy weather.

- Ask students to share what they know about shipwrecks.
- Help students locate the Outer Banks of North Carolina on a map.

Fluency Modeling

Explain that as you read aloud, you will be modeling fluent oral reading. Ask students to listen to your phrasing and expression.

COMPREHENSION SKILL

Sequence of Events

Explain the following:

- Keeping track of the order, or sequence, of events in a story helps readers understand the selection.
- Clue words such as *first, then, finally, after, later,* and *before* help readers keep track of the sequence of events.

Purpose Setting Read the selection aloud, as students listen for clue words. Then use the Guiding Comprehension questions to assess students' understanding. Reread for clarification as needed.

The Wreck of the *E.S. Newman*

by Ruth Ewers

At the turn of the century, the African American crew of the Pea Island Rescue Station, under the helm of Richard Etheridge, saved hundreds of lives on North Carolina's dangerous Outer Banks. Of the crew's many rescues, none was more heroic than its response to the *E.S. Newman*, a three-masted schooner.

Violent winds swept the ocean, and waves thundered to shore, shaking the lookout tower at Pea Island Rescue Station. Surfman Theodore Meekins was on watch that evening of October 11, 1896. A hurricane had struck the Outer Banks of North Carolina, and the tide was so strong that beach patrols had been canceled.

Offshore, the schooner *E.S. Newman* was caught in the storm. The wind ripped the sails from the masts, and mountainous waves smashed onto the decks. The captain, whose wife and child were on board, feared the *Newman* would soon break up. He made the decision to beach his ship, then fired a distress signal, praying that someone onshore would see it.

Meekins, whose eyes were trained to cut through rain and surf mists, thought he saw the signal, but so much spray covered the lookout windows that he could hardly make out the buildings of the station, much less the

❶ horizon offshore. Still, he took no chances. After summoning the station keeper, Captain Richard Etheridge, Meekins set off a coston signal. Together, the two men searched the darkness for a reply. A few moments later, they saw a flash of light to the south and knew a ship was in distress. Even before the return signal burned out, Keeper Etheridge had summoned his men and begun rescue operations.

② Noting the treacherous surf and wind conditions, Captain Etheridge quickly decided the surf boats would be impossible to maneuver. Instead, he instructed his men to load the beach cart with coils of line, powder, shot, and the lyle gun.

The crew set off on the long trek down the beach to the scene of the wreck. Captain Etheridge hoped to fire a line from the gun to the ship's mast. After the ship's crew dragged the line on board, the surfmen would fire a second line. Secured to a spar of the ship, this second line would hold the breeches buoy, a harness for carrying survivors safely to shore. Struggling with the weight of the 185-pound gun, the surfmen crossed three miles of sand and boiling foam to reach the stranded ship. The water was freezing, and the men often sank up to their knees in sand. Captain Etheridge noted in his logbook that "the voice of gladden hearts greeted the arrival of the station crew," but that "it seemed impossible under such circumstances to render any assistance. The team was often brought to a standstill by the sweeping current," and the *Newman* was "rolling and tossing well upon the beach with head sails all blown away."

Even when the rescue equipment proved useless, Etheridge refused to give up. Choosing two of his strongest surfmen, he tied rope lines around their waists and sent them into the surging water. The two men, lashed together and holding a line from shore, waded as far as they could before diving through the waves. Nearly worn out by the exertion of swimming against the tide, they finally made it to the vessel.

③ The first to be rescued were the captain's wife and child. With the two passengers tied to their backs, the surfmen fought their way back to shore. Taking turns, Etheridge and his crew made ten trips to the *Newman*, saving every person on board. It was 1:00 A.M. when the crew and survivors finally made it back to the station. That night, as the exhausted survivors lay sleeping and his lifesaving crew rested, Captain Etheridge picked up his pen, and in the flickering light of an oil lantern, wrote with satisfaction that all the people on board had been saved and were "sheltered in this station"—words he would write for many years to come.

Guiding Comprehension

❶ **SEQUENCE OF EVENTS** What did Meekins do as soon as he realized that someone had sent a distress signal? (He summoned Captain Etheridge, the station keeper, and set off a signal.)

❷ **SEQUENCE OF EVENTS** Why did Captain Etheridge decide not to use surf boats to rescue the people aboard the *Newman*? (He knew that conditions were so bad that he and the crew could not manage the surf boats.)

❸ **SEQUENCE OF EVENTS** What happened once the two surfmen reached the ship? (First, they rescued the captain's wife and child. Then they took turns getting the others on board. Finally, the rescuers made it back to the station.) What clue words helped you follow the order of events? (*first, finally, That night*)

Discussion Options

Personal Response Ask students to tell how they would describe the men who performed the rescue. Ask students how they think they might act in similar circumstances.

⭐ **Connecting/Comparing** Ask students to tell why they think this story was included in the theme *Nature's Fury*.

English Language Learners

Language Development

Write *wreck, shipwreck, hurricane,* and *schooner* on the board, inviting students to give brief meanings for each word. Discuss with students what a *hurricane* is and why it would be so dangerous for ships. If possible, show students illustrations of a schooner and discuss how ships have changed since the late 1800s.

Background and Vocabulary

Key Concept: Causes and Effects of Earthquakes

Remind students that this theme is about the power of nature. Students have just heard a Read Aloud about a terrible storm at sea. Next they will read a story called *Earthquake Terror*.

Discuss the kinds of challenges an earthquake might bring. Then use "Buildup to a Shakeup" on Anthology pages 26–27 to build background and introduce Key Vocabulary.

- Have a volunteer read aloud "Buildup to a Shakeup."

- Use the map to discuss the setting of the story—California. Have students trace the San Andreas fault and discuss how it might affect the story plot.

Vocabulary Preview

The Vocabulary Reader can be used to preteach or reinforce the key vocabulary.

Vocabulary Reader

The San Francisco **Earthquake** by Rob Arego

Get Set to Read

Background and Vocabulary

PEG KEHRET
author of *Terror of the Zoo*

EARTHQUAKE TERROR

It started as an adventure and turned into a nightmare

Earthquake Terror

Genre Realistic Fiction

Key Vocabulary

devastation
earthquake
fault
jolt
undulating
upheaval

Vocabulary Reader

The San Francisco **Earthquake** by Rob Arego

e Glossary

26

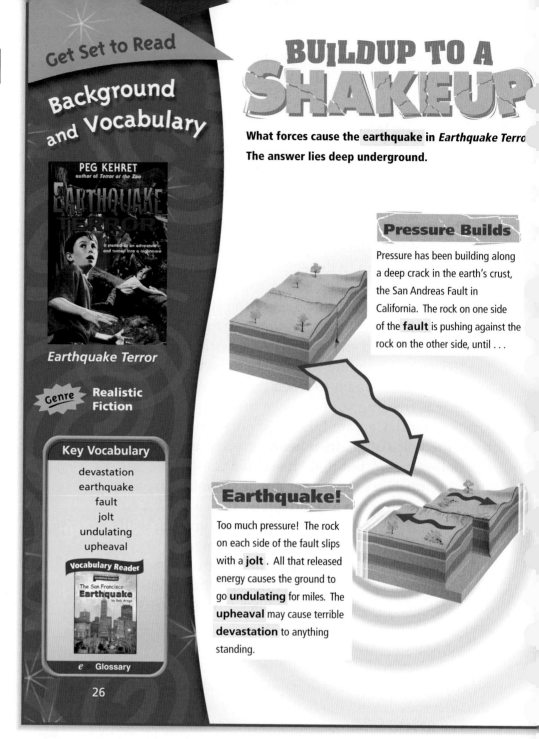

BUILDUP TO A SHAKEUP

What forces cause the **earthquake** in *Earthquake Terror*? The answer lies deep underground.

Pressure Builds

Pressure has been building along a deep crack in the earth's crust, the San Andreas Fault in California. The rock on one side of the **fault** is pushing against the rock on the other side, until . . .

Earthquake!

Too much pressure! The rock on each side of the fault slips with a **jolt**. All that released energy causes the ground to go **undulating** for miles. The **upheaval** may cause terrible **devastation** to anything standing.

English Language Learners

Supporting Comprehension

Beginning/Preproduction Have students listen to the article. Then ask them to point to the illustrations that show the causes and the effects of earthquakes.

Early Production and Speech Emergence Have students repeat the Key Vocabulary words after you. Use the illustrations to help students understand *debris*, *devastation*, and *fault*. Explain *susceptible*, and mime the meaning of the remaining words.

Intermediate and Advanced Fluency Have students work in small groups to read and then restate in their own words the causes and effects of earthquakes.

The San Andreas Fault runs from southern California to just north of San Francisco. The author puts Magpie Island, the fictional setting of *Earthquake Terror*, in its path.

A road in California's Santa Cruz Mountains, south of San Francisco, shows extensive damage from the "World Series Earthquake" that struck part of the San Andreas Fault in October, 1989.

27

Introducing Vocabulary

Key Vocabulary

These words support the Key Concept and appear in the selection.

debris the remains of something broken or destroyed

devastation destruction or ruin

earthquake a trembling or shaking of the ground caused by movements far below the earth's surface

fault a break in a rock mass caused by a shifting of the earth's crust

impact the striking of one body against another

jolt a sudden jerk or bump

shuddered shook or vibrated

susceptible easily affected

undulating moving in waves or with a smooth, wavy motion

upheaval a lifting or upward movement of the earth's crust

 e • Glossary
e • WordGame

See Vocabulary notes on 30, 32, and 40 for additional words to preview.

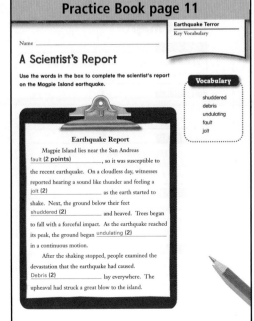

Transparency 1–1

Earthquake Words

Interviewer: Today I am happy to welcome Isaac Ramstein, an expert on earthquakes. Mr. Ramstein, help readers of the *California Daily* understand why earthquakes leave so much <u>debris</u> in their wake.

Mr. Ramstein: Earthquakes cause a tremendous amount of <u>devastation</u> because of the great <u>upheaval</u> of the ground itself.

Interviewer: Tell us what it feels like to be in an earthquake.

Mr. Ramstein: First, you may sense that the ground has <u>shuddered</u> ever so slightly beneath your feet. Next, you may feel a powerful <u>jolt</u> that can knock you down with a terrific <u>impact</u> if the quake is forceful enough. As the quake builds, the ground can feel like it is <u>undulating</u> up and down.

Interviewer: Why is California so <u>susceptible</u> to earthquakes?

Mr. Ramstein: A major <u>fault</u> runs through California, so when the crust of the earth shifts, it often shifts along that crack. Residents of the state should take precautions so they are not caught unprepared.

Interviewer: We appreciate your talking with us today, Mr. Ramstein. I'm sure our readers will take your suggestion to heart.

Practice Book page 11

Name _____

A Scientist's Report

Use the words in the box to complete the scientist's report on the Magpie Island earthquake.

Vocabulary
shuddered
debris
undulating
fault
jolt

Earthquake Report

Magpie Island lies near the San Andreas **fault (2 points)** _____, so it was susceptible to the recent earthquake. On a cloudless day, witnesses reported hearing a sound like thunder and feeling a **jolt (2)** _____ as the earth started to shake. Next, the ground below their feet **shuddered (2)** _____ and heaved. Trees began to fall with a forceful impact. As the earthquake reached its peak, the ground began **undulating (2)** _____ in a continuous motion.

After the shaking stopped, people examined the devastation that the earthquake had caused. **Debris (2)** _____ lay everywhere. The upheaval had struck a great blow to the island.

Display Transparency 1–1.

- Model how to figure out the meaning of *debris* from clues in the first two paragraphs.

- Ask students to use context clues to figure out the meaning of each remaining Key Vocabulary word. Have them explain how they figured out each.

- Ask students to look for these words as they read and to use them to discuss the causes and effects of earthquakes.

Practice/Homework Assign **Practice Book** page 11.

Introducing Vocabulary 27

COMPREHENSION STRATEGY
Predict/Infer

Teacher Modeling Ask a student to read aloud the Strategy Focus. Then have students read the introduction. Explain that in order to make a good prediction or inference, students should use text clues and their own knowledge.

Think Aloud *From the title and cover, I can predict that the two children will get caught in an earthquake. The introduction says that Jonathan is looking after his sister, and he feels uneasy. I infer that he may be worried about looking after his sister by himself.*

Test Prep Tell students to use the Predict/Infer strategy before reading each test passage. Suggest that they use the title and any illustrations to predict whether the passage is fiction or nonfiction. Then they should predict what will happen or what they will learn.

COMPREHENSION SKILL
Sequence of Events

Introduce the Graphic Organizer. Tell students that an Event Map can help them focus on the sequence of events in *Earthquake Terror.* Explain that as they read, students will fill out the Event Map on **Practice Book** page 12.

- Display **Transparency 1–2.** Have students read Anthology pages 29–30, stopping after *"I'm hot,"* Abby said. *"It's too hot to eat."*

- Model how to complete the first box on the Event Map. Monitor students' work as needed.

28 **THEME 1: Nature's Fury**

Selection 1

PEG KEHRET
author of *Terror at the Zoo*

EARTHQUAKE TERROR

It started as an adventure— and turned into a nightmare

Strategy Focus

Think about the selection title and cover illustration. What do you **predict** Jonathan will do to protect himself and his younger sister when a powerful earthquake strikes?

28

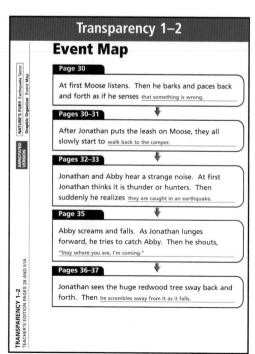

Transparency 1–2
Event Map

Page 30
At first Moose listens. Then he barks and paces back and forth as if he senses that something is wrong.

Pages 30–31
After Jonathan puts the leash on Moose, they all slowly start to walk back to the camper.

Pages 32–33
Jonathan and Abby hear a strange noise. At first Jonathan thinks it is thunder or hunters. Then suddenly he realizes they are caught in an earthquake.

Page 35
Abby screams and falls. As Jonathan lunges forward, he tries to catch Abby. Then he shouts, "Stay where you are, I'm coming."

Pages 36–37
Jonathan sees the huge redwood tree sway back and forth. Then he scrambles away from it as it falls.

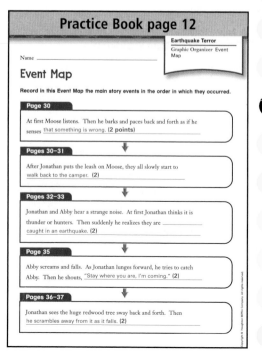

Practice Book page 12

Earthquake Terror
Graphic Organizer Event Map

Name _____

Event Map

Record in this Event Map the main story events in the order in which they occurred.

Page 30
At first Moose listens. Then he barks and paces back and forth as if he senses that something is wrong. **(2 points)**

Pages 30–31
After Jonathan puts the leash on Moose, they all slowly start to walk back to the camper. **(2)**

Pages 32–33
Jonathan and Abby hear a strange noise. At first Jonathan thinks it is thunder or hunters. Then suddenly he realizes they are _____ caught in an earthquake. **(2)**

Page 35
Abby screams and falls. As Jonathan lunges forward, he tries to catch Abby. Then he shouts, "Stay where you are, I'm coming." **(2)**

Pages 36–37
Jonathan sees the huge redwood tree sway back and forth. Then he scrambles away from it as it falls. **(2)**

A family vacation begins peacefully in the woods of Magpie Island. Then Jonathan and Abby's mom breaks her ankle, and their dad has to rush her to the hospital. He promises to return in three hours, leaving Jonathan, age twelve, in charge of his six-year-old sister, whose legs are partially paralyzed. Moose, the family's dog, is with them. But Jonathan is uneasy.

In his mind, Jonathan could see his father unhitching the small camping trailer. He pictured the car going along the narrow, winding road that meandered from the campground through the woods. He saw the high bridge that crossed the river, connecting the island campground to the mainland.

He imagined his father driving across the bridge, faster than usual, with Mom lying down in the back seat. Or maybe she wouldn't lie down. Maybe, even with a broken ankle, she would wear her seat belt. She always did, and she insisted that Jonathan and Abby wear theirs.

29

Extra Support/Intervention

Selection Preview

pages 29–31 As Jonathan and Abby start back to their campsite, their dog, Moose, begins to act strangely. Why might Moose act that way?

pages 32–35 Jonathan hears loud noises and feels a sudden jolt. What's happening in the illustrations? What do you think happens next?

pages 36–39 By now Jonathan is certain they're caught in an earthquake. He's learned what to do inside his school, but now they're outdoors. Look at the illustrations. What do you think the children will do?

pages 40–44 What do you think happens after the earthquake stops? Do you think the children will be safe?

Purpose Setting

- Remind students that they will read a story called *Earthquake Terror*.

- Have students preview the selection by looking at the illustrations. Ask students to predict what they might learn about earthquakes.

- Have students read to confirm or change their predictions as the story unfolds.

- Ask students to pay attention to the order in which story events happen.

- You may want to preview with students the Responding questions on Anthology page 46.

Journal ▶ Students can record any revisions they made to their predictions and explain what made them change their minds.

STRATEGY REVIEW

Phonics/Decoding

Remind students to use the Phonics/Decoding Strategy as they read.

Modeling Write this sentence from *Earthquake Terror* on the board: *"Mommy!" Abby's shrill cry rose above the <u>thundering</u> noise.* Point to *thundering*.

Think Aloud *To figure out this word, I'll drop the -ing and try to break the rest of the word into syllables. The word starts with t-h followed by un. That might sound like thuhn. The second syllable probably sounds like dur. If I blend all the sounds together, I'll get THUHN-dur-ihng. That word makes sense in the sentence.*

CRITICAL THINKING

Guiding Comprehension

1 **DRAWING CONCLUSIONS** What do Jonathan's thoughts of home tell you about how he feels in his present situation? (He is nervous about being in the woods, far from help.)

2 **DRAWING CONCLUSIONS** What does the author mean by the passage that begins *Time had a way of evaporating instantly...?* (Time passes quickly for Jonathan when he is doing things he enjoys.)

3 **WRITER'S CRAFT** How does the author reveal Jonathan's feelings about Abby? (By telling how Jonathan makes sure to walk behind Abby, the author shows that Jonathan is caring and protective.)

Moose cocked his head, as if listening to something. Then he ran toward the trail, sniffing the ground.

"Moose," Jonathan called. "Come back."

Moose paused, looked at Jonathan, and barked.

"Come!"

Moose returned but he continued to smell the ground and pace back and forth.

"Moose wants Mommy," Abby said.

Moose suddenly stood still, his legs stiff and his tail up. He barked again.

"Silly old dog," Abby said.

He knows something is wrong, Jonathan thought. Dogs sense things. He knows I'm worried about Mom. Jonathan patted Moose's head. "It's all right, Moose. Good dog."

Moose barked again.

"I'm hot," Abby said. "It's too hot to eat."

"Let's start back. It'll be cooler in the shade and we can finish our lunch in the camper."

Maybe he could relax in the camper. Here he felt jumpy. He didn't like being totally out of communication with the rest of the world. Whenever he stayed alone at home, or took care of Abby, there was always a telephone at his fingertips or a neighbor just down the street. If he had a problem, he could call his parents or Mrs. Smith next door or even nine-one-one.

Here he was isolated. I wouldn't do well as a forest ranger, Jonathan thought. How do they stand being alone in the woods all the time?

He rewrapped the uneaten food, buckled the backpack over his shoulders, and put the leash on Moose. The goofy way Moose was acting, he might bolt down the trail and not come back.

30

Extra Support/Intervention

Demonstrate the Concept

Place two paperback books flat on a desk next to each other so their pages touch and their spines face outward. Push on the spines until the books shift or buckle. Explain that a similar thing happens along a fault line.

Vocabulary

isolated separated from others

Jonathan helped Abby stand up and placed her walker in position. Slowly, they began the journey across the sand and into the woods, to follow the trail through the trees.

Jonathan wished he had worn a watch. It seemed as if his parents had been gone long enough to get partway to town, but it was hard to be sure. Time had a way of evaporating instantly when he was engrossed in an interesting project, such as cataloging his baseball cards, or reading a good mystery. But time dragged unbearably when he was in the dentist's office or waiting for a ride. It was hard to estimate how much time had passed since his parents waved good-bye and walked away. Forty minutes? An hour?

2

Abby walked in front of him. That way he could see her and know if she needed help, and it kept him from going too fast. When he was in the lead, he usually got too far ahead, even when he tried to walk slowly.

3

31

Realistic Fiction

Teach

- Explain that realistic fiction always includes a realistic problem and solution and characters who speak, think, feel, and act as real people do.

- Point out that events that occur in realistic fiction could happen in real life, even though the author created them.

Practice

- Point out how Jonathan's worries about being far from help make him seem like a real person.

- Then ask students to identify other details that make *Earthquake Terror* realistic fiction. (the realistic campground setting, the children's reactions to the earthquake)

Apply

- Have small groups create a chart like the one below to show how Jonathan behaves like a real person.

- Have groups compare their work.

Realistic Story Elements

Problem The children and dog are alone during an earthquake.

Solution Jonathan remembers what to do from drills at school.

Extra Support/Intervention

Strategy Modeling: Predict/Infer

Use this example to model the strategy.

On page 31, I see that Jonathan walks behind his sister so he can see if she needs help. I can use this clue to infer that he does this because he cares for Abby. I predict that if Abby runs into trouble later in the story, Jonathan will try to help her.

CRITICAL THINKING

Guiding Comprehension

④ MAKING INFERENCES Why does the author say that Jonathan *felt as if he were on a surfboard?* (to help readers understand what it feels like to experience an earthquake)

COMPREHENSION STRATEGY

Predict/Infer

Teacher/Student Modeling Discuss clues on page 32 that can help students predict that trouble is on the way. (Sample answer: From the sentence *Jonathan noticed again how quiet it was,* readers can infer that the quiet is not normal.)

Ask students what they can infer and predict from the sentence *The noise came closer; it was too sharp to be thunder.* (There is a storm coming, but it is not a thunderstorm.)

Vocabulary

stifling very hot or stuffy; suffocating

frantic very excited, as from fear or worry

jolt a sudden jerk or bump

earthquake a trembling or shaking of the ground caused by movements far below the earth's surface

---

While they walked Jonathan planned what he would do when they got back to the camper. As soon as he got Abby settled on her bed, he would turn on the radio and listen to the ball game. That would give him something to think about. The San Francisco Giants were his favorite baseball team and he hoped they would win the World Series.

Jonathan noticed again how quiet it was. No magpies cawed, no leaves rustled overhead. The air was stifling, with no hint of breeze.

Moose barked. Jonathan jumped at the sudden noise. It was Moose's warning bark, the one he used when a stranger knocked on the door. He stood beside Jonathan and barked again. The dog's eyes had a frantic look. He was shaking, the way he always did during a thunderstorm.

"What's wrong, boy?" Jonathan asked. He reached out to pet Moose but the dog tugged toward Abby and barked at her.

"Hush, Moose," Abby said.

Jonathan looked in all directions. He saw nothing unusual. There were still no people and no animals that would startle Moose and set him off. Jonathan listened hard, wondering if Moose had heard something that Jonathan couldn't hear.

Abby stopped walking. "What was that?" she said.

"What was what?"

Jonathan listened. He heard a deep rumbling sound in the distance.

Thunder? He looked up. The sky was bright and cloudless. The noise came closer; it was too sharp to be thunder. It was more like several rifles being fired at the same time.

Hunters! he thought. There are hunters in the woods and they heard us move and they've mistaken us for deer or pheasant. Moose must have seen them or heard them or possibly smelled them.

32

English Language Learners

Supporting Comprehension

After they read page 32, ask students to summarize what has happened so far. Guide them with these questions: Who are the children, and where are they? Why aren't their parents there? In what ways is the dog's behavior strange?

"Don't shoot!" he cried.

As he yelled, Jonathan felt a jolt. He stumbled forward, thrusting an arm out to brace himself against a tree. Another loud noise exploded as Jonathan lurched sideways.

He dropped the leash.

Abby screamed.

A bomb? Jonathan thought. Who would bomb a deserted campground?

The noise continued, and the earth moved beneath his feet. As he felt himself lifted, he knew that the sound was not hunters with guns. It was not a bomb, either.

Earthquake! The word flashed across his brain as if he had seen it blazing on a neon sign.

He felt as if he were on a surfboard, catching a giant wave, rising, cresting, and sliding back down again. Except he was standing on dry land.

4

33

ASSIGNMENT CARD 3

The Way I See It

Character's Perspective

This story is told from Jonathan's perspective. The reader experiences the same sounds, smells, memories, and sensations as Jonathan. How would the story be different if it were told from the perspective of Abby or Moose?

- For Abby, consider her age, her physical limitations, and her feelings toward her brother.

- For Moose, consider his extrasensitive senses of smell and hearing, and his inability to speak to Abby and Jonathan.

Theme 1: Nature's Fury

Teacher's Resource BLM page 48

 Sequence of Events

Teach

- Explain that sequence of events is the order in which events happen.

- Point out that an author may tell events in chronological order, the order in which the events happened.

- Review words that help signal sequence, such as *while, as soon as, and, ever since,* and *then.*

Practice

- Have students reread pages 32–33.

- Ask students to describe the order in which events happen. (Sample answer: As the children walk, Jonathan notices how quiet it is. Then Moose starts to bark. The children hear a rumbling noise. Finally, they feel the earthquake.)

- Have students identify any words that signal sequence. (page 32: *while, as soon as*; page 33: *as*)

Apply

- Have students work in pairs to determine the sequence of events in other parts of the story. (Sample answer: On page 38, Jonathan drags Abby to the redwood tree. Then he tells Abby to get under the tree.) Ask students to identify any signal words they see. (*finally, began, as, when*)

Target Skill Trace	
Preview; Teach	pp. 25E, 28, p. 33; p. 51A
Reteach	p. R8
Review	pp. M35–M35; p. 71; Theme 2, p. 213

Reading the Selection **33**

CRITICAL THINKING
Guiding Comprehension

⑤ NOTING DETAILS Why do you think the author includes Jonathan's memories about school earthquake drills? (to explain how Jonathan knows about earthquakes and earthquake safety procedures)

⑥ MAKING INFERENCES What does the author mean in the passage *That was school. This was Magpie Island?* (Jonathan only knows what to do inside the school building, not out in the woods.)

34

Vocabulary

fault a break in a rock mass caused by a shifting of the earth's crust

susceptible easily affected

 Extra Support/ Intervention

Review (pages 28–34)
Before students who need extra support join the whole class for Stop and Think on page 35, have them

- check predictions
- take turns modeling Predict/Infer and other strategies they used
- help you add to **Transparency 1–2**
- check and revise their Event Map on **Practice Book** page 12, and use it to summarize

English Language Learners

Language Development
Have students locate the word *unable* in the last paragraph on page 35.

- Tell students to place their finger over the letters *un.*
- Remind them that *able* means "can." Say that *un-* is a prefix that means "not."
- Write *important* and *comfortable* on the board. Write *un* before each word. Ask students to give the meanings of these words.

"Jonathan!" Abby's scream was lost in the thunderous noise. He saw her fall, her walker flying off to one side as she went down. Jonathan lunged forward, arms outstretched, trying to catch Abby before she hit the ground. He couldn't get there fast enough.

The ground dropped away beneath his feet as if a trapdoor had opened. His legs buckled and he sank to his knees. He reached for a tree trunk, to steady himself, but before his hand touched it, the tree moved.

Jonathan's stomach rose into his throat, the way it sometimes did on a fast elevator.

Ever since first grade, when the Palmers moved to California, Jonathan had practiced earthquake drills in school each year. He knew that most earthquakes occur along the shores of the Pacific Ocean. He knew that the San Andreas fault runs north and south for hundreds of miles in California, making that land particularly susceptible to earthquakes. He knew that if an earthquake hit while he was in school, he was supposed to crawl under his desk or under a table because injury was most likely to be caused by the roof caving in on him.

That was school. This was Magpie Island. How should he protect himself in the woods? Where could he hide?

He struggled to his feet again. Ahead of him, Abby lay whimpering on the ground. Moose stood beside her, his head low.

"Put your hands over your head," Jonathan called.

The ground shook again, and Jonathan struggled to remain on his feet.

"I'm coming," he shouted. "Stay where you are. I'm coming!"

But he did not go to her. He couldn't.

He staggered sideways, unable to keep his balance. He felt as if he were riding a roller coaster standing up, except the ground rocked back and forth at the same time that it rolled up and down.

(5)

(6)

35

Stop and Think

Critical Thinking Questions

1. **MAKING GENERALIZATIONS** Using Jonathan's experience, describe how it feels to be in an earthquake. (Sample answer: like being on a surfboard or a fast elevator)

2. **PREDICTING OUTCOMES** Will Jonathan be able to use what he learned in school earthquake drills? Explain. (He has learned how to protect himself in a building, so maybe that will give him clues about how to protect himself in the woods.)

Strategies in Action

Have students take turns modeling Predict/Infer and other strategies they used.

Discussion Options

You may wish to bring the entire class together to do one or more of the following activities.

- **Review Predictions/Purpose** Discuss students' predictions. Record any changes and new predictions.

- **Share Group Discussions** Have students share their questions and literature discussions.

- **Summarize** Help students use their Event Maps to summarize the story so far.

ASSIGNMENT CARD 2

Literature Discussion

Discuss your own questions and the following questions with a group of your classmates:

- How does the story remind you of any real-life experiences?

- How is Jonathan protective of Abby?

- What would you like to ask Jonathan about his experience? What would you like to ask Abby?

Theme 1: Nature's Fury

Teacher's Resource BLM page 47

Monitoring Student Progress

If . . .	Then . . .
students have successfully completed the Extra Support activities on page 34,	have them read the rest of the selection cooperatively or independently.

CRITICAL THINKING

Guiding Comprehension

7 **NOTING DETAILS** Which details on page 36 tell you that this earthquake is a strong rather than weak one? (The author calls it a *big one*; This earthquake is strong enough to knock over trees, including a huge redwood.)

8 **CAUSE AND EFFECT** What causes Jonathan to scramble across the ground away from the redwood tree? (The tree starts to fall toward him.)

A clump of small birch trees swayed like dancers and then fell.

The rumbling noise continued, surrounding him, coming from every direction at once. It was like standing in the center of a huge orchestra, with kettle drums pounding on all sides.

Abby's screams and Moose's barking blended with the noise.

Although there was no roof to cave in on him, Jonathan put his arms over his head as he fell. The school's earthquake drills had taught him to protect his head and he did it the only way he could.

Earthquake.

He had never felt an earthquake before and he had always wondered how it would feel. He had questioned his teacher, that first year. "How will I know it's an earthquake?" he asked. "If it's a big one," the teacher said, "you'll know."

His teacher had been right. Jonathan knew. He knew with a certainty that made the hair rise on the back of his neck. He was in the middle of an earthquake now. A big one.

7 The ground heaved, pitching Jonathan into the air.

Jonathan hit the ground hard, jarring every bone in his body. Immediately, the earth below him moved, tossing him into the air again.

As he dropped back down, he saw the trunk of a giant redwood tree tremble. The huge tree swayed back and forth for a few moments and then tilted toward Jonathan.

8 Frantically, he crawled to his left, rushing to get out of the tree's path.

The roots ripped loose slowly, as if not wanting to relinquish their century-long hold on the dirt.

As Jonathan scrambled across the unsteady ground, he clenched his teeth, bracing himself for the impact.

36

Vocabulary

impact the striking of one body against another

shuddered shook or vibrated

The tree fell. Air whizzed across Jonathan as the tree trunk dropped past, and branches brushed his shoulder, scratching his arms. The redwood crashed beside him, missing him by only a few feet. It thudded down, landing at an angle on another fallen tree. Dirt and dry leaves whooshed into the air, and then settled slowly back down.

The earth shuddered, but Jonathan didn't know if it was from the impact of the tree or another jolt from the earthquake.

With his heart in his throat, Jonathan crept away from the redwood tree, toward Abby. Beneath him, the ground swelled and retreated, like ocean waves. Twice he sprawled facedown in the dirt, unable to keep his balance. The second time, he lay still, with his eyes closed. How much longer would this go on? Maybe he should just lie there and wait until this earthquake was over.

37

Noting Details

Review

- Remind students that noting details can help them to understand important information about characters.

- It can also help them picture the setting and visualize what happens during story events.

Practice

- Read aloud this sentence from page 36: *Jonathan hit the ground hard, jarring every bone in his body.*

- Ask: What does this detail tell you? (exactly how Jonathan fell)

Apply

- Have students note details about the characters, events, and setting in a chart like the one below. (Sample answers shown.)

Story Details

Characters: Jonathan holds Moose and is relieved that the dog is not hurt. (p. 40)

Events: The earthquake has stopped as suddenly as it had started. (p. 40)

Setting: After the earthquake, it is so quiet Jonathan doesn't hear animals or even wind. (p. 41)

Review Skill Trace	
Teach	Theme 4, p. 391A
Reteach	Theme 4, p. R12
▶ Review	p. 37; Theme 2, p. 197; Theme 5, p. 481

Guiding Comprehension

READ & COMPREHEND

9 MAKING INFERENCES Why do you think Jonathan tells Abby *"It's only an earthquake"*? (He doesn't want Abby to worry or know that he is afraid; He is trying to convince himself they'll be okay.)

10 MAKING INFERENCES Why do you think the author describes Jonathan's memory about earthquakes here? (to emphasize that the danger is serious; to connect the story to real life)

11 NOTING DETAILS Describe how the fallen tree provides shelter for Jonathan and Abby. (When the giant redwood falls, it lands on the trunk of another fallen tree, creating a space beneath it which the children use for shelter.)

"Mommy!" Abby's shrill cry rose above the thundering noise.

Jonathan struggled toward her again, his heart racing. When he finally reached her, he lay beside her and wrapped his arms around her. She clung to him, sobbing.

9 "We'll be okay," he said. "It's only an earthquake."

Only an earthquake. He remembered magazine pictures of terrible devastation from earthquakes: homes toppled, highways **10** buckled, cars tossed upside down, and people crushed in debris. Only an earthquake.

"We have to get under shelter," he said. "Try to crawl with me." Keeping one arm around Abby's waist, he got to his hands and knees and began crawling forward on the undulating ground.

"I can't!" Abby cried. "I'm scared. The ground is moving."

Jonathan tightened his grip, dragging her across the ground. A small tree crashed beside them. Dust rose, filling their noses.

"I want Mommy!" Abby shrieked.

He pulled her to the trunk of the huge redwood tree that had uprooted.

"Get under the tree," he said, as he pushed her into the angle of **11** space that was created because the center of the redwood's trunk rested on the other tree.

When Abby was completely under the tree, Jonathan lay on his stomach beside her, with his right arm tucked beneath his stomach and his left arm thrown across Abby. He pulled himself in as close as he could so that both he and Abby were wedged in the space under the big tree.

"What's happening?" Abby sobbed. Her fingernails dug into Jonathan's bare arm.

"It's an earthquake."

"I want to go home." Abby tried to push Jonathan away.

"Lie still," Jonathan said. "The tree will protect us."

38

Vocabulary

devastation destruction or ruin

debris the remains of something broken or destroyed

undulating moving in waves or with a smooth, wavy motion

Extra Support/Intervention

Strategy Modeling: Predict/Infer

Use this example to model the strategy.

Jonathan says that it is only an earthquake. But he remembers seeing pictures of the devastation that earthquakes can cause. In spite of what Jonathan tells Abby, I predict that this earthquake will cause a great deal of damage and make it very hard for the children to reach a safe place.

39

Mood

Teach

- Explain that writers use details and descriptive language to create the mood, or emotional tone, in a selection.

- Discuss examples of moods that an author might create, such as fear, panic, happiness, sadness, or mystery.

Practice

- Write the sentences from page 38 shown below on the board.

- Point out *his heart racing, shrieked,* and the image of Abby's nails digging into Jonathan's arm.

- Ask students what mood this language and these details help to create. (a mood of fear and panic)

> Jonathan struggled toward her again, his heart racing.
>
> "I want Mommy!" Abby shrieked.
>
> Her fingernails dug into Jonathan's bare arm.

Apply

- Have students list other scenes in the story that have a similar mood of fear or alarm. (Sample answer: page 36, when Jonathan realizes they're caught in an earthquake)

- Ask them to list details that help create this mood. (*Abby's screams, that made the hair rise on the back of his neck, frantically*)

English Language Learners

Language Development

Have students look for action verbs, such as *crawl* and *pulled,* on page 38.

- List the verbs on the board.

- Have volunteers demonstrate the action that each verb describes.

- If students are unsure about a verb's meaning, have them look up the definition in the dictionary before they demonstrate the meaning.

CRITICAL THINKING
Guiding Comprehension

12 DRAWING CONCLUSIONS What does the sentence *Anxiety tied a tight knot in Jonathan's stomach* say about Jonathan's situation? (He is nervous and worried that the quake may cause the tree to slip and crush them.)

13 MAKING INFERENCES What does the author mean by *the silence seemed both comforting and ominous?* (It seems comforting because the quake has ended, but also ominous because it is unusually quiet.)

14 SEQUENCE OF EVENTS How can you tell that Grandma Whitney's call happened in the past? (clue words such as *had called* and *had seen*)

The dry forest floor scratched his cheek as he inhaled the pungent scent of dead leaves. He felt dwarfed by the enormous redwood and tried not to imagine what would have happened if it had landed on him.

"Moose!" he called. "Come, Moose."

Beneath him, the ground trembled again. Jonathan tightened his grip on Abby and pushed his face close to hers. A sharp crack rang out beside them as another tree hit the ground. Jonathan turned his head enough to peer out; he saw the redwood branches quivering from the impact.

What if the earthquake caused the redwood to move again? What if it slipped off the tree it rested on and crushed them beneath it? **12** Anxiety tied a tight knot in Jonathan's stomach.

The earth shuddered once more. Abby buried her face in Jonathan's shoulder. His shirt grew wet from her tears. The jolt did not seem as severe this time, but Jonathan thought that might be because he was lying down.

Moose, panting with fear, huddled beside Jonathan, pawing at Jonathan's shoulder. Relieved that the dog had not been injured, Jonathan put his right arm around Moose and held him close.

As suddenly as it had begun, the upheaval stopped. Jonathan was unsure how long it had lasted. Five minutes? Ten? While it was happening, time seemed suspended and Jonathan had thought the shaking might go on for days.

The woods were quiet.

He lay motionless, one arm around Abby and the other around Moose, waiting to see if it was really over. The air was completely still. After the roar of the earthquake, the silence seemed both **13** comforting and ominous.

Earlier, even though there were no other people in the area, he'd heard the magpies cawing, and a squirrel had complained when Jonathan tossed a rock.

40

English Language Learners

Language Development

Read aloud this phrase from page 40: *a squirrel had complained.* Remind students that the squirrel complained before the earthquake happened. Tell students that *had* as a helping verb means "before something else" in the past. Ask students what else had happened before the earthquake.

Vocabulary

upheaval a lifting or upward movement of the earth's crust

ominous threatening

Now he heard nothing. No birds. No squirrels. Not even wind in the leaves.

He wondered if his parents had felt the quake. Sometimes, he knew, earthquakes were confined to fairly small areas.

Once Grandma Whitney had called them from Iowa. She had seen news reports of a violent California earthquake less than one hundred miles from where the Palmers lived.

"Are you all right?" Grandma cried, when Mrs. Palmer answered the phone. "Was anyone hurt?"

Grandma had been astonished when none of the Palmers knew anything about an earthquake.

After several minutes of quiet, Jonathan eased out from under the tree. He sat up and looked around. Moose, still trembling, licked his hand.

41

Fluency Practice

Rereading for Fluency Have students choose a favorite part of the story to reread to a partner, or suggest that they read page 41. Encourage students to read expressively.

Extra Support/Intervention

Strategy Modeling: Phonics/Decoding

Use *violent* on page 41 to model the strategy.

I can try sounding this word out. First, I'll look for any word parts I know. I see vi *and the letter* o. *I also see* lent. *I'll try blending these sounds together:* VY-oh-lehnt. *Now I'll check whether* violent *makes sense in the sentence. It does—in this sentence it means that the California earthquake was very strong and forceful.*

> **VY-oh-lehnt**

CRITICAL THINKING
Guiding Comprehension

⓯ MAKING INFERENCES Why do you think the author includes Jonathan's memories of Moose? (to explain why Moose is an important part of Jonathan's life and why Jonathan is so glad that Moose is safe)

COMPREHENSION STRATEGY
Predict/Infer

Student Modeling Ask students to model their predictions about what Jonathan and Abby might do after the earthquake stops. Offer this prompt:

- Based on the children's actions and decisions so far, what might they do after the earthquake to get themselves and Moose to safety?

42

English Language Learners

Supporting Comprehension

Some students may be unfamiliar with camping as a cultural pastime. Explain that camping means spending time outdoors and staying in temporary shelters such as tents, trailers, or cabins. Invite students to discuss why someone might enjoy camping outdoors.

Jonathan put his cheek on the dog's neck and rubbed his ears. He had chosen Moose at the animal shelter, more than six years ago. The Palmers had planned to get a small dog but the moment Jonathan saw the big golden retriever, who was then one year old, he knew which dog he wanted.

Mrs. Palmer had said, "He's too big to be a house dog."

Mr. Palmer said, "I think he's half moose."

Jonathan laughed and said, "That's what I'll name him. Moose."

His parents tried unsuccessfully to interest Jonathan in one of the other, smaller dogs, before they gave in and brought Moose home.

Despite his size, Moose was a house dog from the start, and he slept beside Jonathan's bed every night. They played fetch, and their own version of tag, and Jonathan took Moose for long walks in the county park. In the summer, they swam whenever they had a chance.

When Abby had her accident and Jonathan's parents focused so much of their attention on her, Moose was Jonathan's comfort and companion.

Now, in the devastation of the earthquake, Jonathan again found comfort in the dog's presence. He let go of Moose and looked around. "Wow!" he said, trying to keep his voice steady. "That was some earthquake."

"Is it over?" Abby's voice was thin and high.

"I think so."

He grasped Abby's hand and pulled her out from under the tree. She sat up, apparently uninjured, and began picking leaves out of her hair.

"Are you okay?" he asked.

"My knee is cut." She touched one knee and her voice rose. "It's bleeding," she said, her lip trembling. "You pushed me under the tree too hard."

15

43

ASSIGNMENT CARD 4

Create a Different Picture

Similes

Sometimes, in order to describe an object, person, or event, an author compares it to something else, using words such as *like* or *as*. This comparison is called a simile. For example, the simile "the ground swelled and retreated, like ocean waves" creates a vivid picture of the earth's movements.

- Find other instances in the story where the author has used similes.

- Choose one of the similes, and change it. For example, what picture is created if "the ground swelled and retreated" like ripples on a pond?

Theme 1: Nature's Fury

Teacher's Resource BLM page 48

Story Structure

Review

- Review the elements of story structure:
  - characters: people or animals in a story
  - setting: time and place in which a story occurs
  - plot: sequence of events, which often includes a problem and solution
- Tell students that using a story map can help them identify story structure.

Practice/Apply

- Begin a story map similar to the one below. Point out clues to the story's setting and add these details to the story map.
- Have students provide story details to complete the story map. Write their responses on the board.

Story Map

Setting: woods on Magpie Island, California	Characters: Jonathan, Abby, Moose

Plot	
Problem:	The children get caught in an earthquake.
Events:	Jonathan senses something is wrong. Jonathan dodges a falling tree. He finds shelter.
Solution:	The earthquake ends. They are safe.

Review Skill Trace

Teach	Theme 2, p. 181A
Reteach	Theme 2, p. R12
▶ Review	p. 43; Theme 2, p. 173; Theme 3, p. 295; Theme 4, p. 355

Reading the Selection **43**

CRITICAL THINKING

Guiding Comprehension

16 **MAKING INFERENCES** What does the author mean by saying that Abby will get upset if Jonathan makes a fuss about her cut? (If Jonathan reacts like Abby's cut is a big problem, Abby will react the same way. If he stays calm, she will also stay calm.)

17 **STORY STRUCTURE** How does the author solve the story problem for Jonathan and Abby? (The earthquake stops.) What problem do they still face? (They must take care of themselves until their parents return.)

16 Jonathan examined her knee. It was a minor cut. He knew that if he made a fuss over it, Abby would cry. He had seen it happen before; if his mother showed concern about a small injury, Abby got practically hysterical, but if Mom acted like it was no big deal, Abby relaxed, too. It was as if she didn't know whether she hurt or not until she saw how her parents reacted.

"It's all right," he said. "If that tiny little scrape is all you got, you are lucky, and so am I. We could have been killed."

"We could?" Abby's eyes grew round.

17 Quickly Jonathan said, "But we weren't, and the earthquake is over now."

44

**Extra Support/
Intervention** | **On Level** | **Challenge**

Selection Review

Before students join in Wrapping Up on page 45, have them

• review and discuss the accuracy of their predictions

• take turns modeling the reading strategies they used

• help you complete **Transparency 1–2** and their Event Map on **Practice Book** page 12

• summarize the whole selection

Literature Discussion

Have small groups of students discuss the story, using their own questions or the questions in Think About the Selection on Anthology page 46.

Meet the Author
Peg Kehret

Favorite outfit: Jeans and sweatshirt

Favorite dish: Spaghetti

When not writing: Reads, plays her player piano, bakes bread, volunteers at The Humane Society

Home: An eighty-year-old house in the state of Washington with apple and pear trees, blueberry and blackberry bushes, and a big vegetable garden

Popularity: Kehret has won children's choice awards in fifteen states. Twice a year she and her husband travel across the country in their motor home so that she can speak in schools and meet her readers.

More Kehret books: *Volcano Disaster, Blizzard Disaster, Nightmare Mountain, The Richest Kids in Town, Shelter Dogs: Amazing Stories of Adopted Strays*

Meet the Illustrator
Phil Boatwright

Lone Star boyhood: Boatwright grew up in Mesquite, Texas, a suburb of Dallas.

Favorite children's book: *Treasure Island,* by Robert Louis Stevenson

Favorite illustrators: Gennady Spirin, Jerry Pinkney, John Collier, and N. C. Wyeth

Tips for success: "You have to love to draw, take all the art classes possible, read all the art books available, and study the artists you admire."

Internet

For more information about Peg Kehret and Phil Boatwright, visit Education Place. **www.eduplace.com/kids**

45

Wrapping Up
Critical Thinking Questions

1. **MAKING JUDGMENTS** Do you think it is a good idea for Jonathan to take Abby and crawl under the redwood tree? Explain. (Sample answer: yes, because it protects them from other falling things)

2. **CAUSE AND EFFECT** How do Jonathan's memories help him during the earthquake? (He uses what he has learned about earthquakes to figure out how to stay safe.)

Strategies in Action

Have students model when and how they used the Predict/Infer strategy.

Discussion Options

Bring the entire class together to do one or more of the activities below.

Review Predictions/Purpose Discuss students' predictions and any revisions they made.

Share Group Discussions Have students share their reactions to Jonathan's problem and solution.

Summarize Ask students to summarize the main events of the story using their Event Map.

Comprehension Check

Use **Practice Book** page 13 to assess students' comprehension of the selection.

Monitoring Student Progress

If . . .	Then . . .
students score 6 or below on **Practice Book** page 13,	have them form small groups and refer to their Event Maps to retell parts of the story.

REACHING ALL LEARNERS

English Language Learners

Language Development

Point out the expression *make a fuss over* on page 44. Ask students if Abby's cut is big or small. Explain that because it is small, Jonathan doesn't worry or act frightened—he doesn't make a fuss over it.

Practice Book page 13

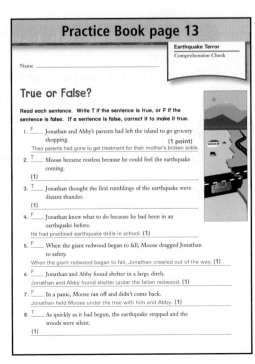

Earthquake Terror
Comprehension Check

Name _____

True or False?

Read each sentence. Write T if the sentence is true, or F if the sentence is false. If a sentence is false, correct it to make it true.

1. _F_ Jonathan and Abby's parents had left the island to go grocery shopping.   **(1 point)**
   Their parents had gone to get treatment for their mother's broken ankle.

2. _T_ Moose became restless because he could feel the earthquake coming.
   (1)

3. _T_ Jonathan thought the first rumblings of the earthquake were distant thunder.
   (1)

4. _F_ Jonathan knew what to do because he had been in an earthquake before.
   He had practiced earthquake drills in school. (1)

5. _F_ When the giant redwood began to fall, Moose dragged Jonathan to safety.
   When the giant redwood began to fall, Jonathan crawled out of the way. (1)

6. _F_ Jonathan and Abby found shelter in a large ditch.
   Jonathan and Abby found shelter under the fallen redwood. (1)

7. _F_ In a panic, Moose ran off and didn't come back.
   Jonathan held Moose under the tree with him and Abby. (1)

8. _T_ As quickly as it had begun, the earthquake stopped and the woods were silent.
   (1)

Responding

Think About the Selection

READ & COMPREHEND

Have students discuss or write their answers. Sample answers are provided; accept reasonable responses.

1. **KNOWLEDGE** The San Andreas Fault is hundreds of miles long on the California coastline, so the entire area, including Magpie Island, is likely to be affected by earthquakes.

2. **APPLYING** Jonathan is caring, considerate, and protective of Abby. He keeps her safe during the earthquake. Abby relies on him for help and comfort.

3. **ANALYZING** Moose senses danger before the children do. On page 30 Moose paces and sniffs. On page 32 he uses his warning bark.

4. **GENERATING** Answers may vary.

5. **INTEGRATING** Jonathan puts his hands over his head to protect himself and tells Abby to do the same; He finds shelter under a fallen tree.

6. **EVALUATING** yes, because they explain Jonathan's past; no, because they take away from the story suspense

 7. **Connections** yes, because an earthquake is a violent, uncontrollable natural event

---

Responding

Think About the Selection

1. **Knowledge** What did you learn about the San Andreas fault?

2. **Applying** How would you describe Jonathan's relationship with his sister? Give examples that show how they feel about each other.

3. **Analyzing** How does the author create suspense before the earthquake hits? Find examples from the story.

4. **Generating** Jonathan notes how time goes fast when he's interested and slowly when he's not. Give examples of that from your own life.

5. **Integrating** Summarize what Jonathan does to protect himself and Abby from the earthquake.

6. **Evaluating** Sometimes the author interrupts the action with events that happened earlier. Does this add to the story? Why?

7. **Connections** Do you think *Earthquake Terror* is a good way to begin a theme called *Nature's Fury*? Why or why not?

Write an Adventure Story

Use what you learned about Jonathan and Abby in *Earthquake Terror* to write an adventure story with them as characters. Your story can tell how they escape from another natural disaster, such as a fire, a flood, or a storm.

Tips
- Begin by thinking about the problem the characters face and write down details.
- Show how the characters feel.
- Include details of the setting.

46

English Language Learners

Supporting Comprehension

Beginning/Preproduction Have students use the pictures to identify the characters. Then have them work in small groups to role-play their favorite scenes from the story.

Early Production and Speech Emergence Have students work in pairs to ask each other questions about the story. Ask partners to take turns answering the questions.

Intermediate and Advanced Fluency Ask students to think about the story's setting. How would the story have been different if it took place in a city?

Additional Responses

Personal Response Invite students to share their personal responses to *Earthquake Terror.*

 Journal ▸ Ask students to write in their journals about how they might feel and act during an earthquake.

Selection Connections Remind students to add to **Practice Book** pages 9–10.

Health and Safety

Demonstrate Earthquake Safety

On pages 35 and 36 of the selection, Jonathan remembers what he learned in school about earthquake safety. Use that information to demonstrate for classmates what to do in case an earthquake strikes.

Listening and Speaking

Deliver a Newscast

With a partner, present a newscast about the earthquake on Magpie Island. You might wish to take on the roles of a television anchorperson and an on-the-scene reporter. Use information from the selection to give details.

Tips

- Plan the order in which you will present your information.
- Write notes on cards or slips of paper.
- Use exact details.

Internet

Post a Review

Write a review of *Earthquake Terror.* Tell others what you liked or didn't like about it. Visit Education Place. **www.eduplace.com/kids**

47

Monitoring Student Progress

End-of-Selection Assessment

Selection Test Use the test on page 113 in the **Teacher's Resource Blackline Masters** to assess selection comprehension and vocabulary.

Student Self-Assessment Have students assess their reading with additional questions such as

- Which parts of this selection were difficult for me? Why?
- What strategies helped me understand the story?
- Would I recommend this story to my friends? Why?

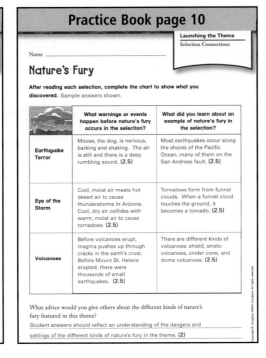

Practice Book page 9

Launching the Theme
Selection Connections

Name

Nature's Fury

After reading each selection, complete the chart below and on the next page to show what you discovered. Sample answers shown.

	What is the setting or settings for the action or descriptions in the selection?	What dangers do people face in the selection?
Earthquake Terror	Magpie Island, in California (2.5 Points)	Jonathan and Abby are stranded on Magpie Island when an earthquake strikes, toppling trees all around them. (2.5)
Eye of the Storm	Tucson, Arizona and Tornado Alley (Amarillo, Texas and towns in Texas, Oklahoma and Kansas) (2.5)	Warren Faidley faces danger from lightning bolts and spiders while photographing from an underpass. He and Tom Willett face danger from tornadoes forming around them in Tornado Alley. (2.5)
Volcanoes	Hawaii, Washington state, Iceland, Guatemala, California, Oregon (2.5)	People face danger from the eruption of Mount St. Helens; people on the island of Heimaey, Iceland, face danger from a volcano; people in Hawaii face danger to their houses from quick-moving lava. (2.5)

Practice Book page 10

Launching the Theme
Selection Connections

Name

Nature's Fury

After reading each selection, complete the chart to show what you discovered. Sample answers shown.

	What warnings or events happen before nature's fury occurs in the selection?	What did you learn about an example of nature's fury in the selection?
Earthquake Terror	Moose, the dog, is nervous, barking and shaking. The air is still and there is a deep rumbling sound. (2.5)	Most earthquakes occur along the shores of the Pacific Ocean, many of them on the San Andreas fault. (2.5)
Eye of the Storm	Cool, moist air meets hot desert air to cause thunderstorms in Arizona. Cool, dry air collides with warm, moist air to cause tornadoes. (2.5)	Tornadoes form from funnel clouds. When a funnel cloud touches the ground, it becomes a tornado. (2.5)
Volcanoes	Before volcanoes erupt, magma pushes up through cracks in the earth's crust. Before Mount St. Helens erupted, there were thousands of small earthquakes. (2.5)	There are different kinds of volcanoes: shield, strato-volcanoes, cinder cone, and dome volcanoes. (2.5)

What advice would you give others about the different kinds of nature's fury featured in this theme?

Student answers should reflect an understanding of the dangers and settings of the different kinds of nature's fury in the theme. (2)

Responding 47

Science Link

Skill: How to Read a Science Article

- **Introduce** "El Niño," a nonfiction science article from *Muse* magazine. Since it is nonfiction rather than fiction, students should read to understand facts and ideas, not a story plot.

- **Discuss** the Skill Lesson on Anthology page 48. Point out that titles, captions, and illustrations provide information about the topic.

- **Model** for students how to follow the steps on the Skill Lesson to identify the topic, share what they already know about it, and predict what they will learn.

- **Explain** that using a K-W-L Chart can help students follow the steps for reading a science article. Then start a chart on the board. Point out that the steps in the lesson correspond to various parts of the chart.

- **Set a purpose** for reading. Tell students to read "El Niño," and have them complete their own K-W-L Charts. Remind them to use the Predict/Infer strategy as they read.

K	W	L
What I Know	**What I Want to Learn**	**What I Learned**
Stormy weather from El Niño caused landslides in California.	How often does El Niño occur? What causes El Niño?	
El Niño caused forest fires in Indonesia.		

Vocabulary

drought a long period of time with little or no rainfall

Science Link

Genre

Science Article

Skill: How to Read a Science Article

Before you read . . .

❶ Look at the title, captions, and illustrations.

❷ Identify the **topic** and ask what you already know about it.

❸ Predict what you will learn in the article.

While you read . . .

❶ Identify the **main idea** and **supporting details** in each paragraph.

❷ When you don't understand something, ask yourself questions and then reread.

48

El Niño

by Fred Pearce

In the winter of 1998, heavy rains caused mudslides in California that washed houses off cliffs. Ice storms on the eastern seaboard from Maine to Quebec downed so many power lines that thousands of people had to live in the dark and cold for weeks. Indonesia's rain forests got no rain, and the months of dry weather turned the forests into the world's largest pile of firewood. At the same time, the worst drought in a hundred years hit neighboring New Guinea, killing crops and leaving some of the most isolated people on Earth starving. On the other side of the globe, lack of rain left the water level in the Panama Canal so low that large ships couldn't make it through.

Mudslides in California

Early 1998 also saw intense storms in places not used to them. Kenya suffered the worst floods in 40 years — in the middle of the *dry* season. Neighboring Uganda was cut off for several days, when both road and rail links were washed away. In South America, floods made half a million Peruvians homeless along a coastline that often has no rain for years at a time. Neighboring Ecuador said it would take 10 years to repair the damage. And in northern Tibet, the worst snow in 50 years starved or froze to death hundreds of Mongol tribesmen.

Was it just bad luck that there was so much bad weather in so many parts of the world at around the same time? Fifty years ago, most people would have said yes.

Flash floods in Ecuador, South America

Forest fires in Indonesia, Southeast Asia

Floods in Kenya, East Africa

49

English Language Learners

Supporting Comprehension

Have students work with partners or in small groups to practice reading a science article. First, have them look at the title, captions, and illustrations. Remind them to use the photos and illustrations to help figure out the meaning of unfamiliar words. Ask students what this article is about. Then ask: Have you heard of El Niño? Ask Spanish speakers: What does *niño* mean? ("child" or "boy")

Expository Nonfiction

Teach

- Explain to students that expository nonfiction gives information about real topics. It often explains the way things are, what they mean, how they work, and why they are important.

- Expository nonfiction is often organized by main ideas and supporting details.

Practice/Apply

- Tell students that "El Niño" is an example of expository nonfiction.

- Help students to identify elements of expository nonfiction in the article. (The topic is El Niño, a real weather system. The article explains how El Niño works, why it is important, and its effects on weather around the world.)

- Ask partners to list examples of main ideas and supporting details. (Sample answer: Supporting details on page 48 help the reader infer the main idea, that intense storms occurred around the world in the winter of 1998.)

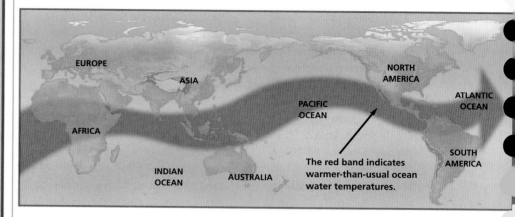

EUROPE

ASIA

NORTH AMERICA

ATLANTIC OCEAN

PACIFIC OCEAN

AFRICA

SOUTH AMERICA

INDIAN OCEAN

AUSTRALIA

The red band indicates warmer-than-usual ocean water temperatures.

But today, meteorologists (scientists who study weather) blame most of 1998's weather disasters on a giant blip in the weather system called *El Niño*. Many years ago, Spanish-speaking Peruvian fishermen noticed that the fish suddenly disappeared whenever warm waters flowed in from the west. They called the warming El Niño (Spanish for "the child") because it usually happened around Christmas. El Niño is caused by a sudden shift in the winds and ocean currents in the Pacific Ocean that pushes a layer of warm water across the ocean, taking weather systems with it.

El Niño is rather like a wave in your bathtub, only the tub is huge and the wave takes months to go from one end to the other. The huge bathtub in this case is the Pacific, the world's largest ocean.

Most of the time, winds and ocean currents at the equator move from east to west across the Pacific — from the Americas to Asia. The winds and currents push the ocean's water toward Asia. After a few years of this, the sea level around the islands of Indonesia is actually over a foot higher than on the American side. This can't go on forever. And it doesn't. Eventually, like a wave reaching the far end of your bathtub, the water bounces back, moving toward the Americas. Scientists have clocked this wave moving about 125 miles a day.

The water around Indonesia is the hottest in the world — usually warmer than 80° F, which is as warm as many swimming pools. As the wave moves toward the Americas, it spreads a layer of the warm Indonesian water across the

50

REACHING ALL LEARNERS

Extra Support/Intervention

Demonstrate the Concept

To help students understand El Niño's effects on the Pacific Ocean, try this activity.

- Fill a plastic dishpan with water, and use your hand to slowly move the water from one side of the pan to the other.

- Point to both coasts of the Pacific Ocean on a map.

- Explain that El Niño has a similar effect in the Pacific, causing a huge wave of warm water to move from one coast to the other.

Vocabulary

equator the imaginary line that divides the earth into the Northern and Southern hemispheres *(Show on a globe if there is one available in the classroom.)*

pollen the fine powderlike material produced by flowering plants

ocean. And because ocean currents and winds are connected, the Indonesian weather follows, too. This means that the heavy rains that normally hit Indonesia for most of the year get moved thousands of miles east, soaking the Pacific Islands and normally dry coastlands from Peru to California. Meanwhile, normally wet Indonesia and its surrounding areas suffer drought.

No one is really sure how long El Niño has been around. Dan Sandweiss of the University of Maine has found telltale signs of sudden El Niño-style floods in old *sediments* in Peru. (Sediments are the solid stuff that settles out of water at places like the mouth of a river.) When it doesn't rain, few plants grow, and there isn't much pollen in the sediments. But when El Niño occurs in these normally dry regions, more plants grow and more pollen shows up. From the amount of pollen in the sediments, Sandweiss can tell that "El Niño has been around for at least 5000 years. Before that there seems to have been a gap."

El Niño isn't just about some rainstorm in California in 1998; it's about wild weather around the world through recorded history.

Episode Two: La Niña Strikes Back!

El Niño typically lasts some 18 months, and usually returns every three to seven years, probably when enough warm water has built up again in the western Pacific. But when El Niño's warm water retreats, it's sometimes followed by a *cool* water wave. Scientists call this cooling of the Pacific *La Niña*. La Niña's effect on the weather is harder to predict than El Niño's. But during La Niña years, the normal weather in some regions becomes *exaggerated*: it gets extra wet in wet Indonesia, extra dry in dry Peru. That's also when we get big droughts in the American Midwest. The great Dust Bowl drought of 1930s America is thought to have been caused by a decade of La Niña-like conditions.

Photo by Arthur Rothstein, *Dust Storm, Cimarron County, 1936.*

Wrapping Up

Critical Thinking Questions

Ask students to use the selection to answer these questions.

1. **CAUSE AND EFFECT** What causes El Niño? (a giant "wave" that creates a shift in ocean and air currents in the Pacific Ocean, which pushes unusually warm water and weather thousands of miles eastward)

2. **CAUSE AND EFFECT** How does El Niño create weather extremes? (As warm tropical weather is pushed farther east, heavy rains flood areas that are usually dry. Normally wet areas are left without rain, so they experience drought.)

3. **MAKING INFERENCES** How are some scientists able to draw conclusions about how long El Niño has been affecting the weather? (They study the amount of pollen in sediments.)

4. **COMPARE AND CONTRAST** How are earthquakes and El Niño alike? How are they different? (Alike: Both are natural disasters that cause destruction in large areas. Different: Earthquakes are caused by pressure on the earth's crust. El Niño is caused by unusually warm water and weather.)

Challenge

Weather Extremes

Have volunteers use reference materials such as encyclopedias or the Internet to collect, compare, and display facts that relate to weather extremes in their region, the nation, and the world. Suggest that they include facts such as highest and lowest recorded temperatures, most or least amounts of rain, and wind speeds.

OBJECTIVES

- Identify the order of story events.
- Identify words that signal sequence.
- Identify when an author shifts from the present action to past events.
- Learn academic language: *signal words, sequential order.*

Target Skill Trace

Preview; Teach	p. 25G; p. 28; p. 33; p. 51A
Reteach	p. R8
Review	pp. M34–M35; p. 71; Theme 2, p. 213
See	*Extra Support Handbook,* pp. 16–17; pp. 22–23

Transparency 1–2

Event Map

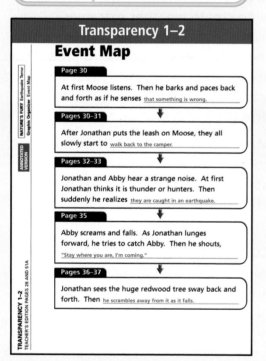

Page 30

At first Moose listens. Then he barks and paces back and forth as if he senses <u>that something is wrong.</u>

Pages 30–31

After Jonathan puts the leash on Moose, they all slowly start to <u>walk back to the camper.</u>

Pages 32–33

Jonathan and Abby hear a strange noise. At first Jonathan thinks it is thunder or hunters. Then suddenly he realizes <u>they are caught in an earthquake.</u>

Page 35

Abby screams and falls. As Jonathan lunges forward, he tries to catch Abby. Then he shouts, <u>"Stay where you are, I'm coming."</u>

Pages 36–37

Jonathan sees the huge redwood tree sway back and forth. Then <u>he scrambles away from it as it falls.</u>

Practice Book page 12

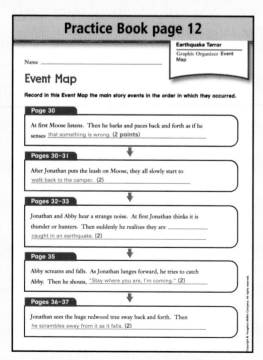

Name _____

Earthquake Terror
Graphic Organizer Event Map

Event Map

Record in this Event Map the main story events in the order in which they occurred.

Page 30

At first Moose listens. Then he barks and paces back and forth as if he senses <u>that something is wrong.</u> **(2 points)**

Pages 30–31

After Jonathan puts the leash on Moose, they all slowly start to <u>walk back to the camper.</u> **(2)**

Pages 32–33

Jonathan and Abby hear a strange noise. At first Jonathan thinks it is thunder or hunters. Then suddenly he realizes they are <u>caught in an earthquake.</u> **(2)**

Page 35

Abby screams and falls. As Jonathan lunges forward, he tries to catch Abby. Then he shouts, <u>"Stay where you are, I'm coming."</u> **(2)**

Pages 36–37

Jonathan sees the huge redwood tree sway back and forth. Then <u>he scrambles away from it as it falls.</u> **(2)**

COMPREHENSION: Sequence of Events

❶ Teach

Review the sequence of events in *Earthquake Terror*. Complete the Graphic Organizer on **Transparency 1–2** with students. They can refer to the selection and to **Practice Book** page 12. Discuss the following:

- the main story events and their sequence
- words that signal sequential order (*at first, then, after*)
- words that signal events that happen at the same time (*as, while*)

Explain time shifts. Tell students that authors can shift from present events to past events. Discuss how time shifts can give readers extra information such as the thoughts, feelings, or history of a character.

Model using signal words to identify time shifts. Have students reread the last three paragraphs on page 30 as you think aloud.

Think Aloud *The author begins in the present by telling how Jonathan feels in the woods. (Here he felt jumpy.) Then she tells how he remembers feeling in the past. (whenever he stayed alone at home) Later, the word* here *signals to me that Jonathan's thoughts shift back to the present. (Here he was isolated.)*

❷ Guided Practice

Have students practice identifying time shifts. Have students find and record examples of time shifts on Anthology pages 35, 36, 38, 41, and 43. Ask them also to record the words or phrases that signal the time shifts.

Page	Present Event	Past Event	Words That Signal the Time Shift
35	The ground drops away beneath Jonathan's feet.	He practiced earthquake drills in school.	Ever since first grade; That was school. This was Magpie Island.
36	Jonathan scrambles to get away from a falling tree.	He asked his teacher how he'd recognize an earthquake.	that first year

❸ Apply

Assign Practice Book pages 14–15. Also have students apply this skill as they read their **Leveled Readers** for this week. You may also select books from the Leveled Bibliography for this theme (pages 23E–23F).

✓ **Test Prep** Remind students that when answering test questions about sequence of events, they should scan the passage for time-order words such as *first, next, last, then, now, tomorrow,* and *yesterday.*

Leveled Readers and Leveled Practice

Students at all levels apply the comprehension skill as they read their Leveled Readers. See lessons on pages 51O–51R.

● **BELOW LEVEL** ▲ **ON LEVEL** ■ **ABOVE LEVEL** ◆ **LANGUAGE SUPPORT**

Reading Traits

Teaching students how to identify sequence of events is one way of encouraging them to "read the lines" of a selection. This comprehension skill supports the reading trait **Establishing Comprehension.**

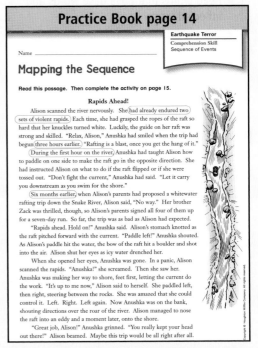

Practice Book page 14

Earthquake Terror
Comprehension Skill
Sequence of Events

Name _____

Mapping the Sequence

Read this passage. Then complete the activity on page 15.

Rapids Ahead!

Alison scanned the river nervously. She had already endured two sets of violent rapids. Each time, she had grasped the ropes of the raft so hard that her knuckles turned white. Luckily, the guide on her raft was strong and skilled. "Relax, Alison," Anushka had smiled when the trip had begun three hours earlier. "Rafting is a blast, once you get the hang of it."

During the first hour on the river, Anushka had taught Alison how to paddle on one side to make the raft go in the opposite direction. She had instructed Alison on what to do if the raft flipped or if she were tossed out. "Don't fight the current," Anushka had said. "Let it carry you downstream as you swim for the shore."

Six months earlier, when Alison's parents had proposed a whitewater rafting trip down the Snake River, Alison said, "No way." Her brother Zack was thrilled, though, so Alison's parents signed all four of them up for a seven-day run. So far, the trip was as bad as Alison had expected.

"Rapids ahead. Hold on!" Anushka said. Alison's stomach knotted as the raft pitched forward with the current. "Paddle left!" Anushka shouted. As Alison's paddle hit the water, the bow of the raft hit a boulder and shot into the air. Alison shut her eyes as icy water drenched her.

When she opened her eyes, Anushka was gone. In a panic, Alison scanned the rapids. "Anushka!" she screamed. Then she saw her. Anushka was making her way to shore, feet first, letting the current do the work. "It's up to me now," Alison said to herself. She paddled left, then right, steering between the rocks. She was amazed that she could control it. Left. Right. Left again. Now Anushka was on the bank, shouting directions over the roar of the river. Alison managed to nose the raft into an eddy and a moment later, onto the shore.

"Great job, Alison!" Anushka grinned. "You really kept your head out there!" Alison beamed. Maybe this trip would be all right after all.

Practice Book page 15

Earthquake Terror
Comprehension Skill
Sequence of Events

Name _____

Mapping the Sequence continued

Write each story event from page 14 in the sequence map below. Put the events in order.

▶ Alison successfully guides the raft to shore.
▶ Anushka tells Alison to relax.
▶ The raft hits a boulder and Anushka falls overboard.
▶ Anushka teaches Alison how to steer the raft.
▶ Alison's parents suggest a raft trip on the Snake River.

Alison's parents suggest a raft trip on the Snake River. **(2 points)**
↓
Anushka tells Alison to relax. **(2)**
↓
Anushka teaches Alison how to steer the raft. **(2)**
↓
The raft hits a boulder and Anushka falls overboard. **(2)**
↓
Alison successfully guides the raft to shore. **(2)**

Now go back to the passage. Circle the words that helped you understand the following:

▶ when the family plans the trip **(1 point)**
▶ when Anushka tells Alison that rafting is fun **(1)**
▶ when Anushka teaches Alison some basic rafting techniques **(1)**
▶ whether Anushka's spill occurs during the first, second, or third set of rapids that she and Alison encounter **(1)**

Monitoring Student Progress

If . . .	Then . . .
students score 10 or below on **Practice Book** page 15,	use the Reteaching lesson on Teacher's Edition page R8.
students have successfully met the lesson objectives,	have them do the Challenge/Extension activities on Teacher's Edition page R9.

OBJECTIVES

- Read words that have base words and inflected forms.
- Use the Phonics/Decoding Strategy to decode longer words.
- Learn academic language: *base word, prefix, suffix.*

Target Skill Trace

Teach	p. 51C
Reteach	p. R14
Review	pp. M36–M37
See	*Handbook for English Language Learners,* p. 19; *Extra Support Handbook,* pp. 14–15; pp. 18–19

STRUCTURAL ANALYSIS/ VOCABULARY: Base Words

❶ Teach

Introduce base words. Write *He saw the high bridge that <u>crossed</u> the river, <u>connecting</u> the island to the mainland.*

- Point to the words *crossed* and *connecting.* Identify *cross* and *connect* as base words. Identify *-ed* and *-ing* as endings.
- Explain that a base word can stand alone.
- Explain that endings and other word parts such as prefixes and suffixes can be added to a base word.

Discuss spelling changes in base words. Write *Jonathan was <u>worried</u> by the way Moose was <u>shaking</u>.*

- Identify the base words *worry* and *shake* in *worried* and *shaking.*

- Point out that the spelling of a base word sometimes changes when an ending is added.

Model the Phonics/Decoding Strategy. Write: *Jonathan spent time <u>surveying</u> the forest after the earthquake.* Then model decoding *surveying.*

Think Aloud *I don't recognize the underlined word. I'll try taking away the ending -ing. Now I'll try breaking the word into syllables: sur-VAY. I recognize the word* survey, *which means "to look at carefully." So* surveying *must mean "looking at carefully." This makes sense in the sentence. Jonathan would do that after the earthquake.*

Practice Book page 16

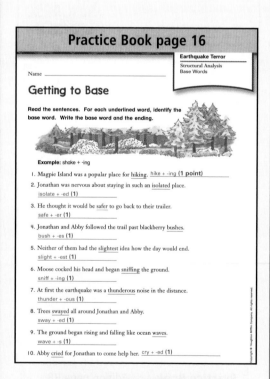

Earthquake Terror
Structural Analysis
Base Words

Name _____

Getting to Base

Read the sentences. For each underlined word, identify the base word. Write the base word and the ending.

Example: shake + -ing

1. Magpie Island was a popular place for <u>hiking</u>. hike + -ing **(1 point)**

2. Jonathan was nervous about staying in such an <u>isolated</u> place.
   isolate + -ed **(1)**

3. He thought it would be <u>safer</u> to go back to their trailer.
   safe + -er **(1)**

4. Jonathan and Abby followed the trail past blackberry <u>bushes</u>.
   bush + -es **(1)**

5. Neither of them had the <u>slightest</u> idea how the day would end.
   slight + -est **(1)**

6. Moose cocked his head and began <u>sniffing</u> the ground.
   sniff + -ing **(1)**

7. At first the earthquake was a <u>thunderous</u> noise in the distance.
   thunder + -ous **(1)**

8. Trees <u>swayed</u> all around Jonathan and Abby.
   sway + -ed **(1)**

9. The ground began rising and falling like ocean <u>waves</u>.
   wave + -s **(1)**

10. Abby <u>cried</u> for Jonathan to come help her. cry + -ed **(1)**

❷ Guided Practice

Have students find base words and endings. Display the sentences below. Have students decode and define the underlined words, using base words. Then have students work in pairs to find other base words and endings in the selection. Check students' work.

Air <u>whizzed</u> across his face.   A branch <u>brushed</u> his arm.

The tree trunk <u>dropped</u>.   The ground was <u>vibrating</u>.

❸ Apply

Assign Practice Book page 16.

Monitoring Student Progress

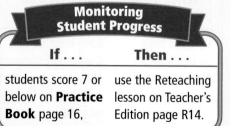

If . . .	Then . . .
students score 7 or below on **Practice Book** page 16,	use the Reteaching lesson on Teacher's Edition page R14.

PHONICS REVIEW:
Short Vowels

OBJECTIVES

- Read words and syllables that have a short vowel sound.
- Use the Phonics/Decoding Strategy to decode longer words.

❶ Teach

Review short vowel sounds. Discuss these points.

- Short vowel sounds are usually spelled with a vowel followed by a consonant: *run, ton, fun*.

- When a syllable ends with a vowel followed by a consonant, the syllable usually has a short vowel sound: *trump<u>et</u>, att<u>ic</u>*.

Model the Phonics/Decoding Strategy. Write this sentence: <u>Frantically</u> *he crawled to his left, rushing to get out of the tree's path.* Then model how to decode *frantically*.

Think Aloud *I see a short vowel pattern in the first syllable,* fran. *The next part could either be* tihk *or* tyk. *FRAN-tyk is not a word I know. Let's try FRAN-tihk. I've heard that. It means "very frightened." That leaves* -ally. *I'll put all the parts together: FRAN-tihk-lee. Adding* -ally *to* frantic *makes a word that means "in a very frightened way." This makes sense in the sentence.*

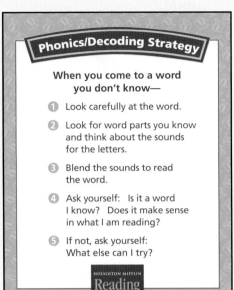

Phonics/Decoding Strategy

When you come to a word you don't know—

1. Look carefully at the word.
2. Look for word parts you know and think about the sounds for the letters.
3. Blend the sounds to read the word.
4. Ask yourself: Is it a word I know? Does it make sense in what I am reading?
5. If not, ask yourself: What else can I try?

HOUGHTON MIFFLIN
Reading

❷ Guided Practice

Help students identify short vowel sounds. Display the sentences below. Ask students to circle the short vowel pattern(s) in the underlined words, pronounce the word, and see if it makes sense in the sentence. Individuals can model their work at the board.

1. The rumbling came from every <u>direction</u>.

2. A branch fell and smashed on <u>impact</u>.

3. Finding shelter was a <u>problem</u>.

❸ Apply

Have students decode words with short vowels. Ask students to decode these words from *Earthquake Terror* and discuss their meanings.

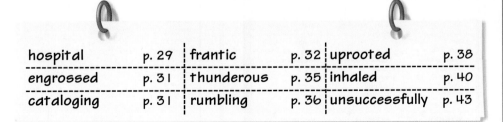

hospital	p. 29	frantic	p. 32	uprooted	p. 38
engrossed	p. 31	thunderous	p. 35	inhaled	p. 40
cataloging	p. 31	rumbling	p. 36	unsuccessfully	p. 43

SPELLING: Short Vowels

OBJECTIVES

- Write Spelling Words with short vowel patterns.

SPELLING WORDS

Basic

bunk	fond
staff	crush*
dock	grasp*
slept*	dwell
mist	fund
bunch	ditch
swift	split
stuck	swept
breath†	deaf†
tough†	rough†

Review	Challenge
trunk*	trek
skill	frantic*
track	summit
fresh	rustic
odd	mascot

*Forms of these words appear in the literature.

† These words are exceptions to the principle.

Extra Support/ Intervention

Basic Word List You may want to use only the left column of Basic Words with students who need extra support.

Challenge

Challenge Word Practice Students can use the Challenge Words to create crossword puzzles. Have them draw the puzzle, write clues, and trade with a partner.

DAY 1 — INSTRUCTION

Short Vowels

Pretest Use the Day 5 Test sentences.

Teach Write *staff, slept, mist, dock, bunk, breath,* and *tough* on the board.

- Say each word. Have students repeat it and name its vowel sound.

- Underline the single vowel in *staff, slept, mist, dock,* and *bunk.* Explain that a short vowel sound is usually spelled with a single vowel followed by a consonant sound.

- Underline *ea* in *breath.* Point out that this is a less common spelling pattern for the short *e* sound. Underline *ou* in *tough* and explain that this is a less common spelling pattern for the short *u* sound.

- Erase the board. Write as column heads /ă/, /ĕ/, /ĭ/, /ŏ/, and /ŭ/. Ask students to identify each sound.

- Say each Basic Word and ask a student to name its vowel sound. Write the word below its symbol.

Practice/Homework Assign **Practice Book** page 265.

Practice Book page 265

Take-Home Word List	Take-Home Word List	Take-Home Word List

Eye of the Storm

The /ā/, /ē/, and /ī/ Sounds
/ā/ → male, claim, stray
/ē/ → leaf, fleet
/ī/ → strike, thigh, sign

Spelling Words
1. speech 11. mild
2. claim 12. waist
3. strike 13. sway
4. stray 14. beast
5. fade 15. stain
6. sign 16. fleet
7. leaf 17. stride
8. thigh 18. praise
9. thief 19. slight
10. height 20. niece

Challenge Words
1. campaign
2. describe
3. cease
4. sacrifice
5. plight

My Study List
Add your own spelling words on the back.

Nature's Fury Reading-Writing Workshop

Look for familiar spelling patterns in these words to help you remember their spellings.

Spelling Words
1. enough 9. there
2. caught 10. there's
3. brought 11. know
4. thought 12. knew
5. every 13. o'clock
6. ninety 14. we're
7. their 15. people
8. they're

Challenge Words
1. decent
2. stationery
3. stationary
4. correspond
5. reversible

My Study List
Add your own spelling words on the back.

Earthquake Terror

Short Vowels
/ă/ → staff
/ĕ/ → slept
/ĭ/ → mist
/ŏ/ → dock
/ŭ/ → bunk

Spelling Words
1. bunk 11. fond
2. staff 12. crush
3. dock 13. grasp
4. slept 14. dwell
5. mist 15. fund
6. bunch 16. ditch
7. swift 17. split
8. stuck 18. swept
9. breath 19. deaf
10. tough 20. rough

Challenge Words
1. trek
2. frantic
3. summit
4. rustic
5. mascot

My Study List
Add your own spelling words on the back.

Take-Home Word List

DAY 2 — REVIEW & PRACTICE

Reviewing the Principle

Go over the spelling patterns for short vowels with students.

Practice/Homework Assign **Practice Book** page 17.

Practice Book page 17

Earthquake Terror
Spelling Short Vowels

Name _____

Short Vowels

Remember that a short vowel sound is usually spelled by one vowel and followed by a consonant sound. This is the **short vowel pattern.** These vowels usually spell short vowel sounds:
/ă/ a /ĕ/ e /ĭ/ i /ŏ/ o /ŭ/ u

► The short vowel sounds in the starred words do not have the usual short vowel spelling patterns. The /ĕ/ sound is spelled *ea* in *breath* and *deaf.* The /ŭ/ sound is spelled *ou* in *tough* and *rough.*

Write each Spelling Word under its vowel sound.
Order of answers for each category may vary.

/ă/ Sound
staff (1 point)   dock (1)
grasp (1)   fond (1)

/ĕ/ Sound   **/ŏ/ Sound**
slept (1)   bunk (1)
breath (1)   bunch (1)
dwell (1)   stuck (1)
swept (1)   tough (1)
deaf (1)   crush (1)
   fund (1)
/ĭ/ Sound   rough (1)
mist (1)
ditch (1)
swift (1)
split (1)

Spelling Words
1. bunk
2. staff
3. dock
4. slept
5. mist
6. bunch
7. swift
8. stuck
9. breath*
10. tough*
11. fond
12. crush
13. grasp
14. dwell
15. fund
16. ditch
17. split
18. swept
19. deaf*
20. rough*

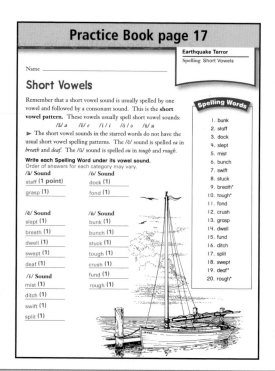

Definitions

Assign a different Basic Word to each student.

- Tell students to take turns looking up their assigned word's meaning in a dictionary.
- List each Basic Word on the board and ask the appropriate student to add the word's meaning.
- Have students use each Basic Word from the board orally in a sentence.

Practice/Homework For spelling practice, assign **Practice Book** page 18.

Game: Word Hunt

Have students do a word hunt. Set a time limit of 5–10 minutes and provide books, magazines, and newspapers.

- Have students form small groups and follow these steps:
  - Each student hunts for words with short vowel spelling patterns and lists the words.
  - When time is called, each group meets to pool and record its words.
  - Each group makes certain that all words have short vowel patterns.
  - The groups save words that do not have short vowel patterns in a special list.
- Select students to list each group's words on the board or on a chart. The group that has the most words with short vowel patterns wins.

Practice/Homework For proofreading and writing practice, assign **Practice Book** page 19.

Spelling Test

Say each underlined word, read the sentence, and then repeat the word. Have students write only the underlined word.

Basic Words

1. I will sleep on the top **bunk**.
2. The **staff** welcomed the new campers.
3. The boat was left at the **dock**.
4. Have you ever **slept** in a tent?
5. The **mist** changed to rain.
6. Ann picked a **bunch** of flowers.
7. The **swift** runner won the race.
8. The car is **stuck** in the mud.
9. I took a **breath** of air.
10. Outdoor clothing must be **tough**.
11. Maria is **fond** of her dog.
12. Do not **crush** the bug with your foot.
13. Please **grasp** the rope tightly.
14. Do bears **dwell** in your state?
15. Is there any money in the birthday **fund**?
16. The car slid into the **ditch**.
17. Can we **split** that sandwich in two?
18. He **swept** the floor with a broom.
19. The **deaf** cat cannot hear the bell.
20. Today the sea is too **rough** for sailing.

Challenge Words

21. Our hike turned into a long **trek**.
22. The dog had a **frantic** look in its eyes.
23. We saw the sunset from the **summit**.
24. The **rustic** house was built from wood.
25. The **mascot** attends every game.

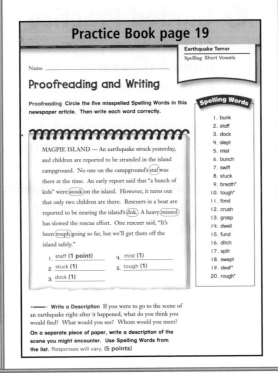

Practice Book page 18

Earthquake Terror
Spelling Short Vowels

Name _____

Spelling Spree

Letter Math Add and subtract letters from the words below to make Spelling Words. Write the new words.

Spelling Words
1. bunk
2. staff
3. dock
4. slept
5. mist
6. bunch
7. swift
8. stuck
9. breath*
10. tough*
11. fond
12. crush
13. grasp
14. dwell
15. fund
16. ditch
17. split
18. swept
19. deaf*
20. rough*

1. b + dunk – d = <u>bunk</u> **(1 point)**
2. sl + kept – k = <u>slept</u> **(1)**
3. f + pond – p = <u>fond</u> **(1)**
4. burn – r + ch = <u>bunch</u> **(1)**
5. st + duck – d = <u>stuck</u> **(1)**
6. dw + shell – sh = <u>dwell</u> **(1)**
7. cr + mush – m = <u>crush</u> **(1)**
8. d + rock – r = <u>dock</u> **(1)**
9. m + wrist – wr = <u>mist</u> **(1)**
10. sw + lift – l = <u>swift</u> **(1)**
11. spl + bit – b = <u>split</u> **(1)**
12. t + cough – c = <u>tough</u> **(1)**
13. d + leaf – l = <u>deaf</u> **(1)**
14. gr + clasp – cl = <u>grasp</u> **(1)**

Phrase Fillers Write the Spelling Word that best completes each phrase.

15. to take a deep <u>breath</u> **(1)**
16. as <u>rough</u> **(1)** as sandpaper
17. to put money into a <u>fund</u> **(1)**
18. to dig a <u>ditch</u> **(1)**
19. <u>swept</u> **(1)** with a broom
20. to join a company's <u>staff</u> **(1)**

Practice Book page 19

Earthquake Terror
Spelling Short Vowels

Name _____

Proofreading and Writing

Proofreading Circle the five misspelled Spelling Words in this newspaper article. Then write each word correctly.

Spelling Words
1. bunk
2. staff
3. dock
4. slept
5. mist
6. bunch
7. swift
8. stuck
9. breath*
10. tough*
11. fond
12. crush
13. grasp
14. dwell
15. fund
16. ditch
17. split
18. swept
19. deaf*
20. rough*

MAGPIE ISLAND — An earthquake struck yesterday, and children are reported to be stranded in the island campground. No one on the campground's (staf) was there at the time. An early report said that "a bunch of kids" were (stouk) on the island. However, it turns out that only two children are there. Rescuers in a boat are reported to be nearing the island's (dok.) A heavy (missed) has slowed the rescue effort. One rescuer said, "It's been (touph) going so far, but we'll get them off the island safely."

1. staff **(1 point)**   4. mist **(1)**
2. stuck **(1)**   5. tough **(1)**
3. dock **(1)**

Write a Description If you were to go to the scene of an earthquake right after it happened, what do you think you would find? What would you see? Whom would you meet?
On a separate piece of paper, write a description of the scene you might encounter. Use Spelling Words from the list. Responses will vary. **(5 points)**

OBJECTIVES

- Use a thesaurus to find synonyms for specific words.
- Learn academic language: *thesaurus, synonym, antonym, index, entry word, subentry word.*

Target Skill Trace

▶ Teach	p. 51G
Review	pp. M38–M39
Extend	Challenge/Extension Activities, p. R15
See	*Handbook for English Language Learners,* p. 23

VOCABULARY: Using a Thesaurus

❶ Teach

Introduce using a thesaurus. Explain that a thesaurus helps writers to find synonyms, words with similar meanings. It also helps writers find antonyms, words with opposite meanings.

Display Transparency 1–3. Explain that this shows a sample index and a sample main entry for one type of thesaurus.

- Discuss main entry words, antonyms, and subentry words.
- Identify main entries, antonyms, and subentries in the index.
- Point out the main entry, *devastation.* Point out the part of speech, the definition, and the sample sentence.
- Point out the subentry words. Explain that these are synonyms for the main entry word.
- Point out the antonyms for the main entry word.

Model using a thesaurus. Write: *The worst part of the earthquake was the <u>devastation</u> of a bridge.* Then model finding a synonym for *devastation.*

Think Aloud Devastation *isn't quite right in this sentence. I need a different word. First I look up* devastation *in the index of my thesaurus. It is a main-entry word, so next I look up the main entry. There I find several subentries, all synonyms of* devastation. *These words all have slightly different meanings.* Destruction *best fits what I am trying to say. I'll use that.*

❷ Guided Practice

Give students practice in using a thesaurus. Have partners write sentences for each of these words: *evaporating, engrossed, cataloging.* Then have them use a thesaurus to find synonyms for each of these words. Have them rewrite each sentence, using the synonyms.

❸ Apply

Assign Practice Book page 20.

Transparency 1–3

Using a Thesaurus

Thesaurus Index

Main entry words are shown in dark print. For example, *information* is a main entry.

Antonyms are shown in regular print. For example, *decrease* is an antonym.

Subentries are shown in italic dark print. For example, *deny* is a subentry.

    D
data **information** n.
decline v.

decrease **grow** v.
dedicated **earnest** adj.
defeat **surrender** v.
deny **decline** v.
desire **wish** v.
determine **think** v.
devastation n.
dim **bright** adj.

Thesaurus Entry

devastation n. The state of being destroyed; ruin; destruction. *It took years to repair the* **devastation** *caused by the earthquake.*

destruction The act or process of destroying. *The fires in California caused the* **destruction** *of several campsites.*

havoc The state of being destroyed. *The tropical storm caused* **havoc** *across the islands.*

ruin Total destruction or collapse. *The rainy season could easily* **ruin** *the harvest this year.*

wreck To cause the destruction of in a collision. *The demolition team can* **wreck** *that old building in a few hours.*
antonyms: create, produce

Monitoring Student Progress

If . . .	Then . . .
students score 8 or below on **Practice Book** page 20,	have them work with partners to correct the items they missed.

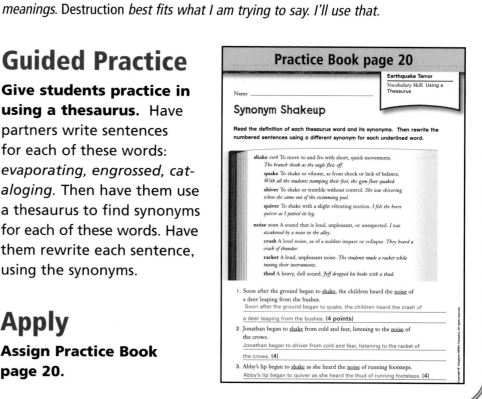

Practice Book page 20

Earthquake Terror
Vocabulary Skill Using a Thesaurus

Name _____

Synonym Shakeup

Read the definition of each thesaurus word and its synonyms. Then rewrite the numbered sentences using a different synonym for each underlined word.

shake *verb* To move to and fro with short, quick movements. *The branch shook as the eagle flew off.*
  quake To shake or vibrate, as from shock or lack of balance. *With all the students stamping their feet, the gym floor quaked.*
  shiver To shake or tremble without control. *She was shivering when she came out of the swimming pool.*
  quiver To shake with a slight vibrating motion. *I felt the horse quiver as I patted its leg.*

noise *noun* A sound that is loud, unpleasant, or unexpected. *I was awakened by a noise in the alley.*
  crash A loud noise, as of a sudden impact or collapse. *They heard a crash of thunder.*
  racket A loud, unpleasant noise. *The students made a racket while tuning their instruments.*
  thud A heavy, dull sound. *Jeff dropped his books with a thud.*

1. Soon after the ground began to <u>shake</u>, the children heard the <u>noise</u> of a deer leaping from the bushes.
  Soon after the ground began to quake, the children heard the crash of a deer leaping from the bushes. (**4 points**)

2. Jonathan began to <u>shake</u> from cold and fear, listening to the <u>noise</u> of the crows.
  Jonathan began to shiver from cold and fear, listening to the racket of the crows. (**4**)

3. Abby's lip began to <u>shake</u> as she heard the <u>noise</u> of running footsteps.
  Abby's lip began to quiver as she heard the thud of running footsteps. (**4**)

STUDY SKILL: Using Reference Sources

OBJECTIVES

- Identify the appropriate reference source to answer a specific question.
- Use printed or electronic reference sources to locate information.
- Use guide words and cross-references to find information in encyclopedias.
- Learn academic language: *topic, guide word, cross-reference, category, subcategory.*

❶ Teach

Introduce using print encyclopedias.

- Display one volume of a print encyclopedia.
- Explain that subjects are listed alphabetically. Model looking up a topic, using the letter with which the topic begins.
- Explain that guide words at the top of each page indicate what subjects the page contains. Model using guide words to find a topic.
- Explain that cross-references list related subjects that may be looked up elsewhere in the encyclopedia. Model finding cross-references at the end of an article.

Introduce using electronic encyclopedias.

- Explain that electronic encyclopedias have the same kind of information as print encyclopedias.
- Explain that electronic encyclopedias often list information in general categories, such as Art, History, and Science.
- Explain that when students open a category, they will find an alphabetical listing of subcategories. For instance, the category Science might contain the subcategories Biology and Chemistry.
- Explain that an alternate way for students to locate information is to type a word into the electronic encyclopedia's Search feature.

Model selecting a reference source to answer questions.

Think Aloud *I want to find out what causes hurricanes. I can look up hurricanes in the H volume of a print encyclopedia. I can also type the word hurricane into the Search feature of an electronic encyclopedia. If I want to find out about a hurricane that is occurring right now, I'd have better luck using a newspaper or searching the Internet, since the Internet contains up-to-the-minute information about current events.*

INDONESIA, Republic of

Capital: Jarkarta sometimes spelled (Djakarta)
Population: 220,788,000 34% urban
66% rural
Area: 741,052 square miles
Elevation: highest 16,503 ft lowest sea level
Language: Bahasa Indonesia (official)
Monetary unit: Rupiah
Government: Republic
National anthem: Indonesia Raya
(Great Indonesia)
Economy: Agriculture, forestry,
manufacturing, fishing, mining
Religion: Mostly Muslim
National Holiday: Independence Day,
August 17

INDONESIA 319

Flag of Indonesia

❷ Practice/Apply

Have partners use reference sources to answer these questions.

- What are three instruments used to predict the weather?
- How is the weather in California different from the weather in Kansas?
- What is the weather forecast for tomorrow?

GRAMMAR: Sentence Kinds and Parts

OBJECTIVES

- Identify the four kinds of sentences.
- Identify complete and simple subjects and complete and simple predicates.
- Proofread and correct sentences with grammar and spelling errors.
- Combine subjects and combine predicates to improve writing.
- Learn academic language: *declarative, interrogative, imperative, exclamatory.*

DAY 1 INSTRUCTION

Kinds of Sentences

Teach Go over the following:

- A declarative sentence tells something. It ends with a period.

- An interrogative sentence asks a question. It ends with a question mark.

- An imperative sentence gives a request or an order. It usually ends with a period.

- An exclamatory sentence expresses strong feeling. It ends with an exclamation point.

- Display **Transparency 1–5.** Identify the sentence type for each of the four example sentences at the top.

- Ask volunteers to write the sentence type for Sentences 1–6.

- Have students find examples of the different types of sentences in *Earthquake Terror.*

Daily Language Practice
Have students correct Sentences 1 and 2 on **Transparency 1–4.**

DAY 2 PRACTICE

Independent Work

Practice/Homework Assign **Practice Book** page 21.

Daily Language Practice
Have students correct Sentences 3 and 4 on **Transparency 1–4.**

Transparency 1–4
Daily Language Practice

Sidebar: NATURE'S FURY Earthquake Terror | Grammar Skill Subjects and Predicates | Spelling Skill Short Vowels | ANNOTATED VERSION

Correct two sentences each day.

1. Did you tie the boat to the doct
   Did you tie the boat to the dock?

2. take a deep breeth before you begin.
   Take a deep breath before you begin.

3. The mayor will set up a fuhnd for the flood victims!
   The mayor will set up a fund for the flood victims.

4. watch out for that dich!
   Watch out for that ditch!

5. The two boys slept until noon?
   The two boys slept until noon.

6. Who swepped the leaves under the fence.
   Who swept the leaves under the fence?

7. Be careful not to cresh your fingers in the car door?
   Be careful not to crush your fingers in the car door. (or door!)

8. Justin and amanda shared a buhch of bananas.
   Justin and Amanda shared a bunch of bananas.

9. Did the staf tell you when your puppy could come home
   Did the staff tell you when your puppy could come home?

10. is she fonde of chocolate chip cookies?
    Is she fond of chocolate chip cookies?

Sidebar: TRANSPARENCY 1-4 | TEACHER'S EDITION PAGE 51I

Monitoring Student Progress

If . . .	Then . . .
students score 7 or below on **Practice Book** page 21 or 11 or below on **Practice Book** page 22,	use the Reteaching lessons on Teacher's Edition pages R20 and R21.

Transparency 1–5
Kinds of Sentences

Sidebar: NATURE'S FURY Earthquake Terror | Grammar Skill Kinds of Sentences | ANNOTATED VERSION

An earthquake can be very dangerous.
Have you ever felt the ground move?
Stay calm during an earthquake.
What a scary feeling that must be!

1. Do you know what to do during an earthquake?
   interrogative sentence

2. What can you do to prepare ahead of time?
   interrogative sentence

3. Try to find shelter as quickly as possible.
   imperative sentence

4. What a roaring sound the earth can make!
   exclamatory sentence

5. An earthquake can stop as suddenly as it can start.
   declarative sentence

6. How silent it is right after an earthquake!
   exclamatory sentence

Sidebar: TRANSPARENCY 1-5 | TEACHER'S EDITION PAGE 51I

Practice Book page 21

Header box: Earthquake Terror | Grammar Skill Kinds of Sentences

Name _____

Sensing Danger

Kinds of Sentences There are four kinds of sentences:
1. A declarative sentence tells something and ends with a period.
   Earthquakes occur along fault lines in the earth.
2. An interrogative sentence asks a question and ends with a question mark.
   Can earthquakes be predicted?
3. An imperative sentence gives a request or an order and usually ends with a period.
   Protect your head in an earthquake.
4. An exclamatory sentence expresses strong feeling and ends with an exclamation mark.
   How frightening an earthquake is!

Add the correct punctuation mark to each sentence below. Then write what kind of sentence each one is.

1. Why is the dog barking? **(1 point)**
   interrogative sentence **(1)**

2. Put him on his leash. **(1)**
   imperative sentence **(1)**

3. Some animals can sense a coming earthquake. **(1)**
   declarative sentence **(1)**

4. How frightened I am! **(1)**
   exclamatory sentence **(1)**

5. The earth has stopped shaking at last. **(1)**
   declarative sentence **(1)**

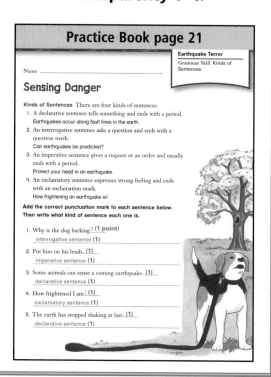

DAY 3 INSTRUCTION

Subjects and Predicates

Teach Go over the following:

- The subject tells whom or what the sentence is about.

- The predicate tells what the subject is or does.

- The complete subject includes all the words in the subject. The simple subject includes just the main word or words.

- The complete predicate includes all the words in the predicate. The simple predicate includes just the main word or words.

- Display **Transparency 1–6.** Point out the complete subject, simple subject, complete predicate, and simple predicate in the sample sentence at the top.

- Have students identify complete and simple subjects and predicates in Sentences 1–6.

Daily Language Practice
Have students correct Sentences 5 and 6 on **Transparency 1–4.**

Transparency 1–6

Subjects and Predicates

The tornado caused a great deal of damage.

1. Many tornadoes happen during the months of April, May, and June.
2. Thunderstorms do not always produce tornadoes.
3. Certain weather conditions cause these storms.
4. Sometimes, several tornadoes will develop from a thunderstorm.
5. Tornadoes can destroy very heavy objects in their path.
6. A funnel-shaped cloud is the characteristic shape of a tornado.

1. complete subject: Many tornadoes/simple subject: tornadoes/complete predicate: happen during the months of April, May, and June/simple predicate: happen
2. complete subject: Thunderstorms/simple subject: Thunderstorms/complete predicate: do not always produce tornadoes/simple predicate: do produce
3. complete subject: Certain weather conditions/simple subject: conditions/complete predicate: cause these storms/simple predicate: cause
4. complete subject: Sometimes, several tornadoes/simple subject: tornadoes/complete predicate: will develop from a thunderstorm/simple predicate: will develop
5. complete subject: Tornadoes/simple subject: Tornadoes/complete predicate: can destroy very heavy objects in their path/simple predicate: can destroy
6. complete subject: A funnel-shaped cloud/simple subject: cloud/complete predicate: is the characteristic shape of a tornado/simple predicate: is

---

DAY 4 PRACTICE

Independent Work

Practice/Homework Assign **Practice Book** page 22.

Daily Language Practice
Have students correct Sentences 7 and 8 on **Transparency 1–4.**

Practice Book page 22

Name _____

Earthquake Terror
Grammar Skill
Subjects and Predicates

On Vacation

Subjects and Predicates Every sentence has a subject. It tells whom or what the sentence is about. The complete subject includes all the words in the subject, and the simple subject is the main word or words in the complete subject.

Every sentence has a predicate too. It tells what the subject is or does. The complete predicate includes all the words in the predicate, and the simple predicate is the main word or words in the complete predicate.

Draw a slash mark (/) between the complete subject and the complete predicate in the sentences below. Then circle the simple subject and underline the simple predicate. (3 points each sentence)

1. The whole family/travels in our new camper.
2. Everybody/helps to pitch the tent under a tree.
3. They/will use a compass on their hike.
4. A good fire/is difficult to build.
5. The smell of cooking/is delicious to the hungry campers.

DAY 5 IMPROVING WRITING

Sentence Combining

Teach Tell students that a good writer avoids using choppy sentences.

- Model combining subjects to form a compound subject:
    - Jonathan saw the bridge. Abby saw the bridge.
    - *Improved:* <u>Jonathan and Abby</u> saw the bridge.

- Model combining predicates to form a compound predicate:
    - The bridge crossed the river. The bridge connected two islands.
    - *Improved:* The bridge <u>crossed the river and connected two islands</u>.

- Have students review their writing to see if they can improve it by combining sentences.

Practice/Homework Assign **Practice Book** page 23.

Daily Language Practice
Have students correct Sentences 9 and 10 on **Transparency 1–4.**

Practice Book page 23

Name _____

Earthquake Terror
Grammar Skill Compound
Subjects and Compound
Predicates

Sentence Combining

A **compound subject** is made up of two or more simple subjects that have the same predicate. Use a connecting word such as *and* or *or* to join the simple subjects.

Jonathan yelled. Abby yelled.   Jonathan and Abby yelled.
Combine two simple subjects into one compound subject, as shown above, to make your writing clearer and less choppy.

A **compound predicate** is made up of two or more simple predicates that have the same subject. Use a connecting word such as *and* or *or* to join the simple predicates.

Moose barked. Moose howled.   Moose barked and howled.
Combine simple predicates into compound predicates, as shown above, to make your writing smoother.

Suppose Jonathan wrote a draft of a letter to his aunt about his vacation. Revise his letter by combining sentences. Each new sentence will have either a compound subject or a compound predicate. Only Jonathan's first sentence will remain the same.

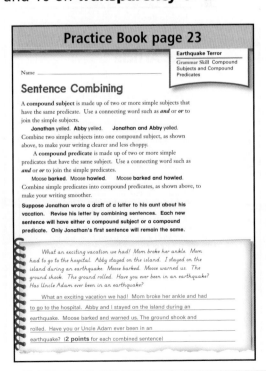

What an exciting vacation we had! Mom broke her ankle. Mom had to go to the hospital. Abby stayed on the island. I stayed on the island during an earthquake. Moose warned us. The ground shook. The ground rolled. Have you ever been in an earthquake? Has Uncle Adam ever been in an earthquake?

What an exciting vacation we had! Mom broke her ankle and had to go to the hospital. Abby and I stayed on the island during an earthquake. Moose barked and warned us. The ground shook and rolled. Have you or Uncle Adam ever been in an earthquake? (**2 points** for each combined sentence)

WRITING: News Article

OBJECTIVES

- Identify the characteristics of a news article.
- Write a news article.
- Add details to improve writing.

Writing Traits

Ideas Emphasize the importance of ideas as you teach the lesson on Day 3. Students can ask these questions about their own writing.

- What do I want my reader to understand?
- Have I written in a way that will help my reader understand this?
- Do I need to add any words or details? Do I need to delete any words or details?

DAY 1 PREWRITING

Introducing the Format

Introduce writing a news article.

- A news article informs readers about interesting or unusual events, such as the earthquake that Jonathan and Abby experienced.
- A news article tells facts about what happened. It does not tell opinions.
- It answers the questions Who, What, When, Where, Why, and How.

Start students thinking about news articles.

- Ask students to list three interesting or unusual events that happened in their neighborhood, at school, or in town.
- Have them save their notes.

DAY 2 DRAFTING

Discussing the Model

Display Transparency 1–7. Ask:

- What is the news article about? (the rescue of a puppy)
- What facts answer the questions Who, What, and When? (Who: firefighters, puppy; What: rescue of puppy; When: October 11)
- What facts answer the questions Where, Why, and How? (Where: storm drain on Main Street; Why: puppy fell in drain opening; How: cut into drain pipe)
- Did the beginning of the article capture your interest? Why or why not?
- Did the headline grab your attention? Why or why not?

Display Transparency 1–8, and discuss the guidelines.

Have students draft a news article.

- Have them write about an interesting event, using their notes from Day 1.
- Assign **Practice Book** page 24 to help students organize their writing.
- Provide support as needed.

Transparency 1–7
A News Article

The Dog Days of Summer

When Roberto Garrigues and Robin Foster became firefighters, little did they know what creative thinking skills they would be called upon to use. For on October 11, a small puppy managed to fall into a storm drain on Main Street. How the puppy got into the drainpipe is not clear. It was even less clear how to get it out. But Roberto and Robin were assigned to solve the problem, and solve it they did.

The pipe was too small for either firefighter to crawl into. Likewise, the puppy wouldn't come when it was called, so the firefighters could not lift a storm grate and grab the puppy from above as it approached. Finally, Robin had an idea. "I realized that if we cut a puppy-sized hole in the side of the pipe," she said, "the dog would probably come out on its own." The clever solution worked. With the added incentive of a bowl of puppy food near the hole, the hungry puppy eventually poked its head out, and the firefighters grabbed it.

Within an hour, the puppy was reunited with its grateful owner. "I didn't even know Tornado was missing," said owner Jerry Emerson of his aptly named pup, who had just caused a whirlwind of trouble. "Somehow Tornado must have slipped out when I was carrying in my groceries. I'm certainly glad he had a dog license, so he could be quickly returned. And I'll be forever grateful to the firefighters for their ingenious rescue."

ANNOTATED VERSION
NATURE'S FURY Earthquake Terror / Writing Skill News Article
TRANSPARENCY 1–7 / TEACHER'S EDITION PAGE 51K

Transparency 1–8
Guidelines for Writing a News Article

- Write about an interesting or unusual event.
- Write facts, not opinions.
- Use the facts to answer the questions *Who? What? When? Where? Why? How?*
- Write the most important facts at the beginning of the article.
- Write your beginning in a way that captures the reader's attention.
- Use quotations to make the article come alive. Make sure the quotations are exactly what people said.
- Write a short, attention-grabbing headline for the article.

ANNOTATED VERSION
NATURE'S FURY Earthquake Terror / Writing Skill News Article
TRANSPARENCY 1–8 / TEACHER'S EDITION PAGE 51K

Practice Book page 24

Earthquake Terror
Writing Skill News Article

Name _____

Writing a News Article

Jonathan and Abby Palmer experience firsthand an unforgettable event — the terror of an earthquake. Imagine you are a reporter for the *Daily Gazette*. Use the chart below to gather details for a news article about an interesting or unusual event at your school, in your neighborhood, or in your town. Answer these questions: What happened? Who was involved? When, where, and why did this event occur? How did it happen?

Who? (2 points)
What? (2)
When? (2)
Where? (2)
Why? (2)
How? (2)

Now use the details you gathered to write your news article on a separate sheet of paper. Include a headline and a beginning that will capture your reader's attention. Present facts in order of importance, from most to least important. Try to use quotations from eyewitnesses to bring this news event to life. (3)

DAY 3 REVISING

Improving Writing: Adding Details

Discuss the importance of adding details.

- Details add information to an article.
- They tell more about who was there, when and where the event happened, what caused it, and how it occurred.
- Details should always be accurate.
- See Writing Traits on page 51K.

Display Transparency 1–9.

- Point out that Passage 2 is a revised version of Passage 1.
- Ask volunteers to underline the new details added to Passage 2.
- Discuss how these details tell who, what, when, where, why, and how.

Assign Practice Book page 25.

Have students revise their drafts.

- Display **Transparency 1–8** again.
- Have partners discuss the guidelines to decide how to make their writing better.
- Have students look for places to add details to their news articles.

DAY 4 PROOFREADING

Checking for Errors

Have students proofread for errors in grammar, spelling, punctuation, or usage.

- Students can use the proofreading checklist on **Practice Book** page 281 to help them proofread their news article.
- Students can also use the proofreading marks on **Practice Book** page 282.

DAY 5 PUBLISHING

Sharing News Articles

Consider these publishing options.

- Ask students to read their news articles or some other piece of writing from the Author's Chair.
- Encourage students to collect their news articles into a class newspaper.

Portfolio Opportunity

Save students' news articles as samples of their writing development.

Transparency 1–9

Adding Details

An Earthshaking Experience

Passage 1

Two hikers on Magpie Island felt the ground swell and retreat beneath their feet. The devastating quake harmed or trapped many on the island, but Jonathan managed to pull his sister Abby to safety.

Passage 2

Two hikers, <u>Jonathan and Abby Palmer</u>, on Magpie Island <u>for a camping trip</u>, felt the ground swell and retreat beneath their feet <u>during yesterday's quake</u>. The devastating quake harmed or trapped many on the island, but Jonathan, <u>crawling on hands and knees</u>, managed to pull his sister Abby to safety <u>beneath a fallen redwood tree</u>.

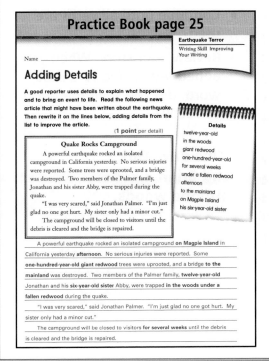

Practice Book page 25

Earthquake Terror
Writing Skill Improving Your Writing

Name _____

Adding Details

A good reporter uses details to explain what happened and to bring an event to life. Read the following news article that might have been written about the earthquake. Then rewrite it on the lines below, adding details from the list to improve the article.

(1 point per detail)

Quake Rocks Campground

A powerful earthquake rocked an isolated campground in California yesterday. No serious injuries were reported. Some trees were uprooted, and a bridge was destroyed. Two members of the Palmer family, Jonathan and his sister Abby, were trapped during the quake.

"I was very scared," said Jonathan Palmer. "I'm just glad no one got hurt. My sister only had a minor cut."

The campground will be closed to visitors until the debris is cleared and the bridge is repaired.

Details

twelve-year-old
in the woods
giant redwood
one-hundred-year-old
for several weeks
under a fallen redwood
afternoon
to the mainland
on Magpie Island
his six-year-old sister

A powerful earthquake rocked an isolated campground **on Magpie Island** in California yesterday **afternoon**. No serious injuries were reported. Some **one-hundred-year-old giant redwood** trees were uprooted, and a bridge **to the mainland** was destroyed. Two members of the Palmer family, **twelve-year-old** Jonathan and his **six-year-old sister** Abby, were trapped **in the woods under a fallen redwood** during the quake.

"I was very scared," said Jonathan Palmer. "I'm just glad no one got hurt. My sister only had a minor cut."

The campground will be closed to visitors **for several weeks** until the debris is cleared and the bridge is repaired.

Monitoring Student Progress

If . . .	Then . . .
students' writing does not follow the guidelines on **Transparency 1–8**,	work with students to improve specific parts of their writing.

Independent Activities

Language Center

VOCABULARY

Building Vocabulary

👥 Groups	🕐 20 minutes
Objective	Make a web of earthquake words.
Materials	Dictionary

Scientists who study earthquakes use specialized terms to identify and describe features of earthquakes. Create a word web that shows vocabulary related to earthquakes. Start with the web below.

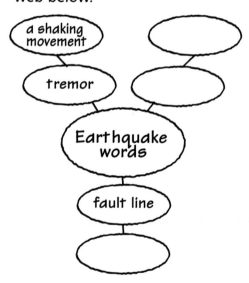

- Work together to find additional words. Write the word meaning in another bubble on the word web. Look up unfamiliar words in a dictionary.

- Share your words with other groups. Then create a class web that includes all the terms.

PHONICS/SPELLING

Trading Bases

👥 Pairs	🕐 15 minutes
Objective	Write sentences using base words and endings.

With a partner, add different endings to base words. Use the words to write a story about an earthquake.

- First, make a list of 10 verbs that can help you tell the story. Examples: *roll, shiver, crash.*

- Take turns adding the *-ed* or *-ing* ending to a verb from the list. Use that word in a complete sentence that helps to tell the story.

- Continue until all verbs are used.

- Review your story: When you added *-ed* or *-ing* to a base word, did you spell the word correctly?

One day, Tina and Brian <u>hiked</u> into the woods.

Tina heard something that sent her heart <u>thumping</u>.

VOCABULARY

Vocabulary Game

👥 Pairs	🕐 30 minutes
Objective	Match Key Vocabulary words with synonyms.
Materials	Activity Master 1–1, scissors

Use the Key Vocabulary words to create a "Concentration" word game.

- Cut out the Key Vocabulary words and synonyms on Activity Master 1–1.

- Place the word cards facedown on a table and scramble them. Then arrange them in a square. You will now try to match each Key Vocabulary word with the appropriate synonym.

- Take turns flipping over two cards. If no match is made, flip the cards back over. After making a match, a player can remove the cards and take an extra turn.

- Continue playing until all matches have been found.

	debris		
			remains

Consider copying and laminating these activities for use in centers.

LISTENING/SPEAKING

Panel Discussion

👥👥👥 Groups	🕐 45 minutes
Objective	Hold a panel discussion.

Have a formal discussion about how Jonathan handled the earthquake emergency.

- First, review the story to find examples that show Jonathan's leadership abilities.

- In groups of three, present opinions on the subject. Have one person act as a moderator to keep the discussion on track.

- Remember to follow the rules for good discussion.

Discussion Tips
- Stick to the topic of discussion.
- Speak clearly.
- Give reasons for your opinions.
- Respect the opinions of others.
- Listen carefully to what others say.
- Allow others to speak without interrupting them.

GRAMMAR

Safety Sentences

👥👥 Pairs	🕐 30 minutes
Objective	Write a list of safety tips.

Make a list of six suggestions for staying safe during earthquakes and storms. Write each suggestion as a sentence. Include each type of sentence listed in the chart.

Sentence Type	Definition	Rule
declarative	tells something	ends with period
interrogative	asks questions	ends with question mark
imperative	gives a request or order	usually ends with period
exclamatory	expresses strong feelings	ends with exclamation mark

Suggestions:

- Review *Earthquake Terror* and other stories about storms. Note ways the characters stayed safe.
- Note problems that could have been prevented.
- Use your own experience.
- Look for advice on the Internet.

Riding Out the Storm

Summary *In* Riding Out the Storm, *young Raylee finds herself trapped in her home with her dog Chomper during a hurricane. Through misunderstandings, she has not been picked up by family members and taken to a nearby shelter. She must ride out the storm on her own. Raylee and her dog endure power outages, shrieking wind, and flooding. They end up in the attic, where they are finally rescued.*

Vocabulary

Introduce the Key Vocabulary and ask students to complete the BLM.

shelter a place that provides protection, *p. 3*

splattered splashed forcefully, as heavy rain in a storm, *p. 4*

fixed attached or fastened securely, *p. 12*

rescue to save from danger, *p. 20*

● BELOW LEVEL

Building Background and Vocabulary

Ask students about experiences they may have had during a terrible storm. Make sure they understand that hurricanes are tropical ocean storms that can hit land with powerful winds and heavy rains, causing damage and even death. Preview the story with students, using the story vocabulary when possible.

Comprehension Skill: Sequence of Events

Have students read the Strategy Focus on the book flap. Remind students to use the strategy and to keep track of the sequence of events as they read the book. (See the Leveled Readers Teacher's Guide for **Vocabulary and Comprehension Practice Masters**.)

Responding

Have partners discuss how to answer the questions on the inside back cover.

Think About the Selection Sample answers:

1. a hurricane

2. making do until the storm is over

3. She runs outside and waves at the car, yells at her dog, and then hugs him.

4. Possible responses: scared, brave, courageous

Making Connections Responses will vary.

Building Fluency

Model Read aloud pages 3 and 4. Point out the heading and explain that headings tell about the paragraphs that follow them.

Practice Have students find and read aloud each heading in the story. Then they can read the paragraphs that follow the heading and explain why the heading is appropriate.

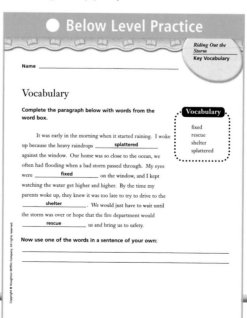

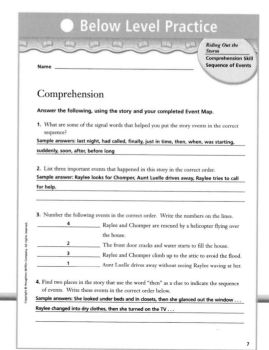

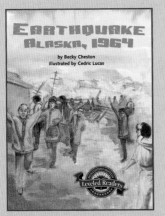

Earthquake Alaska, 1964

Summary *When an earthquake hits her village, Kaya must leave all her belongings behind and flee. From a nearby hillside, she watches two tsunamis wash over the village. Then, Kaya's father races back home to save what he can. The third tsunami crashes onto the village as Kaya looks on, horrified. When her father returns from the wreckage of the village, Kaya realizes that out of all her belongings, her family is the one thing that cannot be replaced.*

Vocabulary

Introduce the Key Vocabulary and ask students to complete the BLM.

journal a diary, *p. 4*

jiggle tremble, *p. 5*

tremors vibrations, especially during an earthquake, *p. 7*

traction grip, *p. 9*

interval time between two events, *p. 12*

volunteered offered a service without reward, *p. 12*

retrieve to get back, *p. 12*

Building Background and Vocabulary

Invite students to think about what possessions they would want to rescue during a catastrophe. Preview the story with students, using the story vocabulary when possible.

🌀 Comprehension Skill: Sequence of Events

Have students read the Strategy Focus on the book flap. Remind students to use the strategy and to keep track of the sequence of events as they read the book. (See the Leveled Readers Teacher's Guide for **Vocabulary and Comprehension Practice Masters**.)

Responding

Have partners discuss how to answer the questions on the inside back cover.

Think About the Selection Sample answers:

1. The possessions make her feel safe and secure.

2. Possible response: She helps Kaya out of the house. Josie understands that people are more important than objects.

3. The tremors cause their homes to collapse. Falling rocks threaten them. Because they live on the coast, tsunamis can destroy what's left.

4. Kaya is relieved that her father is still alive.

Making Connections Responses will vary.

🌀 Building Fluency

Model Read aloud page 7 at a fast rate and then page 16 more slowly. Explain that knowing the action in these passages can help people understand how quickly, or slowly, they should read.

Practice Partners can take turns reading the two passages.

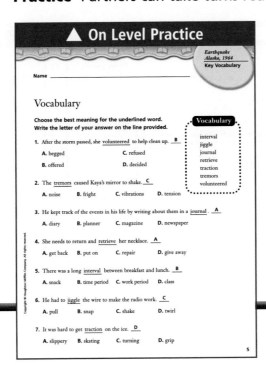

Leveled Readers

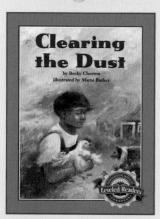

Clearing the Dust

Summary
Twelve-year-old Aaron Oakes's dreams of keeping the family farm are in danger. His father is in town on business when a bad dust storm blows through. Aaron takes charge, securing the farm and the animals.

Vocabulary

Introduce the Key Vocabulary and ask students to complete the BLM.

generations the time between the birth of parents and children, *p. 3*

abandoned deserted, *p. 4*

languished neglected, *p. 4*

terrified full of fear, *p. 5*

warble a song of quavering trills, *p. 6*

galvanized stimulated, *p. 9*

debris* the remains of something broken or destroyed, *p. 10*

hoisted pulled up, *p. 10*

shuddered shook, vibrated, or quivered, *p. 11*

*Forms of these words are Anthology Key Vocabulary words.

■ ABOVE LEVEL

Building Background and Vocabulary

Invite students to share stories about storms. Preview the story with students, using the story vocabulary when possible.

Comprehension Skill: Sequence of Events

Have students read the Strategy Focus on the book flap. Remind students to use the strategy and to keep track of the sequence of events as they read the book. (See the Leveled Readers Teacher's Guide for **Vocabulary and Comprehension Practice Masters**.)

Responding

Have partners discuss how to answer the questions on the inside back cover.

Think About the Selection Sample answers:

1. He wants to take over the farm one day. He worries about losing it.

2. He gets the animals to shelter. He helps his mother up and secures the windows.

3. the descriptions of the farm and storm; Aaron's wishes for the future

4. He arrives with a man who can help the Oakes family keep their farm.

Making Connections Responses will vary.

Building Fluency

Model Read aloud page 3. Tell how the phrase *But now, at age twelve* signals a change in time in the story.

Practice Have students look for other examples of phrases that change the time of the story. Students can read these phrases to partners. If they have difficulty finding more phrases, ask them to look on pages 4 and 7.

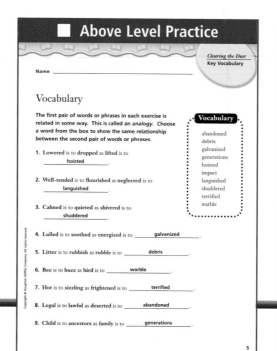

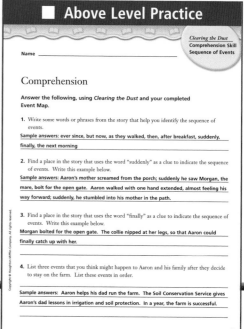

Leveled Readers

Alone in the Storm

Summary *Raylee is alone in the house during a hurricane. She has to ride out the storm with her frightened dog, Chomper. When water fills the house, Raylee and Chomper go to the attic. After the storm, Raylee breaks a hole in the roof and she and Chomper are rescued by a helicopter.*

Vocabulary

Introduce the Key Vocabulary and ask students to complete the BLM.

hurricane a very powerful storm with extremely strong winds and heavy rains, *p. 3*

frightened filled with fear; alarmed, *p. 6*

ride out the storm to keep safe until a storm is over, *p. 8*

shrieking making a shrill, high noise, *p. 11*

attic the room just under the roof, *p. 14*

debris* the remains of something broken or destroyed, *p. 15*

*Forms of these words are Anthology Key Vocabulary words.

◆ LANGUAGE SUPPORT

Building Background and Vocabulary

Define *hurricane*, and discuss basic safety information for storms and emergencies. Then distribute the **Build Background Practice Master**. Read aloud the sentences and discuss whether each action on the list should be taken before, during, or after a hurricane.

Comprehension Skill: Sequence of Events

Have students read the Strategy Focus on the book flap. Remind students to use the strategy and to notice the sequence of events as they read the book. (See the Leveled Readers Teacher's Guide for **Build Background, Vocabulary, and Graphic Organizer Masters**.)

Responding

Have partners discuss how to answer the questions on the inside back cover.

Think About the Selection Sample answers:

1. A hurricane hits the town.

2. It means staying safe until the storm has passed.

3. Strong winds can tear off the roof.

4. Responses will vary.

Making Connections Responses will vary.

Building Fluency

Model Have students follow along in their books as they listen to page 3 of the recording of *Alone in the Storm* on audio CD.

Practice Have partners read along with the recording until they can read the text on their own accurately and with expression.

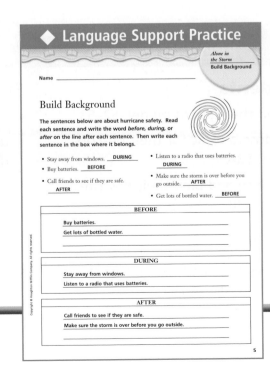

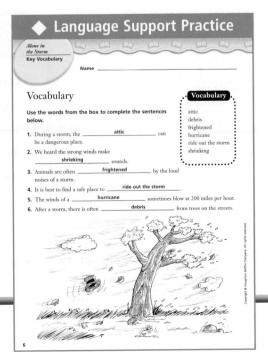

Reading-Writing Workshop

Description

In the Reading-Writing Workshop for Theme 1, *Nature's Fury,* students read Dena's description, "By the Sea," on Anthology pages 52–53. Then they follow the five steps of the writing process to write a description.

Meet the Author

Dena S.
Grade: five
State: New York
Hobbies: ice skating, singing, and basketball
What she'd like to be when she grows up: a singer

Theme Skill Trace

Writing
- Adding Details, 51L
- Capitalizing and Punctuating Sentences, 81L
- Correcting Sentence Fragments, 105L

Grammar
- Sentence Combining: Compound Subjects and Compound Predicates, 51J
- Avoiding Run-ons, 81J
- Exact Nouns, 105J

Spelling
- Short Vowels, 51E
- The /ā/, /ē/, and /ī/ Sounds, 81E
- The /ō/, /o͞o/, and /yo͞o/ Sounds, 105E

Pacing the Workshop

Here is a suggestion for how you might pace the workshop within one week or on five separate days across the theme.

DAY 1 PREWRITING

Students

- read the student model, 52–53
- choose a topic for their description, 53A
- explore and plan their description, 53B 4.04, 4.05

Spelling Frequently Misspelled Words, 53F; *Practice Book,* 265 5.05

DAY 2 DRAFTING

Students

- brainstorm sensory language, 53C
- draft their description, telling details in order, 53D 4.03, 4.04, 4.05, 4.06, 4.07

Spelling *Practice Book,* 28

Focus on Writing Traits: Description

The workshop for this theme focuses on the traits of word choice and sentence fluency. However, students should think about all of the writing traits during the writing process.

WORD CHOICE Your students can make strong word choices without above-grade-level vocabularies. Teach them to sort through the words they already know and choose the one that most closely expresses what they mean. When they are having trouble choosing an exact word, try following these steps:

- Ask them to list at least two or three words they might use. Suggest using a thesaurus.

- Then ask them to read over their list and choose the best word.

SENTENCE FLUENCY Many students have difficulty starting a sentence with something other than the subject. Suggest these strategies.

- Start with a word or phrase that tells where (*Next to my dresser . . .*).

- Start with a word or phrase that tells when (*In the morning . . .*).

- Start with a word or phrase that tells how (*Brightly, it shines . . .*).

- Start with a word or phrase that tells why (*To make taller . . .*).

Emphasize that all sentences must have a subject and a predicate.

Tips for Teaching the Writing Traits

- Teach one trait at a time.

- Discuss examples of the traits in the literature students are reading.

- Encourage students to talk about the traits during a writing conference.

- Encourage students to revise their writing for one trait at a time.

DAY 3 REVISING

Students

- evaluate their description, 53E
- revise their description, 53E
- have a writing conference, 53E 4.08a-c

Spelling *Practice Book,* 29

DAY 4 PROOFREADING

Students

- proofread their description, 53E
- improve their writing by checking for complete sentences, 53E
- correct frequently misspelled words in their description, 53F 5.06, 5.07

Spelling *Practice Book,* 30

DAY 5 PUBLISHING

Students

 publish their description, 53G

- reflect on their writing experience, 53G 4.09, 4.10, 5.08

Spelling Assessment, 53F 5.05

Description

Discussing the Guidelines

Display **Transparency RWW1–1,** and discuss what makes a great description.

- Remember that students should think about all the writing traits as they write: ideas, organization, voice, word choice, sentence fluency, conventions, and presentation.

Discussing the Model

Have students read the Student Writing Model on Anthology pages 52–53.

- Discuss with students what the writer did to make her description interesting to read.
- Use the Reading As a Writer questions on the next page.

Student Writing Model

A Description

A description is a picture in words that helps the reader share the writer's experience. Use this student's writing as a model when you write a description of your own.

By the Sea

The **beginning** tells what the description is about.

> My grandfather has an apartment that we visit every summer for a few days. My favorite place is a beach where my family goes to play and walk along the shore.

Imagery lets readers visualize how something looks, sounds, smells, tastes, and feels.

> When the weather is nice, the sky is blue and the clouds are pure white. The ocean is greenish blue and when the waves crash, the foam is white. Along the water's edge, there are clam shells, crabs, baby shrimp, and once my brother found a starfish! The seagulls walk around like scavengers, looking for clams and crabs to eat. Sometimes I feel like a seagull, because we are both walking around trying to find something special. The seaweed washes up along the shore. It's green and long, and when it wraps around your leg it is ticklish. When we play in the water, we are always careful of the jellyfish. Some are red and some are clear, but they all sting.

Similes give the reader a clear mental picture.

52

Transparency RWW1–1

What Makes a Great Description?

A **description** is a picture in words that helps the reader see, hear, taste, smell, or feel something that the writer has experienced.

Follow these guidelines when you write your description.

- Introduce your topic in an interesting way.
- Use at least three of your five senses to brainstorm details about your topic.
- Include many details to give your readers a clear picture of what you are describing.
- Order details so that readers can easily follow them.
- Provide crisp and vivid descriptions, using sensory language.
- Sum up your thoughts and feelings about your topic in the ending.

TRANSPARENCY RWW 1–1
TEACHER'S EDITION PAGE 52

NATURE'S FURY
Reading-Writing Workshop Description

ANNOTATED VERSION

When the weather is cloudy and stormy, the skies are gray and the waves crash along the shore. It sounds like thunder or like a roaring lion. We don't walk along the shore during a storm, but we can watch from the boardwalk.

> A good description puts **details** in time order, in spatial order, or in order of importance.

The prettiest part of the day is when the sun sets over the bay. It seems as if every time we look up, the colors in the sky change. At first, there is pink, blue, and some green. Then the colors darken to red, orange, blue-gray, and purple. Finally the sky goes dark blue and the sun sets.

I love my grandfather's beach house!

> A good **ending** wraps up the description.

Meet the Author

Dena S.

Grade: five
State: New York
Hobbies: ice skating, singing, and basketball
What she'd like to be when she grows up: a singer

53

Reading As a Writer

1. What scene does this writer paint a description of? (the beach near her grandfather's apartment)

2. What sights does the writer describe? Give some examples of this sense. (Sample answers: blue sky, pure white clouds, greenish blue ocean, white foam)

3. What details tell about the writer's sense of touch? (Sample answer: the ticklish feel of the seaweed)

4. What sounds does the writer describe? (Sample answer: waves crashing)

5. How does the writer sum up her description? (She says she loves her grandfather's beach house.)

Choosing a Topic

1 **Explain how to choose a topic for a description.** Tell students they are going to write their own description of a place or thing that they know about. Have students list three or more ideas for descriptions that they could write. Explain that they should be able to describe their topic using at least three of their five senses.

2 **Offer these prompts** if students are having trouble thinking of a topic.

- What is your favorite place?

- What is your most important possession?

- What is the most amazing thing you've seen lately?

3 **Have students answer these questions** as they choose a topic, either in a writing journal or on a sheet of paper:

- Whom do you see as your audience: classmates? friends? people who share your enthusiasm for your topic?

- What is your purpose for writing: to make readers laugh? to inform them? to share your feelings?

- How will you publish your description: on the Internet? by reading it aloud? in a letter that you will send?

4 **Have students discuss their ideas with a partner** and decide which topic would be the best one to write about. Then review these tips with students.

Tips for Getting Started with a Topic

- Discuss the topic you chose with a partner. Is your topic too big? Can it be narrowed?

- Draw a picture of your topic. Label parts of the picture and list details.

- Think of details that use at least three of your five senses.

Exploring and Planning

1 **Explain that students can brainstorm details** by conducting an inventory of their memories and impressions of the topic. Emphasize that a good description uses many details to paint a vivid picture of a place or thing. Discuss these strategies for brainstorming details.

- Picture yourself near what you're describing. What would you see if you were there?
- If your topic is an object, think about what it does. If it is a place, think about what happens there.
- Remember what you know about your topic. Can you think of some facts and figures that will help your readers picture it?

2 **Display Transparency RWW1–2.** Work with students to brainstorm details for a description of a topic that is familiar to everyone.

- Conduct an inventory of their memories by completing the Description Web.
- You can use the sample answers shown below to complete the transparency.

Details For Description Web

- **Topic:** The schoolyard during recess
- **Sights:** tons of kids; shiny metal slide; trampled grass; black plastic swings
- **Actions:** play kickball; talk with friends; go on swings; have a snack
- **Facts and Figures:** 200 square feet of blacktop; six swings; four-foot chain link fence; 100-year-old oak tree

3 **Distribute copies of Transparency RWW1–2,** and have students use the Description Web to explore and plan their descriptions.

- They should leave out any details not directly related to their topic.
- They should put a star next to the details that seem most important.
- They should number their details in the order they will write about them.

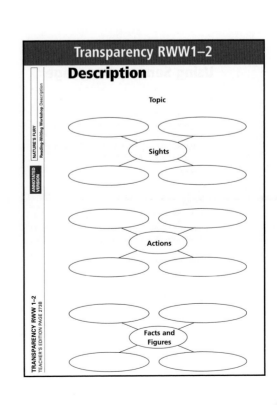

Using Sensory Language

READING-WRITING WORKSHOP

Writing Traits

WORD CHOICE Discuss the following points with students.

- Good writers choose words that say exactly what they mean.
- A good description uses words that help readers see, taste, hear, feel, or smell what is being described.
- Words that appeal to the five senses are called sensory words or sensory language.
- Writers often use comparisons, called similes, to make sensory words more vivid. For example, *the show dog's tail stood straight and tall, like a ship's mast.*

1 **Display Transparency RWW1–3,** and model using sensory language.

- Read the first phrase aloud. Go over the sample response. Discuss how much more vivid the sentence is with sensory words.
- Then ask the students to come up with their own sensory words that might describe a bouquet of flowers. Have them write a sentence that uses these words.
- Instruct students to complete the rest of the transparency with a partner, writing their answers on a separate sheet of paper.

2 **Encourage students to use sensory language** in their own writing.

- Encourage them to close their eyes and picture their topic, focusing on how it looks, feels, tastes, smells, and what it may sound like.
- Remind them to choose words and phrases that show how they feel about their topic: tell them to let readers see how spooky the house looks or hear how much a dog is loved.

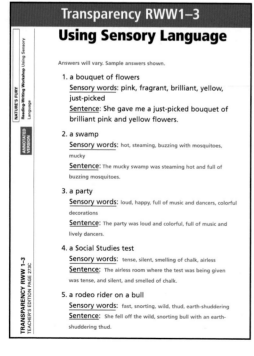

Transparency RWW1–3

Using Sensory Language

Answers will vary. Sample answers shown.

1. a bouquet of flowers
   Sensory words: pink, fragrant, brilliant, yellow, just-picked
   Sentence: She gave me a just-picked bouquet of brilliant pink and yellow flowers.

2. a swamp
   Sensory words: hot, steaming, buzzing with mosquitoes, mucky
   Sentence: The mucky swamp was steaming hot and full of buzzing mosquitoes.

3. a party
   Sensory words: loud, happy, full of music and dancers, colorful decorations
   Sentence: The party was loud and colorful, full of music and lively dancers.

4. a Social Studies test
   Sensory words: tense, silent, smelling of chalk, airless
   Sentence: The airless room where the test was being given was tense, and silent, and smelled of chalk.

5. a rodeo rider on a bull
   Sensory words: fast, snorting, wild, thud, earth-shuddering
   Sentence: She fell off the wild, snorting bull with an earth-shuddering thud.

TRANSPARENCY RWW 1–3
TEACHER'S EDITION PAGE 273C

Organizing Details

1 **Explain that ordering details helps the reader** picture clearly what is being described. Review three ways to organize a description.

Ways to Organize a Description

- **Time Order** A description of a boat race might begin at the start of the race and end at the finish line.

- **Spatial Order** A description of a car might begin at the hood in front and end at the fender in back.

- **Order of Importance** A description of your adorable dog might begin with your dog's most adorable features and end with her least adorable features.

2 **Display Transparency RWW1–4.** Point out that these exercises have no single correct order.

- Have students suggest possible orders for Exercise 1. Ask them to explain their answers.

- Instruct students to complete Exercise 2 on a separate sheet of paper.

3 **Have students look back at their planning webs** and decide which organization scheme they will use.

- Tell students to number the details to show the order they will write about them.

- Remind them to delete any details that are not directly related to their topic.

4 **Have students draft their descriptions.** Tell them to follow these steps.

- Have them refer to their Description Web and add additional details that occur to them as they write.

- Remind them to begin by telling their readers what they are describing and to end in a way that wraps up their description.

- Remind them to use vivid sensory words.

- Encourage them to write freely. Remind them that they can fix spelling and punctuation at the proofreading stage.

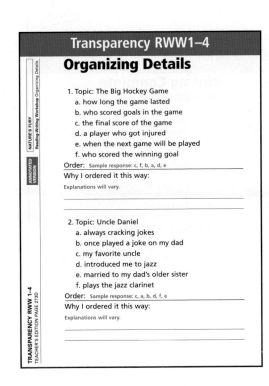

Transparency RWW1–4

Organizing Details

1. Topic: The Big Hockey Game
   a. how long the game lasted
   b. who scored goals in the game
   c. the final score of the game
   d. a player who got injured
   e. when the next game will be played
   f. who scored the winning goal
   Order: Sample response: c, f, b, a, d, e
   Why I ordered it this way:
   Explanations will vary.

2. Topic: Uncle Daniel
   a. always cracking jokes
   b. once played a joke on my dad
   c. my favorite uncle
   d. introduced me to jazz
   e. married to my dad's older sister
   f. plays the jazz clarinet
   Order: Sample response: c, a, b, d, f, e
   Why I ordered it this way:
   Explanations will vary.

Reading-Writing Workshop: Description **53D**

READING-WRITING WORKSHOP

Practice Book page 26

Name _____

Revising Your Description

Reread your description. Put a checkmark in the box for each sentence that describes your paper. Use this page to help you revise.

Rings the Bell
- The beginning tells my topic. The ending is satisfying.
- Sensory words and exact details create vivid pictures.
- My details are well organized and related to my topic.
- Voice is strong; you can tell how I feel about my topic.
- Sentences flow smoothly. There are almost no mistakes.

Getting Stronger
- The beginning and ending may be somewhat weak.
- More exact words and sensory details are needed.
- My details could be easier to follow. A few are unrelated.
- My voice doesn't come through clearly.
- Some sentences are awkward. There are a few mistakes.

Try Harder
- The beginning and ending are missing.
- There are no details. My word choices are confusing.
- The order is unclear. Many details are unrelated.
- My writing sounds flat. You can't tell how I feel.
- Most sentences are choppy. There are lots of mistakes.

Practice Book page 27

Name _____

Writing Complete Sentences

Make each incomplete sentence complete. Change words or add extra words if you need to. Answers will vary. Sample answers given.

1. Being a photographer
   Being a photographer can be exciting. **(1 point)**

2. Photographing nature
   Photographing nature can be dangerous. **(1)**

3. Lightning flashing in the sky
   You can take pictures of lightning flashing in the sky. **(1)**

4. Chasing storms
   You could travel the world while chasing storms. **(1)**

5. Tornadoes in the distance
   You could take pictures of tornadoes in the distance. **(1)**

6. The black funnel is impressive, even far away.
   Complete. **(1)**

7. Planes in storms
   Planes can get tossed about in storms. **(1)**

8. A bumpy ride
   Turbulence can create a bumpy ride for passengers. **(1)**

9. Dangerous to be out in some storms
   It's dangerous to be out in some storms. **(1)**

10. Don't stand under a tree when there's lightning.
    Complete. **(1)**

Transparency RWW1–5

Writing Complete Sentences

Answers will vary. Sample answers shown.

1. My family saw the new movie *President Pooch*.
2. A brown and white beagle named Looie.
   Looie is a brown and white beagle.
3. Looie, the President of the United States.
   Looie becomes the President of the United States.
4. Runs all over the White House.
   Looie runs all over the White House.
5. Most of the people.
   Most of the people loved Looie.
6. The angry vice president and Congress.
   The angry vice president and Congress try to get rid of Looie.
7. The scrappy and smart pooch.
   The scrappy and smart pooch outsmarts them all.
8. Slowly shows his marvelous talents.
   Looie slowly shows his marvelous talents.
9. In the end, the great dog-president.
   In the end, everyone cheers for the great dog-president.

Revising

Have students use **Practice Book** page 26 to help them evaluate and then revise their description. Students should also discuss their drafts in a writing conference with one or more classmates. (Distribute the Conference Master on page R30. Discuss the sample thoughts and questions before students have their conferences.) Remind students to keep in mind their listeners' comments and questions when they revise.

Writing Traits

SENTENCE FLUENCY Remind students that they should try varying the way their sentences begin. Encourage them to begin some sentences with time-order words (*When, After*) or place words (*Where, There*).

Proofreading

Have students proofread their papers to correct capitalization, punctuation, spelling, and usage. They can use the proofreading checklist and proofreading marks on **Practice Book** pages 281–282.

Improving Writing: Writing Complete Sentences

Tell students that good writers use complete sentences.

- A sentence tells a complete thought. It has a subject and a predicate.
- The subject is the person, place, or thing that the sentence is about.
- The predicate contains the verb and the words that go with it.

Display **Transparency RWW1–5,** and model writing complete sentences.

- Read the first two sentences aloud. Show that the first is complete because it has a subject and a predicate. (*My family; saw the new movie President Pooch*)
- Show that the second is not a complete sentence because it does not have a verb. Read the suggested answer. Have students suggest other acceptable answers.
- Have students work together to complete the transparency.

Assign **Practice Book** page 27. Then have students see whether they can improve their descriptions by correcting sentence fragments.

Frequently Misspelled Words

Write the Spelling Words on the board, or distribute the list on **Practice Book** page 265. Help students identify the part of the word likely to be misspelled.

Spelling Pretest/Test

Basic Words

1. I can never do **enough** hiking.
2. I **caught** poison ivy on a hike.
3. I **brought** medicine on the hike.
4. I **thought** I might have to go home.
5. I put cream on **every** two hours.
6. Once, I waited **ninety** minutes.
7. I used **their** shower to clean up.
8. **They're** afraid of bears.
9. **There** are some bears up here.
10. **There's** a beautiful waterfall, too.
11. I **know** the best hikes.
12. I **knew** they would like this hike.
13. We got home at six **o'clock**.
14. **We're** not worried about bears.
15. Most bears leave **people** alone.

Challenge Words

16. A **decent** hike lasts four hours.
17. I even bought some hiking **stationery**.
18. When I can't hike, I ride a **stationary** bike.
19. I **correspond** with other hikers.
20. I just bought a **reversible** jacket.

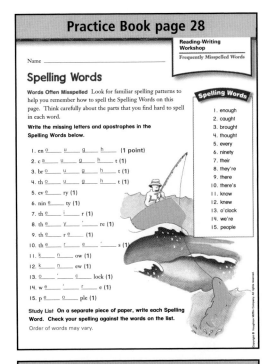

Practice Book page 28

Name _____

Reading-Writing Workshop
Frequently Misspelled Words

Spelling Words

Words Often Misspelled Look for familiar spelling patterns to help you remember how to spell the Spelling Words on this page. Think carefully about the parts that you find hard to spell in each word.

Write the missing letters and apostrophes in the Spelling Words below.

1. en o u g h (1 point)
2. c a u g h t (1)
3. br o u g h t (1)
4. th o u g h t (1)
5. ev e ry (1)
6. nin e ty (1)
7. th e i r (1)
8. th e y ' re (1)
9. th e r e (1)
10. th e r e s (1)
11. k n ow (1)
12. k n ew (1)
13. o ' clock (1)
14. w e ' r e (1)
15. p e o ple (1)

Study List On a separate piece of paper, write each Spelling Word. Check your spelling against the words on the list.
Order of words may vary.

Spelling Words
1. enough
2. caught
3. brought
4. thought
5. every
6. ninety
7. their
8. they're
9. there
10. there's
11. know
12. knew
13. o'clock
14. we're
15. people

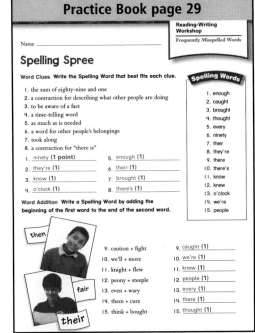

Practice Book page 29

Name _____

Reading-Writing Workshop
Frequently Misspelled Words

Spelling Spree

Word Clues Write the Spelling Word that best fits each clue.

1. the sum of eighty-nine and one
2. a contraction for describing what other people are doing
3. to be aware of a fact
4. a time-telling word
5. as much as is needed
6. a word for other people's belongings
7. took along
8. a contraction for "there is"

1. ninety (1 point)
2. they're (1)
3. know (1)
4. o'clock (1)
5. enough (1)
6. their (1)
7. brought (1)
8. there's (1)

Word Addition Write a Spelling Word by adding the beginning of the first word to the end of the second word.

then
fair
their

9. caution + fight
10. we'll + more
11. knight + flew
12. peony + steeple
13. even + wary
14. them + cure
15. think + bought

9. caught (1)
10. we're (1)
11. knew (1)
12. people (1)
13. every (1)
14. there (1)
15. thought (1)

Spelling Words
1. enough
2. caught
3. brought
4. thought
5. every
6. ninety
7. their
8. they're
9. there
10. there's
11. know
12. knew
13. o'clock
14. we're
15. people

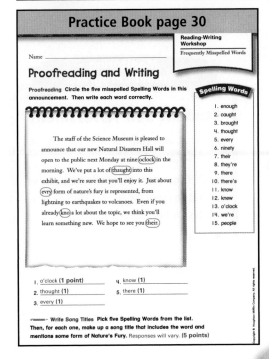

Practice Book page 30

Name _____

Reading-Writing Workshop
Frequently Misspelled Words

Proofreading and Writing

Proofreading Circle the five misspelled Spelling Words in this announcement. Then write each word correctly.

The staff of the Science Museum is pleased to announce that our new Natural Disasters Hall will open to the public next Monday at nine (oclock) in the morning. We've put a lot of (thaught) into this exhibit, and we're sure that you'll enjoy it. Just about (evry) form of nature's fury is represented, from lightning to earthquakes to volcanoes. Even if you already (kno) a lot about the topic, we think you'll learn something new. We hope to see you (their.)

Spelling Words
1. enough
2. caught
3. brought
4. thought
5. every
6. ninety
7. their
8. they're
9. there
10. there's
11. know
12. knew
13. o'clock
14. we're
15. people

1. o'clock (1 point)
2. thought (1)
3. every (1)
4. know (1)
5. there (1)

Write Song Titles Pick five Spelling Words from the list. Then, for each one, make up a song title that includes the word and mentions some form of Nature's Fury. Responses will vary. (5 points)

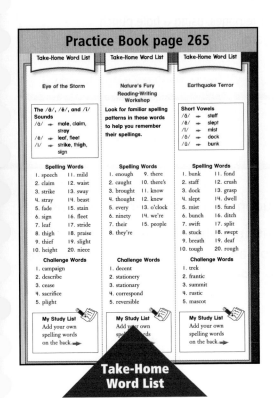

Practice Book page 265

Take-Home Word List	Take-Home Word List	Take-Home Word List
Eye of the Storm	**Nature's Fury** Reading-Writing Workshop	**Earthquake Terror**

Eye of the Storm

The /ā/, /ē/, and /ī/ Sounds
/ā/ → male, claim, stray
/ē/ → leaf, fleet
/ī/ → strike, thigh, sign

Spelling Words
1. speech
2. claim
3. strike
4. stray
5. fade
6. sign
7. leaf
8. thigh
9. thief
10. height
11. mild
12. waist
13. sway
14. beast
15. stain
16. fleet
17. stride
18. praise
19. slight
20. niece

Challenge Words
1. campaign
2. describe
3. cease
4. sacrifice
5. plight

Nature's Fury
Reading-Writing Workshop

Look for familiar spelling patterns in these words to help you remember their spellings.

Spelling Words
1. enough
2. caught
3. brought
4. thought
5. every
6. ninety
7. their
8. they're
9. there
10. there's
11. know
12. knew
13. o'clock
14. we're
15. people

Challenge Words
1. decent
2. stationery
3. stationary
4. correspond
5. reversible

Earthquake Terror

Short Vowels
/ă/ → staff
/ě/ → slept
/ĭ/ → mist
/ŏ/ → dock
/ŭ/ → bunk

Spelling Words
1. bunk
2. staff
3. dock
4. slept
5. mist
6. bunch
7. swift
8. stuck
9. breath
10. tough
11. fond
12. crush
13. grasp
14. dwell
15. fund
16. ditch
17. split
18. swept
19. deaf
20. rough

Challenge Words
1. trek
2. frantic
3. summit
4. rustic
5. mascot

My Study List
Add your own spelling words on the back.

My Study List
Add your own spelling words on the back.

My Study List
Add your own spelling words on the back.

Take-Home Word List

READING-WRITING WORKSHOP

Portfolio Opportunity

Save students' final copy of their description as an example of the development of their writing skills.

Publishing

Have students publish their descriptions.

- Ask them to look back at the publishing ideas they noted when they chose a topic. Discuss the Ideas for Sharing box below.
- Then ask students to decide how they want to publish their writing.
- Tell them to make a neat final copy of their description. Remind them to use good penmanship and to be sure that they have fixed all mistakes.

Ideas for Sharing

Write It

- Turn your paper into a book. Add pictures and a cover.
- Send your paper to a magazine, newspaper, or Internet site that publishes student writing.

Say It

- Record your paper on tape. Add sound effects.
- Read your paper aloud from the Author's Chair.

Show It

- Make a poster to display with your paper.

Tips for Making a Book

- Think of an attention-grabbing title.
- Put an interesting photo or a drawing of what you are describing on the cover.
- Plan which words go on each page.
- Draw pictures or choose photographs that illustrate what you are describing.
- Bind the pages, using a hole punch and yarn.

Monitoring Student Progress

Student Self-Assessment

- What was your favorite part of your description?
- Did you meet the goals that you set out to meet when you started this description?
- What would you change in this description if you wrote it over again?
- What did you learn from your readers' response to your description?

Evaluating

Have students write responses to the Student Self-Assessment questions.

Evaluate students' writing, using the Writing Traits Scoring Rubric. This rubric is based on criteria in this workshop and reflects criteria students used in Revising Your Description on **Practice Book** page 26.

Description

Writing Traits Scoring Rubric

4

IDEAS	The description is focused on a single, clear topic. Many vivid details tell what the writer saw, heard, tasted, smelled, or felt.
ORGANIZATION	The details are organized and presented in a clear order. The beginning introduces the topic, and the ending wraps up the description.
VOICE	Words and phrases clearly show the writer's feelings about the topic.
WORD CHOICE	Many exact words, including sensory words, help create a vivid picture.
SENTENCE FLUENCY	The writing flows well. Sentence length and structure vary.
CONVENTIONS	There are almost no errors in spelling, punctuation, capitalization, or usage.
PRESENTATION	The final copy is neat and legible.

3

IDEAS	The description is focused on a topic. The writing needs more details that address at least three of the five senses.
ORGANIZATION	The organization is generally clear. The beginning and the ending may be somewhat weak.
VOICE	The writer's feelings about the topic are sometimes unclear.
WORD CHOICE	The writer could have used more exact words and more sensory words.
SENTENCE FLUENCY	The paper would benefit from greater sentence variety.
CONVENTIONS	There are a few mistakes, but they do not affect understanding.
PRESENTATION	The final copy is messy in a few places but still legible.

2

IDEAS	The description may not be clearly focused on a topic. Few details are included.
ORGANIZATION	Details are not clearly organized. The beginning and ending may be missing.
VOICE	The writer's feelings about the topic are often unclear.
WORD CHOICE	The writer used few exact words and few sensory words.
SENTENCE FLUENCY	The paper lacks sentence variety.
CONVENTIONS	Mistakes sometimes make the paper hard to understand.
PRESENTATION	The final copy is messy. It may be illegible in a few places.

1

IDEAS	The description may not be focused. There are no details, or they are inappropriate.
ORGANIZATION	Details are disorganized. The beginning and ending are missing.
VOICE	The writer shows no feelings about the topic.
WORD CHOICE	Word choice is vague or uninteresting. It may be confusing.
SENTENCE FLUENCY	Sentences are short, unclear, or repetitive.
CONVENTIONS	Many mistakes make the paper hard to understand.
PRESENTATION	The final copy is messy. It may be illegible in many places.

Lesson Overview

Literature

Eye of the Storm

CHASING STORMS WITH WARREN FAIDLEY

STEPHEN KRAMER

PHOTOGRAPHS BY
WARREN FAIDLEY

Selection Summary

Warren Faidley discusses the challenges involved in photographing tornadoes, lightning, and hurricanes.

Vocabulary Reader

Nonfiction

1 Background and Vocabulary

2 Main Selection

Eye of the Storm: Chasing Storms with Warren Faidley
Genre: Nonfiction

3 Career Link

Instructional Support

Planning and Practice

- Planning and classroom management
- Reading instruction
- Skill lessons
- Materials for reaching all learners

Teacher's Resource Blackline Masters

- Newsletters
- Selection Summaries
- Assignment Cards
- Observation Checklists
- Selection Tests

Practice Book

- Independent practice for skills

Instruction Transparencies/Masters and Strategy Posters

- Transparencies
- Strategy Posters
- Blackline Masters

Reaching All Learners

Intervention Strategies for **Extra Support**

Instructional Activities for **Challenge**

Instructional Strategies for **English Language Learners**

Independent Activities for **Classroom Management**

Coordinated lessons, activities, and projects for additional reading instruction

For
- Classroom Teacher
- Extended Day
- Pull Out
- Resource Teacher
- Reading Specialist

Technology

Audio Selection

Eye of the Storm: Chasing Storms with Warren Faidley

Get Set for Reading CD-ROM

- Background building
- Vocabulary support
- Selection Summary in English and Spanish

Accelerated Reader

- Practice quizzes for the selection

www.eduplace.com

Log on to Education Place for more activities related to the selection.

e•**Glossary**
e•**WordGame**

Leveled Books for Reaching All Learners

Leveled Readers and Leveled Practice

- Independent reading for building fluency

- Topic, comprehension strategy, and vocabulary linked to main selection

- Lessons in Teacher's Edition, pages 81O–81R

- Leveled practice for every book

Technology

Leveled Readers
Audio available

Book Adventure

- Practice quizzes for the Leveled Theme Paperbacks

www.eduplace.com

Log on to Education Place® for activities related to the Leveled Theme Paperbacks.

● BELOW LEVEL

White Dragon:
Anna Allen in the Face of Danger

by Maryann Dobeck
illustrations by Todd Leonardo

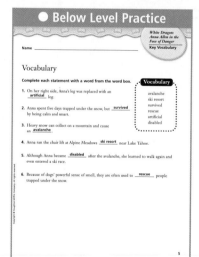

● Below Level Practice

White Dragon: Anna Allen in the Face of Danger
Key Vocabulary

Name _____

Vocabulary

Complete each statement with a word from the word box.

Vocabulary
avalanche
ski resort
survived
rescue
artificial
disabled

1. On her right side, Anna's leg was replaced with an __artificial__ leg.

2. Anna spent five days trapped under the snow, but __survived__ by being calm and smart.

3. Heavy snow can collect on a mountain and cause an __avalanche__.

4. Anna ran the chair lift at Alpine Meadows __ski resort__, near Lake Tahoe.

5. Although Anna became __disabled__ after the avalanche, she learned to walk again and even entered a ski race.

6. Because of dogs' powerful sense of smell, they are often used to __rescue__ people trapped under the snow.

5

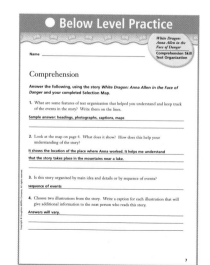

● Below Level Practice

White Dragon: Anna Allen in the Face of Danger
Comprehension Skill
Text Organization

Name _____

Comprehension

Answer the following, using the story *White Dragon: Anna Allen in the Face of Danger* and your completed Selection Map.

1. What are some features of text organization that helped you understand and keep track of the events in the story? Write them on the lines.
Sample answer: headings, photographs, captions, maps

2. Look at the map on page 4. What does it show? How does this help your understanding of the story?
It shows the location of the place where Anna worked. It helps me understand that the story takes place in the mountains near a lake.

3. Is this story organized by main idea and details or by sequence of events?
sequence of events

4. Choose two illustrations from the story. Write a caption for each illustration that will give additional information to the next person who reads this story.
Answers will vary.

7

▲ ON LEVEL

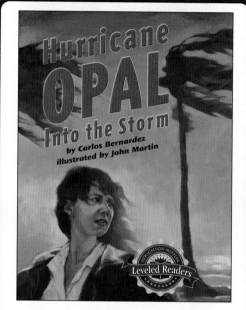

Hurricane OPAL Into the Storm
by Carlos Bernardez
illustrated by John Martin

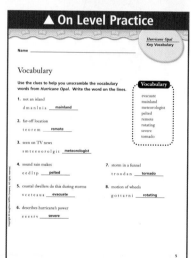

▲ On Level Practice

Hurricane Opal
Key Vocabulary

Name _____

Vocabulary

Use the clues to help you unscramble the vocabulary words from *Hurricane Opal*. Write the word on the lines.

Vocabulary
evacuate
mainland
meteorologist
pelted
remote
rotating
severe
tornado

1. not an island
d l m a n l n i a __mainland__

2. far-off location
t e o r e m __remote__

3. seen on TV news
s m t e e o o r o l g i r __meteorologist__

4. sound rain makes
e e d l t p __pelted__

5. coastal dwellers do this during storms
v c e t e u a a __evacuate__

6. describes hurricane's power
e e e s r v __severe__

7. storm in a funnel
t r o o d a n __tornado__

8. motion of wheels
g o t t a r n i __rotating__

5

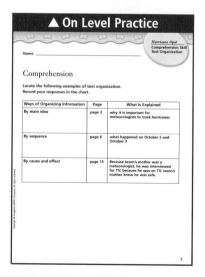

▲ On Level Practice

Hurricane Opal
Comprehension Skill
Text Organization

Name _____

Comprehension

Locate the following examples of text organization. Record your responses in the chart.

Ways of Organizing Information	Page	What Is Explained
By main idea	page 3	why it is important for meteorologists to track hurricanes
By sequence	page 6	what happened on October 2 and October 3
By cause and effect	page 15	Because Jason's mother was a meteorologist, he was interviewed for TV; because he was on TV, Jason's mother knew he was safe.

7

Leveled Theme Paperbacks

- Extended independent reading in theme-related trade books
- Lessons in Teacher's Edition, pages R2–R7

■ ABOVE LEVEL

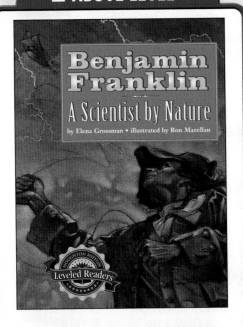

Benjamin Franklin
A Scientist by Nature
by Elena Grossman • illustrated by Ron Mazellan

HOUGHTON MIFFLIN
Leveled Readers

■ Above Level Practice

Benjamin Franklin: A Scientist by Nature
Key Vocabulary

Name _____

Vocabulary

Complete the paragraphs by writing the appropriate word on the lines.

Young Benjamin Franklin learned the publishing trade as an __apprentice__ in his brother's printing shop at the age of 12. It wasn't until later in life that Franklin became __intrigued__ by the idea of electricity.

Franklin __corresponded__ with other scientists all over the world to learn more about electricity. He had a theory that flashes of __lightning__ contained the same power as electricity. One night in 1752, during a particularly __severe__ thunderstorm, Franklin conducted his famous kite experiment with a key and silk string.

It would be many years before electricity was truly __harnessed__ into a useful tool. But Franklin's experiments did lead to his invention of the lightning rod, which __coaxed__ electricity away from people's homes and down into the ground. For the rest of his life, Franklin helped to __foster__ creative thinking and scientific experimentation.

Vocabulary
apprentice
coaxed
corresponded
foster
harnessed
intrigued
lightning
severe

■ Above Level Practice

Benjamin Franklin: A Scientist by Nature
Comprehension Skill
Text Organization

Name _____

Comprehension

Locate the following examples of text organization. Record your responses in the chart.

Ways of Organizing Information	Page	What Is Explained
By main idea and details	Page 14	Sample answer: People and universities honored Franklin, and his work helped spread scientific thinking.
By sequence	Pages 5–6	These pages describe, in order, Franklin's childhood, his work as an apprentice in his brother's print shop, and his early discoveries.
By cause and effect	Page 7	Because Philadelphia was a city of crowded wooden buildings, fire was a constant danger. Because he recognized that cooking in open fireplaces was dangerous, Franklin invented a safer, more efficient stove.

◆ LANGUAGE SUPPORT

Anna Allen Faces the
White Dragon

HOUGHTON MIFFLIN
Leveled Readers

by Maryann Dobeck
illustrations by Todd Leonardo

◆ Language Support Practice

Anna Allen Faces the White Dragon
Build Background

Name _____

Build Background

Draw four things that someone trapped in an avalanche should have. Then complete the sentence below to tell why one of these things is important.

I think that it is important to have _____ in an avalanche because _____

Answers will vary.

◆ Language Support Practice

Anna Allen Faces the White Dragon
Key Vocabulary

Name _____

Vocabulary

Use the words from the box to complete the sentences.

Vocabulary
artificial
avalanche
blast
disabled
hurry
prevent
severe

1. Workers prepared to __blast__ snow to keep the slopes safe for skiers.

2. They were trying to __prevent__ an accident.

3. Anna wanted to get her clothes and __hurry__ home.

4. An __avalanche__ of snow crashed down the mountain.

5. Anna's leg was injured by the __severe__ cold.

6. When Anna left the hospital, she had an __artificial__ leg.

7. Anna entered a race for __disabled__ skiers.

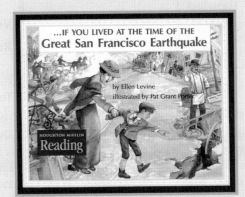

...IF YOU LIVED AT THE TIME OF THE
Great San Francisco Earthquake
by Ellen Levine
illustrated by Pat Grant Porter

HOUGHTON MIFFLIN
Reading

Below Level

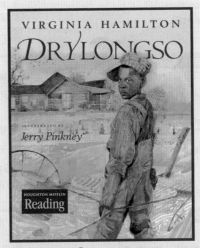

VIRGINIA HAMILTON
DRYLONGSO
ILLUSTRATED BY
Jerry Pinkney

HOUGHTON MIFFLIN
Reading

On Level

HURRICANES
EARTH'S MIGHTIEST STORMS • PATRICIA LAUBER

HOUGHTON MIFFLIN
Reading

Challenge

Daily Lesson Plans

T Skill tested on Weekly or Theme Skills
Test and/or Integrated Theme Test

 North Carolina Competency
Goals indicated in blue.

Technology

Lesson Planner CD-ROM allows you to customize the chart below to develop your own lesson plans.

DAILY LESSON PLANS

50–60 minutes

Reading
Comprehension

Vocabulary Reader
Day of the Tornadoes

Leveled Readers
• Fluency Practice
• Independent Reading

20–30 minutes

Word Work

Phonics/Decoding
Vocabulary
Spelling

20–30 minutes

Writing and Oral Language

Writing
Grammar
Listening/Speaking/Viewing

DAY 1

Teacher Read Aloud, 53S–53T
Hurricanes: Weather at Its Wildest

Background and Vocabulary, 54 2.02a, d, f

Key Vocabulary, 55 1.02
collide	lightning	severe
funnel cloud	prairies	sizzling
jagged	rotate	tornadoes

Vocabulary Reader 1.02

Reading the Selection, 56–75

Comprehension Skill, 56
Text Organization T

Comprehension Strategy, 56 2.01, 2.02a
Question

Leveled Readers
White Dragon: Anna Allen in the Face of Danger
Hurricane Opal: Into the Storm
Benjamin Franklin, A Scientist by Nature
Anna Allen Faces the White Dragon

Lessons and Leveled Practice, 81O–81R
1.05a, 2.02d, f, 2.03a–b, 4.01

Phonics/Decoding, 57 1.01
Phonics/Decoding Strategy

Vocabulary, 56–75 1.02
Selection Vocabulary

Spelling, 81E 5.05
/ā/, /ē/, and /ī/ T

Writing, 81K 4.05
Prewriting a Response to a Prompt

Grammar, 81I 5.03c
Conjunctions T

Daily Language Practice 5.06, 5.07
1. the crowd cheered when the spech was over. (The; speech)
2. The beest walked quickly but it did not run. (beast; quickly,)

2.02d, f, 2.09c
Listening/Speaking/Viewing, 53S–53T, 69
Teacher Read Aloud, Stop and Think

DAY 2

Reading the Selection, 56–75

Comprehension Check, 75

Responding, 76 3.01f–g, 3.02
Think About the Selection

Vocabulary Reader 1.02

Comprehension Skill Preview, 73
Text Organization T

Leveled Readers
White Dragon: Anna Allen in the Face of Danger
Hurricane Opal: Into the Storm
Benjamin Franklin, A Scientist by Nature
Anna Allen Faces the White Dragon

Lessons and Leveled Practice, 81O–81R
1.05a, 2.02d, f, 2.03a–b, 4.01

Structural Analysis, 81C 1.01
Syllabication T

Vocabulary, 56–75 1.02
Selection Vocabulary

Spelling, 81E 5.05
/ā/, /ē/, and /ī/ Review and Practice T

Writing, 81K 4.06, 4.07
Drafting a Response to a Prompt

Grammar, 81I 5.03c
Conjunctions Practice T

Daily Language Practice 5.06, 5.07
3. I will call my neice, or i will write to her. (niece,; I)
4. The weather has been maild all winter (mild; winter.)

Listening/Speaking/Viewing, 75, 76 4.02a, c
Wrapping Up, Responding

DAY 3

Rereading the Selection 2.04

Rereading for Writer's Craft, 61
Suspense

Rereading for Visual Literacy, 63 2.07
Photographs

Vocabulary Reader 1.02

Comprehension Skill, 81A–81B
Text Organization **T**

Leveled Readers

White Dragon: Anna Allen in the Face of Danger
Hurricane Opal: Into the Storm
Benjamin Franklin, A Scientist by Nature
Anna Allen Faces the White Dragon

Lessons and Leveled Practice, 81O–81R
1.05a, 2.02d, f, 2.03a–b, 4.01

Phonics Review, 81D 1.01
Long Vowels: /ā/, /ē/, /ī/

Vocabulary, 81G 1.04
Dictionary Guide Words **T**

Spelling, 81F 5.05
Vocabulary: Classifying; /ā/, /ē/, and /ī/ Practice **T**

Writing, 81L 4.08a, 5.01
Revising a Response to a Prompt

Grammar, 81J 5.01, 5.03c
Compound Sentences **T**

Daily Language Practice 5.06, 5.07
5. The theef jumped up but he could not climb the fence. (thief; up,)
6. The spill on the rug left a huge stane (stain.)

DAY 4

Reading the Career Link,
78–81 2.03b
"Storm Warning"
Skill: How to Read a
Sequence Chart 2.07

Rereading for Visual Literacy, 80 2.07
Communicating Information

Comprehension Skill Review, 65 2.01, 3.07a
Fact and Opinion

Leveled Readers

White Dragon: Anna Allen in the Face of Danger
Hurricane Opal: Into the Storm
Benjamin Franklin, A Scientist by Nature
Anna Allen Faces the White Dragon

Lessons and Leveled Practice, 81O–81R
1.05a, 2.02d, f, 2.03a–b, 4.01

Phonics/Decoding 78–81
Apply Phonics/Decoding Strategy to Link

Vocabulary, 81M 1.03b
Language Center: Building Vocabulary

Spelling, 81F 5.06
Spelling Game, Proofreading **T**

Writing, 81L 5.01, 5.07
Proofreading a Response to a Prompt
Capitalizing and Punctuating Sentences **T**

Grammar, 81J 5.01, 5.03c
Compound Sentences Practice **T**

Daily Language Practice 5.06, 5.07
7. this backpack has a belt that fits around my wast. (This; waist.)
8. Can you read the words on that sine (sign?)

Listening/Speaking/Viewing, 81 3.01g, 3.02
Discuss the Link

DAY 5

Rereading for Fluency, 67
4.01
3.01f–g, 3.02

Responding Activities, 76–77
Write a Job Description 4.07
Cross-Curricular Activities

Information and Study Skills, 81H 3.06
Using Library Catalogs

Comprehension Skill Review, 71 2.04b, 3.01a
Sequence of Events
Other Cross-Curricular Activities, 23I–23J and 53Q–53R SC4.01, SS1.03

Leveled Readers

White Dragon: Anna Allen in the Face of Danger
Hurricane Opal: Into the Storm
Benjamin Franklin, A Scientist by Nature
Anna Allen Faces the White Dragon

Lessons and Leveled Practice, 81O–81R
1.05a, 2.02d, f, 2.03a–b, 4.01

Phonics, 81N 1.01
Language Center: Word Break-Up

Vocabulary, 81M 1.03b
Language Center: Vocabulary Game

Spelling, 81F 5.05
Test: /ā/, /ē/, and /ī/ **T**

Writing, 81L 4.04, 4.09
Publishing a Response to a Prompt

Grammar, 81J, 81M 5.03c
Avoiding Run-ons
Language Center: Writing Forecasts

Daily Language Practice 5.06, 5.07
9. do you see that large flet of boats in the harbor? (Do; fleet)
10. The hite of the shelf is ten feet but my cat can reach the top. (height; feet,)

Listening/Speaking/Viewing, 81N 2.06, 4.02a–c
Language Center: Literature Discussion Other Cross-Curricular Activities, 23I–23J and 53Q–53R SC4.01, SS1.03

Managing Flexible Groups

Leveled Instruction and Leveled Practice

		DAY 1	**DAY 2**
WHOLE CLASS		• Teacher Read Aloud (TE pp. 53S–53T) • Building Background, Introducing Vocabulary (TE pp. 54–55) • Comprehension Strategy: Introduce (TE p. 56) • Comprehension Skill: Introduce (TE p. 56 • Purpose Setting (TE p. 57) **After reading first half of *Eye of the Storm*** • Stop and Think (TE p. 69)	**After reading *Eye of the Storm*** • Wrapping Up (TE p. 75) • Comprehension Check (Practice Book p. 33) • Responding: Think About the Selection (TE p. 76) • Comprehension Skill: Preview (TE p. 73)
SMALL GROUPS	**Extra Support**	**TEACHER-LED** • Preview vocabulary; support reading with Vocabulary Reader. • Preview *Eye of the Storm* to Stop and Think (TE pp. 56–69). • Support reading with Extra Support/Intervention notes (TE pp. 57, 64, 67, 68, 74).	**Partner or Individual Work** • Reread first half of *Eye of the Storm* (TE pp. 56–69). • Preview, read second half (TE pp. 70–75). • Comprehension Check (Practice Book p. 33)
	Challenge	**Individual Work** • Begin "Emergency!" (Challenge Handbook p. 4) • Extend reading with Challenge Note (TE p. 74).	**Individual Work** • Continue work on activity (Challenge Handbook p. 4).
	English Language Learners	**TEACHER-LED** • Preview vocabulary; support reading with Vocabulary Reader. • Preview *Eye of the Storm* to Stop and Think (TE pp. 56–69). • Support reading with English Language Learners notes (TE pp. 54, 59, 62, 70, 73).	**TEACHER-LED** • Review first half of *Eye of the Storm* (TE pp. 56–69). ✔ • Preview, read second half (TE pp. 70–75). • Begin Comprehension Check together (Practice Book p. 33).

Independent Activities

• Get Set for Reading CD-Rom
• Journals: selection notes, questions
• Complete, review Practice Book pages (31–35) and Leveled Readers Practice Blackline Masters (TE pp. 81O–81R).
• Assignment Cards (Teachers Resource Blackline Masters, pp. 49–51)
• Leveled Readers (TE pp. 81O–81R), Leveled Theme Paperbacks (TE pp. R2–R7), or book from Leveled Bibliography (TE pp. 23E–23F)

✔ Opportunity to informally assess oral reading rate

DAY 3

- Rereading: Lessons on Writer's Craft, Visual Literacy (TE pp. 61, 63)
- Comprehension Skill: Main lesson (TE pp. 81A–81B)

DAY 4

- Reading the Career Link (TE pp. 78–81): Skill lesson (TE p. 78)
- Rereading the Link: Visual Literacy lesson (TE p. 80)
- Comprehension Skill: First Comprehension Review lesson (TE p. 65)

DAY 5

- Responding: Select from Activities (TE pp. 76–77)
- Information and Study Skills (TE p. 81H)
- Comprehension Skill: Second Comprehension Review lesson (TE p. 71)

TEACHER-LED

- Reread, review Comprehension Check (Practice Book p. 33).
- Preview Leveled Reader: Below Level (TE p. 81O), or read book from Leveled Bibliography (TE pp. 23E–23F). ✔

Partner or Individual Work

- Reread Career Link (TE pp. 78–81).
- Complete Leveled Reader: Below Level (TE p. 81O), or read book from Leveled Bibliography (TE pp. 23E–23F).

TEACHER-LED

- Comprehension Skill: Reteaching lesson (TE p. R10)
- Reread Leveled Theme Paperback: Below Level (TE pp. R2–R3), or read book from Leveled Bibliography (TE pp. 23E–23F). ✔

TEACHER-LED

- Teacher check-in: Assess progress (Challenge Handbook p. 4).
- Preview Leveled Reader: Above Level (TE p. 81Q), or read book from Leveled Bibliography (TE pp. 23E–23F). ✔

Individual Work

- Complete activity (Challenge Handbook p. 4).
- Complete Leveled Reader: Above Level (TE p. 81Q), or read book from Leveled Bibliography (TE pp. 23E–23F).

TEACHER-LED

- Evaluate activity and plan format for sharing (Challenge Handbook p. 4).
- Reread Leveled Theme Paperback: Above Level (TE pp. R6–R7), or read book from Leveled Bibliography (TE pp. 23E–23F). ✔

Partner or Individual Work

- Complete Comprehension Check (Practice Book p. 33).
- Begin Leveled Reader: Language Support (TE p. 81R), or read book from Leveled Bibliography (TE pp. 23E–23F).

TEACHER-LED

- Reread the Career Link (TE pp. 78–81) ✔ and review Link Skill (TE p. 78).
- Complete Leveled Reader: Language Support (TE p. 81R), or read book from Leveled Bibliography (TE pp. 23E–23F). ✔

Partner or Individual Work

- Reread book from Leveled Bibliography (TE pp. 23E–23F).

- Responding activities (pp. 76–77)
- Language Center activities (TE pp. 81M–81N)
- **Fluency Practice:** Reread *Eye of the Storm; Earthquake Terror.* ✔
- Activities relating to *Eye of the Storm* at Education Place www.eduplace.com

Turn the page for more independent activities.

Classroom Management

Independent Activities

Assign these activities while you work with small groups.

Differentiated Instruction for Small Groups

- **Handbook for English Language Learners**, pp. 28–37

- **Extra Support Handbook**, pp. 24–33

Independent Activities

- Language Center, pp. 81M–81N

- Challenge/Extension Activities, Resources, pp. R11, R17

- **Classroom Management Handbook**, Activity Masters CM1-5–CM1-8

- **Challenge Handbook**, Activity Masters CH1-3–CH1-4

Look for more activities in the Classroom Management Kit.

Social Studies

Tornado Safety

Pairs	30 minutes
Objective	Create a tornado safety poster.
Materials	Reference sources, art materials, poster board

In *Eye of the Storm*, Warren Faidley describes how dangerous a tornado can be. Create a poster that tells about tornado safety.

- Work with a partner to research tornado safety tips, using reference sources such as an encyclopedia or the Internet.

- Take notes about what people could do to stay safe from a tornado. Be specific.

- Write your list of safety tips onto poster board. Then illustrate your poster.

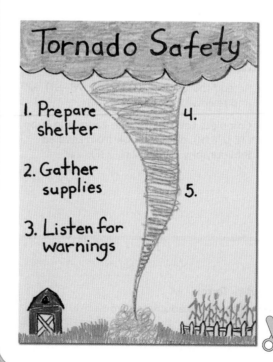

Poetry

From Pictures to Words

Singles	25 minutes
Objective	Write a poem about nature.
Materials	Books or magazines with nature photographs

Look at photographs of nature to get ideas for writing a poem.

- Look carefully at the photographs in *Eye of the Storm*.

- Write down words or phrases that come to mind as you study the pictures.

- Use these words and others to write a poem about natural events, such as lightning or tornadoes.

- Include descriptive words and sensory details.

Consider copying and laminating these activities for use in centers.

Social Studies

Tornado Touchdowns

👥 **Pairs**	🕐 **40 minutes**
Objective	Create a tornado map.
Materials	Reference sources, tracing paper, paper, pencils, markers

Create a map that labels the areas where most tornadoes occur.

- Trace an outline map of the United States.

- Check reference sources such as an encyclopedia, almanac, and the Internet for places where major tornadoes have occurred. Find and label these places on your map.

- Use a marker or colored pencil to connect places that follow a definite path.

- Be sure to include a title and a key that explains the symbols on your map.

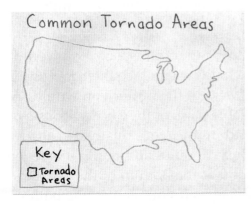

Science

The Doppler Effect

👤 **Singles**	🕐 **45 minutes**
Objective	Learn about the Doppler Effect.
Materials	Reference sources

Have you ever wondered why a train whistle sounds higher-pitched as the train approaches but lower-pitched as it moves further away? This change is called the Doppler Effect. Write a short report about what it is and why it occurs.

- Use reference sources such as an encyclopedia or the Internet to learn about the Doppler Effect.

- Take notes on the most important information you learn. Be sure to include important dates along with definitions of the key terms, such as *sound waves, frequency,* and *Doppler radar*.

- Write a one-page report to summarize what you've learned.

Art

Color Up a Storm

👥 **Pairs**	🕐 **20 minutes**
Objective	Create a storm picture.
Materials	Art materials, drawing paper

How does a dramatic storm make you feel? Create a picture that conveys your experience or emotions.

- Think about storms you have experienced, or look at pictures of storms.

- Visualize the sights and sounds of a storm, such as the brightness of lightning, the crash of thunder, or the feel of heavy rain. Take notes to help you remember your experience or emotions.

- Create a picture using paints, colored pencils, or other art materials.

- Share your picture with a partner. Explain why you included certain images or colors.

Listening Comprehension

OBJECTIVES
- Listen to identify the organization of information in nonfiction text.

Building Background

Tell students that you are going to read aloud a nonfiction selection about one of nature's most powerful forces—hurricanes.

- Ask students to share what they know about hurricanes.
- Invite students who have experienced or seen hurricanes to describe them.

Fluency Modeling

Explain that as you read aloud, you will be modeling fluent oral reading. Ask students to listen carefully to your phrasing and your expression, or tone of voice and emphasis.

COMPREHENSION SKILL

Text Organization

Explain that authors may organize the information in a nonfiction text

- by main idea and details
- by sequence of events
- by cause and effect

Purpose Setting Read the selection aloud, asking students to pay attention to how the text is organized as they listen. Then use the Guiding Comprehension questions to assess understanding. Reread the selection for clarification as needed.

Teacher Read Aloud

Hurricanes: Weather at Its Wildest
by Fran Hodgkins

❶ What Is a Hurricane?

Hurricanes are among the most damaging storms on earth. With wind speeds of over 150 miles per hour, hurricanes can become spinning wheels of wind and water 300 to 500 miles wide. These massive storms can rip the roofs off buildings, wash seaside homes into the ocean, and turn streets into rivers. Hurricanes can cost millions of dollars in damages and disrupt thousands of lives.

Every year, about six hurricanes form in the Atlantic Ocean. Since 1953, scientists have given these hurricanes human names. There are six alphabetical lists of names, and each list is reused every six years. Especially damaging storms may have their names retired from the list.

How Do Hurricanes Form?

Hurricanes are born over warm ocean water, such as the water near the equator. This warm water evaporates into the atmosphere, adding heat and moisture to the air. As ocean winds spiral this moist air upward and inward, the storm gains energy. Clouds and winds increase, and thunderstorms may occur. Once the storm's spiraling winds reach 74 miles an hour, it is officially a hurricane.

Journey of a Hurricane

❷ If you observed a hurricane from space, you would see a gigantic wheel of clouds rotating counterclockwise, traveling from east to west. In the center you would see one of the most remarkable parts of the hurricane: its eye. Unlike the storm around it, the eye is relatively calm, with winds reaching only 15 miles an hour. It may even be cloudless. If you stood at the bottom of the eye and looked up, you would feel as if you were at the bottom of a giant well. The eyewall (the part of the hurricane that surrounds the eye) can tower 50,000 feet into the sky.

Hurricanes are always on the move, swept along over the ocean by the prevailing winds. Hurricanes that form in the southern Atlantic move at a speed of five to fifteen miles per hour. Most Atlantic hurricanes that threaten the United States are pushed by the Bermuda High, a high-pressure zone that pulls the storms away from the coast and back over the ocean. When pulled back over the cold North Atlantic, the hurricane loses its energy and dissipates. A strong hurricane, however, can resist the influence of a high-pressure zone, and that's when people on shore find themselves in the path of the storm.

Hurricane Danger and Protective Measures

❸ Millions of people living along the East and Gulf Coasts of the United States can be in serious danger when a storm threatens. High winds can uproot trees, knock down power lines, and hurl loose objects through windows and walls. High waves and torrential rainfall can cause flooding, washing out roads and even sweeping buildings off their foundations. In 1992, Hurricane Andrew hit southern Florida and Louisiana and destroyed thousands of homes and businesses, causing more than $15 to $25 billion in damage.

❹ To help prevent this type of disaster from happening again, scientists try to learn as much as they can about hurricanes. The National Aeronautics and Space Administration (NASA), for example, has developed a system of satellites that the National Oceanic and Atmospheric Administration (NOAA) uses to help track hurricanes and predict their movements. With the help of accurate tracking systems, timely hurricane warnings, and efficient evacuations, people can better dodge the paths of these dangerous storms.

CRITICAL THINKING
Guiding Comprehension

❶ **TEXT ORGANIZATION** What details in the section "What Is a Hurricane?" help you understand how destructive hurricanes can be? (Hurricanes can rip roofs off buildings, wash away homes, and turn streets into rivers.)

❷ **TEXT ORGANIZATION** What is the first paragraph under "Journey of a Hurricane" about? (a hurricane's eye) How is the text organized? How can you tell? (by main idea and details; Most of the sentences tell what a hurricane's eye is like.)

❸ **TEXT ORGANIZATION** What three things make hurricanes a dangerous threat to people and property? (high winds, high waves, and torrential rains)

❹ **TEXT ORGANIZATION** What cause and effect are in the second paragraph under "Hurricane Danger and Protective Measures"? (Cause: to help prevent huge disasters; Effect: Scientists try to learn about hurricanes.)

Discussion Options

Personal Response Ask students which hurricane facts they find most interesting? Why?

⭐ **Connecting/Comparing** Have students compare hurricanes with the earthquake in *Earthquake Terror*.

English Language Learners

Supporting Comprehension

Ask volunteers to name the word for a hurricane in their native language. Explain that the eye of a hurricane is the center of the storm where the wind is calm. If possible, show the eye in a satellite view of a hurricane.

Background and Vocabulary

Key Concept: Lightning Storms and Tornadoes

Tell students that they will now read about Warren Faidley, who photographs lightning storms and tornadoes, two more examples of nature's power. Discuss some of the dangers Warren might face in his job. Then use "Photographing Wild Weather" on Anthology pages 54–55 to build background and introduce Key Vocabulary.

- Ask volunteers to read aloud "Photographing Wild Weather."
- Point out the route that Warren follows. Have students suggest places along the route where Warren might be found in spring and summer.

Vocabulary Preview

The Vocabulary Reader can be used to preteach or reinforce the key vocabulary.

Vocabulary Reader

Day of the Tornadoes
by Gary Miller

Eye of the Storm

STEPHEN KRAMER
PHOTOGRAPHS BY
WARREN FAIDLEY

Eye of the Storm: Chasing Storms with Warren Faidley

Genre Nonfiction

Key Vocabulary

collide
funnel clouds
lightning
rotate
sizzling
tornadoes

Vocabulary Reader

Day of the Tornadoes
by Gary Miller

e Glossary

54

Photographing Wild Weather

Eye of the Storm tells about Warren Faidley, professional weather photographer and storm chaser. Here's a look at where he goes and the dangers he faces on the job.

The Risks

Lightning Danger

▶ Lightning heats the air around it to a **sizzling** 50,000 degrees Fahrenheit.

▶ Each bolt carries hundreds of millions of volts of electricity.

▶ Lightning kills an average of 100 people each year in the United States.

REACHING ALL LEARNERS

English Language Learners

Supporting Comprehension

Beginning/Preproduction Have students listen to the article. Then ask them to point to the illustrations that show what lightning looks like and the damage that tornadoes may cause.

Early Production and Speech Emergence Have students repeat the Key Vocabulary words after you. Mime *collide*, *rotate*, and *sizzling*. Invite students to discuss lightning storms and tornadoes using Key Vocabulary words.

Intermediate and Advanced Fluency In small groups, have students read and then restate in their own words the information provided in selected paragraphs from the article.

The Route

Every spring, Warren brings his cameras to "Tornado Alley" in the central United States, where warm and cool air **collide** to form **funnel clouds** that might become **tornadoes**. For the summer, Warren returns to his home state of Arizona to photograph **lightning** storms.

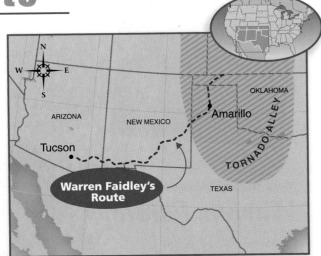

Tornado Danger

▶ The winds inside a killer tornado may **rotate** at jet speed — spinning up to 300 miles per hour.

▶ Tornadoes kill an average of 80 people per year in the United States.

55

Introducing Vocabulary

Key Vocabulary

These words support the Key Concept and appear in the selection.

collide to bump into another mass with force

funnel cloud tornado cloud that is wide at the top and narrow where it touches the ground

jagged having a sharp, pointed edge or outline

lightning the flash of light in the sky when electricity passes between clouds or between a cloud and the ground

prairies flat, open grasslands

rotate to swirl in a circular motion

severe serious or extreme in nature

sizzling crackling with intense heat

tornadoes rotating columns of air accompanied by whirling funnel-shaped downspouts

e • Glossary
e • WordGame

See Vocabulary notes on pages 58, 62, 64, 68, 70, 72, and 74 for additional words to preview.

Display Transparency 1–10.

- Model how to figure out the meaning of *prairies* from sentence clues.

- For each remaining sentence, ask students to use context clues to figure out the Key Vocabulary words.

- Ask students to look for these words as they read and to use them to discuss lightning storms and tornadoes.

Practice/Homework Assign **Practice Book** page 31.

Introducing Vocabulary 55

TRANSPARENCY 1–10
TEACHER'S EDITION PAGE 55

ANNOTATED VERSION   NATURE'S FURY Eye of the Storm   Key Vocabulary

Transparency 1–10

News Flash

Tornado Warning Issued for Texas and Oklahoma

Every spring, warm air from the Gulf of Mexico and cool air from Alaska <u>collide</u> over the Midwest. Powerful weather can brew over the flat <u>prairies</u> when these air masses meet. Today the National Weather Service issued a <u>severe</u> storm warning for northern Texas and Oklahoma. <u>Tornadoes</u> are likely to touch down in this region throughout the weekend. Residents are urged to be on the lookout. These signs show that a tornado may be forming:

- A dense, inky cloud forms over the land.

- Air at the bottom of the cloud begins to <u>rotate</u>. This swirling air is a breeding ground for twisters.

- One or more <u>funnel clouds</u> descend toward the ground like dragon necks.

Tornadoes are often accompanied by <u>sizzling</u> electrical storms. It is not unusual to see <u>jagged</u> bolts of <u>lightning</u>.

Practice Book page 31

Eye of the Storm
Key Vocabulary

Name _____

Stormy Weather

Use words from the box to complete the diary entry below.

May 10, 2000
Dear Diary,

    Today was by far the scariest day of my trip. Everything was fine as I crossed the border into Oklahoma. The highway stretched out over a prairie **(1 point)** *that seemed to go on forever. As I looked into my rear-view mirror, I spotted some dense clouds forming behind me. "I hope they aren't* funnel clouds **(1)** *" I thought. Then I spotted a flash of lightning* **(1)** *. The clouds started to* rotate **(1)** *slowly at first, and then faster and faster. A couple of* tornadoes **(1)** *were forming right before my eyes! I realized that a* severe **(1)** *storm had formed behind me, and it was moving fast in my direction. The* jagged **(1)** *bolts of lightning were getting closer. One of the tornadoes lifted a tractor into the air, spun it around, and dropped it. I watched it* collide **(1)** *with a shed on the ground. Lightning struck a dry bush behind me. It turned into a* sizzling **(1)** *ball of flames.*

Vocabulary

sizzling
collide
funnel clouds
tornadoes
lightning
rotate
jagged
prairie
severe

Write a sentence to end the diary entry.

Answers will vary. **(1)**

TARGET SKILL
COMPREHENSION STRATEGY
Question

Teacher Modeling Have a student read aloud the Strategy Focus. Tell students that asking themselves questions that might be answered as they read can help them understand the selection. Then ask students to read the introduction. Model the strategy.

Think Aloud *The title, photographs, and headings help me figure out that this selection is about chasing and photographing storms. I have these questions about the topic: How does Warren chase storms? What kind of storms does he chase? Maybe I'll find answers to these questions as I read.*

Test Prep Many students get nervous and become distracted when taking a test. Tell them to use the Question strategy to check their understanding and stay focused on what they are reading.

TARGET SKILL
COMPREHENSION SKILL
Text Organization

Introduce the Graphic Organizer.
Tell students that a Selection Map can help them understand how the text is organized. Explain that as they read *Eye of the Storm*, students will fill in the Selection Map on **Practice Book** page 32.

• Display **Transparency 1–11.** Have students read Anthology pages 59–68.

• Model how to complete the first item by writing a sentence telling what the first section of text is about. Monitor students' work as needed.

56 THEME 1: Nature's Fury

Meet the Author
Stephen Kramer

Stephen Kramer teaches at an elementary school near Vancouver, Washington. He has written several other books on nature topics, such as *Avalanche, Caves, Tornado,* and *Lightning. Lightning* features the photographs of Warren Faidley.

Meet the Photographer
Warren Faidley

Warren Faidley's dramatic weather photographs appear not only in books, but in movies, videos, calendars, magazines, and museums. Faidley also served as a consultant and cinematographer for the movie *Twister.* He and his cat, Megamouth, live in Tucson, Arizona.

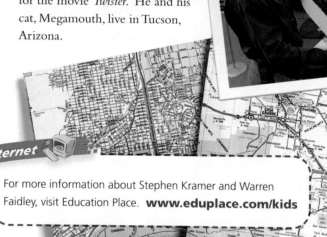

Internet For more information about Stephen Kramer and Warren Faidley, visit Education Place. **www.eduplace.com/kids**

56

Transparency 1–11
Selection Map

Pages 59–68

Page 59	Storm Chasing	how Warren chases a lightning storm
Page 60	Warren Faidley: Storm Chaser	how Warren was interested in storms since he was a child
Page 64	What Happens to Warren's Photos After He Takes Them?	how Warren created a stock photo agency, where people can go and buy his photos
Page 65	Storm Seasons and Chasing	how tornadoes form and how storm chasers follow weather patterns that form tornadoes
Page 67	Chasing Tornadoes	how Warren knows where to go to get the best pictures of tornadoes

Pages 69–75

One Day in the Life of a Storm Chaser
Morning Check the weather, get Shadow Chaser ready for the day, test the equipment, pack supplies
Afternoon Get an update on the weather conditions, change the oil in Shadow Chaser, check maps
Evening Look at the map, call the National Weather Service, head north following the storm, follow the tornadoes from Texas into Oklahoma, shoot the photos

NATURE'S FURY Eye of the Storm
Graphic Organizer Selection Map
ANNOTATED VERSION
TRANSPARENCY 1–11
TEACHER'S EDITION PAGES 56 AND 81A

Practice Book page 32

Eye of the Storm
Graphic Organizer Selection Map

Name _____

Selection Map

Fill in this selection map.

Pages 59–68

Page 59	Storm Chasing	how Warren chases a lightning storm **(2 points)**
Page 60	Warren Faidley: Storm Chaser	how Warren was interested in storms since he was a child **(2)**
Page 64	What Happens to Warren's Photos After He Takes Them? how Warren created a stock photo agency, where people can go and buy his photos **(2)**
Page 65	Storm Seasons and Chasing	how tornadoes form and how storm chasers follow weather patterns that form tornadoes **(2)**
Page 67	Chasing Tornadoes	how Warren knows where to go to get the best pictures of tornadoes **(2)**

Pages 69–75

One Day in the Life of a Storm Chaser
Morning Check the weather, get Shadow Chaser ready for the day, test the equipment, pack supplies **(2 points)**
Afternoon Get an update on the weather conditions, change the oil in Shadow Chaser, check maps **(2)**
Evening Look at the map, call the National Weather Service, head north following the storm, follow the tornadoes from Texas into Oklahoma, shoot the photos **(2)**

Selection 2

Eye of the Storm

CHASING STORMS WITH WARREN FAIDLEY

STEPHEN KRAMER

PHOTOGRAPHS BY

WARREN FAIDLEY

Strategy Focus

Warren Faidley's job takes him all over the country, getting close-up shots of dangerous storms. As you read the selection, think of **questions** about his job to discuss with your classmates.

57

REACHING ALL LEARNERS

Extra Support/Intervention

Selection Preview

pages 59–60 The author describes Warren Faidley as he photographs an intense lightning storm. What might be exciting about Warren's job?

pages 60–65 How might Warren make money with his pictures?

pages 65–68 Warren travels to follow storm patterns. He photographs tornadoes in spring, thunderstorms in summer, and hurricanes in fall. What characteristics and equipment might Warren need as he chases storms?

pages 69–75 Warren writes about his storm chases in a diary. What do you think he will see and do while chasing tornadoes on May 5, 1993?

Purpose Setting

- Remind students that this selection presents information about lightning storms and tornadoes.

- Have students preview the selection by looking at the illustrations. Ask them to predict what they might learn about lightning storms and tornadoes.

- Have students note and write down any questions they have as they read.

- Ask students to pay attention to how well specific text features such as headings, graphic aids, and captions present and organize information.

- You may wish to preview with students the Responding questions on Anthology page 76.

Journal ▸ Have students use their journals to record their predictions and add new ones. They might also record their questions, any answers they find, and new questions that come to mind as they read.

STRATEGY REVIEW

Phonics/Decoding

Remind students to use the Phonics/Decoding Strategy as they read.

Modeling Write this sentence from *Eye of the Storm* on the board: *He slid a few feet down the rough concrete embankment, using his hands and the soles of his shoe as brakes.* Point to *embankment.*

Think Aloud *To figure out this word, I'll look for word parts I know. I see the word* bank *and the prefix* em-. *At the end is the suffix* -ment. *I can blend these sounds and get* ehm-BANGK-muhnt. *I know that* bank *can mean "the edge of a river." I'll find* embankment *in the dictionary to make sure I understand its meaning.*

Guiding Comprehension

1 **DRAWING CONCLUSIONS** Based on the details in the section titled "Storm Chasing," what do you think it would be like to photograph a lightning storm up close? (scary and exciting)

2 **WRITER'S CRAFT** Why do you think the author included information about how ancient peoples viewed the sky? (to show readers that people have always been fascinated by weather; to help readers connect Warren's story to real life)

58

Vocabulary

saguaros tall cactuses native to the American Southwest

jagged having a sharp, pointed edge or outline

lightning the flash of light in the sky when electricity passes between clouds or between a cloud and the ground

prairies flat, open grasslands

conditions circumstances that affect a situation such as weather

Storm Chasing

In the evening shadows, a dusty black truck rolls along a dirt road. A rattlesnake feels the vibrations, lifts its head, and crawls off into the rocks. Giant saguaros sprout from the hillsides, arms held high. Somewhere in the distance, a cactus wren calls. But Warren Faidley isn't looking for rattlesnakes, saguaros, or cactus wrens.

He stares through the windshield, eyes glued to a cauliflower-shaped cloud. Behind the cloud, the setting sun turns the sky the color of a ripe peach. Warren has been watching this cloud, and hoping, for almost thirty minutes. The truck heads toward a hill with a clear view of the sky.

Suddenly, a jagged bolt of lightning shoots from the cloud.

"That's it," says Warren.

The truck speeds to the top of the hill and Warren jumps out, arms full of photographic equipment. His fingers fly as he unfolds tripods, mounts his cameras, and points them toward the cloud. Before the road dust has settled, the cameras are clicking.

For twenty minutes, lightning erupts from the cloud. Warren moves back and forth between the cameras — peering through viewfinders, changing film, switching lenses. Tomorrow, when the film is developed, Warren will know whether he had a successful night. In the meantime, he stands and watches, hoping his cameras are capturing the spectacular lights and colors of the evening thunderstorm.

Watching the Sky

From earliest times, people have watched the sky. Astrologers used the positions of the stars to predict the future. Storytellers used rainbows, winds, the sun and moon to weave tales about the past. Farmers, shepherds, and sailors have all watched the clouds, wondering what tomorrow's weather will be like.

The spectacular storms that sometimes appear in the sky have helped to make weather one of the most mysterious of all natural forces. Myths **2** and legends from around the world describe the fear and awe people felt as they watched lightning explode from a cloud or a tornado appear on the horizon, or listened to the howling winds of a hurricane.

For some people, storms have an irresistible call. These storm chasers head for the mountains, prairies, or seacoasts whenever weather conditions are right.

People chase storms for many reasons. Some storm chasers are scientists, who use video cameras, Doppler radar, and other instruments to learn about

59

English Language Learners

Supporting Comprehension

Point out the words *myths* and *legends* in the second column on page 59. Explain that long ago, people told myths and legends to help explain things about nature. Ask students if they know a legend or myth from their parents' home country about weather or nature. Encourage students to share the story with the class.

CRITICAL THINKING

Guiding Comprehension

❸ MAKING INFERENCES Why do you think the author tells about Warren riding into the middle of a dust whirlwind? (to show readers that storms have always fascinated Warren)

❹ NOTING DETAILS Which details on page 60 tell readers that Warren enjoyed taking pictures of lightning? (He spent his free time taking photos and reading about weather.)

❺ MAKING INFERENCES Why do you think Warren set up his camera near an underpass to photograph the lightning? (probably because it was safer and drier there)

what happens in a tornado or a thunderstorm. Photographers follow storms to try to capture the beauty of wind and sky on film. Still other people chase storms in order to catch a brief glimpse of the awesome power of nature.

Warren Faidley: Storm Chaser

Warren Faidley lives in Tucson, Arizona, with a one-toothed cat named Megamouth. He has been interested in storms for almost as long as he can remember.

Warren still remembers the tremendous thunderstorms he saw as a boy in Tucson. Tucked safely in bed, he watched the lightning and listened to the thunder. After the storms had passed, he fell asleep to the smell of wet creosote bushes outside his window.

Warren also had his first encounter with windstorms when he was a boy. Dust whirlwinds — spinning columns of wind that look like small tornadoes — often formed in the dusty vacant lots of his

60

neighborhood. One day Warren decided to put on safety goggles and a heavy jacket, and ride his bike into the center of a dust whirlwind. He'll never forget the excitement he felt when he rode through the wall of swirling winds:

"The inside was still and almost dust free. The light was orange, filtered, I guess, by the wall of dirt that was spinning around me. This rotating wall was filled with all kinds of debris, including tumbleweeds and newspaper pages. Looking up, I could see the very blue sky."

Becoming a Storm Chaser

Warren hadn't always planned to be a storm chaser. He enjoyed studying science in school, and he loved being outside. But he didn't really become interested in taking pictures of the sky until he was working as a photographer for a newspaper.

Warren began by trying to take pictures of lightning from the balcony of his apartment. Although the pictures didn't turn out very well, he soon found himself spending more and more time taking pictures of lightning on summer evenings. Warren read everything he could about weather, and he began to dream about making a living as a weather photographer.

The storm that started Warren's career arrived in Tucson long after the end of the summer thunderstorm season. On that October afternoon, Warren glanced out the back window of his apartment and saw the sharp edges of the storm cloud. He grabbed his equipment, loaded his car, and drove toward a highway underpass on the east side of town.

When Warren reached the underpass, lightning was flashing just a few miles from it. Snatching up his equipment, he scrambled up the steep bank toward a dry ledge where he could set up his cameras. As he set up his tripods, a huge lightning bolt leaped from a cloud about a mile away, striking the ground next to an air traffic control tower.

But the storm was moving quickly. Suddenly, the air was filled with wind and rain, cutting off the view of any lightning to the east. Warren looked overhead and saw small lightning bolts leaping between the clouds. He knew there was about to be another large bolt — and he was pretty sure that the next big flash would be to the west, on the other side of the underpass.

Warren knew he had to get to the other side of the underpass right away. There wasn't enough room between the ledge and the top of the underpass to walk upright, so he scooted along on his knees. He grabbed hold of overhead rain gutters to keep his balance in the darkness.

Suddenly, Warren stuck his hand into a tangle of thick cobwebs. He quickly pulled his hand back. Then he pointed

61

Suspense

Review

- Remind students that writers often build suspense by describing rising action, a chain of events that moves the action forward.

- The suspense usually ends at a climax, or the highest point of tension.

Practice

- Have students reread "Becoming a Storm Chaser" on pages 60–64 to identify the rising action before Warren gets his photograph of the lightning bolt.

- Record students' responses on the board in a diagram like the one below.

Warren gets his lightning bolt photograph.

↑ **climax**

blinding flash of pure, white light

Ka-boom!

angry black widow spiders

lightning bolt leaps from a cloud to a nearby spot

Warren reaches the underpass.

rising action

Apply

- Ask students to work in pairs to diagram other examples of rising action on pages 69–75.

CRITICAL THINKING

Guiding Comprehension

6 **NOTING DETAILS** Which details help the author create a sense of excitement and danger as he describes the events leading up to Warren's astonishing photo? (Sample answers: *angry black widow spiders, Ka-boom!* and *The air was sizzling*)

7 **DRAWING CONCLUSIONS** How can you tell that Warren was amazed by his own experience beneath the underpass? (He stayed there thinking about what had happened.)

8 **MAKING INFERENCES** How do you think Warren felt when he viewed the photo of the lightning bolt? (proud and excited; maybe surprised that it came out so well)

his penlight toward the ledge and gutters. The whole walkway was lined with webs, and rainwater washing through cracks in the concrete overhead was **6** driving out hundreds of angry black widow spiders!

Ka-boom! A huge bolt of lightning flashed overhead. Warren knew the next bolt would strike somewhere on the west side of the underpass, and he knew he had one chance to capture it. Pushing ahead in the darkness, he used the legs of his tripod as a broom, sweeping aside the cobwebs and trying to brush off any spiders that landed on his clothes.

Near the end of the underpass, and clear of the spider webs, he decided to set up his cameras. The air was sizzling, and Warren could feel that something was about to happen. He slid a few feet down the rough concrete embankment, using his hands and the soles of his shoes as brakes. When the cameras were set up, Warren quickly wiped the raindrops off the lenses. Then he moved back up the slope to a safer place to wait.

Seconds later, he heard a loud crackling, and at the same time he saw a blinding flash of pure, white light. It sounded as if the sky were being torn apart. Next came the boom of a thunderclap roaring through the underpass. It had the energy of a bomb blast, and it lifted Warren's body right off the ground.

Warren lost his hold on the slope and began sliding downhill toward his cameras. He knew that he had to close the shutters on them without bumping the tripods — or the film with the lightning would blur and be ruined. Using his hands and feet and the seat of his pants as brakes on the concrete, Warren slid to a stop just above his tripods. Carefully, he reached up and closed the shutters on the cameras. Then he looked down at his palms and saw that they were covered with blood.

Warren stayed under the underpass long after the storm had passed, thinking about what had just happened. He knew the lightning strike had been close, because when he closed his eyes he could still see its jagged outline.

The next morning, when Warren had his film developed, he was astonished by what he saw. In the center of one of the rolls was an incredible image of a lightning bolt hitting a light pole in front of some metal storage tanks. The picture had been taken from less than four hundred feet. Warren knew that he was holding the closest good picture ever taken of a lightning bolt hitting an object.

The lightning picture changed Warren's life. It was analyzed and written about by Dr. E. Philip Krider, a lightning scientist at the University of

62

REACHING ALL LEARNERS

English Language Learners

Supporting Comprehension

Point out the words *tripod, lenses, shutters, developed,* and *rolls* on page 62. Explain the meaning of each word, using camera equipment or photographs if possible. Ask what these words have in common. (All relate to cameras and photography.) Invite students to share their own knowledge or experiences with photography.

Vocabulary

sizzling crackling with intense heat

63

Visual Literacy

Photographs

Teach

- Tell students that illustrations, maps, and photographs can support text by visually presenting information discussed in the text.

- Explain that authors and illustrators must decide whether illustrations or photographs would provide the best visual support for a particular selection.

Practice/Apply

- Have a volunteer read aloud the last full paragraph on page 62. Then ask students to study the photograph on page 63.

- Ask students to answer the following questions:

  – Compare the description of the photograph with the photograph itself. What do you learn from the text? (what objects are on the photograph) How does the photograph support the text? (It shows the actual colors, sizes, and shapes of the objects.)

  – Why do photographs work well with nonfiction selections? (Both show or tell about real objects or events.)

CRITICAL THINKING
Guiding Comprehension

⑨ DRAWING CONCLUSIONS Why might a stock photo agency be useful? (It lets people find and use pictures they can't easily take themselves.)

⑩ DRAWING CONCLUSIONS What led Warren to photograph tornadoes and hurricanes in addition to lightning? (He realized that people also wanted to buy pictures of these storms.)

COMPREHENSION STRATEGY
Question

Teacher/Student Modeling Model using the Question strategy with "Storm Seasons and Chasing" on pages 63–64.

- When do most storms take place? (spring to fall)

- How do storm seasons affect Warren? (He must travel to find storms.)

Ask students to formulate a question of their own. (Sample question: Where do many storms happen?)

64

Arizona. *Life* magazine printed the picture, calling Warren a storm chaser. *National Geographic* called, wanting to film a special program about his work. The *National Enquirer* ran an article about Warren, calling him a "fearless spider-fighting photog." He even got a call from a Japanese game show that wanted to feature him on a TV program in which contestants try to guess a mystery guest's occupation. Warren began making enough money from selling his pictures that he could think about being a full-time storm chaser.

What Happens to Warren's Photos After He Takes Them?

You've probably seen some of Warren's photographs. His pictures of lightning, tornadoes, and hurricanes have appeared in books, magazines, newspapers, advertisements, and scientific films. One of his lightning pictures was even used on stage passes for rock concerts by singer Paul McCartney.

Warren's business is called a stock photo agency. It's like a library of sky and storm photographs. People pay him for the use of his photos.

Suppose, for example, that you are a magazine editor. If you need a lightning

Vocabulary

occupation job a person does to make a living

tornadoes rotating columns of air accompanied by whirling funnel-shaped downspouts that can cause great destruction

collide to bump into another mass with force

Extra Support/Intervention

Strategy Modeling: Phonics/Decoding

Model the strategy with the word *occupation*.

I see the familiar ending -tion in this word. I can try dividing the first part of the word between the two c's. The first syllable is ahk. The next part might be either kuh or kyuh. The next part is probably PAY. When I blend the sounds together, ahk-kuh-PAY-shuhn doesn't sound right, but ahk-kyuh-PAY-shuhn does. That word means "a job." It makes sense in the sentence.

photo for an article, you could go out and try to take a picture of lightning yourself. But you might have to wait a very long time for the right kind of storm, and unless you have lots of practice your lightning photograph probably won't be very good.

An easier way of getting a good lightning photo is to write to Warren. He'll send you samples, and you can select the one you like. Then, after sending Warren a fee, you can use the photo in your magazine.

When Warren began selling his lightning photos, he found that people were also asking for pictures of tornadoes and hurricanes. He didn't have photographs of these kinds of storms, so he read everything he could find about tornadoes and hurricanes —

and he made plans to photograph them as well.

Storm Seasons and Chasing

Storms are caused by certain kinds of weather patterns. The same patterns are found in the same areas year after year. For example, every spring, large areas of cool, dry air and warm, moist air collide over the central United States. If the winds are right, tornado-producing thunderstorms appear. That's why tornadoes in the south central United States are most likely to happen in spring. During July and August, shifting winds push moisture from the south up into the Arizona desert. When the cool, moist air is heated by the hot desert, storm clouds form. That's why Tucson has summer thunderstorms. In the late

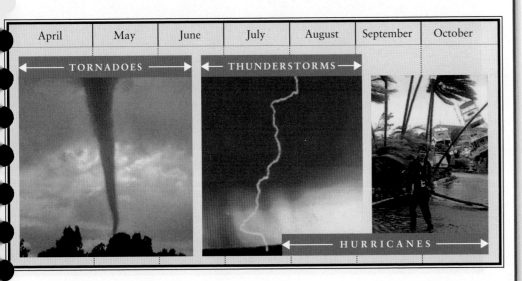

April	May	June	July	August	September	October

TORNADOES

THUNDERSTORMS

HURRICANES

65

Fact and Opinion

Review

- Remind students that a fact is information that can be proven. An opinion is a statement that tells what someone thinks, feels, or believes. An opinion cannot be proven.

- Point out that facts and opinions in a selection can help the reader infer an author's viewpoint.

Practice

- Read aloud the paragraph that begins on page 62 and ends on page 64. Point out that some people thought Warren was *fearless;* this was their opinion.

- Read aloud the first paragraph under "Storm Seasons and Chasing" on page 65.

- Then have students identify a fact in the paragraph. (Sample answer: *Storms are caused by certain kinds of weather patterns.*) Ask them to name a reference source in which they could check the fact. (encyclopedia)

Apply

- Ask students to work in pairs to find other facts and opinions that show the author's viewpoint about Warren Faidley and storm chasing.

- Have students list the facts in one column and the opinions in another column. Monitor students' work as needed.

Review Skill Trace	
Teach	Theme 2, p. 157A
Reteach	Theme 2, p. R10
▶ Review	p. 65; Theme 6, p. 613

CRITICAL THINKING
Guiding Comprehension

11 **NOTING DETAILS** Based on the photograph on page 66, how would you describe a tornado? (like a huge black cloud connected to the ground by a small funnel)

12 **DRAWING CONCLUSIONS** Why does Warren spend so much of the year traveling? (so that he can follow the storms, which occur in different places at different times of year)

13 **MAKING JUDGMENTS** Do you think that Warren's life follows a predictable pattern? Why or why not? (Sample answer: no, because you can't always tell exactly when storms will hit)

14 **DRAWING CONCLUSIONS** What does the author mean by the phrase *a promising storm* on page 67? (a storm that looks as if it will produce tornadoes)

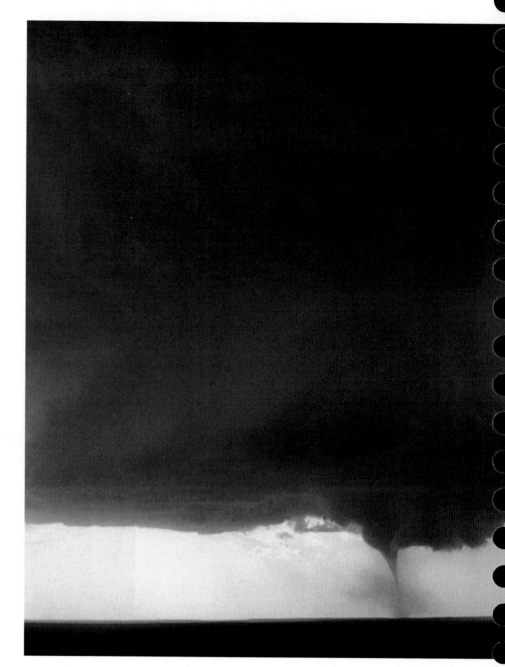

66

ASSIGNMENT CARD 7
Picture This!

Descriptive Language

The author uses descriptive language to tell the readers about lightning and tornadoes. For example, he refers to a "jagged bolt" of lightning. Locate these terms in the selection, and use them to create your own descriptions.

Theme 1: Nature's Fury

Teacher's Resource BLM page 50

summer and early fall, when oceans in the northern Atlantic are warmest, tropical storms form off the west coast of Africa. A few of these turn into the hurricanes that sometimes batter the east and gulf coasts of North America.

Because Warren is a storm chaser, his life also follows these weather patterns. Each spring, Warren goes on the road, traveling through parts of the United States likely to be hit by tornadoes. During the summer, he stays near Tucson so he can photograph the thunderstorms that develop over the desert. In the late summer and fall, he keeps an eye on weather activity in the Atlantic Ocean, ready to fly to the east coast if a hurricane appears.

Chasing Tornadoes

One of Warren's favorite tornado photos is a picture he took near Miami, Texas. Most of the sky is filled by the lower end of a huge storm cloud. A tornado hangs from the cloud, kicking up dust from the empty prairie, while the blue and yellow sky seems to go on forever.

In some ways, this wasn't a difficult picture for Warren to take. He's an experienced photographer. But before he could shoot this picture, he had to be in the right place at the right time — and that's what makes photographing tornadoes such hard work.

On a spring day, dozens of thunderstorms may develop over thousands of square miles in Texas, Oklahoma, and Kansas, but usually only a few will produce tornadoes. Since many tornadoes are on the ground only a few minutes, they will disappear before Warren can photograph them unless he is nearby. Other times, he will follow a promising storm, only to have it head off into an area where there are no roads. Tornadoes may be hidden by falling rain, making it impossible to take a picture of them. Still other storms may produce tornadoes at night, when it's too dark for Warren to take pictures and too dangerous for him to be out chasing because he can't see what's happening.

A successful tornado photographer needs patience, a good understanding of

67

Fluency Practice

Rereading for Fluency Have students choose a favorite part of the selection to reread to a partner, or suggest that they read the first three paragraphs of "Chasing Tornadoes" on page 67. Encourage students to read expressively.

Extra Support/Intervention

Strategy Modeling: Question

Use this example to model the strategy.

I have this question about storm chasing: What are the best seasons for chasing each type of storm? The diagram on page 65 shows seven months and three kinds of storms. I wonder if its purpose is to show when different storms take place. I'll read to try to find the answers.

What are the best seasons for chasing each type of storm?

CRITICAL THINKING

Guiding Comprehension

15 **TOPIC, MAIN IDEA, AND SUPPORTING DETAILS** What is the main idea in the first paragraph of the second column on page 68? (*Getting ready to go tornado chasing takes lots of time and work.*)

16 **CATEGORIZE AND CLASSIFY** Into what categories could you group the different types of chase preparations described on pages 68 and 69? (Sample answer: photography supplies, travel plans, pet care, Storm Chaser, local weather)

weather, up-to-the-minute forecasts, and lots of experience watching the sky. Even so, days, weeks, or even whole years can go by without a chance to see a tornado.

Every spring, Warren makes a trip to an area called Tornado Alley. This area stretches from northern Texas up into Oklahoma, Kansas, and Missouri. Warren and his tornado chase partner, Tom Willett, spend about six weeks tracking down giant storms and searching for tornadoes.

68

Getting ready to go tornado chasing takes lots of time and work. Warren checks all his cameras and buys plenty of film. He makes sure he has up-to-date copies of road maps for all the states he'll be traveling through. He arranges for friends to take care of Megamouth.

Finally, toward the end of April, Warren and Tom stow all their equipment in Shadow Chaser, Warren's black four-wheel-drive vehicle. Warren designed Shadow Chaser to help him find tornadoes and chase them safely. It is packed with electronic equipment, including radios, radio scanners, and a weather center that can take many different kinds of measurements. Shadow Chaser has emergency flashing lights, a long-range cellular phone, and special cabinets for storing equipment. It even has a front-mounted video camera that can make videotapes through the windshield.

As Warren and Tom drive toward Tornado Alley, their hopes are high. They know that they'll cover thousands of miles before returning to Tucson. They know they'll chase storms that never produce tornadoes and they'll probably hear about nearby tornadoes they can't get to in time. But with hard work, careful study of weather data, and a little luck, sometimes they'll have a day like the one they had on May 5, 1993.

Extra Support/Intervention

Review (pages 57–68)

Before students who need extra support join the whole class for Stop and Think on page 69, have them

- check predictions

- take turns modeling Question and other strategies they used

- help you add to **Transparency 1–11**

- check and revise their Selection Map on **Practice Book** page 32, and use it to summarize

Vocabulary

severe serious or extreme in nature

Tornado Chase Diary: May 5, 1993

Warren keeps a diary, in which he writes about his storm chases. Here are some of the things that happened on May 5, 1993, a remarkable day.

Amarillo, Texas — Morning

I awaken in a motel in Tornado Alley. As I walk to the window to peek out the drapes, I remember that last night's weather forecast showed that this might be a good chase day. Tom climbs out of bed and turns on The Weather Channel.

Later in the morning, Tom and I get the Shadow Chaser ready for the day. I test the radios, check under the hood, make sure the tires are inflated and the lights and wipers are working. We clean, pack, and return each piece of equipment to its usual place. During a chase, there isn't time to look around for a roll of film or lens for a camera.

Finally, we check out of the motel and head for a nearby restaurant for breakfast. Then we drive into town to fill the gas tank and get a few supplies.

National Weather Service Office — Early Afternoon

We arrive at the Amarillo office of the National Weather Service. Here I get an update on local weather conditions, as well as a chance to see a satellite picture of the area. I use current weather information to draw a map of where today's thunderstorms are likely to form. The reports are saying that there is a moderate chance of severe weather in our area, and some of the thunderstorms will probably produce tornadoes. Since the storms aren't expected to develop until later in the afternoon, we take some time off and drive to a nearby garage to have the oil changed in Shadow Chaser.

A couple hours later, we're back at the National Weather Service office to make our final chase decisions. It's beginning to look like the area north of town is our best bet. We pull out the highway maps and start looking at possible routes.

As we leave town, I call a friend and fellow chaser who gives weather reports for a local TV station. He confirms that severe storm clouds are building right where we're headed. He also says that a

69

Stop and Think

Critical Thinking Questions

1. **MAKING JUDGMENTS** Does the author succeed in building suspense throughout the selection? Why or why not? (Answers will vary.)

2. **COMPARE AND CONTRAST** Warren Faidley and the characters from *Earthquake Terror* both experience storms. Compare and contrast how Warren reacts with how Jonathan and Abby react. (Sample answer: Warren is excited by storms and enjoys them, while Jonathan and Abby are frightened by the earthquake.)

Strategies in Action

Have students take turns modeling Question and other strategies they used.

Discussion Options

You may wish to bring the entire class together to do one or more of the activities below.

- **Review Predictions/Purpose** Discuss with students their predictions and any revisions they made. Record any new predictions.

- **Share Group Discussions** Have students share their questions and literature discussions.

- **Summarize** Ask students to use their Selection Maps to summarize the selection so far.

ASSIGNMENT CARD 6

Literature Discussion

Discuss your own questions and the following questions with a group of your classmates:

- What traits and skills does a storm chaser need? Does Warren Faidley seem to have these? Give examples that support your answer.

- Why do you think people were so amazed by Warren's photo of the lightning bolt hitting the pole?

- Do you think this photo was worth the risks Warren took to get it? Why or why not?

- How do you think Warren felt when he realized that there was a strong demand for storm photos? Why might he have felt that way?

Theme 1: Nature's Fury

Teacher's Resource BLM page 49

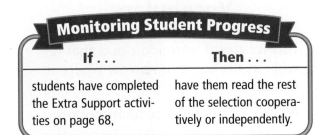

Monitoring Student Progress

If . . .	Then . . .
students have completed the Extra Support activities on page 68,	have them read the rest of the selection cooperatively or independently.

Reading the Selection 69

CRITICAL THINKING

Guiding Comprehension

17 NOTING DETAILS What clues does Warren look for to learn if a tornado might be forming? How does he go about chasing a tornado? (large, dark clouds that rotate; He watches where the storm goes and follows it.)

18 MAKING GENERALIZATIONS How can tornado chasers and other weather experts help people who are traveling through tornado country? (by telling them what the forecast is and whether it is safe to travel)

19 MAKING INFERENCES What does the author mean when he says that chasing a storm is *like playing a huge game of chess*? (Chess players must predict what their opponents might do in order to outmaneuver them. Storm chasers must predict a storm's movement and move first.)

---

news team from his station is already headed there.

Near Panhandle, Texas — Late Afternoon

The sky is hazy, but in the distance we can see the tops of anvil-shaped storm clouds. We stop the truck to pick up the TV report. My forecaster friend is on. He's pointing to an area on his map about fifty miles north of our location. "It looks like we're going to have some severe storms in this area!" he says. We get back into the truck and drive north.

Near Gruver, Texas — Early Evening

The overcast skies clear enough to show a giant thunderstorm just ahead. Then our radio scanner locks onto a message from the TV crew's chase unit. "There's a large funnel cloud coming from this storm," says the message. While the crew describes its location, I look at the map. "They're only eight miles from here," I tell Tom. "Let's go and find it!"

As we approach Gruver, we see the red TV van parked on the side of the road. A cameraman is pointing his camera at a huge, gray-white funnel cloud hanging from the base of a dark cloud. As Tom parks the truck, I use the radio to call in a weather report to the National Weather Service station in Amarillo. The funnel cloud pulls back up into the storm.

We head north, following the storm. As we drive, watching the back of the storm, we can see the clouds darkening and beginning to rotate. The white clouds at the top of the storm take on the shape of a giant mushroom. I'm excited, but I'm worried too. I know that anyone in the path of this storm is in terrible danger.

We follow the storm down the highway. Gradually, it turns and heads back toward the road. We pull over and wait for the storm to cross. While we're waiting, a large semi truck pulls up beside us. The driver opens his window and leans out.

"Hey, are you guys tornado chasers? Is that a tornado forming? Is it safe for me to drive under it?"

"We're not sure if it's going to turn into a tornado, but I'd wait here and let it pass," I answer.

We all watch as the swirling mass crosses the highway. A small funnel cloud reaches down from the storm cloud — and then quickly disappears. I reach for the microphone and call Amarillo:

"This is Warren. I'm about eight miles north of Gruver, just west of Highway 207. Tom and I are looking at a large cloud mass that is organizing and rotating."

"Roger, Warren," replies the spotter coordinator. "We're watching the same area on radar. Thanks."

70

English Language Learners

Supporting Comprehension

Teach the compass points north, south, east, and west.

- Draw lines pointing in these directions, and label the points appropriately at the end of each line.

- Then have students locate your state on a map. Name each compass point as you point to states that are north of, south of, east of, and west of your state.

- Have students locate the places mentioned in the selection and their compass points in relation to your state. Ask students to use *north, south, east,* and *west* as they talk about places and compass points.

Vocabulary

funnel cloud tornado cloud that is wide at the top and narrow where it touches the ground

rotate to swirl in a circular motion

Now we begin to worry about losing the storm. There aren't very many roads in this area, and most of them run north–south or east–west. Since most storms don't continue for long in these directions, following a storm is a little like playing a huge game of chess. Tom loads his cameras back into the truck while I check the road map.

We make our way along a tangle of unmarked farm roads a few miles from the Oklahoma border. Since the storm is on our west side, and it's moving northeast, we can safely stay quite close

71

ASSIGNMENT CARD 8

Warren's Eventful Day

Organize Information Visually

How could you summarize the events of May 5, 1993? Create a graphic organizer, such as a schedule or a logbook entry with sketches, that gives an at-a-glance view of that day's events.

May 5, 1993 Amarillo, Texas	6:00 AM:	Awake in motel room in Tornado Alley; check weather on TV
	12:15 PM:	Arrive at National Weather Service; get update on conditions
	2:00 PM:	Final chase decisions made

Theme 1: Nature's Fury

Teacher's Resource BLM page 50

Sequence of Events

Review

- Remind students that sequence of events refers to the order in which events happen.

- Tell students that words such as *first, next, then, finally, now,* and *at the same time* often signal sequence.

Practice

- Have students read "Amarillo, Texas—Morning" on page 69. Ask, What do Tom and Warren do first? (clean and pack) Have students identify words that signal this order. (*Later in the morning, Finally*)

- Next, remind students that some events can happen at the same time. Point out that Tom walks to the window and remembers a weather forecast. Ask students to identify the signal word. (*As*)

Apply

- Have students identify the order in which the remaining events on page 69 occurred. (They drive into town for supplies. They arrive at the Amarillo office. They drive to a nearby garage. They return to the office. They leave town.)

- Ask students to write down signal words on page 69. (*Morning, As, last night's, Later in the morning, During, Finally, Then, A couple hours later, start*)

Review Skill Trace	
Teach	p. 51A
Reteach	p. R8
▶ Review	p. 71; Theme 2, p. 213

Guiding Comprehension

20 **NOTING DETAILS** Which details on page 72 show that tornadoes have tremendous destructive force? (They suck up soil from fields and rip up fences.)

21 **MAKING INFERENCES** Why is it so difficult for Warren and Tom to photograph the tornado? (It keeps moving, and they can't chase it everywhere because the roads sometimes don't go in the same direction.)

COMPREHENSION STRATEGY

Question

Student Modeling Ask students to share some of the questions they formed about the selection. Offer these prompts:

- What should I look for when I try to spot a cloud that might produce a tornado?

- How can the description on page 72 help me answer this question?

Vocabulary

updraft upwardly moving current of air

vortices whirlpools made of rotating air or water; plural of vortex

multivortex having many vortices at once

---

to the updraft without getting in the direct path of a tornado.

Near the Oklahoma/Texas Border — Evening

We keep an eye on the swirling clouds as we drive along. Suddenly, from the center of the clouds, a large white funnel appears.

"Look, Tom! Another tornado!" I exclaim. "That thing is less than a mile away!"

I reach for the microphone and call in another report. The funnel cloud begins to stretch. Soon it looks like the trunk of a huge elephant, wiggling over the green fields below. Then it touches down, officially becoming a tornado. When the funnel touches the ground, wispy little vortices appear around the main cloud of wind. As these mini-tornadoes spin, they kick up dust of their

72

own. I grab the microphone and send another message to the spotter coordinator:

"We're about three or four miles south of the Texas/Oklahoma state line," I explain. "And we're looking at a large, multivortex tornado on the ground."

Just inside the Oklahoma state line, the road turns slightly toward the northwest. The tornado begins to cross the road a little ahead of us. We stop to try and get some pictures, but the light isn't good. It's hard to see the tornado clearly against the background of the cloud. The air is hazy, and another storm to the west is blocking the sunlight.

"We've got a great tornado here," I say to Tom, "but the light is terrible." We load our gear back into the truck and roll down a bumpy dirt road, looking for better light, while the tornado swirls along beside us.

As Tom drives, he keeps glancing at the tornado. Suddenly he yells, "Warren! There's another tornado forming!" I peer through the window and see a debris cloud forming, sucking up soil from a field.

"Wow," Tom says. "Look what it's doing to that fence!" We watch as it rips a section of barbed-wire fence out of the ground and scatters it across the field. The small area of spinning wind, with no

---

ASSIGNMENT CARD 9

It Looks Like. . .

Comparing by Shape

The author compares the shapes of the tornadoes to various objects, including an elephant's trunk, an anvil, a wedge, and a funnel. Make a list of all the shapes the author uses. Next to each shape name, draw what that type of tornado might look like.

Theme 1: Nature's Fury

Teacher's Resource BLM page 51

visible funnel cloud above, tears across the fields.

"Slow down, Tom," I say. "I can't see the funnel cloud connected to that thing — and we sure don't want to get hit by it." A few seconds later, the debris cloud disappears.

We follow a maze of unmarked dirt roads until we reach a dead end. As we turn around and drive back toward the highway, we watch as the edges of the storm cloud wrap around the tornado, hiding it from sight. Many sightings of "our" tornado, as well as others in the area, are being reported over the radio. I'm happy to hear that so far the tornadoes haven't hit any populated areas.

East of Guymon, Oklahoma — Evening

It's about 7:30 p.m. when we pull back onto the highway. As we head east, we see a long, thin tornado crossing the road a few miles ahead.

"I bet that's our tornado," I tell Tom. "It looks like it's weakening. We've got to shoot it now!" When Tom stops, I jump out the door, set my camera on the hood to steady it, and go through another roll of film. As we watch, the funnel pulls back up into the dark clouds.

West of Hooker, Oklahoma — Evening

Traveling along the highway, we're joined again by the crew from the TV

73

English Language Learners

Supporting Comprehension

Remind students that on page 73 Warren says *"Slow down, Tom."* On page 75, the author uses *slows down* to describe the tornado's movement. Explain that to *slow down* means "to move more slowly." Tell students that the opposite of *slow down* means "speed up."

Text Organization

Teach

- Explain that nonfiction is often organized by main ideas or sequence of events.
- Remind students that main ideas are the most important information about the topic. Sequence of events is the order in which events happen.

Practice

- Have students review Anthology pages 57–68. Ask: Is this section organized by main ideas or sequence of events? How can you tell? (main ideas; The headings describe the most important ideas in each section.)
- Ask: How are pages 69–75 organized? How can you tell? (Sequence of events; The headings organize events by the order and location in which they happened.)
- Discuss with students why authors might use each type of text organization. (to help readers understand the most important ideas; to build suspense and keep readers interested)

Apply

- Have students work in pairs to find examples of both types of text organization in other nonfiction selections.
- Have them share their examples with the class.

Target Skill Trace	
Preview; Teach	p. 53S; p. 56; p. 73; p. 81A
Reteach	p. R10
Review	pp. M34–M35; p. 95; Theme 2, p. 147

CRITICAL THINKING

Guiding Comprehension

22 **WRITER'S CRAFT** Why do you think the author includes so much dialogue in the description of the storm chase? (to make the passage more exciting; to make the people seem real)

23 **DRAWING CONCLUSIONS** Why does Warren decide to stop photographing for the day, even though tornadoes are still forming? (It's dangerous to try to chase tornadoes at night.)

24 **MAKING INFERENCES** Why do you think Warren and Tom were still shaking their heads that night? (They were still surprised by how many tornadoes they saw in one day.)

74

Vocabulary

fortunate lucky

 Extra Support/ Intervention

On Level **Challenge**

Selection Review

Before students join in Wrapping Up on page 75, have them

- check predictions

- take turns modeling Question and other strategies they used

- help you complete **Transparency 1–11**

- complete their Selection Maps on **Practice Book** page 32 and use them to summarize

Literature Discussion

Have small groups of students discuss the selection using their own questions or the Responding questions on Anthology page 76.

station. Down the road, I see a huge wedge-shaped tornado on the ground.

"Stop!" I yell to Tom. Tom hits the brakes and we stare through the windshield. The tornado looks like it's about seven or eight miles from us, moving away, although the fading light makes it hard to be sure. As we watch, the funnel slows down, and then it disappears. We continue on and I spot another tornado. This one looks like a long stovepipe.

"This is incredible," I say to Tom. "We've got two large thunderstorms here, and they're dropping tornadoes everywhere!"

The stovepipe tornado swirls into the clouds before we can get close enough for pictures. As we watch it disappear, I realize that it's getting too dark for any more photos. I know the storms are still active, and I'm worried that the fading light could hide any newly forming tornadoes. Chasing any more tornadoes today would be too dangerous.

Near the Oklahoma/Kansas Border — Evening

As the last of the light disappears, we see two more tornadoes in the distance. One is headed north, rolling into Kansas. As we drive back to Amarillo, we listen to news reports on the radio. "With as many tornadoes as we have had on the ground tonight," says a reporter, "it's a

miracle that none of them have hit a town. We do have at least one report of a farm being destroyed, with no injuries so far. But beyond that, we have been extremely fortunate."

Amarillo, Texas — Night

It's 11:00 p.m. by the time we finally pull back into the motel parking lot. As Tom and I unload Shadow Chaser, we're still shaking our heads about what we've seen. The tornadoes we saw caused some damage, but there have been no reports of any deaths or injuries. That makes it easier to celebrate our seven-tornado day.

75

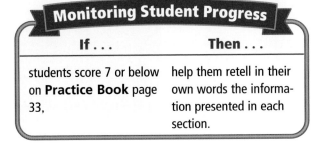

Practice Book page 33

An Interview with Warren Faidley

Practice Book page 33 comprehension check reproduction

Wrapping Up

Critical Thinking Questions

1. **CAUSE AND EFFECT** How has Warren Faidley turned his interests and skills into a profitable career? (He combined his interest in storms and his photography skills to become a storm chaser and a stock photo agency owner.)

2. **MAKING JUDGMENTS** In what ways do you think Warren Faidley's work as a storm chaser is helpful to people? (His work might help people avoid or prepare for dangerous storms.)

Strategies in Action

Have students take turns modeling how and where they used the Question strategy.

Discussion Options

Bring the entire class together to do one or more of the activities below.

Review Predictions/Purpose Ask students to share their predictions.

Share Group Discussions Have students share any answers they found to questions they formulated. Have them refer to the selection to describe the good and bad parts of being a storm chaser.

Summarize Ask students to use their Selection Maps on **Practice Book** page 32 to summarize.

Comprehension Check

Use **Practice Book** page 33 to assess students' comprehension of the selection.

Monitoring Student Progress

If . . .	Then . . .
students score 7 or below on **Practice Book** page 33,	help them retell in their own words the information presented in each section.

Responding

Think About the Selection

Have students discuss or write their answers. Sample answers are provided; accept reasonable responses.

1. **ANALYZING** The headings helped me understand what each section is about. The calendar helped me understand storm seasons.

2. **ANALYZING** He means that the air was filled with the sizzling sound of lightning.

3. **GENERATING** He is adventurous and curious about whirlwinds.

4. **GENERATING** No. He stopped taking pictures of tornadoes when it became unsafe.

5. **INTEGRATING** Answers will vary.

6. **EVALUATING** Answers will vary.

7. **Connections** Alike—Both face dangerous situations caused by forces of nature. Both try to follow safety procedures; Different—Warren is prepared for dangerous situations, but Jonathan is taken by surprise.

READ & COMPREHEND

Think About the Selection

1. **Analyzing** How did the section headings help you understand *Eye of the Storm?* How did the calendar on page 65 help you understand Warren's job.

2. **Analyzing** On page 62, the author writes, "The air was sizzling" before Warren took his famous underpass photograph. What do you think he means?

3. **Generating** Think about Warren Faidley's decision to ride his bike into a whirlwind. What does this action tell you about him?

4. **Generating** Do you think Warren would face any danger in order to get a spectacular storm shot? Use facts from the selection to support your answer.

5. **Integrating** Warren's interest in storms led to his career as a weather photographer. What interests do you have that might lead to a career?

6. **Evaluating** Would you want to accompany Warren on a storm chase? Why or why not? If so, which kind of storm would you want to see and why?

7. **Connections** Compare Warren's risk from tornadoes and lightning with Jonathan's risk in *Earthquake Terror.* How are their situations alike and different?

Write a Job Description

Think about what a storm chaser does. Then write a job description for a storm chaser. Include the character traits and skills a storm chaser should have. Note any special equipment a storm chaser should be able to use.

Tips

- List the job requirements in two categories: traits and skills.
- In the skills category, include special equipment.

76

English Language Learners

Supporting Comprehension

Beginning/Preproduction Help students create a word web for types of weather. Students can copy the webs and add drawings for the words.

Early Production and Speech Emergence Ask students to tell or write about the types of storms that have happened in your area.

Intermediate and Advanced Fluency Ask: What is the most frightening storm you have experienced? Describe the storm and how you felt.

Math

Estimate Mileage

Estimate the number of miles Warren Faidley drove from his home to where he began his tornado chase diary for May 5, 1993. Use the map on page 55, a ruler, and this scale — one inch equals 300 miles.

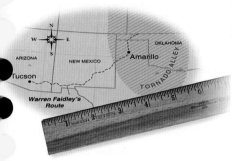

Viewing

Compare Photographs

Choose two photographs from the selection and write a caption that compares and contrasts them. Choose two lightning photographs, two tornado photographs, or one of each kind. Tell about both the details and the mood of each photograph.

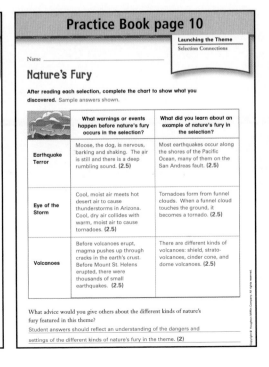

Internet

Take an Online Poll

Have you ever seen a lightning strike or a tornado? What kind of storm have you been in? Do you enjoy books about the weather? Take our online poll and let us know. Visit Education Place. **www.eduplace.com/kids**

77

Additional Responses

Personal Response Invite students to share their personal responses to *Eye of the Storm*.

Journal ▸ Ask students to write their thoughts and opinions about storm chasing in their journals.

Selection Connections Remind students to add to **Practice Book** pages 9–10.

Practice Book page 9

Name _____

Launching the Theme
Selection Connections

Nature's Fury

After reading each selection, complete the chart below and on the next page to show what you discovered. Sample answers shown.

	What is the setting or settings for the action or descriptions in the selection?	What dangers do people face in the selection?
Earthquake Terror	Magpie Island, in California (2.5 Points)	Jonathan and Abby are stranded on Magpie Island when an earthquake strikes, toppling trees all around them. (2.5)
Eye of the Storm	Tucson, Arizona and Tornado Alley (Amarillo, Texas and towns in Texas, Oklahoma and Kansas) (2.5)	Warren Faidley faces danger from lightning bolts and spiders while photographing from an underpass. He and Tom Willett face danger from tornadoes forming around them in Tornado Alley. (2.5)
Volcanoes	Hawaii, Washington state, Iceland, Guatemala, California, Oregon (2.5)	People face danger from the eruption of Mount St. Helens; people on the island of Heimaey, Iceland, face danger from a volcano; people in Hawaii face danger to their houses from quick-moving lava. (2.5)

Practice Book page 10

Name _____

Launching the Theme
Selection Connections

Nature's Fury

After reading each selection, complete the chart to show what you discovered. Sample answers shown.

	What warnings or events happen before nature's fury occurs in the selection?	What did you learn about an example of nature's fury in the selection?
Earthquake Terror	Moose, the dog, is nervous, barking and shaking. The air is still and there is a deep rumbling sound. (2.5)	Most earthquakes occur along the shores of the Pacific Ocean, many of them on the San Andreas fault. (2.5)
Eye of the Storm	Cool, moist air meets hot desert air to cause thunderstorms in Arizona. Cool, dry air collides with warm, moist air to cause tornadoes. (2.5)	Tornadoes form from funnel clouds. When a funnel cloud touches the ground, it becomes a tornado. (2.5)
Volcanoes	Before volcanoes erupt, magma pushes up through cracks in the earth's crust. Before Mount St. Helens erupted, there were thousands of small earthquakes. (2.5)	There are different kinds of volcanoes: shield, strato-volcanoes, cinder cone, and dome volcanoes. (2.5)

What advice would you give others about the different kinds of nature's fury featured in this theme?
Student answers should reflect an understanding of the dangers and settings of the different kinds of nature's fury in the theme. (2)

Monitoring Student Progress

End-of-Selection Assessment

Selection Test Use the test on page 115 of the **Teacher's Resource Blackline Masters** to assess selection comprehension and vocabulary.

Student Self-Assessment Have students assess their reading with additional questions such as

- Which parts of the selection were difficult for me? Why?

- What strategies helped me understand the selection?

- Would I recommend this selection to my friends? Why?

Responding 77

Career Link

Skill: How to Read a Sequence Chart

- **Introduce** "Storm Warning," a nonfiction article about how a meteorologist gathers data for a weather forecast. Ask students what they know about a weather forecaster's job. Invite them to describe different images they have seen on TV weather reports, such as satellite photos and computer-generated weather maps.

- **Discuss** the Skill Lesson on Anthology page 78. Explain that a sequence chart presents the steps in a process.

- **Model** how to identify the three steps of the sequence chart on page 79 by pointing to each step in order.

- **Explain** that this sequence chart is read from top to bottom. Have a volunteer point to the arrows that indicate this sequence. Help students identify the process shown on the chart. (the process of collecting weather data) Ask students to read each step.

- **Set a purpose** for reading. Tell students to read the article and study the photographs, map, and the sequence chart. Remind them to use the Question strategy as they read.

Vocabulary

meteorologist scientist who studies the weather

atmosphere layer of air that surrounds the earth, where weather systems occur

---

Career Link

Genre

Biography

Skill: How to Read a Sequence Chart

❶ Read the **title** of the sequence chart. It tells what **process** is being shown.

❷ Read the **steps** in the process by following the **arrows** from top to bottom or left to right.

❸ Look for **order words**, such as *next, then, resulting,* and *now.*

78

Mishelle Michaels was formerly a weather forecaster at 7 News in Boston. When TV viewers tuned in, they saw the result of a long day of data collection and weather analysis — the job of the meteorologist.

Forecasters like Mishelle rely on information collected at thousands of points around the world. These "eyes" and "ears" that scout the weather include radar satellites, surface sites, and weather balloons

Mishelle Michaels, meteorologist, analyzes computer models to prepare for her evening broadcast.

Collecting the Data

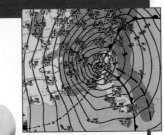

Weather satellites 22,000 miles up take photographs of clouds to show the movement of weather systems.

Surface observing sites report the current weather conditions every hour of every day of every year.

Through a network of NEXRAD (Next Generation Radar) stations, radar images display the motion and intensity of rain or snow.

Weather balloons take measurements of the atmosphere from ground level to thousands of feet above the earth.

The National Weather Service's supercomputer then processes this information, making sixteen billion calculations per second.

The resulting charts and weather images are made available to meteorologists around the United States to help them create their forecasts.

79

Extra Support/Intervention

Scientific Terms

Some students may need help reading some of the scientific terms in this article. Read aloud and explain the boxed vocabulary words before students read. Ask students to write down words they do not recognize as they read. Help students to find and understand the meanings of these terms in a reference source.

radar: a method of detecting and measuring objects by means of reflected radio waves

Communicating Information

Teach

- Tell students that identifying the purposes of visual formats—such as text, photographs, graphs, charts, or illustrations—can help them understand why information is presented in different ways.

- Point out that some information may be easier to understand when presented in text while other information might be easier to understand in charts, graphs, or other formats.

Practice/Apply

- Have students describe the images on page 79. (a computer-generated image of weather patterns; people with a weather balloon; photographs of a weather station and Earth)

- Have students view the photographs on pages 80–81. Ask them to list the different types of visual formats Mishelle Michaels uses to gather information. (computer models, charts, radar images)

- Ask: What might be the purpose for each format? (Sample answer: to make complex weather information easier to understand at a glance)

Vocabulary

analyze think critically and carefully about information in order to interpret it

atmospheric science the study of the air that surrounds the earth

---

Analyzing the Weather

Reviewing Conditions

To begin her forecast, Mishelle checks the current conditions — temperatures, winds, and weather patterns — for the city of Boston, its surrounding communities, and much of New England.

Observing Radar Images

Enhanced Doppler radar provides Mishelle with images of thunderstorms moving toward Boston from the west. Next Generation Radar can detect dangerous shifts in wind direction that may result in tornadoes.

Meteorologists analyze the many charts and images that the National Weather Service provides. But that is only part of the studying and interpreting they have to do before they can create a forecast. The data gathered from the radar and satellites requires the explaining abilities of the meteorologist so that it makes sense to the rest of us.

80

English Language Learners

Supporting Comprehension

Tell students that the word *career* means "what a person does; one's profession." Say: I am a teacher; teaching is my career. Ask: What is Warren's career? (storm chasing) Have students name careers that they find interesting.

Hearing from Weather Watchers

Local volunteers of all ages phone in detailed weather reports from their communities. These observations are often invaluable in helping Mishelle put together the pieces of the forecasting puzzle.

Analyzing Computer Models

By analyzing weather charts and maps created by the National Weather Service from computer models, Mishelle develops a four- to five-day forecast for Greater Boston and New England. She relies on her education and experience to accurately predict how the atmosphere will change.

Career File

Meteorologist

Are you interested in following the weather professionally? You'll need a four-year college degree in Meteorology or Atmospheric Science. It also helps if you enjoy . . .

- watching clouds and chasing storms (from a safe distance)
- the challenge of problem-solving
- communicating your knowledge with others

Meanwhile, contact your local television station about becoming a volunteer weather observer.

81

Challenge

Science

Invite students to set up an outdoor classroom weather station and keep a log book that shows weather conditions and air temperatures over the course of several days. They can compare their findings with the weather report in the local newspaper. For an additional challenge, ask students to find the average temperature at different times of day and communicate this information in a graph or chart.

Wrapping Up

Critical Thinking Questions

Ask students to use the selection and their understanding of charts to answer these questions.

1. **SUMMARIZING** Where does a meteorologist get the information needed to prepare a weather forecast? (from the National Weather Service's charts and images; from weather volunteers' eyewitness accounts)

2. **MAKING INFERENCES** Why is it important for a meteorologist to be able to interpret information that is presented in different forms? (because he or she has to interpret charts, graphs, radar pictures, computer images, and satellite photos)

3. **NOTING DETAILS** Do meteorologists rely only on data collected by machines? Explain. (No. They also rely on information from weather volunteers, who call and tell them what the weather is like.)

4. **COMPARE AND CONTRAST** How is the work Warren Faidley does similar to the work Mishelle Michaels does? How is it different? (Alike: Both study the weather and rely on different sources of information; Different: Warren studies the weather so he can get pictures of storms, but Mishelle studies it so she can prepare weather forecasts.)

OBJECTIVES

- Identify different ways in which authors organize text.
- Use text features as a guide to the organization of information.
- Learn academic language: *text organization, main idea, sequence of events.*

Target Skill Trace

Preview; Teach	p. 53S; p. 56; p. 73; p. 81A
Reteach	p. R10
Review	pp. M34–M35; p. 95; Theme 2, p. 147
See	*Extra Support Handbook,* pp. 26–27; pp. 32–33

Transparency 1–11

Selection Map

Pages 59–68

Page 59	Storm Chasing	how Warren chases a lightning storm
Page 60	Warren Faidley: Storm Chaser	how Warren was interested in storms since he was a child
Page 64	What Happens to Warren's Photos After He Takes Them?	how Warren created a stock photo agency, where people can go and buy his photos
Page 65	Storm Seasons and Chasing	how tornadoes form and how storm chasers follow weather patterns that form tornadoes
Page 67	Chasing Tornadoes	how Warren knows where to go to get the best pictures of tornadoes

Pages 69–75

Morning	One Day in the Life of a Storm Chaser Check the weather, get Shadow Chaser ready for the day, test the equipment, pack supplies
Afternoon	Get an update on the weather conditions, change the oil in Shadow Chaser, check maps
Evening	Look at the map, call the National Weather Service, head north following the storm, follow the tornadoes from Texas into Oklahoma, shoot the photos

TRANSPARENCY 1–11
TEACHER'S EDITION PAGES 56 AND 81A

Practice Book page 32

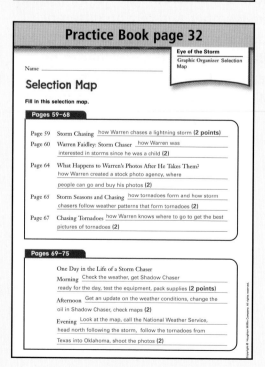

Eye of the Storm
Graphic Organizer Selection Map

Name _____

Selection Map

Fill in this selection map.

Pages 59–68

Page 59	Storm Chasing	how Warren chases a lightning storm **(2 points)**
Page 60	Warren Faidley: Storm Chaser	how Warren was interested in storms since he was a child **(2)**
Page 64	What Happens to Warren's Photos After He Takes Them?	how Warren created a stock photo agency, where people can go and buy his photos **(2)**
Page 65	Storm Seasons and Chasing	how tornadoes form and how storm chasers follow weather patterns that form tornadoes **(2)**
Page 67	Chasing Tornadoes	how Warren knows where to go to get the best pictures of tornadoes **(2)**

Pages 69–75

Morning	One Day in the Life of a Storm Chaser Check the weather, get Shadow Chaser ready for the day, test the equipment, pack supplies **(2 points)**
Afternoon	Get an update on the weather conditions, change the oil in Shadow Chaser, check maps **(2)**
Evening	Look at the map, call the National Weather Service, head north following the storm, follow the tornadoes from Texas into Oklahoma, shoot the photos **(2)**

TARGET SKILL COMPREHENSION: Text Organization

❶ Teach

Review text organization in *Eye of the Storm*. Remind students that authors organize information in a variety of ways to suit different purposes and audiences. Complete the Graphic Organizer on **Transparency 1–11** with students. Have students refer to the selection and to **Practice Book** page 32. Discuss two types of text organization:

- Text can be organized by main ideas.
- Text can be organized according to sequence of events.

Model identifying different types of text organization. Ask a student to identify the main idea in the section under the heading "Chasing Tornadoes" (page 67). (photographing tornadoes) Next, have a volunteer read the first paragraph on page 69. Model identifying how the text organization changes for the second part of the selection.

Think Aloud *The first part is organized by main idea. This is a good way to give general information about this topic, such as the season for chasing tornadoes. On page 69 the author switches to organizing by sequence of events. Why? This way he can show us a typical day in which Warren follows tornadoes, step by step.*

❷ Guided Practice

Have students identify different types of text organization. Have students work in pairs to locate examples of both types of text organization in *Eye of the Storm*: main ideas and sequence of events. Have them record their responses in a chart like the one below.

Type of Organization	Page	Information
by main idea	page 65	when tornadoes, hurricanes, and thunderstorms happen
by sequence	page 69	what happened the morning of May 5, 1993

❸ Apply

Assign Practice Book pages 34–35. Also have students apply this skill as they read their **Leveled Readers** for this week. You may also select books from the Leveled Bibliography for this theme (pages 23E–23F).

Test Prep Tell students that thinking about text organization will help them find details to answer to test questions. They can scan the title, the byline, the headings, and the captions.

Leveled Readers and Leveled Practice

Students at all levels apply the comprehension skill as they read their Leveled Readers. See lessons on pages 81O–81R.

● BELOW LEVEL — White Dragon: Anna Allen in the Face of Danger

▲ ON LEVEL — Hurricane OPAL Into the Storm by Carlos Bernardes, illustrated by John Martin

■ ABOVE LEVEL — Benjamin Franklin A Scientist by Nature by Elena Grossman • illustrated by Ron Mazellan

◆ LANGUAGE SUPPORT — Anna Allen Faces the White Dragon by Maryann Dobeck, illustrations by Todd Leonardo

Reading Traits

Teaching students how to recognize test organization is one way of encouraging them to "read the lines" of a selection. This comprehension skill supports the reading trait **Decoding Conventions.**

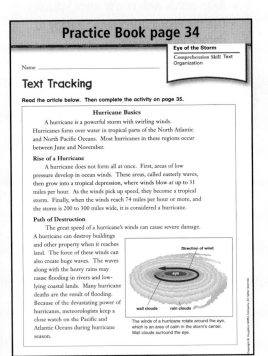

Practice Book page 34

Eye of the Storm
Comprehension Skill Text Organization

Name _____

Text Tracking

Read the article below. Then complete the activity on page 35.

Hurricane Basics

A hurricane is a powerful storm with swirling winds. Hurricanes form over water in tropical parts of the North Atlantic and North Pacific Oceans. Most hurricanes in these regions occur between June and November.

Rise of a Hurricane

A hurricane does not form all at once. First, areas of low pressure develop in ocean winds. These areas, called easterly waves, then grow into a tropical depression, where winds blow at up to 31 miles per hour. As the winds pick up speed, they become a tropical storm. Finally, when the winds reach 74 miles per hour or more, and the storm is 200 to 300 miles wide, it is considered a hurricane.

Path of Destruction

The great speed of a hurricane's winds can cause severe damage. A hurricane can destroy buildings and other property when it reaches land. The force of these winds can also create huge waves. The waves along with the heavy rains may cause flooding in rivers and low-lying coastal lands. Many hurricane deaths are the result of flooding. Because of the devastating power of hurricanes, meteorologists keep a close watch on the Pacific and Atlantic Oceans during hurricane season.

The winds of a hurricane rotate around the eye, which is an area of calm in the storm's center. Wall clouds surround the eye.

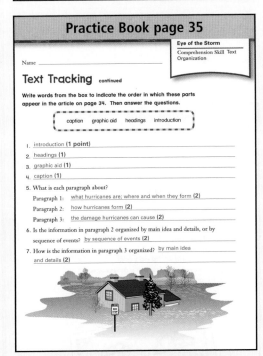

Practice Book page 35

Eye of the Storm
Comprehension Skill Text Organization

Name _____

Text Tracking continued

Write words from the box to indicate the order in which these parts appear in the article on page 34. Then answer the questions.

> caption   graphic aid   headings   introduction

1. introduction **(1 point)**
2. headings **(1)**
3. graphic aid **(1)**
4. caption **(1)**
5. What is each paragraph about?
   Paragraph 1: what hurricanes are; where and when they form **(2)**
   Paragraph 2: how hurricanes form **(2)**
   Paragraph 3: the damage hurricanes can cause **(2)**
6. Is the information in paragraph 2 organized by main idea and details, or by sequence of events? by sequence of events **(2)**
7. How is the information in paragraph 3 organized? by main idea and details **(2)**

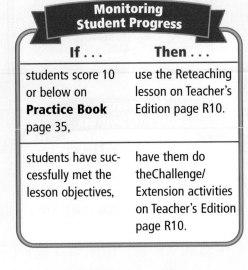

Monitoring Student Progress

If . . .	Then . . .
students score 10 or below on **Practice Book** page 35,	use the Reteaching lesson on Teacher's Edition page R10.
students have successfully met the lesson objectives,	have them do the Challenge/ Extension activities on Teacher's Edition page R10.

OBJECTIVES

- Read words with two or more syllables.
- Use the Phonics/Decoding Strategy to decode longer words.

Target Skill Trace

Teach	p. 81C
Reteach	p. R16
Review	pp. M36–M37
See	*Handbook for English Language Learners,* p. 29; *Extra Support Handbook,* pp. 24–25; pp. 28–29

Practice Book page 36

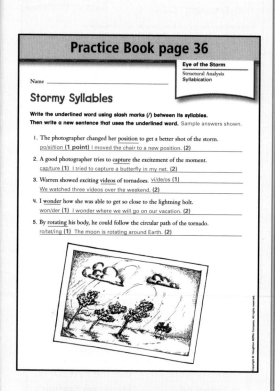

Eye of the Storm
Structural Analysis
Syllabication

Name _____

Stormy Syllables

Write the underlined word using slash marks (/) between its syllables.
Then write a new sentence that uses the underlined word. Sample answers shown.

1. The photographer changed her position to get a better shot of the storm.
   po/si/tion **(1 point)** I moved the chair to a new position. **(2)**
2. A good photographer tries to capture the excitement of the moment.
   cap/ture **(1)** I tried to capture a butterfly in my net. **(2)**
3. Warren showed exciting videos of tornadoes. vi/de/os **(1)**
   We watched three videos over the weekend. **(2)**
4. I wonder how she was able to get so close to the lightning bolt.
   won/der **(1)** I wonder where we will go on our vacation. **(2)**
5. By rotating his body, he could follow the circular path of the tornado.
   ro/tat/ing **(1)** The moon is rotating around Earth. **(2)**

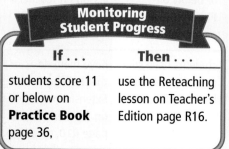

Monitoring Student Progress

If . . .	Then . . .
students score 11 or below on **Practice Book** page 36,	use the Reteaching lesson on Teacher's Edition page R16.

STRUCTURAL ANALYSIS/ VOCABULARY: Syllabication

❶ Teach

Discuss the VCCV syllable pattern. Explain that a syllable is a word part that has one sound. Write *looking for <u>cactus</u> wrens.*

- Write *V* under *a* and *u* of *cactus.* Write *C* under the second *c* and the *t.* Point to the VCCV pattern.
- Explain that words with this pattern break between the consonants. Divide the word between the *c* and *t*: *CAC-tuss.*
- Explain that when two or more consonants stand for a single sound, the consonants stay together: *to-GETH-er, TA-ble.*

Discuss the VCV syllable pattern. Write *the fury of <u>nature</u>.*

- Write *V* under *a* and *u* of *nature.* Write *C* under *t.*
- Point to the VCV pattern. Note that to decode a word with this pattern, students should first try dividing it after the consonant and pronouncing the syllable with a short vowel sound: *NAT-yur.*
- If that doesn't sound like a familiar word, they should divide the word after the vowel and use a long sound: *NAY-chuhr.*

Discuss the CVVC syllable pattern. Write *keeps a <u>diary</u>.* Point out the CVVC pattern in *diary.* Explain that in this word, the *i* and *a* each stand for a separate sound, and the word is divided *DI-a-ry.*

Model the Phonics/Decoding Strategy. Write *Warren focuses his camera.* Point to *camera.* Write *V* under the first *a* and the *e.* Write *C* under the *m.* Model how to divide this word.

Think Aloud *This word has a VCV pattern. I'll try the first* a *with a long vowel sound.* CAY-muh-ruh *doesn't sound right. I'll try the short vowel sound.* CAM-uh-ruh *sounds right and makes sense in the sentence.*

❷ Guided Practice

Have students divide words into syllables. Display the phrases below. Have students identify and circle the syllables in each underlined word. Ask partners to discuss their work.

a <u>radio</u> report   a huge <u>tornado</u>   used a <u>scanner</u>

❸ Apply

Assign Practice Book page 36.

PHONICS REVIEW:
Long Vowels: /ā/, /ē/, /ī/

OBJECTIVES

- Read words with long vowel sounds.
- Use the Phonics/Decoding Strategy to decode longer words.

❶ Teach

Review long vowels. Tell students that understanding long vowel sounds can help them decode unfamiliar words. Discuss:

- The letters *a*-consonant-*e*, *ai*, and *ay* can stand for the /ā/ sound as in *claim*.

- The letters *ea* and *ee* can stand for the /ē/ sound as in *knee*.

- The letters *i*-consonant-*e*, *igh*, and *i* can stand for the /ī/ sound as in *flight*.

Model the Phonics/Decoding Strategy. Write *The wind of the hurricane howled.* Model how to decode *hurricane*.

Think Aloud *The first syllable looks like the beginning of the word* hurry, *or* hur. *I see the pattern* a-consonant-e *at the end of the word, so the third syllable is probably* kayn. *Is the second syllable long or short? I'll try a short vowel:* HUR-ih-kayn. *That word makes sense in the sentence.*

❷ Guided Practice

Help students find long vowel sounds. Display the sentences below. Have partners circle the long vowel sounds in each underlined word, pronounce the word, and check if it makes sense in the sentence. Call on individuals to model at the board.

1. In the <u>meantime</u>, he stands and watches.

2. "Another tornado!" I <u>exclaimed</u>.

3. There were many <u>sightings</u> of our tornado.

4. Warren hadn't always planned to be a storm <u>chaser</u>.

5. I reached for the <u>microphone</u>.

❸ Apply

Have students find words with long vowels. Ask students to decode these selection words and discuss their meanings.

lightning	p. 59	concrete	p. 62	excited	p. 70
tripods	p. 61	feature	p. 64	highway	p. 73

Phonics/Decoding Strategy

When you come to a word you don't know—

❶ Look carefully at the word.

❷ Look for word parts you know and think about the sounds for the letters.

❸ Blend the sounds to read the word.

❹ Ask yourself: Is it a word I know? Does it make sense in what I am reading?

❺ If not, ask yourself: What else can I try?

HOUGHTON MIFFLIN
Reading

SPELLING: /ā/, /ē/, /ī/

OBJECTIVES

- Write Spelling Words with long vowel patterns.

SPELLING WORDS

Basic

speech	mild
claim	waist
strike*	sway
stray	beast
fade*	stain
sign*	fleet
leaf	stride
thigh	praise
thief†	slight*
height†	niece†

Review	Challenge
free*	campaign
twice	describe*
gray*	cease
least*	sacrifice
safe*	plight

* Forms of these words appear in the literature.

† These words are exceptions to the principle.

Extra Support/Intervention

Basic Word List You may want to use only the left column of Basic Words with students who need extra support.

Challenge

Challenge Word Practice Have students write Challenge Words across, down, or diagonally in a grid, filling in other letters to complete the grid. Tell them to trade puzzles and circle the Challenge Words they find.

DAY 1 — INSTRUCTION

/ā/, /ē/, and /ī/

Pretest Use the Day 5 Test sentences.

Teach Write these symbols and Basic Words on the board in three columns: /ā/: *fade, claim, stray*; /ē/: *leaf, speech, thief*; /ī/: *strike, thigh, sign, height*.

- Point to each symbol and ask students to identify its sound.

- Say each word in the first column with students. Have them name its vowel sound. (/ā/) Underline *ade, ai,* and *ay*. Explain that *a-consonant-e, ai,* and *ay* are three patterns for spelling the /ā/ sound.

- Repeat the procedure for the other two columns. Explain that the /ē/ sound can be spelled with the patterns *ea, ee,* and *ie*. The /ī/ sound can be spelled with the patterns *i-consonant-e, igh, i,* and *eigh*.

- Say each remaining word in the Basic Word list. Have a student name its vowel sound. Write the word in the correct column.

Practice/Homework Assign **Practice Book** page 265.

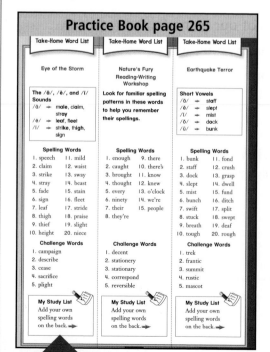

Practice Book page 265

DAY 2 — REVIEW & PRACTICE

Reviewing the Principle

Go over the spelling patterns for /ā/, /ē/, and /ī/ sounds with students.

Practice/Homework Assign **Practice Book** page 37.

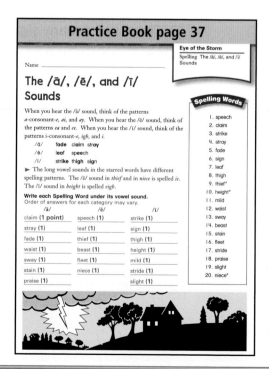

Practice Book page 37

Take-Home Word List

DAY 3 — VOCABULARY

Classifying

Write the Basic Words on the board.

- Dictate each word group below and have students write the Basic Word that completes the group.

  – flower, stem, (*leaf*)

  – reward, honor, (*praise*)

  – hit, punch, (*strike*)

  – herd, team, (*fleet*)

  – step, walk, (*stride*)

  – cousin, uncle, (*niece*)

  – spot, smudge, (*stain*)

  – small, little, (*slight*)

  – monster, dragon, (*beast*)

  – length, width, (*height*)

- Have students use each Basic Word from the board orally in a sentence.

Practice/Homework For spelling practice, assign **Practice Book** page 38.

Practice Book page 38

Eye of the Storm
Spelling The /ā/, /ē/, and /ī/ Sounds

Name _____

Spelling Spree

Find a Rhyme For each sentence write a Spelling Word that rhymes with the underlined word and makes sense in the sentence.

1. On what day did you last see the stray (1 point) cat?
2. It looks like the stain (1) _____ got washed out by the rain.
3. She liked to stride (1) _____ down the beach at low tide.
4. They swam out to meet the fleet (1) _____ of ships.
5. How high on the thigh (1) _____ did the ball hit you?
6. His niece (1) _____ asked for another piece of pie.
7. The police chief took credit for catching the thief (1) _____
8. The young child liked mild (1) _____ food better than spicy food.

Crack the Code Some Spelling Words have been written in the code below. Use the code to figure out each word. Then write the word correctly. (1 point each)

CODE:	R	V	L	O	C	A	D	X	P	T	Y	Q	J	N	E	I	M
LETTER:	a	b	c	e	f	g	h	i	l	m	n	p	r	s	t	w	y

9. LPRXT claim
10. IRXNE waist
11. VORNE beast
12. NQOOLD speech
13. NXAY sign
14. DOXADE height
15. NPXADE slight
16. NJRM sway
17. QJRXNO praise
18. PORC leaf

Spelling Words
1. speech
2. claim
3. strike
4. stray
5. fade
6. sign
7. leaf
8. thigh
9. thief*
10. height*
11. mild
12. waist
13. sway
14. beast
15. stain
16. fleet
17. stride
18. praise
19. slight
20. niece*

Copyright © Houghton Mifflin Company. All rights reserved.

DAY 4 — PROOFREADING

Game: Treasure Map

Have students work in small groups. Each group will make a treasure map game board and 25 index cards with a Basic or Review Word on one side and its definition on the other. They will also need game markers and a spinner.

- Students place the cards in a pile, with the definitions facing up.
- A player picks up the top card, reads the definition aloud, and spells the word that fits it.
- If the spelling is correct, the player spins the spinner and moves the number of spaces shown.
- Players take turns until one "finds" the treasure.

Practice/Homework For proofreading and writing practice, assign **Practice Book** page 39.

Practice Book page 39

Eye of the Storm
Spelling The /ā/, /ē/, and /ī/ Sounds

Name _____

Proofreading and Writing

Proofreading Circle the five misspelled Spelling Words in this weather log entry. Then write each word correctly.

May 20 — There was a report today of a lightning streik at the shopping mall outside town. The same storm passed over our house, with heavy winds. It made the trees sweigh so much that I was sure at least one would fall. The winds started to faide before that happened, though. On the news, the reporter said that the base of the storm clouds was actually at hight of over 5,000 feet. The weather tomorrow is supposed to be mild, with a slite chance of rain.

1. strike (1 point)
2. sway (1)
3. fade (1)
4. height (1)
5. slight (1)

Spelling Words
1. speech
2. claim
3. strike
4. stray
5. fade
6. sign
7. leaf
8. thigh
9. thief*
10. height*
11. mild
12. waist
13. sway
14. beast
15. stain
16. fleet
17. stride
18. praise
19. slight
20. niece*

Write a Storm Warning Storm chasers are able to provide firsthand, "you are there" reports of storms because they chase the storms.

On a separate sheet of paper, write the script of a storm warning that a storm chaser might issue by radio. Use Spelling Words from the list. Responses will vary. (5 points)

DAY 5 — ASSESSMENT

Spelling Test

Say each underlined word, read the sentence, and then repeat the word. Have students write only the underlined word.

Basic Words

1. Did you hear the **speech** about litter?
2. The boys **claim** that they did not cheat.
3. Do not **strike** anything with that stick.
4. We found a **stray** cat.
5. Some colors can **fade** in the wash.
6. Did you see the name on the **sign**?
7. This **leaf** fell from that oak tree.
8. The ball hit my **thigh**.
9. The police caught the **thief**.
10. You and I are the same **height**.
11. The weather is clear and **mild**.
12. The pants are too big around the **waist**.
13. The trees **sway** in the wind.
14. The **beast** looked like a bear.
15. The ink **stain** would not wash out.
16. The **fleet** of ten boats will sail today.
17. That man walks with a long **stride**.
18. Be sure to **praise** Mary's good work.
19. The difference between the twins is **slight**.
20. My sister's daughter is my **niece**.

Challenge Words

21. Her **campaign** will begin next week.
22. Can you **describe** what your house looks like?
23. The sun will come out when the rains **cease**.
24. It was a **sacrifice** for Tom to miss the show in order to help his sister.
25. Is there any news about the **plight** of the people caught in the storm?

OBJECTIVES

- Use alphabetical order to locate words in a dictionary.
- Use pairs of guide words to locate the page of specific entry words.
- Learn academic language: *entry words, guide words.*

Target Skill Trace	
Teach	p. 81G
Extend	p. R17
Review	pp. M38–M39
See	*Handbook for English Language Learners,* p. 33

Transparency 1–12

Dictionary Guide Words

NATURE'S FURY *Eye of the Storm* — Vocabulary Skill Dictionary Guide Words — ANNOTATED VERSION

antiquity / anywhere

anvil (ăn′ vĭl) *n.* A heavy block of iron or steel with a smooth flat top on which metals are shaped by hammering.

picket fence / pie chart
pied / pile
Philippines / phony
phosphate / physical

adrift / adventure: adult, among, account, advance, adverb

frankfurter / freedom: frame, fortune, free, fraud, formal

live / loaf: load, long, lizard, llama, level, lie

top hat / tort: total, torch, talk, tornado, trail

Monitoring Student Progress

If . . .	Then . . .
students score 11 or below on **Practice Book** page 40,	have them work in small groups to correct the items they missed.

VOCABULARY: Dictionary Guide Words

❶ Teach

Discuss alphabetical order and guide words in dictionaries. Note that words defined in a dictionary are called **entry words**.

- Explain that entry words are arranged in alphabetical order.
- Tell students that they can use guide words to quickly locate the page on which a particular entry word appears.

Display Transparency 1–12. Show only the top.

- Point out the entry word *anvil* and its definition.
- Point out the guide words *antiquity* and *anywhere*.
- Explain that the first guide word shows the first entry word on a page and the second guide word shows the last entry word.
- Emphasize that all other entry words on the page fall in alphabetical order between the two guide words.

Model how to use guide words. Model finding *photograph.*

Think Aloud *Entry words are in alphabetical order, so* photograph *must be on a page with guide words that start with* ph. *I see two pairs of guide words that start with* ph, *so I have to look at the next few letters in the word. I see that* photograph *would come after* phosphate, *but before* physical. *It must be on the page with those guide words.*

❷ Guided Practice

Give students practice in using guide words. Display the next section of the transparency. Point out the pairs of guide words in boldface. Point out the possible entry words following them. For each pair, ask: Which entry word would appear on a page with these guide words?

❸ Apply

Assign Practice Book page 40.

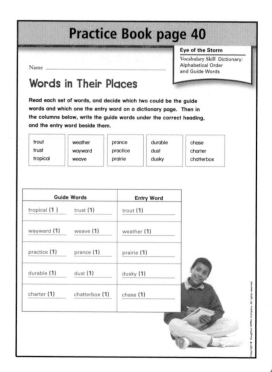

Practice Book page 40

Eye of the Storm — Vocabulary Skill Dictionary: Alphabetical Order and Guide Words

Name _____

Words in Their Places

Read each set of words, and decide which two could be the guide words and which one the entry word on a dictionary page. Then in the columns below, write the guide words under the correct heading, and the entry word beside them.

trout	weather	prance	durable	chase
trust	wayward	practice	dust	charter
tropical	weave	prairie	dusky	chatterbox

Guide Words		Entry Word
tropical (1)	trust (1)	trout (1)
wayward (1)	weave (1)	weather (1)
practice (1)	prance (1)	prairie (1)
durable (1)	dust (1)	dusky (1)
charter (1)	chatterbox (1)	chase (1)

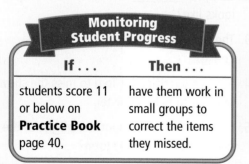

STUDY SKILL:
Using Library Catalogs

OBJECTIVES
- Use a library card catalog or electronic catalog to locate call numbers and other information.
- Use call numbers to locate books.

❶ Teach

Explain how to use card catalogs.

- All the books, videotapes, and other materials in a library are listed in either a card catalog or an electronic catalog.

- A card catalog has three types of cards for each book: a title card, a subject card, and an author card.

- The cards are filed alphabetically by the first letter of the first word, not including *a, an,* or *the.*

- A call number in one corner of the card matches the number on the book's spine. It tells the location of the book in the library.

- The card may also show suggestions for related titles or subjects.

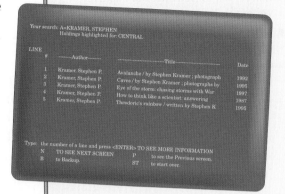

Explain how to use electronic catalogs.

- The first screen in an electronic catalog lets you search for a book.

- You can search for a book by its author, its title, or its subject.

- When a search finds many books, the screen shows a numbered list of choices. You type in the number of a book and press enter.

- The screen for a particular book will show the same information as in a card catalog. It will also tell whether the book is checked out.

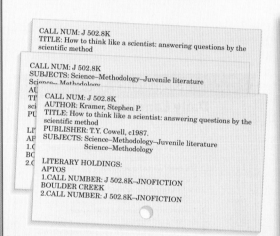

Display Transparency 1–13, and model using an electronic catalog.

Think Aloud *Does my library have other books by Stephen Kramer? I type A= to search by author. Then I type* Kramer, Stephen, *putting his last name first, and press* Enter. *The screen that comes up shows me five books that he wrote.* How to Think Like a Scientist *sounds interesting. That is number 4 on the list. I type 4 and press* Enter. *The screen that comes up next shows me the call number: J502.8K. It also tells me that the book is on the shelves in two branches, and it provides subject headings I can use to find books on similar topics.*

❷ Practice/Apply

Give students practice in using library catalogs.

- Have partners select a book from the classroom library. Ask them to discuss the different ways they could search for this book in a public library: by title, by author, and by subject.

- Have students to use a library catalog to check out a book on extreme weather conditions or one by a favorite author.

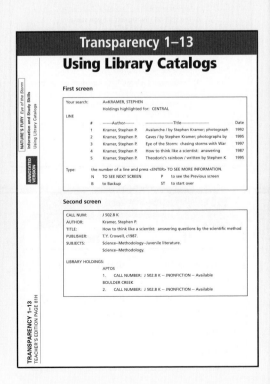

GRAMMAR: Longer Sentences

OBJECTIVES

- Identify conjunctions.
- Identify compound sentences.
- Proofread and correct sentences with grammar and spelling errors.
- Correct run-on sentences to improve writing.
- Learn academic language: *conjunction, compound sentence.*

DAY 1 INSTRUCTION

Conjunctions

Teach Go over the following:

- A conjunction may be used to join words in a sentence.
- A conjunction may be used to join sentences.

- Display **Transparency 1–15**. Point out the conjunctions *and, but,* and *or* in the three example sentences at the top.

- Ask volunteers to look at Sentences 1–5, identify the conjunctions, and tell whether they join words or sentences.

- Have students find sentences with *and, but,* or *or* in *Eye of the Storm* and identify what each conjunction joins.

Daily Language Practice
Have students correct Sentences 1 and 2 on **Transparency 1–14.**

DAY 2 PRACTICE

Independent Work

Practice/Homework Assign **Practice Book** page 41.

Daily Language Practice
Have students correct Sentences 3 and 4 on **Transparency 1–14.**

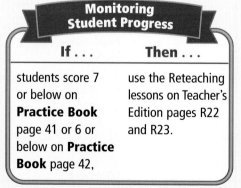

Transparency 1–14

Daily Language Practice

Correct two sentences each day.

1. the crowd cheered when the spech was over.
   The crowd cheered when the speech was over.
2. The beest walked quickly but it did not run.
   The beast walked quickly, but it did not run.
3. I will call my neice, or i will write to her.
   I will call my niece, or I will write to her.
4. The weather has been maild all winter.
   The weather has been mild all winter.
5. The theef jumped up but he could not climb the fence.
   The thief jumped up, but he could not climb the fence.
6. The spill on the rug left a huge stane
   The spill on the rug left a huge stain.
7. this backpack has a belt that fits around my wast.
   This backpack has a belt that fits around my waist.
8. Can you read the words on that sine
   Can you read the words on that sign?
9. do you see that large flet of boats in the harbor?
   Do you see that large fleet of boats in the harbor?
10. The hite of the shelf is ten feet but my cat can reach the top.
    The height of the shelf is ten feet, but my cat can reach the top.

Monitoring Student Progress

If . . .	Then . . .
students score 7 or below on **Practice Book** page 41 or 6 or below on **Practice Book** page 42,	use the Reteaching lessons on Teacher's Edition pages R22 and R23.

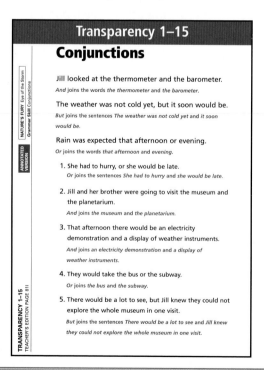

Transparency 1–15

Conjunctions

Jill looked at the thermometer and the barometer.
And joins the words the thermometer and the barometer.

The weather was not cold yet, but it soon would be.
But joins the sentences The weather was not cold yet and it soon would be.

Rain was expected that afternoon or evening.
Or joins the words that afternoon and evening.

1. She had to hurry, or she would be late.
   Or joins the sentences She had to hurry and she would be late.

2. Jill and her brother were going to visit the museum and the planetarium.
   And joins the museum and the planetarium.

3. That afternoon there would be an electricity demonstration and a display of weather instruments.
   And joins an electricity demonstration and a display of weather instruments.

4. They would take the bus or the subway.
   Or joins the bus and the subway.

5. There would be a lot to see, but Jill knew they could not explore the whole museum in one visit.
   But joins the sentences There would be a lot to see and Jill knew they could not explore the whole museum in one visit.

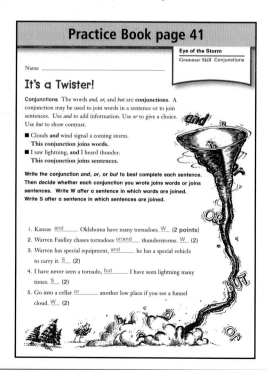

Practice Book page 41

Eye of the Storm
Grammar Skill Conjunctions

Name _____

It's a Twister!

Conjunctions The words *and, or,* and *but* are **conjunctions.** A conjunction may be used to join words in a sentence or to join sentences. Use *and* to add information. Use *or* to give a choice. Use *but* to show contrast.

■ Clouds **and** wind signal a coming storm.
   This conjunction joins words.
■ I saw lightning, **and** I heard thunder.
   This conjunction joins sentences.

Write the conjunction *and, or,* or *but* to best complete each sentence. Then decide whether each conjunction you wrote joins words or joins sentences. Write W after a sentence in which words are joined. Write S after a sentence in which sentences are joined.

1. Kansas _and_ Oklahoma have many tornadoes. _W_ (2 points)
2. Warren Faidley chases tornadoes _or/and_ thunderstorms. _W_ (2)
3. Warren has special equipment, _and_ he has a special vehicle to carry it. _S_ (2)
4. I have never seen a tornado, _but_ I have seen lightning many times. _S_ (2)
5. Go into a cellar _or_ another low place if you see a funnel cloud. _W_ (2)

811I   **THEME 1: Nature's Fury**

DAY 3 | INSTRUCTION

Compound Sentences

Teach Go over the following:

- If two sentences are related, they can be combined to make one compound sentence.

- Use a comma and the conjunction *and, but,* or *or* to combine the sentences.

- Display **Transparency 1–16.** Point out that the first sentence at the top is a compound sentence because it contains two complete sentences joined by *and.* Ask students if the second sentence is a compound sentence. (no)

- Ask volunteers to read Sentences 1–5 and tell whether each is a compound sentence.

- Have students find compound sentences in *Earthquake Terror* or *Eye of the Storm.*

Daily Language Practice
Have students correct Sentences 5 and 6 on **Transparency 1–14.**

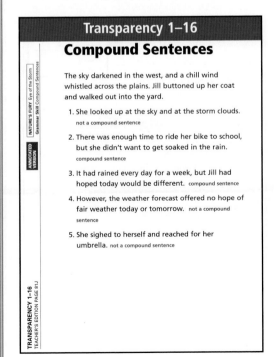

DAY 4 | PRACTICE

Independent Work

Practice/Homework Assign **Practice Book** page 42.

Daily Language Practice
Have students correct Sentences 7 and 8 on **Transparency 1–14.**

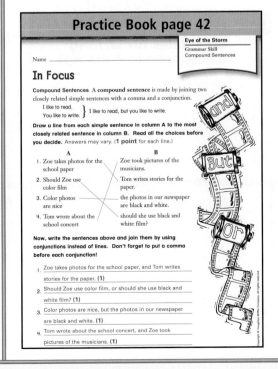

DAY 5 | IMPROVING WRITING

Avoiding Run-ons

Teach Tell students that a good writer joins short sentences with a comma and a conjunction, rather than letting them run together.

– *Run-on:* Jill usually rode her bike to soccer practice, in this weather she would get a ride.

– *Corrected:* Jill usually rode her bike to soccer practice, <u>but</u> in this weather she would get a ride.

– *Run-on:* The lights were out at the Carltons' house there was no car in the driveway.

– *Corrected:* The lights were out at the Carltons' house, <u>and</u> there was no car in the driveway.

- Have students proofread a piece of their own writing for run-ons.

Practice/Homework Assign **Practice Book** page 43.

Daily Language Practice
Have students correct Sentences 9 and 10 on **Transparency 1–14.**

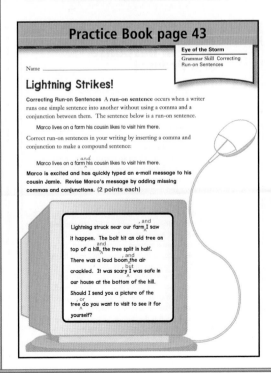

WRITING: A Response to a Prompt

OBJECTIVES

- Identify the characteristics of a good written response.
- Write a response to a prompt.
- Learn academic language: *writing prompt.*
- Correct capitalization and punctuation to improve their writing.

Writing Traits

Voice As students draft their response to a prompt on Day 2, emphasize the importance of voice on tests. Discuss these points.

- Writing that sounds unique or distinctive will improve your score.
- Avoid writing in a way that sounds like you don't care.
- Try to express your thoughts and feelings about the topic in the prompt.

DAY 1 PREWRITING

Introducing the Format

Introduce writing a response to a prompt.

- Writing prompts direct students to write a paper. They are a part of many tests.
- A prompt tells the topic to write about and the kind of writing to use. The paper students write has to fit the prompt.
- A prompt might ask students to write a story, give an opinion, write instructions, or persuade readers to do something.

Start students thinking about writing prompts.

- Read aloud the prompts below.
  – What job do you think is the most difficult or dangerous? Explain your choice.
  – Think about how Warren Faidley customized Shadow Chaser for chasing tornadoes. Describe how you would customize a vehicle for a specific task.
- Have students list some ideas for a paper they might write to one of these prompts.
- Have them save their notes.

DAY 2 DRAFTING

Discussing the Model

Display Transparency 1–17. Ask:

- What does the prompt ask you to do? (explain why photographing tornadoes is hard)
- Which response answers the prompt most completely? (Response #2)
- Which sentences in Response #1 do not fit the prompt? (third, fourth, and fifth sentences)
- Which sentences in Response #2 make the main ideas clear? (first, third, fourth, and sixth sentences)
- Which sentences in Response #2 tell details about the main ideas? (second, fifth, and seventh sentences)

Display Transparency 1–18 and discuss the guidelines.

Have students write a response to a prompt.

- Assign **Practice Book** page 44.
- Have them use their notes from Day 1.
- See Writing Traits on this page.
- Provide additional support as needed.

Transparency 1–17

Write in Response to a Prompt

NATURE'S FURY Eye of the Storm
Writing Skill Write in Response to a Prompt

ANNOTATED VERSION

Prompt:
Explain why photographing tornadoes is difficult.

Response #1
Tornadoes are powerful forces that can cause great destruction. A tornado photographer never knows exactly when or where a tornado will touch down. Tornadoes are often accompanied by severe thunderstorms. Tornadoes happen when cool, dry air collides with warm, moist air. The results can be astonishing and dangerous. It's hard to get a good photo.

Response #2
Photographing a tornado is difficult because it takes luck, skill, and courage. No one can predict where and when a tornado will touch down. To photograph a tornado, a photographer must be in the right place at the right time. Even when a tornado comes into sight, following it is difficult. Tornado photographers can drive fast along roads, but they cannot cross fields and rivers the way a tornado does. Photographing tornadoes is also difficult because it is dangerous. Storm photographers must drive safely in bad weather, and they must stay a safe distance away from the tornadoes they are chasing.

TRANSPARENCY 1–17
TEACHER'S EDITION PAGE 81K

Transparency 1–18

Guidelines for Writing a Response to a Prompt

NATURE'S FURY Eye of the Storm: Chasing Storms with Warren Faidley
Writing Skill Response to a Prompt

ANNOTATED VERSION

- Carefully read the prompt. Find the key words that tell the topic and the kind of writing. Restate in your own words what you need to do.
- Decide what to write about. List main ideas and details. Make sure your ideas fit the prompt.
- Plan your paper. Organize your main ideas and details.
- Draft your paper. Begin by restating the prompt. Follow the plan you made.
- State each main idea clearly. Support each main idea with specific details.
- Revise your paper. Look for places to add exact words and details.
- Proofread your paper to correct errors.

Key Word	Meaning
narrative	a story
opinion	your thoughts or feelings
explain why	give reasons supported by details
explain how	give steps and details for doing or making something
describe	give details to create a picture in your reader's mind
persuade	convince your reader to take action
compare and contrast	point out similarities and differences

TRANSPARENCY 1–18
TEACHER'S EDITION PAGE 81K

Practice Book page 44

Eye of the Storm
Writing Skill Response to a Prompt

Name _____

Responding to a Prompt

A **prompt** is a direction that asks for a written answer of one or more paragraphs. Read the following prompts.

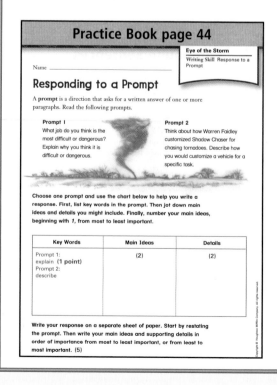

Prompt 1
What job do you think is the most difficult or dangerous? Explain why you think it is difficult or dangerous.

Prompt 2
Think about how Warren Faidley customized Shadow Chaser for chasing tornadoes. Describe how you would customize a vehicle for a specific task.

Choose one prompt and use the chart below to help you write a response. First, list key words in the prompt. Then jot down main ideas and details you might include. Finally, number your main ideas, beginning with 1, from most to least important.

Key Words	Main Ideas	Details
Prompt 1: explain (1 point) Prompt 2: describe	(2)	(2)

Write your response on a separate sheet of paper. Start by restating the prompt. Then write your main ideas and supporting details in order of importance from most to least important, or from least to most important. (5)

Copyright © Houghton Mifflin Company. All rights reserved.

DAY 3 — REVISING

Evaluating to Revise

Display Transparency 1–18 again.

- Ask students to use the guidelines to decide how to make their writing better. Encourage students to turn each point into a question: "Did I…?"

- Students may work with a partner in a writing conference.

- Ask students to revise any parts of their writing that still need work.

DAY 4 — PROOFREADING

Improving Writing: Capitalizing and Punctuating Sentences

Review capitalizing and punctuating sentences.

- Every sentence should begin with a capital letter.

- Every sentence should end with a period, a question mark, or an exclamation point.

- See Writing Traits on page 81K.

Display Transparency 1–19.

- Have students read the sample response.

- Work together to identify the errors in the capitalization and punctuation of the sentences.

- Model using proofreading marks to fix each error.

Assign Practice Book page 45.

- Then have students review their responses to the writing prompt and correct capitalization and punctuation as needed.

DAY 5 — PUBLISHING

Sharing Responses to a Prompt

Consider these publishing options.

- Ask students to read their responses to a prompt from the Author's Chair. They can also read aloud some other piece of writing.

- Students can create a bulletin board of their responses to a prompt.

Portfolio Opportunity

Save students' responses to a prompt as samples of their writing development.

Transparency 1–19

Capitalizing and Punctuating Sentences

I think firefighters are true heroes. they rush inside burning buildings and they can never be sure what dangers they will meet? these dangers include exposure to poisonous fumes, collapsing floors, and extreme heat. Firefighters risk becoming trapped by flames, and they may also suffer smoke inhalation. in addition to courage, fighting fires requires great strength. Have you ever thought about how strong a person must be to carry a victim down a ladder or to break down a door. Firefighting is certainly one of the most dangerous and challenging jobs of all

I think firefighters are true heroes. They rush inside burning buildings, and they can never be sure what dangers they will meet. These dangers include exposure to poisonous fumes, collapsing floors, and extreme heat. Firefighters risk becoming trapped by flames, and they may also suffer smoke inhalation. In addition to courage, fighting fires requires great strength. Have you ever thought about how strong a person must be to carry a victim down a ladder or to break down a door? Firefighting is certainly one of the most dangerous and challenging jobs of all!

TRANSPARENCY 1–19
TEACHER'S EDITION PAGE 81L

NATURE'S FURY *Eye of the Storm*
Writing Skill Improving Your Writing

ANNOTATED VERSION

Practice Book page 45

Name _____

Eye of the Storm
Writing Skill Improving Your Writing

Capitalizing and Punctuating Sentences

A fifth-grade class was given this writing prompt: **Warren Faidley is a storm chaser. Summarize what he does for a living.** One fifth grader wrote the response below but forgot to check for capitalization and punctuation errors.

Use these proofreading marks to add the necessary capital letters and end punctuation. (1 point each)

⊙ Add a period.   ∧! Add an exclamation point.
≡ Make a capital letter.   ∧? Add a question mark.

what does Warren Faidley do for a living? He follows dangerous storms. for example, he tracks down tornadoes and hurricanes. then he photographs lightning striking the earth and funnel clouds whirling in the sky. if he has been successful, he can sell his dramatic photos to magazines, newspapers, and other publications. What a risky but exciting job storm chasers have!

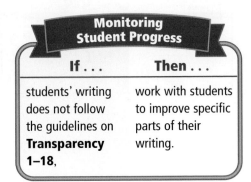

Monitoring Student Progress

If . . .	Then . . .
students' writing does not follow the guidelines on **Transparency 1–18**,	work with students to improve specific parts of their writing.

Language Center

VOCABULARY

Building Vocabulary

👥👥👥 Groups	🕐 20 minutes
Objective	Find origins of weather words.
Materials	Dictionary, encyclopedia, world atlas

Many English words used to describe weather came from other languages. For example, the word *typhoon* came from a Chinese word meaning "great wind." Find and map the origins of other weather words.

- Make a list of the following weather words: *tornado, hurricane, monsoon, cyclone, tsunami.*

- Use a dictionary or encyclopedia to discover where these words came from.

- Trace a world map. Write each weather word on the country from which it came. Label the country.

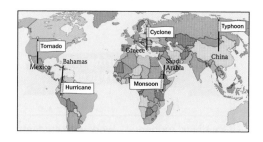

GRAMMAR

Writing Forecasts

👥 Pairs	🕐 20 minutes
Objective	Write a fictional weather forecast.

Write a one-page weather report that summarizes an imaginary day's weather and gives the next day's forecast.

- Vary the length of your sentences as you write. Create longer compound sentences by using conjunctions such as *and, or,* and *but* to join shorter sentences together.

- Check your weather report for correct grammar and punctuation.

- Trade papers with a partner. Underline each compound sentence and circle each conjunction that you find. Write the letter *W* by each conjunction that joins words in a sentence, and write *S* by each conjunction that joins sentences.

VOCABULARY

Vocabulary Game

👥👥👥 Groups	🕐 20 minutes
Objective	Play a vocabulary game.
Materials	Activity Master 1–2, scissors, timer

Play a "Beat the Clock" game with the Key Vocabulary words.

- Cut out the word cards on Activity Master 1–2. Place the cards in a basket.

- Sit with your group in a circle. Assign one person to be the timekeeper.

- Players take turns drawing a card from the basket. After drawing a card, each player has 30 seconds in which to use the word as directed on the card.

- Play until each player has taken at least four turns.

tornadoes
(Define the word.)

collide
(Use in a sentence.)

rotate
(Name a synonym.)

severe
(Name an antonym.)

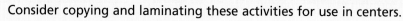

Consider copying and laminating these activities for use in centers.

LISTENING/SPEAKING

Literature Discussion

Groups	⏱ 40 minutes
Objective	Hold a literature discussion.

Use the discussion questions below to discuss *Eye of the Storm* with your classmates.

- Choose a moderator to help the group stay focused on the topic.
- During the discussion, support your statements with evidence from the text.
- Make sure that everyone takes a turn speaking.

Discussion Questions

- What is the author's purpose for writing? How well does the author achieve this purpose, and why?
- What passage do you like best, and why?
- What do you think the author means in this part of the selection?
- Would you like to read another book by this author? Why or why not?

PHONICS/SPELLING

Word Break-Up

👥 Pairs	⏱ 20 minutes
Objective	Identify syllable patterns.

How many long words can you decode and define?

- With a partner, go through the selection and make a list of eight words with three or more syllables.
- Take turns breaking each word into syllables. Write the word broken up into syllables. Write the syllable that is stressed in capital letters.
- Write a brief definition for each word. Check your definition in a dictionary, and make changes to your definitions as needed.

| encounter | en/COUN/ter | "a brief or unexpected meeting" |
| moderate | MOD/er/ate | "not extreme" |

Leveled Readers

White Dragon:
Anna Allen in the Face of Danger

by Maryann Dobeck
illustrations by Todd Leonardo

White Dragon: Anna Allen in the Face of Danger

Summary White Dragon: Anna Allen in the Face of Danger *is the true story of Anna Allen, who was trapped in an avalanche at a California ski resort. The book describes a series of events in March, 1982, when an avalanche, sometimes called a White Dragon, struck the lodge where she worked. The book describes how Anna was trapped below the surface of the snow, where she fought cold and hunger for five days.*

Vocabulary

Introduce the Key Vocabulary and ask students to complete the BLM.

avalanche a large mass of snow or ice that slides down a mountain, *p. 7*

ski resorts ski areas, *p. 3*

survived lived through, *p. 11*

rescue to save from danger or harm, *p. 13*

artificial not natural, *p. 20*

disabled not fully functioning, *p. 20*

● BELOW LEVEL

Building Background and Vocabulary

Ask students what they know about avalanches. Preview the story with students, using the story vocabulary when possible.

Comprehension Skill: Text Organization

Have students read the Strategy Focus on the book flap. Remind students to use the strategy and to think about the elements of text organization as they read the book. (See the Leveled Readers Teacher's Guide for **Vocabulary and Comprehension Practice Masters**.)

Responding

Have partners discuss how to answer the questions on the inside back cover.

Think About the Selection Sample answers:

1. Anna had just missed getting caught in the blasting of an avalanche.

2. In deep snow, sound easily travels down, but not up.

3. Anna wanted to be sure that she was awake when the searchers came back.

4. The headings organize the story by topic in sequence.

Making Connections Responses will vary.

Building Fluency

Model Read aloud the caption on page 4. Point out that the caption helps explain the pictures above it and to the right of it.

Practice Have partners find other examples of captions in the book and take turns reading them aloud to each other as they look at the pictures.

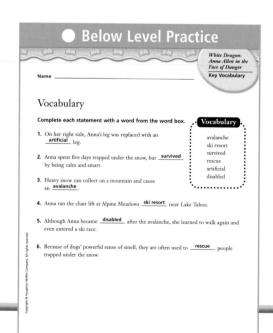

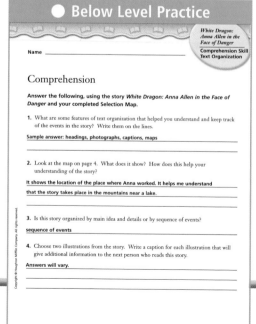

Hurricane Opal: Into the Storm

Summary
Dana Everhart, a meteorologist, tracks unpredictable tropical storms. When Hurricane Opal changes course and heads toward her home on the Florida coast, Dana urges her father and son to drive inland to a safer place.

Vocabulary

Introduce the Key Vocabulary and ask students to complete the BLM.

tornado* violent, funnel-shaped windstorm, *p. 3*

rotating* circular, swirling motion, *p. 3*

meteorologist one who studies weather, *p. 3*

severe* serious or extreme in nature, *p. 4*

mainland the main part of a continent, *p. 6*

pelted beat against, *p. 9*

evacuate to leave a threatened area, *p. 11*

remote distant, *p. 12*

*Forms of these words are Anthology Key Vocabulary words.

▲ ON LEVEL

Building Background and Vocabulary
Discuss some of the tasks a meteorologist has to perform. Preview the story with students, using the story vocabulary when possible.

◉ Comprehension Skill: Text Organization
Have students read the Strategy Focus on the book flap. Remind students to use the strategy and to think about the elements of text organization as they read the book. (See the Leveled Readers Teacher's Guide for **Vocabulary and Comprehension Practice Masters**.)

Responding
Have partners discuss how to answer the questions on the inside back cover.

Think About the Selection Sample answers:

1. October 2

2. People depend on her forecasts to prepare for dangerous storms.

3. They gather information about hurricanes by flying into the storms.

4. Possible response: Students might mention taping windows or knowing where to find shelter.

Making Connections Responses will vary.

◉ Building Fluency

Model Read aloud page 5. Explain that an introductory phrase like *The next morning at work* establishes the time and place.

Practice Have students work in pairs to find other introductory phrases that define time or place. Have them take turns reading the introductory phrases to each other.

▲ On Level Practice

Hurricane Opal
Key Vocabulary

Name _____

Vocabulary

Use the clues to help you unscramble the vocabulary words from *Hurricane Opal*. Write the word on the lines.

Vocabulary
- evacuate
- mainland
- meteorologist
- pelted
- remote
- rotating
- severe
- tornado

1. not an island

d m a n l n i a **mainland**

2. far-off location

t e o r e m **remote**

3. seen on TV news

s m t e e o o r o l g i t **meteorologist**

4. sound rain makes

e e d l t p **pelted**

7. storm in a funnel

t r o o d a n **tornado**

5. coastal dwellers do this during storms

v c e t e a u a **evacuate**

8. motion of wheels

g o t t a r n i **rotating**

6. describes hurricane's power

c e e s r v **severe**

5

▲ On Level Practice

Hurricane Opal
Comprehension Skill
Text Organization

Name _____

Comprehension

Locate the following examples of text organization. Record your responses in the chart.

Ways of Organizing Information	Page	What Is Explained
By main idea	page 3	why it is important for meteorologists to track hurricanes
By sequence	page 6	what happened on October 2 and October 3
By cause and effect	page 15	Because Jason's mother was a meteorologist, he was interviewed for TV; because he was on TV, Jason's mother knew he was safe.

7

8

LEVELED READERS

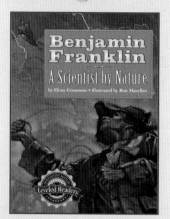

Ben Franklin: A Scientist

Summary *This biography of Benjamin Franklin focuses on his career as a scientist. His curiosity and intelligence, along with his interest in natural forces, motivated him to discover practical ways of solving problems. He established the first fire insurance company and invented the cast iron stove and the lightning rod.*

Vocabulary

Introduce the Key Vocabulary and ask students to complete the BLM.

intrigued fascinated, *p. 4*

apprentice a student of a trade, *p. 5*

harnessed tamed, *p. 6*

corresponded communicated, usually through letters, *p. 9*

lightning* the flash of light in the sky when electricity passes between clouds or between a cloud and the ground, *p. 10*

severe* serious or extreme in nature, *p. 11*

foster encourage, *p. 14*

coaxed persuaded, *p. 16*

*Forms of these words are Anthology Key Vocabulary words.

Building Background and Vocabulary

Ask what students know about Franklin's experiments with electricity. Preview the story with students, using the story vocabulary when possible.

◉ Comprehension Skill: Text Organization

Have students read the Strategy Focus on the book flap. Remind students to use the strategy and to think about the elements of text organization as they read the book. (See the Leveled Readers Teacher's Guide for **Vocabulary and Comprehension Practice Masters**.)

Responding

Have partners discuss how to answer the questions on the inside back cover.

Think About the Selection Sample answers:

1. Possible response: He rigged up a kite that helped him swim faster.

2. Possible response: Ben founded the first fire company and the first fire prevention company. He invented the Franklin stove, a safer way to heat buildings with fire.

3. Possible response: It proved that lightning is a form of electricity.

4. His inventions and experiments made him a symbol of those times.

Making Connections Responses will vary.

◉ Building Fluency

Model Read aloud page 5. Point out that the word *newspaper* is hyphenated and appears on two different lines. Point out that sometimes words are hyphenated at the end of a line. Demonstrate that it should still be read as one word.

Practice Students should find other examples of words that are divided in the same way. Have them practice reading each divided word as one word.

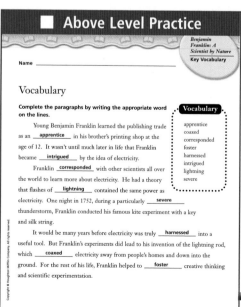

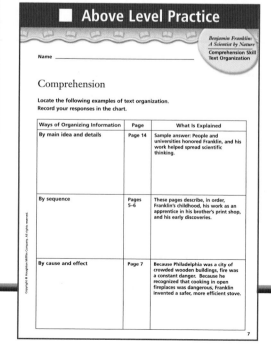

Leveled Readers

Anna Allen
Faces the
White Dragon

by Maryann Dobeck
illustrations by Todd Leonardo

Anna Allen Faces the White Dragon

Summary *Anna Allen loves her job at a ski lodge and she loves to ski. But one day she is buried alive in an avalanche. Rescuers find her five days later. She loses a leg, but that doesn't stop Anna. She learns to ski with an artificial leg and works at a ski resort where she teaches children about safety.*

Vocabulary

Introduce the Key Vocabulary and ask students to complete the BLM.

avalanche a large amount of snow, ice, or earth that falls down a mountain, *p. 7*

blast to blow up with an explosive, *p. 7*

prevent to keep from happening, *p. 8*

hurry to act or move quickly, *p. 9*

artificial made by human beings, *p. 20*

disabled unable to use a physical ability, *p. 20*

severe* very serious, *p. 20*

*Forms of these words are Anthology Key Vocabulary words.

◆ LANGUAGE SUPPORT

Building Background and Vocabulary

Explain that this story is about a girl who gets trapped in an avalanche and spends five days under the snow. Use the picture on the book cover to spark a discussion of avalanches, and what a person would need to have in order to survive in the snow for five days. Then distribute the **Build Background Practice Master** and have students complete the activity.

Comprehension Skill: Text Organization

Have students read the Strategy Focus on the book flap. Remind students to use the strategy and to look for chapter headings, topics, and main ideas as they read the book. (See the Leveled Readers Teacher's Guide for **Build Background, Vocabulary, and Graphic Organizer Masters**.)

Responding

Have partners discuss how to answer the questions on the inside back cover.

Think About the Selection Sample answers:

1. She skied on the main road, near the blasting.

2. The snow that covered Anna kept the sound from reaching the searchers.

3. She loves to ski, and she wants to keep on going.

4. Responses will vary.

Making Connections Responses will vary.

Building Fluency

Model Read aloud pages 17–18. Point out *yelled* and *said weakly,* and remind students that these words tell how each character speaks.

Practice Ask partners to take turns reading aloud the same text to each other three times, or until they are able to read it accurately and with expression.

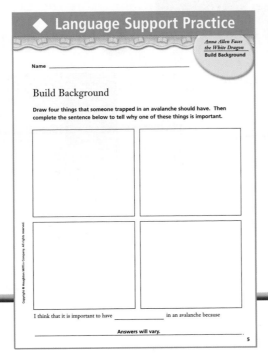

Lesson Overview

Literature

VOLCANOES
S E Y M O U R   S I M O N

Nonfiction

1 Background and Vocabulary

2 Main Selection

Volcanoes
Genre: Nonfiction

Selection Summary

Science writer Seymour Simon explains the characteristics of volcanoes and describes the aftermath of some well-known eruptions.

3 Folktale Link

Instructional Support

Planning and Practice

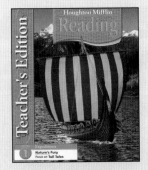

Practice Book

- Planning and classroom management
- Reading instruction
- Skill lessons
- Materials for reaching all learners

- Independent practice for skills

Teacher's Resource Blackline Masters

Instruction Transparencies/Masters and Strategy Posters

- Newsletters
- Selection Summaries
- Assignment Cards
- Observation Checklists
- Selection Tests

- Transparencies
- Strategy Posters
- Blackline Masters

Reaching All Learners

Intervention Strategies for Extra Support

Instructional Activities for Challenge

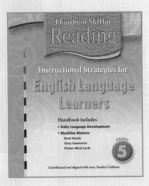

Instructional Strategies for English Language Learners

Independent Activities for Classroom Management

Coordinated lessons, activities, and projects for additional reading instruction

For
- Classroom Teacher
- Extended Day
- Pull Out
- Resource Teacher
- Reading Specialist

Technology

Audio Selection

Volcanoes

Get Set for Reading CD-ROM
- Background building
- Vocabulary support
- Selection Summary in English and Spanish

Accelerated Reader
- Practice quizzes for the selection

www.eduplace.com
Log on to Education Place for more activities related to the selection.

e•Glossary
e•WordGame

Leveled Books for Reaching All Learners

Leveled Readers and Leveled Practice

- Independent reading for building fluency
- Topic, comprehension strategy, and vocabulary linked to main selection
- Lessons in Teacher's Edition, pages 105O–105R
- Leveled practice for every book

Technology

Leveled Readers
Audio available

Book Adventure

- Practice quizzes for the Leveled Theme Paperbacks

www.eduplace.com

Log on to Education Place® for activities related to the Leveled Theme Paperbacks.

● BELOW LEVEL

FLOODS
by Barbara Brooks Simons

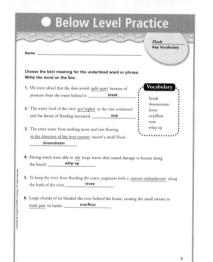

● Below Level Practice

● Below Level Practice

▲ ON LEVEL

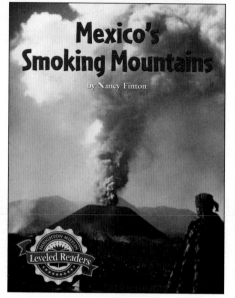

Mexico's Smoking Mountains
by Nancy Finton

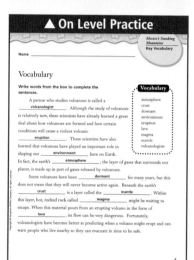

▲ On Level Practice

▲ On Level Practice

■ ABOVE LEVEL

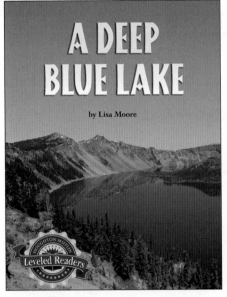

A DEEP BLUE LAKE

by Lisa Moore

HOUGHTON MIFFLIN
Leveled Readers

◆ LANGUAGE SUPPORT

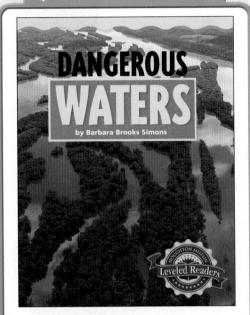

DANGEROUS WATERS

by Barbara Brooks Simons

HOUGHTON MIFFLIN
Leveled Readers

Leveled Theme Paperbacks

- Extended independent reading in theme-related trade books
- Lessons in Teacher's Edition, pages R2–R7

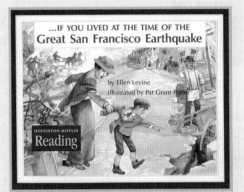

...IF YOU LIVED AT THE TIME OF THE
Great San Francisco Earthquake

by Ellen Levine
illustrated by Pat Grant Porter

HOUGHTON MIFFLIN
Reading

Below Level

■ Above Level Practice

Name _____

A Deep Blue Lake
Key Vocabulary

Vocabulary

Choose a word from the box that best completes each sentence. Write it on the line.

Vocabulary
cradles
crater
eruptions
glistening
lava
minerals
molten
national park
preserve
scorched

1. Volcanic **eruptions** are caused when the pressure beneath the earth can no longer be contained.

2. **molten** rock flowed down the mountain, destroying everything in its path.

3. The force of the explosion left a huge **crater** in the ground.

4. Many organizations seek to **preserve** the natural environment.

5. The water in the lake was **glistening** in the sunlight.

Now use the remaining words in a paragraph.
Answers will vary.

◆ Language Support Practice

Name _____

Dangerous Waters
Build Background

Build Background

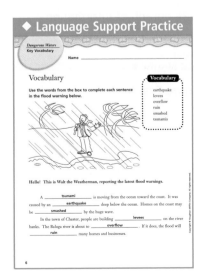

Use the picture to answer the questions.

1. What is making the water in the river rise?
rain

2. What are the people doing to keep the river from overflowing?
Sample answer: They are making the side of the river higher.

3. What will happen if the water floods the land?
The houses and the playground will be under water.

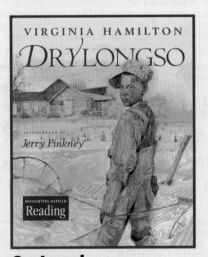

VIRGINIA HAMILTON
DRYLONGSO

ILLUSTRATED BY
Jerry Pinkney

HOUGHTON MIFFLIN
Reading

On Level

■ Above Level Practice

Name _____

A Deep Blue Lake
Comprehension Skill
Categorize and
Classify

Comprehension

Use information from your category chart and the selection to answer the following questions.

1. What are some strategies you can use to help you categorize information you read?
Sample answer: re-read or use illustrations to clarify understanding; draw a chart to help sort information presented in a selection; look for similarities and differences between the categories.

2. What categories did you use to help you understand this selection?
Sample answer: Types of volcanoes, discovery of volcanoes, size of volcanoes.

3. Give some examples of how classifying and categorizing helped you keep track of information presented in *A Deep Blue Lake*.
Sample answer: I was able to keep track of the different volcanoes by categorizing them by type.

4. Several categories of people are mentioned in the selection. Choose two of these categories and describe their similarities or differences.
Sample answer: Native people and early settlers are two categories of people. Neither group had seen the lake. The native people were afraid, and the settlers didn't know it was there.

◆ Language Support Practice

Dangerous Waters
Key Vocabulary

Name _____

Vocabulary

Use the words from the box to complete each sentence in the flood warning below.

Vocabulary
earthquake
levees
overflow
ruin
smashed
tsunamis

Hello! This is Walt the Weatherman, reporting the latest flood warnings.

A **tsunami** is moving from the ocean toward the coast. It was caused by an **earthquake** deep below the ocean. Homes on the coast may be **smashed** by the huge wave.

In the town of Chester, people are building **levees** on the river banks. The Baluga river is about to **overflow**. If it does, the flood will **ruin** many homes and businesses.

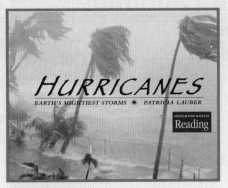

HURRICANES
EARTH'S MIGHTIEST STORMS ● PATRICIA LAUBER

HOUGHTON MIFFLIN
Reading

Challenge

Daily Lesson Plans

  Technology
Lesson Planner CD-ROM allows you to customize the chart below to develop your own lesson plans.

T Skill tested on Weekly or Theme Skills Test and/or Integrated Theme Test

 North Carolina Competency Goals indicated in blue.

	DAY 1	**DAY 2**
⏱ 50–60 minutes **Reading** **Comprehension**  **Vocabulary Reader** 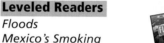 **Leveled Readers** • Fluency Practice • Independent Reading	**Teacher Read Aloud,** 81CC–81DD *Making Waves!* Background and Vocabulary, 82 2.02a, f, 2.03b **Key Vocabulary,** 83 1.02 cinders eruption molten crater lava summit crust magma **Vocabulary Reader** 1.02 **Reading the Selection,** 84–99 **◎ Comprehension Skill,** 84 3.02 Categorize and Classify **T** **◎ Comprehension Strategy,** 84 2.01 Monitor/Clarify ⋯⋯⋯⋯⋯⋯⋯⋯⋯⋯⋯⋯⋯⋯⋯ **Leveled Readers** *Floods* *Mexico's Smoking Mountains* *A Deep Blue Lake* *Dangerous Waters* Lessons and Leveled Practice, 105O–105R 2.02d, f, 2.03b, 3.02, 4.01	**Reading the Selection,** 84–99 Comprehension Check, 99 Responding, 100 3.01f–g, 3.02 Think About the Selection **Vocabulary Reader** 1.02 **◎ Comprehension Skill Preview,** 97 3.02 Categorize and Classify **T** ⋯⋯⋯⋯⋯⋯⋯⋯⋯⋯⋯⋯⋯⋯⋯ **Leveled Readers** *Floods* *Mexico's Smoking Mountains* *A Deep Blue Lake* *Dangerous Waters* Lessons and Leveled Practice, 105O–105R 2.02d, f, 2.03b, 3.02, 4.01
⏱ 20–30 minutes **Word Work** **Phonics/Decoding** **Vocabulary** **Spelling**	**Phonics/Decoding,** 85 1.01 Phonics/Decoding Strategy **Vocabulary,** 84–99 1.02 Selection Vocabulary **Spelling,** 105E 5.05 /ō/, /o͞o/, and /yo͞o/ **T**	**◎ Structural Analysis,** 105C 1.01 Word Roots *rupt* and *struct* **T** **Vocabulary,** 84–99 1.02 Selection Vocabulary **Spelling,** 105E 5.05 /ō/, /o͞o/, and /yo͞o/ Review and Practice **T**
⏱ 20–30 minutes **Writing and Oral Language** **Writing** **Grammar** **Listening/Speaking/Viewing**	**✎ Writing,** 105K 4.05 Prewriting a Paragraph of Information **Grammar,** 105I Singular/Plural Nouns **T** **Daily Language Practice** 5.06, 5.07 1. The boxs were thron out by mistake. (boxes; thrown) 2. In my yuth I loved storys about dragons. (youth; stories) 2.02d, f, 2.09b–c **Listening/Speaking/Viewing,** 81CC–81DD, 91 Teacher Read Aloud, Stop and Think	**✎ Writing,** 105K 4.06, 4.07 Drafting a Paragraph of Information **Grammar,** 105I Singular/Plural Nouns Practice **T** **Daily Language Practice** 5.06, 5.07 3. Why do i chuse to wear my red hat every day? (I; choose) 4. being sick puts me in a bad moud. (Being; mood.) **Listening/Speaking/Viewing,** 99, 100 4.02a, c Wrapping Up, Responding

DAILY LESSON PLANS

Target Skills of the Week

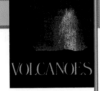

Comprehension	Monitor/Clarify; Categorize and Classify
Vocabulary	Dictionary Definitions
Phonics/Decoding	Word Roots *rupt* and *struct*
Fluency	Leveled Readers

DAY 3

Rereading the Selection, 84–99

Vocabulary Reader 1.02

 **Comprehension Skill,** 105A–105B 3.02
Categorize and Classify **T**

Leveled Readers
Floods
Mexico's Smoking Mountains
A Deep Blue Lake
Dangerous Waters

Lessons and Leveled Practice, 105O–105R
2.02d, f, 2.03b, 3.02, 4.01

Phonics Review, 105D 1.01
Long Vowel Sounds /ō/, /o͞o/, and /yo͞o/

 **Vocabulary,** 105G 1.04
Dictionary Definitions **T**

Spelling, 105F 5.05
Vocabulary: Exact Words; /ō/, /o͞o/, and /yo͞o/
Practice **T**

✏ **Writing,** 105L 4.08c
Revising a Paragraph of Information

Grammar, 105J
More Plural Nouns **T**

Daily Language Practice 5.06, 5.07
5. Look at the loos peachs all over the road! (loose; peaches)
6. The two thiefs stoal all the food in the kitchen. (thieves; stole)

DAY 4

Reading the Folktale Link, 102–105 2.03a
"The Princess and the Warrior"
Skill: How to Read a Folktale

Comprehension Skill Review, 89
Topic, Main Idea, and Details

Leveled Readers
Floods
Mexico's Smoking Mountains
A Deep Blue Lake
Dangerous Waters

Lessons and Leveled Practice, 105O–105R
2.02d, f, 2.03b, 3.02, 4.01

Phonics/Decoding, 102–105 1.01
Apply Phonics/Decoding Strategy to Link

Vocabulary, 105M 1.03b
Language Center: Building Vocabulary

Spelling, 105F 5.06
Spelling Game, Proofreading **T**

✏ **Writing,** 105L 5.01, 5.07
Proofreading a Paragraph of Information
Correcting Sentence Fragments **T**

Grammar, 105J
More Plural Nouns Practice **T**

Daily Language Practice 5.06, 5.07
7. When she fell, Pam got a bruse on her knee and lost two tooths. (bruise; teeth)
8. The cruse was filled with relaxed mans and women. (cruise; men)

Listening/Speaking/Viewing, 105 3.01g, 3.02
Discuss the Link

DAY 5

 **Rereading for Fluency,** 93 4.01
3.01f–g, 3.02
Responding Activities, 100–101
Write a Travel Brochure 4.07
Cross-Curricular Activities

Information and Study Skills, 105H 2.07
Using Graphic Aids **T**

Comprehension Skill Review, 95
Text Organization
Other Cross-Curricular Activities, 23I–23J and 81AA–81BB SC3.02a–e

Leveled Readers
Floods
Mexico's Smoking Mountains
A Deep Blue Lake
Dangerous Waters

Lessons and Leveled Practice, 105O–105R
2.02d, f, 2.03b, 3.02, 4.01

Structural Analysis, 105N 1.01
Language Center: Sentence Con-STRUCT-ion

Vocabulary, 105M 1.03b
Language Center: Vocabulary Game

Spelling, 105F, 105M 5.05
Test: /ō/, /o͞o/, and /yo͞o/ **T**
Language Center: End Rhymes

✏ **Writing,** 105L 4.04, 4.09
Publishing a Paragraph of Information

Grammar, 105J
Exact Nouns

Daily Language Practice 5.06, 5.07
9. My parents love to bost about their three childs. (boast; children.)
10. The five womans took a stroal along the bank of the river. (women; stroll)

Listening/Speaking/Viewing, 105N 2.07, 4.02a–c
Language Center: Discuss Favorite Photos
Other Cross-Curricular Activities, 23I–23J and 81AA–81BB

Managing Flexible Groups

Leveled Instruction and Leveled Practice

	DAY 1	**DAY 2**
WHOLE CLASS	• Teacher Read Aloud (TE pp. 81CC–81DD) • Building Background, Introducing Vocabulary (TE pp. 82–83) • Comprehension Strategy: Introduce (TE p. 84) • Comprehension Skill: Introduce (TE p. 84) • Purpose Setting (TE p. 85) **After reading first half of Volcanoes** • Stop and Think (TE p. 91)	**After reading Volcanoes** • Wrapping Up (TE p. 99) • Comprehension Check (Practice Book p. 48) • Responding: Think About the Selection (TE p. 100) • Comprehension Skill: Preview (TE p. 97)

SMALL GROUPS

Extra Support	**TEACHER-LED** • Preview vocabulary; support reading with Vocabulary Reader. • Preview *Volcanoes* to Stop and Think (TE pp. 84–91). • Support reading with Extra Support/Intervention notes (TE pp. 85, 86, 89, 90, 93, 98, 99).	**Partner or Individual Work** • Reread first half of *Volcanoes* (TE pp. 84–91). • Preview, read second half (TE pp. 92–99). • Comprehension Check (Practice Book p. 48)
Challenge	**Individual Work** • Begin "Volcano Terror" (Challenge Handbook p. 6). • Extend reading with Challenge Note (TE p. 98).	**Individual Work** • Continue work on activity (Challenge Handbook p. 6).
English Language Learners	**TEACHER-LED** • Preview vocabulary; support reading with Vocabulary Reader. • Preview *Volcanoes* to Stop and Think (TE pp. 84–91). • Support reading with English Language Learners notes (TE pp. 82, 88, 92, 95).	**TEACHER-LED** • Review first half of *Volcanoes* (TE pp. 84–91). ✔ • Preview, read second half (TE pp. 92–99). • Begin Comprehension Check together (Practice Book p. 48).

Independent Activities

- Get Set for Reading CD-Rom
- Journals: selection notes, questions
- Complete, review Practice Book (pp. 46–50) and Leveled Readers Practice Blackline Masters (TE pp. 105O–105R).
- Assignment Cards (Teacher's Resource Blackline Masters pp. 52–53)
- Leveled Readers (TE pp. 105O–105R), Leveled Theme Paperbacks (TE pp. R2–R7), or book from Leveled Bibliography (TE pp. 23E–23F)

✔ Opportunity to informally assess oral reading rate

DAY 3

- Rereading (TE pp. 84–99)
- Comprehension Skill: Main lesson (TE pp. 105A–105B)

TEACHER-LED

- Reread, review Comprehension Check (Practice Book p. 48).
- Preview Leveled Reader: Below Level (TE p. 105O), or read book from Leveled Bibliography (TE pp. 23E–23F). ✔

TEACHER-LED

- Teacher check-in: Assess progress (Challenge Handbook p. 6).
- Preview Leveled Reader: Above Level (TE p. 105Q), or read book from Leveled Bibliography (TE pp. 23E–23F). ✔

Partner or Individual Work

- Complete Comprehension Check (Practice Book p. 48).
- Begin Leveled Reader: Language Support (TE p. 105R), or read book from Leveled Bibliography (TE pp. 23E–23F).

DAY 4

- Reading the Folktale Link (TE pp. 102–105): Skill lesson (TE p. 102)
- Rereading the Link (TE pp. 102–105)
- Comprehension Skill: First Comprehension Review lesson (TE p. 89)

Partner or Individual Work

- Reread Folktale Link (TE pp. 102–105).
- Complete Leveled Reader: Below Level (TE p. 105O), or read book from Leveled Bibliography (TE pp. 23E–23F).

Individual Work

- Complete activity (Challenge Handbook p. 6).
- Complete Leveled Reader: Above Level (TE p. 105Q), or read book from Leveled Bibliography (TE pp. 23E–23F).

TEACHER-LED

- Reread the Folktale Link (TE pp. 102–105) ✔ and review Link Skill (TE p. 102).
- Complete Leveled Reader: Language Support (TE p. 105R), or read book from Leveled Bibliography (TE pp. 23E–23F). ✔

DAY 5

- Responding: Select from Activities (TE pp. 100–101)
- Information and Study Skills (TE p. 105H)
- Comprehension Skill: Second Comprehension Review lesson (TE p. 95)

TEACHER-LED

- Comprehension Skill: Reteaching lesson (TE p. R12)
- Reread Leveled Theme Paperback: Below Level (TE pp. R2–R3), or read book from Leveled Bibliography (TE pp. 23E–23F). ✔

TEACHER-LED

- Evaluate activity and plan format for sharing (Challenge Handbook p. 6).
- Reread Leveled Theme Paperback: Above Level (TE pp. R6–R7), or read book from Leveled Bibliography (TE pp. 23E–23F). ✔

Partner or Individual Work

- Reread book from Leveled Bibliography (TE pp. 23E–23F).

- Responding activities (TE pp. 100–101)
- Language Center activities (TE pp. 105M–105N)
- **Fluency Practice:** Reread *Volcanoes; Eye of the Storm; Earthquake Terror.* ✔
- Activities relating to *Volcanoes* at Education Place www.eduplace.com

Turn the page for more independent activities.

Classroom Management

Independent Activities

Assign these activities while you work with small groups.

Differentiated Instruction for Small Groups

- **Handbook for English Language Learners**, pp. 38–47

- **Extra Support Handbook**, pp. 34–43

Independent Activities

- Language Center, pp. 105M–105N

- Challenge/Extension Activities, Resources, pp. R13, R19

- **Classroom Management Handbook**, Activity Masters CM1-9–CM1-12

- **Challenge Handbook**, Challenge Masters CH1-5–CH1-6

Look for more activities in the Classroom Management Kit.

Writing

Volcano Myths

🧍 Singles	🕐 45 minutes	
Objective	Retell a myth.	
Materials	Reference sources, paper, pencil	

In *Volcanoes*, the author refers to gods and goddesses of fire. Write a story about one of these mythical characters.

- Find out more about one volcano god or goddess, such as Vulcan or Pele. If possible, read a myth about that god or goddess.

- Write a short story about why the god or goddess caused a volcano to erupt. Be sure to add dialogue and description to your story.

- Hint: To get started, think about these questions: How do you think a god or goddess would act? What happens during a volcano? What did ancient people think caused volcanoes?

Math

Rings of Lava

👥 Pairs	🕐 20 minutes	
Objective	Make a diagram showing how fast lava spreads.	
Materials	Paper, pencil	

Lava can travel 30 miles per hour. Make a diagram that shows how far and how fast lava from a volcano could spread.

- Draw a volcano. To the right of the volcano, draw 10 vertical lines, spaced equally as in the diagram below.

- Label the first line *12*, the second *24*, and so on, adding *12* (minutes) to each line.

- Then calculate how many miles lava would travel in each time interval. (Hint: In 12 minutes the lava would travel 6 miles.)

- Write the times below the diagram.

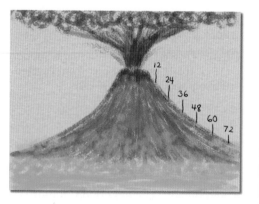

Consider copying and laminating these activities for use in centers.

Science

Fire and Quake

👤 Singles	🕐 15 minutes
Objective	Compare two natural events.
Materials	Anthology, reference sources

Use a Venn Diagram to compare and contrast volcanoes and earthquakes.

- Label the left section of the diagram *Earthquakes*. Label the right side *Volcanoes*.

- Label the intersecting section *Both*.

- Use reference materials to research volcanoes and earthquakes.

- Under *Earthquakes*, write characteristics that are true only of earthquakes. Under *Volcanoes*, write characteristics that are true only of volcanoes.

- Under *Both*, write characteristics that are true of both.

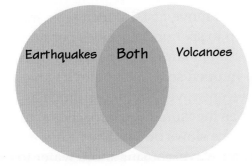

Earthquakes   Both   Volcanoes

Language Arts

Volcano Glossary

👥 Groups	🕐 30 minutes
Objective	Make a volcano glossary.
Materials	Anthology, dictionary

A glossary is a list of specialized words and their definitions. Make a glossary that gives the meanings of volcano terms.

- Reread *Volcanoes* and list important words and terms. Some examples are *magma, lava,* and *crater*. Put the words into alphabetical order.

- Divide the list of words so that each group member has an equal number. Then work to find definitions for them, using the selection, a dictionary, or both.

- Create the glossary. Add pictures or diagrams to help explain some of the words.

- Put the pages together to make a book, or create a bulletin board display.

Career Link

Could I Be a Volcanologist?

👤 Singles	🕐 20 minutes
Objective	Learn what volcanologists do.
Materials	Reference sources

Write a job description for a volcanologist, an earth scientist who studies volcanoes.

- Using a reference source such as an encyclopedia or the Internet, find out what volcanologists do.

- Then, write a job description for a volcanologist in your own words. Be sure to include what types of skills and education are needed to become a volcanologist.

Listening Comprehension

OBJECTIVES
- Listen to categorize and classify information.

Building Background

Tell students that you will read aloud a selection about one of nature's most incredible and powerful forces, the tsunami.

- Ask volunteers to explain what a tsunami is. (a giant ocean wave that forms from an earthquake or volcanic eruption)
- Tell students that the largest recorded tsunami wave was 210 feet high.

Fluency Modeling

Explain that as you read aloud, you will be modeling fluent oral reading. Ask students to listen carefully to your phrasing and your expression, or tone of voice and emphasis.

COMPREHENSION SKILL

Categorize and Classify

Explain that

- a category is a group of people, animals, things, or ideas that are alike
- grouping facts in a category can help readers better understand and remember information

Purpose Setting Read the selection aloud, asking students to think about how the facts can be grouped together. Then use the Guiding Comprehension questions to assess understanding. Reread the selection for clarification as needed.

81CC   **THEME 1: Nature's Fury**

Teacher Read Aloud

Making Waves
by Gail Skroback Hennessey

On the open seas, this monster can travel as fast as a 747 jetliner. Approaching the shore, the destructive giant's loud sucking and hissing sounds and rumblings echo through the air like a speeding train. As it attacks, its height can reach a staggering one hundred feet.

No, we're not talking about Godzilla. This monster is real—and even scarier. But it's not a living thing. This killer of the sea is a giant wave called a tsunami.

A Tsunami Is Born

❶ Tsunamis aren't like waves you normally see at the beach. Those are usually caused by winds blowing across the surface of the water. Tsunamis occur when disturbances like earthquakes, volcanoes, and landslides happen underwater. Even huge meteorites crashing into the ocean can cause a tsunami. "Think of a rock hitting the end of a pond," says Eddie Bernard, director of the Pacific Marine Environmental Laboratory, part of the National Oceanic and Atmospheric Administration. "It creates a series of waves that go in all directions away from where it initially hit."

The waves in a tsunami move fast. In open seas, they can travel at speeds of up to six hundred miles per hour. But surprisingly, deep-sea tsunami waves aren't much more than a foot high. In open seas, a tsunami's wave length, or distance between waves, can be as much as one hundred miles. But as the tsunami approaches shallower waters, the first wave slows down. The next wave catches up with the earlier wave, causing more water to be crowded into a smaller area. This creates larger and larger waves. "Think of a Slinky being pushed," says Bernard. "The pulse goes through the whole thing, bunching up and expanding."

Wave Warning

2 Unlike earthquakes, hurricanes, and other natural disasters, tsunamis aren't easy to predict and track. One reason is that they're tough to spot in the deep ocean. Another is that they move incredibly fast. A tsunami can cross the Pacific Ocean—a distance of up to eleven thousand miles—in less than a day. Because of that, there's little time for scientists to warn people that the waves are approaching.

That hasn't stopped scientists from trying to protect people from the deadly waves. About fifty years ago, experts from twenty-six nations banded together to form the Tsunami Warning System (TWS). The group monitors tsunami-prone areas throughout the Pacific Ocean. Sensor instruments placed on the sea floor measure the weight of increased water bunching up—a sign of an approaching tsunami. If necessary, a warning is issued for the area in the path of the approaching tsunami.

A tsunami's unpredictable nature makes it all the more dangerous—and deadly. Last year, people heard rumbling sounds along the shore of Papua, New Guinea, and went to investigate. Within ten minutes of the roaring thunder (caused by water rushing back over shells, rocks, and semi-dry sand), a forty-foot wave appeared. It took the lives of about three thousand people.

Tsunami in the U.S.?

According to Bernard, a monster of a tsunami along the shores of Hawaii, Alaska, California, Oregon, or Washington is a real possibility. "Scientists think there is a ten to thirty percent probability of a large earthquake in the next thirty to fifty years along this section of the U.S. coast," he says.

3 After a tsunami hit Cape Mendocino, California, in 1992, the National Tsunami Hazard Mitigation Program (NTHMP) was formed. The group educates people about the warning signs of tsunamis. Eddie Bernard and other scientists hope groups like the NTHMP can prevent nature's ultimate "wipeout" from doing harm.

CRITICAL THINKING
Guiding Comprehension

1 **CATEGORIZE AND CLASSIFY** How are tsunamis different from the waves you normally see at the beach? (Tsunamis are caused by volcanic eruptions, earthquakes, landslides, or meteorites; regular ocean waves are caused by the wind. Also, tsunamis are much bigger than regular waves.)

2 **CATEGORIZE AND CLASSIFY** According to the author, in what way are tsunamis unlike other natural disasters, such as earthquakes and hurricanes? (Other natural disasters are easier to predict and track than tsunamis.)

3 **CATEGORIZE AND CLASSIFY** For what purpose was the National Tsunami Hazard Mitigation Program (NTHMP) formed? (to educate people about warning signs of tsunamis)

Discussion Options

Personal Response Have students discuss what they learned about tsunamis from the selection.

⭐ **Connecting/Comparing** Ask students to compare tsunamis with hurricanes and other storms they have read about in this theme.

English Language Learners

Supporting Comprehension

Explain to students that *tsunami* is a Japanese word for the giant waves described in this article. Invite students to share words in their native languages for waves or giant waves.

Background and Vocabulary

Key Concept: How Volcanoes Form

Ask students to name the forces of nature they have read about so far. (earthquakes, tornadoes, lightning, and thunderstorms) Explain that the next selection is about volcanoes.

Discuss what volcanoes are, and ask students to name any volcanoes they have heard of. Then use "The World of Volcanoes" on Anthology pages 82–83 to build background and introduce Key Vocabulary.

- Have a volunteer read "The World of Volcanoes."
- Point out the map of the earth's surface, and have students locate volcanic regions on a globe or map of the world.

Vocabulary Preview

The Vocabulary Reader can be used to preteach or reinforce the key vocabulary.

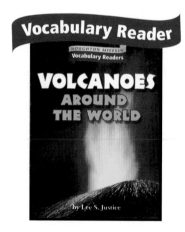

Get Set to Read

Background and Vocabulary

The World of Volcanoes

Volcanoes

Genre Nonfiction

Key Vocabulary

cinders
crater
crust
lava
molten

Vocabulary Reader

VOLCANOES AROUND THE WORLD

e Glossary

From Hawaii to the Pacific Northwest, from Guatemala to Iceland, Seymour Simon's *Volcanoes* will take you on a world tour. You'll see more than mountain peaks. The heart of the story is about the part of the earth that's deep underground, where the heat turns the earth's **crust** into **molten** rock.

Mauna Loa
Molten rock erupts as flowing **lava** from Hawaii's Mauna Loa.

82

English Language Learners

Supporting Comprehension

Beginning/Preproduction Have students listen to the article. Then ask students to point out the volcanoes in the photographs. Have students point first to the example of an erupting volcano. (Mauna Loa)

Early Production and Speech Emergence Have students repeat these Key Vocabulary words after you: *cinders, crater, crust, eruption, lava, magma, molten,* and *summit.* Use the illustrations on pages 82–83 to help students understand the meaning of each word.

Intermediate and Advanced Fluency Have students work in small groups to read and then restate in their own words the information provided in selected paragraphs from the article.

Mount St. Helens
One of many volcanoes in the Pacific Northwest, Mount St. Helens cooled down to form a hard lava dome in its **crater**.

Surtsey
An undersea volcano near Iceland created a new island, Surtsey.

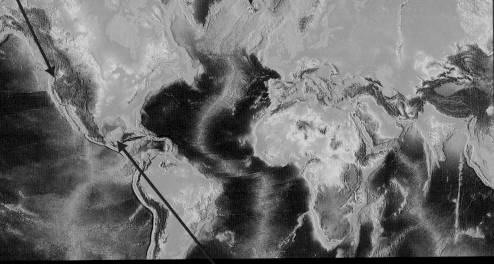

Fuego and Acatenango
These volcanoes in Guatemala are built of **cinders** and ash.

Introducing Vocabulary

Key Vocabulary
These words support the Key Concept and appear in the selection.

cinders charred bits of rock; ashes

crater a bowl-shaped depression

crust the solid outer layer of earth

eruption a volcanic explosion or large flow of lava

lava hot melted rock that flows from a volcano

magma hot melted rock underneath the earth's surface

molten made liquid by heat

summit the top of a mountain

 e • Glossary
e • WordGame

See Vocabulary notes on pages 86, 90, 92, 94, and 96 for additional words to preview.

Display Transparency 1–20.

- Model how to figure out the meaning of *cinders* from clues in the sentence.

- Have students use sentence clues and the diagram to figure out the meanings of Key Vocabulary words. Have students explain how they figured out each word.

- Ask students to look for these words as they read and to use them to discuss volcanoes.

Practice/Homework Assign **Practice Book** page 46.

Transparency 1–20

TRANSPARENCY 1–20
TEACHER'S EDITION PAGE 83

ANNOTATED VERSION

NATURE'S FURY Volcanoes
Key Vocabulary

Volcanic Vocabulary

1. Volcanoes often produce <u>cinders</u>, charred bits of rock and ash that can coat the ground.
2. When a volcano blows its top, a huge hole or <u>crater</u> may be formed.
3. The force will break through the earth's <u>crust</u>, or solid outer layer of earth.
4. <u>Magma</u> is hot melted rock that lies deep under the earth's surface.
5. Sometimes magma is forced upward toward the earth's surface. This <u>molten</u> rock can melt the rock around it, turning it into liquid.
6. In a volcanic <u>eruption</u>, magma flows upward through an opening inside the earth.
7. Then <u>lava</u> flows out of the opening in the earth. This hot liquid rock can flow slowly or quickly.
8. A volcano can blast away the <u>summit</u>, or the very top of a mountain.

Practice Book page 46

Name _____

Volcanoes
Key Vocabulary

Volcanic Activity

Write each word from the box under the correct category below.

Vocabulary
molten
lava
crater
crust
cinders
eruption
magma
summit

Description of Hot Lava
molten **(1 point)**

Earth Layer
crust **(1)**

Materials in a Volcano
lava **(1)**
magma **(1)**
cinders **(1)**

Volcano Parts
crater **(1)**
summit **(1)**

Event
eruption **(1)**

Now choose at least four words from the box. Use them to write a short paragraph describing an exploding volcano.

(1 point for each word)

_____
_____
_____
_____

Introducing Vocabulary **83**

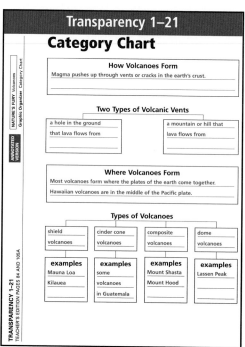

Selection 3

Strategy Focus

In this selection, Seymour Simon gives you lots of information about volcanoes and how they form. As you read, **monitor** your understanding, and reread or use the photos and the map to **clarify**.

84

COMPREHENSION STRATEGY
Monitor/Clarify

Teacher Modeling Have a volunteer read aloud the Strategy Focus. Then have students read the introduction. Model the strategy.

 **Think Aloud** *I'm not sure why the Romans thought that Vulcan worked at a hot forge. I've reread this section, so I'll look at the photographs on pages 84–85. Now I see why the Romans might think of a forge when they see volcanoes. Erupting lava looks like hot sparks in a forge.*

Test Prep Remind students that many reading tests are timed. Caution them, however, not to rush. In particular, students should take time to monitor and clarify their understanding.

COMPREHENSION SKILL
Categorize and Classify

Introduce the Graphic Organizer. Tell students that grouping information into categories will help them understand it. Explain that as students read, they will group facts about volcanoes using the Category Chart on **Practice Book** page 47.

- Display **Transparency 1–21.** Have students read the last two paragraphs on Anthology page 85.

- Model how to complete the first chart item. Monitor students' work as needed.

Vocabulary

molten made liquid by heat

84   **THEME 1: Nature's Fury**

Transparency 1–21

NATURE'S FURY Volcanoes
Graphic Organizer Category Chart

ANNOTATED VERSION

Category Chart

How Volcanoes Form
Magma pushes up through vents or cracks in the earth's crust.

Two Types of Volcanic Vents

| a hole in the ground that lava flows from | a mountain or hill that lava flows from |

Where Volcanoes Form
Most volcanoes form where the plates of the earth come together.
Hawaiian volcanoes are in the middle of the Pacific plate.

Types of Volcanoes

| shield volcanoes | cinder cone volcanoes | composite volcanoes | dome volcanoes |
| examples Mauna Loa Kilauea | examples some volcanoes in Guatemala | examples Mount Shasta Mount Hood | examples Lassen Peak |

TRANSPARENCY 1–21
TEACHER'S EDITION PAGES 84 AND 105A

Practice Book page 47

Volcanoes
Graphic Organizer
Category Chart

Name _____

Category Chart

Fill in the boxes in each category.

How Volcanoes Form
Magma pushes up through vents or cracks in the earth's crust. **(1 point)**

Two Types of Volcanic Vents

| a hole in the ground that lava flows from **(1)** | a mountain or hill that lava flows from **(1)** |

Where Volcanoes Form
Most volcanoes form where the plates of the earth come together. Hawaiian volcanoes are in the middle of the Pacific plate.

Types of Volcanoes

| shield volcanoes **(1)** | cinder cone volcanoes **(1)** | composite volcanoes **(1)** | dome volcanoes **(1)** |
| examples Mauna Loa Kilauea **(1)** | examples some volcanoes in Guatemala **(1)** | examples Mount Shasta Mount Hood **(1)** | examples Lassen Peak **(1)** |

Throughout history, people have told stories about volcanoes. The early Romans believed in Vulcan, their god of fire. They thought that Vulcan worked at a hot forge, striking sparks as he made swords and armor for the other gods. It is from the Roman god Vulcan that we get the word *volcano*. **1**

The early Hawaiians told legends of the wanderings of Pele, their goddess of fire. Pele was chased from her homes by her sister Namaka, goddess of the sea. Pele moved constantly from one Hawaiian island to another. Finally, Pele settled in a mountain called Kilauea, on the big island of Hawaii. Even though the islanders tried to please Pele, she burst forth every few years. Kilauea is still an active volcano.

In early times, no one knew how volcanoes formed or why they spouted fire. In modern times, scientists began to study volcanoes. They still don't know all the answers, but they know much about how a volcano works.

Our planet is made up of many layers of rock. The top layers of solid rock are called the crust. Deep beneath the crust, it is so hot that some rock melts. The melted, or molten, rock is called magma.

Volcanoes are formed by cracks or holes that poke through the earth's crust. Magma pushes its way up through the cracks. This is called a volcanic eruption. **2** When magma pours forth on the surface it is called lava. In the above photograph of an eruption, you can see great fountains of boiling lava forming fiery rivers and lakes. As lava cools, it hardens to form rock.

85

Extra Support/Intervention

Selection Preview

pages 85–90 Scientists know how volcanoes form and why they occur where they do. What type of information is shown in the diagram on page 89?

pages 91–93 Most volcanoes are on the edges of the earth's plates, but Hawaii's are in the middle of the Pacific plate. What do Hawaiian eruptions look like?

pages 94–96 Scientists divide volcanoes into four groups: shield, cinder cone, composite, and dome. Look at the photographs on pages 94–96. What group might each one belong to?

pages 97–98 Looking at the photographs on pages 97–98, what do you think often happens after a volcano stops erupting?

Purpose Setting

- Ask students what they would like to learn about volcanoes.

- Have students preview the selection by looking at the illustrations. Ask students to predict what they might learn about volcanoes from this selection.

- As they read, have students monitor and clarify their understanding about volcanoes.

- Ask students to try grouping selection details into categories that will help them understand and remember what they read.

- You may wish to preview with students the Responding questions on Anthology page 100.

Journal ▶ Students can record predictions, questions, and key facts about volcanoes.

STRATEGY REVIEW

Phonics/Decoding

Remind students to use the Phonics/Decoding Strategy as they read.

Modeling Write this sentence from *Volcanoes* on the board: *Ten years after the explosion that formed Surtsey, another volcano erupted near Iceland.* Point to *explosion*.

Think Aloud   *First, I'll look for word parts I know. I see ex- at the beginning. I also see -sion, which comes at the end of many nouns. This ending is pronounced zhuhn. I think the middle syllable has the long o sound. If I blend the sounds together, I get ihk-SPLOH-zhuhn. This word makes sense in the sentence.*

Guiding Comprehension

1 **WRITER'S CRAFT** Why do you think the author begins the selection by writing about Vulcan and Pele? (to show that people have been fascinated by volcanoes for a long time; to interest readers)

2 **SEQUENCE OF EVENTS** Describe the sequence of events before, during, and after a volcanic eruption. (Magma pushes up through a crack in the earth's crust. Lava flows out. Lava cools and hardens into rock.)

3 **MAKING INFERENCES** What do you think the author means when he says that Mount St. Helens *awakened from its long sleep*? (The mountain seemed to be sleeping when it was quiet; It seemed to wake when it erupted.)

A volcano can be two things: a hole in the ground that lava comes through, or a hill or mountain formed by the lava. Mount Rainier in the state of Washington is a volcano even though it has not erupted since 1882.

Not far from Mount Rainier (top, right) is Mount St. Helens (bottom, left). Native Americans and early settlers in the Northwest had seen Mount St. Helens puff out some ashes, steam, and lava in the mid-1800s. Yet for more than a century, the mountain seemed quiet and peaceful.

3 In March 1980 Mount St. Helens awakened from its long sleep. First there were a few small earthquakes that shook the mountain. Then on March 27 Mount St. Helens began to spout ashes and steam. Each day brought further quakes, until by mid-May more than ten thousand small quakes had been recorded. The mountain began to swell up and crack.

Sunday May 18 dawned bright and clear. The mountain seemed much the same as it had been for the past month. Suddenly, at 8:32 A.M., Mount St. Helens erupted with incredible force. The energy released in the eruption was equal to ten million tons of dynamite.

86

Vocabulary

lava hot melted rock that flows from a volcano

century one hundred years

Extra Support/Intervention

Strategy Modeling: Phonics/Decoding

Model the strategy for *dynamite*.

The first part of this word must be DYE, since the letter y stands for the long i sound when it acts as a vowel. The next part is either nay or nuh. The last part is probably myt. When I first try to blend the parts, I get DYE-nay-myt. No, that's not right. When I try again, I get DYE-nuh-myt. That word makes sense in the sentence.

DYE-nuh-myt

87

ASSIGNMENT CARD 12

Take Another Look

Comparisons

On page 96, the author compares a plugged-up dome volcano to a bottle of soda water with a cork in it. Find some other comparisons the author has used to help readers understand volcanoes. Look on pages 88, 89, and 94. Then make up a new comparison in place of each one the author has used. Try to make your comparison as vivid as you can.

Theme 1: Nature's Fury

Teacher's Resource BLM page 53

CRITICAL THINKING
Guiding Comprehension

④ MAKING INFERENCES Do you think the suddenness of Mount St. Helens's eruption surprised people? Why? (Yes. If they had expected it, everyone would have moved away.)

⑤ DRAWING CONCLUSIONS What do you think happened to the rest of Mount St. Helens's summit? (It was probably blown into small pieces.)

⑥ TEXT ORGANIZATION Why do you think the author included a diagram on page 89? (to make clear where the earth's plates fit together)

COMPREHENSION STRATEGY
Monitor/Clarify

Teacher/Student Modeling Model how to monitor and clarify as you read.

- If you weren't sure why Mount St. Helens was dedicated as a national monument, how could rereading page 88 help clarify your understanding?

- How might viewing the photographs of Mount St. Helens clarify understanding?

Have students reread or view photographs to monitor their understanding.

Vocabulary

eruption a volcanic explosion or large flow of lava

crater a bowl-shaped depression

crust the solid outer layer of earth

magma hot melted rock underneath the earth's surface

---

④ The eruption of Mount St. Helens was the most destructive in the history of the United States. Sixty people lost their lives as hot gases, rocks, and ashes covered an area of two hundred thirty square miles. Hundreds of houses and cabins were destroyed, leaving many people homeless. Miles of highways, roads, and railways were badly damaged. The force of the eruption was so great that entire forests were blown down like rows of matchsticks.

⑤ Compare the way Mount St. Helens looked before and after the eruption. The entire top of the mountain was blown away. In its place is a huge volcanic crater. In 1982 the mountain and the area around it were dedicated as the Mount St. Helens National Volcanic Monument. Visitor centers allow people to view the volcano's astonishing power.

88

English Language Learners

Supporting Comprehension

Draw on the board or show an example of a bicycle chain or a necklace. Point out that chains are made of many connected links. Then read aloud the phrase *a chain of underwater volcanoes* on page 89. Help students to visualize this phrase.

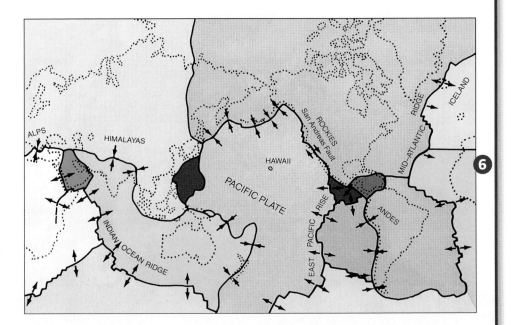

V olcanoes don't just happen anyplace. The earth's crust is broken into huge sections like a giant cracked eggshell. The pieces of the crust are called plates. The United States, Canada, and Mexico and part of the North Atlantic Ocean are all on the North American plate. Almost all the volcanoes in the world erupt in places where two plates meet.

Down the middle of the North Atlantic Ocean, two plates are slowly moving apart. Hot magma pushes up between them. A chain of underwater volcanoes runs along the line where the two plates meet. Some of the underwater volcanoes have grown so high that they stick up from the ocean floor to make islands.

89

Extra Support/Intervention

Strategy Modeling: Monitor/Clarify

Use this example to model the strategy.

At first I didn't understand the explanation that the earth's crust is broken up into huge sections called plates. So I reread page 89 and looked at the diagram. The diagram helped me see that the plates are like giant puzzle pieces. Some are pushing away from each other. Most volcanoes happen along the lines where these pieces meet.

Topic, Main Idea, and Details

Teach

- Remind students that the topic is the main subject that is being written about. It can be named in one word or a brief phrase.

- Explain that the main idea is the most important idea about the topic. Sometimes authors state a main idea in a heading or key sentence.

Practice

- Ask students to name the topic of this selection. (volcanoes)

- Ask a volunteer to read aloud the first paragraph on page 88. Then ask students to find its main idea. (the first one)

Apply

- Have students reread page 89 and complete a chart like the one below.

Topic	the earth's plates
Main Idea	Most volcanoes occur where the earth's plates meet.

Review Skill Trace	
Teach	Theme 2, p. 229A
Reteach	Theme 2, p. R14
▶ Review	p. 89; Theme 3, p. 273; Theme 6, p. 611

Reading the Selection 89

Guiding Comprehension

7 **MAKING INFERENCES** Why do you think the people of Heimaey came back to their island after a year? (Sample answers: They didn't expect another eruption; It was their home.)

Iceland is a volcanic island in the North Atlantic. In 1963, an area of the sea near Iceland began to smoke. An undersea volcano was exploding and a new island was being formed. The island was named Surtsey, after the ancient Norse god of fire.

Ten years after the explosion that formed Surtsey, another volcano erupted near Iceland. It was off the south coast of Iceland on the island of Heimaey. Within six hours of the eruption, more than 5,000 people were taken off the island to safety. After two months, hundreds of buildings had burned down and dozens more had been buried in the advancing lava. Then the volcano stopped erupting. **7** After a year's time, the people of Heimaey came back to reclaim their island with its new 735-foot volcano.

90

Extra Support/Intervention

Review (pages 84–90)

Before students who need extra support join the whole class for Stop and Think on page 91, have them

- take turns modeling Monitor/Clarify and other strategies they used
- add to **Transparency 1–21**
- check and revise their Category Chart on **Practice Book** page 47, and use it to summarize

Vocabulary

Norse having to do with the ancient Scandinavians

advancing moving forward

Most volcanoes and earthquakes are along the edges of the large Pacific plate. There are so many that the shoreline of the Pacific Ocean is called the "Ring of Fire." But a few volcanoes are not on the edge of a plate. The volcanoes in the Hawaiian Islands are in the middle of the Pacific plate.

A million years ago, magma pushed up through cracks in the Pacific plate. Over the years, eruption followed eruption. Little by little, thin layers of lava hardened, one atop another. Thousands of eruptions were needed to build mountains high enough to reach from the deep sea bottom and appear as islands.

The largest Hawaiian volcano is Mauna Loa. It is seventy miles long and rises thirty thousand feet from the ocean floor. It is still growing. Every few years, Mauna Loa erupts again.

Hawaiian volcano lava usually bubbles out quietly to form rivers or lakes, or spouts a few hundred feet in the air in a fiery fountain. Hawaiian volcanoes erupt much more gently than did Surtsey or Mount St. Helens. Only rarely does a Hawaiian volcano throw out rock and high clouds of ash.

91

READ & COMPREHEND

Volcanoes

Stop and Think

Critical Thinking Questions

1. **TEXT ORGANIZATION** Diagrams and photographs help present information in *Volcanoes*. What other text features might help readers learn and remember information easily? (Sample answers: section headings, photograph captions)

2. **COMPARE AND CONTRAST** How are volcanic eruptions similar to earthquakes? (Sample answer: Both are caused by pressures in the ground, are unpredictable, and cause damage.) How are volcanic eruptions unlike earthquakes? (Sample answer: Volcanic eruptions have hot lava while earthquakes do not.)

Strategies in Action

Have students take turns modeling Monitor/Clarify and other strategies.

Discussion Options

Bring the entire class together to do one or more of the activities below.

- **Review Predictions/Purpose** Ask students to share their predictions. Have them record new predictions or additional questions about volcanoes.

- **Share Group Discussions** Have students share their literature discussions.

- **Summarize** Have students use their Category Charts to summarize what they have read.

ASSIGNMENT CARD 11
Reading Routines

Before You Read . . .

Preview the selection. Read the first page. Then look at all the photographs in the selection.

As You Read . . .

- **Monitor your understanding**. If you come to a part you don't understand, pause for a moment. Reread or look at the photos to clarify.

- **Think of questions** to discuss with your classmates when you finish reading.

- **Fill in your Category Map** to help you understand what causes volcanoes of various kinds.

Theme 1: Nature's Fury

Teacher's Resource BLM page 52

Monitoring Student Progress	
If . . .	**Then . . .**
students have completed the Extra Support activities on page 90,	have them read the rest of the selection cooperatively or independently.

Guiding Comprehension

8 COMPARE AND CONTRAST How is Hawaiian lava different from the lava produced by volcanic eruptions elsewhere? (It can bubble out quietly to form rivers. Some of it is thin and flows quickly.)

9 DRAWING CONCLUSIONS How can scientists tell what kind of eruption occurred by studying cooled lava formations? (The rough, sharp *aa* formations tell scientists that the lava was thick and slow moving. The smooth *pahoehoe* formations tell them that the lava was thin, hot, and fast moving.)

10 MAKING INFERENCES Why do you think the author included the lava's Hawaiian names? (to show how common lava is in Hawaii; to add interest)

Steam clouds billow as a flow of hot lava enters the sea. Hawaii is constantly changing as eruptions add hundreds of acres of new land to the islands. In other parts of the shoreline, old lava flows are quickly weathered by the waves into rocks and black sand.

Hawaiian lava is thin and flows quickly. In some lava rivers, speeds as high as thirty-five miles per hour have been measured. In an eruption in 1986, a number of houses were threatened by the quick-moving lava. Fire fighters sprayed water on the lava to slow down its advance.

92

Vocabulary

weathered changed because of being exposed to the weather

billowy rising in a great wave

English Language Learners

Supporting Comprehension

Draw a line on the board, and write the word *line* next to it. Have students read page 92 and find the word *shoreline*. Explain that the shore is where land and water meet. Point out that where land and water meet a line is created, the shoreline.

READ & COMPREHEND

W hen lava cools and hardens, it forms volcanic rocks. The kinds of rocks formed are clues to the kind of eruption. The two main kinds have Hawaiian names. Thick, slow-moving lava called *aa* (AH-ah) hardens into a rough tangle of sharp rocks. Thin, hot, quick-moving lava called *pahoehoe* (pah-HO-ee-ho-ee) forms a smooth, billowy surface. **9** **10**

93

Fluency Practice

Rereading for Fluency Have students choose a favorite part of the selection to reread to a partner, or suggest that they read pages 92–93. Encourage students to read expressively.

Extra Support/Intervention

Strategy Modeling: Monitor/Clarify

Use this example to model the strategy.

The text says that pahoehoe forms a smooth, billowy surface. It's hard for me to picture this. The photo shows puffy, black, swirling rock. That helps me understand what the flowing lava might look like.

CRITICAL THINKING

Guiding Comprehension

11 **MAKING INFERENCES** Why do you think scientists divide volcanoes into groups? (Maybe it helps them study volcanoes and make predictions about them.)

12 **COMPARE AND CONTRAST** Why do you think the author compares volcanoes to warriors' shields and upside-down ice cream cones? (to help readers picture volcanoes' shapes more easily; to give readers familiar objects to compare them to)

13 **DRAWING CONCLUSIONS** Based on the information on page 95, what do you think an active volcano is? (one that can still erupt but doesn't necessarily erupt for many years)

11 Earth scientists have divided volcanoes into four groups. Shield volcanoes, such as Mauna Loa and Kilauea, have broad, gentle slopes shaped like an ancient warrior's shield.

12 Cinder cone volcanoes look like upside-down ice cream cones. They erupt explosively, blowing out burning ashes and cinders. The ashes and cinders build up to form the cone shape. The cinder cone volcano to the near left erupted in Guatemala, Central America, in 1984. The cinder cone volcanoes in the background are still smoking from earlier eruptions.

94

Vocabulary

cinders charred bits of rock; ashes

composite made up of different substances or parts

M ost of the volcanoes in the world are composite or strato-volcanoes. Strato-volcanoes are formed by the lava, cinders, and ashes of an eruption. During an eruption, ashes and cinders fall to the ground. The eruption quiets down and lava slowly flows out, covering the layer of ashes and cinders. Further eruptions add more layers of ashes and cinders, followed by more layers of lava. Mount Shasta (above) in California and Mount Hood in Oregon are strato-volcanoes. They are still active even though they have not erupted for many years.

13

95

Text Organization

Review

- Remind students that information in nonfiction selections is often organized either by main ideas or by sequence of events.

Practice

- Point out that the information on pages 94–96 is organized by main idea. Ask students to identify the main idea. (first sentence on page 94) Then have them identify its supporting details. (remaining sentences)

- Next, ask a volunteer to read aloud the last three paragraphs on page 86 and tell what they are about. (the 1980 eruption of Mount St. Helens) Ask students how this passage is organized. (by sequence of events)

Apply

- Have students reread page 90 and distinguish whether this information is organized by main ideas or by sequence of events. (sequence of events)

- Ask students to explain how they might display this information. (in an event map)

Review Skill Trace	
Teach	p. 81A
Reteach	p. R10
▶ Review	p. 73, p. 95; Theme 2, p. 147

English Language Learners

Supporting Comprehension

Have students look at page 95. Point to the two-word verb *flows out*. Ask students what happens when too much water is poured into a glass. Explain that the water flows out of, or spills over, the top of the glass. Then ask students to look for another two-word verb in the same sentence. (quiets down)

Guiding Comprehension

14 **COMPARE AND CONTRAST** How does the author help readers understand the way pressure builds up in a dome volcano? (by comparing the plugged-up dome volcano to a corked bottle of soda water)

15 **DRAWING CONCLUSIONS** Why do you think Crater Lake is so deep? (Volcanoes originate below the surface of the earth, so when the volcano collapsed, it formed a deep crater.)

COMPREHENSION STRATEGY
Monitor/Clarify

Student Modeling Have students model the strategy by sharing how they monitored and clarified their understanding. Offer these prompts:

- How could rereading page 97 help you understand more clearly how Crater Lake was formed?

- How do the photographs on pages 94–96 help you understand the four types of volcanoes?

14 The fourth kind of volcano is called a dome volcano. Dome volcanoes have thick, slow-moving lava that forms a steep-sided dome shape. After an eruption, the volcano may be plugged with hardened lava. The plug prevents the gases from escaping, like a cork in a bottle of soda water. As the pressure builds up, the volcano blows its top, as Mount St. Helens did. Lassen Peak in California is a dome volcano that erupted violently in 1915. You can see the huge chunks of volcanic rock near the summit.

96

Vocabulary

summit the top of a mountain

extinct no longer active; extinguished

collapsed suddenly fell inward

caldera a crater formed by a collapsed volcano

ASSIGNMENT CARD 13
Volcanic History

Make a Time Line

Use the information about Mount St. Helens the author gives, as well as the photos of the mountain, to create an illustrated time line showing Mount St. Helens's recent volcanic history. Begin the time line in the mid-1800s, and end it in the present.

Mid–1800s   Today

Theme 1: Nature's Fury

Teacher's Resource BLM page 53

round the world there are many very old volcanoes that no longer erupt. These dead volcanoes are called **extinct**. Crater Lake in Oregon is an extinct volcano. Almost seven thousand years ago, Mount Mazama in Oregon erupted, sending out a thick blanket of ashes that covered the ground for miles around. Then the entire top of the volcano **collapsed**. A huge crater, called a **caldera**, formed and was later filled with water. Crater Lake reaches a depth of two thousand feet, the deepest lake in North America.

97

Categorize and Classify

Teach

- Tell students that *classify* means to arrange similar items into a group.
- Explain that *categorize* means to find a name describing all the items in a group.

Practice

- Have students reread pages 94–96. Point out that these pages explain how scientists have categorized and classified volcanoes.
- Ask students to name the four categories of volcanoes and describe each one.

Apply

- Write the names of these volcanoes on the board: *Lassen Peak, Mount Shasta, Mount Hood, Mauna Loa, Kilauea.*
- Have students work in pairs to classify and categorize these volcanoes using a chart like the one below.

shield	cinder cone	composite	dome
Mauna Loa, Kilauea		Mount Shasta, Mount Hood	Lassen Peak

Target Skill Trace

Preview; Teach	p. 81CC; p. 84; p. 97; p. 105A
Reteach	p. R12
Review	pp. M34–M35; Theme 2, pp. 149, 217

Reading the Selection 97

CRITICAL THINKING
Guiding Comprehension

16 **NOTING DETAILS** How does the author end the selection? (He describes how life returns after a volcano erupts; He tells some of the good things volcanoes do.)

17 **MAKING INFERENCES** Why do you think the author ends the selection in this way? (Maybe he wants people to understand that both good and bad things happen as a result of volcanoes.)

After a volcano erupts, everything is buried under lava or ashes. Plants and animals are nowhere to be found. But in a few short months, life renews itself. Plants grow in the cracks between the rocks. Insects and other animals return. Volcanoes do not just destroy. They bring new mountains, new islands, and new soil to the land. Many good things can come from the fiery explosions of volcanoes.

16

17

98

REACHING ALL LEARNERS **Extra Support/ Intervention**	**On Level** **Challenge**
Selection Review Before students join in Wrapping Up on page 99, have them <ul><li>take turns modeling the reading strategies they used;</li><li>help you to complete **Transparency 1–21;**</li><li>complete their Category Charts and summarize the entire selection.</li></ul>	**Literature Discussion** In mixed-ability groups of five or six, students can discuss their own questions about the selection as well as the Responding questions on Anthology page 100.

Meet the AUTHOR

Seymour Simon

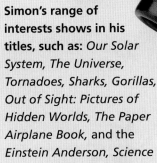

"Many of the books I write are really in the nature of guidebooks to unknown territories. Each territory has to be discovered again by children venturing into it for the first time."

"I'm always working on several books at the same time. I may be writing a book and researching another book and writing for information about a third book and thinking about plans for still a fourth book."

FACT FILE

- Graduated from the Bronx High School of Science
- President of the Junior Astronomy Club at New York's Museum of Natural History
- Taught science and creative writing in New York City public schools, 1955–1979
- First published work: a magazine article about the moon
- Author of more than two hundred books in thirty years

Simon's range of interests shows in his titles, such as: *Our Solar System, The Universe, Tornadoes, Sharks, Gorillas, Out of Sight: Pictures of Hidden Worlds, The Paper Airplane Book,* and the *Einstein Anderson, Science Detective* series.

 Internet

For more information about Seymour Simon, visit Education Place.
www.eduplace.com/kids

99

Wrapping Up

Critical Thinking Questions

1. **MAKING JUDGMENTS** Do you think it is important for scientists to study volcanoes? Why? (yes, so that they can predict them)

2. **DRAWING CONCLUSIONS** Based on what you've learned so far, how well do you think scientists can predict when and where volcanoes will happen? (They can predict that new volcanoes will happen where the earth's plates meet. They can't predict exactly when.)

Strategies in Action

Have students take turns modeling how they used the Monitor/Clarify strategy.

Discussion Options

Bring the entire class together to do one or more of the activities below.

Review Predictions/Purpose Ask students to share their predictions for the selection and any answers they found to questions they had about volcanoes. Have students describe any information that surprised them.

Share Group Discussions Have students share their literature discussions.

Summarize Have students use their Category Charts to summarize *Volcanoes*.

Comprehension Check

Use **Practice Book** page 48 to assess students' comprehension of the selection.

REACHING ALL LEARNERS

Extra Support/ Intervention

Review Prefix *re-*

Point out the word *renews* on page 98. Explain that this word begins with the prefix *re-*, which can add the meaning "again" to a base word. Ask students what *renews* means. ("becomes new again")

Practice Book page 48

Volcanoes
Comprehension Check

Name _____

Show What You Know!

The following questions ask about volcanoes. Answer each question by writing the letter of the correct answer in the space provided.

B (1) 1. Where does the word *volcano* come from?
  A. the Hawaiian name for the goddess of fire, Pele
  B. the name for the Roman god of fire, Vulcan
  C. the scientific name for mountains that spout fire and ash
  D. the name for a race of mythological creatures called Vulcans

A (1) 2. How are volcanoes formed?
  A. Hot magma beneath the earth's crust pushes up through cracks or holes.
  B. The earth's crust melts and forms rivers of hot lava.
  C. Wood and other materials catch fire and cause explosions that melt mountaintops.
  D. Glaciers melt, leaving craters through which magma can escape.

B (1) 3. What happened when Mt. St. Helens erupted in 1980?
  A. The first of the Hawaiian islands was formed in the Pacific Ocean.
  B. Homes, roads, and forests were destroyed, and 60 people were killed.
  C. Ash spewed into the air, but no real damage was done.
  D. A new volcanic island appeared in the North Atlantic Ocean.

D (1) 4. Where in the earth's crust do most volcanoes erupt?
  A. in the weakest parts of the earth's plates, near the center
  B. in the Atlantic Ocean
  C. wherever mountains or mountain ranges are found
  D. in places where two of the earth's plates meet

C (1) 5. How have volcanoes helped to create the Hawaiian Islands?
  A. Eruptions destroyed much of the land area, leaving only islands.
  B. Eruptions caught the attention of explorers, who settled there.
  C. Eruptions built up the islands, and new eruptions add lava to the shoreline.
  D. Ash and cinders from thousands of eruptions have mixed with seawater to help form new land.

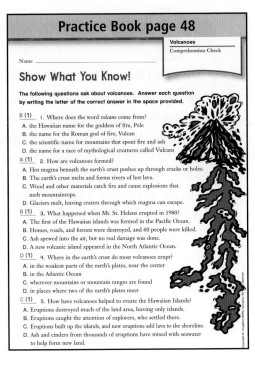

Monitoring Student Progress

If . . .	Then . . .
students score 3 or below on **Practice Book** page 48,	work with them to review the sections that describe the earth's plates.

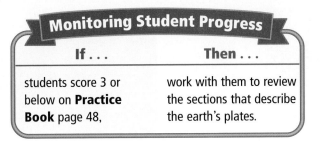

Responding

Think About the Selection

Have students discuss or write their answers. Sample answers are provided; accept reasonable responses.

1. **ORGANIZING** Helpful: Volcanoes create new land and beautiful lakes; Harmful: They destroy homes and cause loss of life.

2. **ANALYZING** Answers will vary.

3. **GENERATING** People did not know the scientific explanation for volcanoes, so they made up stories to explain them.

4. **GENERATING** Before a volcanic eruption, the earth probably moves as magma pushes upward, causing an earthquake.

5. **EVALUATING** Answers will vary.

6. **EVALUATING** Worst: It might be dangerous and scary; Best: It would be exciting to see volcanoes up close.

7. **Connections** Volcanoes are caused by forces deep underground, but tornadoes are caused by weather patterns in the atmosphere. Volcanoes happen mostly where the earth's plates meet, but tornadoes happen mostly in the Midwest. Both can give warning signs.

Responding

Think About the Selection

1. **Organizing** Find examples in the selection of both the helpful and harmful things that volcanoes do.

2. **Analyzing** Which word best describes a volcano for you: *beautiful, scary, exciting, ugly,* or some other word? Explain why.

3. **Generating** Why did people use folktales to explain volcanoes?

4. **Generating** Why might earthquakes occur just before eruptions?

5. **Evaluating** Of the different volcanoes mentioned in the selection, which one impressed you the most? Why?

6. **Evaluating** What do you think would be the best and worst things about studying volcanoes for a living?

7. **Connections** Compare the conditions that cause a volcanic eruption with those that cause a tornado. Think about how, where, and when they happen, and how much warning people have.

 **Explaining**

Write a Travel Brochure

Use information from the selection to create a travel brochure for a tour of the world's volcanoes. Explain where the tour will go and what volcanoes you will see.

Tips
- Fold a sheet of paper into three panels.
- Describe the tour on the inside panels and illustrate the outside panels.
- Check your spelling and capitalize all proper nouns.

100

English Language Learners

Supporting Comprehension

Beginning/Preproduction Ask students to draw different types of volcanoes and to label them using the words they learned in this selection.

Early Production and Speech Emergence Have students work in small groups to describe one type of volcanic eruption. Suggest that students refer to one of the illustrations to guide their descriptions.

Intermediate and Advanced Fluency Have partners discuss the different types of volcanoes. Suggest that they list the characteristics of each type.

Science

Create a Poster

Use information from Seymour Simon's *Volcanoes* to make a poster. You might show how magma rises to erupt as lava, or show the four different kinds of volcanoes.

Social Studies

Create a Fact File

With classmates, create a volcano fact file. Using the information in *Volcanoes*, each person chooses a country or state, such as Iceland or Hawaii, and lists the volcanoes for that place, along with a brief description of the volcanoes and a small map.

Bonus: Find information about the volcanoes of a country not mentioned in the selection, such as Italy or Japan. Add a fact file about that place.

Additional Responses

Personal Response Invite students to share their personal responses to the selection.

Journal ▶ Ask students to write in their journals about the most interesting information they have learned about volcanoes.

Selection Connections Remind students to add to **Practice Book** pages 9–10.

Internet

Go on a Web Field Trip

Connect to Education Place and explore a weather center, science museum, and other places to observe nature's fury. **www.eduplace.com/kids**

101

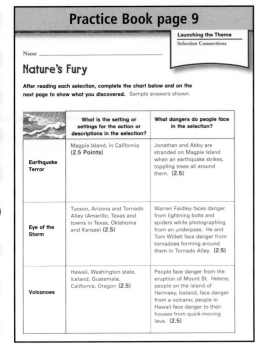

Practice Book page 9

Launching the Theme
Selection Connections

Name _____

Nature's Fury

After reading each selection, complete the chart below and on the next page to show what you discovered. Sample answers shown.

	What is the setting or settings for the action or descriptions in the selection?	What dangers do people face in the selection?
Earthquake Terror	Magpie Island, in California **(2.5 Points)**	Jonathan and Abby are stranded on Magpie Island when an earthquake strikes, toppling trees all around them. **(2.5)**
Eye of the Storm	Tucson, Arizona and Tornado Alley (Amarillo, Texas and towns in Texas, Oklahoma and Kansas) **(2.5)**	Warren Faidley faces danger from lightning bolts and spiders while photographing from an underpass. He and Tom Willett face danger from tornadoes forming around them in Tornado Alley. **(2.5)**
Volcanoes	Hawaii, Washington state, Iceland, Guatemala, California, Oregon **(2.5)**	People face danger from the eruption of Mount St. Helens; people on the island of Heimaey, Iceland, face danger from a volcano; people in Hawaii face danger to their houses from quick-moving lava. **(2.5)**

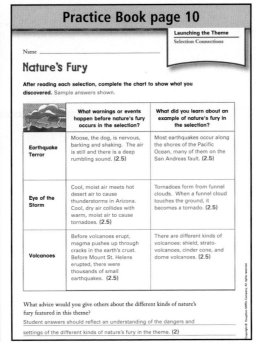

Practice Book page 10

Launching the Theme
Selection Connections

Name _____

Nature's Fury

After reading each selection, complete the chart to show what you discovered. Sample answers shown.

	What warnings or events happen before nature's fury occurs in the selection?	What did you learn about an example of nature's fury in the selection?
Earthquake Terror	Moose, the dog, is nervous, barking and shaking. The air is still and there is a deep rumbling sound. **(2.5)**	Most earthquakes occur along the shores of the Pacific Ocean, many of them on the San Andreas fault. **(2.5)**
Eye of the Storm	Cool, moist air meets hot desert air to cause thunderstorms in Arizona. Cool, dry air collides with warm, moist air to cause tornadoes. **(2.5)**	Tornadoes form from funnel clouds. When a funnel cloud touches the ground, it becomes a tornado. **(2.5)**
Volcanoes	Before volcanoes erupt, magma pushes up through cracks in the earth's crust. Before Mount St. Helens erupted, there were thousands of small earthquakes. **(2.5)**	There are different kinds of volcanoes: shield, strato-volcanoes, cinder cone, and dome volcanoes. **(2.5)**

What advice would you give others about the different kinds of nature's fury featured in this theme?
Student answers should reflect an understanding of the dangers and settings of the different kinds of nature's fury in the theme. **(2)**

Monitoring Student Progress

End-of-Selection Assessment

Selection Test Use the test on page 117 in the **Teacher's Resource Blackline Masters** to assess selection comprehension and vocabulary.

Student Self-Assessment Have students assess their reading with additional questions such as

- What parts of the selection were difficult for me? Why?

- What strategies helped me understand the selection?

- Would I recommend this selection to my friends? Why?

Responding 101

Folktale Link

Skill: How to Read a Folktale

- **Introduce** "The Princess and the Warrior," a traditional folktale from Mexico.

- **Discuss** the Skill Lesson on Anthology page 102. Remind students that folktales are stories that explain how something came to be.

- **Model** how to identify what this folktale explains and write it on the board in a chart like the one below.

- **Explain** that folktales feature simple characters who represent ideals or types, rather than real people.

- **Set a purpose** for reading. Have students read "The Princess and the Warrior" and decide which characters are good and which are bad. Have them add their responses to their charts.

Folktale Title: "The Princess and the Warrior"

What It Explains: how the volcanoes Ixtaccihuatl and Popocatépetl came to be

How It Explains This: tells a sad love story about a brave warrior and a princess who are transformed into volcanoes

Characters

Good:	Bad:
emperor, princess, brave warrior	jealous warrior

Vocabulary

beloved much loved

brutal violent and ugly

Genre

Folktales

Skill: How to Read a Folktale

❶ Notice that the **characters** are simple — good or bad, wise or foolish.

❷ Notice that the **action** moves quickly, in brief episodes.

❸ Look for information about the **country** the folktale comes from.

THE PRINCESS AND

A Mexican Folktale

Not far from Mexico City, two mountains, only five miles apart, rise more than 17,000 feet into the sky. One is an inactive volcano, Ixtaccihuatl (ees-tah-SEE-wah-tul). Its outline is said to resemble that of a sleeping woman. The other is Popocatépetl (poh-puh-CAT-uh-pet-ul), an active volcano that regularly sends up clouds of smoke and ash. This ancient Mexican folktale tells the story of how the two companion volcanoes came to be.

Many centuries ago, there was an Aztec emperor who had a good and beautiful daughter named Ixtaccihuatl.

One day the emperor received word that his enemies were preparing to attack his lands. He called his brave young warriors to the

102

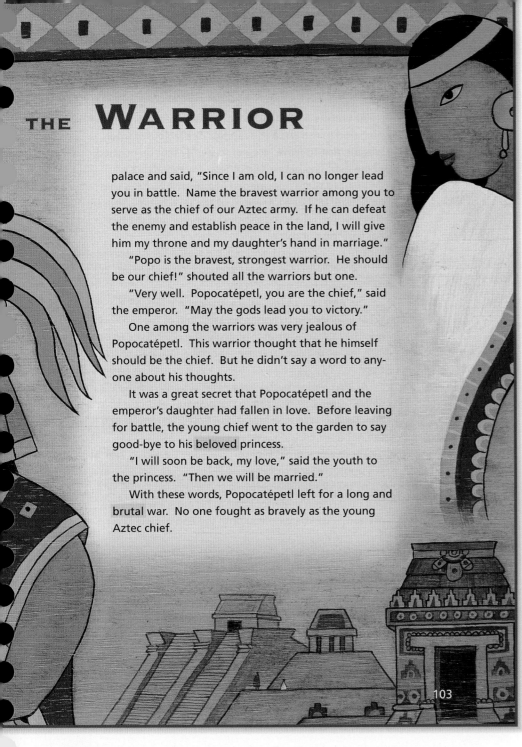

THE **WARRIOR**

palace and said, "Since I am old, I can no longer lead you in battle. Name the bravest warrior among you to serve as the chief of our Aztec army. If he can defeat the enemy and establish peace in the land, I will give him my throne and my daughter's hand in marriage."

"Popo is the bravest, strongest warrior. He should be our chief!" shouted all the warriors but one.

"Very well. Popocatépetl, you are the chief," said the emperor. "May the gods lead you to victory."

One among the warriors was very jealous of Popocatépetl. This warrior thought that he himself should be the chief. But he didn't say a word to anyone about his thoughts.

It was a great secret that Popocatépetl and the emperor's daughter had fallen in love. Before leaving for battle, the young chief went to the garden to say good-bye to his beloved princess.

"I will soon be back, my love," said the youth to the princess. "Then we will be married."

With these words, Popocatépetl left for a long and brutal war. No one fought as bravely as the young Aztec chief.

103

Extra Support/Intervention

REACHING ALL LEARNERS

Making Inferences About Folktale Characters

Help students interpret the actions of the jealous warrior. Read aloud the third complete paragraph on page 103 and discuss the warrior's refusal to support Popocatépetl as leader. Have students use this behavior to predict what the jealous warrior might do. Make sure students understand that he is the same jealous warrior who returns to the capital ahead of the other warriors after the battle.

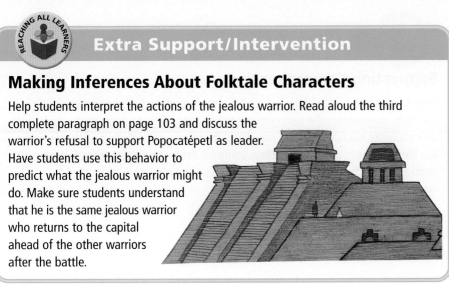

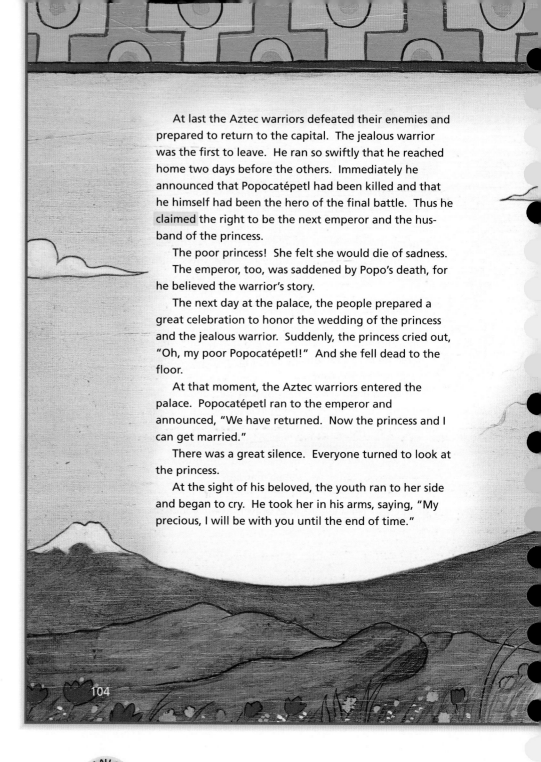

At last the Aztec warriors defeated their enemies and prepared to return to the capital. The jealous warrior was the first to leave. He ran so swiftly that he reached home two days before the others. Immediately he announced that Popocatépetl had been killed and that he himself had been the hero of the final battle. Thus he claimed the right to be the next emperor and the husband of the princess.

The poor princess! She felt she would die of sadness.

The emperor, too, was saddened by Popo's death, for he believed the warrior's story.

The next day at the palace, the people prepared a great celebration to honor the wedding of the princess and the jealous warrior. Suddenly, the princess cried out, "Oh, my poor Popocatépetl!" And she fell dead to the floor.

At that moment, the Aztec warriors entered the palace. Popocatépetl ran to the emperor and announced, "We have returned. Now the princess and I can get married."

There was a great silence. Everyone turned to look at the princess.

At the sight of his beloved, the youth ran to her side and began to cry. He took her in his arms, saying, "My precious, I will be with you until the end of time."

104

English Language Learners

Supporting Comprehension

Remind students that folktales, which tell a story, and nonfiction selections, which use facts, may explain the same information in very different ways. Invite students to suggest other folktales they are familiar with, or help students find examples from the library or from their own reading. Invite students to compare these folktales with nonfiction selections from their textbooks about the same topics.

Vocabulary

claimed declared with force

transformed changed

Then the brave chief carried her body to the highest mountains. He laid her gently in a bed of beautiful flowers and sat down beside her.

Days passed. Finally, one of the good gods transformed the warrior and the princess into two volcanoes. Ixy remains quiet. But from time to time, Popo trembles and tears of fire flow from his heart. Then all of Mexico knows that Popo is crying for his beloved princess.

105

Wrapping Up

Critical Thinking Questions

Ask students to use their charts and the selection to answer these questions.

1. **MAKING JUDGMENTS** Which characters in this folktale are good? What actions make them so? (the warrior, because he is brave and true; the princess, because she honors her father's promise and is loyal to the brave warrior)

2. **MAKING JUDGMENTS** Which character or characters are bad? Why? (the jealous warrior, because he lies and causes the princess's death)

3. **MAKING INFERENCES** According to the folktale, what is happening when Popo *trembles and tears of fire flow from his heart*? (The volcano named after him is erupting.)

4. **COMPARE AND CONTRAST** Think about the original tellers of "The Princess and the Warrior" and about Seymour Simon, the author of *Volcanoes*. How are their purposes for storytelling and writing alike? (Both try to explain how volcanoes originated and why volcanic eruptions occur.) How are their purposes different? (One uses stories while the other uses facts.)

Challenge

REACHING ALL LEARNERS

Researching Volcanoes

Have students locate the companion volcanoes Ixtaccihuatl and Popocatépetl in an atlas. Also have them look up the volcanoes in an encyclopedia or nonfiction book about volcanoes. Then ask students to write a brief profile of each volcano that includes the volcano's type, location, height, and origin.

OBJECTIVES

- Determine that writers often categorize information to make it easier for readers to understand.
- Categorize and classify information.
- Learn academic language: *categorize, classify.*

Target Skill Trace

Preview; Teach	p. 81CC; p. 84, p. 97; p. 105A
Reteach	p. R12
Review	pp. M34–M35; Theme 2, p. 217
See	*Extra Support Handbook,* pp. 36–37; pp. 42–43

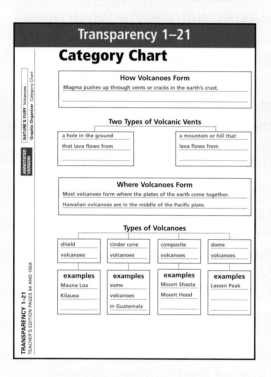

Transparency 1–21

Category Chart

How Volcanoes Form
Magma pushes up through vents or cracks in the earth's crust.

Two Types of Volcanic Vents

| a hole in the ground that lava flows from | a mountain or hill that lava flows from |

Where Volcanoes Form
Most volcanoes form where the plates of the earth come together. Hawaiian volcanoes are in the middle of the Pacific plate.

Types of Volcanoes

| shield volcanoes | cinder cone volcanoes | composite volcanoes | dome volcanoes |
| **examples** Mauna Loa Kilauea | **examples** some volcanoes in Guatemala | **examples** Mount Shasta Mount Hood | **examples** Lassen Peak |

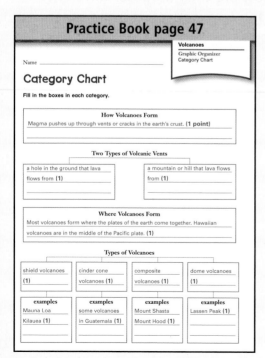

Practice Book page 47

Name

Category Chart

Fill in the boxes in each category.

How Volcanoes Form
Magma pushes up through vents or cracks in the earth's crust. **(1 point)**

Two Types of Volcanic Vents

| a hole in the ground that lava flows from **(1)** | a mountain or hill that lava flows from **(1)** |

Where Volcanoes Form
Most volcanoes form where the plates of the earth come together. Hawaiian volcanoes are in the middle of the Pacific plate. **(1)**

Types of Volcanoes

| shield volcanoes **(1)** | cinder cone volcanoes **(1)** | composite volcanoes **(1)** | dome volcanoes **(1)** |
| **examples** Mauna Loa Kilauea **(1)** | **examples** some volcanoes in Guatemala **(1)** | **examples** Mount Shasta Mount Hood **(1)** | **examples** Lassen Peak **(1)** |

COMPREHENSION: Categorize and Classify

❶ Teach

Review categorizing and classifying in *Volcanoes*. Complete the Graphic Organizer on **Transparency 1–21** with students. (Sample answers are shown.) Have students refer to the selection and to **Practice Book** page 47. Discuss these points:

- A category is group of people, animals, things, or ideas that are alike. When you categorize, you identify groups, such as Vehicles.

- When you classify, you put items in groups according to their similarities. You can classify cars and trucks in the category Vehicles.

Model categorizing and classifying to remember information. Review the four categories of volcanoes. Explain that thinking about these categories can help students remember information about volcanoes.

Think Aloud *I can remember information about different volcanoes by remembering the category in which scientists have classified it. For example, I remember that Mauna Loa has broad, gentle slopes because Mauna Loa is a shield volcano, and volcanoes in this category have broad, gentle slopes. I remember that Mount Shasta was formed by layers of lava, ashes, and cinders because it is a composite volcano, and that is how volcanoes in this category are formed.*

❷ Guided Practice

Have students classify volcanoes by the way they erupt. Ask students to complete a chart like the one below, based on selection.

Gentle Eruptions	Violent Eruptions
What they are like:	What they are like:
Lava bubbles out quietly.	Lava explodes from the cone.
Lava moves quickly or slowly.	Hot ash bursts out.
Examples:	Examples:
Mauna Loa Kilauea	Mt. St. Helens Lassen Peak

❸ Apply

Assign Practice Book pages 49–50. Also have students apply this skill as they read their **Leveled Readers** for this week. You may also select books from the Leveled Bibliography for this theme (pages 23E–23F).

Test Prep Explain that categorizing and classifying can help students remember information they read for a test. It will also help them to locate the information they need in a test passage to answer a question correctly.

Leveled Readers and Leveled Practice

Students at all levels apply the comprehension skill as they read their Leveled Readers. See lessons on pages 105O–105R.

● BELOW LEVEL   ▲ ON LEVEL   ■ ABOVE LEVEL   ◆ LANGUAGE SUPPORT

Reading Traits

As students develop the ability to categorize and classify, they are learning how to "read beyond the lines" of a selection. This comprehension skill supports the reading trait **Integrating for Synthesis**.

Practice Book page 49

Volcanoes
Comprehension Skill
Categorize and Classify

Name _____

Classifying Clouds

Read the article. Then complete the activity on page 50.

Clouds

Clouds come in a variety of forms and colors. They occur at different heights. Some are made of water and some of ice. With all these differences, a good way to identify clouds is by their groups.

Clouds are grouped by how high above the earth they are found. Low clouds are usually not more than 6,000 feet above sea level. They include stratus and stratocumulus clouds. A stratus cloud looks like a smooth sheet, while stratocumulus clouds are lumpy. They look like fluffy gray piles of cotton.

Middle clouds form between 6,000 and 20,000 feet. They include altostratus, altocumulus, and nimbostratus clouds. An altostratus cloud forms a white or gray sheet. Altocumulus clouds appear as fluffy piles that may be separated or connected in a lumpy mass. Nimbostratus clouds look like a smooth, gray layer. Rain or snow often falls from them, making them hard to see.

High clouds form above 20,000 feet. Unlike other kinds of clouds, which are made of water droplets, these clouds consist of ice crystals. Cirrus, cirrostratus, and cirrocumulus are types of high clouds. Cirrus clouds are very high in the sky and have a feathery appearance. A cirrostratus cloud is a very thin cloud layer. Cirrocumulus clouds look like millions of bits of fluff high in the sky.

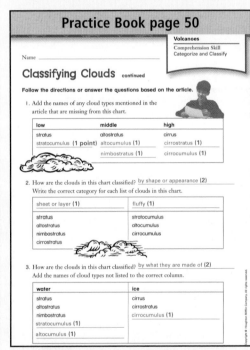

Practice Book page 50

Volcanoes
Comprehension Skill
Categorize and Classify

Name _____

Classifying Clouds continued

Follow the directions or answer the questions based on the article.

1. Add the names of any cloud types mentioned in the article that are missing from this chart.

low	middle	high
stratus	altostratus	cirrus
stratocumulus (1 point)	altocumulus (1)	cirrostratus (1)
	nimbostratus (1)	cirrocumulus (1)

2. How are the clouds in this chart classified? by shape or appearance (2)
Write the correct category for each list of clouds in this chart.

sheet or layer (1)	fluffy (1)
stratus	stratocumulus
altostratus	altocumulus
nimbostratus	cirrocumulus
cirrostratus	

3. How are the clouds in this chart classified? by what they are made of (2)
Add the names of cloud types not listed to the correct column.

water	ice
stratus	cirrus
altostratus	cirrostratus
nimbostratus	cirrocumulus (1)
stratocumulus (1)	
altocumulus (1)	

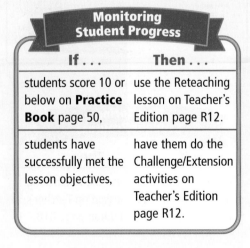

Monitoring Student Progress

If . . .	Then . . .
students score 10 or below on **Practice Book** page 50,	use the Reteaching lesson on Teacher's Edition page R12.
students have successfully met the lesson objectives,	have them do the Challenge/Extension activities on Teacher's Edition page R12.

OBJECTIVES

- Read words with the roots *rupt* and *struct*.
- Use the Phonics/Decoding Strategy to decode longer words.
- Learn academic language: *word root*.

Target Skill Trace

Teach	p. 105C
Reteach	p. R18
Review	pp. M36–M37
See	*Handbook for English Language Learners,* p. 39; *Extra Support Handbook,* pp. 34–35; pp. 38–39

Practice Book page 51

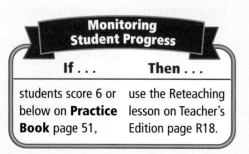

Monitoring Student Progress

If . . .	Then . . .
students score 6 or below on **Practice Book** page 51,	use the Reteaching lesson on Teacher's Edition page R18.

STRUCTURAL ANALYSIS/ VOCABULARY: Word Roots *rupt* and *struct*

❶ Teach

Introduce word roots. Explain that a word root is a part of a word that has meaning but cannot stand alone.

Explain the word root *rupt*. Write *Mount St. Helens erupted*.

- The word root *rupt* is from a Latin word that means "break" or "burst."
- The word part *e-* means "out of."
- The word *erupt* means "to burst out."

Explain the word root *struct*. Write *The lava was <u>destructive</u>*.

- The word root *struct* is from a Latin word that means "build."
- The word part *de-* means "undo."
- The word *destructive* means "unbuilding" or "destroying."

Find word roots within words. Write *abrupt* and *construction*. Have a student underline the word root in each word.

Model the Phonics/Decoding Strategy. Write *The damaged railway lines had to be <u>reconstructed</u> after the blast*. Model decoding *reconstructed*.

> **Think Aloud**
> *I recognize the word root* struct *in* reconstructed, *so I think the word has to do with building. The word describes something done to damaged railway lines. Maybe it means "rebuilt." I'll see if that makes sense in the sentence. If I'm still not sure, I'll look it up.*

❷ Guided Practice

Have students use words roots. Display the phrases below. Ask partners to decode and define the underlined words, using word roots. Have students share their work.

<u>structures</u> collapsed

<u>interrupted</u> a television show

<u>instructions</u> on where to go

<u>disrupted</u> traffic

stopped <u>abruptly</u>

<u>ruptured</u> the ground

❸ Apply

Assign Practice Book page 51.

PHONICS REVIEW:
Long Vowel Sounds /ō/, /o͞o/, and /yo͞o/

OBJECTIVES

- Read words with long vowel sounds /ō/, /o͞o/, and /yo͞o/.
- Use the Phonics/Decoding Strategy to decode longer words.

❶ Teach

Review long vowel sounds. Explain the following.

- The letters o-consonant-e, *oa, ow,* and *o* can stand for the /ō/ sound as in *show.*

- The letters u-consonant-e, *ue, ew, u, ui, ou,* and *oo* can stand for the sound /o͞o/ as in *flew.*

- The letters u-consonant-e, *ue, ew, u,* and *eau* can stand for the /yo͞o/ sound as in *skew.*

Model the Phonics/Decoding Strategy. Write *The melted, or molten, rock is called magma.* Then model how to decode *molten.*

Think Aloud *I see the vowel* o *in this word. If I try the short o sound, I get* MAHL-ten. *That doesn't sound right. I know that* o *can also have long vowel sound. I'll try that:* MOHL-ten. *That sounds like a word I've heard, and it makes sense in the sentence.*

❷ Guided Practice

Help students identify long vowel sounds. Display the sentences below. Have students circle the long vowel sounds in each underlined word, pronounce the word, and see if it makes sense in the sentence. Have individuals model at the board.

1. Lava began <u>flowing</u> down the mountainside.

2. There was another <u>episode</u> of rumbling.

3. The volcano was <u>spewing</u> ash.

4. In a few short months, life <u>renews</u> itself.

❸ Apply

Have students find long vowel sounds. Ask students to decode these words from *Volcanoes* and discuss their meanings.

through	p. 86	billow	p. 92	dome	p. 96
smoke	p. 90	strato-volcanoes	p. 95	soda	p. 96
explosion	p. 90	slowly	p. 95	nowhere	p. 98

Phonics/Decoding Strategy

When you come to a word you don't know—

❶ Look carefully at the word.

❷ Look for word parts you know and think about the sounds for the letters.

❸ Blend the sounds to read the word.

❹ Ask yourself: Is it a word I know? Does it make sense in what I am reading?

❺ If not, ask yourself: What else can I try?

HOUGHTON MIFFLIN
Reading

SPELLING: /ō/, /o͞o/, and /yo͞o/

OBJECTIVES

- Write Spelling Words with long vowel patterns.

SPELLING WORDS

Basic

thrown*	mood
stole	loaf
clue*	growth*
dew	youth
choose	slope*
rule	bruise
boast	loose
cruise	rude
stroll	flow*
route	flute

Review	Challenge
group*	subdue
goal	pursuit
fruit	molten*
blew*	reproach
broke*	presume

Forms of these words appear in the literature.

Extra Support/Intervention

Basic Word List You may want to use only the left column of Basic Words with students who need extra support.

Challenge

Challenge Word Practice Have students make rebus puzzles, using both small drawings and word parts, for the Challenge Words. Ask them to trade papers and solve their partners' puzzles.

DAY 1 INSTRUCTION

/ō/, /o͞o/, and /yo͞o/

Pretest Use the Day 5 Test sentences.

Teach Write these Basic Words on the board in two columns: (1) *stole, boast, thrown, stroll;* (2) *rule, clue, dew, choose, cruise, route.*

- Say each word in the first column. Have students repeat the words and identify the vowel sound. (/ō/)

- Explain that the long o sound can be spelled o-consonant-e, *oa, ow,* or *o.* Underline: *ole* in *stole, oa* in *boast, ow* in *thrown, o* in *stroll.*

- Repeat the process with column 2. After students identify the vowel sounds (/o͞o/ or /yo͞o/), underline and discuss the spelling patterns: *u-consonant-e, ue, ew, oo, ui, ou.*

- Add symbols to the column heads: (1) /ō/ and (2) /o͞o/ or /yo͞o/. Then say the remaining Basic Words. Have students name the vowel sounds. Write the words in the columns.

Practice/Homework Assign **Practice Book** page 267.

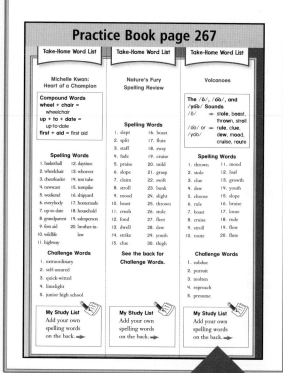

DAY 2 REVIEW & PRACTICE

Reviewing the Principle

Go over the spelling patterns for /ō/, /o͞o/, and /yo͞o/ sounds with students.

Practice/Homework Assign **Practice Book** page 52.

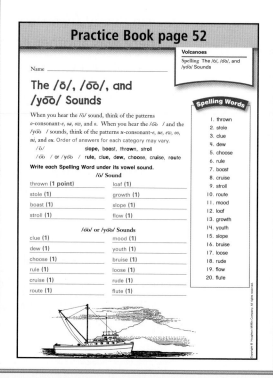

Take-Home Word List

Exact Words

Write the following sentence pairs on the board. Select students to tell which underlined word in each pair is more exact and why.

– I can play the <u>flute</u>.
  I can play an <u>instrument</u>.

– They like to <u>talk</u> about their grades.
  They like to <u>boast</u> about their grades.

– We took a <u>walk</u> through the park.
  We took a <u>stroll</u> through the park.

– Rivers <u>flow</u> to the ocean.
  Rivers <u>go</u> to the ocean.

(The words *flute, boast, stroll, flow* are more exact. Sample explanation: They paint clearer pictures.)

- List the Basic Words on the board, and have students use each Basic Word orally in a sentence.

Practice/Homework For spelling practice, assign **Practice Book** page 53.

Game: What's the Question?

Tell pairs of students to make a word card for each list word and stack the cards face-down. Explain these game rules:

- Player 1 draws a card and gives a clue for the word on it. The clue must be a statement, such as "It might be black and blue."

- Player 2 tries to earn a point by asking a question that includes the spelling word and by spelling the word correctly (For example, "What is a bruise? b-r-u-i-s-e").

- Players take turns, and the one who ends the game with more points wins.

Practice/Homework For proofreading and writing practice, assign **Practice Book** page 54.

Spelling Test

Say each underlined word, read the sentence, and then repeat the word. Have students write only the underlined word.

Basic Words

1. The pitcher has **thrown** a fastball.
2. Someone **stole** the book.
3. We need a **clue** to guess the secret word.
4. The grass is wet with **dew**.
5. I will **choose** two books from this list.
6. This class has a **rule** against shouting.
7. Do not **boast** about your score.
8. Shall we **cruise** around the block?
9. Let's **stroll** through the park.
10. What **route** do you take to school?
11. I am in a happy **mood** today.
12. Please buy a **loaf** of bread.
13. The city's **growth** has been quick.
14. My mother looked like me in her **youth**.
15. The seats **slope** down to the field.
16. I got a **bruise** when I bumped the table.
17. Tighten the lid so that it is not **loose**.
18. It is **rude** to talk back to someone.
19. Which way does the river **flow**?
20. Jane plays the **flute** in the band.

Challenge Words

21. Please **subdue** the crowd.
22. The judge is in **pursuit** of the truth.
23. Steam rose from the **molten** lead.
24. Do not **reproach** them for being late.
25. I **presume** that you are ready for the test.

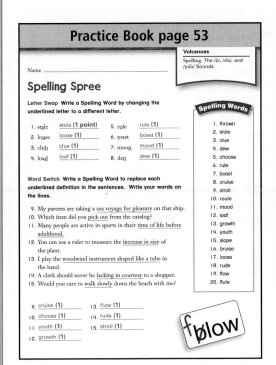

Practice Book page 53

Spelling Spree

Letter Swap Write a Spelling Word by changing the underlined letter to a different letter.

1. sta<u>l</u>e — stole (1 point)
2. lo<u>u</u>se — loose (1)
3. cl<u>u</u>b — clue (1)
4. lo<u>a</u>d — loaf (1)
5. r<u>o</u>le — rule (1)
6. <u>t</u>oast — boast (1)
7. mo<u>o</u>n — mood (1)
8. d<u>e</u>n — dew (1)

Word Switch Write a Spelling Word to replace each underlined definition in the sentences. Write your words on the lines.

9. My parents are taking a <u>sea voyage for pleasure</u> on that ship. — cruise (1)
10. Which item did you <u>pick out</u> from the catalog? — choose (1)
11. Many people are active in sports in their <u>time of life before adulthood</u>. — youth (1)
12. You can use a ruler to measure the <u>increase in size</u> of the plant. — growth (1)
13. I play the <u>woodwind instrument shaped like a tube</u> in the band. — flute (1)
14. A clerk should never be <u>lacking in courtesy</u> to a shopper. — rude (1)
15. Would you care to <u>walk slowly</u> down the beach with me? — stroll (1)

Spelling Words
1. thrown
2. stole
3. clue
4. dew
5. choose
6. rule
7. boast
8. cruise
9. stroll
10. route
11. mood
12. loaf
13. growth
14. youth
15. slope
16. bruise
17. loose
18. rude
19. flow
20. flute

Practice Book page 54

Proofreading and Writing

Proofreading Circle the five misspelled Spelling Words in this paragraph from a personal narrative. Then write each word correctly.

Our (roote) led us up the side of the volcano. We had just reached an old area of lava (flo) when we heard a rumbling noise from above. Hikers ahead of us on the trail had knocked some rocks loose! The avalanche was heading down the (sloap) of the mountain, straight for us. In the rush to reach safety, I tripped and was (thron) off the trail. Luckily, the mass of rocks passed me by, and all I got was a (bruise) on my leg.

1. route (2 points)
2. flow (2)
3. slope (2)
4. thrown (2)
5. bruise (2)

Spelling Words
1. thrown
2. stole
3. clue
4. dew
5. choose
6. rule
7. boast
8. cruise
9. stroll
10. route
11. mood
12. loaf
13. growth
14. youth
15. slope
16. bruise
17. loose
18. rude
19. flow
20. flute

Write a List of Safety Tips What safety tips would it be good to keep in mind when exploring a volcano?

On a separate sheet of paper, list some tips for volcano explorers. Use Spelling Words from the list. Responses will vary. (5 points)

SPELLING

Volcanoes

Spelling **105F**

OBJECTIVES

- Use definitions to understand the meaning of entry words in a dictionary.
- Use sample phrases or sentences to understand how entry words are used in context.
- Learn academic language: *entry word, definition, context.*

Target Skill Trace

Teach	p. 105G
Extend	p. R19
Review	pp. M38–M39
See	*Handbook for English Language Learners,* p. 43

Transparency 1–22

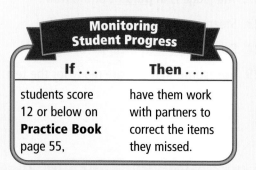

Graphic Aids

Table

Six Active Volcanoes of the Aleutian Islands

Volcano Name	Height in Meters	Date of Last Eruption*	Number of Recorded Eruptions
Akutan	1,303	1989	32
Makushin	2,036	1987	20
Okmok	1,072	1988	18
Pavlof	2,519	1988	41
Shishaldin	2,856	1987	35
Trident	1,864	1968	15

*As of 2000

Graph

Number of Recorded Eruptions of Six Aleutian Volcanoes

Akutan Makushin Okmok Pavlof Shishaldin Trident

NATURE'S FURY Volcanoes
Information and Study Skills Graphic Aids
ANNOTATED VERSION

TRANSPARENCY 1–23
TEACHER'S EDITION PAGE 105H

Monitoring Student Progress

If . . .	Then . . .
students score 12 or below on **Practice Book** page 55,	have them work with partners to correct the items they missed.

VOCABULARY: Dictionary Definitions

TARGET SKILL

❶ Teach

Explain dictionary entries. Tell students that in a dictionary, each entry word shows the following information:

- a phonetic respelling that tells how to pronounce the word
- an abbreviation that tells what part of speech the word is
- a definition, or statement that explains the word's meaning
- a sample sentence that shows how the word is used in context

Display Transparency 1–22. Cover the lower part, showing only the dictionary entry for *destructive.*

- Point out the phonetic respelling and the part of speech.
- Point out the definition. Read it aloud.
- Point out the italicized sentence that follows the definition. Read it aloud.

Model how to use a dictionary entry. Uncover the dictionary entry for *eruption* on **Transparency 1–22,** and model how to figure out its meaning.

Think Aloud *I see the definition for* eruption: *"The act of forcing out or releasing violently." I'm having a little trouble understanding what that means. Maybe the sample sentence can help. It says,* With the eruption of the geyser, steam shot out of the ground. *An eruption is when something shoots up or bursts out.*

❷ Guided Practice

Give students practice in finding definitions. Display the rest of **Transparency 1–22.** Have students work in pairs to figure out the meaning of each word. Ask them to discuss how the sample sentences helped them.

❸ Apply

Assign Practice Book page 55.

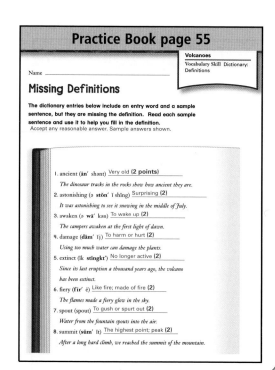

Practice Book page 55

Volcanoes
Vocabulary Skill Dictionary: Definitions

Name _____

Missing Definitions

The dictionary entries below include an entry word and a sample sentence, but they are missing the definition. Read each sample sentence and use it to help you fill in the definition.
Accept any reasonable answer. Sample answers shown.

1. ancient (ān' shənt) Very old **(2 points)** _____
   The dinosaur tracks in the rocks show how ancient they are.
2. astonishing (ə stŏn' ĭ shĭng) Surprising **(2)** _____
   It was astonishing to see it snowing in the middle of July.
3. awaken (ə wā' kən) To wake up **(2)** _____
   The campers awaken at the first light of dawn.
4. damage (dăm' ĭj) To harm or hurt **(2)** _____
   Using too much water can damage the plants.
5. extinct (ĭk stĭngkt') No longer active **(2)** _____
   Since its last eruption a thousand years ago, the volcano has been extinct.
6. fiery (fīr' ē) Like fire; made of fire **(2)** _____
   The flames made a fiery glow in the sky.
7. spout (spout) To gush or spurt out **(2)** _____
   Water from the fountain spouts into the air.
8. summit (sŭm' ĭt) The highest point; peak **(2)** _____
   After a long hard climb, we reached the summit of the mountain.

STUDY SKILL: Using Graphic Aids

OBJECTIVES

- Use a table to find information.
- Use a graph to find information.
- Locate sites and interpret information on a map.
- Learn academic language: *compass rose, map key, map scale, political maps, specialized maps.*

❶ Teach

Introduce maps and globes.

- Display a flat map. Discuss these map features: a **compass rose** for showing compass directions; a **map key** for showing the meaning of symbols; and a **map scale** for showing distance.

- Explain that **political maps** show countries, states, and cities.

- Explain that **specialized maps** show population, rainfall, and so on. Discuss the specialized map on Anthology page 89.

- Compare a flat map of the world with a globe. Invite volunteers to trace the same route on each.

Display Transparency 1–23 and model finding information in tables.

- Point out the table, or chart. Explain that a table lists information about two or more things. Read the title.

- Read the column headings. Explain what each column shows.

- Model finding the number of times Okmok has erupted. (18)

- Model the height of Shishaldin. (2,856 meters)

Use Transparency 1–23 to model finding information in graphs.

- Point out the bar graph. Note that it shows the same information as in the last column of the table. Read the title. Explain that a bar graph helps readers compare amounts.

- Model finding the number of times Akutan has erupted. (32)

- Model finding which volcano has erupted the most times (Pavlof) and which has erupted the fewest times. (Trident)

❷ Practice/Apply

Give students practice in using graphic aids.

- Have students use **Transparency 1–23** to answer these questions: Which volcano has the second highest number of eruptions? Which volcano is the tallest? Which has erupted most recently?

- Have partners research five volcanoes. Have them put a dot and a name on a blank world map to show the location of each volcano.

- Have partners create a table or chart that shows this information about each volcano: its name, its location, and its height.

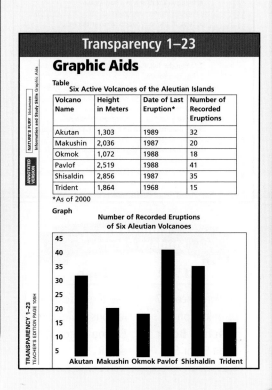

Transparency 1–23

Graphic Aids

Table
Six Active Volcanoes of the Aleutian Islands

Volcano Name	Height in Meters	Date of Last Eruption*	Number of Recorded Eruptions
Akutan	1,303	1989	32
Makushin	2,036	1987	20
Okmok	1,072	1988	18
Pavlof	2,519	1988	41
Shisaldin	2,856	1987	35
Trident	1,864	1968	15

*As of 2000

Graph

Number of Recorded Eruptions of Six Aleutian Volcanoes

GRAMMAR: Singular/Plural Nouns

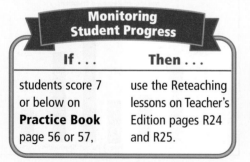

OBJECTIVES

- Identify singular nouns.
- Identify plural nouns.
- Determine the plural forms of nouns with regular and irregular plurals.
- Proofread and correct sentences with grammar and spelling errors.
- Replace general nouns with specific nouns to improve writing.
- Learn academic language: *singular nouns, plural nouns, exact nouns.*

DAY 1 INSTRUCTION

Singular/Plural Nouns

Teach Go over these rules:

- A noun names a person, place, thing, or idea.
- To form the plural of most nouns, add -s or -es.
- To form the plural of a noun ending with x, s, ch, sh, or ss, add -es.
- To form the plural of a noun ending with a consonant + y, change the y to i and add -es.
- To form the plural of a noun ending in a vowel + y, add -s.

- Display **Transparency 1–25.** Ask volunteers to find plural nouns in the four sentences at the top to illustrate each rule.
- Ask other students to write the plurals of singular nouns in the sentences and tell which rule each plural illustrates. Have them give other examples of plural nouns.

Daily Language Practice
Have students correct Sentences 1 and 2 on **Transparency 1–24.**

DAY 2 PRACTICE

Independent Work

Practice/Homework Assign **Practice Book** page 56.

Daily Language Practice
Have students correct Sentences 3 and 4 on **Transparency 1–24.**

Transparency 1–24

Daily Language Practice

Correct two sentences each day.

1. The boxs were thron out by mistake.
   The boxes were thrown out by mistake.
2. In my yuth I loved storys about dragons.
   In my youth I loved stories about dragons.
3. Why do i chuse to wear my red hat every day?
   Why do I choose to wear my red hat every day?
4. being sick puts me in a bad moud.
   Being sick puts me in a bad mood.
5. Look at the loos peachs all over the road!
   Look at the loose peaches all over the road!
6. The two thiefs stoal all the food in the kitchen.
   The two thieves stole all the food in the kitchen.
7. When she fell, Pam got a bruse on her knee and lost two tooths.
   When she fell, Pam got a bruise on her knee and lost two teeth.
8. The cruse was filled with relaxed mans and women.
   The cruise was filled with relaxed men and women.
9. My parents love to bost about their three childs.
   My parents love to boast about their three children.
10. The five womans took a stroal along the bank of the river.
    The five women took a stroll along the bank of the river.

Monitoring Student Progress

If . . .	Then . . .
students score 7 or below on **Practice Book** page 56 or 57,	use the Reteaching lessons on Teacher's Edition pages R24 and R25.

Transparency 1–25

Singular and Plural Nouns

The forest stretched between two deep valleys.
singular noun forest/plural noun valleys
Slim birches grew beside an eddy in the stream.
singular nouns eddy, stream/plural noun birches
The hiker had an impulse to make a sketch of the ferns and mosses.
singular nouns hiker, impulse, sketch/plural nouns ferns, mosses
A bear was eating wild blackberries while a bluejay scolded him.
singular nouns bear, bluejay/plural noun blackberries

- A noun names a person, place, thing, or idea.
  plural nouns valleys, birches, ferns, mosses, blackberries
- To form the plural of most nouns, add -s or -es.
  plural nouns valleys, birches, ferns, mosses; singular nouns to plural forests, streams, hikers, impulses, bears, bluejays
- To form the plural of a noun ending with x, s, ch, sh, or ss, add -es.
  plural nouns birches, mosses; singular noun to plural sketches
- To form the plural of a noun ending with a consonant + y, change the y to i and add -es.
  eddies, blackberries; singular noun to plural eddies
- To form the plural of a noun ending with a vowel + y, add -s.
  valleys; singular noun to plural bluejays

Additional plural nouns will vary.

Practice Book page 56

Volcanoes
Grammar Skill Singular and Plural Nouns

Name _____

Finding Your Way

Singular and Plural Nouns A **singular noun** names one person, one place, one thing, or one idea. A **plural noun** names more than one person, place, thing, or idea. To decide how to form a plural, look at the end of the singular noun. Here are four rules to study:

1. To most singular nouns, add -s to form the plural.
2. If a singular noun ends in s, ss, x, ch, or sh, add -es to form the plural.
3. For singular nouns ending with a vowel plus y, add -s to form the plural.
4. If a singular noun ends in a consonant plus y, change the y to i and add -es.

| bench |
| table |
| tree |
| fox |
| fireplace |
| tent |
| daisy |
| bush |
| bus |
| pathway |

Conrad and Carmen have drawn a map of a campground they are visiting. Label each landmark on the map with a plural noun. Use nouns from the list. (1 point each)

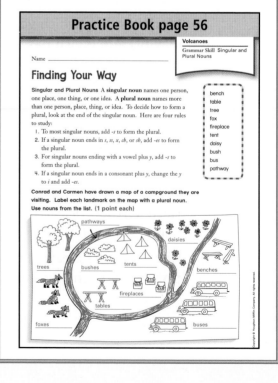

105I **THEME 1: Nature's Fury**

DAY 3 INSTRUCTION

More Plural Nouns

Teach Go over these rules:

- – In some nouns that end in *f* or *fe*, the *f* changes to a *v* before *-s* or *-es* is added.

- – In nouns that end in *o*, the plural may be formed by adding either *-s* or *-es*.

- – Some nouns have plural forms that do not end in *-s* or *-es*.

- – Some nouns have the same singular and plural form.

- Display **Transparency 1–26.** Have students identify plural nouns in the sentence at the top, noting which one does not end in *-s* or *-es*.

- Ask volunteers to identify the plural nouns in Sentences 1–7 and tell which rule each noun illustrates. Have students think of other plural nouns that follow each rule.

Daily Language Practice
Have students correct Sentences 5 and 6 on **Transparency 1–24.**

Transparency 1–26

More Plural Nouns

All the children had their own guidebooks. plural nouns *children, guidebooks; Children* does not end in *-s* or *-es*.

- In some nouns that end in *f* or *fe*, the *f* changes to a *v* before *-s* or *-es* is added.

- In nouns that end in *o*, the plural may be formed by adding either *-s* or *-es*.

- Some nouns have plural forms that do not end in *-s* or *-es*.

- Some nouns have the same singular and plural form.

1. There are many active volcanoes in the world. rule: Nouns that end in *o* add *-s* or *-es*.

2. Volcanic eruptions usually happen where plates of the earth's crust meet. rule: Add *-s* or *-es* to most nouns.

3. These sections are like the broken halves of a dish. rules: Add *-s* or *-es* to most nouns; change *f* to *v* before adding *-s* or *-es*.

4. Undersea volcanoes that explode can form new islands. rule: Nouns that end in *o* add *-s* or *-es*; add *-s* or *-es* to most nouns.

5. Many people are fascinated by these natural formations. rules: Some plural nouns do not end in *-s* or *-es*; add *-s* or *-es* to most nouns.

6. Pieces of volcanic rock may be sold as mementos. rules: Add *-s* or *-es* to most nouns; nouns that end in *o* add *-s* or *-es*.

7. The lives of animals such as wolves, moose, deer, and bears are affected by volcanic eruptions. rules: Change *f* to *v* before adding *-s* or *-es*; add *-s* or *-es* to most nouns; some nouns have the same singular and plural form.

Additional plural nouns will vary.

DAY 4 PRACTICE

Independent Work

Practice/Homework Assign **Practice Book** page 57.

Daily Language Practice
Have students correct Sentences 7 and 8 on **Transparency 1–24.**

Practice Book page 57

Volcanoes
Grammar Skill More Plural Nouns

Name _____

Science Fair

More Plural Nouns Here are a few more rules for forming plurals:

1. To form the plural of some nouns ending in *f* or *fe*, change the *f* to *v* and add *-es*. For others ending in *f*, simply add *-s*.
2. To form the plural of nouns ending with a vowel plus *o*, add *-s*.
3. To form the plural of nouns ending with a consonant plus *o*, add *-s* or *-es*.
4. Some nouns have special plural forms.
5. Some nouns are the same in the singular and the plural.

For the science fair, Jody made a model of the volcano Mount Saint Helens and wrote a report about it. Jody isn't sure how to form the plural of some words in her report. She made a list of these words.

Write the plural next to each word on Jody's list. Check your dictionary if you are unsure of a plural.

leaf	leaves **(1 point)**
child	children **(1)**
volcano	volcanoes **(1)**
man	men **(1)**
ash	ashes **(1)**
home	homes **(1)**
deer	deer **(1)**
woman	women **(1)**
plant	plants **(1)**
mouse	mice **(1)**

DAY 5 IMPROVING WRITING

Exact Nouns

Teach Tell students that a good writer uses specific singular or plural nouns rather than general ones in a description or an explanation.

- Model replacing general nouns with exact ones:

  - – We saw a lot of animals on our trip to British Columbia.

  - – *Improved:* We saw <u>several moose, a herd of buffalo, three bighorn sheep, and a pack of wolves</u> on our trip to British Columbia.

- Have students review a piece of their own writing to see if they can improve it by replacing general nouns with exact nouns.

Practice/Homework Assign **Practice Book** page 58.

Daily Language Practice
Have students correct Sentences 9 and 10 on **Transparency 1–24.**

Practice Book page 58

Volcanoes
Writing Skill Using Exact Nouns

Name _____

Roaming Through the Woods

Using Exact Nouns You can make your writing more lively and interesting by replacing general nouns with more specific ones. Here is an example of writing with a general noun:

For my birthday, I received **several things**.

A reader does not know what the person received. Here is the same sentence revised to use more specific nouns:

For my birthday, I received **a book** about sports legends, a basketball, and basketball shoes.

Read the following paragraph. Revise the general nouns in bold type by replacing them with a more specific noun from the box. (1 point each)

> a rabbit
> dragonfly
> maples and oaks
> Duck Pond
> minnows
> peanut butter
> sandwiches
> my ankles
> mint
> bark
> sneakers

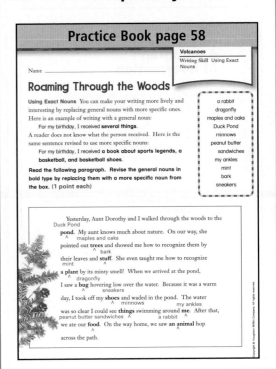

Yesterday, Aunt Dorothy and I walked through the woods to the **Duck Pond** **pond.** My aunt knows much about nature. On our way, she pointed out **trees** and showed me how to recognize them by **maples and oaks** their leaves and **stuff**. She even taught me how to recognize **bark** **a plant** by its minty smell! When we arrived at the pond, **mint** I saw a **bug** hovering low over the water. Because it was a warm **dragonfly** day, I took off my **shoes** and waded in the pond. The water **sneakers** was so clear I could see **things** swimming around me. After that, **minnows** **my ankles** we ate our **food**. On the way home, we saw **an animal** hop **peanut butter sandwiches** **a rabbit** across the path.

WRITING: Paragraph of Information

OBJECTIVES

- Identify the characteristics of a good paragraph of information.
- Write a paragraph of information.
- Improve writing by correcting sentence fragments.
- Learn academic language: *topic, topic sentence, supporting details.*

Writing Traits

Conventions As you teach the lesson on Day 3, emphasize the importance of conventions. Discuss these points:

- Conventions make it easier for others to read what you have written.
- Paying attention to capitalization, punctuation, spelling, and usage is part of making your ideas clear.

DAY 1 PREWRITING

Introducing the Format

Introduce paragraphs of information.

- A paragraph of information gives facts.
- Tell students that they can write a paragraph to share facts they have learned.

Start students thinking about writing an informational paragraph.

- Remind students that they learned many facts about volcanoes and volcanic eruptions.
- Ask students to list three topics about volcanoes for an informational paragraph.
- They might write about one of the volcanoes in *Volcanoes* or about a certain type of volcano.
- Have them save their notes.

DAY 2 DRAFTING

Discussing the Model

Display Transparency 1–27. Ask:

- What is the topic of the paragraph? (Mauna Loa)
- Which sentence states the topic? (the first sentence.)
- What information do the supporting sentences give about Mauna Loa? (size, eruptions, how it was formed)

Discuss fact and opinion.

- An informational paragraph should include only facts, not opinions.
- Facts can be proven. Opinions tell how the writer thinks or feels.

Display Transparency 1–28 and discuss the guidelines.

Have students draft a paragraph of information.

- They should write about volcanoes, using their prewriting notes from Day 1.
- Assign **Practice Book** page 59 to help students organize their writing.
- Provide support as needed.

Transparency 1–27

A Paragraph of Information

Mauna Loa is located on the big island of Hawaii. It is the world's largest active volcano, rising more than 13,000 feet above sea level. Mauna Loa has a long history of volcanic activity. In 1855 and 1856, it erupted continuously for eighteen months. In 1926, lava from an eruption destroyed a fishing village. In 1950, the city of Hilo was threatened by a river of lava, which stopped only four miles from the city. Mauna Loa continues to erupt every few years, and as it erupts, it continues to grow. Thousands of overlapping lava flows have dried one atop another to form Mauna Loa.

NATURE'S FURY *Volcanoes*
Writing Skill A Paragraph of Information
ANNOTATED VERSION

TRANSPARENCY 1–27
TEACHER'S EDITION PAGE 105K

Transparency 1–28

Guidelines for Writing a Paragraph of Information

- Select an interesting topic that you know something about.
- Include a topic sentence that tells what the whole paragraph is about. The topic sentence is usually the first sentence in the paragraph.
- Include several supporting sentences that give more information about the topic. Make sure your sentences are in a logical order.
- Leave out any sentences that don't give more information about your topic.
- Include facts only — don't include your opinions.
- Remember to indent the first sentence of the paragraph.

NATURE'S FURY *Volcanoes*
Writing Skill Paragraph of Information
ANNOTATED VERSION

TRANSPARENCY 1–28
TEACHER'S EDITION PAGE 105K

Practice Book page 59

Name _____

Volcanoes
Writing Skill Paragraph of Information

Writing a Paragraph of Information

Read the following paragraph of information from page 87 of *Volcanoes*.

Volcanoes are formed by cracks or holes that poke through the earth's crust. Magma pushes its way up through the cracks. This is called a volcanic eruption. When magma pours onto the surface it is called lava. . . . As lava cools, it hardens to form rock.

Now get ready to write your own paragraph of information about volcanoes. Use the following graphic organizer to help you organize your paragraph. (5 points)

Topic

Topic Sentence

Supporting Sentences

Now, write your paragraph of information on a separate sheet of paper. Arrange your supporting sentences in a logical order, and make sure all of the sentences contain facts about the topic. (5 points)

DAY 3 REVISING

Evaluating to Revise

Display Transparency 1–28 again.

- Ask students to use the guidelines to decide how to make their writing better. Encourage students to turn each point into a question: "Did I...?"
- Students may work with a partner in a writing conference.
- Ask students to revise any parts of their writing that still need work.

Transparency 1–29

TRANSPARENCY 1–29
TEACHER'S EDITION PAGE 105L

ANNOTATED VERSION

NATURE'S FURY Volcanoes
Writing Skill Improving Your Writing

Correcting Sentence Fragments

Italy's Mount Vesuvius. One of the world's most famous volcanoes. Its best-known eruption occurred on August 24, A.D. 79. On that day, a violent explosion of rocks, ash, and lava. A river of lava swiftly buried the cities that lay beneath. In the centuries that followed, many destructive eruptions occurred. People around the world, fascinated by Vesuvius. In the early part of the twentieth century, thousands of visitors came to Vesuvius each year for a firsthand look at flowing lava. A cable railway. Took visitors down into the cone. There they could view a red stream of glowing lava. The cable railway was destroyed in 1944 by an eruption. Vesuvius has been frequently studied by scientists. Because it erupts often and is easy to reach. In fact, Vesuvius is the most carefully studied volcano in the world.

Answers will vary. Sample answers shown.

Italy's Mount Vesuvius is one of the world's most famous volcanoes. Its best-known eruption occurred on August 24, A.D. 79. On that day, a violent explosion of rocks, ash, and lava spewed from the volcano. A river of lava swiftly buried the cities that lay beneath. In the centuries that followed, many destructive eruptions occurred. People around the world were fascinated by Vesuvius. In the early part of the twentieth century, thousands of visitors came to Vesuvius each year for a firsthand look at flowing lava. A cable railway took visitors down into the cone. There they could view a red stream of glowing lava. The cable railway was destroyed in 1944 by an eruption. Vesuvius has been frequently studied by scientists because it erupts often and is easy to reach. In fact, Vesuvius is the most carefully studied volcano in the world.

DAY 4 PROOFREADING

Improving Writing: Correcting Sentence Fragments

Review complete sentences.

- A complete sentence has a subject that tells who or what the sentence is about.
- It also has a predicate that tells what the subject did or what the subject is like.
- A sentence fragment lacks a subject or a predicate.

Display Transparency 1–29.

- Underline the first two sentence fragments. (Italy's Mount Vesuvius; One of the world's most famous volcanoes.)
- Model rewriting these as one complete sentence. (Italy's Mount Vesuvius is one of the world's most famous volcanoes.)
- Have volunteers identify the remaining fragments and rewrite each as a complete sentence.

Assign Practice Book page 60.

- Have students review their paragraphs of information, correcting any sentence fragments and proofreading for other errors.
- See Writing Traits on this page.

Practice Book page 60

Name _____

Volcanoes
Writing Skill Improving Your Writing

Correcting Sentence Fragments

A sentence fragment is a group of words that is missing either a subject or a predicate. The following groups of words are sentence fragments. Turn them into complete sentences by adding either a subject or a predicate. Write the complete sentence on the lines. Responses will vary.

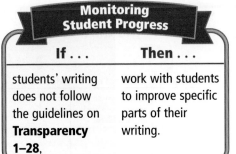

1. Many of the world's active volcanoes.
   Many of the world's active volcanoes are destructive. **(3 points)**

2. Clouds of hot ash.
   Clouds of hot ash fill the air. **(3)**

3. Buries plants and animals.
   Quick-moving lava buries plants and animals. **(3)**

4. The blast of an eruption.
   The blast of an eruption topples trees and buildings. **(3)**

5. Are seriously injured or killed.
   Hundreds of people are seriously injured or killed. **(3)**

DAY 5 PUBLISHING

Sharing Paragraphs of Information

Consider these publishing options.

- Ask students to read their informational paragraphs or some other piece of writing from the Author's Chair.
- Encourage students to create a class book about volcanoes.

Portfolio Opportunity

Save students' informational paragraphs as samples of their writing development.

Monitoring Student Progress

If . . .	Then . . .
students' writing does not follow the guidelines on **Transparency 1–28,**	work with students to improve specific parts of their writing.

Independent Activities

Language Center

VOCABULARY
Building Vocabulary

👤👤👤 Groups	🕐 45 minutes
Objective	Learn words from mythology.
Materials	Poster board or chart paper, dictionary or encyclopedia

The word *volcano* comes from the name of the Roman god of fire, Vulcan. Many other words have origins in Roman or Greek mythology—the stories they told about their ancestors and heroes.

- On a poster board make three columns. Write these headings: *Word, Character,* and *Meaning.*

- Write these words in the first column: *atlas, jovial, mercurial, panic, siren, tantalize, titanic,* and *volcano.*

- Use a dictionary or encyclopedia to find the Roman or Greek mythological characters who inspired these words. Write their names in the second column.

- Write the meaning of each word in the third column.

Word	Character	Meaning
atlas	Atlas: Roman god who carried world on shoulders	book of world maps
jovial		

SPELLING
End Rhymes

👤👤 Pairs	🕐 30 minutes
Objective	Write a poem.
Materials	Activity Master 1–3, scissors

Write a poem using words with the /ō/, /o͞o/, and /yo͞o/ sounds.

- Review the Spelling Words on Activity Master 1–3.

- Cut out all the cards and place them face-down in the center of the table. Mix them up.

- Have each person choose six words.

- Work together to think of words that rhyme with each word. The rhyming words must contain the /ō/, /o͞o/, and /yo͞o/ sounds. Write the new words on the cards next to the spelling words.

- Use these words to create a rhyming poem.

> If I could sail the ocean on a <u>cruise</u>,
>
> I'd stretch out in a deck chair, and take a <u>snooze.</u>

VOCABULARY
Vocabulary Game

👤👤👤 Groups	🕐 20 minutes
Objective	Use body language to create and interpret meaning.

Use the Key Vocabulary words to play a "Charades" game.

- One player selects a Key Vocabulary word, then acts it out in front of the group. For example, someone might demonstrate the word *summit* by pretending to climb to a mountaintop and place a flag proudly in the ground.

- The player who guesses the word correctly must then give its definition.

- Players take turns at "Charades" until all the Key Vocabulary words have been performed.

- *Tip:* Players cannot speak as they demonstrate the words. However, they may act out individual syllables if they wish.

Consider copying and laminating these activities for use in centers.

LISTENING/SPEAKING/VIEWING

Discuss Favorite Photos

👤👤👤 Groups	🕐 30 minutes
Objective	Hold a conversation.

Which photograph in *Volcanoes* do you like the best? The eruption cloud or the swirly, hardened lava? The snowy mountaintop or the deep blue lake? Choose your favorite, and discuss it with your group.

- Begin by spending a few minutes silently reviewing the photographs.
- Meet with two or three other students and have a conversation about your favorite photograph.
- Make sure to explain why you like that particular photograph.

Rules for Effective Conversations

1. Take turns speaking.
2. Ask each other's opinions, and listen carefully to the answer.
3. Ask questions if you don't understand something.
4. Remember that it's all right to disagree.

STRUCTURAL ANALYSIS

Sentence Con-STRUCT-ion

👤👤 Pairs	🕐 30 minutes
Objective	Write sentences.

How many words do you know that contain the word roots *struct* and *rupt*? Write sentences that show your knowledge.

- With a partner, make a list of words that combine *struct* and *rupt* with the prefixes *de-, dis-, con-, e-, inter-, in-,* and *re-* and the suffixes *-ive, -or, -ion,* and *-ure*. Try to think of eight words.
- Discuss the meaning of each word, using a dictionary if needed.
- Divide the list with your partner and write a sentence for each of your words.

Leveled Readers

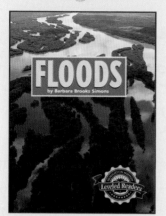

FLOODS
by Barbara Brooks Simons

Floods

Summary Floods *focuses on the causes of and damage resulting from river and ocean floods. After discussing flood prevention, the author charts ten floods in U.S. history.*

Vocabulary

Introduce the Key Vocabulary and ask students to complete the BLM.

overflow to run over the banks, *p. 6*

downstream the direction in which the river current moves, *p. 7*

break to split apart from force or pressure, *p. 8*

levee a bank of earth built to keep a river from flooding, *p. 9*

rose got higher, *p. 14*

whip up stir up, *p. 17*

● BELOW LEVEL

Building Background and Vocabulary

Invite students to tell what they know about floods from personal experience or news reports. Preview the story with students, using the story vocabulary when possible.

◉ Comprehension Skill: Categorize and Classify

Have students read the Strategy Focus on the book flap. Remind students to use the strategy and to categorize and classify ideas as they read the book. (See the Leveled Readers Teacher's Guide for **Vocabulary and Comprehension Practice Masters**.)

Responding

Have partners discuss how to answer the questions on the inside back cover.

Think About the Selection Sample answers:

1. a river flood

2. Rushing water from floods can cause damage to land, buildings, and people.

3. river and ocean floods

4. build dams and levees to hold back water, dig canals to carry away floodwaters, build homes far from water to cut down on damage

Making Connections Responses will vary.

◉ Building Fluency

Model Read aloud the word *tsunamis* on page 19. Explain how to use the pronunciation guide following the word.

Practice Have students look for another word in the story that has a pronunciation guide. Have volunteers read the word, using the pronunciation guide.

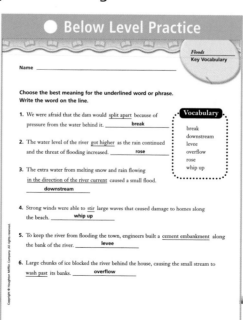

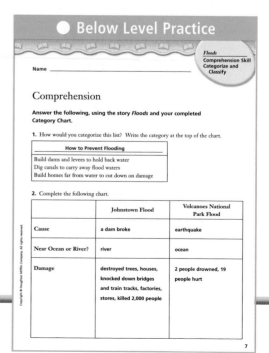

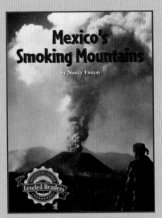

Mexico's Smoking Mountains

Summary *El Popo is one of Mexico's most dangerous volcanoes. This and other volcanoes are discussed in this book.*

Vocabulary

Introduce the Key Vocabulary and ask students to complete the BLM.

eruption* a volcanic explosion or large flow of lava, *p. 4*

dormant inactive, *p. 6*

lava* hot melted rock that flows from a volcano, *p. 6*

volcanologists scientists who study volcanoes, *p. 10*

environment surroundings, *p. 11*

atmosphere layer of gases surrounding the earth, *p. 11*

crust* the solid outer layer of earth, *p. 12*

mantle layer beneath earth's crust, *p. 12*

magma* hot melted rock underneath the earth's surface, *p. 12*

*Forms of these words are Anthology Key Vocabulary words.

Building Background and Vocabulary

Have students share what they know about volcanoes. Explain that volcanic eruptions occur when pressure builds up beneath the earth's surface. Preview the story with students, using the story vocabulary when possible.

Comprehension Skill: Categorize and Classify

Have students read the Strategy Focus on the book flap. Remind students to use the strategy and to categorize and classify ideas as they read the book. (See the Leveled Readers Teacher's Guide for **Vocabulary and Comprehension Practice Masters.**)

Responding

Have partners discuss how to answer the questions on the inside back cover.

Think About the Selection Sample answers:

1. Today, scientists have developed tools to help predict eruptions.

2. Students might point out that living near a volcano is not always dangerous.

3. It is a chain of volcanoes that encircles much of the Pacific Ocean.

4. More people live near volcanoes today than ever before.

Making Connections Responses will vary.

Building Fluency

Model Read aloud pages 3 and 4. Explain that headings tell about the paragraphs that come after them.

Practice Ask students to find and read aloud other headings in the story. Have them predict what the paragraphs after each heading will be about. Then students can read the paragraphs that follow the heading and explain to a partner why a heading is appropriate.

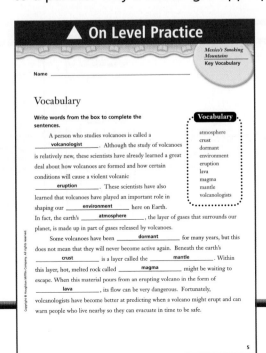

▲ **On Level Practice**

Mexico's Smoking Mountains
Key Vocabulary

Name _____

Vocabulary

Write words from the box to complete the sentences.

> **Vocabulary**
> atmosphere
> crust
> dormant
> environment
> eruption
> lava
> magma
> mantle
> volcanologists

A person who studies volcanoes is called a **volcanologist**. Although the study of volcanoes is relatively new, these scientists have already learned a great deal about how volcanoes are formed and how certain conditions will cause a violent volcanic **eruption**. These scientists have also learned that volcanoes have played an important role in shaping our **environment** here on Earth. In fact, the earth's **atmosphere**, the layer of gases that surrounds our planet, is made up in part of gases released by volcanoes.

Some volcanoes have been **dormant** for many years, but this does not mean that they will never become active again. Beneath the earth's **crust** is a layer called the **mantle**. Within this layer, hot, melted rock called **magma** might be waiting to escape. When this material pours from an erupting volcano in the form of **lava**, its flow can be very dangerous. Fortunately, volcanologists have become better at predicting when a volcano might erupt and can warn people who live nearby so they can evacuate in time to be safe.

5

▲ **On Level Practice**

Mexico's Smoking Mountains
Comprehension Skill
Categorize and Classify

Name _____

Comprehension

The items in the box fall into three categories. Study the list and decide what each category is. Then classify the items, listing them in the correct category.
Accept reasonable category heads.

> Paricutin
> Crust
> Wear protective suits
> Andes Mountains
> Check for ground tremors
> Mount St. Helens
> Predict eruptions
> Lava
> El Popo
> Measure gas levels in air

Ring of Fire	Volcanologists	Volcano Basics
Paricutin	wear protective suits	lava
Andes Mountains	check for ground tremors	crust
Mount St. Helens	predict eruptions	magma
El Popo	measure gas levels in air	mantle

7

10

LEVELED READERS

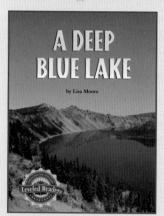

A Deep Blue Lake

Summary *This book is about Crater Lake, a lake in Oregon.*

Vocabulary

Introduce the Key Vocabulary and ask students to complete the BLM.

cradles supports, shelters, *p. 3*

glistening sparkling, *p. 4*

molten* made liquid by heat, *p. 4*

seethed bubbled, as if boiling, *p. 4*

lava* hot melted rock that flows from a volcano, *p. 4*

eruptions* volcanic explosions or lava flows, *p. 4*

crater* a bowl-shaped depression, *p. 6*

national park federally protected public land, *p. 9*

preserve keep safe from injury or destruction, *p. 13*

minerals natural, solid substances, *p. 13*

*Forms of these words are Anthology Key Vocabulary words.

■ ABOVE LEVEL

Building Background and Vocabulary

Have students share what they know about volcanoes and national parks. Preview the story with students, using the story vocabulary when possible.

Comprehension Skill: Categorize and Classify

Have students read the Strategy Focus on the book flap. Remind students to use the strategy and to categorize and classify ideas as they read the book. (See the Leveled Readers Teacher's Guide for **Vocabulary and Comprehension Practice Masters**.)

Responding

Have partners discuss how to answer the questions on the inside back cover.

Think About the Selection Sample answers:

1. constant 39°F; sits in a caldera; crystal blue; deepest lake in North America

2. Mt. Mazama is the name of the volcanic mountain that erupted, leaving a huge crater that filled with water. The lake that formed is called Crater Lake.

3. They believed that if they looked at it they would die.

4. The park was created to preserve Crater Lake in all its natural splendor.

Making Connections Responses will vary.

Building Fluency

Model Read aloud page 9, asking students to pay attention to the list of animals in the park. Then draw on the chalkboard four or more blank lines with commas between them. Elicit from students animals that probably wouldn't live in the park and write the animal names on the lines.

Practice Have partners find other lists in the story and read them aloud.

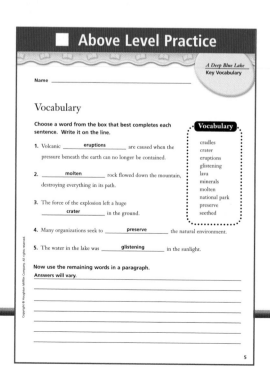

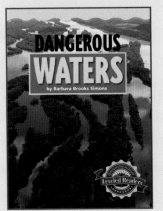

Dangerous Waters

Summary
Rivers and oceans provide food and a means to travel, but people who live near water face the dangers of floods. River floods occur when melting snow causes rivers to rise. Ocean floods are caused when storms create huge waves that damage nearby homes and towns.

Vocabulary

Introduce the Key Vocabulary and ask students to complete the BLM.

ruin to cause great damage or destruction, *p. 4*

earthquake a trembling or shaking of the ground caused by sudden movements in the rocks far below the Earth's surface, *p. 5*

overflow run freely over the top of something, *p. 6*

levees walls built along rivers to keep them from flooding, *p. 9*

smashed destroyed; crushed completely, *p. 15*

tsunamis very big ocean waves caused by earthquakes under the ocean floor, *p. 19*

Building Background and Vocabulary

Explain that this story is about floods. Use the story illustrations to lead a discussion about what happens in a flood, and what people do during a flood. Then distribute the **Build Background Practice Master**. Read aloud the questions and have pairs of students answer them.

Comprehension Skill: Categorize and Classify

Have students read the Strategy Focus on the book flap. Remind students to use the strategy and to think about how the author groups information in categories as they read the book. (See the Leveled Readers Teacher's Guide for **Build Background, Vocabulary, and Graphic Organizer Masters**.)

Responding

Have partners discuss how to answer the questions on the inside back cover.

Think About the Selection Sample answers:

1. River floods are the most common kind of floods.

2. Floods can ruin houses and towns and drown people and animals.

3. A big river flood could come down and ruin where you live.

4. Responses will vary.

Making Connections Responses will vary.

Building Fluency

Model Read aloud pages 10–11. Point out the question marks on page 10, and model the correct emphasis for reading a question.

Practice Lead students in an echo reading of the same text. Repeat several times until students can read accurately and with appropriate emphasis.

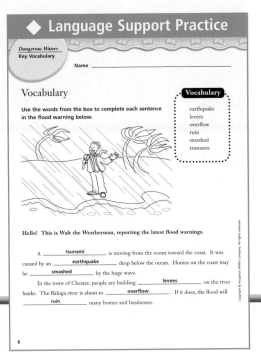

Connecting and Comparing Literature

Check Your Progress

Use these Paired Selections to help students make connections with other theme literature and to wrap up the theme.

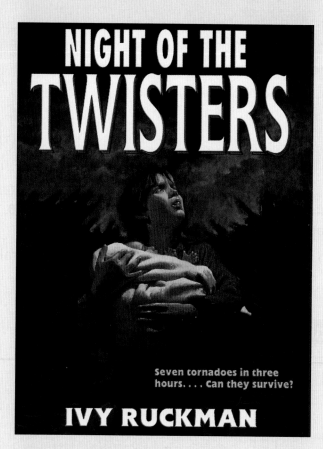

Night of the Twisters
Genre: Fiction

As a tornado threatens his home, Dan Hatch rushes his best friend and baby brother to a safe spot in the basement.

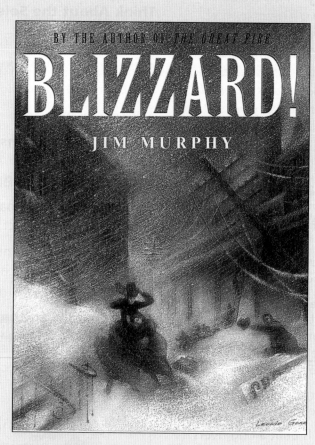

Blizzard!
Genre: Nonfiction

When the East River in New York City freezes over, thousands cross the new ice bridge. Soon the ice starts to break, putting the people in danger.

Preparing for Tests

Taking Tests: Test Categories

Use this material to practice for North Carolina EOG tests and question categories.

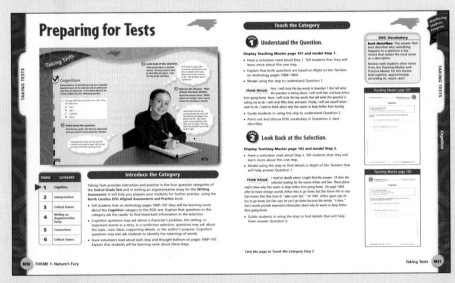

Skill Review

Use these lessons and supporting activities to review tested skills in this theme.

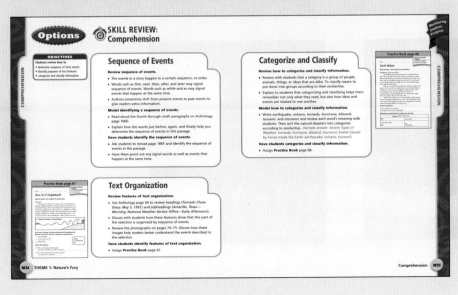

- Independent practice for skills

- Transparencies
- Strategy Posters
- Blackline Masters

Technology

Audio Selections
Night of the Twisters

Blizzard!

www.eduplace.com
Log on to Education Place for vocabulary support—
e•Glossary
e•WordGame

Theme Connections

Anthology Literature

Activities to help students think critically

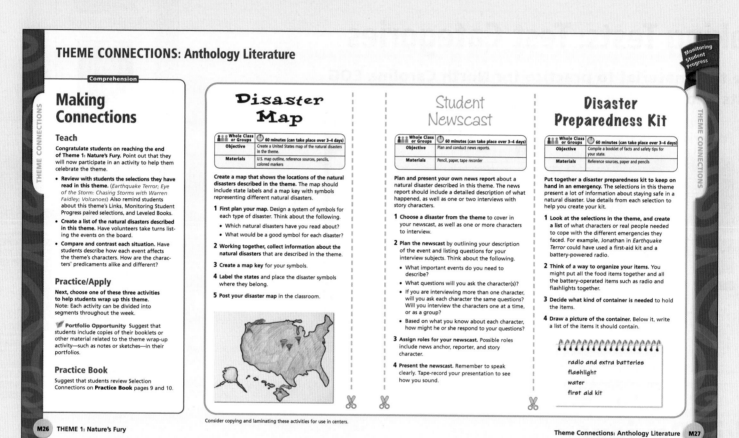

THEME CONNECTIONS: Anthology Literature

Monitoring Student Progress

Comprehension

Making Connections

Teach

Congratulate students on reaching the end of Theme 1: Nature's Fury. Point out that they will now participate in an activity to help them celebrate the theme.

- **Review** with students the selections they have read in this theme. (*Earthquake Terror; Eye of the Storm: Chasing Storms with Warren Faidley; Volcanoes*) Also remind students about this theme's Links, Monitoring Student Progress paired selections, and Leveled Books.
- **Create a list** of the natural disasters described in this theme. Have volunteers take turns listing the events on the board.
- **Compare and contrast** each situation. Have students describe how each event affects the theme's characters. How are the characters' predicaments alike and different?

Practice/Apply

Next, choose one of these three activities to help students wrap up this theme. Note: Each activity can be divided into segments throughout the week.

Portfolio Opportunity Suggest that students include copies of their booklets or other material related to the theme wrap-up activity—such as notes or sketches—in their portfolios.

Practice Book

Suggest that students review Selection Connections on **Practice Book** pages 9 and 10.

Disaster Map

Whole Class or Groups	60 minutes (can take place over 3–4 days)
Objective	Create a United States map of the natural disasters in the theme.
Materials	U.S. map outline, reference sources, pencils, colored markers

Create a map that shows the locations of the natural disasters described in the theme. The map should include state labels and a map key with symbols representing different natural disasters.

1 **First plan your map.** Design a system of symbols for each type of disaster. Think about the following.
- Which natural disasters have you read about?
- What would be a good symbol for each disaster?

2 **Working together,** collect information about the natural disasters that are described in the theme.

3 **Create a map key** for your symbols.

4 **Label the states** and place the disaster symbols where they belong.

5 **Post** your disaster map in the classroom.

Student Newscast

Whole Class or Groups	60 minutes (can take place over 3–4 days)
Objective	Plan and conduct news reports.
Materials	Pencil, paper, tape recorder

Plan and present your own news report about a natural disaster described in this theme. The news report should include a detailed description of what happened, as well as one or two interviews with story characters.

1 **Choose a disaster from the theme** to cover in your newscast, as well as one or more characters to interview.

2 **Plan the newscast** by outlining your description of the event and listing questions for your interview subjects. Think about the following.
- What important events do you need to describe?
- What questions will you ask the character(s)?
- If you are interviewing more than one character, will you ask each character the same questions? Will you interview the characters one at a time, or as a group?
- Based on what you know about each character, how might he or she respond to your questions?

3 **Assign roles** for your newscast. Possible roles include news anchor, reporter, and story character.

4 **Present the newscast.** Remember to speak clearly. Tape-record your presentation to see how you sound.

Disaster Preparedness Kit

Whole Class or Groups	60 minutes (can take place over 3–4 days)
Objective	Compile a booklet of facts and safety tips for your state.
Materials	Reference sources, paper and pencils

Put together a disaster preparedness kit to keep on hand in an emergency. The selections in this theme present a lot of information about staying safe in a natural disaster. Use details from each selection to help you create your kit.

1 **Look at the selections** in the theme, and create a list of what characters or real people needed to cope with the different emergencies they faced. For example, Jonathan in *Earthquake Terror* could have used a first-aid kit and a battery-powered radio.

2 **Think of a way to organize your items.** You might put all the food items together and all the battery-operated items such as radio and flashlights together.

3 **Decide what kind of container** is needed to hold the items.

4 **Draw a picture of the container.** Below it, write a list of the items it should contain.

radio and extra batteries
flashlight
water
first aid kit

Consider copying and laminating these activities for use in centers.

M26 THEME 1: Nature's Fury

Theme Connections: Anthology Literature M27

Three Main Selections

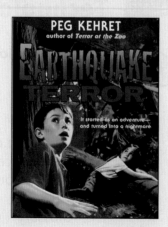

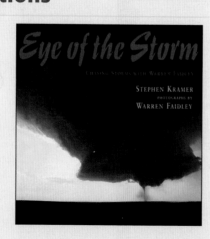

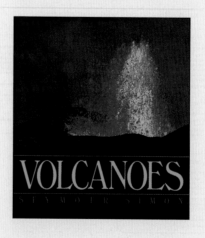

Leveled Books

Activities to help students connect and compare

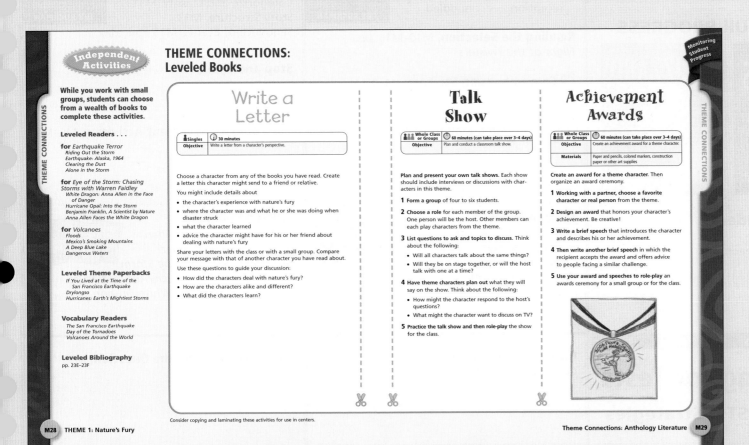

Independent Activities

THEME CONNECTIONS:
Leveled Books

While you work with small groups, students can choose from a wealth of books to complete these activities.

Leveled Readers . . .

for *Earthquake Terror*
Riding Out the Storm
Earthquake: Alaska, 1964
Clearing the Dust
Alone in the Storm

for *Eye of the Storm: Chasing Storms with Warren Faidley*
White Dragon: Anna Allen in the Face of Danger
Hurricane Opal: Into the Storm
Benjamin Franklin, A Scientist by Nature
Anna Allen Faces the White Dragon

for *Volcanoes*
Floods
Mexico's Smoking Mountains
A Deep Blue Lake
Dangerous Waters

Leveled Theme Paperbacks
If You Lived at the Time of the San Francisco Earthquake
Drylongso
Hurricanes: Earth's Mightiest Storms

Vocabulary Readers
The San Francisco Earthquake
Day of the Tornadoes
Volcanoes Around the World

Leveled Bibliography
pp. 23E–23F

Write a Letter

👤 Singles	🕐 30 minutes
Objective	Write a letter from a character's perspective.

Choose a character from any of the books you have read. Create a letter this character might send to a friend or relative.

You might include details about

- the character's experience with nature's fury
- where the character was and what he or she was doing when disaster struck
- what the character learned
- advice the character might have for his or her friend about dealing with nature's fury

Share your letters with the class or with a small group. Compare your message with that of another character you have read about.

Use these questions to guide your discussion:

- How did the characters deal with nature's fury?
- How are the characters alike and different?
- What did the characters learn?

Talk Show

👥 Whole Class or Groups	🕐 60 minutes (can take place over 3–4 days)
Objective	Plan and conduct a classroom talk show.

Plan and present your own talk shows. Each show should include interviews or discussions with characters in this theme.

1 **Form a group** of four to six students.

2 **Choose a role** for each member of the group. One person will be the host. Other members can each play characters from the theme.

3 **List questions** to ask and topics to discuss. Think about the following:

- Will all characters talk about the same things?
- Will they be on stage together, or will the host talk with one at a time?

4 **Have theme characters plan out** what they will say on the show. Think about the following:

- How might the character respond to the host's questions?
- What might the character want to discuss on TV?

5 **Practice the talk show** and then role-play the show for the class.

Achievement Awards

👥 Whole Class or Groups	🕐 60 minutes (can take place over 3–4 days)
Objective	Create an achievement award for a theme character.
Materials	Paper and pencils, colored markers, construction paper or other art supplies

Create an award for a theme character. Then organize an award ceremony.

1 **Working with a partner,** choose a favorite character or real person from the theme.

2 **Design an award** that honors your character's achievement. Be creative!

3 **Write a brief speech** that introduces the character and describes his or her achievement.

4 **Then write another brief speech** in which the recipient accepts the award and offers advice to people facing a similar challenge.

5 **Use your award and speeches** to role-play an awards ceremony for a small group or for the class.

Consider copying and laminating these activities for use in centers.

Twelve Leveled Readers

Three Leveled Theme Paperbacks

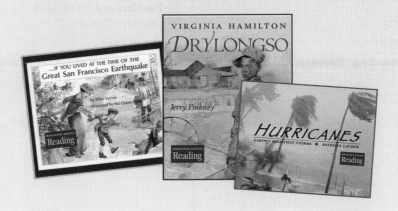

Daily Lesson Plans

 Technology
Lesson Planner CD-ROM allows you to customize the chart below to develop your own lesson plans.

 North Carolina Competency Goals indicated in blue.

50–60 minutes

Connecting and Comparing Literature

CHECK YOUR PROGRESS

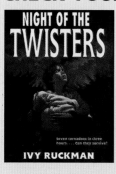 

Leveled Readers
• Fluency Practice
• Independent Reading

40–60 minutes

Preparing for Tests

TAKING TESTS: Strategies

SKILL REVIEW OPTIONS
Comprehension
Structural Analysis
Vocabulary
Spelling
Grammar
Prompts for Writing

DAY 1

Introducing Paired Selections

Key Vocabulary, M9 1.02

alert	bolting
flickering	lull
reception	huddled

Reading the Selection, M10–M16 2.03a
Night of the Twisters

Comprehension Strategy, M10 3.01g
Predict/Infer **T**

Classroom Management Activities, M6–M7
SC4.04, SS1.01, SS1.03

Leveled Readers
Riding Out the Storm
Earthquake: Alaska, 1964
Clearing the Dust
Alone in the Storm

Introduce the Strategy, M30
Choosing the Best Answer

Comprehension, M34–M35 2.04b, 3.01a, 3.02
Skill Review Options **T**

Structural Analysis, M36–M37 1.01
Skill Review Options **T**

Vocabulary, M38–M39 1.03c, 1.04
Skill Review Options **T**

Spelling, M40 5.05
Short Vowels **T**

Grammar, M42
Kinds of Sentences **T**

Prompts for Writing, M44 4.09
News Article/Adding Details

DAY 2

Reading the Selection
Night of the Twisters

Connecting and Comparing
Categorize and Classify, M11 2.01
Story Structure, M13
Sequence of Events, M15 2.04b, 3.01a

Stop and Think, M17 3.01g, 3.02, 3.03

Classroom Management Activities, M6–M7
SC4.04, SS1.01, SS1.03

Leveled Readers
White Dragon: Anna Allen in the Face of Danger
Hurricane Opal: Into the Storm
Benjamin Franklin, A Scientist by Nature
Anna Allen Faces the White Dragon

Step 1: Understand the Question, M31

Comprehension, M34–M35 2.04b, 3.01a, 3.02
Skill Review Options **T**

Structural Analysis, M36–M37 1.01
Skill Review Options **T**

Vocabulary, M38–M39 1.03c, 1.04
Skill Review Options **T**

Spelling, M40 5.05
ā, ē, and ī **T**

Grammar, M42
Subjects and Predicates **T**

Prompts for Writing, M44 4.02a, c, 5.01
Response to a Prompt/Capitalizing and Punctuating Sentences **T**

Target Skills of the Week

TARGET SKILL

Comprehension
Vocabulary
Phonics/Decoding
Fluency

Monitoring Student Progress

DAILY LESSON PLANS

DAY 3

Key Vocabulary, M18 1.02

immense   floes
treacherous   ominous
stranded   desperate

Reading the Selection, M19–M24 2.03a
Blizzard!

🎯 **Comprehension Strategy,** M20 3.01g

Predict/Infer **T**

Classroom Management Activities, M6–M7
SC4.04, SS1.01, SS1.03

Leveled Readers

Floods
Mexico's Smoking Mountains
A Deep Blue Lake
Dangerous Waters

Step 2: Look Back at the Selection, M31

🎯 **Comprehension,** M34–M35 2.04b, 3.01a, 3.02
Skill Review Options **T**

🎯 **Structural Analysis,** M36–M37 1.01
Skill Review Options **T**

🎯 **Vocabulary,** M38–M39 1.03c, 1.04
Skill Review Options **T**

Spelling, M41 5.05
/ō/, /o͞o/, and /yo͞o/ **T**

Grammar, M43 5.03c
Longer Sentences **T**

Prompts for Writing, M45 4.07
Paragraph of Information/Correcting
Sentence Fragments **T**

DAY 4

Reading the Selection,
Blizzard!

Connecting and Comparing
Text Organization, M21
Sequence of Events, M23 2.04b, 3.01a

Think and Compare, M25 3.01g, 3.02

Theme Connections: Anthology Literature,
M26–M27 3.02, 303

Classroom Management Activities, M6–M7
SC4.04, SS1.01, SS1.03

Leveled Readers
Theme Connections:
Leveled Books, M28–M29
3.01b, d, g, 3.02, 4.07

Step 3: Narrow the Choices. Then Choose the Best Answer, M32

🎯 **Comprehension,** M34–M35 2.04b, 3.01a, 3.02
Skill Review Options **T**

🎯 **Structural Analysis,** M36–M37 1.01
Skill Review Options **T**

🎯 **Vocabulary,** M38–M39 1.03c, 1.04
Skill Review Options **T**

Spelling, M41 5.05
Silent Consonants

Grammar, M43
Singular/Plural Nouns **T**

Prompts for Writing, M45 4.07
Taking Notes/Choosing What's Important

DAY 5

Theme Connections:
Anthology Literature,
M26–M27 3.02, 3.03

🎯 **Rereading for Fluency,**
M15, M23 4.01

NIGHT OF THE TWISTERS

IVY RUCKMAN

Classroom Management Activities, M6–M7
SC4.04, SS1.01, SS1.03

Leveled Readers
Theme Connections:
Leveled Books, M28–M29
3.01b, d, g, 3.02, 4.07

Multiple-Choice Test Practice, M33

🎯 **Comprehension,** M34–M35 2.04b, 3.01a, 3.02
Skill Review Options **T**

🎯 **Structural Analysis,** M36–M37 1.01
Skill Review Options **T**

🎯 **Vocabulary,** M38–M39 1.03c, 1.04
Skill Review Options **T**

Spelling Test, M41 5.05

Grammar, M43
More Plural Nouns **T**

Prompts for Writing, M45 4.07, 5.04
Description **T**/Writing Complete Sentences

Daily Lesson Plans **M5**

DAILY LESSON PLANS

Classroom Management

Independent Activities

Assign these activities while you work with small groups.

 Suggest that students include copies of their work in their portfolios.

Media

TV vs. Radio

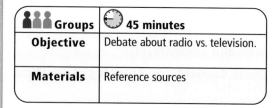

👥👥👥 Groups	🕐 45 minutes
Objective	Debate about radio vs. television.
Materials	Reference sources

In *Night of the Twisters,* Dan and Arthur listen to both TV and radio. With a few classmates, have a debate about which broadcast medium you think is better.

- Have one team support TV, the other radio.

- Team members brainstorm the strong points of their medium and the weak points of the other, writing notes on index cards.

- Teams can use an encyclopedia, the Internet, or other reference sources to find facts supporting TV or radio.

- Each team takes five minutes to argue for TV or radio.

- Discuss which argument "won" and why.

Science

Will It Float?

👥 Pairs	🕐 45 minutes
Objective	Experiment with buoyancy.
Materials	Plastic container, water, small objects

In *Blizzard!,* the author describes how ice floes jammed together, clogging the river. Why does ice float, rather than sink? With a partner, find out about *buoyancy,* the quality that makes an object sink or float.

- Fill a small plastic or metal container with water.

- Gather a variety of small objects. Examples might include: coin, cotton ball, small pencil, piece of candy, candy wrapper, paper clip, eraser, chalk, stone.

- Drop each object into the water. Write down what happens each time.

- Discuss the results. What do you think are the reasons why an object sinks or floats?

Look for more activities in the **Classroom Management Kit.**

Consider copying and laminating these activities for use in centers.

Folktale

Once Upon a Tornado

👤 Singles	🕐 30 minutes
Objective	Write a folktale about nature's fury.

The folktale "The Princess and the Warrior" tells how two volcanoes came to exist. Write a brief folktale about the origin of another kind of nature's fury from the theme: earthquake, tornado, hurricane, lightning, or blizzard.

- Brainstorm ideas about what created the kind of nature's fury you choose. For example, did a character get angry? Did a character transform? Did the storm happen by accident?

- Go back to the selection to jot down details about the upheaval.

- Write and illustrate your folktale and share it with your classmates.

Social Studies

A World of Fury

👥 Pairs	🕐 45 minutes
Objective	Create a map of theme settings.
Materials	Atlas, drawing and writing materials, colored pencils

In this theme, you traveled to California, Oklahoma, Nebraska, Hawaii, Iceland, and New York City. With a partner, make a world map showing all the geographical settings of the theme selections.

- Use an atlas to trace a world map.

- Revisit the maps on Anthology pages 27, 55, 82–83, and 89 for details.

- Use the atlas to find other map details.

- Color or illustrate your map and label the settings from the theme.

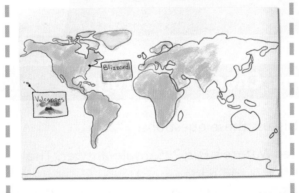

Writing

The Scare-o-meter

👤 Singles	🕐 30 minutes
Objective	Compare examples of nature's fury.

In *Nature's Fury*, you have read about earthquakes, electrical storms, tornadoes, blizzards, and volcanic eruptions. Which storm or disaster in the theme do you think is the scariest?

- Write an essay that describes which natural disaster rates highest on your "scare-o-meter," and why.

- In your essay, tell what elements of the event you find most frightening. Describe these elements (for example: lightning, lava, funnel cloud).

- Also write about how you think you might react if you were caught in this storm or disaster.

Connecting and Comparing Literature

Theme Wrap-Up

Check Your Progress

In this theme you have read about nature's most powerful displays, from earthquakes to lightning to volcanoes. Now read and compare two new examples of nature's fury and practice your test-taking skills.

Start by looking back at the letter from Warren Faidley on pages 23–24 of your book. Think about how his account of his experiences during Hurricane Andrew gets you ready for looking at nature in a new way.

As you read the next two selections about a tornado and a blizzard, compare the way they show people coping with the power of nature.

106

Read and Compare

NIGHT OF THE TWISTERS
seven tornadoes in three hours.... Can they survive?
IVY RUCKMAN

Realistic Fiction

In a small town, three boys are at home alone during a monster tornado.

Try these strategies:
Question
Evaluate

BLIZZARD!
JIM MURPHY

Nonfiction

Read about the terrible Blizzard of 1888 in New York City.

Try these strategies:
Summarize
Monitor and Clarify

Strategies in Action *Make use of all your reading strategies as you read the selections.*

106 A

Use Paired Selections: Check Your Progress

Have students read page 106. Discuss these questions:

- Why do you think this theme is called *Nature's Fury*? (Sample answer: The stories describe how nature can be fierce and dangerous.)

- Which selection looks most exciting? Why? (Answers will vary.)

Have students read page 106A. Ask these questions:

- How might *Night of the Twisters* and *Blizzard!* be similar to some of the other selections in *Nature's Fury*? (Like the main selections, these are about dangerous or violent natural events.)

Strategies in Action Remind students to use all their reading strategies as they read these Paired Selections.

Transparency 1–30

NATURE'S FURY *Night of the Twisters*
Monitoring Student Progress
Key Vocabulary

ANNOTATED VERSION

Weather Warning Words

alert flickering reception bolting lull huddled

Interviewer: Emergency Manager Bill Parker is here to talk about twisters. Mr. Parker, can you tell listeners what to do as a tornado approaches?
Mr. Parker: When people notice their lights _____flickering_____ off and on, they should immediately check for a weather _____alert_____. If they are getting any _____reception_____ at all on their radio or television, they will hear the emergency signal. These warnings give important information.
Interviewer: Where should people go to be safe?
Mr. Parker: Some people get hurt by _____bolting_____ out the door into the storm. The best way to stay safe is to head for the basement. If possible, remain _____huddled_____ under a heavy blanket to protect yourself from broken glass.
Interviewer: Any other tips for our listeners?
Mr. Parker: Sometimes as a tornado approaches, everything becomes quiet. This _____lull_____ can fool people into thinking that the storm has passed, when in fact it is just about to hit.
Interviewer: Thank you for talking to KBAB today, Mr. Parker. I'm sure our listeners will be able to use your tips to better protect themselves.

TRANSPARENCY 1–30
TEACHER'S EDITION PAGE M9

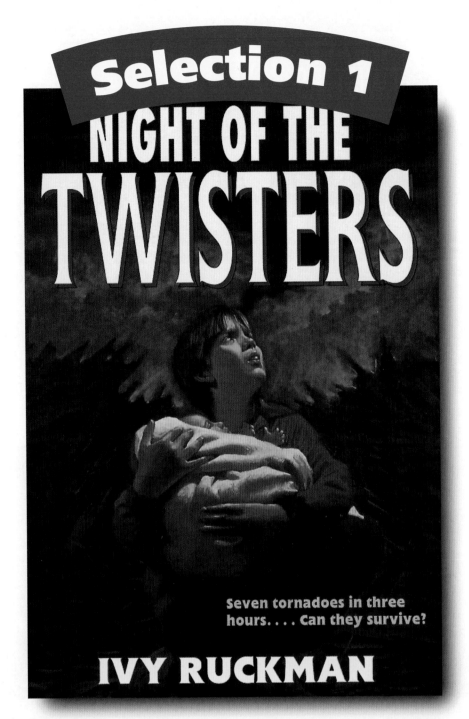

Selection 1
NIGHT OF THE TWISTERS

Seven tornadoes in three hours. . . . Can they survive?

IVY RUCKMAN

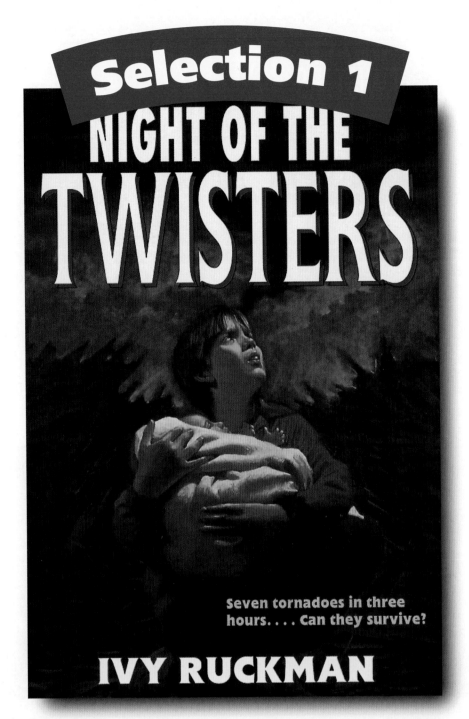

Selection 1
NIGHT OF THE TWISTERS

Seven tornadoes in three hours. . . . Can they survive?

IVY RUCKMAN

Introducing Vocabulary

Key Vocabulary
These words appear in the selection.

alert a warning signal

flickering shining unsteadily

reception converting electrical signals into sound or light, as in a radio or TV

bolting moving suddenly

lull a calm period

huddled crowded together

 e • Glossary
e • WordGame

See Vocabulary notes on pages M10, M12, and M16 for additional words to preview.

Have students locate Key Vocabulary words in the story.

- Have volunteers read aloud each sentence containing a highlighted Key Vocabulary word in the selection.

Display Transparency 1–30.

- Model how to use context clues to choose the correct word to fill in the first blank.

- For each remaining sentence, have students use context clues to choose the correct Key Vocabulary word.

Practice/Homework Assign **Practice Book** page 61.

Introduce the Graphic Organizer.

Tell students to fill in **Practice Book** page 62 as they read the Paired Selections.

Practice Book page 61

Name _____

Monitoring Student Progress
Key Vocabulary Night of the Twisters

Tornado Report

Use the words in the box to complete this news report about a tornado.

Vocabulary

alert   flickering   reception   bolting   lull   huddled

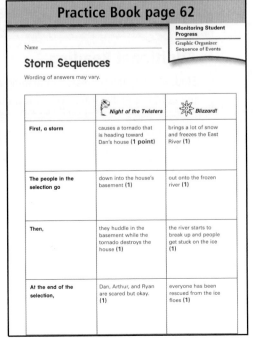

A Category 4 tornado touched down in central Nebraska at approximately 4:30 P.M. yesterday. A severe weather alert **(2 points)** ____ was issued by the National Weather Service before the storm struck. However, many residents lost power and had no reception **(2)** ____ on their radios or televisions at the time.

Witnesses who still had power reported that their lights were flickering **(2)** ____ on and off as the twister approached. One man remembered bolting **(2)** ____ for the basement of his house as he heard the storm draw nearer. A local woman recalled a period of absolute stillness right before the tornado hit. During this lull **(2)** ____, she wondered if the tornado had passed by. Most local residents huddled **(2)** ____ in the center of their basements until the storm passed, following safety guidelines published in yesterday's newspaper.

Practice Book page 62

Name _____

Monitoring Student Progress
Graphic Organizer
Sequence of Events

Storm Sequences

Wording of answers may vary.

	Night of the Twisters	Blizzard!
First, a storm	causes a tornado that is heading toward Dan's house (1 point)	brings a lot of snow and freezes the East River (1)
The people in the selection go	down into the house's basement (1)	out onto the frozen river (1)
Then,	they huddle in the basement while the tornado destroys the house (1)	the river starts to break up and people get stuck on the ice (1)
At the end of the selection,	Dan, Arthur, and Ryan are scared but okay. (1)	everyone has been rescued from the ice floes (1)

Guiding Comprehension

❶ STORY STRUCTURE Who is telling this story? (Dan Hatch)

❷ DRAWING CONCLUSIONS Why does Dan turn to go back to Ryan's room? (He wants to keep his brother safe.)

COMPREHENSION STRATEGY

Predict/Infer

Teacher Modeling Remind students that making predictions and inferences as they read can help them better understand a story. Read aloud page 106C. Then model the strategy.

Think Aloud *This part of the story tells me that the radio is dead, the TV is showing an emergency signal, and the lights are flickering. Because of this, I predict that the tornado is very close, and Dan will quickly try to get to a safe place with Arthur and Ryan.*

Vocabulary

alert a warning signal

flickering shining unsteadily

reception converting electrical signals into sound or light, as in a radio or TV

Civil Defense Emergency a situation in which people must take steps to protect themselves from a natural disaster or other emergency

NIGHT OF THE TWISTERS

Seven tornadoes in three hours.... Can they survive?

IVY RUCKMAN

NIGHT OF THE TWISTERS

BY IVY RUCKMAN, ILLUSTRATED BY MIKE ADAMS

106**B**

REACHING ALL LEARNERS

Challenge

Additional Reading

Students may be interested in reading more of Ivy Ruckman's stories. To learn about the author and illustrator, visit Education Place at **www.eduplace.com/kids**.

A siren has been sounding a tornado alert for the town of Grand Island, Nebraska. Dan Hatch's parents are away, leaving Dan and his friend Arthur alone in the house with Dan's baby brother, Ryan. While Arthur listens to the radio, Dan checks on Ryan. Maybe the storm will blow over, he thinks as he leaves Ryan's room.

Quietly, I closed the door behind me.

That's when the lights started flickering.

In the hallway, I practically had a head-on with Arthur, who was coming at me real fast. The look on his face scared me.

"There's no ... there's no ..."

"What?"

"There's no radio reception anymore. It just went dead! This guy.... He kept saying, 'Tornado alert, tornado alert!' Then it went dead."

We rushed back to the living room. The TV was flashing these big letters that filled the entire screen: CD ... CD ... CD ...

"What's it mean?" Arthur cried.

"Civil Defense Emergency!" I whirled around. "I'm getting Ryan!"

The lights flickered again.

At the same time we heard these really strange sounds that stopped us in our tracks. They were coming from the bathroom and the kitchen. Sucking sounds. The drains were sucking! I felt this awful pulling in my ears, too, as if there were vacuums on both sides of my head.

1

2

106C

REACHING ALL LEARNERS

Extra Support/Intervention

Selection Preview

page 106C A tornado alert has been given. The main character, Dan Hatch, is home with only his friend Arthur and his baby brother Ryan. What do you think Dan will do as the tornado gets closer?

pages 106D–106E Dan struggles to pull Ryan from his crib. How do you think Dan is feeling now?

pages 106F–106H Dan, Arthur, and Ryan take shelter in the bathroom. Why do they cover themselves with a blanket? What seems to be happening to the house around them?

Connecting and Comparing

Categorize and Classify

- Have students classify the selections in this theme into the categories *Related to Storms* and *Related to the Earth*. (Related to Storms: *Eye of the Storm, Night of the Twisters, Blizzard!*; Related to the Earth: *Earthquake Terror, Volcanoes*)

- How else could you classify the stories in this theme? What stories would be in each category? (Sample answer: Fiction: *Earthquake Terror, Night of the Twisters*; Nonfiction: *Eye of the Storm, Volcanoes, Blizzard!*)

Guiding Comprehension

③ COMPARE AND CONTRAST How do Arthur and Dan each react to the storm? (Arthur seems more scared and confused. He tries to go home even though that decision would put him in greater danger. Dan is scared, but he gets Arthur and Ryan to safety.)

④ WRITER'S CRAFT How does the author create a mood of fear and alarm? (Sample answer: by including details about the tornado alert, losing radio reception, Dan's and Arthur's fear, and Dan's struggles to free Ryan from the crib)

⑤ NOTING DETAILS Where do the three characters go when the storm hits? (They go to the downstairs bathroom.)

Vocabulary

bolting moving suddenly

mobile a hanging toy with moving parts

"I've got to go home!" Arthur cried all of a sudden, bolting for the door.

I ran after him. "You're not — you can't!" I grabbed the back of his T-shirt, hauled him around, and pushed him toward the stairs. "Get **③** down there. I have to get Ryan! Now go!"

I don't know what I'd have done if he hadn't minded me. We were catching the fear from each other, and even though the siren was screaming on and off again, so I didn't know what it was telling us, I knew we had to take cover fast.

The lights went out for good just before I reached Ryan's room.

I smashed face first into Ryan's butterfly mobile. That's how I knew I was at the crib. I felt for him, got my hands under his nightshirt and diaper, rolled him over. I lifted him, but we didn't get far. He was caught in the mobile, his arm or his head . . . I couldn't see . . . I couldn't get him loose. . . .

"Mom!" I yelled, though I knew she wasn't there.

I tried to lay him down again, but he was so tangled, part of him was still up in the air. He started to cry.

④ "Wait, Ryan, I'll get you out!" But I couldn't.

Finally, holding him with my left arm, I climbed onto the side of the crib. My right hand followed the string up the mobile, way up to the hook. I yanked it loose. The whole thing came crashing down on top of us as I jumped backward off the crib.

The plastic butterfly poking me was poking Ryan, too, but I didn't care. The tornado was close, and I knew it. Both my ears had popped, and I had this crazy fear that those drains, sucking like monsters now, would get us if the storm didn't.

Arthur was at the bottom of the stairs, waiting. He'd found the flashlight! I jumped the last half-flight to the floor.

⑤ "Hurry!" I screamed. I swung into the doorway of the bathroom, with Arthur right behind me. We crouched under the towel rack.

"Shine it here, on Ryan," I gasped. "He's caught in this thing." By now Ryan was kicking and screaming, and his eyes were big in the light.

106**D**

Extra Support/ Intervention

Why Ears "Pop"

Explain to students that Dan's ears *popped* because of the low air pressure in the tornado. As air pressure goes down, the air inside the head pushes outward. The body lets this air out through small tubes connected to the throat. When the pressure releases, you hear a "pop."

English Language Learners

Language Development

Explain to students that *minded* means "obeyed," and *take cover* means "get to a safe place."

106E

Connecting and Comparing

Story Structure

- Have students discuss which characters in *Night of the Twisters* and *Earthquake Terror* are most alike, and why. (Sample answer: Dan in *Night of the Twisters* is like Jonathan in *Earthquake Terror.* Both of them have to take charge in a scary situation.)

- How is the problem in *Earthquake Terror* similar to and different from the problem in *Night of the Twisters?* (Sample answer: Similar—In both stories, the main characters must protect themselves and others in a natural disaster; Different—In *Night of the Twisters,* the characters are indoors, but in *Earthquake Terror,* they are outside.)

Guiding Comprehension

 6 MAKING INFERENCES Why does Arthur say *"Your mom's back!"*? (He hears noises that make him think Dan's mom is moving the chair upstairs, when it is really the tornado moving furniture.)

7 DRAWING CONCLUSIONS Why do the characters cover themselves with a blanket? (to protect themselves from flying glass)

COMPREHENSION STRATEGY
Predict/Infer

Teacher/Student Modeling Have students read the first two paragraphs on page 106F. Discuss clues that will help them to make a prediction or inference about what the characters might do next.

Once we got the mess of strings free of Ryan's sweaty nightshirt, Arthur kicked the mobile against the wall by the toilet.

"I have to go home!" he cried. "They won't go to the basement. Mama never does."

The beam of light bounced around the blackness of the bathroom as Arthur scrambled to his feet, but I grabbed and held on to him.

"You can't go! It's here! Can't you feel it?"

The siren quit again as I pulled him back down and threw my leg over him. The flashlight clattered to the floor and rolled away from us.

We heard it next. The lull. The deadliest quiet ever, one that makes you think you might explode. The heat in that room built until I couldn't get my breath.

Then I began to hear noises. A chair scraping across the kitchen floor upstairs.

6 "Your mom's back!" Arthur said, pushing at my leg.

I knew it wasn't my mother moving the chair.

The noises got worse. It seemed as if every piece of furniture was moving around up there . . . big, heavy things, smashing into each other.

106F

English Language Learners

Language Development

Explain to students that just as Dan's ears *popped* on page 106D to relieve air pressure in his head, the window shatters on page 106G due to air pressure.

Vocabulary

lull a calm period

huddled crowded together

A window popped.

Crash! Another.

Glass, shattering — everywhere — right next to us in the laundry room.

I pulled a towel down over Ryan and held him tight. If he was still crying, I didn't know it because I was feeling the sucking this time. It was like something trying to lift my body right up off the floor.

Arthur felt it, too. "We're going to die!"

Ten seconds more and that howling, shrieking tornado was upon us.

"The blanket!" I screamed at Arthur's ear.

He pulled it down from the countertop and we covered ourselves, our hands shaking wildly. I wasn't worrying about my mom then or my dad or Mrs. Smiley. Just us. Ryan and Arthur and me, huddled together there on the floor.

7

106**G**

Connecting and Comparing

Sequence of Events

- Ask students the following: At the beginning of both *Earthquake Terror* and *Night of the Twisters,* the characters are warned of danger. What do they each do next? (Jonathan puts Moose on a leash. Dan rushes to protect his brother.)

- How are the sequences of events alike and different in *Earthquake Terror* and *Night of the Twisters?* (Alike: Both stories tell about what happens before, during, and after a natural disaster strikes; Different: At the beginning of *Earthquake Terror* no one knows that an earthquake is coming, while at the beginning of *Night of the Twisters* there is a tornado alert.)

TARGET SKILL Fluency Practice

Rereading for Fluency Have students reread page 106G. Encourage students to read expressively.

CRITICAL THINKING

Guiding Comprehension

8 **MAKING JUDGMENTS** Do you think Arthur is lucky to have a friend like Dan? Why or why not? (Sample answer: Yes. Dan keeps Arthur from leaving the house and protects him when the tornado hits.)

9 **DRAWING CONCLUSIONS** Do the characters make it through the storm? How do you know? (Yes. Dan survives to say that neither he nor Arthur will ever be that scared again.)

Summarize Have students use what they wrote on their Sequence of Events Graphic Organizers to summarize *Night of the Twisters*.

The roaring had started somewhere to the east, then came bearing down on us like a hundred freight trains. Only that twister didn't move on. It stationed itself right overhead, making the loudest noise I'd ever heard, whining worse than any jet. There was a tremendous crack, and I felt the wall shudder behind us. I knew then our house was being ripped apart. Suddenly chunks of ceiling were falling on our heads.

We'll be buried! was all I could think.

At that moment, as plain as anything above that deafening roar, I heard my dad's voice: The shower's the safest place.

I didn't question hearing it. Holding Ryan against me with one arm, I began crawling toward the shower stall. I reached back and yanked at Arthur's shirt. Somehow we got inside with the blanket. Another explosion, and the glass shower door shattered all over the bathroom floor.

We pulled the blanket over our heads. I could feel Ryan's heart beating through his undershirt against mine. Outside those places where our bodies touched, there was nothing but terror as the roar of that tornado went on and on. I thought the world was coming to an end, had come to an end, and so would we, any minute.

Then I felt Ryan's fat fingers close around one of mine. He pulled my hand to his mouth and started sucking on my finger. It made me cry. The tears ran down my cheeks and onto his head. With the whole world blowing to pieces around us, Ryan took my hand and made me feel better.

Afterward, neither Arthur nor I was able to say how long we huddled there in the basement shower.

8

"A tornado's forward speed is generally thirty to fifty miles an hour," the meteorologist had told us.

Our tornado's forward speed was zero. It parked right there on Sand Crane Drive. Five minutes or ten, we couldn't tell, but it seemed like an hour. Roaring and humming and shrieking, that twister was right on top of us. I'll never be that scared again as long as I live. Neither will Arthur.

9

106**H**

Vocabulary

stationed set in a fixed spot

meteorologist scientist who studies weather

Challenge

Create a Tornado Flow Chart

Tornadoes are twisting funnel clouds that violently suck air upward in a circular pattern. Have students research how a tornado forms and create an illustrated flow chart.

1. Giant storms high in the atmosphere form large clouds.

2. The high storms draw in warm air from below.

3. The warm air cools off and sinks.

4. The rising and sinking motion forms a rotating column of air.

5. The spinning column descends, and tornadoes develop from it.

Stop and Think

Critical Thinking Questions

1. **MAKING JUDGMENTS** Do you think the characters should have acted differently during the tornado? Explain why or why not. (Sample answers: Yes, Arthur should have stayed calm; No, they managed to survive the tornado.)

2. **COMPARE AND CONTRAST** How is Ryan like Abby in *Earthquake Terror?* (His older brother protects him during a natural disaster.)

3. **PREDICTING OUTCOMES** What do you think will happen next? (When the tornado passes, the characters will meet up with their families.)

Strategies in Action Have students model how they used Predict/Infer and other strategies to help them understand this selection.

Connecting and Comparing

Compare and Contrast

- Remind students that authors use vivid verbs, sensory details, and figurative language to add excitement to a story.

- Ask volunteers to find and read aloud a specific detail or description in *Night of the Twisters* that they find exciting. Record examples on the board.

- Point out that a fiction story gives different information and views about tornadoes than a nonfiction selection about the same topic. Have students use **Practice Book** page 63 to compare and contrast the descriptions of tornadoes in *Night of the Twisters* and *Eye of the Storm.* Ask students to think about what they learned from reading each selection.

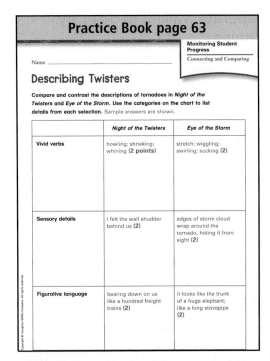

Practice Book page 63

Monitoring Student Progress
Connecting and Comparing

Name _____

Describing Twisters

Compare and contrast the descriptions of tornadoes in *Night of the Twisters* and *Eye of the Storm.* Use the categories on the chart to list details from each selection. Sample answers are shown.

	Night of the Twisters	*Eye of the Storm*
Vivid verbs	howling; shrieking; whining (**2 points**)	stretch; wiggling; swirling; sucking (2)
Sensory details	I felt the wall shudder behind us (2)	edges of storm cloud wrap around the tornado, hiding it from sight (2)
Figurative language	bearing down on us like a hundred freight trains (2)	it looks like the trunk of a huge elephant; like a long stovepipe (2)

Extra Support/Intervention

Review Predictions

Have students discuss the predictions and inferences they made about what would happen when the tornado struck Dan's house. How do their predictions compare to the story events?

Monitoring Student Progress

If . . .	Then . . .
students have difficulty answering Guiding Comprehension questions,	guide them in reading aloud relevant portions of the text and discussing their answers.

Introducing Vocabulary

READ & COMPARE

Key Vocabulary
These words appear in the selection.

immense very large

floes masses of floating ice

treacherous dangerous

ominous signaling trouble or danger

stranded left in a difficult position

desperate willing to do or try anything

e • Glossary
e • WordGame

See Vocabulary notes on pages M20 and M22 for additional words to preview.

Have students locate Key Vocabulary words in the selection.

- Have volunteers read aloud each sentence containing a highlighted Key Vocabulary word in the selection.

Display Transparency 1–31.

- Work with students to complete the sentences, using Key Vocabulary words.

Practice/Homework Assign **Practice Book** page 64.

Selection 2

BY THE AUTHOR OF *THE GREAT FIRE*

BLIZZARD!

JIM MURPHY

Transparency 1–31

Powerful Blizzard to Strike Northeast

NATURE'S FURY *Blizzard!*
Monitoring Student Progress
Key Vocabulary

ANNOTATED VERSION

immense	floes	treacherous
ominous	stranded	desperate

BOSTON — A winter storm warning was issued this morning as a huge blizzard made its way eastward. This ____immense____ snowstorm stretches from Illinois to Texas, and it is moving toward the East Coast. The first signs of the storm appeared over Pennsylvania late last night as dark, ____ominous____ clouds rolled in and snow began to fall.

Yesterday in Chicago, freezing temperatures and falling snow made roads very dangerous. Due to the ____treacherous____ conditions, drivers were urged to stay off the streets. Many drivers were ____stranded____ in the freezing cold for hours after getting stuck in the snow. Emergency trucks and plows worked through the night to bring these ____desperate____ folks to safety.

Weather experts are also concerned about how the storm will affect cities with rivers. As rivers freeze, chunks of ice can form and break away. Large ice ____floes____ could heavily damage piers and docked boats.

TRANSPARENCY 1–31
TEACHER'S EDITION PAGE M18

Practice Book page 64

Monitoring Student Progress
Key Vocabulary *Blizzard!*

Name _____

Emergency Response Words

Write each word from the box in the space next to its meaning.

Vocabulary		
immense	treacherous	desperate
ominous	stranded	floes

1. unable to reach safety stranded **(1 point)**
2. very, very dangerous treacherous **(1)**
3. frantic and willing to try anything desperate **(1)**
4. chunks of floating ice floes **(1)**
5. signaling danger or trouble ominous **(1)**
6. huge immense **(1)**

Now choose four words from the box. Use them to write a short paragraph describing a winter storm you have experienced or read about. Answers will vary, but should include four vocabulary words.
(1 point for each word used correctly.)

_____
_____
_____
_____

BLIZZARD!

BY JIM MURPHY

On March 12, 1888, one of the most destructive blizzards in history struck the eastern United States from Virginia to Maine. By the following day, snow, wind, and ice posed great danger for people trying to go back to work, especially in the city of New York.

106I

CRITICAL THINKING

Guiding Comprehension

Monitoring Student Progress

❶ CAUSE AND EFFECT What problems do you think the snow, wind, and ice caused in New York? (Sample answer: The icy streets became dangerous for people walking or riding to work, and the winds and ice may have damaged boats.)

Extra Support/Intervention

Selection Preview

page 106I A powerful blizzard struck the eastern United States on March 12, 1888. Based on the picture, why might a powerful blizzard be dangerous for people?

pages 106J–106K The air is so cold that the East River in New York City freezes over. People are amazed by this, and many people decide to walk from the island of Manhattan to Brooklyn. Would you have crossed the ice bridge?

pages 106L–106M As the tide comes in, the water under the ice starts to move, and the ice breaks. People become trapped on floating pieces of ice!

page 106N The stranded people are in great danger. A tugboat rescues some of them. How do you think the others reach safety?

CRITICAL THINKING
Guiding Comprehension

❷ MAKING JUDGMENTS Do you think it was a good idea to walk out onto the ice? Why or why not? (Sample answer: no, because only one boy had tested the thickness of the ice)

❸ NOTING DETAILS What two parts of New York City are separated by the East River? (Manhattan and Brooklyn)

❹ MAKING INFERENCES Why do you think the police tried to stop people from crossing the ice? (Sample answer: They thought it was unsafe.)

COMPREHENSION STRATEGY
Predict/Infer

Student Modeling Have students model their predictions about what will happen to the people on the ice. If necessary, use these prompts: Is it dangerous for thousands of people to walk on ice at the same time? What could happen to them?

Vocabulary

immense very large

floes masses of floating ice

pedestrians people walking

entrepreneurs people who start businesses

treacherous very dangerous

In New York City and Brooklyn, the early-morning commuters were shocked when they saw the East River. It looked like a solid sheet of ice.

People immediately rushed to the riverbanks and began to speculate on how thick the ice might be and whether it was safe to walk on. Up close, the distance across looked immense and the ice was clearly not a single sheet, but many big and small ice floes jammed together. No one rushed to be first on the ice.

It was then that a Brooklyn boy of eighteen lowered a ladder onto the ice. Cautiously he climbed down, then proceeded to jump up and down several times. As he came back toward his ladder, he announced that "She's safe as the United States Mint!" ❷

Instantly, many onlookers announced that they wanted to cross the ice bridge. On the Brooklyn side, the boy gladly held his ladder as one hardy soul after another came down, though he made it clear that the fee to use his ladder would be five cents. ❸

"His pockets bulged with coins," one observer noted. "Soon a long file of pedestrians surely numbering at least two hundred were slowly edging toward the Manhattan shore." Similar business operations were set up on the Manhattan side, and in no time at all, the ice swarmed with people.

106J

English Language Learners

Language Development

Explain to students that *commuters* are "people going to work" and that *speculate* means "to wonder hard about something." Tell them that *import* is a multiple-meaning word. In this case, it means "importance."

Another group of ice-crossers also appeared. The unnamed observer recalled that "all the dogs in Brooklyn . . . came barking and bounding onto the [ice] field as well. The pooches were of all sizes, shapes, and varieties. . . . Perhaps they, too, had sensed the drama and historic import of the occasion."

More than just men and dogs crossed the ice bridge. Several women were spotted making the journey, while hordes of boys slid down the icy pilings and raced across the expanse. And at least one horse was hoisted over the side in a sling-harness and ridden to Brooklyn by its owner.

Police on both sides of the river tried to halt the stream of adventurers, but with little success. Other ladder entrepreneurs had appeared, and now there were more spots where a person could get onto the ice than policemen to block them. **4**

Not everyone had an easy crossing. Many slipped on the treacherous ice or were blown over by the still-fierce wind. A few of the elderly adventurers had to be carried to shore. For over an hour and a half, people and animals paraded from one shore to the other. While no one kept an official count, the policemen on duty that day estimated that between 1,500 and 3,000 walked across the river.

106**K**

Connecting and Comparing

Text Organization

- Remind students that nonfiction selections can be organized in different ways. Two of these are by main ideas and by sequence of events.

- Have students look back at pages 106J–106K. Ask them how this section of *Blizzard!* is organized, and how they can tell. (by sequence of events; Signal words and phrases like *immediately, then, instantly, soon, in no time at all, now,* and *for over an hour and a half* tell me that the story is organized by time order.)

- Have students compare the organization of *Blizzard!* with that of *Eye of the Storm* (p. 56) and *Volcanoes* (p. 84). Ask them which selection is organized more like *Blizzard!* (*Eye of the Storm*)

- Then have students identify some text features in *Eye of the Storm* that are not found in *Blizzard!* Ask them what kinds of information these features add to the selection. (headings, subheadings, photographs; Headings and subheadings guide the reader, and photographs show more details.)

Reading the Paired Selections **M21**

CRITICAL THINKING
Guiding Comprehension

5 **DRAWING CONCLUSIONS** Why did the ladder operators raise their prices? (because everyone had to get off the ice soon, and the ladder operators wanted to get as much money as they could quickly)

6 **MAKING JUDGMENTS** What do you think would be the best way for the people trapped on the moving ice to get to safety? (Answers will vary.)

The cheerful mood of the crowd began to subside just after 9 A.M. That was when a deep, ominous grumbling began coming from the ice. The tide was beginning to shift, pushing at the ice to shove it downriver. Meanwhile, three powerful tugs had been ordered out to batter and break the floe in order to free up the river for navigation. When those operating the ladder-climbing concessions noticed this, they raised their prices to twenty-five cents.

Those on the ice realized the danger they were in and hurried to the closest shore. All of the dogs must have sensed something also, because they fled the ice as well. A large squad of police arrived and began ordering the ladders pulled up and watchers away from the ice. "Very many refused to obey," a reporter for the *Sun* noted. "When the ladders were taken away, they let themselves down from the piers. . . . They thirsted for glory."

5

106L

English Language Learners

Supporting Comprehension

Students may need help with several expressions on these pages. These include *tugs* ("small, strong boats that push or tow larger ships"), *thirsted for glory* ("wished for fame or praise"), *cake of ice* ("ice floe"), *pilings* ("wood beams supporting a pier"), and *keep their hearts* ("remain hopeful").

Vocabulary

ominous signaling trouble or danger

concessions businesses

stranded left in a difficult position

Just then, the tide turned and began exerting immense pressure downriver. The giant cake of ice began to move very slowly. "There were over a hundred persons on the ice at this moment," the *Sun* reporter went on. "Most of them broke into a run. Loud were the cries [by those on the riverbank] to get to the shore."

When the ice broke free and began moving seaward, there were between forty and fifty people still on it. The ice came close to the Fulton Ferry pier and some of the stranded tried to grab hold, but the pilings were too slippery. They were close enough that the *Sun* reporter could see that "some exchanged cool jokes with those on the docks. One quietly asked to have a tug sent down for him; another requested a stove; still another shouted that he'd cable from Europe. . . . One man sank down on his knees and prayed."

The ice inched along and collided with a collection of piers on the New York City side. There was a horrible crunching sound as ice met wood, and then the floe came to a shivering stop. In the few minutes it was lodged there, men on the docks lowered down ladders and ropes and managed to pull almost everyone up to safety. Then the floe broke free and continued downriver.

There were still a number of men trapped on smaller chunks of ice heading toward New York Bay and the open sea. Three bobbed about near the Brooklyn shore, while five were close to Manhattan.

The *Sun* reporter took up the story of the three Brooklyn men. "The ice cracked merrily. Then it bulged up, separated and each young man was launched upon a separate cake of ice. The men shouted frantically and waved their arms. . . . Two of the men were on neighboring ice cakes. One finally made a dangerous jump to the cake nearer the shore on which the other stood. The crowd shouted approval, [and] told them to keep their hearts."

106M

Connecting and Comparing

Sequence of Events

- Have students compare the sequence of events described on pages 106J–106L of *Blizzard!* with the events described on pages 69–75 of *Eye of the Storm*.

- When does each selection take place? (*Blizzard!* takes place on March 13, 1888; *Eye of the Storm* takes place on May 5, 1993.)

- How long does the sequence of events last in each selection? (In *Blizzard!*, the events last about one and a half to two hours in the morning. In *Eye of the Storm*, they last the entire day.)

- Do the selections describe events that happened before, during, or after storms? Explain your answer. (*Eye of the Storm* describes tornadoes as they happen during storms, while *Blizzard!* describes events that happened the day after a storm.)

TARGET SKILL Fluency Practice

Rereading for Fluency Have students reread the first two paragraphs on page 106M. Encourage students to read expressively.

Guiding Comprehension

7 NOTING DETAILS How did the people get off the ice after it broke free? (Some scrambled up onto a pier, others were pulled to shore by a rope with a rock attached, and the last few were rescued by tugboat.)

8 NOTING DETAILS How did the onlookers feel after the last men were rescued? How do you know? (Sample answer: They were happy and relieved; they cheered and applauded.)

Finish the Graphic Organizer Have students share and discuss their completed Sequence of Events Graphic Organizers.

A rope with a rock attached to it was eventually tossed to these men and they were hauled to shore and rescued.

"The other young man, who was irreproachably dressed and carried a satchel, was on a cake scarcely twenty-five feet in diameter. He ran from edge to edge, till each time he nearly slipped in the water, and showed such terror that terror was communicated to those on shore."

Farther and farther out the desperate man drifted, and many watchers felt he would be lost. Then the tugboat *S.E. Babcock* managed to plow through a large chunk of ice and swing in close enough for the man to be brought on board. **7**

Meanwhile, the five men near Manhattan were floating out rapidly. Three were on a rather large slab of ice, while two were each on cakes that the *Sun* reporter said were "the size of door mats."

First, a tug nudged the large floe into shore until it hit a wharf and the three men leaped off. Then the tug went after the two last floaters. When they were finally hauled up and safe "the thousands of men on the riverside and the Bridge yelled their applause in rounds of cheers and screams." **8**

106N

Challenge

Research Icebreakers

Today icebreaking ships usually push their bows up onto ice until it collapses, but sometimes they have to back up and ram thick ice. These boats can break through ice that is more than 23 feet thick. Have students work together to create a labeled diagram of an icebreaker that describes its parts and functions.

Vocabulary

desperate willing to do or try anything

Think and Compare

1. **Analyzing** Compare the danger of the tornado in *Night of the Twisters* with the danger of the ice floes in *Blizzard!* How are the two situations similar and different?

2. **Analyzing** Compare Dan in *Night of the Twisters* and Jonathan in *Earthquake Terror*. How are the characters alike and different?

3. **Generating** How have *Night of the Twisters* and *Blizzard!* added to or changed your feelings about nature at its most dangerous?

4. **Integrating** How well-prepared do you think people were in 1888 to face a natural disaster compared to people today?

5. **Evaluating** Both *Night of the Twisters* and *Eye of the Storm* give details about tornadoes. Which selection seems scarier or more realistic? Use examples to explain why.

Strategies in Action Which reading strategies did you use most while reading this theme? How did they help?

Write a Weather Report

Write a paragraph telling about a fictional thunderstorm, blizzard, or tornado. Include details about what will happen and how people can stay safe.

Tips
- Think about the damage the storm might cause to land and buildings.
- Think about the movement in the storm, such as its speed and direction.
- Think about how long the storm will last.

106O

Extra Support/ Intervention	**English Language Learners**
Review Predictions Have students discuss the predictions they made about the people on the ice. How do their predictions compare to the actual story events?	**Language Development** **Beginning/Preproduction** Ask students how people trapped on the ice felt before and after they were rescued. Help students create simple word webs to describe how the people felt. **Early Production and Speech Emergence** Have students work in pairs to retell in their own words one of the Paired Selections they have just read. **Intermediate and Advanced Fluency** Ask students to write a summary of one of the Paired Selections. Ask them to use words that provide a clear description of key information.

Think and Compare

Discuss or Write Have students discuss or write their answers. Sample answers are provided; accept reasonable responses.

1. **ANALYZING** The tornado was fast-moving, and everything happened in a matter of minutes. The ice floes took much longer to form and become dangerous to people. Both situations are examples of how a storm can put people in danger.

2. **ANALYZING** Both boys bravely protect their younger siblings despite their fear. Dan knows how to stay safe inside during a tornado, but Jonathan has never experienced an earthquake outside before and is not sure what to do.

3. **GENERATING** Answers will vary.

4. **INTEGRATING** People today are warned through emergency alerts, and they are taught how to deal with natural disasters. There was less information for people in 1888.

5. **EVALUATING** *Eye of the Storm* is realistic because it explains when tornadoes occur and what causes them. It isn't as scary as *Night of the Twisters*, where the characters are almost killed by a tornado that destroys the house they are in.

Strategies in Action Have students take turns modeling how and where they used Predict/Infer and other strategies.

Monitoring Student Progress

If . . .	Then . . .
students have difficulty answering more than two Think and Compare questions,	guide them in reading aloud relevant portions of the text and discussing their answers.

THEME CONNECTIONS: Anthology Literature

Making Connections

Teach

Congratulate students on reaching the end of Theme 1: Nature's Fury. Point out that they will now participate in an activity to help them celebrate the theme.

- **Review with students the selections they have read in this theme.** (*Earthquake Terror; Eye of the Storm: Chasing Storms with Warren Faidley; Volcanoes*) Also remind students about this theme's Links, Monitoring Student Progress paired selections, and Leveled Books.

- **Create a list of the natural disasters described in this theme.** Have volunteers take turns listing the events on the board.

- **Compare and contrast each situation.** Have students describe how each event affects the theme's characters. How are the characters' predicaments alike and different?

Practice/Apply

Next, choose one of these three activities to help students wrap up this theme. Note: Each activity can be divided into segments throughout the week.

📗 **Portfolio Opportunity** Suggest that students include copies of their booklets or other material related to the theme wrap-up activity—such as notes or sketches—in their portfolios.

Practice Book

Suggest that students review Selection Connections on **Practice Book** pages 9 and 10.

Disaster Map

👤👤👤 Whole Class or Groups	🕐 60 minutes (can take place over 3–4 days)
Objective	Create a United States map of the natural disasters in the theme.
Materials	U.S. map outline, reference sources, pencils, colored markers

Create a map that shows the locations of the natural disasters described in the theme. The map should include state labels and a map key with symbols representing different natural disasters.

1 First plan your map. Design a system of symbols for each type of disaster. Think about the following.

- Which natural disasters have you read about?
- What would be a good symbol for each disaster?

2 Working together, collect information about the natural disasters that are described in the theme.

3 Create a map key for your symbols.

4 Label the states and place the disaster symbols where they belong.

5 Post your disaster map in the classroom.

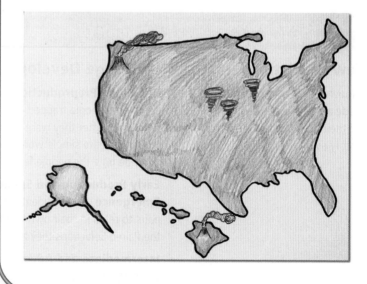

Consider copying and laminating these activities for use in centers.

Student Newscast

👥👥 Whole Class or Groups	🕐 60 minutes (can take place over 3–4 days)
Objective	Plan and conduct news reports.
Materials	Pencil, paper, tape recorder

Plan and present your own news report about a natural disaster described in this theme. The news report should include a detailed description of what happened, as well as one or two interviews with story characters.

1 Choose a disaster from the theme to cover in your newscast, as well as one or more characters to interview.

2 Plan the newscast by outlining your description of the event and listing questions for your interview subjects. Think about the following.

- What important events do you need to describe?

- What questions will you ask the character(s)?

- If you are interviewing more than one character, will you ask each character the same questions? Will you interview the characters one at a time, or as a group?

- Based on what you know about each character, how might he or she respond to your questions?

3 Assign roles for your newscast. Possible roles include news anchor, reporter, and story character.

4 Present the newscast. Remember to speak clearly. Tape-record your presentation to see how you sound.

Disaster Preparedness Kit

👥👥 Whole Class or Groups	🕐 60 minutes (can take place over 3–4 days)
Objective	Compile a booklet of facts and safety tips for your state.
Materials	Reference sources, paper and pencils

Put together a disaster preparedness kit to keep on hand in an emergency. The selections in this theme present a lot of information about staying safe in a natural disaster. Use details from each selection to help you create your kit.

1 Look at the selections in the theme, and create a list of what characters or real people needed to cope with the different emergencies they faced. For example, Jonathan in *Earthquake Terror* could have used a first-aid kit and a battery-powered radio.

2 Think of a way to organize your items. You might put all the food items together and all the battery-operated items such as radio and flashlights together.

3 Decide what kind of container is needed to hold the items.

4 Draw a picture of the container. Below it, write a list of the items it should contain.

radio and extra batteries

flashlight

water

first aid kit

Independent Activities

THEME CONNECTIONS:
Leveled Books

While you work with small groups, students can choose from a wealth of books to complete these activities.

Leveled Readers . . .

for *Earthquake Terror*
Riding Out the Storm
Earthquake: Alaska, 1964
Clearing the Dust
Alone in the Storm

for *Eye of the Storm: Chasing Storms with Warren Faidley*
White Dragon: Anna Allen in the Face of Danger
Hurricane Opal: Into the Storm
Benjamin Franklin, A Scientist by Nature
Anna Allen Faces the White Dragon

for *Volcanoes*
Floods
Mexico's Smoking Mountains
A Deep Blue Lake
Dangerous Waters

Leveled Theme Paperbacks

If You Lived at the Time of the San Francisco Earthquake
Drylongso
Hurricanes: Earth's Mightiest Storms

Vocabulary Readers

The San Francisco Earthquake
Day of the Tornadoes
Volcanoes Around the World

Leveled Bibliography

pp. 23E–23F

Write a Letter

👤 Singles	🕐 30 minutes
Objective	Write a letter from a character's perspective.

Choose a character from any of the books you have read. Create a letter this character might send to a friend or relative.

You might include details about

- the character's experience with nature's fury
- where the character was and what he or she was doing when disaster struck
- what the character learned
- advice the character might have for his or her friend about dealing with nature's fury

Share your letters with the class or with a small group. Compare your message with that of another character you have read about.

Use these questions to guide your discussion:

- How did the characters deal with nature's fury?
- How are the characters alike and different?
- What did the characters learn?

Consider copying and laminating these activities for use in centers.

THEME CONNECTIONS

Selling Safety

👥 Pairs	🕐 30 minutes
Objective	Create an advertisement for a product.
Materials	Colored markers, reference materials

Think about the books you have read. What equipment do the characters in them use to protect themselves from nature's fury?

Pick a piece of equipment from one of the books. Then write and illustrate an advertisement to sell the equipment to people.

Think about

- how the character uses the equipment in the story
- when else it might be useful
- what the character might say about it

In your advertisement, include

- a picture of what you are selling
- a recommendation from the character in the book

Act Out a Scene

👥 Pairs	🕐 40 minutes
Objective	Plan and act out a story scene.
Materials	Props and costumes (optional)

Choose a scene from a book you have read. Then act out the scene with a partner. To refresh your memory, reread the scene several times. Take notes and outline a simple script for you and your partner to act out.

As you plan your scene, think about

- each character's personality, strengths, and weaknesses
- how the setting and events affect the characters

Act out your scene for the class or for a small group.

Preparing for Tests

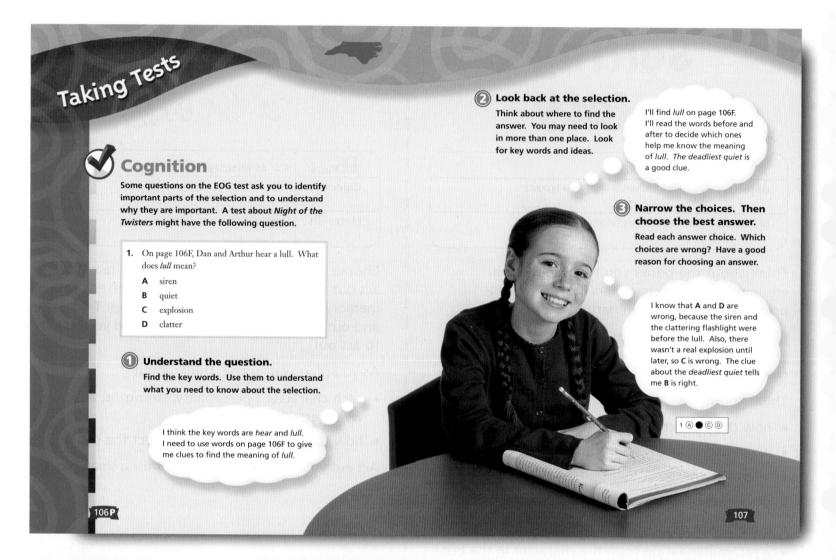

Taking Tests

✓ **Cognition**

Some questions on the EOG test ask you to identify important parts of the selection and to understand why they are important. A test about *Night of the Twisters* might have the following question.

> 1. On page 106F, Dan and Arthur hear a lull. What does *lull* mean?
>
> A siren
>
> B quiet
>
> C explosion
>
> D clatter

① **Understand the question.**
Find the key words. Use them to understand what you need to know about the selection.

I think the key words are hear and lull. I need to use words on page 106F to give me clues to find the meaning of lull.

② **Look back at the selection.**
Think about where to find the answer. You may need to look in more than one place. Look for key words and ideas.

I'll find lull on page 106F. I'll read the words before and after to decide which ones help me know the meaning of lull. The deadliest quiet is a good clue.

③ **Narrow the choices. Then choose the best answer.**
Read each answer choice. Which choices are wrong? Have a good reason for choosing an answer.

I know that A and D are wrong, because the siren and the clattering flashlight were before the lull. Also, there wasn't a real explosion until later, so C is wrong. The clue about the deadliest quiet tells me B is right.

1 Ⓐ ● Ⓒ Ⓓ

106P   107

THEME	CATEGORY
▶ **1**	**Cognition**
2	**Interpretation**
3	**Critical Stance**
4	**Writing an Argumentative Essay**
5	**Connections**
6	**Critical Stance**

Introduce the Category

Taking Tests provides instruction and practice in the four question categories of the **End-of-Grade Test** and in writing an argumentative essay for the **Writing Assessment.** It will help you prepare your students for further practice, using the **North Carolina EOG Aligned Assessments and Practice** book.

- Tell students that on Anthology pages 106P–107 they will be learning more about the **Cognition** category in the EOG test. Explain that questions in this category ask the reader to find important information in the selection.

- Cognition questions may ask about a character's problem, the setting, or important events in a story. In a nonfiction selection, questions may ask about the topic, main ideas, supporting details, or the author's purpose. Cognition questions may also ask students to identify the meanings of words.

- Have volunteers read aloud each step and thought balloon on pages 106P–107. Explain that students will be learning more about these steps.

Teach the Category

 Understand the Question.

Display Teaching Master page 101 and model Step 1.

- Have a volunteer read aloud Step 1. Tell students that they will learn more about this one step.
- Explain that both questions are based on *Night of the Twisters* on Anthology pages 106B–106H.
- Model using the step to understand Question 1.

Think Aloud *First, I will circle the key words in Question 1 that tell what the question is asking about. I will circle* Dan *and* keep Arthur from going home. *Next, I will circle the key words that tell what the question is asking me to do. I will circle* Why does *and* want. *Finally, I will ask myself what I need to do. I need to think about why Dan wants to keep Arthur from leaving.*

- Guide students in using the step to understand Question 2.
- Point out and discuss EOG vocabulary in Question 2: *best describes*.

 Look Back at the Selection.

Display Teaching Master page 102 and model Step 2.

- Have a volunteer read aloud Step 2. Tell students that they will learn more about this one step.
- Model using the step to find details in *Night of the Twisters* that will help answer Question 1.

Think Aloud *I need to decide where I might find the answer. I'll skim the selection looking for the names Arthur and Dan. Those places might show why Dan wants to keep Arthur from going home. On page 106D, after he hears strange sounds, Arthur tries to go home, but Dan forces him to stay. Dan knows that they have to "take cover fast." On 106F, Arthur again says he has to go home, but Dan says he can't go home because the twister "is here." Dan's words provide important information about why he wants to keep Arthur from going home.*

- Guide students in using the step to find details that will help them answer Question 2.

Turn the page to Teach the Category Step 3.

EOG Vocabulary

best describes: The answer that *best describes* why something happens in a selection is the choice that makes the most sense as a description.

Review with students other terms from the Teaching Master and Practice Master for this theme: *best explains, approximately, according to, result, react.*

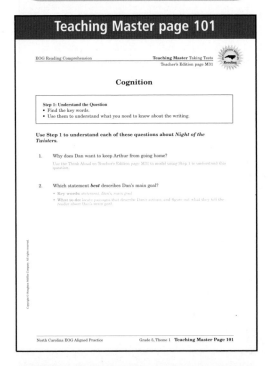

Teaching Master page 101

Teaching Master page 102

Teaching Master page 103

Copyright © Houghton Mifflin Company. All rights reserved.

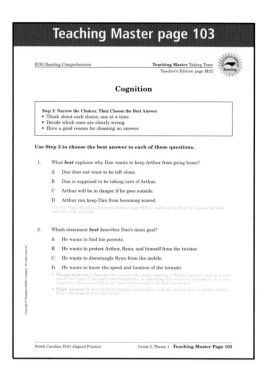

EOG Reading Comprehension   **Teaching Master** Taking Tests
                                             Teacher's Edition page M32

Cognition

Step 3: Narrow the Choices. Then Choose the Best Answer
- Think about each choice, one at a time.
- Decide which ones are clearly wrong.
- Have a good reason for choosing an answer.

Use Step 3 to choose the best answer to each of these questions.

1. What *best* explains why Dan wants to keep Arthur from going home?

    A   Dan does not want to be left alone.

    B   Dan is supposed to be taking care of Arthur.

    C   Arthur will be in danger if he goes outside.

    D   Arthur can keep Dan from becoming scared.

    Use the Think Aloud on Teacher's Edition page M32 to model using Step 3 to choose the best answer to the question.

2. Which statement *best* describes Dan's main goal?

    A   He wants to find his parents.

    B   He wants to protect Arthur, Ryan, and himself from the twister.

    C   He wants to disentangle Ryan from the mobile.

    D. He wants to know the speed and location of the tornado.

    • **Wrong answers:** A because Dan never talks about wanting to find his parents and he is safer inside the house. C because even though this is something Dan wants to accomplish, it is less important. D because this is not important enough to be Dan's main goal.

    • **Right answer:** B because Dan's helpful actions show that his main goal is to protect Arthur, Ryan, and himself from the twister.

North Carolina EOG Aligned Practice   Grade 5, Theme 1   **Teaching Master Page 103**

Narrow the Choices.
Then Choose the Best Answer.

Display Teaching Master page 103 and model Step 3.

- Have a volunteer read aloud Step 3. Tell students that they will learn more about this one step.

- Model how to narrow the answer choices and then choose the best answer for Question 1.

Think Aloud *I will start by narrowing the choices. Which answers are obviously wrong? I know B is wrong because it never says in the selection that Dan is supposed to be taking care of Arthur. A is wrong too. The author never says that Dan doesn't want to be alone. That leaves C and D. D doesn't seem right. Arthur can't keep himself from being scared, so I don't think he can keep Dan calm. I think the correct answer is C. I know that the twister is happening outside, and that Arthur will be in danger if he tries to go home.*

- Guide students in using the step to narrow the answer choices and choose the best answer for Question 2.

English Language Learners

Review in detail any test-specific language that your students might not understand.

- Many tests use essentially the same direction lines every year.

- Other supporting material, such as a list of criteria for answering open-response questions, is often quite similar from year to year.

Using published samples, make sure that students understand as much of this language as possible. They will be less anxious and more focused if they are confident that they understand what is expected of them.

Apply the Category

Cognition Test Practice

Review Cognition questions with students.

- In Cognition questions, the reader locates important information in the selection.

- A question may ask the reader to restate the main idea or purpose of the selection.

- Sometimes a question will ask the reader to find the meaning of a word in the selection using context clues.

- A question may ask how the selection is organized or why a specific text feature is used in the selection.

Assign Practice Master pages 104 and 105.

- Tell students that these Cognition questions are based on *Blizzard!* on Anthology pages 106I–106N.

- Remind students to use all three steps to choose the best answer for each question.

- Point out the answer box at the bottom of each Practice Master. Remind students that this is where they are supposed to mark their answers.

- When students are finished, review and discuss each item on the Practice Master pages.

Remind students how to mark and check answers.

- Make sure that you mark your answer in the right place. Be sure to fill in the answer bubble correctly.

- When you change an answer, be sure to erase it completely.

- Check answers for questions that gave you trouble, not answers that you feel confident about.

Practice Master page 104

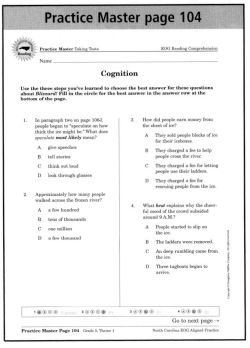

Practice Master page 105

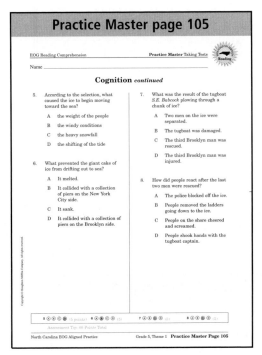

Additional Resources

North Carolina EOG Aligned Assessments and Practice

Provides students with more opportunities for practice and assessment in EOG questions and Writing Assessment prompts

 **Options**

COMPREHENSION

OBJECTIVES

Students review how to
- determine sequence of story events
- identify purposes of text features
- categorize and classify information

Sequence of Events

Review sequence of events.

- The events in a story happen in a certain sequence, or order.
- Words such as *first, next, then, after,* and *later* may signal sequence of events. Words such as *while* and *as* may signal events that happen at the same time.
- Authors sometimes shift from present events to past events to give readers extra information.

Model identifying a sequence of events.

- Read aloud the fourth through ninth paragraphs on Anthology page 106D.
- Explain how the words *just before, again,* and *finally* help you determine the sequence of events in this passage.

Have students identify the sequence of events.

- Ask students to reread page 106F and identify the sequence of events in the passage.
- Have them point out any signal words as well as events that happen at the same time.

Practice Book page 67

Name _____

Monitoring Student Progress
Comprehension Skill
Text Organization

How Is It Organized?

Read the article. Then complete the activity below.

Tsunamis[1]

A tsunami (tsoo NAH mee)[2] is a giant ocean wave produced by an undersea earthquake, landslide, or volcanic eruption. Most tsunamis occur in the Pacific Ocean. The wave may only be a few feet high in the open ocean, but as it approaches a coastline it can rise to a height of over 100 feet. How fast a tsunami travels depends on the depth of the water it is traveling through. In deep waters, a tsunami can travel 600 miles per hour. As it nears shore, however, the wave might slow to about 100 miles per hour.

3 **Energy Compression of Tsunami Waves**

Use a word or phrase in the box to label each of the numbered text features in the article. Write your responses on the lines below.

1. title **(2 points)**
2. pronunciation key **(2)**
3. diagram **(2)**

diagram
pronunciation key
title

Answer the questions.

4. What is the heading of the diagram?
   Energy Compression of Tsunami Waves **(2)**
5. How is the information in the article organized?
   by main idea and details **(2)**

Text Organization

Review features of text organization.

- Use Anthology page 69 to review headings (*Tornado Chase Diary: May 5, 1993*) and subheadings (*Amarillo, Texas— Morning; National Weather Service Office—Early Afternoon*).
- Discuss with students how these features show that this part of the selection is organized by sequence of events.
- Review the photographs on pages 74–75. Discuss how these images help readers better understand the events described in the selection.

Have students identify features of text organization.

- Assign **Practice Book** page 67.

COMPREHENSION

Categorize and Classify

Review how to categorize and classify information.

- Review with students that a *category* is a group of people, animals, things, or ideas that are alike. To *classify* means to put items into groups according to their similarities.

- Explain to students that categorizing and classifying helps them remember not only what they read, but also how ideas and events are related to one another.

Model how to categorize and classify information.

- Write *earthquake, volcano, tornado, hurricane, blizzard, tsunami,* and *monsoon* and review each word's meaning with students. Then sort the natural disasters into categories according to similarities. (Sample answer: Severe Types of Weather: *tornado, hurricane, blizzard, monsoon;* Events Caused by Forces Inside the Earth: *earthquake, volcano, tsunami*)

Have students categorize and classify information.

- Assign **Practice Book** page 68.

Practice Book page 68

Name _____

Earth Waves

Read the article. Then complete the activity below.

Earthquakes and Seismic Waves

An earthquake occurs when huge masses of rock shift and break below and on the surface of the earth. This movement releases energy that travels in all directions in the form of vibrations called seismic waves. These waves are classified according to how they travel. Fast vibrations known as **body waves** move through the earth. Slower **surface waves** move along the earth's surface.

Body waves travel faster deep within the earth than near the earth's surface. However, body waves usually cause the most damage during an earthquake. As body waves pass through the earth, they cause rock to move in different ways. One type of body wave, known as a compressional wave, pushes and pulls the rock. Another type, called a shear wave, makes rocks move from side to side.

Surface waves are long, slow waves that usually cause little damage. The two main kinds of surface waves are Love waves and Rayleigh waves. Love waves move the ground from side to side. Rayleigh waves make the surface of the earth roll like waves on the ocean.

Answer the questions.

How are seismic waves classified?
according to how they travel **(2 points)** _____

Add names or categories that are missing from this chart.

Types of Seismic Waves **(2)**	
Body	Surface **(2)**
compressional **(2)**	Love
shear	Rayleigh **(2)**

SKILL REVIEW:
Structural Analysis/Vocabulary

OBJECTIVES

Students review how to

- decode words that have base words and affixes or are inflected forms
- identify syllables in longer words
- decode words with *struct* and *rupt*

Base Words

Review base words.

- A base word can stand alone.
- Endings and other word parts such as prefixes and suffixes can be added to base words. The spelling of a base word sometimes changes when an ending is added.

Model how to identify base words.

- Display this phrase: <u>hurried</u> *to the door.* Model decoding *hurried.*

Think Aloud *I see the ending -ed. If I cover it, the part that remains looks like* hurry. *I recall that* y *sometimes changes to* i *when an ending is added.* Hurried *must mean "went fast." It makes sense in the phrase.*

Have students identify base words.

- Display *whispered, surprising, squeezes, flopped, terrified.*
- Have partners take turns identifying the base words.

Syllabication

Review how to divide words into syllables.

- A syllable is a word part with just one vowel sound.
- In the VCCV pattern, syllables usually break between the two consonants.
- If the first vowel in a VCV pattern has the long sound, the syllable may break before the consonant.
- In the CVVC pattern, break the syllables between the two vowels if each vowel stands for a separate sound.

Model how to divide words into syllables.

- Display and pronounce *observation.*
- Rewrite *ob-ser-va-tion* as separate syllables, pointing out the syllable breaks between consonant pairs and after the long vowel.
- Model dividing *vol-can-ic, e-rup-tion,* and *vid-e-o* into syllables.

Have students divide words into syllables.

- Assign **Practice Book** page 69.

Practice Book page 69

Monitoring Student Progress
Structural Analysis Review

Name _____

Decide Where to Divide

Read each sentence. Rewrite the underlined word with a slash or slashes to divide the syllables. After the word, write which of the following patterns helped you decide where to divide.

VCCV   VCV (long first vowel)
CVVC   VCV (short first vowel)

1. The sunset <u>glimmered</u> orange on the sparkling waves.
   glim-mered, VCCV **(2 points)**

2. A <u>giant</u> wave gathered strength and smashed into the shore.
   gi-ant, CVVC **(2)**

3. A <u>funnel</u> cloud threatened to reach the ground.
   fun-nel, VCCV **(2)**

4. The family took <u>shelter</u> in their basement.
   shel-ter, VCCV **(2)**

5. The tornado left the house with several <u>broken</u> windows.
   bro-ken, VCV (long first vowel) **(2)**

6. The <u>reporter</u> wrote an eyewitness account of the storm.
   re-por-ter, VCV/VCCV (long first vowel) **(2)**

Word Roots *struct* and *rupt*

Review word roots *rupt* and *struct*.

- A word root has meaning, but is not a word by itself.
- *Rupt* means "break" and *struct* means "build."

Model how to decode a word with *rupt*.

- Display this phrase: *annoying* <u>*interruptions*</u>. Model decoding *interruptions*.

Think Aloud *II recognize the prefix* inter-, *which means "between," and the word root* rupt, *which means "break." Interruptions must be times when someone breaks in on something that is happening. That makes sense in the phrase.*

Have students decode words.

- Display *destruction, instructor, reconstruct, bankrupt, corruption, disruptive.*
- Have partners decode each word and tell its meaning.

OBJECTIVES

Students review how to
- use a thesaurus
- use dictionary guide words
- use dictionary definitions

Using a Thesaurus

Review the reasons for using a thesaurus.

- A thesaurus lists synonyms and antonyms for words.

- A thesaurus may be organized alphabetically or it may have an index that tells how to find more information.

- It is useful in finding the right word to express your thoughts.

Model how to use a thesaurus.

- Display *An earthquake <u>shook</u> the building.*

- Discuss these thesaurus subentries under **shake**: *quiver, rattle, shiver, shudder, tremble, vibrate.* **Antonyms**: *rest, keep still.*

- Substitute the past tense of each subentry, demonstrating that *rattled* or *vibrated* are the best synonyms to replace *shook.*

Have students practice using a thesaurus.

- Have students look up synonyms for *earthquake* and *building*, and then write sentences using each synonym correctly.

Dictionary Guide Words

Review alphabetical order and the use of guide words.

- Dictionary entry words are listed in alphabetical order.

- Pairs of guide words at the top of each dictionary page show the first and last entry words on that page.

Model how to find entry words using guide words.

- Display these guide words: *lastly/laugh* and *laughable/lawn.*

- Demonstrate identifying the page on which you would find *latitude* by using the third letter in each guide word to locate it alphabetically. (between *lastly* and *laugh*)

Have students use alphabetical order and guide words.

- Display these pairs of guide words: *range/rascal* and *kick/kin.*

- Have students identify which of these entry words would be found between each pair: *raptor, rancher, rasp, ransom* (*raptor, ransom*); *khaki, kickoff, kindling, kimono* (*kickoff, kimono*).

Dictionary Definitions

Review the parts of dictionary entries.

- Each entry word has a phonetic respelling that shows how the word is pronounced.
- An abbreviation shows what part of speech the word is.
- Each entry has at least one definition.
- A sample sentence gives an example of a word's meaning in context.

Model how to use a sample sentence to figure out meaning.

- Display *He <u>trimmed</u> some limbs off the tree.*
- Display these definitions and sample sentences for *trim:*

    1. make tidy by clipping: *Barbers trim men's beards.*
    2. remove or reduce by cutting: *Trim the pie crust.*
    3. decorate: *We will trim the Christmas tree.*

- Explain why the second definition makes the most sense in this context.

Have students practice identifying correct definitions.

- Assign **Practice Book** page 70.

Practice Book page 70

Monitoring Student Progress

Name _____

Vocabulary Skill Review

Meaning Match

Read the definitions and the four sentences at the bottom of the page. In the blank space after each sentence, write the correct meaning for the underlined word.

fragment (frăg´ mənt) *n.* **1.** A piece or part broken off or separated from a whole: *She picked up a fragment of the broken plate.* **2.** Something incomplete or not finished. *The note contained only a sentence fragment.* —*v.* to break into pieces. *The thin ice will fragment at the slightest pressure.*

particular (pər tĭk´ yə lər) *adj.* **1.** Of or for a single person, group, or thing. *Each group did its particular job.* **2.** Unique; having to do only with a certain person or thing. *The dog has a particular whine when it is hungry.* **3.** Demanding close attention to detail. *My aunt is very particular about housekeeping.* —*n.* a single item, fact, or detail.

vent (vĕnt) *n.* An opening through which liquid or gas can pass through or escape. *Hot air from the dryer flows through a hose to a vent in the wall.* —*v.* to express; give utterance to. *People vented their frustrations about the long ticket lines.*

1. Ash, rock, and fumes spewed outward through a <u>vent</u> in the side of the volcano. An opening through which liquid or gas can pass through or escape. **(2 points)**

2. The blast left a <u>particular</u> track of devastation. Unique; having to do only with a certain person or thing. **(2)**

3. The eruption sent <u>fragments</u> of rock flying in all directions. Pieces or parts broken off or separated from a whole. **(2)**

4. Sam had to <u>vent</u> his anger that we were not taking the volcano threat seriously. To express. **(2)**

Options

SKILL REVIEW: Spelling

OBJECTIVES

Students review

- words with short vowel patterns
- words with /ā/, /ē/, and /ī/ sounds
- words with /ō/, /o͞o/, and /yo͞o/ sounds
- words with silent consonants

SPELLING WORDS

Basic

slept	boast
split	flute
staff	sway
fade	cruise
praise	mild
slope	grasp
claim	swift
stroll	bunk
mood	slight
beast	thrown
crush	stole
fond	fleet
dwell	dew
strike	youth
clue	thigh

Challenge

frantic	rustic
trek	describe
cease	campaign
molten	subdue
pursuit	reproach

DAY 1 — SHORT VOWELS

Pretest Use the Day 5 Test sentences.

Review words with short vowel patterns.

- Display *staff, swept, dock, ditch,* and *bunch.*
- Read each word aloud, emphasizing its short vowel sound.
- Underline the letter in each word that spells the short vowel sound.
- Explain that a short vowel sound is usually spelled by a single vowel and followed by a consonant sound.

Have students identify short vowel patterns in words.

- Say *dwell, fond, swift, bunk, slept, split, crush,* and *grasp.*
- Have students write each word and underline the letter that makes the short vowel sound.
- Repeat with the Challenge Words *frantic, trek, rustic, describe,* and *campaign,* if appropriate.

Practice/Homework Assign **Practice Book** page 267.

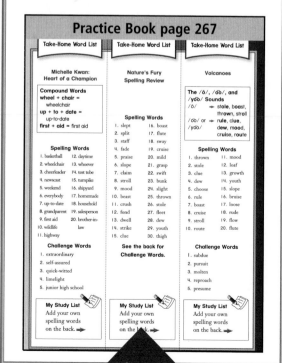

Practice Book page 267

DAY 2 — /ā/, /ē/, AND /ī/

Review words with /ā/, /ē/, and /ī/.

- Display *fade, waist,* and *stray.* Read each word aloud.
- Point out the ways to spell /ā/: *a*-consonant-*e, ai,* and *ay.*
- Display *leaf* and *speech.* Read each word aloud.
- Point out ways to spell /ē/: *ea, ee.*
- Display *strike, mild, sign,* and *slight.* Read each word aloud.
- Point out ways to spell /ī/: *i*-consonant-*e, i, igh.*

Have students identify words with /ā/, /ē/, and /ī/.

- Have students make a three-column chart with these headings: /ā/, /ē/, and /ī/.
- Have them write each Basic Spelling Word in the appropriate column and underline the letter or letters that make the vowel sound.

Practice/Homework Assign **Practice Book** page 71.

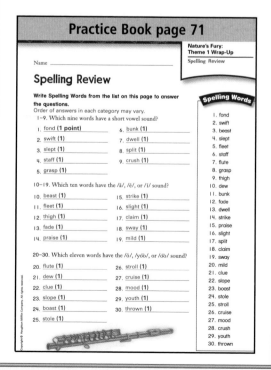

Practice Book page 71

Take-Home Word List

DAY 3 — /ō/, /o͞o/, AND /yo͞o/

Review words with /ō/, /o͞o/, and /yo͞o/.

- Display *slope*, *loaf*, *flow*, and *stroll*. Read each word aloud.
- Point out the ways of spelling /ō/: *o-consonant-e*, *oa*, *ow*, *o*.
- Display *loose*, *clue*, *route*, *bruise*, *dew*, and *rule*.
- Point out the ways of spelling /o͞o/ or /yo͞o/: *oo*, *ue*, *ou*, *ui*, *ew*, and *u-consonant-e*.

Have students review words with /ō/, /o͞o/, and /yo͞o/.

- Display *youth*, *stole*, *thrown*, *boast*, *flute*, *cruise*, *slope*, *dew*, *stroll*, *clue*, and *mood*.
- Have students list words with /ō/, and underline the letter or letters in each that make the long *o* sound.
- Have students do the same for words with /o͞o/ or /yo͞o/.

Practice/Homework Assign **Practice Book** page 72.

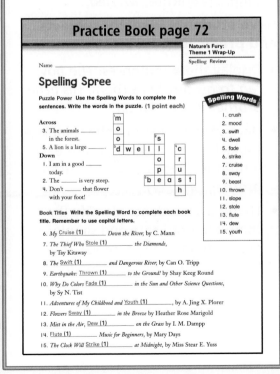

Practice Book page 72

Nature's Fury:
Theme 1 Wrap-Up
Spelling Review

Name _____

Spelling Spree

Puzzle Power Use the Spelling Words to complete the sentences. Write the words in the puzzle. (1 point each)

Spelling Words
1. crush
2. mood
3. swift
4. dwell
5. fade
6. strike
7. cruise
8. sway
9. beast
10. thrown
11. slope
12. stole
13. flute
14. dew
15. youth

Across
3. The animals _____ in the forest.
5. A lion is a large _____

Down
1. I am in a good _____ today.
2. The _____ is very steep.
4. Don't _____ that flower with your foot!

Book Titles Write the Spelling Word to complete each book title. Remember to use capital letters.

6. *My Cruise (1) _____ Down the River*, by C. Mann
7. *The Thief Who Stole (1) _____ the Diamonds*, by Tay Kitaway
8. *The Swift (1) _____ and Dangerous River*, by Can O. Tripp
9. *Earthquake: Thrown (1) _____ to the Ground!* by Shay Keeg Round
10. *Why Do Colors Fade (1) _____ in the Sun and Other Science Questions*, by Sy N. Tist
11. *Adventures of My Childhood and Youth (1) _____*, by A. Jing X. Plorer
12. *Flowers Sway (1) _____ in the Breeze* by Heather Rose Marigold
13. *Mist in the Air, Dew (1) _____ on the Grass* by I. M. Dampp
14. *Flute (1) _____ Music for Beginners*, by Mary Days
15. *The Clock Will Strike (1) _____ at Midnight*, by Miss Stear E. Yuss

DAY 4 — SILENT CONSONANTS

Review words that have silent consonants.

- Explain that some words have consonants that are not pronounced.
- Display *climb*, *kneel*, *listen*, *wrist*, and *calf*.
- Read each word aloud.
- Underline the silent consonant in each. (*b*, *k*, *t*, *w*, *l*)

Have students identify silent consonants.

- Display *knight*, *honor*, *soften*, *thumb*, and *handsome*.
- Have partners read each word and tell which consonant is silent. (*k*, *h*, *t*, *b*, *d*)

Practice/Homework Assign **Practice Book** page 73.

Practice Book page 73

Nature's Fury:
Theme 1 Wrap-Up
Spelling Review

Name _____

Proofreading and Writing

Proofreading Circle the six misspelled Spelling Words in this newspaper article. Then write each word correctly.

Spelling Words
1. slept
2. praise
3. fond
4. clue
5. staff
6. thigh
7. stroll
8. slight
9. claim
10. fleet
11. mild
12. grasp
13. split
14. bunk
15. boast

At 11:30 last night, a (milde) earthquake gently rocked the city. Little damage was reported, and some people (sleept) right through it. This morning Helen and Joe Dalton (boste) that they were not afraid. There was only (slite) damage downtown. With (prayse) for his workers, the mayor said, "My (staf) responded quickly to all questions."

1. mild **(1 point)** _____   4. slight **(1)** _____
2. slept **(1)** _____   5. praise **(1)** _____
3. boast **(1)** _____   6. staff **(1)** _____

In the News A reporter takes notes after an earthquake. Complete his ideas by writing Spelling Words in the blanks.

- No one is fond **(1)** _____ of surprises like this.
- Scientists have no clue **(1)** _____ about why this quake occurred at night.
- It is a strange time to stroll **(1)** _____ through town!
- A man has cuts on his thigh **(1)** _____ and ankle.
- A large fleet **(1)** _____ of fire trucks roars by.
- Large crevice in ground. Oak street is split **(1)** _____ in two!
- It's hard to fully grasp **(1)** _____ the power of a quake.
- Some people claim **(1)** _____ that animals can predict earthquakes.

Write a Safety Plan On a separate sheet of paper, write about what you should do in an earthquake. Use the Spelling Review Words.

DAY 5 — TEST

Say each underlined word, read the sentence, and then repeat the word. Have students write only the underlined words.

Basic Words

1. We watched a **fleet** of **swift** ships.
2. Ralph **slept** all through the **cruise**.
3. If the trees start to **sway**, **grasp** a strong limb.
4. We took a **stroll** while the grass was wet with **dew**.
5. The pitch was a **strike**, but Ella **stole** second base.
6. Gus offered to **split** gold from the **claim** with Pablo.
7. That **beast** will **crush** the plants.
8. The **youth** has a **slight** headache.
9. Notes played by a **flute** do not **fade** quickly.
10. Larry is **fond** of **mild** curries.
11. A **clue** was found on a steep **slope**.
12. Hearing Victor **boast** puts me in a sour **mood**.
13. Who has **thrown** away my hiking **staff**?
14. People who **dwell** in this area **praise** its parks.
15. Jenna bruised her **thigh** after climbing to the upper **bunk**.

Challenge Words

16. Kyle became **frantic** during his **pursuit** of the runaway puppy.
17. We will **trek** to a **rustic** cabin.
18. If you **reproach** Fran, she may **cease** her troublesome behavior.
19. The writer tried to **describe** the color of **molten** lava.
20. The army's **campaign** to **subdue** the enemy was successful.

SKILL REVIEW: Grammar

OBJECTIVES

Students review how to
- identify kinds of sentences
- identify complete and simple subjects and predicates
- identify conjunctions and compound sentences
- identify and write singular and plural nouns

DAY 1 — KINDS OF SENTENCES

Review the four kinds of sentences and display the examples.

- A declarative sentence tells something and ends with a period: *The lights are flickering.*

- An interrogative sentence asks a question and ends with a question mark: *Why is a siren sounding?*

- An imperative sentence gives a request or an order and usually ends with a period: *Go down to the basement.*

- An exclamatory sentence expresses strong feeling and ends with an exclamation mark: *A tornado is approaching!*

Have students identify kinds of sentences.

- Assign **Practice Book** page 74.

Practice Book page 74

Name _____

Monitoring Student Progress
Grammar Skill Review

The Twister Is Right on Top of Us!

Write what kind of sentence each is—declarative, interrogative, imperative, or exclamatory.

1. The windows are breaking! exclamatory **(1 point)**
2. Cover your face with a towel. imperative **(1)**
3. We must stay together. declarative **(1)**
4. Has the tornado passed? interrogative **(1)**

Identify each sentence type. Then rewrite it as the type shown below. Sample answers are shown.

5. You should help your brother. declarative **(1)**
   Imperative: Help your brother. **(1)**
6. The rain will stop soon. declarative **(1)**
   Interrogative: Will the rain stop soon? **(1)**
7. Does someone have a flashlight? interrogative **(1)**
   Declarative: Someone has a flashlight. **(1)**
8. The police are outside. declarative **(1)**
   Exclamatory: The police are outside! **(1)**

DAY 2 — SUBJECTS/PREDICATES

Review subjects and predicates and display the examples.

- The subject tells whom or what the sentence is about.

- The predicate tells what the subject is or does.

- The complete subject includes all the words in the subject. The simple subject includes just the main word or words.

- The complete predicate includes all the words in the predicate. The simple predicate includes just the main word or words.

Identify subjects and predicates.

- Display this sentence: *A huge tornado whirled across the fields.*

- Underline the complete subject, *A huge tornado.* Circle the simple subject, *tornado.*

- Draw a vertical line after *tornado* to separate the subject and the predicate.

- Underline the complete predicate, *whirled across the fields.* Circle the simple predicate, *whirled.*

Have students identify subjects and predicates.

- Display these sentences: *The boy ran to his brother's room. His little brother wailed loudly.*

- Have students identify the complete subject and simple subject in each sentence. (*The boy, boy; His little brother, brother*)

- Then have students identify the complete predicate and simple predicate in each sentence. (*ran to his brother's room, ran; wailed loudly, wailed*)

DAY 3 — LONGER SENTENCES

Review conjunctions and compound sentences and display the examples.

- A conjunction may be used to join words in a sentence: *Men and women crossed the ice bridge.*
- A conjunction may be used to join sentences: *The sky was blue, and the earth was white.*
- If two sentences are related, they can be combined to make one compound sentence.
- Use a comma and the conjunction *and*, *but*, or *or* to combine sentences.

Have students identify conjunctions and compound sentences.

- Assign **Practice Book** page 75.

Practice Book page 75

Monitoring Student Progress
Grammar Skill Review

Name _____

Conjunction Functions

Circle each conjunction in the sentences below. Write *compound sentence* after each compound sentence.

1. A blanket of snow covered Manhattan and Brooklyn.
   (2 points)
2. The ice on the river looked thick, but no one walked out on it.
   compound sentence (2)
3. A boy put a ladder onto the ice and jumped up and down.
   (2)
4. The boy held the ladder, and people climbed down to the ice.
   compound sentence (2)
5. People stepped carefully onto the ice, but dogs ran onto it recklessly.
   compound sentence (2)
6. Were there more dogs or more people on the ice?
   (2)

DAY 4 — SINGULAR/PLURAL NOUNS

Review singular and plural nouns.

- A noun names a person, a place, a thing, or an idea.
- To form the plural of most nouns, add *-s* or *-es*.
- To form the plural of a noun ending with *x*, *s*, *ch*, *sh*, or *ss*, add *-es*.
- To form the plural of a noun ending with a consonant + *y*, change the *y* to *i* and add *-es*.
- To form the plural of a noun ending in a vowel + *y*, add *-s*.

Identify singular and plural nouns.

- Display these sentences: *Careless folks slip on patches of ice. Smoke rises from chimneys in cities.*
- Circle the singular nouns. (*ice, smoke*)
- Underline the plural nouns. (*folks, patches, chimneys, cities*)
- Point out the plural formed by adding *-s* (*folks*), adding *-es* (*patches*), changing *y* to *i* and adding *-es* (*cities*), and adding *-s* after a vowel + *y* (*chimneys*).

Have students identify and form plural nouns.

- Display these nouns: *church, armies, dishes, ladder, party, snowflakes, monkey, valleys.*
- Have students list the plural nouns. (*armies, dishes, snowflakes, valleys*)
- Have students write the plural forms of the singular nouns. (*churches, ladders, parties, monkeys*)

DAY 5 — MORE PLURAL NOUNS

Review more plural nouns.

- For some nouns that end in *f* or *fe*, the *f* changes to a *v* before *-s* or *-es* is added to form the plural. (*life, lives*)
- For nouns that end in *o*, the plural may be formed by adding either *-s* or *-es*. (*hero, heroes; auto, autos*)
- Some nouns have plural forms that do not end in *-s* or *-es*. (*mouse, mice*)
- Some nouns have the same form for both the singular and plural. (*sheep, sheep*)

Identify plural nouns.

- Display these sentences: *Wolves and deer can survive in deep snow, but geese must fly to warmer regions. After the tornado, many people could hear the echoes of sirens on their radios.*
- Underline the plural nouns. (*wolves, deer, geese, regions, people, echoes, sirens, radios*)
- Point out the plural formed by adding *-s* after *o* (*radios*), by adding *-es* after *o* (*echoes*), and by changing *f* to *v* and adding *-es*. (*wolves*)
- Point out the special plural forms (*geese, people*) and the plural form that is the same as the singular form (*deer*).

Have students form plural nouns.

- Display these nouns: *tomato, piano, woman, knife, moose.*
- Have students write the plural of each word. (*tomatoes, pianos, women, knives, moose*)

SKILL REVIEW:
Prompts for Writing

OBJECTIVES

Students review how to

- write a news article that includes specific details
- write a response to a prompt
- write a paragraph of factual information
- take notes
- write a description

News Article

👤 **Singles**	🕐 **30 minutes**
Objective	Write a news article.

When a natural disaster strikes, such as the one in *Earthquake Terror*, people seek out news articles to learn facts and details about what happened.

Choose one event from this theme to write a news article about. Write a news article that

- informs readers about the event
- answers the questions *Who? What? When? Where? Why?* and *How?*
- includes interesting and unusual facts
- does not include opinions

Include a headline and opening statement that will grab a reader's attention, and make sure the article answers each of the six questions.

Remember to include specific, accurate, and interesting details that answer the questions more fully.

TORNADO HITS NEBRASKA TOWN

The three boys were home alone when the twister struck.

Response to a Prompt

👤 **Singles**	🕐 **30 minutes**
Objective	Write a response to a prompt.

In this theme you have read about an earthquake, powerful storms, volcanic eruptions, tornadoes, and blizzards. Think about what happens during each type of natural disaster.

Which event do you think is the most dangerous? Explain why you have this opinion.

To respond to this writing prompt,

- answer each part of the prompt completely
- begin your response by restating the prompt
- organize each section of your response with a clear main idea
- include interesting details to explain and support each main idea
- review your writing to remove information that does not fit the prompt

Remember to proofread your work for correct capitalization and punctuation.

Consider copying and laminating these activities for use in centers.

WRITING

Paragraph of Information

👤 Singles	🕐 30 minutes
Objective	Write a paragraph of information.

Selections like *Volcanoes* contain many different types of facts, such as stories of historic eruptions, information about different types of volcanoes, and details about the causes and effects of volcanoes.

Choose an event covered by one of the selections in this theme as a topic for a paragraph of information. Then write a paragraph that

- includes a topic sentence that tells what the paragraph is about
- includes several supporting sentences that give more information about the topic
- presents information in logical order
- includes facts and not opinions

Remember to make sure that your paragraph contains complete sentences.

Taking Notes

👤 Singles	🕐 30 minutes
Objective	Take notes.

The selections and features in this theme present a great deal of information about interesting and unusual events. Taking notes is a good way to remember information or to collect information on a topic for a research report.

Choose a few pages in the theme that are interesting to you. Take notes on the passage you selected, using the following plan:

- Identify the topic and write its name.
- Write a specific question about the topic to answer as you take notes.
- Restate the information you find in your own words.
- Record both main ideas and supporting details.

Remember when noting details to include only those that support or tell more about a main idea, or that help answer your research question.

Description

👤 Singles	🕐 30 minutes
Objective	Write a description.

Have you ever experienced a natural disaster? What powerful weather events, such as storms, have you witnessed?

To answer the question, write a description of your experience.

- Include sensory images that convey how things look, feel, sound, taste, and smell.
- Choose descriptive words that are clear and vivid.
- Organize details in a meaningful order.
- Leave out details that don't add to your main idea.
- Wrap up your description with a satisfying conclusion.

Remember to make sure that each sentence has both a subject and a predicate.

A Description of Hurricane Bob

The sky looked very milky that morning.

Assessing Student Progress

Monitoring Student Progress

Preparing for Testing

Throughout the theme your students have had opportunities to read and think critically, connect and compare, and practice and apply new and reviewed skills and reading strategies.

Monitoring Student Progress

For Theme 1, *Nature's Fury*, students have read the paired selections—*Night of the Twisters* and *Blizzard!*—and made connections between these and other selections in the theme. They have practiced strategies for choosing the best answer, and they have reviewed all the tested skills taught in this theme, as well as some tested skills taught in earlier themes. Your students are now ready to have their progress formally assessed in both theme assessments and standardized tests.

Testing Options

The **North Carolina EOG Aligned Assessments** and the **Weekly Skills Test** are formal group assessments used to evaluate student performance on theme objectives. In addition to administering one or both of these tests, you may wish to assess students' oral reading fluency.

North Carolina EOG Aligned Assessments
- Measures student performance on objectives tested on the North Carolina EOG Reading Tests or Writing Assessments and taught in Houghton Mifflin Reading
- Gathers information that allows teachers to modify instruction to help students reach Proficiency and higher
- Matches formats used on the North Carolina EOG Tests and Writing Assessments

Weekly Skills Test
- Assesses students' mastery of discrete reading and language arts skills taught in the week: comprehension skills, word skills, spelling, grammar, writing, and information and study skills
- Consists of individual skill subtests, which can be administered separately
- **Theme Skills Tests** are also available.

Fluency Assessment

Oral reading fluency is a useful measure of a student's development of rapid automatic word recognition. Students who are on level in Grade 5 should be able to read, accurately and with expression, an appropriate level text at the approximate rates shown in the table below.

Early Grade 5	Mid-Grade 5	Late Grade 5
106–132 words correct per minute	118–143 words correct per minute	128–151 words correct per minute

- You can use the **Leveled Reading Passages Assessment Kit** to assess fluency or a **Leveled Reader** from this theme at the appropriate level for each student.

- For some students you may check their oral fluency rate three times during the year. If students are working below level, you might want to check their fluency rate more often. Students can also check their own fluency by timing themselves reading easier text.

- Consider decoding and comprehension, as well as reading rate, when evaluating students' reading development.

- For information on how to select appropriate text, administer fluency checks, and interpret results, see the **Teacher's Assessment Handbook** pages 25–28.

Using Multiple Measures

In addition to the tests mentioned on page M46, multiple measures might include the following:

- Observation Checklist from this theme
- Description writing from the Reading-Writing Workshop
- Other writing, projects, or artwork
- One or more items selected by the student

Student progress is best evaluated through multiple measures. Multiple measures of assessment can be collected in a portfolio. The portfolio provides a record of student progress over time and can be useful when conferencing with the student, parents, or other educators.

Technology

Managing Assessment

The *Learner Profile*® **CD-ROM** lets you record, manage, and report your assessment of student progress electronically.

You can

- record student progress on objectives in Theme 1

- add or import additional objectives, including your state standards, and track your students' progress against these

- record and manage results from the **Integrated Theme Test** and the **Theme Skills Test** for Theme 1, as well as results from other reading assessments

- organize information about student progress and generate a variety of student assessment reports

- use *Learner Profile to Go*® to record student progress throughout the day on a hand-held computer device and then upload the information to a desktop computer

Turn the page to continue

Using Assessment to Plan Instruction

You can use the results of theme assessments to determine individual students' needs for additional skill instruction and to modify instruction during the next theme. For more detail, see the test manuals or the **Teacher's Assessment Handbook**.

This chart shows Theme 1 resources for customizing additional instruction. As you look ahead to Theme 2, you can plan to use the corresponding Theme 2 resources.

Differentiating Instruction

Assessment Shows	Use These Resources	
Difficulty with Comprehension **Emphasize** Oral comprehension, strategy development, story comprehension, vocabulary development	• **Get Set for Reading CD-ROM** • Reteaching: Comprehension, *Teacher's Edition,* pp. R8; R10: R12 • Selection Summaries in *Teacher's Resource Blackline Masters,* pp. 21–23 • *Reader's Library Blackline Masters,* pp. 1A–36A	• *Extra Support Handbook,* pp. 16–17, 22–23; 26–27, 32–33; 36–37, 42–43
Difficulty with Word Skills Structural Analysis Phonics Vocabulary **Emphasize** Word skills, phonics, reading for fluency, phonemic awareness	• **Get Set for Reading CD-ROM** • Reteaching: Structural Analysis, *Teacher's Edition,* pp. R14; R16; R18 • *Extra Support Handbook,* pp. 14–15, 18–19; 24–25, 28–29; 34–35, 38–39	• *Handbook for English Language Learners,* pp. 18–19, 20, 22–23, 24, 26; 28–29, 30, 32–33, 34, 36; 38–39, 40, 42–43, 44, 46 • **Lexia Quick Phonics Assessment CD-ROM** • **Lexia Phonics CD-ROM: Intermediate Intervention**
Difficulty with Fluency **Emphasize** Reading and rereading of independent level text, vocabulary development	• Leveled Bibliography, *Teacher's Edition,* pp. 23E–23F • Below Level **Theme Paperback** • Below Level **Leveled Readers**	• Leveled Readers: Below Level lesson, *Teacher's Edition,* pp. 51O; 81O; 105O
Difficulty with Writing **Emphasize** Complete sentences, combining sentences, choosing exact words	• *Handbook for English Language Learners,* pp. 27; 37; 47 • Reteaching: Grammar Skills, *Teacher's Edition,* pp. R20–R25	• Improving Writing, *Teacher's Edition,* pp. 51J, 51L; 53E; 81J, 81L; 105J, 105L
Overall High Performance **Emphasize** Independent reading and writing, vocabulary development, critical thinking	• Challenge/Extension Activities: Comprehension, *Teacher's Edition,* pp. R9; R11; R13 • Challenge/Extension Activities: Vocabulary, *Teacher's Edition,* pp. R15; R17; R19 • Reading Assignment Cards, *Teacher's Resource Blackline Masters,* pp. 47–53	• Above Level **Theme Paperback** • Above Level **Leveled Readers** • Leveled Readers: Above Level lesson, *Teacher's Edition,* pp. 51Q; 81Q; 105Q • Challenge Activity Masters, *Challenge Handbook,* CH1–1 to CH1–6

TALL TALES

Literature

Vocabulary Reader

TALL TALES

❶ Background and Genre Vocabulary
Nonfiction

❷ Main Selections

❸ Write a Tall Tale

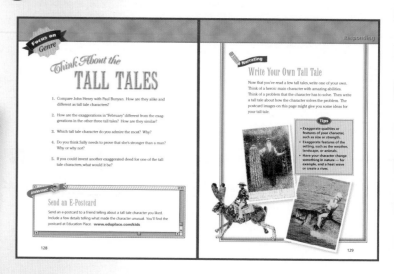

Instructional Support

Planning and Practice

- Planning and classroom management
- Reading instruction
- Skill lessons
- Materials for reaching all learners

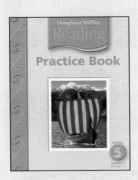

- Independent practice for skills, Level 5.1

- Transparencies
- Strategy Posters
- Blackline Masters

Technology

Audio Selections

Paul Bunyan, the Mightiest Logger of Them All

John Henry Races the Steam Drill

Sally Ann Thunder Ann Whirlwind

February, from McBroom's Almanac

www.eduplace.com

Log on to Education Place for vocabulary support—
- e•Glossary
- e•WordGame

Leveled Books for Reaching All Learners

Leveled Readers and Leveled Practice

- Independent reading for building fluency
- Topic, comprehension strategy, and comprehension skill linked to selections
- Lessons in Teacher's Edition, pages 129O–129R
- Leveled practice for every book

Technology

Leveled Readers
Audio available

● BELOW LEVEL

Apples for America

by Tim Johnson
illustrated by Alexandra Wallner

● Below Level Practice

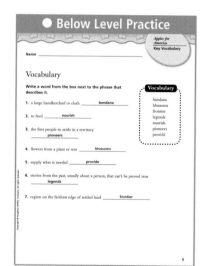

Name _____

Apples for America
Key Vocabulary

Vocabulary

Write a word from the box next to the phrase that describes it.

Vocabulary
bandana
blossoms
frontier
legends
nourish
pioneers
provide

1. a large handkerchief or cloth   **bandana**
2. to feed   **nourish**
3. the first people to settle in a territory   **pioneers**
4. flowers from a plant or tree   **blossoms**
5. supply what is needed   **provide**
6. stories from the past, usually about a person, that can't be proved true   **legends**
7. region on the farthest edge of settled land   **frontier**

5

● Below Level Practice

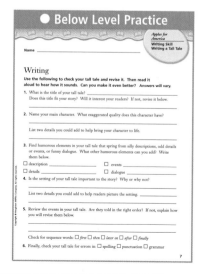

Name _____

Apples for America
Writing Skill
Writing a Tall Tale

Writing

Use the following to check your tall tale and revise it. Then read it aloud to hear how it sounds. Can you make it even better? Answers will vary.

1. What is the title of your tall tale? _____
   Does this title fit your story? Will it interest your readers? If not, revise it below.

2. Name your main character. What exaggerated quality does this character have?
   _____
   List two details you could add to help bring your character to life.

3. Find humorous elements in your tall tale that spring from silly descriptions, odd details or events, or funny dialogue. What other humorous elements can you add? Write them below.
   ☐ description _____   ☐ events _____
   ☐ details _____   ☐ dialogue _____

4. Is the setting of your tall tale important to the story? Why or why not?
   _____
   List two details you could add to help readers picture the setting. _____

5. Review the events in your tall tale. Are they told in the right order? If not, explain how you will revise them below.
   _____

   Check for sequence words: ☐ *first* ☐ *then* ☐ *later on* ☐ *after* ☐ *finally*

6. Finally, check your tall tale for errors in: ☐ spelling ☐ punctuation ☐ grammar

7

▲ ON LEVEL

Grandpa's Rail Tales

by E.C. Hill
illustrated by
Robert Bender

▲ On Level Practice

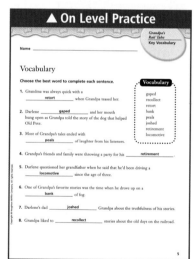

Name _____

Grandpa's Rail Tales
Key Vocabulary

Vocabulary

Choose the best word to complete each sentence.

Vocabulary
gaped
recollect
retort
bank
peals
joshed
retirement
locomotive

1. Grandma was always quick with a _____ **retort** _____ when Grandpa teased her.
2. Darlene _____ **gaped** _____ and her mouth hung open as Grandpa told the story of the dog that helped Old Pete.
3. Most of Grandpa's tales ended with _____ **peals** _____ of laughter from his listeners.
4. Grandpa's friends and family were throwing a party for his _____ **retirement**
5. Darlene questioned her grandfather when he said that he'd been driving a _____ **locomotive** _____ since the age of three.
6. One of Grandpa's favorite stories was the time when he drove up on a _____ **bank** _____ of fog.
7. Darlene's dad _____ **joshed** _____ Grandpa about the truthfulness of his stories.
8. Grandpa liked to _____ **recollect** _____ stories about the old days on the railroad.

5

▲ On Level Practice

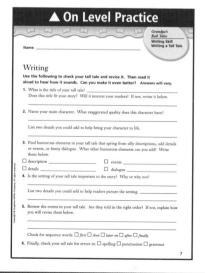

Name _____

Grandpa's Rail Tales
Writing Skill
Writing a Tall Tale

Writing

Use the following to check your tall tale and revise it. Then read it aloud to hear how it sounds. Can you make it even better? Answers will vary.

1. What is the title of your tall tale? _____
   Does this title fit your story? Will it interest your readers? If not, revise it below.

2. Name your main character. What exaggerated quality does this character have?
   _____
   List two details you could add to help bring your character to life.

3. Find humorous elements in your tall tale that spring from silly descriptions, odd details or events, or funny dialogue. What other humorous elements can you add? Write them below.
   ☐ description _____   ☐ events _____
   ☐ details _____   ☐ dialogue _____

4. Is the setting of your tall tale important to the story? Why or why not?
   _____
   List two details you could add to help readers picture the setting. _____

5. Review the events in your tall tale. Are they told in the right order? If not, explain how you will revise them below.
   _____

   Check for sequence words: ☐ *first* ☐ *then* ☐ *later on* ☐ *after* ☐ *finally*

6. Finally, check your tall tale for errors in: ☐ spelling ☐ punctuation ☐ grammar

7

■ ABOVE LEVEL

Davy Crockett: Frontier Hero
by E.C. Hill
illustrated by Val Paul Taylor

◆ LANGUAGE SUPPORT

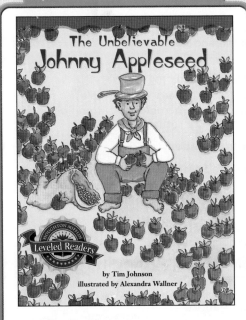

The Unbelievable Johnny Appleseed
by Tim Johnson
illustrated by Alexandra Wallner

Suggestions for Independent Reading

- Recommended trade books for independent reading in the genre

Swamp Angel
(Dutton)
by Anne Isaacs

The Gullywasher
(Northland)
by Joyce Rossi

Pecos Bill
(Morrow)
by Steven Kellogg

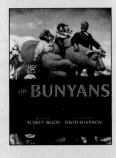

The Bunyans
(Scholastic)
by Audrey Wood

Cut From the Same Cloth
(Philomel)
by Robert San Souci

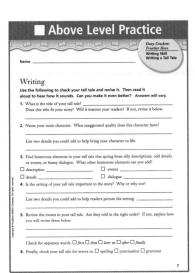

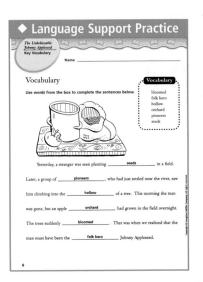

Daily Lesson Plans

 **Technology**
Lesson Planner CD-ROM allows you to customize the chart below to develop your own lesson plans.

Reading
Comprehension

50–60 minutes

Vocabulary Reader
Tall Tales

Leveled Readers
• Fluency Practice
• Independent Reading

DAY 1

Teacher Read Aloud, 107K–107L
Bess Call

Background and Vocabulary, 108 2.02d, f

Genre Vocabulary, 109 1.02
deeds	hero	tale
exaggerate	heroine	tradition
frontier	settler	

Vocabulary Reader 1.02

Reading the Selections, 110–118
Paul Bunyan, the Mightiest Logger of Them All; John Henry Races the Steam Drill

Comprehension Skill, 110 3.01e
Understanding Tall Tales

Comprehension Strategy, 110 2.01
Summarize

Leveled Readers
Apples for America
Grandpa's Rail Tales
Davy Crockett, Frontier Hero
The Unbelievable Johnny Appleseed

Lessons and Leveled Practice, 129O–129R
2.02d, f, 2.03a, 3.01e, 4.01

DAY 2

2.03a
Reading Selections, 119–127
Sally Ann Thunder Ann Whirlwind; February, from *McBroom's Almanac*

Comprehension Check, 127

Responding, 128 3.01f–g
Think About the Selections

Vocabulary Reader 1.02

Comprehension Strategy, 113, 124 2.01
Summarize

Leveled Readers
Apples for America
Grandpa's Rail Tales
Davy Crockett, Frontier Hero
The Unbelievable Johnny Appleseed

Lessons and Leveled Practice, 129O–129R
2.02d, f, 2.03a, 3.01e, 4.01

Word Work
Phonics/Decoding
Vocabulary
Spelling

20–30 minutes

Phonics/Decoding, 111 1.01
Phonics/Decoding Strategy

Vocabulary, 110–118 1.02
Selection Vocabulary

Spelling, 129E 5.05
Long to Short Vowels

Structural Analysis, 129C 1.01
Word Roots *vis* and *vid*

Vocabulary, 119–127 1.02
Selection Vocabulary

Spelling, 129E 5.05
Long to Short Vowels Review and Practice

Writing and Oral Language
Writing
Grammar
Listening/Speaking/Viewing

20–30 minutes

Writing, 129K 4.05
Prewriting a Tall Tale

Grammar, 129I
Varying Sentence Types

Daily Language Practice 5.06
1. did a criminel steel Heck's sock! (Did; criminal; steal; sock?)
2. The loggers slept in a camp in the willderness (wilderness.)

Listening/Speaking/Viewing,
107K–107L, 118 2.05, 3.01g, 4.02b
Teacher Read Aloud, Stop and Think

Writing, 129K 4.06, 4.07
Drafting a Tall Tale

Grammar, 129I
Varying Sentence Types Practice

Daily Language Practice 5.06
3. Be wize and rest in the shade on hot dayes (wise; days.)
4. The wolfs howled and the sound took my breathe away. (wolves; howled,; breath)

Listening/Speaking/Viewing, 127, 128 3.01f–g, 3.02
Wrapping Up, Responding

DAILY LESSON PLANS

Target Skills of the Week

Comprehension	Summarize; Understanding Tall Tales
Vocabulary	Slang and Informal Language
Phonics/Decoding	Word Roots *vis* and *vid*
Fluency	Leveled Readers

Focus On Genre

DAILY LESSON PLANS

Focus on Tall Tales

DAY 3

Rereading the Selections 2.01

Rereading for Writer's Craft, 115
Retelling

Responding, 128 3.01f–g, 3.02, 3.03
Preparing for Literature Discussion

Vocabulary Reader 1.02

Comprehension Skill, 129A–129B 3.01e
Understanding Tall Tales

Leveled Readers

Apples for America
Grandpa's Rail Tales
Davy Crockett, Frontier
  Hero
The Unbelievable Johnny Appleseed

Lessons and Leveled Practice, 129O–129R
2.02d, f, 2.03a, 3.01e, 4.01

Phonics Review, 129D 1.01
The Vowel Pair *ea*

Vocabulary, 129G 1.03b
Slang and Informal Language

Spelling, 129F 5.05
Vocabulary: Synonyms; Long to Short Vowels
Practice

Writing, 129L 4.08a
Revising a Tall Tale

Grammar, 129J 5.01
Appositives

Daily Language Practice 5.06
5. Mike Fink used stelth to surprise Sally when she
was looking for berrys. (stealth; berries.)
6. The two men, Canadian lumberjacks saw a scary
shaddow. (lumberjacks,; shadow.)

DAY 4

Rereading the Selections

Rereading for Writer's Craft,
117 3.01a, f
Identifying Character
Descriptions

Responding, 128 3.02, 4.02a, c
Literature Discussion

Comprehension Skill, 121 2.04b, 3.01a
Visualizing

Leveled Readers

Apples for America
Grandpa's Rail Tales
Davy Crockett, Frontier
  Hero
The Unbelievable Johnny Appleseed

Lessons and Leveled Practice, 129O–129R
2.02d, f, 2.03a, 3.01e, 4.01

Structural Analysis, 129M 1.01
Language Center: Word Root Puzzle

Vocabulary, 129M 1.03b
Language Center: Building Vocabulary

Spelling, 129F 5.05, 5.06
Spelling Game, Proofreading

Writing, 129L 5.06, 5.07
Proofreading a Tall Tale
Using Exact Nouns

Grammar, 129J 5.01
Appositives Practice

Daily Language Practice 5.06
7. Sally delt bravely. With any problem. (dealt;
bravely; with)
8. Why did he revize the storys when he told
them. (revise; stories; them?)

Listening/Speaking/Viewing, 128 3.02, 4.02a, c
Literature Discussion

DAY 5

Rereading for Fluency, 113 4.01

Rereading for Writer's Craft, 123
Humor 2.04b, 3.01a

Responding, 128 3.01f, g, 3.02
Internet Activity

Information and Study Skills, 129H 3.06
Using an Atlas

Leveled Readers

Apples for America
Grandpa's Rail Tales
Davy Crockett, Frontier
  Hero
The Unbelievable Johnny Appleseed

Lessons and Leveled Practice, 129O–129R
2.02d, f, 2.03a, 3.01e, 4.01

Phonics, 129N 1.01
Language Center: Tall Tale Word Pairs

Vocabulary, 129M 1.03b
Language Center: Vocabulary Game

Spelling, 129F 5.05
Test: Long to Short Vowels

Writing, 129L 4.04, 4.09
Publishing a Tall Tale

Grammar, 129J 5.01
Using Commas with Appositives

Daily Language Practice 5.06
9. Sally an atheletic woman was very strong. (Sally,;
athletic; woman,)
10. The dentist a tiny man checked the logger's
teeth for a cavety. (dentist,; man,; cavity.)

Listening/Speaking/Viewing, 129N 2.07
Language Center: Comparing Art Styles

Managing Flexible Groups

Leveled Instruction and Leveled Practice

	DAY 1	**DAY 2**
WHOLE CLASS	• Teacher Read Aloud (TE pp. 107K–107L) • Building Background, Introducing Vocabulary (TE pp. 108–109) • Comprehension Strategy: Introduce (TE p. 110) • Comprehension Skill: Introduce (TE p. 110) • Purpose Setting (TE p. 111) **After reading** *Paul Bunyan* and *John Henry Races the Steam Drill* • Stop and Think (TE p. 118)	• Building Background (TE pp. 118, 125) • Comprehension Strategy: Reinforce (TE p. 124) **After reading** *Sally Ann Thunder Ann Whirlwind* and *February* • Wrapping Up (TE p. 127) • Comprehension Check (Practice Book p. 79) • Responding: Think About the Selections (TE p. 128)
SMALL GROUPS		
Extra Support	**TEACHER-LED** • Preview vocabulary; support reading with Vocabulary Reader. • Preview *Paul Bunyan* and *John Henry Races the Steam Drill* to Stop and Think (TE pp. 110–118). • Support reading with Extra Support/ Intervention notes (TE pp. 111, 113, 115, 118, 119, 120, 126).	**Partner or Individual Work** • Reread *Paul Bunyan* and *John Henry Races the Steam Drill* (TE pp. 110–118). • Preview, read *Sally Ann Thunder Ann Whirlwind* and *February* (TE pp. 119–127). • Comprehension Check (Practice Book p. 79)
Challenge	**Individual Work** • Extend reading with Challenge note (TE pp. 118, 124). • See Independent Activities below and Classroom Management (TE pp. 107I–107J).	**Individual Work** • See Independent Activities below and Classroom Management (TE pp. 107I–107J).
English Language Learners	**TEACHER-LED** • Preview vocabulary; support reading with Vocabulary Reader. • Preview *Paul Bunyan* and *John Henry Races the Steam Drill* to Stop and Think (TE pp. 110–118). • Support reading with English Language Learners notes (TE pp. 108, 112, 113, 114, 116, 117, 121, 126).	**TEACHER-LED** • Review *Paul Bunyan* and *John Henry Races the Steam Drill* (TE pp. 110–118). ✔ • Preview, read *Sally Ann Thunder Ann Whirlwind* and *February* (TE pp. 119–127). • Begin Comprehension Check together (Practice Book p. 79).

Independent Activities

• Journals: selection notes, questions
• Complete, review Practice Book (pp. 77–81) and Leveled Readers Practice Blackline Masters (TE pp. 129O–129R).
• Leveled Readers (TE pp. 129O–129R) or Suggestions for Independent Reading (TE p. 107D).

✔ **Opportunity to informally assess oral reading rate**

DAY 3

- Rereading: Lessons on Writer's Craft, Visualizing (TE pp. 115, 117, 123)
- Comprehension Skill: Main lesson (TE pp. 129A–129B)
- Responding: Preparing for Literature Discussion (Practice Book p. 80)

TEACHER-LED

- Review Comprehension Check (Practice Book p. 79).
- Preview Leveled Reader: Below Level (TE p. 129O), or read book from Suggestions for Independent Reading (TE p. 107D). ✔

TEACHER-LED

- Preview Leveled Reader: Above Level (TE p. 129Q), or read book from Suggestions for Independent Reading (TE p. 107D). ✔

Partner or Individual Work

- Complete Comprehension Check (Practice Book p. 79).
- Begin Leveled Reader: Language Support (TE p. 129R), or read book from Suggestions for Independent Reading (TE p. 107D).

DAY 4

- Rereading: Comprehension Skill lesson (TE p. 121)
- Responding: Literature Discussion (TE p. 128)

Partner or Individual Work

- Complete Leveled Reader: Below Level (TE p. 129O), or read book from Suggestions for Independent Reading (TE p. 107D).

Individual Work

- Complete Leveled Reader: Above Level (TE p. 129Q), or read book from Suggestions for Independent Reading (TE p. 107D).

TEACHER-LED

- Complete Leveled Reader: Language Support (TE p. 129R), or continue book from Suggestions for Independent Reading (TE p. 107D). ✔

DAY 5

- Responding: Select from Activities (TE pp. 128–129)
- Information and Study Skills (TE p. 129H)

TEACHER-LED

- Read or reread book from Suggestions for Independent Reading (TE p. 107D). ✔

TEACHER-LED

- Read or reread book from Suggestions for Independent Reading (TE p. 107D). ✔

Partner or Individual Work

- Read or reread book from Suggestions for Independent Reading (TE p. 107D).

- Responding activities (TE pp. 128–129)
- Language Center activities (TE pp. 129M–129N)
- **Fluency Practice:** Reread *Paul Bunyan; John Henry Races the Steam Drill; Sally Ann Thunder Ann Whirlwind, February.* ✔
- Activities relating to *Paul Bunyan, John Henry Races the Steam Drill, Sally Ann Thunder Ann Whirlwind, February* at Education Place www.eduplace.com

Turn the page for more independent activities. ➡

Managing Flexible Groups 107H

Classroom Management

Independent Activities

Assign these activities while you work with small groups.

Differentiated Instruction for Small Groups

- **Leveled Readers**
  Below Level, On Level, Above Level, Language Support

- Lessons and Leveled Practice, pp. 129O–129R

  Audio available

Independent Activities

- Language Center, pp. 129M–129N

Look for more activities in the Classroom Management Kit.

Career

Paul Bunyan, Forester

👥 Pairs	⏱ 45 minutes
Objective	Make an advertisement for Paul Bunyan's company.
Materials	Encyclopedia, scratch paper, poster board, markers

Find out about jobs in forestry, and make an advertisement for a forestry company that Paul Bunyan might own.

- With a partner, look up *forestry* in an encyclopedia. Find out what foresters do, and learn about the tools or equipment foresters use.

- On scratch paper, plan an advertisement showing what Paul Bunyan's company does. Include a catchy company name or slogan.

- Draw and write your finished ad on poster board.

Art

Tall Illustrations

👤 Singles	⏱ 30 minutes
Objective	Draw exaggerations.
Materials	Anthology, paper, crayons, markers

In *Sally Ann Thunder Ann Whirlwind*, Sally brags about her amazing feats, such as carrying a steamboat on her back. She demonstrates a few feats, too! Draw a picture of Sally in action.

- Reread *Sally Ann Thunder Ann Whirlwind* to find descriptions of amazing things Sally does or brags about.

- Choose your favorite feat to illustrate.

- Use the illustrations in the tall tale as a guide to what Sally looks like, or use your own ideas.

Consider copying and laminating these activities for use in centers.

Language Arts

Super Traits and Super Deeds

Pairs	🕐 30 minutes
Objective	Chart exaggerated characters.
Materials	Anthology, chart paper

In tall tales, the main character often has superhuman traits that help him or her perform amazing deeds. For example, the character Pecos Bill is great at roping and riding, and he lassoes a tornado. List on a chart the traits and deeds of the main characters in the four tall tales.

- With a partner, copy the chart shown below.

- Review the four tall tales. Jot down notes on each main character's traits and deeds.

- Compare traits to pick the one you would most like to have!

Character	Superhuman Traits	Amazing Deeds
Paul Bunyan		
John Henry		
Sally Ann Thunder Ann Whirlwind		
McBroom		

Music

The Tale and the Tune

👥 **Groups**	🕐 45 minutes
Objective	Learn a tall-tale ballad.
Materials	Reference sources

Did you know that the song "The Ballad of John Henry" tells a musical version of John Henry's tall tale? Track down the song, and then decide which you prefer—the musical or the prose version of the story.

- With one or two classmates, use an encyclopedia, the Internet, or other reference source to find a copy of "The Ballad of John Henry."

- Listen to a recording of the song, sing the song, or read the words.

- Have each group member tell why he or she prefers the song or prose version.

Drama

To the Rescue!

👥 **Groups**	🕐 30 minutes
Objective	Act like a tall-tale character.
Materials	Anthology, writing materials, scissors, basket

How would Paul Bunyan, John Henry, Sally Ann Thunder Ann Whirlwind, and Josh McBroom solve a problem? Act out the answer!

- Have each student choose one of the characters to portray. Then skim the appropiate selection to review how the character acts.

- Have each student pick one problem listed in the chart below.

- Have each student act out a scene for the rest of the group. Each should show how their character would solve the problem.

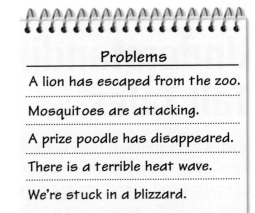

Problems

A lion has escaped from the zoo.

Mosquitoes are attacking.

A prize poodle has disappeared.

There is a terrible heat wave.

We're stuck in a blizzard.

Listening Comprehension

OBJECTIVES
- Listen to identify elements in a tall tale.

Building Background

Tell students that they will read some tall tales in this section. They will learn the elements of a good tall tale and try writing a tall tale of their own. Explain that you will begin by reading aloud a tall tale about a very strong woman named Bess Call and her brother Joe. Ask students what they know about other tall tale characters such as Pecos Bill, John Henry, and Paul Bunyan.

Fluency Modeling

Explain that as you read aloud, you will be modeling fluent oral reading. Ask students to listen carefully to your phrasing and your expression, or tone of voice and emphasis.

COMPREHENSION SKILL
Understanding Tall Tales

Discuss with students how tall tales differ from other stories. (Sample answers: The characters and events are exaggerated; some tall tales explain how a natural phenomenon or event came about.)

Purpose Setting Read the selection aloud, asking students to pay attention to exaggerated characters and actions as they listen. Then use the Guiding Comprehension questions to assess students' understanding. Reread for clarification as needed.

Teacher Read Aloud

Bess Call

Retold by Kevin Supples

You may have heard of Joe Call. He lived in New York two hundred years ago or so. He was the strongest man in the *entire* USA. But do you know about his sis-
❶ ter, Bess? According to my grandma McKinley, Bess had "hands as big as pies and feet bigger than boats." She was tall, too—seven feet or so—and almost as strong as Joe.

One day, a stranger walked out to Call Farm. His name was Dewey D. He found Joe chopping wood and Bess kicking apples. Yes, I said *kicking*. Bess just kicked
❷ each tree and caught the fruit as it fell. When Joe came from the barn, Dewey D.'s eyes opened wider than silver dollars. Joe was carrying oak trees—one under each arm!

When Joe asked what he wanted, Dewey D. asked to buy some apples. So Bess smiled, scooped up a handful —a dozen or so—and sent the stranger on his way. Of course, Dewey D. didn't really want apples. You see, Dewey D. had heard that Joe was the strongest man in the *entire* USA, and he wanted to challenge him to an arm-wrestling contest. But Dewey D. knew he couldn't beat Joe yet, so he went home to lift weights and eat one extra meal every day.

About thirteen months later, Dewey D. returned to Call Farm. Joe and Bess were making cider. Joe held a strainer over a huge jug while Bess squeezed apples with

her bare hands to get the juice. The strainer caught the seeds and skins, which Joe threw to the pigs. (According to my grandma McKinley, the Calls wasted nothing.) Dewey D. shouted hello.

"If you want apples, you're too late," Bess apologized.

"Actually, miss, I've heard your brother is the strongest man in the *entire* USA. I want to challenge him."

Bess wiped her hands. Joe threw the last seeds and skins to the pigs. And Dewey D. took a deep breath. This made him almost as big as Bess, but not nearly as gigantic as Joe.

"I'd love to oblige, but I'm afraid I'm busy at the moment," said Joe. "I've got to get these jugs into the barn."

"Brother Joe," said Bess with a smile, "you know I can do that myself." And with that, she put the jugs in a horse-drawn wagon, picked up the wagon, and carried it away.

Dewey D.'s mouth opened wider than a dinner plate —and his breath whooshed out. He suddenly recalled something he had to do, and he dashed off. Of course, he didn't really have something to do . . . except lift more weights and eat *two* extra meals every day.

About fourteen months later, Dewey D. returned to Call Farm. Bess was reading by the fire. Dewey D. shouted hello. This time, Bess was not surprised to see him. "Joe's gone into town, stranger, but sit down. I just have to put more wood on the fire."

Bess got some wood. But Joe hadn't chopped the oak trees small enough, and the trunks were too long for the fireplace. So Bess split the tree trunks over her knee. Then, brushing splinters off her hands, she offered Dewey D. some hot cider. (According to my grandma McKinley, Bess disliked arm-wrestling *anyone* who had cold hands.)

"If you'd like, we could arm wrestle to pass the time," Bess said, smiling. Dewey D. turned pale as snow. He glanced at his pocket watch, mumbled an apology, and dashed off. This time, Bess didn't expect him to return ❸ to Call Farm. And he never did.

CRITICAL THINKING
Guiding Comprehension

❶ **UNDERSTANDING TALL TALES** What clues tell you that the story is a tall tale? (Sample answer: the exaggeration that Bess has *hands as big as pies and feet bigger than boats*)

❷ **UNDERSTANDING TALL TALES** Which of Bess's and Joe's activities are clues that the story is a tall tale? (Bess kicks apple trees to get the fruit; Joe carries two oak trees.)

❸ **UNDERSTANDING TALL TALES** Why do you think Dewey D. finally leaves, never to return to Call Farm? (He knows he can't beat either of these two larger-than-life characters.)

Discussion Options

Personal Response Have students discuss whether they think that this tall tale has a good ending, and why.

⭐ **Connecting/Comparing** Ask students to compare this tall tale with a tall tale that they already know, such as *Pecos Bill*.

English Language Learners

Language Development

Have students work in pairs to identify the exaggerations in this tall tale. Review some of the more obvious examples, such as *hands as big as pies and feet bigger than boats*. Have students discuss why this description would not really be possible, but makes the characters seem larger than life.

Background and Vocabulary

Key Concept:
Tall Tales

Have students examine the illustration on Anthology pages 108–109.

- Ask students what they think is taking place. (Sample answer: A storyteller is telling a fantastic story.)

- Ask a volunteer to read aloud the text on page 109.

- Remind students that a tall tale is a story that features far-fetched, larger-than-life events or acts.

Ask students to think of a story they might have told or heard in which something was exaggerated, such as a far-fetched story about a dog eating someone's home-work. Then have students discuss reasons for exaggerating in a story, and list them on the board. (Sample answers: to add humor, to create drama, to impress, to gain sympathy)

Vocabulary Preview

The Vocabulary Reader can be used to preteach or reinforce the genre vocabulary.

Focus on Genre

TALL TALES

108

English Language Learners

Supporting Comprehension

Beginning/Preproduction Have students listen to the article. Then ask them to mime or draw a possible character or scene from a tall tale.

Early Production and Speech Emergence Show photographs or illustrations that help students understand the meanings of *frontier* and *settler*. Explain the meanings of the remaining Genre Vocabulary words.

Intermediate and Advanced Fluency Have students work in small groups to read and then restate in their own words the information in the article.

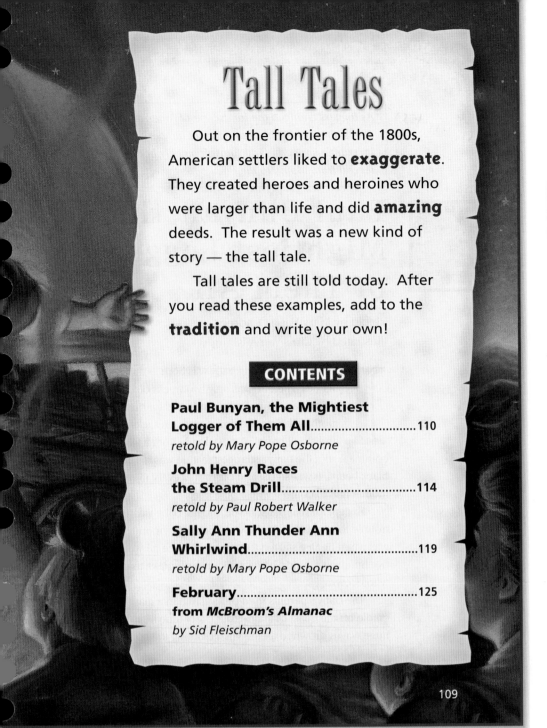

Tall Tales

Out on the frontier of the 1800s, American settlers liked to **exaggerate**. They created heroes and heroines who were larger than life and did **amazing** deeds. The result was a new kind of story — the tall tale.

Tall tales are still told today. After you read these examples, add to the **tradition** and write your own!

CONTENTS

109

Introducing Vocabulary

Focus On Genre

READ & COMPREHEND

Focus on Tall Tales

Genre Vocabulary
These words support the Key Concept.

deeds acts or actions

exaggerate to describe something as being greater or larger than it really is

frontier a remote area beyond which few people live

hero the main male character in a story, poem, or play

heroine the main female character in a story, poem, or play

settler a person who settles in a new region

tale a story, usually an imaginary or made-up one

tradition an idea, custom, or belief that is passed down from one generation to the next

 e•**Glossary**
e•**WordGame**

See Vocabulary notes on pages 112, 114, 116, 120, 122, 124, and 126 for additional words to preview.

Transparency F1–1

Genre Vocabulary

A Reporter's Tale

Use the words in the box to complete the news reporter's memo about Pecos Bill.

Vocabulary		
tale	heroine	settler
frontier	exaggerate	tradition
hero	deeds	

To: *The East Coast Gazette*
From: Gil Ibel, Gazette Staff
Subject: Pecos Bill Story

Last week I took a stagecoach to the Kansas _____frontier_____. Since arriving, I have spoken to every _____settler_____ in town, but have had no luck in getting an interview with Pecos Bill. However, I think I may have heard about every amazing ___deed___ he has ever done. It seems the folks around here have a ___tradition___ of gathering daily to swap Pecos Bill stories. He is unlike any other ___hero___ or ___heroine___ I have ever written about. At yesterday's meeting, I heard one ___tale___ about how Bill was raised by coyotes and another about how he came to use a rattlesnake as a whip. Then someone told me he'd left town on a cyclone headed for Arizona or Wyoming. I'm still not sure how to find him, but I do not ___exaggerate___ when I say that this

---

Practice Book page 77

Focus on Tall Tales
Genre Vocabulary

Name _____

A Reporter's Tale

Use the words in the box to complete the news reporter's memo about Pecos Bill.

Vocabulary
tale
frontier
hero
heroine
exaggerate
deeds
settler
tradition

To: *The East Coast Gazette*
From: Gil Ibel, Gazette Staff
Subject: Pecos Bill Story

Last week I took a stagecoach to the Kansas frontier **(1 point)**. Since arriving, I have spoken to every settler **(1)** in town, but have had no luck in getting an interview with Pecos Bill. However, I think I may have heard about every one of the amazing deeds **(1)** he has ever done. It seems the folks around here have a tradition **(1)** of gathering daily to swap Pecos Bill stories. He is unlike any other hero **(1)** or heroine **(1)** I have ever written about. At yesterday's meeting, I heard one tale **(1)** about how Bill was raised by coyotes and another about how he came to use a rattlesnake as a whip. Then someone told me he'd left town on a cyclone headed for Arizona or Wyoming. I'm still not sure how to find him, but I do not exaggerate **(1)** when I say that this is the best story I have ever followed!

Display Transparency F1–1.

- Model how to use context clues to choose the word *frontier* to fill in the first blank.

- For each remaining sentence, ask students to use context clues to choose the correct Genre Vocabulary word to fill in the blank.

- Ask students to use these words as they discuss tall tales.

Practice/Homework Assign **Practice Book** page 77.

Introducing Vocabulary **109**

TARGET SKILL
COMPREHENSION STRATEGY
Summarize

Teacher Modeling Tell students that summarizing, or retelling the most important ideas in their own words, can help them understand what they are reading. Ask a volunteer to read aloud the first paragraph on page 110. Then model the strategy.

Think Aloud *I could summarize the paragraph this way: "A huge baby with a beard and an enormous appetite was born in Maine." The details about what he ate and how his mother cared for his beard are interesting, but they do not belong in a summary because they are not the most important ideas.*

Remind students to use other strategies as well as they read.

TARGET SKILL
COMPREHENSION SKILL
Understanding Tall Tales

Introduce the Graphic Organizer.
Display **Transparency F1–2,** Discuss the chart, and tell students to fill in the top section ("Character, Setting, Plot") as they read.

- Ask students to complete the chart for *Paul Bunyan, the Mightiest Logger of Them All* as they read.

Focus on Genre
TALL TALES

> As loggers changed the landscape of America in the 1800s, they told tales about a giant lumberjack of incredible strength. Paul Bunyan quickly became a folk legend from Maine to the Pacific Northwest.

Paul Bunyan, the Mightiest Logger of Them All

Retold by Mary Pope Osborne
Illustrated by Chris Van Allsburg

It seems an amazing baby was born in the state of Maine. When he was only two weeks old, he weighed more than a hundred pounds, and for breakfast every morning he ate five dozen eggs, ten sacks of potatoes, and a half barrel of mush made from a whole sack of cornmeal. But the baby's strangest feature was his big, curly black beard. It was so big and bushy that every morning his mother had to comb it with a pine tree.

Except for that black beard, the big baby wasn't much trouble to anybody until he was about nine months old. That was when he first started to crawl, and since he weighed over five hundred pounds, he caused an earthquake that shook the whole town.

The baby's parents tried putting him in a giant floating cradle off the coast of Maine; but every time he rolled over, huge waves drowned all the villages along the coast.

110

Transparency F1–2
Tackle a Tall Tale

Tale _____
Sample answers

Character, Setting, Plot
Main Character(s)
Paul Bunyan
Setting
United States in the nineteenth century
Plot: Important Events in the Tale
Paul is born, outgrows his home, becomes a logger, cuts down forests across the country, builds the Big Onion Lumber Company

Tall Tale Exaggeration
Exaggerated Character Traits
Paul's growth as a baby; his appetite shown by his huge breakfast; his strength "felled ten white pines with a single swing," and dug the Grand Canyon, by mistake, by dragging his pickaxe
Exaggerated or Impossible Setting Elements
a giant floating cradle off the coast of Maine; a mile-long bunkhouse
Exaggerated or Impossible Actions or Events
Paul causing an earthquake when he crawled as a baby; Paul digs ponds to provide drinking water; words freezing into icicles
Realistic Details
locations in the United States; the growth of the lumber industry; the fact that loggers slept in bunkhouse and ate together

For me, the funniest part of this tall tale was _____

Answers will vary.

Practice Book page 78

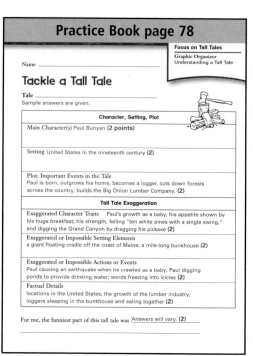

Focus on Tall Tales
Graphic Organizer
Understanding a Tall Tale

Name _____

Tackle a Tall Tale

Tale _____
Sample answers are given.

Character, Setting, Plot
Main Character(s) Paul Bunyan **(2 points)**
Setting United States in the nineteenth century **(2)**
Plot: Important Events in the Tale Paul is born, outgrows his home, becomes a logger, cuts down forests across the country, builds the Big Onion Lumber Company. **(2)**

Tall Tale Exaggeration
Exaggerated Character Traits Paul's growth as a baby; his appetite shown by his huge breakfast; his strength, felling "ten white pines with a single swing," and digging the Grand Canyon by dragging his pickaxe **(2)**
Exaggerated or Impossible Setting Elements a giant floating cradle off the coast of Maine; a mile-long bunkhouse **(2)**
Exaggerated or Impossible Actions or Events Paul causing an earthquake when he crawled as a baby; Paul digging ponds to provide drinking water; words freezing into icicles **(2)**
Factual Details locations in the United States; the growth of the lumber industry; loggers sleeping in the bunkhouse and eating together **(2)**

For me, the funniest part of this tall tale was Answers will vary. **(2)**

Focus On Genre

Paul Bunyan, the Mightiest Logger of Them All

Building Background

- Have a volunteer read aloud the introduction on page 110. Ask why a giant logger might have been a popular "superhero" in the United States. (Many loggers worked in the United States during the 1800s.)

- Compare Paul Bunyan with giants in other folktales, such as the one in *Jack in the Beanstalk*.

Just looking at the picture, what suggests that this is a tall tale? What seems unrealistic.

Purpose Setting

Ask students to predict what might happen in a tall tale about a giant logger. (Sample answer: He may use giant logging tools or chop down many huge trees.)

Journal ▶ Ask students to explain how Paul Bunyan might have created Niagra Falls, the geyser Old Faithful, or some other natural wonder.

111

REACHING ALL LEARNERS

Extra Support/Intervention

Selection Preview

pages 110–113 What do the illustrations tell you about Paul Bunyan, the main character in this tall tale? What events do you think the story will be about?

pages 114–118 What does the illustration on page 114 tell you about the character John Henry?

STRATEGY REVIEW

Phonics/Decoding

Remind students to use the Phonics/ Decoding Strategy as they read.

Guiding Comprehension

❶ AUTHOR'S VIEWPOINT What sentence on page 112 gives a clue about how the author feels about forests? (*It would be nice if those trees could have stayed tall and thick forever.*)

❷ WRITER'S CRAFT The author uses understatement, using a word for something small to describe something much bigger. What are two examples of this technique on pages 112–113? (The author calls the Grand Canyon a *ditch* and the Great Lakes *ponds*.)

❸ STORY STRUCTURE How does the author make the end of this tall tale seem unfinished? (She says that more stories about Paul Bunyan might thaw in the spring.)

COMPREHENSION STRATEGY

Summarize

Teacher/Student Modeling Model how to summarize events in *Paul Bunyan, the Mightiest Logger of Them All.*

- What were the main events and most important information in the second through fourth paragraphs on page 113?

- In summarizing, what would you leave out? Why? (minor details; Only key information needs to be in a summary.)

Have students work with a partner to summarize the entire selection.

Vocabulary

pioneers people who are the first to settle in a region

So his parents hauled the giant toddler to a cave in the Maine woods far away from civilization and said good-bye. His father gave him a fishing pole, a knife, some flint rocks, and an axe. "We'll think of you often, honey," his mother said, weeping. "But you can't come back home — you're just too big."

That's the story of how Paul Bunyan came to take care of himself in the Maine woods. And even though he lived alone for the next twenty years, he got along quite well.

❶ In those times, huge sections of America were filled with dark green forests. It would be nice if those trees could have stayed tall and thick forever. But the pioneers needed them to build houses, churches, ships, wagons, bridges, and barns. So one day Paul Bunyan took a good look at those trees and decided to invent logging.

"Tim-ber!" he yelled, and he swung the bright steel axe his father had given him in a wide circle. There was a terrible crash, and when Paul looked around, he saw he'd felled ten white pines with a single swing.

After that Paul traveled plenty fast through the untamed North Woods. He cut pine, spruce, and red willow in Minnesota, Michigan, and Wisconsin. He cleared cottonwoods out of Kansas so farmers could plant wheat and oaks out of Iowa so farmers could plant corn.

❷ When next heard of, Paul was headed to Arizona. He dragged his pickaxe behind him on the trip, not realizing he was leaving a big ditch in his tracks. Today that ditch is called the Grand Canyon. *understatement*

When Paul got back from the West, he decided to start a logging camp. Word spread fast. Since all the woodsmen had heard of Paul Bunyan, thousands of them hurried to Paul's headquarters at Big Onion on the Big Onion River in Minnesota to be part of his crew.

"There's only two requirements," Paul announced to the men who'd gathered to apply for the job. "All my loggers have to be over ten feet tall and be able to pop six buttons off their shirts with one breath."

Well, about a thousand of the lumberjacks met those requirements, and Paul hired them all. Then he built a gigantic logging camp with

112

English Language Learners

Supporting Comprehension

Explain that logging is the work of cutting down trees and transporting the logs to a mill, to be cut into lumber or made into other products. Ask students to share any knowledge they have about forests, logging, or mills.

READ & COMPREHEND

bunkhouses a mile long and bunks ten beds high. The camp's chow table was so long that it took a week to pass the salt and pepper from one end to the other. Paul dug a few ponds to provide drinking water for everyone. Today we call those ponds the Great Lakes. — understatement

Things went pretty well at the Big Onion Lumber Company until the Year of the Hard Winter. One day Shot Gunderson, the crew boss, complained to Paul, "Boss, it's so cold that the flames for all the lanterns are freezing. And, Boss, when I give orders to the woods crew, all my words freeze in the air and hang there stiff as icicles."

"Well, haul away your frozen words and store them somewhere next to the lantern flames," Paul advised. "They'll both thaw out in the spring."

Sure enough, they did. The only problem was that, come spring, the melting lantern flames started some mean little brush fires. And when Shot's frozen words thawed, old cries of "Timber!" and "Chow time!" started to echo throughout the woods, causing all sorts of confusion. But other than that, things ran pretty smoothly.

Well, there's stories and stories about Paul Bunyan. For many years, old loggers sat around potbellied stoves and told about the good old times with Paul. Those loggers are all gone now, but many of their stories still hang frozen in the cold forest air of the North Woods, waiting to be told. Come spring, when they start to thaw, some of them might just start telling themselves. It's been known to happen.

113

Fluency Practice

Rereading for Fluency Have students choose a favorite part of a tall tale to reread to a partner, or suggest that they read pages 112–113. Encourage students to read expressively.

Handwritten notes:
- They make the character seem "larger than life"
- those "grand" things are nothing compared to Paul Bunyan.

READ & COMPREHEND

Focus on Tall Tales

Extra Support/Intervention	English Language Learners
Strategy Modeling: Summarize Use this example to model the strategy. *I could sum up the events on page 112 this way: Paul grew too big to live at home, so he lived alone in a Maine forest. When Paul grew up, he invented logging and helped clear the West for farmlands, created the Grand Canyon, and started a logging camp. I would not mention that Paul cut red willow trees. It's not one of the most important details.*	**Language Development** Help students to use context clues to define the word *felled* on page 112. Point out that the words *axe, crash, pines,* and *swing* help them infer that the word means "chopped down." Point out how the tree stumps in the illustration on page 113 also offer a clue.

READ & COMPREHEND

John Henry Races the Steam Drill

Building Background

- Have a volunteer read aloud the introduction on page 114. Note that *John Henry Races the Steam Drill* comes from a time when people were worried about new inventions taking the place of human workers.

- Ask students to predict whether John Henry or the steam drill will win the race, and why.

Purpose Setting

Ask students to identify selection details that help them know that this is a tall tale.

Vocabulary

shaker a worker whose job is to shake out loose rock or other material

Focus on Genre

TALL TALES

Volunteer to Read →

> Stories and songs about John Henry have been around since the 1870s. He became famous as the steel driver who hammered faster than a machine. Did John Henry exist? No one knows for sure. But like Paul Bunyan, he stands for the deeds of many others.

John Henry Races the Steam Drill

Retold by Paul Robert Walker

The Big Bend Tunnel was the longest tunnel in America — a mile and a quarter through the heart of the West Virginia mountains. The C & O Railroad started building it back around 1870. There was plenty of hard work for everyone, but the steel-driving men worked the hardest. And the hardest-working steel-driving man of them all was John Henry.

Now, John Henry was a powerful man — six feet tall and two hundred pounds of rippling muscle. He swung his nine-pound hammer from sunup to sundown, driving a steel drill into solid rock. Little Bill, the shaker, turned John Henry's drill between hammer blows and pulled it out when the hole was done. When there were enough holes, the demolition boys filled them with nitroglycerine and blew the rock to kingdom come. Then John Henry drove more steel — day after day in the heat and darkness and stale air of the tunnel.

114

English Language Learners

Language Development

Explain that adding the suffix *-est* turns an adjective into a superlative, such as *longest* and *hardest* on page 114. Have students think of other superlatives that might apply to John Henry. (Sample answers: *strongest, tallest*)

115

Retelling

Teach

- Point out that myths and folktales, including tall tales, were originally passed along orally and retold by memory. List some of the things that a modern-day author tries to do in retelling a tale.

  - Be faithful to the characters and events.

  - Make the story interesting with action, description, and dialogue.

  - Make the story appeal to a new audience.

Practice/Apply

- Reread the first two paragraphs on page 112 to remind students how the Paul Bunyan story is retold in an informal, conversational style.

- Have students look in *John Henry Races the Steam Drill* for examples of action, description, and dialogue that make the tale interesting to a new audience.

Extra Support/Intervention

Fact or Fiction

Have students decide which parts of *John Henry Races the Steam Drill* are exaggerated and which could be fact. Students can work in pairs to create a fact and fiction chart and then share their work.

CRITICAL THINKING

Guiding Comprehension

4 **MAKING INFERENCES** Why does the author have John Henry repeat the phrase "*a man ain't nothin' but a man*" to Captain Tommy and Polly Ann? (Sample answer: John Henry believes a man must try his best.)

5 **DRAWING CONCLUSIONS** Why might it be so important to Captain Tommy and the other steel workers to beat the steam drill? (to show that machines are not better than human workers)

What did John Henry mean?

John Henry always sang while he drove the steel — and at the end of every line he brought that nine-pound hammer down like a crash of thunder.

> *This old hammer* (Bam!)
> *Rings like silver* (Bam!)
> *Shines like gold, boys,* (Bam!)
> *Shines like gold.* (Bam!)
>
> *Ain't no hammer* (Bam!)
> *In these mountains* (Bam!)
> *Rings like mine, boys,* (Bam!)
> *Rings like mine.* (Bam!)

One day, Captain Tommy interrupted John Henry in the middle of his song. "John Henry," he said, "the company wants to test one of those new steam drills. They say a steam drill can do the work of three or four men. But I say a good man can beat the steam. And I say you are the best man I have."

4 John Henry rested his nine-pound hammer on his broad, muscular shoulder. "Captain Tommy," he said, "a man ain't nothin' but a man. Before I let that steam drill beat me down, I'll die with my hammer in my hand."

"Son," offered Captain Tommy, "if you beat that steam drill, I'll give you one hundred dollars and a new suit of clothes."

"That's mighty generous," said John Henry, "but don't you worry about that. Just go to town and buy me a twenty-pound hammer. This nine-pound maul is feeling light."

5 The news of the contest spread through the camp like a strong wind whipping down the mountain. The company men said John Henry was a poor working fool who didn't stand a chance against that mighty steam drill. Some of the working men thought the same. But the steel-driving men knew John Henry — and they believed in the power of a mighty man.

That night, John Henry told his wife, Polly Ann, about the contest. "Don't you strain yourself, honey," said Polly Ann. "'Course we could use that hundred dollars — and you need a new suit of clothes."

116

English Language Learners

Supporting Comprehension

Explain that dialogue is often written to show how people talk informally. Point out that the dialogue may not always follow formal grammar rules. Have students work in mixed-ability groups to rewrite phrases such as *"Course we could use…"* or *"I ain't worried…"* to follow grammar rules.

Vocabulary

maul a heavy, long-handled hammer

John Henry smiled and kissed Polly Ann. "I ain't worried about money or clothes," he said. "Don't y'see sugar — a man ain't nothin' but a man, and a man's got to beat the steam."

The next morning, the steel drivers crowded into the Big Bend Tunnel. It was hot and dusty, and the air was so foul that a man could hardly breathe. The only light was the flickering of lamps burning lard oil and blackstrap molasses.

The company man wheeled the steam drill into the tunnel and set it up against the rock. It was nothing but a machine — all shiny and modern and strange. Then John Henry walked in and stood beside it. He was nothing but a man — all black and fine and natural.

Captain Tommy handed John Henry a brand-new twenty-pound hammer. "There ain't another like it in West Virginia," he said. "Good luck, son."

John Henry held the hammer in his hand and felt its fine natural weight. In the flickering light of the tunnel, the head of that hammer shone like gold. "Gonna call this hammer Polly Ann," he said.

Little Bill sat on the rock, holding the six-foot drill in his hands. John Henry towered above the steel, just waiting to begin. It was so quiet in that tunnel, you could hear the soft breathing of the steel-driving men.

Captain Tommy blew his whistle. The company man turned on the steam drill. John Henry swung his twenty-pound hammer back and brought it down with a crash like thunder. As he swung it back again, he began to sing:

> *This old hammer* (Bam!)
> *Rings like silver* (Bam!)
> *Shines like gold, boys,* (Bam!)
> *Shines like gold.* (Bam!)

John Henry kept driving steel and the steam drill kept drilling. Pretty soon the whole mountain was rumbling and shaking. John Henry's muscles bulged and strained like they never bulged and strained before. Sweat cascaded down his powerful chest, and veins protruded from the sides of his handsome face.

117

English Language Learners

Supporting Comprehension

Students may be confused when Captain Tommy calls John Henry *son* and John Henry calls Polly Ann *sugar*. Explain that these are affectionate terms, not to be understood literally. Ask students to give examples of terms of endearment in their parents' home language.

Identifying Character Descriptions

Teach

- Explain that writers can build the reader's understanding of the characters through
  - the narrator's description
  - descriptions by other characters
  - the character's own dialogue

Practice

- Ask students to find examples of descriptions of John Henry by the narrator. (page 117: *He was nothing but a man—all black and fine and natural.*)

- Ask students to find a description by another character in the story. (page 116: Captain Tommy describes John Henry as *"the best man I have."*)

- Then have students find an example of John Henry's dialogue. Ask: What can you learn about John Henry from what he says here? (page 117, first paragraph: Pride and honor matter more to John Henry than money or new clothes.)

Apply

- Have students work in small groups to find other examples of character descriptions.

Stop and Think

Critical Thinking Questions

1. **DRAWING CONCLUSIONS** Do you think Paul Bunyan is a good character for a tall tale? Why or why not? (Yes. He is larger than life and his physical traits and deeds are exaggerated.)

2. **NOTING DETAILS** How does Paul Bunyan help to change the landscape of the United States? (Sample answer: He clears the forests and creates the Grand Canyon and the Great Lakes.)

3. **MAKING JUDGMENTS** Does the author do a good job of convincing readers that John Henry is larger than life? Why or why not? (Sample answer: Yes. His strength, speed, and deeds are beyond what real people can do.)

Strategies in Action

Have students take turns modeling Summarize and other strategies they used while reading.

"Are you all right, John Henry?" asked Captain Tommy.

"Don't you worry," said John Henry. "A man ain't nothin' but a man — and a man's got to beat the steam." Then he went on singing:

Ain't no hammer (Bam!)
In these mountains (Bam!)
Rings like mine, boys, (Bam!)
Rings like mine. (Bam!)

When they hit the end of the six-foot drill, Little Bill pulled it out and shoved in a longer drill — and then a longer one and a longer one still. John Henry swung his twenty-pound hammer and drove that steel. He swung and drove faster and harder, and faster and harder, until that Polly Ann hammer caught fire. The whole Big Bend Tunnel glowed with the blue flame of John Henry's hammer.

"Time!" shouted Captain Tommy.

"Time!" cried the company man, shutting off the steam drill.

"Time," gasped John Henry, leaning on his hammer. "I need a cool drink of water."

While John Henry drank his water, Captain Tommy and the company man measured the holes. The steam drill had done nine feet; John Henry had drilled fourteen.

"John Henry!" shouted the steel drivers. "John Henry beat the steam!"

"Congratulations, son," said Captain Tommy, slapping him on the back. "I don't care what you say — I'm gonna give you a hundred dollars and a new suit of clothes."

John Henry leaned heavily on his hammer and sucked in the stale air of the tunnel. "That's mighty generous, Captain Tommy. But you give that hundred dollars to Polly Ann. And you bury me in that suit of clothes." Then he slumped to the ground, clutching his hammer in his hand. "I beat the steam," he gasped, "but I broke inside."

As his eyes closed, John Henry lay back against the black earth and whispered, "A man ain't nothin' but a man."

118

REACHING ALL LEARNERS

Extra Support/ Intervention

Review (pages 110–118)

Before students who need extra support join the whole class for Stop and Think on page 118, have them

- check predictions
- add to their Tackle a Tall Tale Chart on **Practice Book** page 78
- summarize the story

On Level   Challenge

Allegory

Explain that an allegory is a tale that works on two levels: as a story and as a symbol for an idea. Encourage students to consider how *John Henry Races the Steam Drill* could be an allegory about the value of people versus technology. Ask: Is this idea still relevant today? Why or why not?

Monitoring Student Progress

If . . .	Then . . .
students have successfully completed the Extra Support activities on page 117,	have them read the rest of the selections cooperatively or independently.

Focus On Genre

The Tennessee frontiersman, Davy Crockett, was the real-life subject of many a tall tale. But there is no truth to the story that he had a wife named Sally Ann Thunder Ann Whirlwind. Good thing for Davy, because in her he would have met his match!

Sally Ann Thunder Ann Whirlwind

Retold by Mary Pope Osborne

One early spring day, when the leaves of the white oaks were about as big as a mouse's ear, Davy Crockett set out alone through the forest to do some bear hunting. Suddenly it started raining real hard, and he felt obliged to stop for shelter under a tree. As he shook the rain out of his coonskin cap, he got sleepy, so he laid back into the crotch of the tree, and pretty soon he was snoring.

Davy slept so hard, he didn't wake up until nearly sundown. And when he did, he discovered that somehow or another in all that sleeping his head had gotten stuck in the crotch of the tree, and he couldn't get it out.

Well, Davy roared loud enough to make the tree lose all its little mouse-ear leaves. He twisted and turned and carried on for over an hour, but still that tree wouldn't let go. Just as he

119

Building Background

- Have a volunteer read aloud the introduction on page 119. Ask students why they think storytellers invented a tall tale wife for Davy Crockett.
- Note that this retelling is by Mary Pope Osborne, who also wrote *Paul Bunyan, the Mightiest Logger of Them All*.

Purpose Setting

Ask students to find examples of both realistic and fantastic qualities in the character Sally Ann Thunder Ann Whirlwind as they read.

READ & COMPREHEND

Focus on Tall Tales

Extra Support/Intervention

Selection Preview

pages 119–124 Look at the illustrations. What exaggerated or improbable events do you expect Sally Ann Thunder Ann Whirlwind to do?

pages 125–127 Look at the title and illustrations. What do you predict this tall tale will be about?

CRITICAL THINKING

Guiding Comprehension

6 **STORY STRUCTURE** Why do you think the author chooses to delay Sally's appearance in her own tall tale? (Sample answer: to create suspense)

7 **MAKING INFERENCES** Why does the author emphasize and repeat the word *sweetie?* (Sample answer: Davy Crockett uses the term condescendingly. Then Sally throws the word back at him defiantly, as if to say she is no stereotype of a "sweet" woman.)

---

6 was about to give himself up for a goner, he heard a girl say, "What's the matter, stranger?"

Even from his awkward position, he could see that she was extraordinary — tall as a hickory sapling, with arms as big as a keelboat tiller's.

7 "My head's stuck, *sweetie,*" he said. "And if you help me get it free, I'll give you a pretty little comb."

"Don't call me sweetie," she said. "And don't worry about giving me any pretty little comb, either. I'll free your old coconut, but just because I want to."

Then this extraordinary girl did something that made Davy's hair stand on end. She reached in a bag and took out a bunch of rattlesnakes. She tied all the wriggly critters together to make a long rope, and as she tied, she kept talking. "I'm not a shy little colt," she said. "And I'm not a little singing nightingale, either. I can tote a steamboat on my back, outscream a panther, and jump over my own shadow. I can double up crocodiles any day, and I like to wear a hornets' nest for my Sunday bonnet."

As the girl looped the ends of her snake rope to the top of the branch that was trapping Davy, she kept bragging: "I'm a streak of lightning set up edgeways and buttered with quicksilver. I can outgrin, outsnort, outrun, outlift, outsneeze, outsleep, outlie any varmint from Maine to Louisiana. Furthermore, sweetie, I can blow out the moonlight and sing a wolf to sleep." Then she pulled on the other end of the snake rope so hard, it seemed as if she might tear the world apart.

The right-hand fork of that big tree bent just about double. Then Davy slid his head out as easy as you please. For a minute he was so dizzy, he couldn't tell up from down. But when he got everything going straight again, he took a good look at that girl. "What's your name, ma'am?"

"Sally Ann Thunder Ann Whirlwind," she said. "But if you mind your manners, you can call me Sally."

From then on Davy Crockett was crazy in love with Sally Ann Thunder Ann Whirlwind. He asked everyone he knew about her, and everything he heard caused another one of Cupid's arrows to jab him in the gizzard.

120

Extra Support/Intervention

Elements of the Genre: Bragging

Explain that outrageous bragging was a common form of entertainment in the 1800s. Point out that bragging is one example of exaggeration in the tall tale. Ask students to make up their own examples of bragging that characters such as Davy Crockett and Sally Ann Thunder Ann Whirlwind might use.

Vocabulary

tiller a lever used to turn the rudder, or steering mechanism, of a boat

varmint wild creature

had a reputation was known for

READ & COMPREHEND

Focus on Tall Tales

"Oh, I know Sally!" the preacher said. "She can dance a rock to pieces and ride a panther bareback!"

"Sally's a good ole friend of mine," the blacksmith said. "Once I saw her crack a walnut with her front teeth."

"Sally's so very special," said the schoolmarm. "She likes to whip across the Salt River, using her apron for a sail and her left leg for a rudder!"

Sally Ann Thunder Ann Whirlwind had a reputation for being funny, too. Her best friend, Lucy, told Davy, "Sally can laugh the bark off a pine tree. She likes to whistle out one side of her mouth while she eats with the other side and grins with the middle!"

121

Visualizing

Teach

- Explain that visualizing is the process of using an author's words to create a mental picture.

- Point out that in *Sally Ann Thunder Ann Whirlwind,* the author describes many incredible acts performed by Sally. By visualizing these scenes, readers can understand how exaggerated Sally's accomplishments must be.

Practice/Apply

- Ask a volunteer to read aloud the schoolmarm's dialogue on page 121. Tell students that many authors of tall tales create these wild exaggerations to make the stories more fun.

- Then ask students to close their eyes and picture a person crossing a river on a boat. You might ask them to picture the person on a sailboat.

- Have students visualize someone crossing a river using an apron as a sail and his or her left leg to steer the boat.

- Ask students to describe or draw their mental images.

English Language Learners

Language Development

Explain that the prefix *out-* before a verb, such as *outrun,* lends the meaning "to be better at" doing whatever the verb describes. Ask students to identify and explain the meanings of verbs with *out-* on page 120. *(Outgrin, outsnort, outrun, outlift, out-sneeze, outsleep, outlie)* Encourage students to think of other examples.

Guiding Comprehension

❽ MAKING INFERENCES What qualities can you infer about Sally from the episode with the Great King Bear? (bravery, cleverness)

❾ STORY STRUCTURE Why does the author tell about Sally's deeds in the order she does, with short descriptions on page 121 followed by the more elaborate stories about the bear and Mike Fink? (maybe to build suspense and the reader's interest)

According to her friends, Sally could tame about anything in the world, too. They all told Davy about the time she was churning butter and heard something scratching outside. Suddenly the door swung open, and in walked the Great King Bear of the Mud Forest. He'd come to steal one of her smoked hams. Well, before the King Bear could say boo, Sally grabbed a warm dumpling from the pot and stuffed it in his mouth.

The dumpling tasted so good, the King Bear's eyes winked with tears. But then he started to think that Sally might taste pretty good, too. So opening and closing his big old mouth, he backed her right into a corner.

❽ Sally was plenty scared, with her knees a-knocking and her heart a-hammering. But just as the King Bear blew his hot breath in her face, she gathered the courage to say, "Would you like to dance?"

As everybody knows, no bear can resist an invitation to a square dance, so of course the old fellow forgot all about eating Sally and said, "Love to."

Then he bowed real pretty, and the two got to kicking and whooping and swinging each other through the air, as Sally sang:

> *We are on our way to Baltimore,*
> *With two behind, and two before:*
> *Around, around, around we go,*
> *Where oats, peas, beans, and barley grow!*

And while she was singing, Sally tied a string from the bear's ankle to her butter churn, so that all the time the old feller was kicking up his legs and dancing around the room, he was also churning her butter!

❾ And folks loved to tell the story about Sally's encounter with another stinky varmint — only this one was a *human* varmint. It seems that Mike Fink, the riverboat man, decided to scare the toenails off Sally because he was sick and tired of hearing Davy Crockett talk about how great she was.

One evening Mike crept into an old alligator skin and met Sally just as she was taking off to forage in the woods for berries. He spread open his gigantic mouth and made such a howl that he nearly scared himself to

122

Vocabulary

forage search

Writer's Craft

Humor

Teach

- Point out that writers use many techniques to make their writing humorous, such as
  - silly descriptions
  - a funny series of events
  - exaggeration
  - odd coincidences
  - nonsensical conversation

Practice

- Ask students to identify examples of humor in *Sally Ann Thunder Ann Whirlwind,* such as Sally's encounter with the Great King Bear.

- Ask them to explain what makes each instance humorous.

Apply

- Have students work in small groups to write a humorous paragraph in the style of *Sally Ann Thunder Ann Whirlwind*. Allow time for students to share their work.

COMPREHENSION STRATEGY
Summarize

Student Modeling Have students model the strategy by summarizing what happened with the bear. If necessary, use the following prompt:

- What are the most important events and information to include in the summary?

death. But Sally paid no more attention to that fool than she would have to a barking puppy dog.

However, when Mike put out his claws to embrace her, her anger rose higher than a Mississippi flood. She threw a flash of eye lightning at him, turning the dark to daylight. Then she pulled out a little toothpick and with a single swing sent the alligator head flying fifty feet! And then to finish him off good, she rolled up her sleeves and knocked Mike Fink clear across the woods and into a muddy swamp.

When the fool came to, Davy Crockett was standing over him. "What in the world happened to you, Mikey?" he asked.

"Well, I — I think I must-a been hit by some kind of wild alligator!" Mike stammered, rubbing his sore head.

Davy smiled, knowing full well it was Sally Ann Thunder Ann Whirlwind just finished giving Mike Fink the only punishment he'd ever known.

That incident caused Cupid's final arrow to jab Davy's gizzard. "Sally's the whole steamboat," he said, meaning she was something great. The next day he put on his best raccoon hat and sallied forth to see her.

When he got within three miles of her cabin, he began to holler her name. His voice was so loud, it whirled through the woods like a hurricane.

Sally looked out and saw the wind a-blowing and the trees a-bending. She heard her name a-thundering through the woods, and her heart began to thump. By now she'd begun to feel that Davy Crockett was the whole steamboat, too. So she put on her best hat — an eagle's nest with a wild-cat's tail for a feather — and ran outside.

Just as she stepped out the door, Davy Crockett burst from the woods and jumped onto her porch as fast as a frog. "Sally, darlin'!" he cried. "I think my heart is bustin'! Want to be my wife?"

"Oh, my stars and possum dogs, why not?" she said.

From that day on, Davy Crockett had a hard time acting tough around Sally Ann Thunder Ann Whirlwind. His fightin' and hollerin' had no more effect on her than dropping feathers on a barn floor. At least that's what *she'd* tell you. *He* might say something else.

124

Challenge

Reader's Theater

The story *Sally Ann Thunder Ann Whirlwind* has plenty of dialogue to make an exciting reader's theater. Have students work in groups to practice performing a reading.

Vocabulary

extract a concentrated form of something

dismal gloomy

Focus on
Genre

Focus
On
Genre

Sid Fleischman has created his own tall tale characters in his stories about farmer Josh McBroom. In this tale, the McBroom family has to cope with unpredictable weather and, as usual, neighbor Heck Jones.

February

by Sid Fleischman

Illustrated by Walter Lorraine

It's not generally known, but I invented air conditioning. I read in the paper the idea has already spread to the big cities.

But, shucks, everyone is welcome to it. Folks around here call it McBroom's Natural Winter Extract & Relief for the Summer Dismals. You can make your own, same as us.

February is about the last month you can lay in a supply of prime Winter Extract.

Wait for an infernal cold day. When the mercury in the thermometer drops to the bottom — you're getting close. But the weather's still a mite too warm.

When the mercury busts the glass bulb and rolls over to the fireplace to get warm — that's Extract weather.

"Will*jill*hester*chester*peter*polly*tim*tom*mary*larry*andlittle*clarinda!*" I shouted to our young'uns. "Bulb's shattered. Fetch the ripsaws, the crosscut saws, and let's get to work!"

Cold? Mercy, it was so cold outside *the wind had frozen solid.*

Didn't we get busy! We began sawing up chunks of frozen wind.

125

February

Building Background

- Have a volunteer read aloud the introduction on page 125. Tell students that *February* is not a retelling, but was created as a written story in *McBroom's Almanac,* a book about the McBroom family over the course of one year.

- Students may be familiar with other books about the character Josh McBroom and his one-acre farm, by author Sid Fleischman.

Purpose Setting

Ask students to find the most outrageous claim made by the narrator of the tale, Josh McBroom.

READ & COMPREHEND

Focus on Tall Tales

CRITICAL THINKING
Guiding Comprehension

 STORY STRUCTURE What personality traits does Josh McBroom seem to have? (McBroom is talkative, confiding, and cheerful.)

 WRITER'S CRAFT What effect does the author's invented language, such as *Summer Dismals, sizzle-hot,* and *scrambly-witted,* create in this tall tale? (Sample answers: It makes the story sound vivid; It gives the narrator a unique way of talking.)

 Now, you got to do the thing right. Wind's got a grain, just like wood. So be positive to use the crosscut saw against the grain, and the ripsaw along with it.

It fell dark before we finished harvesting and hauling that Winter Extract to our icehouse. And there stood our neighbor Heck Jones. That skinflint is so mean and miserly he brands the horseflies over at his place for fear someone will rustle 'em.

"Are you hidin' my left sock, McBroom?" he asked.

"Of course not," I said.

"Someone stole it off the clothesline. My best black sock, too! It only had three holes in it. If I catch the thief, I'll have him in a court of law!"

He loped away, grumbling and snarling.

We finished packing sawdust around the chunks of wind to keep them frozen. "Good work, my lambs," I said. "We're all set for the Summer Dismals."

Well, Heck Jones walked around in one sock the rest of winter, and summer, too.

126

Vocabulary

skinflint someone who is very reluctant to spend money

rustle to steal, especially livestock

instinct knowledge one is born with

REACHING ALL LEARNERS

Extra Support/ Intervention

Review (pages 125–127)

Before students who need extra support join the whole class for Wrapping Up on page 127, have them

- check predictions
- add to their Tackle a Tall Tale Chart on **Practice Book** page 78
- summarize the story

English Language Learners

Language Development

Have students work in mixed-ability groups to understand colloquial sentences, such as *That skinflint is so mean and miserly he brands the horseflies over at his place for fear someone will rustle 'em.*

As soon as the days turned sizzle-hot, we'd set a chunk of Winter Extract in the parlor. In a second or three it would begin to thaw — just a cool breeze at first. But when that February wind really got whistling, it would lift the curtains!

One hot night I fetched in a nice chunk of frozen wind without bothering to scrape off the sawdust. A few minutes later I saw a black thing shoot across the room. Something had got frozen in our Winter Extract.

"Heck Jones's sock!" I declared. "I can smell his feet!"

He was sure to think we'd stolen it. He'd have us in a court of law! I made a grab for it, but the February wind was kicking up such a blow it shot the sock past the curtains and far out the window.

I could see Heck Jones asleep in his hammock, one sock on, the other foot bare. The left sock hoisted its tail like a kite in the air and started down.

I declare, if I didn't see it with my own eyes, I'd think I was scrambly-witted. That holey black sock had the instinct of a homing pigeon. It returned right to Heck Jones's left foot and pulled itself on. I think it navigated by scent.

What Heck Jones thought when he awoke and looked at both feet — I can't reckon.

127

Wrapping Up

Critical Thinking Questions

1. **MAKING JUDGMENTS** Which tall tale did you find the funniest? What did that writer do that made you laugh? (Answers will vary.)

2. **CATEGORIZE AND CLASSIFY** Which main characters from the four stories seem like they are based on real people? Why do you think so? (Sample answer: Paul Bunyan and John Henry seem like they could be based on real people because each one does a job, such as logging or steam drilling, that real people can do.)

Strategies in Action

Have students take turns modeling how and where they used the Summarize strategy.

Comprehension Check

Use **Practice Book** page 79 to assess students' comprehension of the selection.

Practice Book page 79

Name _____

That Could Never Happen!

Each of the four selections in *Focus on Tall Tales* contains at least one exaggerated event. Write the event after each story title.
Sample answers shown.

Paul Bunyan, the Mightiest Logger of Them All
Paul Bunyan chops down ten pine trees with one swing of his axe.

(2 points)

John Henry Races the Steam Drill
John Henry swings his hammer so hard and fast that it catches fire. **(2)**

Sally Ann Thunder Ann Whirlwind
Sally talks the grizzly bear into dancing with her, and at the same time he churns her butter. **(2)**

February
McBroom saws chunks of the frozen wind during the winter and thaws them out during the summer. **(2)**

Monitoring Student Progress

If . . .	Then . . .
students score 7 or below on **Practice Book** page 79,	have them form small groups and reread relevant selection pages to clarify understanding.

Responding

Think About the Selections

Discuss or Write

1. ANALYZING They are both super-strong, hard-working working men. Paul Bunyan's accomplishments seem more fantastic than John Henry's.

2. ANALYZING In the other tales, exaggerations are mostly about the character's qualities and deeds, whereas in *February* they are about natural occurrences. They all have some connection to realistic people, things, and events, but are so exaggerated as to be impossible.

3. GENERATING Answers will vary.

4. EVALUATING Answers will vary.

5. EVALUATING Sample answer: yes, because some people assume that men are always stronger than women

Literature Discussion

To help students prepare for the discussion, assign **Practice Book** page 80. Students may also refer to **Practice Book** page 79.

1. MAKING JUDGMENTS Which tall tale do you find the most fantastic and hard to believe? Why? (Answers will vary.)

2. COMPARE AND CONTRAST How are tall tales different from realistic fiction stories such as *Earthquake Terror*? (Sample answer: The characters and events in a tall tale are highly exaggerated, whereas events in realistic fiction could actually happen in real life.)

Focus on Genre

Think About the

TALL TALES

1. **Analyzing** Compare John Henry with Paul Bunyan. How are they similar and different as tall tale characters?

2. **Analyzing** How are the exaggerations in "February" similar to and different from the ones in the other tall tales?

3. **Generating** If you could invent another exaggerated deed for one of the tall tale characters, what would it be? Explain.

4. **Evaluating** Which tall tale character do you admire most? Why?

5. **Evaluating** Do you think Sally needs to prove that she's stronger than a man? Why or why not?

Send an E-Postcard

Send an e-postcard to a friend telling about a tall tale character you liked. Include a few details telling what made the character unusual. You'll find the postcard at Education Place. **www.eduplace.com/kids**

128

Practice Book page 80

Focus on Tall Tales
Literature Discussion

Name

You'll Never Believe Whom I Just Met.

Think about characters you might find in a tall tale. Describe five tall tale characters by completing each sentence with an exaggeration. Sample answers shown.

1. This character is so tall that he has to duck whenever the space shuttle goes by. **(2 points)**

2. This character is so loud that when she clears her throat it causes an avalanche. **(2)**

3. This character is so old that he used to play hide-and-go-seek with the dinosaurs when he was a little boy. **(2)**

4. This character is so fast that she can run to the store, buy a quart of milk, and be back with the change before her father has finished writing *milk* on the shopping list. **(2)**

5. This character is so strong that when he loses something, he really does turn the house upside down to find it. **(2)**

Write Your Own Tall Tale

Now that you've read a few tall tales, write one of your own. Think of a heroic main character with amazing abilities. Think of a problem that the character has to solve. Then write a tall tale about how the character solves the problem. The postcard images on this page might give you some ideas for your tall tale.

Tips
- Exaggerate qualities or features of your character, such as size or strength.
- Exaggerate features of the setting, such as the weather, landscape, or animals.
- Have your character change something in nature — for example, end a heat wave or create a river.

129

Write a Tall Tale

Have students read and briefly discuss the writing assignment on page 129 of the Anthology. Before students begin their own tall tales, present the writing lesson on pages 129K–129L.

English Language Learners

Supporting Comprehension

If necessary, allow students to write their tall tales as comic strips with captions or dialogue in thought balloons. Remind students that a tall tale includes characters and events that are exaggerated. Provide help as needed as they create their tall tales.

Monitoring Student Progress

End-of-Selection Assessment

Have students assess their reading and writing with questions such as

- Which parts of the selections were difficult to read? Why?
- Which strategies helped me understand the stories?
- Would I recommend these stories to my friends? Why or why not?

OBJECTIVES

- Identify the elements of a tall tale.
- Analyze the exaggerated and realistic elements in tall tales.
- Discuss the humor in tall tales.

Target Skill Trace

▶ Preview; Teach   p. 107K, p. 110; p. 129A–129B

Transparency F1–2

Tackle a Tall Tale

Tale _____
Sample answers

Character, Setting, Plot
Main Character(s) Paul Bunyan
Setting United States in the nineteenth century
Plot: Important Events in the Tale Paul is born, outgrows his home, becomes a logger, cuts down forests across the country, builds the Big Onion Lumber Company.

Tall Tale Exaggeration
Exaggerated Character Traits Paul's growth as a baby; his appetite shown by his huge breakfast; his strength "felled ten white pines with a single swing," and dug the Grand Canyon, by mistake, by dragging his pickaxe
Exaggerated or Impossible Setting Elements a giant floating cradle off the coast of Maine; a mile-long bunkhouse
Exaggerated or Impossible Actions or Events Paul causing an earthquake when he crawled as a baby; Paul digs ponds to provide drinking water; words freezing into icicles
Realistic Details locations in the United States; the growth of the lumber industry; the fact that loggers slept in bunkhouse and ate together

For me, the funniest part of this tall tale was _____

Answers will vary.

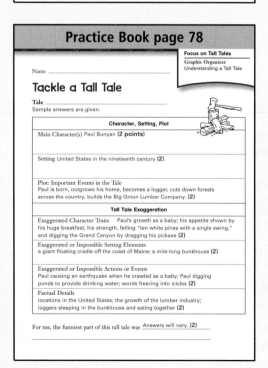

Practice Book page 78

Focus on Tall Tales

Graphic Organizer
Understanding a Tall Tale

Name _____

Tackle a Tall Tale

Tale _____
Sample answers are given.

Character, Setting, Plot
Main Character(s) Paul Bunyan **(2 points)**
Setting United States in the nineteenth century **(2)**
Plot: Important Events in the Tale Paul is born, outgrows his home, becomes a logger, cuts down forests across the country, builds the Big Onion Lumber Company. **(2)**

Tall Tale Exaggeration
Exaggerated Character Traits   Paul's growth as a baby; his appetite shown by his huge breakfast; his strength, felling "ten white pines with a single swing," and digging the Grand Canyon by dragging his pickaxe **(2)**
Exaggerated or Impossible Setting Elements a giant floating cradle off the coast of Maine; a mile-long bunkhouse **(2)**
Exaggerated or Impossible Actions or Events Paul causing an earthquake when he crawled as a baby; Paul digging ponds to provide drinking water; words freezing into icicles **(2)**
Factual Details locations in the United States; the growth of the lumber industry; loggers sleeping in the bunkhouse and eating together **(2)**

For me, the funniest part of this tall tale was Answers will vary. **(2)**

🎯 COMPREHENSION: Understanding Tall Tales

❶ Teach

Review the characteristics of a tall tale. A tall tale

- is a story about exaggerated actions or events
- includes characters, setting, and plot
- includes realistic details
- may feature a larger-than-life main character whose abilities, character traits, or deeds are exaggerated
- is often humorous

Review the characteristics of one tall tale. Display **Transparency F1–2**. Have students discuss the basic story elements of *Paul Bunyan,* referring to **Practice Book** page 78.

- Direct students to Anthology pages 110–113.
- Ask: What parts of the setting are realistic? What parts are exaggerated? (Sample answers: Realistic: names of states, types of trees, settlements built by pioneers; exaggerated: the Grand Canyon and Great Lakes made by Paul, bunkhouses a mile long)
- Students can add to their charts during the discussion.

Model relating tall tales to historical facts. Refer students to page 110. Use the Think Aloud to model relating story elements to historical facts.

Think Aloud *The note before this tall tale tells me that it has something to do with the logging business of the 1800s. I wonder why this tale begins in Maine. Maybe the logging business started in the eastern part of the United States and then moved west, like Paul's movements in the story. Some other facts I know about logging are that loggers have to be strong; they clear trees for farmland; the logging business spread to many places; and loggers live in bunkhouses in the woods. I can see these facts in the tall tale.*

❷ Guided Practice

Have students analyze another tall tale. As a class, analyze the elements of *John Henry Races the Steam Drill.* Ask students about the main character, the exaggerated abilities and actions, and the realistic elements in the tale. Then compare these elements in *Paul Bunyan* and *John Henry Races the Steam Drill.*

❸ Apply

Assign Practice Book page 81. Have students use it to analyze *Sally Ann Thunder Ann Whirlwind* or *February*. Also have students apply this skill as they read their **Leveled Readers** for this week. You may also select books from the **Leveled Bibliography** for this theme (pages 23E–23F).

Test Prep Tell students that questions on reading tests sometimes ask them to identify the genre of a passage they have read. Emphasize that students can identify a tall tale by looking for exaggerated traits, actions or events, a larger-than-life character, and realistic details.

Leveled Readers and Leveled Practice

Students at all levels apply the comprehension skill as they read their **Leveled Readers**. See lessons on pages 129O–129R.

● BELOW LEVEL — Apples for America

▲ ON LEVEL — Grandpa's Tall Tales

■ ABOVE LEVEL — Davy Crockett: Frontier Hero

◆ LANGUAGE SUPPORT — The Unbelievable Johnny Appleseed

Reading Traits

Teaching students to think about genre is one way of encouraging them to "read the lines" of a selection. This comprehension skill supports the reading trait **Decoding Conventions**.

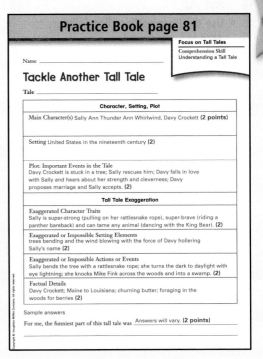

Practice Book page 81

Focus on Tall Tales
Comprehension Skill
Understanding a Tall Tale

Name _____

Tackle Another Tall Tale

Tale _____

Character, Setting, Plot
Main Character(s) Sally Ann Thunder Ann Whirlwind, Davy Crockett **(2 points)**
Setting United States in the nineteenth century **(2)**
Plot: Important Events in the Tale Davy Crockett is stuck in a tree; Sally rescues him; Davy falls in love with Sally and hears about her strength and cleverness; Davy proposes marriage and Sally accepts. **(2)**

Tall Tale Exaggeration
Exaggerated Character Traits Sally is super-strong (pulling on her rattlesnake rope), super-brave (riding a panther bareback) and can tame any animal (dancing with the King Bear). **(2)**
Exaggerated or Impossible Setting Elements trees bending and the wind blowing with the force of Davy hollering Sally's name **(2)**
Exaggerated or Impossible Actions or Events Sally bends the tree with a rattlesnake rope; she turns the dark to daylight with eye lightning; she knocks Mike Fink across the woods and into a swamp. **(2)**
Factual Details Davy Crockett; Maine to Louisiana; churning butter; foraging in the woods for berries **(2)**

Sample answers
For me, the funniest part of this tall tale was _Answers will vary._ **(2 points)** _____

Monitoring Student Progress

If . . .	Then . . .
students are unable to complete **Practice Book** page 81 correctly,	have them work with partners to complete or correct the sections that were not successfully completed.

OBJECTIVES

- Read words with the word roots *vis* and *vid*.
- Use the Phonics/Decoding Strategy to decode longer words.

STRUCTURAL ANALYSIS/ VOCABULARY: Word Roots *vis* and *vid*

❶ Teach

Define the word roots *vis* and *vid*. Both these word parts mean "to see."

- Write *There was <u>evidence</u> of blows from a giant axe on the tree's stump.* Have a volunteer circle the word root *vid*. Tell students that *evidence* is proof that you can see.

- Write *I need to <u>revise</u> my paper.* Have a volunteer circle the word root *vis*. Tell students that *revise* means "to look at again in order to change or modify."

Model using word roots. Write *Pecos Bill was barely <u>visible</u> as he rode the cyclone into the sunset.*

Think Aloud — *I recognize the word root* vis, *which I know means "to see." I also notice that the word ends with the suffix* -ible, *which I know means "able to be." Maybe the word* visible *means "able to be seen." That meaning makes sense in the sentence.*

❷ Guided Practice

Write these phrases on the board, and ask students to copy the underlined words: *captured on <u>videocassette</u>; <u>envision</u> what lies ahead; watched by the <u>supervisor</u>.* Have students circle the word roots in each underlined word. Then ask them to work in pairs to decode the words and figure out their meanings. Have students share their answers.

❸ Apply

Have students complete Practice Book page 82.

Practice Book page 82

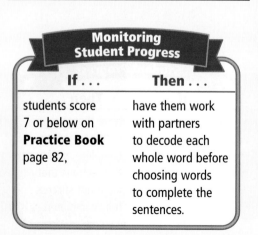

Focus on Tall Tales

Structural Analysis Word Roots *vis* and *vid*

Name _____

Growing Words from their Roots

Vis and *vid* are word roots. They have meaning, but are words by themselves. The Latin word roots *vis* and *vid* mean "to see."

television   videotape   supervision

Complete each sentence. Build a word containing the root *vis* or *vid*.

vis + ion	re + vis + e
e + vid + ent	pro + vid + e
vis + or	in + vis + ible

1. Max put on his visor (1 point) _____ because the sun was in his eyes.

2. We missed the turn because the road sign was almost invisible (1) _____ in the darkness.

3. When Hank slowly shuffled into class with his head down, it was evident (1) _____ that he had not done his homework.

4. The factory has been without power for two days, but the new generator they bought will provide (1) _____ enough energy.

5. The famous actor disliked the original script, so the writer was brought in to make a major revision (1) _____.

Now write sentences using four of the words you constructed.

(1 point for each word)

_____

_____

_____

Monitoring Student Progress

If . . .	Then . . .
students score 7 or below on **Practice Book** page 82,	have them work with partners to decode each whole word before choosing words to complete the sentences.

PHONICS REVIEW:
The Vowel Pair *ea*

❶ Teach

Review long and short e spelling patterns. Discuss how the *ea* vowel pair has different sounds in different words.

• The vowel pair *ea* is pronounced /ē/ in *each*, /ĕ/ in *head*, and /ā/ in *great*.

• To decode an unfamiliar word with the vowel pair *ea*, try using the /ē/, /ĕ/, and /ā/ vowel sounds. You might recognize the word from its sound and the way it is used in the sentence.

• If you cannot figure out the word by trying different sounds, use the dictionary to find its pronunciation and meaning.

Modeling Write *Paul <u>headed</u> for the huge fallen tree, picked it up, and <u>heaved</u> it out of the way.* Then model decoding <u>headed</u> and <u>heaved</u>.

Think Aloud *As I scan the first underlined word, I recognize the short word* head. *I know this word has the short e sound, so I will pronounce* HEHD-ihd *and see that it fits the sentence. When I scan the word* h-e-a-v-e-d, *I don't see a familiar word. It may have a short or long e sound. Since I can't be sure, I look the word up in the dictionary. The word is a form of the word* heave. *It is pronounced* HEEVD *with a long e sound and means "used great effort to lift, throw, pull, or push." It makes sense in the sentence.*

❷ Guided Practice

Write *He <u>spread</u> open his gigantic mouth and made such a howl that he almost scared himself to <u>death</u>.* Then ask volunteers to come to the board and decode the underlined words using the Phonics/Decoding Strategy.

❸ Apply

Have pairs of students decode the following words from *Sally Ann Thunder Ann Whirlwind* and discuss their meanings: *streak*, page 120; *preacher*, page 121; *feather*, page 124.

OBJECTIVES

• Read words and syllables with different vowel sounds for the *ea* spelling pattern.
• Use the Phonics/Decoding Strategy to decode longer words.

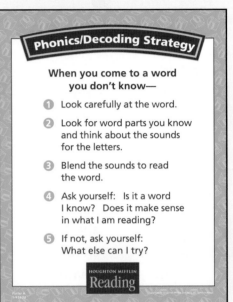

Phonics/Decoding Strategy

When you come to a word you don't know—

❶ Look carefully at the word.

❷ Look for word parts you know and think about the sounds for the letters.

❸ Blend the sounds to read the word.

❹ Ask yourself: Is it a word I know? Does it make sense in what I am reading?

❺ If not, ask yourself: What else can I try?

HOUGHTON MIFFLIN
Reading

SPELLING: Vowel Changes

OBJECTIVE

- Write Spelling Words that are related in spelling and meaning even though the vowel sound changes from long to short.

SPELLING WORDS

Basic

steal*	crime
stealth	criminal
cave*	breathe
cavity	breath*
wise	wild*
wisdom	wilderness
deal	shade
dealt	shadow*
athlete	revise
athletic	revision

Review	Challenge
final*	volcano
finish*	volcanic
heal	cycle
health	bicycle

Forms of these words appear in the literature.

Extra Support/Intervention

Basic Word List You may want to use only the left column of Basic Words with students who need extra support.

Challenge

Challenge Word Practice Have students write four sentences that state tall tale-style exaggerations, using at least one Challenge Word in each sentence.

DAY 1 — INSTRUCTION

Long to Short Vowels

Pretest Use the Day 5 Test sentences.

Teach Write *wise* and *wisdom*.

- Discuss with students the meaning of each word and how the meanings are related. (*wise:* having or showing intelligence and good judgment; *wisdom:* intelligence and good judgment. Both have to do with intelligence and good judgment.)

- Have students compare the spelling and pronunciation of the two words. (first three letters are the same; *wise:* long *i* sound; *wisdom:* short *i* sound)

- Explain that words related in meaning are also often related in spelling, even though a vowel sound may change.

- Write the other pairs of Basic Words. Have students compare the meanings, spellings, and pronunciations of each pair.

Practice/Homework Assign **Practice Book** page 277.

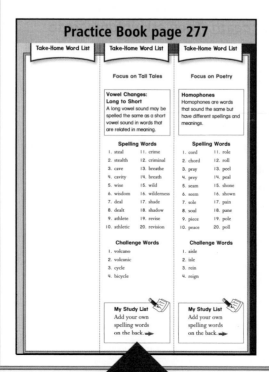

Practice Book page 277

Take-Home Word List

Focus on Tall Tales

Vowel Changes: Long to Short
A long vowel sound may be spelled the same as a short vowel sound in words that are related in meaning.

Spelling Words

1. steal	11. crime
2. stealth	12. criminal
3. cave	13. breathe
4. cavity	14. breath
5. wise	15. wild
6. wisdom	16. wilderness
7. deal	17. shade
8. dealt	18. shadow
9. athlete	19. revise
10. athletic	20. revision

Challenge Words
1. volcano
2. volcanic
3. cycle
4. bicycle

Focus on Poetry

Homophones
Homophones are words that sound the same but have different spellings and meanings.

Spelling Words

1. cord	11. role
2. chord	12. roll
3. pray	13. peel
4. prey	14. peal
5. seam	15. shone
6. seem	16. shown
7. sole	17. pain
8. soul	18. pane
9. piece	19. pole
10. peace	20. poll

Challenge Words
1. aisle
2. isle
3. rein
4. reign

My Study List
Add your own spelling words on the back.

DAY 2 — REVIEW & PRACTICE

Reviewing the Principle

Go over the spelling principle that some words related in meaning are also related in spelling, even though a vowel sound may change.

Practice/Homework Assign **Practice Book** page 83.

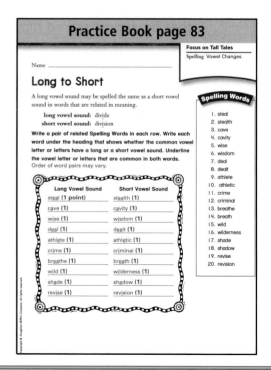

Practice Book page 83

Focus on Tall Tales
Spelling Vowel Changes

Name _____

Long to Short

A long vowel sound may be spelled the same as a short vowel sound in words that are related in meaning.

long vowel sound: di**vide**
short vowel sound: di**vision**

Write a pair of related Spelling Words in each row. Write each word under the heading that shows whether the common vowel letter or letters have a long or a short vowel sound. Underline the vowel letter or letters that are common in both words. Order of word pairs may vary.

Long Vowel Sound	Short Vowel Sound
steal (1 point)	stealth (1)
cave (1)	cavity (1)
wise (1)	wisdom (1)
deal (1)	dealt (1)
athlete (1)	athletic (1)
crime (1)	criminal (1)
breathe (1)	breath (1)
wild (1)	wilderness (1)
shade (1)	shadow (1)
revise (1)	revision (1)

Spelling Words
1. steal
2. stealth
3. cave
4. cavity
5. wise
6. wisdom
7. deal
8. dealt
9. athlete
10. athletic
11. crime
12. criminal
13. breathe
14. breath
15. wild
16. wilderness
17. shade
18. shadow
19. revise
20. revision

Take-Home Word List

DAY 3 VOCABULARY

Synonyms

Write the Basic Words.

- Say each word below. Have students write the Basic Word that means the same or nearly the same.

  savage *(wild)*

  rob *(steal)*

  bargain *(deal)*

  lawbreaker *(criminal)*

  hole *(cavity)*

  secrecy *(stealth)*

  change *(revise)*

- Next, have students use each Basic Word orally in a sentence. (Sentences will vary.)

Practice/Homework For spelling practice, assign **Practice Book** page 84.

Practice Book page 84

Focus on Tall Tales
Spelling Vowel Changes

Name _____

Spelling Spree

Letter Swap Write a Spelling Word by changing the underlined letter or letters to one or more different letters.

Spelling Words

1. revive   revise **(1 point)**   6. wife   wise **(1)**
2. death   breath **(1)**   7. steam   steal **(1)**
3. shape   shade **(1)**   8. wave   cave **(1)**
4. mild   wild **(1)**   9. meal   deal **(1)**
5. shallow   shadow **(1)**   10. wealth   stealth **(1)**

1. steal
2. stealth
3. cave
4. cavity
5. wise
6. wisdom
7. deal
8. dealt
9. athlete
10. athletic
11. crime
12. criminal
13. breathe
14. breath
15. wild
16. wilderness
17. shade
18. shadow
19. revise
20. revision

Analogies An analogy compares word pairs that are related in the same way. An analogy might use pairs of opposites or pairs of synonyms, or it might show word pairs that name a category and an item in that category. Write the Spelling Word that completes each analogy.

Opposites: *Hot* is to *cold* as *last* is to *first.*
Category and item: *Hammer* is to *tool* as *peach* is to *fruit.*

11. *Building is to city as forest is to* wilderness **(1)**
12. *Dentist is to doctor as burglar is to* criminal **(1)**
13. *Sadness is to joy as foolishness is to* wisdom **(1)**
14. *Iron is to rust as tooth is to* cavity **(1)**
15. *Proofread is to correction as edit is to* revision **(1)**

trumble

DAY 4 PROOFREADING

Game: Pair Up

Have students play this game in pairs.

- Have each pair make a word card for each Basic Word. One player shuffles the cards and deals ten cards to each player.

- Each player looks at his or her cards for pairs of cards that are related in spelling and meaning. Players place those cards on the table, face-up.

- Players then try to make more pairs by taking turns and asking each other for a card that would make a pair with another card in their hand. A player must spell the requested word correctly and use it in a sentence in order to get the card.

- When all the cards have been matched, the player with the most pairs wins.

Practice/Homework For proofreading and writing practice, assign **Practice Book** page 85.

Practice Book page 85

Focus on Tall Tales
Spelling Vowel Changes

Name _____

Proofreading and Writing

Proofreading Circle the five misspelled Spelling Words in this paragraph from a tall tale. Then write each word correctly. Order of answers may vary.

Spelling Words

1. steal
2. stealth
3. cave
4. cavity
5. wise
6. wisdom
7. deal
8. dealt
9. athlete
10. athletic
11. crime
12. criminal
13. breathe
14. breath
15. wild
16. wilderness
17. shade
18. shadow
19. revise
20. revision

Back in the Old West, Burl Redwood was known far and wide as the most athletic man who ever walked this planet. He could outrun, outjump, outride, outfight, outwrestle—just plain outdo anyone or anything. With great stealth Burl could sneak up on a grizzly bear, breeth down its neck, and then chase it for miles through the wilderness until the bear dropped from exhaustion. When Burl had a problem, he delt with it by holding a contest, which he always won.

One time, though, Burl committed a crim in a town policed by Wiley Wunn. That wise sheriff was eager to match wits with the famous athleet.

1. athletic **(1 point)**
2. breathe **(1)**
3. dealt **(1)**
4. crime **(1)**
5. athlete **(1)**

Make a Wanted Poster Think of a tall tale character whose special abilities might get him or her in trouble. Think about the character's abilities and what problems they might cause.

On a separate sheet of paper, create a wanted poster for your character. List the character's abilities and reasons why he or she is wanted. Use Spelling Words from the list. Responses will vary. **(5)**

DAY 5 ASSESSMENT

Spelling Test

Say each underlined word, read the sentence, and then repeat the word. Have students write only the underlined word.

Basic Words

1. Do not **steal** my pencil.
2. Cats are known for their **stealth**.
3. The bats slept in the **cave**.
4. I have a **cavity** in one tooth.
5. Try to make **wise** choices.
6. My dad has a lot of **wisdom**.
7. Sam got a **deal** on a used bike.
8. Mom quickly **dealt** the cards.
9. Al wants to be an Olympic **athlete**.
10. Jake is very **athletic**.
11. The thief committed a **crime**.
12. This photo shows the **criminal**.
13. Fish use gills to **breathe**.
14. I took a **breath** of air.
15. Have you seen a **wild** horse?
16. We hiked in the **wilderness**.
17. It is cool in the **shade**.
18. The tree cast a **shadow**.
19. I will **revise** the letter.
20. This **revision** fixed the story.

Challenge Words

21. The **volcano** erupted twice.
22. This dust is **volcanic** ash.
23. The washer finished its **cycle**.
24. Wear a helmet when riding a **bicycle**.

OBJECTIVES

- Learn about informal language.
- Become familiar with some slang from tall tales.

Practice Book page 86

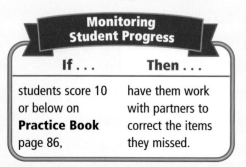

Focus on Tall Tales
Vocabulary Skill Slang and Informal Language

Name _____

Informally Speaking

Tom has written a letter to Marissa, who lives in France. She doesn't know American slang very well and may not understand what Tom is talking about! Help make his letter easier to understand. Replace each underlined slang word or phrase with a proper word or phrase that means the same thing. Write the new word or words on the line that has the same number. Answers may vary. Sample answers are provided.

Dear Marissa,

    I'm <u>psyched</u> to come visit you this summer. Paris sounds so <u>cool</u>, and you're a real <u>pal</u> to invite me. My <u>old man</u> says he's been to France with my mom. He told me it's just as nice as it looks in the French <u>flicks</u> we rented at the video store. I've been watching a French-language show on the <u>tube</u> so I can learn a few words and phrases. I figure if I <u>cram</u> for two weeks, I'll know how say hello and goodbye, and how to order some of that famous French <u>chow</u>. I'm planning to <u>pig out</u> the whole time! If I <u>croak</u> after eating too many French pastries, <u>no sweat</u>!

    Okay, I've got to hop on my <u>wheels</u> and deliver the local <u>rag</u> now, so I can earn some <u>greenbacks</u> for the trip. Talk to you soon!

Your friend,
Tom

1. excited
2. good
3. friend
4. father
5. movies
6. television
7. study hard
8. food
9. eat a lot
10. die
11. no problem
12. bicycle/car
13. newspaper
14. money

English Language Learners

Language Development

Tall tales often contain slang and informal language that English language learners find difficult. Pair students speaking a common first language to discuss examples of slang in their own language, then report in English to the class.

Monitoring Student Progress

If . . .	Then . . .
students score 10 or below on **Practice Book** page 86,	have them work with partners to correct the items they missed.

 TARGET SKILL

VOCABULARY: Slang and Informal Language

❶ Teach

Explain slang and informal language. Write *She tied all the wriggly <u>critters</u> together to make a long rope.*

- Ask students what the underlined word means. (creatures) Explain to students that this word is an example of *informal language*—special words and phrases that are used in place of proper or official language to add humor or effect. Tell students that *slang* is a type of informal language.

Discuss examples of slang. Have students give the meaning of each term below. Have them use context clues from the story. Then challenge students to think of more slang terms from tall tales. Write their ideas on the board.

- *hollerin'*, page 124 (yelling or shouting)
- *young'uns*, page 125 (children)

Model using context clues to understand slang. Have students read this sentence. *Just as he was about to give himself up for a goner, he heard a girl say, "What's the matter, stranger?"*

Think Aloud
I don't know the word goner, *but maybe it is a slang term. The first part of the sentence says he was about to give himself up. The last part of the sentence suggests that something is wrong. The sentence before this one tells me he was caught in a tree.* Goner *may be slang for "a doomed or ruined person." I'll check the dictionary to be sure. Yes, that meaning is correct.*

❷ Guided Practice

Display the following words. Have volunteers match each slang term with its meaning. Have students use dictionaries or their Anthologies to help them figure out the meaning of each term.

❸ Apply

Assign Practice Book page 86.

Slang Term	Meaning
1. bustin', page 124 (c)	a. wild creature
2. chow, page 113 (d)	b. man
3. feller, page 122 (b)	c. breaking
4. varmint, page 120 (a)	d. food

STUDY SKILL:
Using an Atlas

❶ Teach

Introduce the features of an atlas.

- Display an atlas. Tell students that an atlas is a collection of maps.

- Display a map of the world in the atlas, and explain that this map gives "the big picture" but not much detail.

- Display maps with views of regions and countries, and point out that these maps show more detail, such as rivers, mountains, cities, and boundaries between states and countries.

Model how to find items in an atlas.

- Tell students that the detailed maps are typically organized in sections by continent. The table of contents will show the pattern.

- In each section, maps may be arranged as follows:
  - alphabetically (by region or country)
  - geographically (by areas that lie side by side)

- Model how to find a specific country, such as Brazil, by using the table of contents.

- Next, show how to find a specific feature, such as Mount Rainier, by consulting the index and using the letter-and-number map coordinates.

❷ Practice/Apply

Provide practice in using atlas features.

- Have volunteers use an atlas to locate Pittsburgh, the Badlands, and the Ohio River. Prompt and guide them as needed.

- Have students work in small groups. Provide an atlas to each group. Have students locate the places listed below. Tell them to find each place by using the index to find the page number and the coordinates. (Page numbers and coordinates will vary, based on atlas.)

Place	Page, coordinates	Place	Page, coordinates
Baltimore		Mississippi River	
Grand Canyon		Great Lakes	

OBJECTIVES

- Learn about the features of an atlas.
- Navigate an atlas by using the index and map coordinates.

GRAMMAR: Using Sentence Variety

OBJECTIVES

- Vary sentence types to add interest to writing.
- Add appositives to sentences.
- Proofread and correct sentences with grammar, spelling, and punctuation errors.

DAY 1 INSTRUCTION

Varying Sentence Types

Teach Have students give examples of the four types of sentences as well as sentences that include compound elements (subjects, predicates, sentences).

- Explain that writers may use different types of sentences to make their writing more fluent and interesting to read.

- Display **Transparency F1–4**. Ask a volunteer to read aloud the sample paragraphs. Ask students to identify how some sentences in the second example changed. Explain that the second paragraph sounds less choppy and flows more naturally because it uses different types of sentences.

- Help students revise the last paragraph to add sentence variety.

Daily Language Practice
Have students correct Sentences 1 and 2 on **Transparency F1–3**.

DAY 2 PRACTICE

Independent Work

Practice/Homework Assign **Practice Book** page 87.

Daily Language Practice
Have students correct Sentences 3 and 4 on **Transparency F1–3**.

Transparency F1–3
Daily Language Practice

THEME 2 Focus on Tall Tales   Grammar Skill

Correct two sentences each day.

1. did a criminel steel Heck's sock!
   Did a criminal steal Heck's sock?
2. The loggers slept in a camp in the willderness
   The loggers slept in a camp in the wilderness.
3. Be wize and rest in the shade on hot dayes
   Be wise and rest in the shade on hot days.
4. The wolfs howled and the sound took my breathe away. The wolves howled, and the sound took my breath away.
5. Mike Fink used stelth to surprise Sally when she was looking for berrys. Mike Fink used stealth to surprise Sally when she was looking for berries.
6. The two men, Canadian lumberjacks saw a scary shaddow. The two men, Canadian lumberjacks, saw a scary shadow.
7. Sally delt bravely. With any problem. Sally dealt bravely with any problem.
8. Why did he revize the storys when he told them. Why did he revise the stories when he told them?
9. Sally an athletic woman was very strong. Sally, an athletic woman, was very strong.
10. The dentist a tiny man checked the logger's teeth for a cavety. The dentist, a tiny man, checked the logger's teeth for a cavity.

TRANSPARENCY F1–3
TEACHER'S EDITION PAGE 129I

Monitoring Student Progress

If . . .	Then . . .
students score 7 or below on **Practice Book** page 88 or 89,	have them work in small groups to correct the items they missed.

Transparency F1–4
Varying Sentence Types

THEME 2 Focus on Tall Tales   Grammar Skill Varying Sentence Types

In the winter McBroom cut up chunks of frozen wind. His children helped him. They put the chunks in the icehouse. In the summer they thawed the wind to cool off.

One winter Heck Jones lost a sock. He thought the McBrooms stole it. The next summer McBroom and his children saw something black fly by. They wondered what it could be. It was Heck Jones's sock. It had been frozen with the wind. The sock flew back to Heck. It pulled itself right over his foot.

In the winter McBroom and his children cut up chunks of frozen wind and put them in the ice-house. In the summer they thawed the wind to cool off.

One winter Heck Jones lost a sock, and he thought the McBrooms stole it. The next summer McBroom and his children saw something black fly by. What could it be? It was Heck Jones's sock! It had been frozen with the wind. The sock flew back to Heck and pulled itself right over his foot!

McBroom had never seen a sock do that. He wondered how it happened. McBroom thought maybe the smell of Heck's feet attracted the sock. The smell made that sock behave like a homing pigeon.
Sample response:
McBroom had never seen a sock do that. How did it happen? McBroom thought maybe the smell of Heck's feet attracted the sock and made that sock behave like a homing pigeon.

TRANSPARENCY F1–4
TEACHER'S EDITION PAGE 129I

Practice Book page 87

Name _____

Focus on Tall Tales
Grammar Skill Using Sentence Variety

A Hairy Tale

Using Sentence Variety Use different types of sentences to make your writing more interesting and smooth to read. Use declarative, interrogative, imperative, or exclamatory sentences. Use compound sentences or sentences with compound subjects or compound predicates.

Rewrite these paragraphs describing a tall tale character. Change five sentences to introduce more sentence variety. (2 points for each sentence)

Maybe you have heard tales about Hairy Harry. Harry was born with long hair wrapped around him like a cocoon. His parents tied it in a ponytail. It dragged behind him like a king's robe for more than twenty feet.

Harry soon learned that he could use that hair like an extra arm. One time Harry fell down an old well. His sister, Harriet, fell in, too. Harry flipped his hair out of that well. He wrapped it around a tree trunk. Harriet climbed up his hair. Then Harry climbed up his hair. They were out of that well lickety-split.

Sample paragraphs. More than five changes are shown as examples.

Have you heard tales about Hairy Harry? Harry was born with long hair wrapped around him like a cocoon. His parents tied it in a ponytail, and it dragged behind him like a king's robe for more than twenty feet.

Harry soon learned that he could use that hair like an extra arm. One time Harry and his sister, Harriet, fell down an old well. Harry flipped his hair out of that well and wrapped it around a tree trunk. Harriet and Harry climbed up his hair and were out of that well lickety-split!

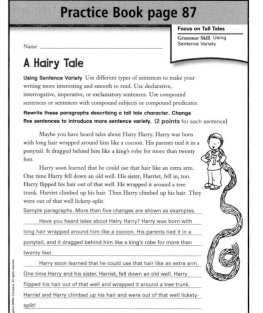

129I   **THEME 1: Focus on Tall Tales**

DAY 3 INSTRUCTION

Appositives

Teach Display **Transparency F1–5**.

- Read the examples. Have students find the phrase added to the second sentence. *(a bearded giant)* Point out that the phrase includes the noun *giant,* which tells more about the first noun, *logger.* Explain that this phrase is an **appositive.** Point out that *a bearded giant* is set off by commas.

- For each numbered sentence, have students add the phrase from the box that describes the underlined noun. Have students find the noun in each appositive. Remind them to set off the appositive with commas. Point out that an appositive that ends a sentence is followed only by end punctuation.

Daily Language Practice
Have students correct Sentences 5 and 6 on **Transparency F1–3**.

Transparency F1–5

THEME 2: Focus on Tall Tales
Grammar Skill Improving Writing

ANNOTATED VERSION

Appositives

The logger, a bearded giant, picked up an axe, a saw, and a chain.

the mightiest logger
the Big Onion Lumber Company
a pickaxe
the Great Lakes
a bushy beard

Nouns in appositives are underlined.

1. Paul Bunyan was born in Maine.
   Paul Bunyan, the mightiest logger, was born in Maine.

2. Paul had a strange feature when he was born.
   Paul had a strange feature, a bushy beard, when he was born.

3. In Arizona one of Pauls' tools created the Grand Canyon.
   In Arizona, one of Paul's tools, a pickaxe, created the Grand Canyon.

4. The loggers' drinking water came from several ponds.
   The loggers' drinking water came from several ponds, the Great Lakes.

5. Paul's logging company was in Minnesota.
   Paul's logging company, the Big Onion Lumber Company, was in Minnesota.

TRANSPARENCY F1–5
TEACHER'S EDITION PAGE 129J

DAY 4 PRACTICE

Independent Work

Practice/Homework Assign **Practice Book** page 88.

Daily Language Practice
Have students correct Sentences 7 and 8 on **Transparency F1–3**.

Practice Book page 88

Focus on Tall Tales
Grammar Skill Appositives

Name _____

Name a Noun

Appositives An appositive is a phrase that includes a noun that tells more about another noun in the same sentence. Use commas to set off an appositive.

Sally Ann Thunder Ann Whirlwind, the title character, was amazing.

Rewrite each sentence. Add the phrase from the box that tells more about the underlined noun. Use commas correctly.

an alligator's skin
an eagle's nest
a muddy swamp
a riverboat man
his rival

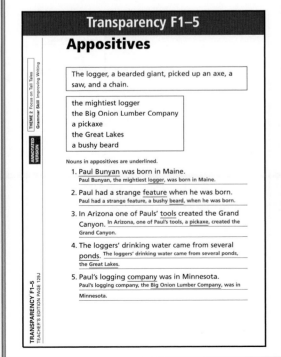

1. Mike Fink wanted to play a mean trick.
   Mike Fink, a riverboat man, wanted to play a mean trick. **(2 points)**

2. He was tired of hearing Davy Crockett praise Sally.
   He was tired of hearing Davy Crockett, his rival, praise Sally. **(2)**

3. Mike decided to wear a disguise.
   Mike decided to wear a disguise, an alligator's skin. **(2)**

4. Sally gave him a whack, and he landed in an uncomfortable place.
   Sally gave him a whack, and he landed in an uncomfortable place, a muddy swamp. **(2)**

5. Sally wore her favorite hat to meet Davy.
   Sally wore her favorite hat, an eagle's nest, to meet Davy. **(2)**

DAY 5 IMPROVING WRITING

Using Commas with Appositives

Teach Remind students to use commas before and after an appositive. If an appositive ends a sentence, it is followed only by the end mark.

- Write the following sentences. Ask volunteers to set off the appositive by adding one or more commas to each sentence.

  – Paul Bunyan, the giant woodsman, started a logging camp.

  – One well-known tall tale tells about John Henry, a steel-driving man.

- Have students review a piece of their writing to see if they can improve it by adding appositives. Ask them to proofread for correct comma placement in all of their sentences.

Practice/Homework Assign **Practice Book** page 89.

Daily Language Practice
Have students correct Sentences 9 and 10 on **Transparency F1–3**.

Practice Book page 89

Focus on Tall Tales
Grammar Skill Using Commas with Appositives

Name _____

Counselor Wanted

Using Commas with Appositives Use commas to set off an appositive. If an appositive ends a sentence, it is followed by only the end mark.

Use proofreading marks to correct ten errors in punctuation and capitalization in this job advertisement.
(1 point for each correction)

Example: this job, a real opportunity, looks interesting

A great opportunity awaits you Camp Timberlake, a wilderness retreat for boys and girls in Minnesota, has an opening for a junior counselor. Do you love the sound of the wind and the smell of campfires? Help our young campers, children from large cities, learn about and appreciate the sights, sounds, and smells of the outdoors. Lead hikes and campfire songs, tell and create tall tales? We offer good pay and plenty of fun. Apply at our office, the first red cabin.

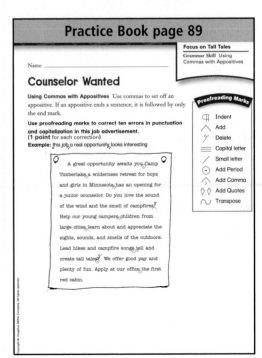

Proofreading Marks

⊓ Indent
∧ Add
ℐ Delete
≡ Capital letter
／ Small letter
⊙ Add Period
∧ Add Comma
∨∨ Add Quotes
∩ Transpose

WRITING: Tall Tale

OBJECTIVES

- Plan a tall tale.
- Create a larger-than-life main character.
- Write the tall tale.
- Use exact nouns to improve writing.

DAY 1 PREWRITING

Introducing the Format

Review the characteristics of a tall tale. A tall tale

- is a story with exaggerated, larger-than-life actions or events;
- includes characters, setting, and plot;
- may feature a larger-than-life main character whose abilities, character traits, or deeds are exaggerated;
- includes enough details about realistic places, things, and activities to seem grounded in reality; and
- uses exaggeration to bring humor to the story.

Start students thinking about tall tales.

- Have students brainstorm ideas for a larger-than-life tall tale character, including what the character looks like and his or her abilities, personality traits, and actions.
- Ask pairs of students to discuss other possible exaggerated elements as well as realistic ones.
- Have students save their notes.

DAY 2 DRAFTING

Discussing the Model

Have students review the tall tales on Anthology pages 110–127. Discuss the steps an author follows in writing a tall tale. An author

- creates a memorable main character, giving details about his or her appearance, abilities, actions, and personality;
- uses exaggeration in describing characters, actions, and setting;
- includes some factual or realistic details; and
- emphasizes the humor in story events.

Display Transparency F1–6, and discuss how to use the graphic organizer.

Have students draft a tall tale.

- Have students choose a tall tale character and exaggerated actions or events.
- Assign **Practice Book** page 90 to help students organize their writing.
- Have them use their notes from Day 1.
- Provide support as needed.

Writing Traits

Word Choice As students revise their paragraphs on Day 3, emphasize the importance of choosing exact nouns.

Without Exact Nouns Bill hitched a ride on a storm, and it dropped him at the contest in a matter of minutes.

With Exact Nouns Bill hitched a ride on a tornado, and it dropped him at the rodeo in a matter of minutes.

Transparency F1–6

Planning a Tall Tale

Character, Setting, Plot

Main Character(s)

Setting

Plot: Important Events in the Tale

Tall Tale Exaggeration

Exaggerated Character Traits

Exaggerated or Impossible Setting Elements

Exaggerated or Impossible Actions or Events

Realistic Details

THEME 2 Focus on Tall Tales
Writing Skill Tall Tale

ANNOTATED VERSION

TRANSPARENCY F1–6
TEACHER'S EDITION PAGES 129K–129L

Practice Book page 90

Focus on Tall Tales
Writing Skill Drafting

Name _____

Planning a Tall Tale

Use the Chart to help plan your tall tale. (2 points each)

Character, Setting, Plot

Main Character(s)

Setting

Plot: Important Events in the Tale

Tall Tale Exaggeration

Exaggerated Character Traits

Exaggerated or Impossible Setting Elements

Exaggerated or Impossible Actions or Events

Realistic Details

DAY 3 · REVISING

Improving Writing: Using Exact Nouns

Review exact nouns.

- Remind students that a noun refers to a person, place, or thing.

- Tall tales usually include funny, exaggerated character traits, places, or objects.

- Exact nouns help the reader see exaggerated elements clearly.

Display Transparency F1–7.

- Have volunteers replace the vague nouns and noun phrases with exact nouns. Suggest that they refer to Anthology pages 110–113 as needed.

- Discuss how the exact nouns create stronger images.

- See Writing Traits on page 129K.

Assign Practice Book page 91.

DAY 4 · PROOFREADING

Checking for Errors

Have students proofread for errors in grammar, spelling, punctuation, or usage.

- Students can use the proofreading checklist on **Practice Book** page 281 and the chart of proofreading marks on **Practice Book** page 282 to help them proofread their tall tales.

- Have students review their tall tales, replacing vague nouns and proofreading for other errors.

DAY 5 · PUBLISHING

Sharing Tall Tales

Consider these publishing options.

- Ask students to read their tall tales or some other piece of writing from the Author's Chair.

- Encourage students to make their tall tales into picture books for younger children.

Portfolio Opportunity

Save students' tall tales as samples of their writing development.

WRITING

Focus on Tall Tales

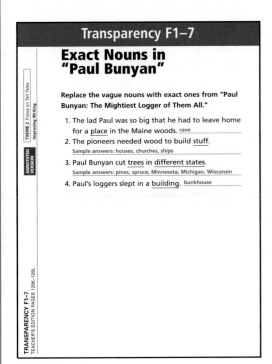

Transparency F1–7

Exact Nouns in "Paul Bunyan"

Replace the vague nouns with exact ones from "Paul Bunyan: The Mightiest Logger of Them All."

1. The lad Paul was so big that he had to leave home for a <u>place</u> in the Maine woods. cave

2. The pioneers needed wood to build <u>stuff</u>.
   Sample answers: houses, churches, ships

3. Paul Bunyan cut <u>trees</u> in <u>different states</u>.
   Sample answers: pines, spruce; Minnesota, Michigan, Wisconsin

4. Paul's loggers slept in a <u>building</u>. bunkhouse

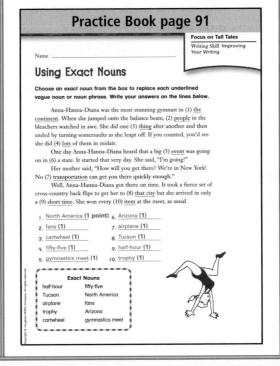

Practice Book page 91

Focus on Tall Tales
Writing Skill Improving Your Writing

Name _____

Using Exact Nouns

Choose an exact noun from the box to replace each underlined vague noun or noun phrase. Write your answers on the lines below.

Anna-Hanna-Diana was the most stunning gymnast in (1) <u>the continent</u>. When she jumped onto the balance beam, (2) <u>people</u> in the bleachers watched in awe. She did one (3) <u>thing</u> after another and then ended by turning somersaults as she leapt off. If you counted, you'd see she did (4) <u>lots</u> of them in midair.

One day Anna-Hanna-Diana heard that a big (5) <u>event</u> was going on in (6) <u>a state</u>. It started that very day. She said, "I'm going!"

Her mother said, "How will you get there? We're in New York! No (7) <u>transportation</u> can get you there quickly enough."

Well, Anna-Hanna-Diana got there on time. It took a fierce set of cross-country back flips to get her to (8) <u>that city</u> but she arrived in only a (9) <u>short time</u>. She won every (10) <u>item</u> at the meet, as usual.

1. North America **(1 point)**   6. Arizona **(1)**
2. fans **(1)**   7. airplane **(1)**
3. cartwheel **(1)**   8. Tucson **(1)**
4. fifty-five **(1)**   9. half-hour **(1)**
5. gymnastics meet **(1)**   10. trophy **(1)**

Exact Nouns

half-hour	fifty-five
Tucson	North America
airplane	fans
trophy	Arizona
cartwheel	gymnastics meet

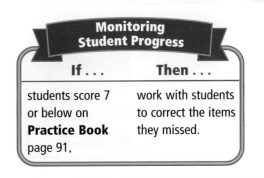

Monitoring Student Progress

If . . .	Then . . .
students score 7 or below on **Practice Book** page 91,	work with students to correct the items they missed.

Language Center

LANGUAGE CENTER

VOCABULARY
Building Vocabulary

👥 Pairs	🕐 30 minutes
Objective	Make a poster showing names of trees.
Materials	Poster board, markers, construction paper, scissors, glue

Paul Bunyan doesn't just cut trees. He clears *cottonwoods*, *oaks*, *spruce*, and *pine*. Grow your own tree vocabulary with a poster that displays tree names.

- With a partner, review "Paul Bunyan" and use an encyclopedia to find tree names.

- List tree names under two categories: *deciduous* (shedding leaves) or *evergreen* (having leaves or needles all year).

- Cut leaf shapes out of green and yellow construction paper.

- Write a tree name on each leaf. Use yellow leaves for deciduous trees and green leaves for evergreen. Glue them to poster board.

- Add a title and a key explaining leaf types.

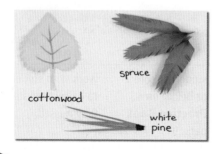

STRUCTURAL ANALYSIS
Word Root Puzzle

👥 Pairs	🕐 30 minutes
Objective	Make a puzzle using words with *vis* or *vid*.
Materials	Dictionary, writing materials, scissors

Some words contain the roots *vis* or *vid,* which mean "to see." How many of these words do you know?

- With a partner, write the following words on a list: *envision, evidence, evident, provide, provisions, supervisor, video, visa, visage, visible, vision, visit, visor, vista.*

- Divide the list in half and have each partner write the meanings of his or her words. Use a dictionary if necessary.

- On another sheet of paper, have each partner write letter blanks for each word, followed by the definition. For example: _ _ _ _ , *a travel permit*

- Exchange lists and try to guess each other's words.

VOCABULARY
Vocabulary Game

👥👥 Groups	🕐 45 minutes
Objective	Write a "patchwork" tall tale.
Materials	Activity Master 1–4, writing materials, scissors, timer

Use the Key Vocabulary words to help you plan and write a patchwork tall tale.

- Read the planner on Activity Master 1–4.

- Cut a blank piece of paper into strips. On each strip, write the elements under the headings **Hero, Heroine, Setting, Style,** and **Plot.**

- Fold the strips and put them in five separate piles. Now, have everyone choose one slip from each pile. These are the elements you must use in your patchwork tall tale.

- Set the timer for twenty minutes and begin writing. When the time is up, read your stories aloud to each other.

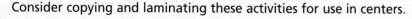

"Mom and the mayor meet at the mall, where they make a discovery."

Consider copying and laminating these activities for use in centers.

VIEWING

Comparing Art Styles

👥 **Pairs**	🕐 **30 minutes**
Objective	Compare visual styles.
Materials	Anthology, writing materials

What's the best style in which to illustrate a story: cartoon, realistic painting, woodcuts, or photography? Of course, the answer is—it depends. Compare different visual styles.

- Review the illustration styles on pages 108–109 and in the tall tales. Pick two styles that seem quite different from one another.

- Compare the illustrations, using the questions shown below. Repeat the questions for Story #2.

Name of Story #1: _____

How would you describe the style of artwork? _____
_____

Does it suit the story? Why or why not? _____
_____

How does this style compare to the one in Story #2? _____
_____

PHONICS/SPELLING

Tall Tale Word Pairs

👥 **Pairs**	🕐 **30 minutes**
Objective	Write a tall tale using spelling words.

With a partner, write a tall tale that uses at least four pairs of related Spelling words. Follow these steps:

- Review the Spelling words.

- Choose four pairs of related words from the list to use in your tall tale.

- Read your tall tale to a classmate and challenge him or her to identify the related words.

- Illustrate your tall tale if you like.

He had a <u>cavity</u> as big as a <u>cave</u>.

LEVELED READERS

by Tim Johnson
illustrated by Alexandra Wallner

Apples for America

Summary *John Chapman was a real person, though more people know him by his legendary name, Johnny Appleseed. Like other tall tales, the stories about Johnny contain some outrageous exaggerations. In this story, the author covers some whoppers about Johnny, all the way back to his first word, which some folks say was* apple. *Johnny's apple-planting adventures are ripe with tall-tale material.*

Vocabulary

Introduce the Key Vocabulary and ask students to complete the BLM.

legends fables, *p. 3*

blossoms flowers from a tree, *p. 4*

provide to supply, *p. 7*

bandana a large brightly colored handkerchief, *p. 9*

frontier a region beyond a settlement, *p. 11*

pioneers the first people to settle new territory, *p. 11*

nourish to feed, *p. 13*

Building Background and Vocabulary

Invite students to share what they know about tall tales. Preview the story with students, using the story vocabulary when possible.

Writing Skill: Writing a Tall Tale

Have students read the Strategy Focus on the book flap. Remind students to use the strategy and to think about the elements of tall tales as they read the book. (See the Leveled Readers Teacher's Guide for **Vocabulary and Writing Masters**.)

Responding

Have partners discuss how to answer the questions on the inside back cover.

Think About the Selection Sample answers:

1. He roped a stream, sprinkled sugar on rain clouds, and grew trees in one hour.

2. Possible responses: He was born in Leominster, Massachusetts, he walked to the frontier, and he loved apples.

3. Students might say that sharing a den with bears would be too dangerous.

4. Responses will vary, but students might name other tall-tale figures like Paul Bunyan.

Making Connections Responses will vary.

Building Fluency

Model Read the first paragraph on page 10. Explain that *sang* and *happy* are clues about how to read the next sentences. Read the next paragraph, showing happiness and showing that the italicized words are part of a song.

Practice Have partners read page 16 and look for clues on how to read the final sentence.

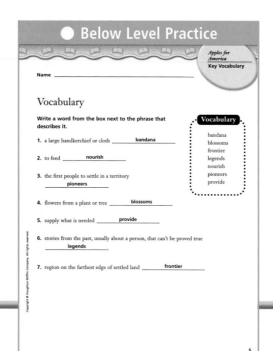

Leveled Readers

Grandpa's Rail Tales

Summary *Seven-year-old Darlene is attending a party for her grandfather, who is retiring from his job on the railroad. Her grandfather clearly loved his work and loves to tell about his life on the rails. Darlene and Grandpa's friends clearly appreciate Grandpa's ability to tell stories.*

Vocabulary

Introduce the Key Vocabulary and ask students to complete the BLM.

retirement end of a career or job, *p. 3*

locomotive a vehicle used to move railroad cars, *p. 6*

bank a mound or pile, *p. 9*

gaped stared at with mouth wide open, *p. 9*

joshed teased or joked, *p. 10*

retort a quick or witty reply, *p. 10*

recollect to recall or remember, *p. 12*

peals loud sounds, *p. 16*

▲ ON LEVEL

Building Background and Vocabulary

Invite students to recall some of the techniques that a good storyteller uses, like humor, detail, and exaggeration. Preview the story with students, using the story vocabulary when possible.

Writing Skill: Writing a Tall Tale

Have students read the Strategy Focus on the book flap. Remind students to use the strategy and to think about the elements of tall tales as they read the book. (See the Leveled Readers Teacher's Guide for **Vocabulary and Writing Masters**.)

Responding

Have partners discuss how to answer the questions on the inside back cover.

Think About the Selection Sample answers:

1. Possible response: Grandpa tells funny and entertaining stories.

2. They are so exaggerated, they could not really be true.

3. Grandpa added that to make the story even more far-fetched.

4. The setting of the stories, like the foggy night or the hot summer day, could be real.

Making Connections Responses will vary.

Building Fluency

Model Read the sixth paragraph on page 10. Explain that *sure* is a conversation word that can take on different meanings. Explain that Grandpa is defending himself, so he may be feeling annoyed as he says it.

Practice Ask students to look for other conversation words (page 14) and to read them appropriately. Students then can explain why they read it the way they did.

▲ On Level Practice

Grandpa's Rail Tales
Key Vocabulary

Name _____

Vocabulary

Choose the best word to complete each sentence.

Vocabulary:
gaped
recollect
retort
bank
peals
joshed
retirement
locomotive

1. Grandma was always quick with a _____ **retort** _____ when Grandpa teased her.

2. Darlene _____ **gaped** _____ and her mouth hung open as Grandpa told the story of the dog that helped Old Pete.

3. Most of Grandpa's tales ended with _____ **peals** _____ of laughter from his listeners.

4. Grandpa's friends and family were throwing a party for his _____ **retirement** _____

5. Darlene questioned her grandfather when he said that he'd been driving a _____ **locomotive** _____ since the age of three.

6. One of Grandpa's favorite stories was the time when he drove up on a _____ **bank** _____ of fog.

7. Darlene's dad _____ **joshed** _____ Grandpa about the truthfulness of his stories.

8. Grandpa liked to _____ **recollect** _____ stories about the old days on the railroad.

5

▲ On Level Practice

Grandpa's Rail Tales
Writing Skill
Writing a Tall Tale

Name _____

Writing

Use the following to check your tall tale and revise it. Then read it aloud to hear how it sounds. Can you make it even better? Answers will vary.

1. What is the title of your tall tale? _____
Does this title fit your story? Will it interest your readers? If not, revise it below.
_____

2. Name your main character. What exaggerated quality does this character have? _____
List two details you could add to help bring your character to life.

3. Find humorous elements in your tall tale that spring from silly descriptions, odd details or events, or funny dialogue. What other humorous elements can you add? Write them below.
☐ description _____   ☐ events _____
☐ details _____   ☐ dialogue _____

4. Is the setting of your tall tale important to the story? Why or why not?
_____
List two details you could add to help readers picture the setting. _____

5. Review the events in your tall tale. Are they told in the right order? If not, explain how you will revise them below.
_____

Check for sequence words: ☐ *first* ☐ *then* ☐ *later on* ☐ *after* ☐ *finally*

6. Finally, check your tall tale for errors in: ☐ spelling ☐ punctuation ☐ grammar

7

■ ABOVE LEVEL

Building Background and Vocabulary

Remind students that Davy Crockett was a real man, but tall tales have been written about him, many of which were exaggerated. Preview the story with students, using the story vocabulary when possible.

Writing Skill: Writing a Tall Tale

Have students read the Strategy Focus on the book flap. Remind students to use the strategy and to think about the elements of tall tales as they read the book. (See the Leveled Readers Teacher's Guide for **Vocabulary and Writing Masters**.)

Responding

Have partners discuss how to answer the questions on the inside back cover.

Think About the Selection Sample answers:

1. Davy became well known as a great hunter and as a storyteller.

2. Davy died a hero's death at the Alamo.

3. Davy couldn't really have taken a ride on the moon.

4. because he wanted to be remembered for doing what he thought was right

Making Connections Responses will vary.

Building Fluency

Model Read the last paragraph on page 6. Explain that the text that comes before Davy Crockett's dialogue helps indicate how Crockett says it. Having read the paragraph, we know that Crockett's voice must show that he has been heartsick many times in his life.

Practice Have students look for other dialogue in the story where there are clues in paragraphs or sentences that show how it should be said.

Davy Crockett: Frontier Hero

Summary *Davy Crockett was a real person who became a legend as a symbol of the American frontier. Born in 1786 in what is now Tennessee, he became famous as a woodsman, hunter, and storyteller.*

Vocabulary

Introduce the Key Vocabulary and ask students to complete the BLM.

circumstances facts, events, details, *p. 4*

marksman a target-shooting expert, *p. 7*

humorist a person noted for humor, *p. 8*

mock humorously false, *p. 8*

frankness honesty, *p. 9*

conscience sense of right and wrong, *p. 11*

boisterous spirited, rowdy, *p. 11*

legislators people who write laws, *p. 13*

garrison troops at a military post, *p. 15*

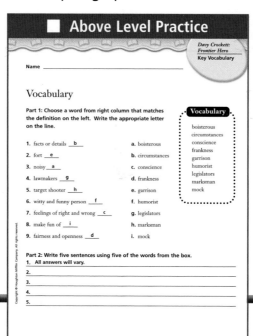

◆ **LANGUAGE SUPPORT**

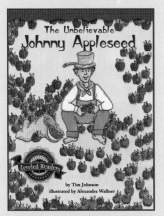

The Unbelievable Johnny Appleseed

Summary *This tall tale recounts some of the incredible stories about American folk hero Johnny Appleseed. These tales are based on the exploits of a real man named John Chapman. John loved apples and went to great lengths to share them with people near and far.*

Vocabulary

Introduce the Key Vocabulary and ask students to complete the BLM.

folk hero a hero of legends and folktales, *p. 3*

bloomed grew; flourished, *p. 4*

seeds parts of plants from which new plants can grow, *p. 8*

orchard an area of land where fruit trees grow, *p. 10*

pioneers people who first settle in a region, *p. 11*

hollow a space or opening inside something, *p. 12*

Building Background and Vocabulary

Explain that in a tall tale a character does things that a real person could not do. Have students give examples of stories about things real people couldn't do. Then distribute the **Build Background Practice Master.** Read the instructions and have students complete the activity in pairs. (See the Leveled Readers Teacher's Guide for **Build Background and Vocabulary Masters**.)

Reading Strategy: Summarize

Have students read the Strategy Focus on the book flap. Remind students to notice what happens at the beginning, middle, and end of the story.

Responding

Have partners discuss how to answer the questions on the inside back cover.

Think About the Selection Sample answers:

1. He walks around the country planting apple seeds.

2. Possible answer: He wants to plant apple trees all over America. Then people will always have food.

3. They wanted to have apple trees grow where they lived.

4. Responses will vary.

Making Connections Responses will vary.

Building Fluency

Model Have students point to each word on page 3 as they follow along with the recording of *The Unbelievable Johnny Appleseed* on audio CD.

Practice Have students read aloud with the recording until they are able to read the text on their own accurately and with expression.

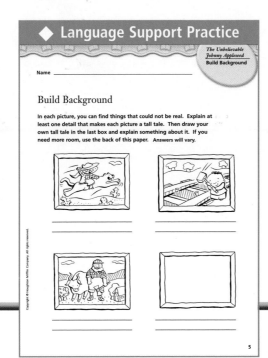

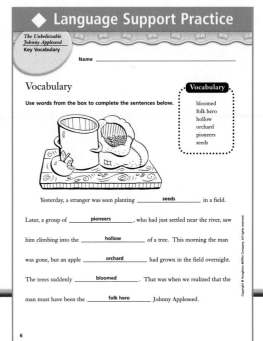

Resources for Theme 1

Contents

If You Lived at the Time of the Great San Francisco Earthquake

Summary *The nonfiction book If You Lived at the Time of the Great San Francisco Earthquake answers many questions about what life was like for people during this incredible natural disaster. Anecdotes throughout the book help readers see the effects of the earthquake through the eyes of the residents of the city.*

Vocabulary

cobblestones rounded stones used for paving streets, *p. 18*

terror an extreme, overpowering fear, *p. 25*

inspector a person whose job is to carefully review or examine, *p. 50*

recover to restore or regain a normal state, *p. 60*

committee a group of people brought together for a special purpose, *p. 63*

Preparing to Read

Building Background Ask students to describe what they know about earthquakes. Be sure they understand that earthquakes are caused by shifts in the earth's crust and can vary greatly in severity. Tell them that this book answers many questions about what happened to people during the 1906 San Francisco earthquake. Remind students to use their reading strategies.

Developing Key Vocabulary Preview with students the meanings of the Key Vocabulary words listed at the left. Also have students pay attention to the many verbs that describe how things looked, sounded, and felt.

Previewing the Text

If You Lived at the Time of the Great San Francisco Earthquake may be read in its entirety or in three segments, pages 4–25, pages 26–45, and pages 46–64. Have students look at the table of contents and the illustrations and ask them what they expect to find out as they read. Remind students to monitor their comprehension as they read.

Supporting the Reading

pages 4–25

- Why did many people run outside in their pajamas when the earthquake struck? (Most people had been asleep and quickly ran outside because they were afraid.)

- What steps did Gloria Hansen follow to determine how many people died in the disaster? (First she read the 1906 newspapers, magazines, and official city books. Then she created her own list of the people who had died. Then she sent letters to newspapers, magazines, and clubs to ask if anyone knew someone who had been in the quake.)

- How does the author help you understand how the earthquake sounded, looked, and felt? (She includes the words of people who were actually there.)

- What words does the author use to describe the sounds and sights? (Sounds: rumbling, roaring, stampede, thunder, a loud clap, firecrackers; Sights: streets splitting open, buildings shook and swayed, cobblestones jumping, treetops touching the ground, ground rolled like ocean waves)

pages 26–45

- Why do you think the author describes actual attempts to rescue people, property, and animals? (These descriptions give an idea of the events and what being in the earthquake was like; they make the disaster seem more real to the reader.)

- What kinds of things did the people of San Francisco try to save during the earthquake? (Examples: things for sleeping, clothing, pets, household items)

- Describe the kinds of shelters people used after the earthquake. (Be sure students understand the terms *refugee camps, tents, barracks, cottages*.)

pages 46–64

- What kinds of things were sent to help the people of San Francisco after the earthquake? (Examples: money, food, clothing, medicine)

- What caused the fires that burned in the city for three days and nights? (damaged gas pipes, water pipes, and electrical systems; no fire alarms or water)

- What sources of heat did people use for cooking after the earthquake? (stoves, circles of stones, metal garbage cans, cooking shacks)

- What human qualities helped people survive after the earthquake? (sense of humor, sense of helping others, support from around the world)

- Why do you think the author begins each section of the book with a question? (This type of organization helps the reader see the big picture by understanding small parts at a time; it also helps the reader locate specific information.)

Responding

Have students tell whether their predictions were accurate and have them tell how they used reading strategies, such as Monitor/Clarify or Question. Then have students summarize the key ideas of *If You Lived at the Time of the Great San Francisco Earthquake*.

Activity Have students reread the description of what San Francisco looked like after the earthquake, and draw a picture of the image they find most striking or amazing.

English Language Learners

Language Development

Be sure students understand the comparisons the author uses to help readers understand what the earthquake felt like, including an elevator going down fast, sinking, *danced* as she was trying to get dressed, two invisible giants wrestling under the hotel, and feeling *like corn in a popper.*

THEME PAPERBACKS

▲ ON LEVEL

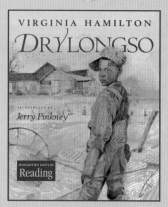

Drylongso

Summary *Drylongso tells the story of a farming family living through a drought in the 1970s, and how an unusual visitor effects great change in their lives. While the story is realistic fiction, it hints at the visitor's special—perhaps mythical—skill for finding water.*

Vocabulary

granules small grains or pellets, *p. 7*

mattock a digging tool, *p. 33*

divining rod or dowser a forked branch or stick that is believed to indicate underground water or minerals by bending downward when held over a source, *p. 36*

cultivate to improve and prepare land for raising crops, *p. 40*

canals man-made waterways used for irrigation, shipping, or travel, *p. 46*

Preparing to Read

Building Background Discuss briefly with students what they know about droughts and explain that this book tells the story of a family trying to farm during a drought. Be sure that students understand the long-term nature of a drought and the damage it can cause. Remind students to use their reading strategies as they read this book.

Developing Key Vocabulary Preview with students the meanings of the Key Vocabulary words listed at the left for each segment of the book, pages 1–28 and pages 29–54.

Previewing the Text

Drylongso may be read in its entirety or in two segments, pages 1–28 and pages 29–54. Encourage students to read the first page and look at the illustrations. Ask them to predict what the story might be about. Explain to students that characters in the story sometimes speak in dialect, or a form of language that is spoken in a particular place or by a particular group of people. For example, Lindy and her father work in his *garden-a-chance* on page 2. Other examples include *drylongso, rain-fella,* and *rag-a-wet.* Encourage students to use context to help them understand how these words and phrases help describe objects, situations, and people in the story.

Supporting the Reading

pages 1–28

- Why did the author choose to begin the story with a description of Lindy and her father planting a tomato plant in the dust? (Possible response: to emphasize the dryness of the land and the difficulty the farmers faced, but also their hope and optimism.)

- How long has there been a drought? How does it affect Lindy? (The drought has been going on for three years. It is a part of Lindy's everyday life; she can't even imagine a heavy rain.)

- What happens just before the dust storm to indicate it is approaching? (Lindy and her father see the dancing grit, the flock of birds squawking by, and then a sudden quiet. All are clues to an abrupt change in the weather.)

- What words and phrases does the author use to describe the dryness caused by the drought? (trail of dust; dirt was fine as powder; dry, packed ground; jumping dirt; grit; brown high wall; bits of dusty ground; misty-dusty; red mist; hazy with a rusty fog)

- What reason does Drylongso give about being alone? (He tells Lindy and her family that he got separated from his family during the dust storm.)

THEME PAPERBACKS

pages 29–54

- **When does Lindy's father decide to plant in the streambed?** (After Drylongso's dowsing indicates water is present, Lindy's father decides he trusts him enough to plant there.)

- **For people living through a drought, the possibility of finding water is exciting. What words and phrases does the author use to describe water?** (streambed, spring, once-a-stream, flood, faint moisture, a trickling steadying stream, springwater, cross canals, the sweetest water, rain, cloudburst)

- **What does Drylongso do that makes him seem like a hero?** (his survival in the dust storm, his discovery of the dowser, his ability to find water when no one else could)

- **How does Drylongso's departure affect Lindy?** (Because she considers him to be like a brother, Lindy misses Drylongso, but she comes to accept that he has to move on and she feels certain that she will meet up with him again.)

- **Why does the author say, "It was as if the forked stick knew there was something underground"?** (Possible response: The author wanted to emphasize that it was the stick, rather than Drylongso, that seemed to have a special power.)

Responding

Have students tell whether their predictions were or were not accurate and have them tell how they used the Predict/Infer or Question strategies as they read. Then have students share their reaction to *Drylongso*. Finally, have students summarize the main events of the book. Take this opportunity to observe how well students are using strategies and comprehending the book.

English Language Learners

Language Development

Be sure students understand the metaphorical reference to the approaching dust storm as "a wall." Discuss the image the author created by describing it in this way. Follow a similar pattern as you point out other figurative language in the selection, including *gravy* (page 2), *whistling in the wind* (page 6), *I'm a baked potato* (page 10), and plants that *grow when your back is turned* (page 48).

■ ABOVE LEVEL

HURRICANES
EARTH'S MIGHTIEST STORMS ● PATRICIA LAUBER
Reading

Hurricanes: Earth's Mightiest Storms

Summary *The nonfiction book* Hurricanes: Earth's Mightiest Storms *gives an in-depth look at hurricanes, from the no-name storm that engulfed New England in 1938 to Hurricane Andrew in 1993. The book explains how these powerful storms begin, how scientists have learned to track them, and their devastating effect on the areas they strike.*

Vocabulary

mooring a place to which a boat or ship can be secured, *p. 7*

condense to reduce the volume of, *p. 19*

air pressure the amount of air that presses onto the earth's surface, *p. 20*

dome a bulge, or rounded extension, *p. 23*

cycle a sequence of events that repeats regularly over time, *p. 55*

sea level the level at the ocean's surface, *p. 59*

Preparing to Read

Building Background Discuss briefly what students know about hurricanes. Tell them that this book describes how hurricanes are formed and traces the paths of several significant hurricanes. Remind students to use their reading strategies as they read this book.

Developing Key Vocabulary Technical terms are introduced with clear explanations in this book. Preview with students the meanings of the Key Vocabulary words listed at the left. Point out the Greek root *meter*, meaning "measure," in the names of the instruments shown on page 26. A *baro<u>meter</u>*, for example, measures air pressure, while a *thermo<u>meter</u>* measures temperature.

Previewing the Text

Hurricanes: Earth's Mightiest Storms may be read in its entirety or in two segments, pages 7–27 and pages 28–61. You may have students look at the section titles and photographs and have them make predictions about what each section will describe.

Supporting the Reading

pages 7–27

- Point out that a *breakwater* is land that slows the force of strong waves. A *storm surge* is a sudden rise in the water level during a hurricane. *Typhoon* and *cyclone* are the names given to hurricanes in some parts of the world.

- Why were people unprepared for the "monster" storm of September, 1938? (They didn't know the storm was coming. There were no weather satellites at that time, and no ships were near the storm as it was developing.)

- What is the order in which events happen when conditions are right to start a hurricane? (First, warm, moist air flows into an area of low-pressure. Then the air rises and condenses into clouds. Next, more warm air is drawn in over the ocean. It spirals up in a counterclockwise direction. Finally, the clusters of thunderstorms that begin a hurricane form.)

- Which of the weather instruments shown on page 26 would be most helpful in predicting a hurricane? Explain your answer. (Accept reasonable responses that students can support with evidence from the text.)

- Why did the author choose to begin the book with a detailed description of the 1938 storm? (Possible response: In describing how the storm developed and took people by surprise, the author was able to give readers a sense of its power and the devastation hurricanes can cause.)

pages 28–61

- How do the headings help you to predict and remember the type of information presented in each section of the book ? ("Into the Eye of the Storm" tells how scientists have learned to analyze and track hurricanes; "Big Winds and Big Damage" tells of the damage caused by the strong winds of Hurricane Andrew; "More Storms Ahead" explains how scientists make long-range predictions about hurricanes.)

- What words and phrases does the author use to describe the strength of Hurricane Andrew's winds? (winds gusting to 195 miles per hour, shrieking, growling like a rushing freight train, snatched at shutters, walls bulged in and out, howling)

- What factors leave the ecology of Everglades National Park in question after Hurricane Andrew? (The hurricane destroyed many of the native plants, and the foreign plants recently brought in have spread quickly. The plant life also affects the ecology of the animal population.)

- What kinds of changes do the diagrams on page 45 illustrate? (Areas that were once swamps, marshes, and flatlands have shrunk considerably, and the east coast of Florida is now heavily populated by humans.)

- Why does the author say that "Today no one who reads a newspaper, listens to radio, or watches television can be taken by surprise when a hurricane strikes"? (With information from hurricane-hunting planes, satellites, and computers, forecasters are able to use all forms of media to warn people of an approaching hurricane.)

Responding

Have students tell whether their predictions were or were not accurate and have them tell how they used the Predict/Infer or Monitor/Clarify strategies as they read. Then have students share their reaction to *Hurricanes: Earth's Mightiest Storms*. Finally, have students summarize the key ideas of the book. Take this opportunity to observe how well students are using strategies and comprehending the book.

Bonus Have students describe an animal that reminds them of a hurricane. Tell them to be prepared to explain the reasons for their comparison.

English Language Learners

Language Development

Be sure students understand the language the author uses to personify the storm and the floods that accompany it. Discuss the images created by phrases such as *the storm was born, dying out over cool water, water crept up around houses, water swallowed houses, the sea swallowed automobiles, the eye of the storm,* and *Andrew came ashore.*

RETEACHING: Comprehension Skills

Sequence of Events

> ### OBJECTIVES
> - Identify order of events.
> - Identify time-order clue words.
> - Place events in sequence on a time line.
>
> ### Target Skill Trace
> - Sequence of Events, pp. 51A–51B

Teach

Ask volunteers to name three things they did before class this morning, in the order in which they did them. Jot down time words that students use, such as *first, next, then, before,* and *after.* Tell students that they have just described a sequence of events—the order in which events happened.

Point out that the story *Earthquake Terror* describes a sequence of exciting events. Draw a time line on a long sheet of paper and display it. Tell students that the left side of the time line is the beginning of the story and the right side is the end.

On the left side of the time line, tack an index card that says, *Jonathan and Abby are left alone in the woods.* On the right side, tack a card that says, *The earthquake ends, and the children are safe.* Show students three index cards with the following story events written on them:

> *Then the rumbling noise comes closer.*
>
> *First, Jonathan hears a rumbling noise in the distance.*
>
> *Finally, Jonathan feels a jolt and stumbles.*

Think aloud as you ask students to help you put these story events in order on the time line.

Think Aloud *I see words that will help me know the order. The sentence that begins with the word* First *must tell the first thing that happened after Jonathan and Abby are left alone. I'll put it after the first card on the time line. Which event should I put next? Which one should I put last?*

Practice

Have students work with a partner to copy the time line with the events you have ordered so far. Then have them add the following events:

> *As Jonathan tries to rescue Abby, a giant tree crashes beside him.*
>
> *When the earthquake begins, Abby falls and screams.*
>
> *Finally, Jonathan reaches Abby and drags her to safety.*

Afterward, have students compare their time lines in a class discussion and point out word clues.

Apply

Have students keep track of sequence of events, with an eye to identifying and using order clue words, such as *first, next, then, before,* and *after,* as they read their **Leveled Readers** for this week. Ask students to complete the questions and activity on the Responding page.

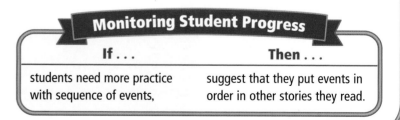

Monitoring Student Progress	
If . . .	**Then . . .**
students need more practice with sequence of events,	suggest that they put events in order in other stories they read.

CHALLENGE/EXTENSION:
Sequence of Events

 ## Sharing Personal Narratives

Partner Activity With a partner, take turns describing what you did last weekend. As one partner speaks, the other should listen carefully to the sequence of events being described. The listener should then try to list the events in order, using time-order words such as *first, next, after, later, on Saturday morning, on Sunday afternoon.*

CHALLENGE

Explaining a Process

Group Activity With a group, show what you know about science. Explain a sequence of events that occurs in nature. For example, you might explain the water cycle; day and night; the seasons; or the growth of a seed. Draw a picture of each step in the process, and write a caption for each one, using time-order words.

| First, the seed sprouts in the soil. | Next, the seedling grows. | Finally, the plant has a stem and leaves. |

Writing a Comic Strip

Partner Activity With a partner, work together to summarize the sequence of events in a newspaper comic strip. Write one sentence for each frame of the strip. Remember to use time-order words such as *first, then, after,* and *finally.*

RETEACHING: Comprehension Skills

Text Organization

OBJECTIVES

- Use headings and visual features to predict the focus of information in a selection or section of text.
- Use headings to recognize important information in a particular section.

Target Skill Trace

- Text Organization, pp. 81A–81B

Teach

Tell students that reading a long nonfiction article is like taking a long car trip. Readers need to know where they are in the article and where the author is taking them next, or they can get lost.

Point out to students that writers of nonfiction often include features such as headings, photographs, and charts to help readers understand the information in an organized way. Add that the headings are like road signs on a highway. They let us know what kinds of information we can expect to find as we read.

Think aloud as you ask students to help you make predictions about the article, based on its headings.

Think Aloud *I know this article is about a man named Warren Faidley, a man who chases storms. The title tells me that. I wonder what I'm going to find out about him. I can look at the headings in this article to get an idea of what it's about.*

On page 59 I see two headings. I'll probably learn how Faidley chases storms in the first section and what he or others learn from watching the sky in the second section.

On page 60 I see two headings. The first one mentions Warren Faidley, so it probably gives some background about him. The second one is "Becoming a Storm Chaser." What do you think this section will be about?

Discuss the headings in the rest of the article. Encourage students to make their own predictions about the article, based on the headings.

Practice

Separate students into three groups. Assign each group one of the following sections of the article to read and discuss the text and visual features: pages 56–59; pages 60–63; pages 64–67.

Have all the groups gather together to discuss what they learned. Write each heading on the board, and ask group members to tell the most important information in the section they read.

Apply

Have students keep track of text organization, with an eye to identifying features authors use, as they read their **Leveled Readers** for this week. Ask students to complete the questions and activity on the Responding page.

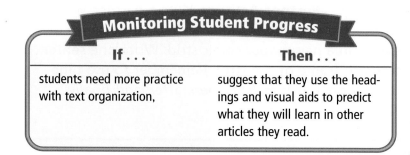

Monitoring Student Progress

If ...	Then ...
students need more practice with text organization,	suggest that they use the headings and visual aids to predict what they will learn in other articles they read.

CHALLENGE/EXTENSION: Text Organization

Interpreting a Graphic Aid

Partner Activity Take turns asking a partner questions about the information in the graphic on page 65. Each partner chooses a month on the calendar and asks the other which type or types of storms are most likely to occur in that month.

Previewing a Textbook Chapter

Partner Activity Work with a partner to preview a chapter in your science textbook that you have not yet read. Take turns choosing a heading from the chapter and predicting what kinds of information you might learn in that section of the text. Also, discuss the purpose of any other text features, such as highlighted words, and visual aids, such as charts and diagrams.

CHALLENGE

Writing a Study Guide

Group Activity Meet in a small group to create a study guide for a chapter the class is currently reading in science or social studies. The study guide should briefly summarize the most important ideas in the chapter and should use text structures such as headings, highlighted terms, and visual aids to help other students remember the key ideas in the chapter. Share your study guide with the rest of the class.

RETEACHING: Comprehension Skills

Categorize and Classify

OBJECTIVES

- Sort items into groups.
- Name categories for groups of items.

Target Skill Trace

- Categorize and Classify, pp. 105A–105B

Teach

Invite students to suggest items that we often group together in our everyday lives in order to organize them. Students might suggest forks, knives, food items, and so on. Discuss the ways in which the items in each group are alike.

Display index cards with the names or pictures of six animals: robin, dog, cat, blue jay, squirrel, cardinal. Ask students to suggest ways to sort, or group, the cards into two stacks.

If students need help with this sorting activity, use a Think Aloud to model the process.

Think Aloud *Let's see. Do I see any animals with something in common? Well, a robin is a bird. It has feathers and wings. Are there any other birds here? Yes, there are. A bluejay and a cardinal are birds too. I'll put the robin, the blue jay, and the cardinal in the same stack. I'll call it the bird stack.*

Discuss the remaining three cards and whether or not they are a group. (Yes, a dog, a cat, and a squirrel all have fur.) Explain that sorting similar things into groups is called classifying.

Ask students what name they might give to the other stack. (furry animals or mammals) Explain that giving a name to all the items in a group is called categorizing.

Tell students that a good way to organize the information in what they read is to classify and categorize facts. Add that this helps readers to remember important information and be able to compare the facts.

Practice

Point out to students that *Volcanoes* gives facts about four different groups of volcanoes. Put the following chart on the board, with the headings only. Have students copy it.

1. Read the first paragraph on page 94 aloud. Ask students what information should be added to the chart for Category 1. Fill in the information on your chart and have students do the same.

2. Repeat the procedure after reading aloud the second paragraph on page 94.

3. Have students work in pairs to read pages 95–96 and fill in the chart for Categories 3 and 4.

Let students compare their charts.

Apply

Have students keep track of categorizing and classifying, with an eye to sorting into groups, as they read their **Leveled Readers** for this week. Ask students to complete the questions and activity on the Responding page.

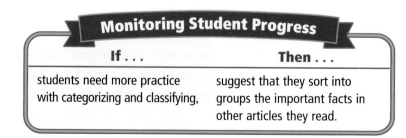

Monitoring Student Progress

If . . .	Then . . .
students need more practice with categorizing and classifying,	suggest that they sort into groups the important facts in other articles they read.

CHALLENGE/EXTENSION:
Categorize and Classify

Play a Map Game

Group Activity Form two teams and display a map of the United States. One student reads aloud different categories of states, and teams take turns naming as many states as possible that fit the category. Possible categories include states bordering the Pacific; states bordering the Atlantic; states starting with the letter *C* or the letter *A;* states east of the Mississippi; and states north of New York.

Make a Poster

Group Activity Work in groups to make posters that classify and categorize foods that make a healthy diet. First, cut out pictures of nutritious foods. Then sort the pictures into groups based on similarities and give each group a name. Finally, glue pictures onto poster board and print the name of each category.

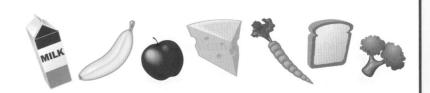

CHALLENGE

Write a Personal Essay

Individual Activity List your ten favorite movies and classify the movies into two or more categories. Then write an essay explaining how the movies in each category are similar and why you enjoy that category of movie.

RETEACHING: Structural Analysis/Vocabulary

Base Words

OBJECTIVES

- Students identify base words.

Target Skill Trace

- Base Words, p. 51C

Teach

Ask students if they have ever taken something apart to find out how it works (for example, a toy, a motor, a kitchen appliance). Tell them that a good way to figure out the meaning of long words is to take them apart.

Explain that the first step in taking a word apart is to look for a shorter word you already know inside the longer word. This shorter word is called the *base word*. Other word parts can be added to the beginning or the end of a base word.

On the board write the following sentence from the selection: *In his mind, Jonathan could see his father unhitching the small camping trailer.*

Think Aloud *If I didn't know the word* unhitching, *I could take it apart to figure out its meaning. First, I'd look for a shorter word within it that I already know. Oh, I see the word* hitch. *I know that* hitch *means "to hook one thing up to another thing." I can take the word apart this way:* un-hitch-ing.

Tell students that if they also know the meanings of the word parts added to the beginning and the end of *hitch*, they can figure out what *unhitching* means. Point out that *un-* can mean "the opposite of." So *unhitching* means "taking apart two things that used to be hooked together."

Practice

Write the following words from the story on the board: *rewrapped, unbearably, comforting, connecting.* Have students copy the words and underline the base word in each.

Apply

Take eight index cards, and write one of the following words on each one: *rewrapped, unbearably, comforting, connecting, unwrapping, bearable, disconnected, uncomfortable.* Have students work in pairs to sort the cards according to their base words. Any cards that have the same base word should be put into the same pile.

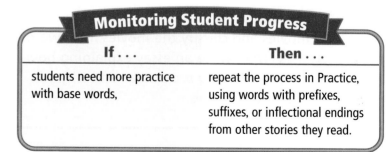

Monitoring Student Progress

If . . .	Then . . .
students need more practice with base words,	repeat the process in Practice, using words with prefixes, suffixes, or inflectional endings from other stories they read.

CHALLENGE/EXTENSION: Vocabulary

Independent Activities

CHALLENGE

Using a Thesaurus

Individual Activity Read the following passage from *Earthquake Terror*:

As he <u>yelled</u>, Jonathan felt a <u>jolt</u>. He <u>stumbled</u> forward, <u>thrusting</u> an arm out to brace himself against a tree. Another loud noise <u>exploded</u> as Jonathan <u>lurched</u> sideways.

Locate the underlined words in a thesaurus. Then rewrite the passage, replacing each underlined word with a synonym. Read your passages aloud and compare your word choices with those of a classmate.

Vocabulary Expansion

Group Activity Review the following specific words for *go* from the story: *meandered, lunged, buckled, swayed*. Look up the definitions and then act out the verbs for classmates to identify.

Continue the activity by listing as many other specific words for *go* as you can find in the story. After you share and compare your lists with others', check the definitions and take turns acting out the verbs.

RETEACHING: Structural Analysis/Vocabulary

Syllabication

OBJECTIVES

- Recognize a shorter word inside a long word.
- Break words into syllables as a way to decode long words.

Target Skill Trace

- Syllabication, p. 81C

Teach

Remind students that sometimes they can recognize a shorter word inside a long word they are trying to figure out. Some long words, however, do not contain shorter words. Point out that a good way to decode a long word is to break it into syllables. A syllable is a word part with just one vowel sound.

To make sure students understand syllables, pronounce these words: *school, kitchen, president, gymnasium.* Have students tell how many vowels sounds they hear in each word and then how many syllables each has.

Write the following sentence from page 59 on the board: *The spectacular storms that sometimes appear in the sky have helped to make weather one of the most mysterious of all natural forces.*

Underline the word *spectacular,* and use a Think Aloud to model the process of syllabication.

Think Aloud *I see that the first vowel in this word is* e. *The letters* spec *form a syllable with one vowel sound. I know that when a vowel is followed by a consonant, the vowel sound is short. I'll pronounce that syllable* speck.

Where is the next vowel sound in the word? Oh, there's the vowel a *between the consonants* t *and* c. *The letters* tac *form another syllable with a short vowel sound. I'll pronounce this* tak .

What's left now? There's the letter u. *A vowel can be a syllable all by itself. Then there are the letters* lar. *I'll try making* u *and* lar *into separate syllables.*

Write *spec-tac-u-lar* on the board. Have students pronounce the syllables and then the whole word.

Practice

Have pairs of students break these words from the article into syllables: *mysterious, tornado, horizon, hurricane.* Discuss with students how they decoded the words.

Apply

Have the same pairs read aloud pages 60–61. Ask them to jot down words they do not know and to try to decode them by breaking them into syllables.

Monitoring Student Progress

If . . .	Then . . .
students need more practice with syllabication,	suggest that they separate words into syllables in other stories they read.

CHALLENGE/EXTENSION: Vocabulary

CHALLENGE

Alphabetical Order/Guide Words

Individual Activity Use alphabetical order and guide words to look up in a dictionary the words you separated into syllables in the syllabication lesson: *mysterious, tornado, horizon, hurricane, irresistible, conditions.* Add other words that you have noted on your own. When you find each entry word, compare the syllables shown for each word with the syllable divisions you made for decoding the words.

ice · idea

ice (īs) *n.* **1.** Water frozen solid. **2.** A frozen water. **3.** Something r

CHALLENGE

Vocabulary Expansion

Group Activity Reread the second paragraph of *Eye of the Storm* on page 59. Note the images of food used to make these comparisons: *a cauliflower-shaped cloud; the sky the color of a ripe peach.*

Create your own descriptions from similar comparisons. Think about what other shapes a cloud might have. What color might the rising sun have?

CHALLENGE / EXTENSION

RETEACHING: Structural Analysis/Vocabulary

Roots: *struct* and *rupt*

OBJECTIVES

- Identify the roots *struct* and *rupt* in words.
- Use the roots *struct* and *rupt* as an aid to decoding and word meaning.

Target Skill Trace

- Roots: *struct* and *rupt*, p. 105C

Teach

Write the following list of words on the board: *erupt, interrupt, disrupted, eruption, rupture.* Ask students if they can see anything alike in all of the words. Underline the root *rupt* in each word.

Tell students that the word part *rupt* is called a root. Explain that recognizing this root in unfamiliar words can help students decode new words. Also point out that most words with this root have a similar meaning. They are related, like members of the same family.

Use a Think Aloud to model the process of figuring out the meaning of the root *rupt*.

Think Aloud *Let's see. When a volcano erupts, it explodes. Erupt means "to explode" or "to break out." When you interrupt someone, you "break into" their conversation. If someone disrupts the class, he or she disturbs, or breaks the flow of, the lesson. It looks like all these words have something to do with breaking things. I think the root* rupt *means "to break."*

Now use a process similar to that above to discuss the root *struct* with the following list of words: *construct, structure, destructive, construction.*

Lead students to recognize that the words all have something to do with building or with taking apart something that has been built. Help students recognize that the root *struct* means "to build, arrange, or put together."

Practice

Have pairs of students work together to read pages 85–88 and look for words containing the roots *rupt* and *struct*. Have them copy the sentences in which the words appear. Then have students share their sentences with the class and discuss the meanings of the words in context.

Apply

Have students write a paragraph in which they include four words with the root *rupt* or four words with the root *struct*. Have students underline the root in each word. Invite students to read their paragraphs aloud in small groups.

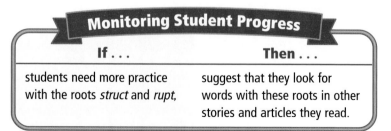

Monitoring Student Progress	
If . . .	**Then . . .**
students need more practice with the roots *struct* and *rupt*,	suggest that they look for words with these roots in other stories and articles they read.

CHALLENGE/EXTENSION: Vocabulary

CHALLENGE

Definitions

Partner Activity With a partner, look up the defini-tions of the following words in a dictionary and then use the words in sentences: *destructible, indestructible, constructive, disruptive, interruption, interrupter*. Then have some fun with the words. Make two cartoon books called "Meet the *struct* Family" and "Meet the *rupt* Family." Each page in the books should include a word, its definition, and a cartoon illustrating its meaning.

Vocabulary Expansion

Group Activity Begin a word web with the word *volcano* in the center. Then look through the selection to find terms associated with a volcano, such as *magma, lava,* and *gases*. Record responses on the word web.

Hold a discussion about the four types of volcanoes, referring to pages 94–96 of the selection. Record responses in a bubble on the word web labeled *four kinds*.

Discuss how each term in the word web adds to your understanding of volcanoes.

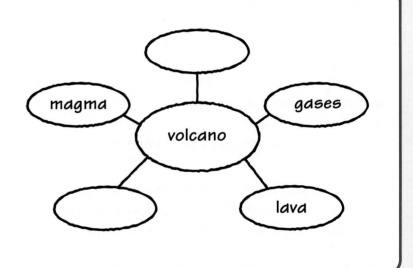

RETEACHING: Grammar

Kinds of Sentences

OBJECTIVES

- Identify sentences as statement, question, exclamation, and command.
- Write example sentences of a statement, question, exclamation, and command.

Target Skill Trace

- Kinds of Sentences, p. 51I

Teach

Tell students that there are four kinds of sentences and that the author of *Earthquake Terror* uses all four kinds in the story.

Read aloud the passage on page 35 that begins "That was school." Continue reading to the end of the page. Ask students to listen to how your voice changes as you read each sentence. After you read, ask: *Did you hear any sentence that simply states, or tells, what is happening?* Write an example on the board and label it Statement. Point out that a statement ends with a period.

> He struggled to his feet again.

Ask: *Did you hear any questions?* Write an example on the board and label it Question. Point out the question mark at the end of the sentence.

> Where could he hide?

Ask: *Did you hear Jonathan give a command, or tell somebody what to do?* Write an example on the board and label it Command. Point out the period at the end of the sentence.

> Stay where you are.

Ask: *Did you hear Jonathan say something with strong feeling?* Write an example on the board and label it Exclamation. Point out the exclamation point at the end of the sentence.

> I'm coming!

Practice

In small groups, have students write each sentence type and its punctuation on an index card. As one student reads page 38 aloud, sentence by sentence, have the other students hold up the appropriate card to identify the kind of sentence.

Apply

Have students work in pairs to read the rest of the story and find more examples of each kind of sentence. Have them write at least two examples of each kind of sentence on a four-column chart labeled Statement, Question, Command, and Exclamation.

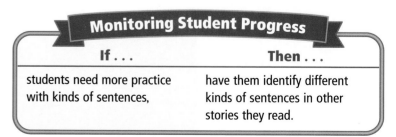

Monitoring Student Progress

If . . .	Then . . .
students need more practice with kinds of sentences,	have them identify different kinds of sentences in other stories they read.

RETEACHING: Grammar

Subjects and Predicates

RETEACHING

OBJECTIVES

- Identify simple and complete subject.
- Identify simple and complete predicate.

Target Skill Trace

- Kinds of Sentences, p. 51J

Teach

Remind students that a sentence is a group of words that expresses a complete thought. Explain that every sentence has two parts: a subject and a predicate. Then write the following sentence on the board:

> Jonathan looked in all directions.

Ask: *Who or what is the sentence about?* Tell students that *Jonathan* is the subject of the sentence. The subject is the sentence part that tells who or what the sentence is about. Ask: *What did Jonathan do?* Tell students that *looked* is the predicate. The predicate is the sentence part that tells what the subject does or is.

Point out that a subject and a predicate can have more than one word. Insert the word *Young* before *Jonathan* in the sentence on the board. Underline the sentence as shown below.

> <u>Young Jonathan</u> <u>looked in all directions.</u>

Clarify that *Jonathan* by itself is the simple subject, and *Young Jonathan* is called the complete subject. A complete subject has one main word as well as others. Point out that *looked* is the simple predicate; *looked in all directions* is the complete predicate.

Make a two-column chart on the board. Label one column Subject and the other Predicate. Write *Young Jonathan* in the Subject column and *looked in all directions* in the Predicate column.

Now write this sentence on the board:

> Moose is Jonathan's dog.

Ask: *Who or what is the sentence about?* Write Moose in the Subject column of the chart. Ask: *What words tell what Moose does or is?* Write *is Jonathan's dog* in the Predicate column.

Practice

Have students copy the chart on a sheet of paper. Then write these sentences on the board:

> A huge tree crashes near Jonathan.
> Abby is very scared.
> Jonathan takes Abby to a safe place.
> The earthquake is finally over.

Have students write the complete subjects and predicates on their charts in the correct columns.

Apply

Have students work in pairs to write four sentences about the story. Have them add the subjects and predicates to the chart.

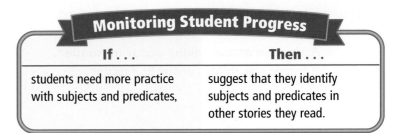

Monitoring Student Progress

If . . .	Then . . .
students need more practice with subjects and predicates,	suggest that they identify subjects and predicates in other stories they read.

RETEACHING: Grammar

Conjunctions

OBJECTIVES

- Use the conjunctions *and* and *or* to combine sentences.
- Identify sentences that contain the conjunction *and* or *or*.

Target Skill Trace

- Conjunctions, p. 811

Teach

Write the following two sentences on the board:

> Warren Faidley photographs tornadoes.
> Warren Faidley photographs lightning.

Ask students if they can think of a way to express both of these ideas in one sentence.

Use a Think Aloud to model a way to combine the ideas.

Think Aloud *The beginnings of both sentences are exactly the same. If Warren Faidley photographs two different things, I could name both things in the same sentence. What would I put in between the two words to show that he photographs both things? I know. I'll put the conjunction* and. *I know that I can use the conjunction* and *or* or *to combine sentences.*

Write the following sentence on the board. Underline the words *tornadoes* and *lightning*, and circle the conjunction *and*.

> Warren Faidley photographs <u>tornadoes</u>
> (and) <u>lightning</u>.

Now write these two sentences on the board:

> A thunderstorm might occur in August.
> A hurricane might occur in August.

Point out that the ends of the two sentences are the same, but the beginnings are different. Ask students to suggest a way to express both of these ideas in one sentence. If necessary, tell students that they can combine the sentences by using the conjunction *or.* Write the sentence on the board: *A <u>thunderstorm</u> or a <u>hurricane</u> might occur in August.*

Practice

Have pairs of students read page 59 together and look for sentences that include the conjunction *and* or the conjunction *or.* Ask students to copy the sentences, circle the conjunction in each one, and underline the words that are joined by the conjunction. Bring students together to share and compare their sentences.

Apply

Have students work in pairs to write three original sentences about thunderstorms, tornadoes, and hurricanes. Warren Faidley photographs tornadoes.

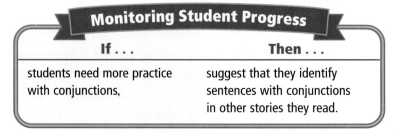

Monitoring Student Progress

If . . .	Then . . .
students need more practice with conjunctions,	suggest that they identify sentences with conjunctions in other stories they read.

Compound Sentences

OBJECTIVES

- Form a compound sentence using a conjunction.
- Separate ideas in a compound sentence by using a comma.

Target Skill Trace

- Compound Sentences, p. 81J

Teach

Remind students that they have already learned how to join words in a sentence by using a conjunction. Now they will learn how to join two complete thoughts by using a conjunction.

Write the following sentences on the board:

> The air is hazy.
> Another storm to the west is blocking the sunlight.

Use the following Think Aloud to model the process of forming a compound sentence.

Think Aloud *I can use a conjunction to join two whole sentences together.*

Combine the two sentences into a compound sentence. Mark the sentence as shown below.

> <u>The air is hazy</u> (and) <u>another storm to the west is blocking the sunlight.</u>

Now I have a sentence that joins two complete thoughts. This kind of sentence is called a compound sentence. *I need to add a comma to show where the first thought ends and the second one begins. I'll add it now.*

Write these two sentences and continue the Think Aloud:

> Warren tries to photograph a huge tornado.
> The light isn't good enough for a picture.

I can't use the conjunction and *to join these sentences because the ideas are different. I can use the conjunction* but *to show a contrast between the first thought and the second thought.*

Write the compound sentence on the board. Circle the conjunction, underline the two complete thoughts, and add a comma.

Practice

On the board, write these compound sentences from the selection:

> We've got two large thunderstorms here and they're dropping tornadoes everywhere.
> The sky is hazy but in the distance we can see the tops of anvil-shaped storm clouds.

Have students copy the sentences and repeat the procedure you used above to mark the two thoughts, the conjunction, and to add the comma.

Apply

Have students form a compound sentence using these sentences:

> Warren Faidley takes amazing pictures.
> His work appears in many magazines.

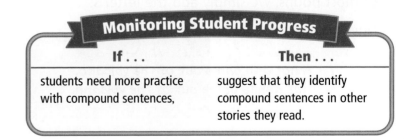

Monitoring Student Progress

If . . .	Then . . .
students need more practice with compound sentences,	suggest that they identify compound sentences in other stories they read.

Singular and Plural Nouns

> ### OBJECTIVES
> - Identify singular and plural nouns.
> - Form plural nouns by adding -s or -es.
>
> ### Target Skill Trace
> - Singular and Plural Nouns, p. 105I

Teach

Write these two sentences on the board:

> A highway, a road, and a railway were destroyed.
> Highways, roads, and railways were destroyed.

Ask students what is different about the nouns in the two sentences. Then ask how the two sentences differ in meaning.

If students need help, use a Think Aloud to model the process.

Think Aloud *Well, first I'll look at the beginnings of the two sentences. The first one begins with the words* A highway; *the second one begins with the word* Highways. Highway *and* highways *are almost the same, except* highways *has an* s *at the end of it. It means more than one* highway.

Underline the *s* in *highways*. Continue in this way until students have found all the differences between the nouns.

Tell students that the nouns *highway, road,* and *railway* are singular. They each name one thing. The nouns *highways, roads,* and *railways* are plural. They each name more than one thing. To form the plural of most nouns, we simply add the letter *s*.

Now display these two sentences:

> A hot ash came out of the volcano.
> Hot ashes came out of the volcano.

Ask students to find the difference between these two sentences. If necessary, model the process, and underline the words *ash* and *ashes*.

Point out that *ash* is singular and *ashes* is plural. Tell students that the plural of *ash* is formed by adding *es*, instead of *s*. Then give them this rule: Add *es* to form the plural of singular nouns ending in *s, ss, x, ch,* or *sh*.

Practice

Write the following sentences on the board. Have students find the nouns and tell whether they are singular or plural.

> The early Hawaiians told legends about two goddesses named Pele and Namaka.
> Pele was the goddess of fire, and Namaka was the goddess of the sea.

Apply

Have students rewrite each sentence, changing each noun from its singular form to its plural form.

> Hot gas, rock, and ash destroyed the home.
> The eruption blew down the tree and formed the crater.

Monitoring Student Progress

If . . .	Then . . .
students need more practice with singular and plural nouns,	suggest that they look for singular and plural nouns in other stories and articles they read.

More Plural Nouns

OBJECTIVES

- Identify plurals of nouns ending in *o* or *y*.
- Form plurals of nouns ending in *o* or *y*.

Target Skill Trace

- More Plural Nouns, p. 105J

Teach

Write these two sentences on the board:

> The volcano destroyed many homes.
> The volcanoes destroyed many homes.

Ask students to find the difference between the two sentences. If necessary, model the process as you did for the sentences on the previous page.

Tell students that many singular nouns ending in *o* add *-es* to form the plural, especially if a consonant comes before the *o*. Give them the following additional examples:

Singular	Plural
tornado	tornadoes
potato	potatoes
tomato	tomatoes

Write these two sentences on the board, and help students identify the difference in them:

> The Hawaiians told a story about the goddess Pele.
> The Hawaiians told stories about the goddess Pele.

Tell students that when a singular noun ends in *y* preceded by a consonant, they must change the *y* to *i* and then add *-es* to form the plural. Give them the following additional examples:

Singular	Plural
party	parties
puppy	puppies
baby	babies

Practice

Have students help you find the nouns in the following sentence and then rewrite the sentence, making each noun plural.

> The tornado and the volcano destroyed the country.

Apply

Have students copy the following list of singular nouns and then write the plural form of each one.

Singular	Plural
hero	
memory	
echo	
dictionary	

Monitoring Student Progress

If . . .	Then . . .
students need more practice with more plural nouns,	suggest that they look for nouns ending in *o* or *y* in other stories they read, and then write the plural form of those nouns.

Name_____

Concentration

debris	**jolt**
remains	**jerk**
devastation	**shuddered**
ruin	**quivered**
earthquake	**susceptible**
tremor	**impressionable**
fault	**undulating**
crack	**wavy**
impact	**upheaval**
collision	**elevation**

Theme 1: **Nature's Fury**

Copyright © Houghton Mifflin Company. All rights reserved.

Consider copying and laminating game pieces for use in centers.

Beat the Clock

collide (Use in a sentence.)	**collide** (Name a synonym.)
funnel cloud (Use in a sentence.)	**funnel cloud** (Define the word.)
jagged (Use in a sentence.)	**jagged** (Name an antonym.)
lightning (Use in a sentence.)	**lightning** (Define the word.)
prairies (Use in a sentence.)	**prairies** (Name an antonym.)
rotate (Use in a sentence.)	**rotate** (Name a synonym.)
severe (Use in a sentence.)	**severe** (Name an antonym.)
sizzling (Use in a sentence.)	**sizzling** (Name a synonym.)
tornadoes (Use in a sentence.)	**tornadoes** (Define the word.)

Copyright © Houghton Mifflin Company. All rights reserved.

Theme 1: **Nature's Fury**

Consider copying and laminating game pieces for use in centers.

Volcanoes

Language Center, p. 105M
Activity Master 1–3

Words with the /ō/, /o͞o/, and /yo͞o/ Sounds

thrown	mood	stole	loaf
clue	growth	dew	youth
choose	slope	rule	bruise
boast	loose	cruise	rude
stroll	flow	route	flute

Theme 1: **Nature's Fury**

Copyright © Houghton Mifflin Company. All rights reserved.

Consider copying vond laminating game pieces for use in centers.

Name _____

Patchwork Tale Planner

For each category below, add your own element on the blank line.
Then use the elements to make a "Patchwork" tale.

HERO (one of the main characters)
Settler
Elf
Mayor

_____

HEROINE (another main character)
Doctor
Computer Expert
Safari Guide

_____

SETTING
Frontier
Submarine
Mall

_____

PLOT (my tale involves . . .)
dangerous deeds
a family tradition
a discovery

_____

STYLE (In my writing, . . .)
exaggerate setting
exaggerate actions
exaggerate characters

_____

Before you write, complete sentences like the ones shown below.

My Patchwork Tale takes place in _____the mall_____. My two main characters
are _____an elf_____ and a _____computer expert_____. They must _____stop some_____
_____dangerous deeds_____. In my writing, I will _____use exaggerated characters and actions_____.

Copyright © Houghton Mifflin Company. All rights reserved.

Theme 1: **Focus on Tall Tales**

Writer _____   Listener _____

Writing Conference
What Should I Say?

In a writing conference, a writer reads a draft to a partner or a small group. A listener can help the writer by discussing the draft and asking questions such as these.

If you're thinking . . .

- I can't really picture what the writer is describing.
- The writer uses the same words over and over.
- I can't follow this description.

You could say . . .

- Could you tell more details about how _____ looked? smelled? felt? tasted? sounded?
- What sensory words could you add?
- Could you group your details about your topic so they belong together?

More Questions a Listener Might Ask

Read these questions before you listen. Take notes on the other side of this paper. Then discuss your thoughts with the writer.

1. What do you like about the writer's description?

2. What is the writer describing? Retell what you heard.

3. What details help paint a clear picture?

4. Are there places where the writer needs to tell more? less? Give examples.

Theme 1: **Nature's Fury**

Copyright © Houghton Mifflin Company. All rights reserved.

TECHNOLOGY RESOURCES

American Melody
P.O. Box 270
Guilford, CT 06437
800-220-5557
www.americanmelody.com

Audio Bookshelf
174 Prescott Hill Road
Northport, ME 04849
800-234-1713
www.audiobookshelf.com

Baker & Taylor
100 Business Center Drive
Pittsburgh, PA 15205
800-775-2600
www.btal.com

BDD Audio/Random House
400 Hohn Road
Westminster, MD 21157
800-733-3000

Big Kids Productions
1606 Dywer Ave.
Austin, TX 78704
800-477-7811
www.bigkidsvideo.com

Books on Tape
P.O. Box 25122
Santa Ana, CA 92799
www.booksontape.com
800-541-5525

Broderbund Company
1 Martha's Way
Hiawatha, IA 52233
www.broderbund.com

Filmic Archives
The Cinema Center
Botsford, CT 06404
800-366-1920
www.filmicarchives.com

Great White Dog Picture Company
10 Toon Lane
Lee, NH 03824
800-397-7641
www.greatwhitedog.com

HarperAudio
10 E. 53rd St.
New York, NY 10022
800-242-7737
www.harperaudio.com

Houghton Mifflin Company
222 Berkeley St.
Boston, MA 02116
800-225-3362

Informed Democracy
P.O. Box 67
Santa Cruz, CA 95063
800-827-0949

JEF Films
143 Hickory Hill Circle
Osterville, MA 02655
508-428-7198

Kimbo Educational
P.O. Box 477
Long Branch, NJ 07740
800-631-2187
www.kimboed.com

Library Video Co.
P.O. Box 580
Wynnewood, PA 19096
800-843-3620
www.libraryvideo.com

Listening Library
P.O. Box 25122
Santa Ana, CA 92799
800-541-5525
www.listeninglibrary.com

Live Oak Media
P.O. Box 652
Pine Plains, NY 12567
800-788-1121
www.liveoakmedia.com

Media Basics
Lighthouse Square
P.O. Box 449
Guilford, CT 06437
800-542-2505
www.mediabasicsvideo.com

Microsoft Corp.
One Microsoft Way
Redmond, WA 98052
800-426-9400
www.microsoft.com

National Geographic School Publishing
P.O. Box 10597
Des Moines, IA 50340
800-368-2728
www.nationalgeographic.com

New Kid Home Video
P.O. Box 10443
Beverly Hills, CA 90213
800-309-2392
www.NewKidhomevideo.com

Puffin Books
345 Hudson Street
New York, NY 10014
800-233-7364

Rainbow Educational Media
4540 Preslyn Drive
Raleigh, NC 27616
800-331-4047
www.rainbowedumedia.com

Recorded Books
270 Skipjack Road
Prince Frederick, MD 20678
800-638-1304
www.recordedbooks.com

Sony Wonder
Dist. by Professional Media Service
19122 S. Vermont Ave.
Gardena, CA 90248
800-223-7672
www.sonywonder.com

Spoken Arts
195 South White Rock Road
Holmes, NY 12531
800-326-4090
www.spokenartsmedia.com

SRA Media
220 E. Danieldale Rd.
DeSoto, TX 75115
800-843-8855
www.sra4kids.com

Sunburst Technology
101 Castleton St.
Suite 201
Pleasantville, NY 10570
800-321-7511
www.sunburst.com

SVE & Churchill Media
6677 North Northwest Highway
Chicago, IL 60631
800-829-1900
www.svemedia.com

Tom Snyder Productions
80 Coolidge Hill Road
Watertown, MA 02472
800-342-0236
www.tomsnyder.com

Troll Communications
100 Corporate Drive
Mahwah, NJ 07430
800-526-5289
www.troll.com

Weston Woods
143 Main St.
Norwalk, CT 06851-1318
800-243-5020
www.scholastic.com/weston-woods

PRONUNCIATION GUIDE

In this book some unfamiliar or hard-to-pronounce words are followed by respellings to help you say the words correctly. Use the key below to find examples of various sounds and their respellings. Note that in the respelled word, the syllable in capital letters is the one receiving the most stress.

Dictionary letter or mark	Respelled as	Example	Respelled word
ă (pat)	a	basket	BAS-kiht
ā (pay)	ay	came	kaym
âr (care)	air	share	shair
ä (father)	ah	barter	BAHR-tur
ch (church)	ch	channel	CHAN-uhl
ĕ (pet)	eh	test	tehst
ē (bee)	ee	heap	heep
g (gag)	g	goulash	GOO-lahsh
ĭ (pit)	ih	liver	LIHV-ur
ī (pie, by)	y	alive	uh-LYV
	eye	island	EYE-luhnd
îr (hear)	eer	year	yeer
j (judge)	j	germ	jurm
k (kick, cat, pique)	k	liquid	LIHK-wihd
ŏ (pot)	ah	otter	AHT-ur
ō (toe)	oh	solo	SOH-loh
ô (caught, paw)	aw	always	AWL-wayz
ôr (for)	or	normal	NOR-muhl
oi (noise)	oy	boiling	BOYL-ihng
ŏŏ (took)	u	pull, wool	pul, wul
ōō (boot)	oo	bruise	brooz
ou (out)	ow	pound	pownd
s (sauce)	s	center	SEHN-tur
sh (ship, dish)	sh	chagrin	shuh-GRIHN
ŭ (cut)	uh	flood	fluhd
ûr (urge, term, firm, word, heard)	ur	earth	urth
		bird	burd
z (zebra, xylem)	z	cows	kowz
zh (vision, pleasure, garage)	zh	decision	dih-SIHZH-uhn
ə (about)	uh	around	uh-ROWND
(item)	uh	broken	BROH-kuhn
(edible)	uh	pencil	PEHN-suhl
(gallop)	uh	connect	kuh-NEHKT
(circus)	uh	focus	FOH-kuhs
ər (butter)	ur	liter	LEE-tur

Glossary

This glossary contains meanings and pronunciations for some of the words in this book. The Full Pronunciation Key shows how to pronounce each consonant and vowel in a special spelling. At the bottom of the glossary pages is a shortened form of the full key.

Full Pronunciation Key

Consonant Sounds

b	**bib**, ca**bb**age	kw	**ch**oir, **qu**ick	t	**t**igh**t**, s**t**opped
ch	**ch**ur**ch**, sti**tch**	l	**l**id, need**l**e, ta**ll**	th	**b**a**th**, **th**in
d	**d**ee**d**, maile**d**, pu**ddl**e	m	a**m**, **m**an, du**mb**	th	**b**a**th**e, **th**is
f	**f**ast, **f**i**f**e, o**ff**, **ph**rase, rough	n	**n**o, su**dd**en	v	ca**v**e, **v**al**v**e, **v**ine
		ng	thi**ng**, i**nk**	w	**w**ith, **w**olf
g	**g**a**g**, **g**et, fin**g**er	p	**p**o**p**, ha**pp**y	y	**y**es, **y**olk, on**i**on
h	**h**at, **wh**o	r	**r**oar, **rh**yme	z	ro**s**e, **s**ize, **x**ylophone, **z**ebra
hw	**wh**ich, **wh**ere	s	mi**ss**, **s**au**c**e, **s**cene, see	zh	gara**g**e, plea**s**ure, vi**si**on
j	**j**ud**g**e, **g**em	sh	**di**sh, **sh**ip, **s**ugar, ti**ss**ue		
k	**c**at, **k**ick, s**ch**ool				

Vowel Sounds

ă	p**a**t, l**au**gh	ŏ	h**o**rrible, p**o**t	ŭ	c**u**t, fl**oo**d, r**ou**gh, some
ā	**a**pe, **ai**d, p**ay**	ō	g**o**, r**ow**, t**oe**, th**ough**		
â	**ai**r, c**a**re, w**ea**r	ô	**a**ll, c**au**ght, f**o**r, p**aw**	û	c**i**rcle, f**u**r, h**ea**rd, term, t**u**rn, **u**rge, w**o**rd
ä	f**a**ther, k**o**ala, y**a**rd	oi	b**oy**, n**oi**se, **oi**l		
ĕ	p**e**t, pl**ea**sure, **a**ny	ou	c**ow**, **ou**t	yōō	c**u**re
ē	b**e**, b**ee**, **ea**sy, p**ia**no	ŏŏ	f**u**ll, b**oo**k, w**o**lf	yōō	**a**buse, **u**se
ĭ	**i**f, p**i**t, b**u**sy	ōō	b**oo**t, r**u**de, fr**ui**t, flew	ə	**a**go, sil**e**nt, penc**i**l, lem**o**n, circ**u**s
ī	r**i**de, b**y**, p**ie**, h**igh**				
î	d**ea**r, d**ee**r, f**ie**rce, mere				

Stress Marks

Primary Stress ´: bi·ol·o·gy [bī **ŏl**´ ə jē]
Secondary Stress ´: bi·o·log·i·cal [bī´ ə **lŏj**´ ĭ kəl]

Pronunciation key and definitions © 1998 by Houghton Mifflin Company. Adapted and reprinted by permission from *The American Heritage Children's Dictionary.*

A

ab·o·li·tion·ist (ăb´ ə **lĭsh**´ ə nĭst) *n.* A person who felt that slavery should be against the law. *Quakers and other **abolitionists** believed that owning slaves was wrong.*

a·bun·dant (ə **bŭn**´ dənt) *adj.* More than enough; plentiful. *Fish and game were **abundant** along the coast.*

ac·com·pa·ni·ment (ə **kŭm**´ pə nĭ mənt) *n.* A musical part, usually played on an instrument, that goes along with the performance of a singer or musician. *Victoria sang to the **accompaniment** of a guitar.*

ad·ven·ture (əd **vĕn**´ chər) *n.* An unusual or exciting experience. *Greg thought that sailing to Africa would be a real **adventure**.*

ag·gres·sive (ə **grĕs**´ ĭv) *adj.* Ready and quick to fight; bold. *The bear cub snarled in an **aggressive** way.*

am·a·teur (**ăm**´ ə chər) *n.* Someone who performs a sport or other activity without being paid. *You must be an **amateur** to compete in high school sports.*

a·maz·ing·ly (ə **mā**´ zĭng lē) *adv.* In a way that causes surprise or wonder. *The test questions were **amazingly** easy.*

ap·plause (ə **plôz**´) *n.* The clapping of hands to show approval. *Adam's speech was greeted with loud **applause**.*

ap·pren·tice (ə **prĕn**´ tĭs) *n.* Someone who works for another person in order to learn a trade. *The blacksmith helped the **apprentice** learn how to use the tools.*

arm (ärm) *v.* To equip with weapons. *The rebels were **arming** themselves as the British troops approached the town.*

ar·ti·fi·cial (är´ tə **fĭsh**´ əl) *adj.* Created by humans rather than occuring in nature. *The zookeepers built an **artificial** den for the lion to live in.*

ar·tis·tic (är **tĭs**´ tĭk) *adj.* Showing imagination and skill in creating something beautiful. *The dancers gave an **artistic** performance.*

as·tro·naut (**ăs**´ trə nôt) *n.* A person trained to fly in a spacecraft. *Neil Armstrong was the first **astronaut** to walk on the moon.*

at·tach·ment (ə **tăch**´ mənt) *n.* A feeling of closeness and affection. *The two cousins have a strong **attachment** to one another.*

amateur
Amateur comes from the Latin word *amare*, which means "to love." Someone who is an amateur takes part in an activity for the love of it.

apprentice
Apprentice comes from the Latin word *apprehendere*, which means "to grasp." An apprentice is a learner who must grasp what to do in a profession.

astronaut
This word was created in 1929 by combining two ancient Greek word parts, *astro-* and *nautes*, which translate as "star sailor."

ōō **boot** / ou **out** / ŭ **cut** / û **fur** / hw **which** / th **thin** / *th* **this** / zh **vision** / ə **ago**, silent, pencil, lemon, circus

675

---

braille
Louis Braille (1809–1852) was a French inventor who lost his sight at the age of three and as a student of fifteen created the unique writing system that bears his name.

canopy
The Greek word *konopeion*, a bed with a netting to keep out mosquitoes, gave us the word for the covering created by treetops in a rain forest.

caribou
Caribou is the Canadian French version of a Native American word — the Micmac *khalibu*, which means "snow scraper."

au·di·ence (**ô**´ dē əns) *n.* People who gather to see and hear a performance. *The **audience** cheered loudly as the singer bowed.*

B

ban·dit (**băn**´ dĭt) *n.* An outlaw, especially one who robs. *The **bandit** demanded that the passengers hand over their wallets.*

bluff (blŭf) *n.* A high cliff or bank. *From the top of the **bluff**, he could see the entire valley.*

braille (brāl) *n.* A system of writing that uses raised dots, for people who are visually impaired. *Angela ran her fingers over the **braille** letters on the page.*

C

cache (kăsh) *n.* A store of hidden goods. *The bear dug up the campers' **cache** of food.*

can·o·py (**kăn**´ ə pē) *n.* The highest layer of a forest, formed by the treetops. *Many kinds of parrots and monkeys live in the dense **canopy** of the rain forest.*

cap·tive (**kăp**´ tĭv) *n.* A prisoner. *The soldiers brought their **captives** back to the fort.* — *adj.* Captured; held against one's will. *The **captive** squirrel managed to escape from the trap.*

car·cass (**kär**´ kəs) *n.* The dead body of an animal. *The wolves fed on the **carcass** of a deer.*

car·go (**kär**´ gō) *n., pl.* **cargoes**. The freight carried by a ship or other vehicle. *The ship's **cargo** included molasses from the West Indies.*

car·i·bou (**kăr**´ ə bōō) *n., pl.* **caribou**. A large deer found in northern North America, related to the reindeer. *The herd of **caribou** swam across the river.*

cau·tious (**kô**´ shəs) *adj.* Careful; not taking chances. *It is best to be **cautious** when crossing a busy street.*

cel·e·bra·tion (sĕl´ ə **brā**´ shən) *n.* A special activity that honors a person, event, or idea. *I invited ten friends to my birthday **celebration**.*

cin·der (**sĭn**´ dər) *n.* A partly burned piece of coal or wood. *A pile of **cinders** lay at the bottom of the fire pit.*

claim (klām) *n.* A piece of land that someone reserves for ownership. *The settlers took a **claim** that bordered on the river.*

col·lide (kə **līd**´) *v.* To come together with forceful impact. *When warm and cold air masses **collide**, the weather becomes stormy.*

ă **rat** / ā **pay** / â **care** / ä **father** / ĕ **pet** / ē **be** / ĭ **pit** / ī **pie** / î **fierce** / ŏ **pot** / ō **go** / ô **paw**, for / oi **oil** / ōō **book**

676

---

col·o·ny (**kŏl**´ ə nē) *n., pl.* **colonies** A territory ruled by or belonging to another country. *The thirteen **colonies** no longer wanted to be taxed by England.*

com·pete (kəm **pēt**´) *v.* To take part in a contest. *The runners hoped to **compete** in the Boston Marathon.*

con·cen·trate (**kŏn**´ sən trāt´) *v.* To give full attention to. *It is difficult to **concentrate** on my book when the television is on.*

con·flict (**kŏn**´ flĭkt´) *n.* A struggle; a war. *The United States had a second **conflict** with England in 1812.*

con·vinced (kən **vĭnsd**´) *adj.* Persuaded; certain. *They were **convinced** that the bridge was strong enough to carry their weight.*

cra·ter (**krā**´ tər) *n.* A hollow bowl-shaped area at the mouth of a volcano. *The hikers peered down into the deep rocky **crater** below.*

crust (krŭst) *n.* The hard outer layer of the earth. *Cracks in the earth's **crust** help create volcanoes.*

cus·tom (**kŭs**´ təm) *n.* Something that members of a group usually do. *One of the **customs** of people in the desert is to offer visitors refreshment and shade.*

D

de·bris (də **brē**´) *n.* The remains of something broken or destroyed; rubble. *The bulldozer pushed the **debris** into the corner of the lot.*

de·but (dā **byōō**´) *n.* First public performance. *The actor made his stage **debut** as Peter Pan.*

dec·o·rate (**dĕk**´ ə rāt´) *v.* To make festive or beautiful. *We will **decorate** the room with flowers and streamers.*

dem·on·stra·tion (dĕm´ ən **strā**´ shən) *n.* A showing and explanation of how something works. *The teacher gave a **demonstration** of how to operate a camera.*

de·scrip·tion (dĭ **skrĭp**´ shən) *n.* A statement that uses words to tell about something. *Debbie wrote an exciting **description** of the game.*

de·tain (dĭ **tān**´) *v.* To delay; to hold back. *If you **detain** us much longer, we will miss the bus.*

de·ter·mi·na·tion (dĭ tûr´ mə **nā**´ shən) *n.* Firmness in carrying out a decision. *The team's **determination** to do better showed in how well they played.*

dev·as·ta·tion (dĕv´ ə **stā**´ shən) *n.* Destruction or ruin. *The floods brought **devastation** to much of the coast.*

crater

ōō **boot** / ou **out** / ŭ **cut** / û **fur** / hw **which** / th **thin** / *th* **this** / zh **vision** / ə **ago**, silent, pencil, lemon, circus

677

Glossary continued

dex·ter·i·ty (dĕk stĕr′ ĭ tē) *n.* Skill in the use of the hands, body, or mind. *The juggler showed great **dexterity** in keeping the oranges in the air.*

di·a·ry (dī′ ə rē) *n., pl.* **diaries.** A daily record of a person's thoughts and experiences. *Every night Marta wrote about the day's events in her **diary.***

dominance
The root of this word is the Latin word *domus*, meaning "house." The head of a household often had control, or dominance, over a large staff of people.

dic·ta·tor (dĭk′ tā tər) *n.* A ruler who has complete power over a country. *The **dictator** would not allow any citizens to travel outside the country.*

di·lem·ma (dĭ lĕm′ ə) *n.* A situation in which one has to choose between two or more difficult options. *Sara's **dilemma** was whether to wake up her father or try to figure out the problem herself.*

dim sum (dĭm′ sŏŏm′) *n.* A type of traditional Chinese meal where small portions of different foods are served one after another. *Many Chinese restaurants serve **dim sum** on Sunday mornings.*

dis·ap·point·ed (dĭs′ ə point′ əd) *adj.* Unhappy because of an unsatisfied hope or wish. *Tanya was **disappointed** when her team lost the game.*

dis·com·fort (dĭs kŭm′ fərt) *n.* A feeling of mild distress. *Noah always feels **discomfort** when people ask him about his famous brother.*

dim sum

dis·cour·aged (dĭ skûr′ ĭjd) *adj.* Not hopeful or enthusiastic. *Sam felt **discouraged** when he learned that he had not won a prize.*

dis·mayed (dĭs mād′) *adj.* Filled with sudden concern or distress. *They were **dismayed** to learn that the bus had left without them.*

dog guide (dôg gīd) *n.* A dog especially trained to lead visually impaired people. *May's **dog guide** waited until it was safe to cross the street.*

dom·i·nance (dŏm′ ə nəns) *n.* The greatest control within a group. *Wolves compete for **dominance** in the pack.*

dread (drĕd) *n.* Great fear. *The panther's roar filled the villagers with **dread.***

drill (drĭl) *v.* To perform training exercises. *The soldiers were **drilling** all morning.*

du·o (dŏŏ′ ō) *n.* Two people performing together. *The sisters performed in the show as a singing **duo.***

E

earth·quake (ûrth′ kwāk′) *n.* A trembling or shaking of the ground caused by sudden movements in rock below the earth's surface. *The **earthquake** caused buildings to topple.*

å rat / ā pay / â care / ä father / ĕ pet / ē be / ĭ pit / ī pie / î fierce / ŏ pot / ō go / ô paw, for / oi oil / ŏŏ book

678

el·e·ment (ĕl′ ə mənt) *n.* A basic part of a whole. *Spirals, spins, and jumps are **elements** of a figure skating program.*

em·bar·rassed (ĕm bâr′ əsd) *adj.* Made to feel self-conscious and ill at ease. *Josh felt **embarrassed** when he realized he had called her by the wrong name.*

en·cour·age (ĕn kûr′ ĭj) *v.* To give support to; to inspire. *Hal's parents **encouraged** him to become a skater.*

en·slave·ment (ĕn slāv′ mənt) *n.* The process by which one person becomes the property of another. *After years of **enslavement** by cruel owners, the men were set free.*

e·rup·tion (ĭ rŭp′ shən) *n.* A volcanic explosion or large flow of lava. *The newspaper showed photos of the **eruption** of a volcano in Nicaragua.*

ex·cite·ment (ĭk sīt′ mənt) *n.* A stirred-up feeling. *The fire caused a lot of **excitement** in our neighborhood.*

ex·pe·ri·ence (ĭk spîr′ ē əns) *n.* An event that someone takes part in or lives through. *Camping was a new **experience** for the children.*

ex·press (ĭk sprĕs′) *adj.* Fast, direct, and often nonstop. ***Express** services promise overnight deliveries.*

ex·tend·ed (ĭk stĕn′ dĭd) *adj.* Including more; broadened. *Your **extended** family includes your aunts, uncles, and cousins.*

ex·tinc·tion (ĭk stĭngk′ shən) *n.* The condition of having died out. *No one knows for sure what caused the **extinction** of the dinosaurs.*

eruption

F

fash·ion (făsh′ ən) *v.* To give a form or shape to; to make. *Ralph was able to **fashion** a waterproof cape from a large plastic bag.*

fault (fôlt) *n.* A break in a rock mass caused by a shifting of the earth's crust. *An active **fault** runs through the center of our town.*

fer·tile (fûr′ tl) *adj.* Rich in material needed to grow healthy plants. *Wheat and corn grew well in the prairie's **fertile** soil.*

fes·tive (fĕs′ tĭv) *adj.* Joyful; merry. *The party guests were in a **festive** mood.*

fierce (fîrs) *adj.* Intense; ferocious. *The lion gave a **fierce** roar.*

for·ty-five re·cord (fôr′ tē fīv′ rĕk′ ərd) *n.* A small phonograph record that is played at forty-five revolutions per minute. *The **forty-five record** has one song on each side.*

fierce
The Latin word *ferus* ("wild and savage") is the origin of the words *ferocious* and *fierce.*

ŏŏ boot / ou out / ŭ cut / û fur / hw which / th thin / th this / zh vision / ə ago, silent, pencil, lemon, circus

679

funnel cloud

fran·tic (frăn′ tĭk) *adj.* Very upset, as from fear or worry. *When she couldn't find her backpack anywhere, Julie became **frantic.***

fright·ened (frīt′ nd) *adj.* Scared, alarmed. *Billy was **frightened** as he stepped out on the diving board.*

fun·nel cloud (fŭn′ əl kloud′) *n.* A storm cloud that is wide at the top and narrow at the bottom, often becoming a tornado. *Whenever the settlers saw **funnel clouds**, they hurried toward storm shelters.*

G

gene (jēn) *n.* A tiny part of a plant or animal cell that determines a characteristic passed on to the next generation. *Lucy has blue eyes like her parents because of their **genes.***

H

hab·i·tat (hăb′ ĭ tăt′) *n.* The type of environment where an animal or plant naturally lives and grows. *Sloths and jaguars live in the rain forest **habitat.***

harsh (härsh) *adj.* Demanding and severe; unpleasant. *Winter is a **harsh** season for most animals.*

har·vest (här′ vĭst) *v.* To gather a crop. *The workers were **harvesting** apples.*

heif·er (hĕf′ ər) *n.* A young cow that has not yet had a calf. *Sally's cow has been winning blue ribbons since it was a **heifer.***

herd (hûrd) *n.* A group of animals of a single kind. *A **herd** of wild horses galloped across the plain.*

her·i·tage (hĕr′ ĭ tĭj) *n.* Traditions, practices, and beliefs passed down from earlier generations. *Yinglan celebrates her Chinese **heritage** in her choice of music, clothes, and food.*

home·stead (hōm′ stĕd′) *n.* A piece of land given to settlers for farming and building a home. *The Andersens' **homestead** lay near Blackberry Creek.*

hon·or (ŏn′ ər) *v.* To show respect for; to accept. *They will **honor** their mother's request to dress up for Thanksgiving dinner.*

hu·mid (hyŏŏ′ mĭd) *adj.* Containing a large amount of water vapor; damp, sticky. *The air is often **humid** before a storm.*

I

im·mi·grant (ĭm′ ĭ grənt) *n.* A person who moves to a new country. *Many **immigrants** from Norway made their homes on the Great Plains.*

å rat / ā pay / â care / ä father / ĕ pet / ē be / ĭ pit / ī pie / î fierce / ŏ pot / ō go / ô paw, for / oi oil / ŏŏ book

680

im·mo·bile (ĭ mō′ bəl) *adj.* Fixed in one place; unable to move. *He stood **immobile** against the cliff face as the hikers passed by.*

im·pact (ĭm′ păkt′) *n.* The striking of one object against another. *The **impact** of the bike hitting the fence knocked the flowerpots to the ground.*

im·press (ĭm prĕs′) *v.* To have a strong, favorable effect on someone's feelings. *His piano playing **impressed** the audience.*

in·flu·en·tial (ĭn′ flŏŏ ĕn′ shəl) *adj.* Having the power to affect events or sway opinions. *The **influential** Women's League brought the problem to the mayor's attention.*

in·her·it (ĭn hĕr′ ĭt) *v.* To receive something from a parent or ancestor. *They **inherited** their mother's talent for music.*

in·stinct (ĭn′ stĭngkt) *n.* An inner feeling or way of behaving that is automatic, not learned. *A newly hatched sea turtle's **instinct** is to crawl toward the water.*

in·tense (ĭn tĕns′) *adj.* Very strong; focused. *Patrice put in hours of **intense** study to get ready for the test.*

J

jag·ged (jăg′ ĭd) *adj.* Having a ragged or pointed edge or outline. *Jamal cut his hand on a **jagged** piece of tin.*

jar (jär) *v.* To bump or cause to shake from impact. *By **jarring** Matthew, I caused him to drop the ball.*

jolt (jōlt) *n.* A sudden jerk or bump. *When the car went over the speed bump, the passengers got quite a **jolt.***

judge (jŭj) *n.* A person who decides who wins a contest. *The **judges** awarded first prize to my grandfather's pumpkin pie.*

just (jŭst) *adj.* Honorable and fair. *It is **just** to listen to both sides of an argument.*

K

kin (kĭn) *n.* Relatives; family. *Your father's cousins are your **kin**, too.*

L

launch (lônch) *v.* To forcefully send upward. *A powerful blast **launches** the rocket into the sky.*

la·va (lä′ və) *n.* Hot melted rock that flows from a volcano. *As the **lava** moved down the hillside, it set fire to the trees in its path.*

lava
People from Naples, Italy, near Mt. Vesuvius, used the Italian word *lava*, meaning "a stream caused suddenly by rain" for the molten rock that flowed down the volcano. It became an English word in 1750.

ŏŏ boot / ou out / ŭ cut / û fur / hw which / th thin / th this / zh vision / ə ago, silent, pencil, lemon, circus

681

lay-out (lā′ out′) *n.* The way something is arranged. *The **layout** of the office building confuses visitors.*

lib-er-ty (lib′ ər tē) *n.* Freedom from the control of others; independence. *The colonists won their **liberty** from England.*

light-ning (līt′ ning) *n.* The flash of light when electricity builds up in storm clouds. *A bolt of **lightning** lit up the night sky.*

lime-light (līm′ līt′) *n.* The center of public attention. *Ana's performance in the play brought her into the **limelight**.*

limelight
In the 1800s, theaters used limelights, made by burning the mineral lime. That bright stage light came to stand for the attention of the public.

M

mag-ma (mag′ mə) *n.* Molten rock underneath the earth's surface. ***Magma** boiled up through cracks deep inside the mountain.*

mare (mâr) *n.* A female horse. *Some of the **mares** were followed by their colts.*

mas-ter (mas′ tər) *v.* To become expert in a skill or art. *Ramón **mastered** the violin through years of practice.*

ma-ture (ma tyŏŏr′) *adj.* Fully grown or mentally developed. *A **mature** dog is calmer than a puppy.*

mem-o-rize (mem′ ə rīz′) *v.* To learn by completely remembering. *The hikers are **memorizing** the landmarks along their route.*

mustang
This word for a wild horse came from the Mexican Spanish word *mestengo,* which means "stray animal."

mi-gra-tion (mī grā′ shən) *n.* A movement of animals to a different habitat, especially in response to the change of seasons. *Scientists have mapped the spring **migration** of the whales.*

mill (mil) *v.* To move around in confusion. *The impatient crowd **milled** in front of the theater doors.*

mis-sion (mish′ ən) *n.* An operation that attempts to achieve certain goals or carry out specific tasks. *The astronauts' **mission** included bringing back samples of moon rocks.*

mol-ten (mōl′ tən) *adj.* Made liquid by heat. *The **molten** lava glowed red-orange.*

mus-tang (mus′ tăng′) *n.* A wild horse of the plains of western North America. *Joe could not ride as fast as the herd of **mustangs**.*

N

no-ble (nō′ bəl) *adj.* Showing greatness of character by unselfish behavior. *It was **noble** of Karen to share her prize money with her teammates.*

no-to-ri-ous (nō tôr′ ē əs) *adj.* Well known for something bad. *Billy the Kid was a **notorious** outlaw.*

ā rat / ā **pay** / â **care** / ä **father** / ĕ **pet** / ē **be** / ĭ **pit** / ī **pie** / î **fierce** / ŏ **pot** / ō **go** / ô **paw, for** / oi **oil** / ŏŏ **book**

682

O

o-be-di-ence (ō bē′ dē əns) *n.* Willingness to follow orders. *Mr. Yee expects **obedience** from his crew.*

ob-ser-va-tion (ŏb′ zûr vā′ shən) *n.* The act of paying careful attention. *You can learn a lot about nature through **observation**.*

ob-sta-cle (ŏb′ sta kəl) *n.* A thing that stands in one's way. *The horse had to jump over such **obstacles** as bushes and fences.*

op-er-a (ŏp′ ə rə) *n.* A form of theater in which the dialogue is sung to musical accompaniment. *The actors in the **opera** wore beautiful costumes.*

op-pose (ə pōz′) *v.* To be against something or someone. *The neighbors **oppose** the plan to turn the park into an office building.*

or-bit (ôr′ bit) *n.* The path of a spacecraft around the earth. *Shannon Lucid spent six months in **orbit** aboard the spacecraft Mir.*

o-ver-take (ō′ vər tāk′) *v.* To catch up with. *If we continue at this pace, we will **overtake** Billie's group.*

P

pan-to-mime (păn′ tə mīm′) *n.* The use of movements and facial expressions instead of words to convey meaning. *Jean used **pantomime** to show us how she caught the fish.*

Pa-tri-ot (pā′ trē ət) *n.* A colonist who was against British rule in the time of the Revolutionary War. *Patrick Henry spoke as a **Patriot** when he said "Give me liberty or give me death!"*

peer (pîr) *v.* To look at with concentration. *Mom **peered** at Paul suspiciously as he told his story.*

pi-o-neer (pī′ ə nîr′) *adj.* Describing a person who is first or among the first to settle in a region. *Our town was settled by three **pioneer** families in the 1800s.*

prai-rie (prâr′ ē) *n.* A large area of flat or rolling grassland. *The treeless **prairie** stretched for miles in all directions.*

pred-a-tor (prĕd′ ə tər) *n.* An animal that hunts other animals for food. *Small lizards must always be on the alert for hungry **predators**.*

pres-en-ta-tion (prĕz′ ən tā′ shən) *n.* Performance. *Although the actor knew his lines, his **presentation** was flat.*

pioneer
This word comes from the French word *peonier,* meaning "foot soldier." Those who marched into unknown territory were often soldiers on an expedition.

ŏŏ **boot** / ou **out** / ŭ **cut** / û **fur** / hw **which** / th **thin** / *th* **this** / zh **vision** / ə **ago**, silent, pencil, lemon, circus

683

pres-sure (prĕsh′ ər) *n.* A strong influence or force. *Sandra felt **pressure** to finish the book over the weekend.*

pri-va-teer (prī′ və tîr′) *n.* A privately owned ship that is ordered by the government to attack enemy ships during a war. *The **privateers** captured several merchant ships without firing a shot.*

pro-gram (prō′ grăm) *n.* In figure skating, the routine that one performs in front of judges or an audience. *The young skater spent hours getting his **program** ready for the competition.*

prose (prōz) *n.* Ordinary spoken or written language, in contrast to poetry. *Most fiction and nonfiction books are written in **prose**.*

R

raid (rād) *n.* A sudden attack, often with the goal of taking property. *The men brought back horses after their **raid** on their neighbors' village.*

ra-vine (rə vēn′) *n.* A narrow, deep valley, usually formed by the flow of water. *A small stream trickled at the bottom of the **ravine**.*

rav-ine

reb-el (rĕb′ əl) *n.* A person who opposes or defies the government in power. *The **rebels** refused to obey King George's laws.*

ref-u-gee (rĕf′ yŏŏ jē′) *n.* A person who flees to find protection from danger. *As the fighting in the hills grew worse, **refugees** streamed into the city.*

re-hear-sal (rĭ hûr′ səl) *n.* A session of practicing for a public performance. *The cast needed one more **rehearsal** before the play opened.*

re-in-tro-duc-tion (rē′ ĭn trə dŭk′ shən) *n.* The process of returning animals to their native habitats. *The zoo's tamarins are doing well since their **reintroduction** into the rain forest.*

re-ject (rĭ jĕkt′) *v.* To refuse to accept. *The magazine **rejected** her poem.*

re-luc-tant (rĭ lŭk′ tənt) *adj.* Unwilling to take an action. *Emily was **reluctant** to get out of the swimming pool.*

re-morse (rĭ môrs′) *n.* A feeling of regret or guilt for having done something wrong. *Jennie felt **remorse** for the trouble she had caused her sister.*

rep-u-ta-tion (rĕp′ yə tā′ shən) *n.* What others think about someone's character, behavior, and abilities. *Alex had a **reputation** for getting along well with everyone.*

re-quired (rĭ kwīrd′) *adj.* Needed. *Kayla has all of the training **required** for this job.*

ā rat / ā **pay** / â **care** / ä **father** / ĕ **pet** / ē **be** / ĭ **pit** / ī **pie** / î **fierce** / ŏ **pot** / ō **go** / ô **paw, for** / oi **oil** / ŏŏ **book**

684

re-spect (rĭ spĕkt′) *n.* A feeling of admiration and approval. *Mr. Garcia won the **respect** of all his students.*

re-us-a-ble (rē yŏŏz′ ə bəl) *adj.* Able to be used again. *April's family never throws away **reusable** paper bags.*

rev-o-lu-tion-ar-y (rĕv′ ə lŏŏ′ sha nĕr′ ē) *adj.* Connected with complete change. *The American colonists fought for their independence from England during the **Revolutionary** War.*

rhyth-mic (rĭth′ mĭk) *adj.* Having a noticeable beat with a pattern to it. *It is easy to dance to **rhythmic** music.*

ro-tate (rō′ tāt) *v.* To turn around on a center or axis. *It takes twenty-four hours for the earth to **rotate** once.*

rug-ged (rŭg′ ĭd) *adj.* Having a very rough and uneven surface. *The valley was surrounded by **rugged** mountains.*

S

sat-el-lite (săt′ l īt′) *n.* A human-made device that orbits a planet. *A weather **satellite** sends weather photos and data back to earth.*

sen-try (sĕn′ trē) *n., pl.,* sentries. A guard who is posted at a spot to keep watch. *Two **sentries** guarded the gates of the city.*

se-vere (sə vîr′) *adj.* Serious or extreme in nature. ***Severe** thunderstorms caused flooding in parts of the Midwest.*

shud-der (shŭd′ ər) *v.* To suddenly shake, vibrate, or quiver. *The house **shuddered** every time a heavy truck drove by.*

siz-zling (sĭz′ lĭng) *adj.* Crackling or hissing with intense heat. *The tree trunk was **sizzling** after the lightning bolt hit it.*

skir-mish (skûr′ mĭsh) *n.* A small, short fight; a minor battle. *The soldiers galloped away after a brief **skirmish** with the rebels.*

skit-ter (skĭt′ ər) *v.* To move lightly and quickly, especially with many changes of direction. *The mice **skittered** across the floor.*

skit-tish (skĭt′ ĭsh) *adj.* Nervous and jumpy. *The cat was **skittish** during the thunderstorm.*

snoop (snŏŏp) *n.* Someone who tries to find out about other people's doings in a sneaky way. *Maria's brother is such a **snoop** that she must keep her diary locked.*

sod (sŏd) *n.* A chunk of grass and soil held together by matted roots. *Settlers built houses out of blocks of **sod** because wood was scarce.*

satellite
In the Middle Ages the French used the word *satellite* to refer to an attendant who waits upon an important person. That same idea is in the modern meaning of a small device circling around a planet.

ŏŏ **boot** / ou **out** / ŭ **cut** / û **fur** / hw **which** / th **thin** / *th* **this** / zh **vision** / ə **ago**, silent, pencil, lemon, circus

685

Glossary **G3**

Glossary continued

sombrero
The name of the broad-brimmed hat that shades the wearer's eyes came from the Spanish word for shade, *sombra.*

shuttle
Shuttle started out as an Old English word, *scytel,* meaning "dart." It came to mean a weaving device that carried thread back and forth, and from that, a vehicle going back and forth over a short route.

som·bre·ro (sŏm brâr′ ō) *n.* A tall hat with a wide brim, worn in Mexico and the American Southwest. *The farmers wore **sombreros** to shade their eyes from the sun.*

space shut·tle (spās shŭt′ l) *n.* A reusable spacecraft that is launched like a rocket and can be landed like a plane. *The **space shuttle** landed safely after a seven-day flight.*

space·craft (spās′ krăft′) *n.* A vehicle designed for travel beyond the earth's atmosphere. *The **spacecraft** carried astronauts to the moon.*

spe·cial·ist (spĕsh′ ə lĭst) *n.* Someone who is an expert in a particular field. *A pediatrician is a medical **specialist** who treats only children.*

spec·ta·tor (spĕk′ tā′ tər) *n.* A person who watches an event or performance. *The **spectators** cheered when Jessie hit a home run.*

splen·did (splĕn′ dĭd) *adj.* Excellent. *The actor gave a **splendid** performance.*

stal·lion (stăl′ yən) *n.* An adult male horse. *Lizzie rode a black **stallion** at the horse show.*

stam·i·na (stăm′ ə nə) *n.* The strength needed to keep doing something tiring or difficult. *A young child lacks the **stamina** for a ten-mile hike.*

store·house (stôr′ hous′) *n.* A place or building where supplies are stored for future use. *The settlers' **storehouse** contained dried fruit and hams.*

sub·mit (səb mĭt′) *v.* To offer one's work to someone for their judgment or approval. *She **submitted** an article to the student newspaper.*

sub·ser·vi·ence (səb sûr′ vē əns) *n.* Willingness to give in to others' power. *Letting the tail drop is a sign of **subservience** in a wolf.*

sum·mit (sŭm′ ĭt) *n.* The top of a mountain. *Carolyn and I cheered when we finally reached the **summit** of Mount Rainier.*

sur·viv·al (sər vī′ vəl) *n.* The preservation or continuation of one's life. *Quick thinking is often necessary for **survival** in the wilderness.*

sus·pect (sə spĕkt′) *v.* To believe without being sure; to imagine. *Scott **suspects** that we are planning a surprise party for him.*

T

tack (tăk) *v.* To change the course of a boat. *The sailing ship was **tacking** in order to return to the harbor.*

ă rat / ā pay / â care / ä father / ĕ pet / ē be / ĭ pit / ī pie / î fierce / ŏ pot / ō go / ô paw, for / oi oil / o͝o book

tal·ent (tăl′ ənt) *n.* A natural ability to do something well. *She has a **talent** for playing the violin.*

tax (tăks) *n.* Money that people must pay in order to support a government. *England insisted that the colonists pay **taxes** on tea, stamps, and many other items.*

tech·ni·cal (tĕk′ nĭ kəl) *adj.* Showing basic knowledge of a complex task. *The acrobat performed the triple somersault with great **technical** skill.*

ter·ri·fy (tĕr′ ə fī′) *v.* To fill with overpowering fear. *The angry bear **terrified** the campers.*

ter·ri·to·ry (tĕr′ ĭ tôr′ ē) *n., pl.* **territories.** An area inhabited by an animal or animal group and defended against intruders. *The mountain lion hunted within its own **territory**.*

To·ry (tôr′ ē) *n., pl.* **Tories.** An American who sided with the British during the American Revolution. *As the British troops departed, most of the city's **Tories** followed.*

tor·na·do (tôr nā′ dō) *n.* A violent, whirling wind in a funnel-shaped cloud that can cause great destruction. *Many **tornadoes** form in Kansas and Oklahoma.*

tra·di·tion (trə dĭsh′ ən) *n.* The passing down of customs and beliefs from one generation to the next. *There is a long **tradition** of helping others in our family.*

train·ing (trā′ nĭng) *n.* The process of learning how to behave or perform. *Guide dogs must go through a long period of **training** before they can help people.*

trans·form (trăns fôrm′) *v.* To change greatly in appearance or form. *The make-up **transformed** the actor into the character of an old man.*

tun·dra (tŭn′ drə) *n.* A treeless Arctic region where very few plants can grow. *Large plants cannot put down roots in the frozen subsoil of the **tundra**.*

U

un·der·stand (ŭn′ dər stănd′) *v.* To get the meaning of. *After the teacher explained it again, Ivan could **understand** the problem.*

un·du·lat·ing (ŭn′ jə lāt′ ĭng) *adj.* Moving in waves or with a smooth, wavy motion. *The **undulating** water raised and lowered the rowboat.*

un·sure (ŭn sho͝or′) *adj.* Not certain; having doubts. *She was **unsure** of whether to bring her umbrella.*

tornado
Tornadoes were unknown and unnamed in Britain, so Americans borrowed and adapted the Spanish word *tronada,* meaning "thunderstorm."

tradition
Our word for the passing down of customs from one generation to another comes from the Latin verb *tradere,* which means "to hand down."

undulate
The Latin word for a wave, *unda,* contributes the sense of rising and falling in *undulate.*

o͞o boot / ou out / ŭ cut / û fur / hw which / th thin / *th* this / zh vision / ə ago, silent, pencil, lemon, circus

wilderness

up·heav·al (ŭp hē′ vəl) *n.* A lifting or upward movement of the earth's crust. *The mountain range was created by a great **upheaval**.*

ur·gent·ly (ûr′ jənt lē) *adv.* In a way that calls for immediate action. *The team **urgently** needs someone to take Kate's place.*

V

vol·un·teer (vŏl′ ən tîr′) *v.* To offer to do something of one's own free will, usually without being paid. *He **volunteered** to make the posters for the show.*

W

war·i·ness (wâr′ ē nĭs) *n.* Extreme caution. *Wild animals show **wariness** with people they don't know.*

weight·less·ness (wāt′ lĭs nĭs) *n.* The condition of experiencing little or no pull of gravity. *Astronauts experience **weightlessness** in outer space.*

wil·der·ness (wĭl′ dər nĭs) *n.* A region in its natural state, unsettled by human beings. *Grizzly bears live in the Alaskan **wilderness**.*

wound (wo͞ond) *n.* Injury in which the skin is cut or broken. *The soldier's **wounds** were not serious.*

ă rat / ā pay / â care / ä father / ĕ pet / ē be / ĭ pit / ī pie / î fierce / ŏ pot / ō go / ô paw, for / oi oil / o͝o book

Acknowledgments

Main Literature Selections

And Then What Happened, Paul Revere? by Jean Fritz, illustrated by Margot Tomes. Text copyright © 1973 by Jean Fritz. Illustrations copyright © 1973 by Margot Tomes. Reprinted by permission of the Putnam & Grosset Group, a division of Penguin Putnam Inc.

Black Cowboy, Wild Horses: A True Story, by Julius Lester, illustrated by Jerry Pinkney. Text copyright © 1998 by Julius Lester. Illustrations copyright © 1998 by Jerry Pinkney. Reprinted by permission of Dial Books for Young Readers, a division of Penguin Putnam Inc.

Selection from *Blizzard!*, by Jim Murphy, published by Scholastic Press, a division of Scholastic Inc. Copyright © 2000 by Jim Murphy. Reprinted by permission of Scholastic Inc.

A Boy Called Slow: The True Story of Sitting Bull, by Joseph Bruchac, illustrated by Rocco Baviera. Text copyright © 1994 by Joseph Bruchac. Illustrations copyright © 1994 by Rocco Baviera. Reprinted by permission of the Putnam Grosset Group, a division of Penguin Putnam Inc.

Selection from *Dear Mr. Henshaw*, by Beverly Cleary, illustrated by Paul O. Zelinsky. Text copyright © 1983 by Beverly Cleary. Reprinted by permission of HarperCollins Publishers.

Selection from *Earthquake Terror*, by Peg Kehret. Copyright © 1996 by Peg Kehret. Reprinted by permission of Dutton Children's Books, a division of Penguin Putnam Inc.

Selection from *Elena*, by Diane Stanley. Copyright © 1996 by Diane Stanley. Reprinted by permission of Hyperion Books for Children.

Eye of the Storm: Chasing Storms with Warren Faidley, by Stephen Kramer, photographs by Warren Faidley. Text copyright © 1997 by Stephen Kramer. Photographs copyright © 1997 by Warren Faidley. Reprinted by permission of G. P. Putnam's Sons, a division of Penguin Putnam Inc.

Selection from *The Fear Place*, by Phyllis Reynolds Naylor. Copyright © 1994 by Phyllis Reynolds Naylor. Reprinted by permission of Atheneum Books for Young Readers, an imprint of Simon & Schuster Children's Publishing Division. Cover copyright © 1994 by Doron Ben Ami. Reprinted by permission of the author and illustrator.

The Golden Lion Tamarin Comes Home by George Ancona. Copyright © 1994 by George Ancona, except photographs of frog, snake and sloth by James M. Dietz and map by Isabel Ancona. All rights reserved. Reprinted with permission of Simon & Schuster Books for Young Readers, an imprint of Simon & Schuster Children's Publishing Division.

The Grizzly Bear Family Book, by Michio Hoshino, translated by Karen Collier-Taylor. Copyright © 1992 by Michio Hoshino. Reprinted by permission of North-South Books Inc., New York. All rights reserved.

Selection from *Iditarod Dream*, by Ted Wood. Copyright © 1996 by Ted Wood. Reprinted by arrangement with Walker & Co.

Selection from *Interrupted Journey*, by Kathryn Lasky, photographs by Christopher Knight. Text copyright © 2001 by Kathryn Lasky. Photographs copyright © 2001 by Christopher Knight. Reproduced by permission of Candlewick Press Inc., Cambridge, MA.

"James Forten" from *Now Is Your Time: The African-American Struggle for Freedom*, by Walter Dean Myers. Copyright © 1991 by Walter Dean Myers. Reprinted by permission of HarperCollins Publishers.

Selection from *Journey to Nowhere*, by Mary Jane Auch. Copyright © 1997 by Mary Jane Auch. Jacket illustration copyright © 1997 by Bob Crofut. Cover and excerpt reprinted by permission of Henry Holt and Company, LLC.

Katie's Trunk, by Ann Turner, illustrated by Ron Himler. Text copyright © 1992 by Ann Turner. Illustrations copyright © 1992 by Ron Himler. All rights reserved. Reprinted by permission of Simon & Schuster Books for Young Readers, an imprint of Simon & Schuster Children's Publishing Division.

"La Bamba" from *Baseball in April and Other Stories*, by Gary Soto. Copyright © 1990 by Gary Soto. Reprinted by permission of Harcourt Inc. The song "La Bamba" adaptation and arrangement by Ritchie Valens © 1958 Picture Our Music (Renewed). All rights for U.S.A. administered by EMI Longitude Music (BMI). All rights for the World except U.S.A. administered by Warner-Tamerlane Publishing Corp. All rights reserved. Reprinted by permission of Warner Bros. Publications U.S. Inc.

Mae Jemison: Space Scientist, by Gail Sakurai. Copyright © 1995 by Gail Sakurai. Reprinted by permission of Childrens Press Inc., a division of Grolier Publishing.

Selection from *Mariah Keeps Cool*, by Mildred Pitts Walter, illustrated by Pat Cummings. Text copyright © 1990 by Mildred Pitts Walter. Cover illustration copyright © 1990 by Pat Cummings. Reprinted by permission of Simon & Schuster Books for Young Readers, an imprint of Simon & Schuster Children's Publishing Division.

"Mary Redmond, John Darragh, and Dicey Langston: Spies" from *We Were There, Too!: Young People in U.S. History*, by Phillip Hoose. Copyright © 2001 by Phillip Hoose. Reprinted by permission of Farrar, Straus and Giroux, LLC.

Selection from *Me, Mop, and the Moondance Kid*, by Walter Dean Myers. Copyright © 1988 by Walter Dean Myers. Used by permission of Random House Children's Books, a division of Random House, Inc.

Selection from *Michelle Kwan: Heart of a Champion, An Autobiography*. Copyright © 1997 by Michelle Kwan Corp. Reprinted by permission of Scholastic Inc. and Momentum Partners Inc.

Mom's Best Friend, by Sally Hobart Alexander, photographs by George Ancona. Text copyright © 1992 by Sally Hobart Alexander. Photographs copyright © 1992 by George Ancona. Text reprinted by permission of the Author and Bookstop Literary Agency. Photographs reprinted by permission of the Photographer.

Selection from *My Side of the Mountain*, by Jean Craighead George. Copyright © 1959 by Jean Craighead George. Reprinted by permission of Dutton Children's Books, a division of Penguin Putnam Inc.

Selection from *Night of the Twisters*, by Ivy Ruckman. Text copyright © 1984 by Ivy Ruckman. Reprinted by permission of HarperCollins Publishers.

Selection from *Pioneer Girl Growing Up on the Prairie,* by Andrea Warren. Copyright © 1998 by Andrea Warren. Reprinted by permission of HarperCollins Publishers.

The Rabbit's Judgment, by Suzanne Crowder Han, illustrated by Yumi Heo. The text was originally published in *Korean Folk and Fairy Tales.* Text copyright © 1991 by Suzanne Crowder Han. Text reprinted by permission of Hollym Corporation, Publishers, Seoul, Korea. Illustrations copyright © 1994 by Yumi Heo. Illustrations reprinted by permission of Henry Holt and Company.

"Robert Farnsworth: Army Post on the Yukon" from *Children of the Gold Rush,* by Claire Rudolf Murphy and Jane G. Haigh. Copyright © 1999 by Claire Rudolf Murphy and Jane G. Haigh. Reprinted by permission of Alaska Northwest Books®.

Selection from *Summer on Wheels,* by Gary Soto. Copyright © 1995 by Gary Soto. Reprinted by permission of Scholastic Inc.

Selection from *Toliver's Secret,* by Esther Wood Brady. Text copyright © 1996 by Esther Wood Brady. Illustrations copyright © 1976 by Richard Cuffari. Used by permission of Crown Children's Books, a division of Random House, Inc.

Volcanoes, by Seymour Simon. Copyright © 1988 by Seymour Simon. Reprinted by permission of HarperCollins Publishers.

Selection from *The Wright Brothers: How They Invented the Airplane,* by Russell Freedman. Copyright © 1991 by Russell Freedman. All rights reserved. Reprinted by permission of Holiday House, Inc.

Selection from *Yang the Second and Her Secret Admirers,* by Lensey Namioka. Copyright © 1998 by Lensey Namioka. Reprinted by permission of Little, Brown and Company (Inc.).

Focus Selections

"Alex Rodriguez" from *Hit a Grand Slam,* by Alex Rodriguez with Greg Brown. Copyright © 1998 by Alex Rodriguez and Greg Brown. Reprinted by permission of Taylor Publishing Company.

"The Bat" from *The Collected Poems of Theodore Roethke,* by Theodore Roethke. Copyright 1938 by Theodore Roethke. Used by permission of Doubleday, a division of Random House, Inc.

"Be Glad Your Nose Is on Your Face" from *The New Kid on the Block,* by Jack Prelutsky. Copyright © 1984 by Jack Prelutsky. Reprinted by permission of HarperCollins Publishers.

Selection from *Bill Peet: An Autobiography.* Copyright © 1989 by William Peet. Reprinted by permission of Houghton Mifflin Company.

"Campfire" from *A Suitcase of Seaweed and Other Poems,* by Janet S. Wong. Copyright © 1996 by Janet S. Wong. Jacket illustration copyright © 1996 by Janet S. Wong. Reprinted with the permission of Margaret K. McElderry Books, an imprint of Simon & Schuster Children's Publishing Division.

The Case of the Runaway Appetite: A Joe Giles Mystery, by Rob Hale, is based upon a work by Hal Ober. Copyright © by Hal Ober. Adaptation and use is by permission of the author.

"Civilization" from *4-Way Stop and Other Poems,* by Myra Cohn Livingston. Copyright © 1976 by Myra Cohn Livingston. Reprinted by permission of Marian Reiner.

"Dinner Together," by Diana Rivera, from *The Invisible Ladder, An Anthology of Contemporary American Poems for Young Readers,* edited by Liz Rosenberg, published by Henry Holt and Company, 1996. Copyright © 1996 by Diana Rivera. Reprinted by permission of the author.

"Dream Variation" from *Collected Poems,* by Langston Hughes. Copyright © 1994 by the Estate of Langston Hughes. Reprinted by permission of Alfred A. Knopf, a division of Random House, Inc.

"Early Spring" from *Navajo: Visions and Voices Across the Mesa,* by Shonto Begay. Copyright © 1995 by Shonto Begay. Reprinted by permission of Scholastic, Inc.

"February" from *McBroom's Almanac,* written by Sid Fleischman, illustrated by Walter Lorraine. Text copyright © 1984 by Sid Fleischman. Illustrations copyright © 1984 by Walter Lorraine. Reprinted by permission of the author and illustrator.

"It's All the Same to the Clam" from *A Light in the Attic,* by Shel Silverstein. Copyright © 1981 by Evil Eye Music, Inc. Reprinted by permission of HarperCollins Publishers.

"Jane Goodall" from *Talking with Adventurers,* by Pat and Linda Cummings, published by the National Geographic Society. Excerpt copyright © 1998 Jane Goodall. Reprinted by permission of the National Geographic Society.

"John Henry Races the Steam Drill" from *Big Men, Big Country, A Collection of American Tall Tales,* by Paul Robert Walker, illustrated by James Bernardin. Text copyright © 1993 by Paul Robert Walker. Illustrations copyright © 1993 by James Bernardin. Reprinted by permission of Harcourt Inc.

"knoxville, tennessee" from *Black Feeling, Black Talk, Black Judgment,* by Nikki Giovanni. Copyright © 1968, 1970 by Nikki Giovanni. Reprinted by permission of HarperCollins Publishers.

"Langston Terrace" from *Childtimes, A Three-Generation Memoir*, by Eloise Greenfield and Lessie Jones Little. Copyright © 1979 by Eloise Greenfield and Lessie Jones Little. Reprinted by permission of HarperCollins Publishers.

"Árbol de limón/Lemon Tree," by Jennifer Clement, translated by Consuelo de Aerenlund. Copyright © 1995 by Jennifer Clement. Reprinted by permission of the author and translator.

"Ode to Pablo's Tennis Shoes" from *Neighborhood Odes,* by Gary Soto. Copyright © 1992 by Gary Soto. Illustrations copyright © 1992 by Harcourt Inc. Reprinted by permission of Harcourt Inc.

"A Patch of Old Snow" from *The Poetry of Robert Frost,* edited by Edward Connery Lathem. Copyright 1939, © 1967, 1969 by Henry Holt and Company, LLC. Reprinted by permission of Henry Holt and Company, LLC. Illustration by Henri Sorensen is reprinted by permission of Evelyn Johnson & Associates. Illustration copyright © 1994 by Henri Sorensen.

"Paul Bunyan, the Mightiest Logger of Them All" from *American Tall Tales,* by Mary Pope Osborne. Text copyright © 1991 by Mary Pope Osborne. Reprinted by permission of Alfred A. Knopf, a division of Random

House, Inc. Illustration by Chris Van Allsburg and book cover of *From Sea to Shining Sea: A Treasury of American Folklore and Folk Songs*, compiled by Amy L. Cohn, are reprinted by permission of Scholastic, Inc. Illustration copyright © 1993 by Chris Van Allsburg. Cover illustration copyright © 1993 by the artists. All rights reserved.

Quote from *Dogs and Dragons, Trees and Dreams,* by Karla Kuskin, published in 1980 by HarperCollins Publishers, New York.

"Reggie" from *Honey I Love and Other Love Poems,* by Eloise Greenfield, pictures by Diane and Leo Dillon. Text copyright © 1978 by Eloise Greenfield. Reprinted by permission of HarperCollins Publishers.

"Sally Ann Thunder Ann Whirlwind" from *American Tall Tales,* by Mary Pope Osborne, wood engravings by Michael McCurdy. Text copyright © 1991 by Mary Pope Osborne. Illustrations copyright © 1991 by Michael McCurdy. Reprinted by permission of Alfred A. Knopf, a division of Random House, Inc.

"The Shark" from *Fast and Slow: Poems,* by John Ciardi. Text copyright © 1975 by John Ciardi. Reprinted by permission of Houghton Mifflin Company. All rights reserved.

"Travel," by Edna St. Vincent Millay from *Collected Poems,* published by HaperCollins. Copyright 1921, 1948 by Edna St. Vincent Millay. All rights reserved. Reprinted by permission of Elizabeth Barnett, literary executor.

"What Are Pockets For?" from *One at a Time,* by David McCord. Copyright © 1974 by David McCord. By permission of Little, Brown and Company (Inc.).

"Whirligig Beetles" from *Joyful Noise: Poems for Two Voices*, by Paul Fleischman. Text copyright © 1988 by Paul Fleischman. Reprinted by permission of HarperCollins Publishers.

Links and Theme Openers

"Above Jackson Pond," by Joseph Bruchac. Copyright © by Joseph Bruchac. Reprinted by permission of the Barbara Kouts Literary Agency.

"Blind to Limitations," by Brent H. Weber from the August 1997 issue of *Highlights for Children.* Copyright © 1997 by Highlights for Children, Inc., Columbus, Ohio. Reprinted by permission.

"El Niño," by Fred Pearce from *MUSE* magazine, October 1988 issue, Vol. 2, No. 5. Copyright © 1998 by Fred Pearce. Reprinted by permission of the author. Cover copyright © 1988 by Carus Publishing Company. Cover is reprinted by permission of MUSE magazine.

"Los ojos de mi gente/The Eyes of My People," by DaMonique Dominguez, age 11, Englewood, CA. Copyright © 1999 by DaMonique Dominguez. Reprinted by permission of *Skipping Stones* magazine, Vol. 11, No. 3.

"Hands & Hearts" adapted from *American Girl,* Volume 6, Issue 6. Copyright © 1998 by Pleasant Company. Reprinted by permission of Pleasant Company.

"Home on the Range," by Johnny D. Boggs. Copyright © by Johnny D. Boggs. Reprinted by permission of the author and *Boy's Life,* June 1998. Published by the Boy Scouts of America.

Excerpt from *I Have Heard of a Land,* by Joyce Carol Thomas. Copyright © 1998 by Joyce Carol Thomas. Reprinted by permission of Joanna Cotler Books, an imprint of HarperCollins Publishers.

"Into the Deep" from the April 26, 1996, issue of *Time for Kids.* Copyright © 1996 by Time Inc. Reprinted by permission of the publisher.

"Maputo Saturday Craft Market," by Rebecca Beatriz Chavez, age 11. Reprinted by permission of *Stone Soup: the magazine by young writers and artists.* Copyright © 1998 by the Children's Art Foundation.

"Monkeys with a Mission" from the April 1999 issue of *National Geographic World.* Copyright © 1999 by the National Geographic Society. Reprinted by permission of the publisher.

"Nicodemus Stakes a Claim in History," by Angela Bates-Tompkins from Cobblestone's February 1999 issue: *African American Pioneers and Homesteaders.* Copyright © 1999 by Cobblestone Publishing Company, Peterborough, NH 03458. All rights reserved. Reprinted by permission of the publisher.

"One Pair of Shoes and a lot of good souls" originally published in the Winter 1995 issue of *ZuZu* magazine. Copyright © 1995 by *ZuZu Magazine/* Restless Youth Press. Reprinted by permission of the publisher.

"The Princess and the Warrior," originally published as *"Los novios,"* by Genevieve Barlow and William Stivers from *Leyendas Mexicanas.* Copyright © 1996 by NTC Publishing Group. Reprinted by permission of NTC/Contemporary Publishing Group.

"Problems," by Kevin A. Zuniga, age 12, Laredo, Texas, from the November/December 1998 issue of *Skipping Stones* magazine. Copyright © 1998 by Kevin A. Zuniga. Reprinted by permission of *Skipping Stones* magazine.

Quote from *Pilgrim at Tinker Creek,* by Annie Dillard. Copyright © 1974 by Annie Dillard. Published by HarperCollins Publishers, New York.

Quote by Florence Joyner. ™ Florence Joyner under license authorized by CMG Worldwide Inc., Indianapolis, Indiana 46255 USA www.cmgww.com.

"Raccoons on the Shore at Paradox Lake," by Joseph Bruchac. Copyright © by Joseph Bruchac. Reprinted by permission of the Barbara Kouts Literary Agency.

"Robin Hughes: Wildlife Doctor," by Susan Yoder Ackerman, reprinted by permission of *Cricket Magazine,* March 1997, Vol. 24, No. 7. Copyright © 1997 by Susan Yoder Ackerman.

"Swish," by Chance Yellowhair. Copyright © 1998 by Chance Yellowhair. Reprinted by permission of *Skipping Stones* magazine, September/October 1998.

"A Thousand Geese," by Joseph Bruchac. Copyright © by Joseph Bruchac. Reprinted by permission of the Barbara Kouts Literary Agency.

"To Mother," by Aaron Wells, age 11, Eugene OR. Copyright © 1999 by Aaron Wells. Reprinted by permission of *Skipping Stones* magazine, March/April 1999.

"Wind Song" from *Four Ancestors: Stories, Songs and Poems from Native North America,* by Joseph Bruchac. Copyright © 1996 by Joseph Bruchac. Published and reprinted by permission of Troll Communications L.L.C.

"Yankee Doodle" from *Songs and Stories of the Revolution,* by Jerry Silverman. Copyright © 1994 by Jerry Silverman. Reprinted by permission of Millbrook Press Inc.

Special thanks to the following teachers whose students' compositions appear as Student Writing Models: Cindy

Cheatwood, Florida; Diana Davis, North Carolina; Kathy Driscoll, Massachusetts; Linda Evers, Florida; Heidi Harrison, Michigan; Eileen Hoffman, Massachusetts; Julia Kraftsow, Florida; Bonnie Lewison, Florida; Kanetha McCord, Michigan.

Credits

Photography

3 (t) © Ed Young/Corbis. (m) Hemera Technologies Inc. (b) C Squared Studios/PhotoDisc Green/Getty Images. **5** © Ed Young/Corbis. **8** Hemera Technologies Inc. **9** (t) © PhotoDisc/Getty Images. **11** Hemera Technologies Inc. **13** Hemera Technologies Inc. **16** © 2001 Werner Forman/Art Resource, NY. **17** (l) Courtesy HarperCollins Publishers. (ml) Hugo Van Lawick/National Geographic Image Collection. (mr) © The Walt Disney Company, courtesy The Kobal Collection. (r) Bill Frakes/Life Magazine © Time Inc. **19** C Squared Studios/Photodisc Green/Getty Images. **20–21** (bkgd) ©Byron Aughenbaugh/ The Image Bank/Getty Images. **21** (m) © Ed Young/ Corbis. **22** (mr) © Warren Faidley/Weather Stock. (b) Aaron Horowitz/Corbis. **22–23** (bkgd) Gary Williams/ Liaison. **23** (m) © Warren Faidly/Weather Stock. **24–25** (m) Gary Williams/Liaison. **24** (t) © Warren Faidly/ Weather Stock. **27** © Kevin Schafer/Allstock/ PictureQuest. **28–9** (bkgd) © Roger Ressmeyer/Corbis. **45** (t) Jeff Reinking/Mercury Pictures. (m) Courtesy Phil Boatwright. (b) © PhotoDisc/Getty Images. **48** ©Vince Streano/CORBIS. **49** (t) Mauro Andino/AP/Wide World Photos. (m) Topi Lyambila/AP/Wide World. (b) Geoff Spencer/AP/Wide World. **51** Library of Congress (LC-USZ62-11491). **52** Digital Vision/PictureQuest. **54** (t) © PhotoDisc/Getty Images. (b) © Johnny Autery. **55** L.M. Otero/AP Photo. **56–7** (bkgd) © Vittoriano Rastelli/ Corbis. **56** (t) Christine Kramer. (b) AP/Wide World Photos./Lennox McLendon. **58–77** Warren Faidley/ WeatherStock. **79** (tl) National Center for Atmospheric Research/University Corporation for Atmospheric Research/National Science Foundation. (tr) National Climactic Data Center. (bl) ©Peter Jarver/Wildscape Australia. (br) ©Mark C. Burnett/Photo Researchers, Inc. **80–1** (bkgd) © Bill Bachman/ Photo Researchers, Inc. **82–3** Dr. Peter W. Sloss/NOAA/NESDIS/NGDC. **82** (b) Photo by J.D. Griggs/U.S. Geological Survey. **83** (tl) Photo by Lyn Topinka, U.S. Geological Survey. (tr) ©Nik Wheeler/CORBIS. (b) © Stephen and Donna O'Meara/ Volcano Watch International. **84–5** (bkgd) © Tom Ives/ Corbis **85** National Park Service, Hawaii Volcanoes National Park. **86** Terraphotographics/BPS. **86–7** Gary Rosenquist/Earth Images. **88** Terraphotographics/BPS. **90** Solarfilma. **91–2** J. D. Griggs/U.S. Geological Survey. **93** Seymour Simon. **94** (t) National Park Service, Hawaii Volcanoes National Park. (b) John K. Nakata/ Terraphotographics/BPS. **95** Terraphotographics/BPS. **96** Carl May/Terraphotographics/BPS. **97** Terraphotographics/BPS. **98** Seymour Simon. **99** (l) Courtesy Seymour Simon. (r) © PhotoDisc/Getty Images. **106–6A** (bkgd) © First Light/CORBIS. **106** (b) © Ed Young/Corbis. **106L–M** Culver Pictures. **128** from *Larger Than Life: The American Tall-Tale Postcard 1905–1915* by Cynthia Elyce Rubin and Morgan Williams. Compilation copyright © 1990 by Abbeville Press, Inc. **130–1** (bkgd) © Zoran Milich/Allsport Concepts/Getty Images. **131** (m) Hemera Technologies Inc. **132** Courtesy of Phyllis R. Naylor. **136** AP/Wide World Photos. **137** (t)Thomas Zimmermann/Stone/Getty Images. (m) © Agence Vandystadt/Allsport. (b) ©Tim Defrisco/Allsport. **138–9** (bkgd) Spike/Stone/Getty Images. **139** Courtesy of the Kwan family. **141** (t) Courtesy of the Kwan family. (b) © Dave Black. **142** © Cindy Lang. **143** Courtesy of the Kwan family. **145** (t) ©Kevin R. Morris/CORBIS. (m) ©Mike Powell/Allsport. (b) Associated Press AP. **146** (l) © Dave Black. (r) ©1997 Gerard Chataigneau. **149** © Dave Black. **151** Momentum Partners, Inc. **154** © 1985 Jose Azel/AURORA. **155** © Photonews/Liaison Agency Inc. **156** (l) © Photonews/ Liaison Agency Inc. (r) ©1985 Jose Azel/AURORA. **157** ©Peter Wouda/Persbureau Noordoost, The Netherlands **162–3** (bkgd) Aaron Jones Studios/Stone/Getty Images. **162** (t) Courtesy Carolyn Soto. (b) Lorraine Parrow/ Mercury Pictures. **178** (t) Archive Photos. (b) U.S. Department of the Interior, National Park Service, Edison National Historic Site/Photo Researchers, Inc. **179** (tl) (tc) Brown Brothers. (tr) Popperfoto/Archive Photos. (mr) © CORBIS. (bl) Smithsonian Institution/National Museum of American History (SI #: 69857). **180** (tl) Archive Photos. (tc) Hulton Getty/Stone/Getty Images. (ml) Comstock Klips. (bl) Archive Photos/John V. Dunigan. (br) © Bettmann/CORBIS. **181** (tc) Leonard Lessin/Peter Arnold, Inc. (r) © PhotoDisc/Getty Images. (bl) Courtesy of Sony Electronics, Inc. **182** © Robert Holmgren/ Stone/Getty Images. **182–3** ©Andrew J.G. Bell, Eye Ubiquitous/CORBIS **183** Stephen Cooper/Allstock/ PictureQuest. **184–5** (bkgd) Norbert Rosing/National Geographic/Getty Images. **184** (t) Dennis Crews/Mercury Pictures. (b) Michael Justice/Mercury Pictures. **188–9** (b) © David Muench/CORBIS. **191** (b) © David Muench/ CORBIS. **194–5** (b) © David Muench/CORBIS. **199** (b) © David Muench/CORBIS. **202** (b) © David Muench/ CORBIS. **204–7** Jamie Bloomquist, American Foundation for the Blind. **208–9** (bkgd) NASA/Ames Research Center. **208–9** (inset) NASA. **208** (bl) NASA. **208** (c) Sovfoto/ Eastfoto. **209** NASA. **210–1** (bkgd) © Pli/Taxi/Getty Images. **211–2** NASA. **214–5** CORBIS-Bettmann/UPI. **216–21** NASA. **222** AP/Wide World Photos. **223** Mike Williams/Mercury Pictures. **226–9** (bkgd) © PhotoDisc/ Getty Images. **227** ©1995 Marty Snyderman. **228–9** © Bruce H. Robison. **230–0A** (bkgd) © PhotoDisc/Getty Images. **230** (b) Hemera Technologies Inc. **230B–D** Ted Wood. **230E** Ted Levin/Animals Animals. **230F–I** Ted Wood. **234** NonStock/PictureQuest. **235** © PhotoDisc/ Getty Images. **236** W.A. Sharman/Milepost 92 1/2 /CORBIS. **237** © PhotoDisc/Getty Images. **238–9** Roy Corral/CORBIS. **240** Craig Lovell/CORBIS. **242** (t) William Amos/Bruce Coleman. (b) Gossi/Bruce Coleman. **243** Gary Meszanos/Bruce Coleman. **245** Telegraph Colour Library/FPGInternational. **246** © PhotoDisc/ Getty Images. **249** © PhotoDisc/Getty Images. **250** NonStock/PictureQuest. **251** Nancy Ney/Corbis. **252** Ron Rovtar/Photonica. **254–5** (bkgd) The Colonial Williamsburg Foundation. **255** (m) Hemera Technologies Inc. **256–8** (bkgd) Siede Preis/Photodisc/Getty Images. **256** (tl) Courtesy of Walter Dean Myers, (mr) Joseph Sohm; Visions of America/Corbis, (bl) Carl & Ann Purcell/

Corbis. **257** (bl) Lynn Stone/Index Stock Imagery, (tm) Bettmann Corbis, (tr) Joseph Sohm; Visions of America/ Corbis, (br) Lester Lefkowitz/Corbis. **258** (t) Photograph courtesy of the Concord Museum, Concord, Massachusets and the Lexington Historical Society, Inc., Lexington, Massachusets Photograph by David Bohl, (b) Bettmann/ Corbis. **260** Colonial Williamsburg Foundation. **260–1** The Granger Collection, New York. **261** (t) The Granger Collection, New York. (b) John Singleton Copley, *Paul Revere.* Gift of Joseph W., William B., and Edward H.R. Revere. Courtesy, Museum of Fine Arts, Boston. Reproduced with permission. ©1999 Museum of Fine Arts, Boston. All Rights Reserved. **262–3** (bkgd) © Robert Holmes/Corbis. **279** Tom Iannuzzi/Mercury Pictures. **281** Courtesy, American Antiquarian Society. **283** American 19th Century, *General Washington on a White Charger*, Gift of Edgar William and Bernice Chrysler Garbisch, Photograph © 1999 Board of Trustees, National Gallery of Art, Washington. **285** © Bettmann/CORBIS. **290** Colonial Williamsburg Foundation. **291** (tl) Bettmann/ CORBIS. (tr) Collection of Mr. and Mrs. Karl T. Molin, photo courtesy Henry Groskinsky. (b) The Granger Collection, New York. **292** (t) Jon Crispin/Mercury Pictures. (b) Tom Spitz/Mercury Pictures. **292–3** (bkgd) © Lee Snider; Lee Snider/Corbis. **306–7** ©Lee Snider/ CORBIS. **308** Chicago Historical Society. **309** detail, James Peachey/National Archives of Canada/C-002001. **310** (r) The Historical Society of Pennsylvania (HSP), watercolor of James Forten from the Leon Gardiner Collection. Frame from Image Farm, Inc. (l) Friends Historical Library of Swarthmore College. **311** (t) AP/ Wide World Photos. (b) Massachusetts Historical Society. **312–3** (bkgd) Tsuneo Nakamua/Index Stock Imagery. **312** (t) Courtesy Walter Dean Myers. (b) Courtesy Leonard Jenkins. **329** (l) Print Collection, Miriam and Ira D. Wallach Division of Art, Prints and Photographs. The New York Public Library. Astor, Lenox and Tilden Foundation. **330** The Granger Collection, New York. **334–4A** (bkgd) © Richard T. Nowitz/National Geographic/ Getty Images. **334** (b) Hemera Technologies Inc. **336–7** (bkgd) © Jim Cummins/Taxi/Getty Images. **337** (m) Hemera Technologies Inc. **338–40** Courtesy of Lensey Namioka. **342** © Skjold/The Image Works **343** © Tommy Dodson/Unicorn Stock Photos **344–5** (bkgd) Chuck Keeler/Stone/Getty Images. **344** (t) Eric Bakke/Mercury Pictures. (b) Courtesy Nneka Bennett. **358** © PhotoDisc/ Getty Images. **359–60** © PhotoDisc/Getty Images. **366** Sonda Dawes/The Images Works. **367** (l) Mark Richards/ PhotoEdit. (tr) San Francisco SPCA Hearing Dog Program. (br) Bob Daemmrich/The Image Works. **368–9** (bkgd) © Ralph A. Clevenger/Corbis. **368** (t) Courtesy Sally Hobart Alexander. (b) Courtesy George Ancona. **369–385** George Ancona. **386** © PhotoDisc/Getty Images. **388** Dan Helms/Compix. **389–90** Paula Lerner/Aurora. **391** Dan Helms/Compix. **392** Zeva Oelbaum/Envision. **392–3** Ric Ergenbright/ CORBIS. **393** (inset) Alison Wright/CORBIS. **394–5** (bkgd) Studio Montage. **407** (t) Courtesy Little, Brown and Company. (b) Courtesy Kees DeKiefte. (bkgd) Jane Dill. **408** © PhotoDisc/Getty Images. **410–1** ©2001 Bruce Zake, All Rights Reserved. **411** E. Silverman. **412** ©Danny Turner. **413** Wade Spees/first published in *American Girl* magazine. **416–7** (bkgd) © Randy Wells/Corbis. **417** © PhotoDisc/Getty Images. **419** © PhotoDisc/Getty Images. **431** (t) Alan McEwen, 1999. (b) Courtesy Nancy Carpenter. (bkgd) © PhotoDisc/Getty Images. **438–8A** (bkgd) © Jose Luis Pelaez/CORBIS. **438** (b) Hemera Technologies Inc. **438I** Wright State University Libraries. **438J–K** Bettmann/Corbis. **438J** (t) Wright State University Libraries. **438L** (b) Smithsonian Institution. **460** © PhotoDisc/Getty Images. **462–3** (bkgd) © David Hiser/Stone/Getty Images. **463** (m) © 2001 Werner Forman/Art Resource, NY. **464** Courtesy of Joseph Bruchac. **466** (tr) Lynton Gardiner/American Museum of Natural History. **466–7** Kevin Alexander/Index Stock Imagery. **468** (l) LH Benschneider. (r) Photo by O.S. Goff, the Denver Public Library, Western History Department. **469** National Museum of American Art, Washington, D.C./Art Resource, NY. **470–1** (bkgd) Eric Meola/The Image Bank/Getty Images. **485** (t) Mike Greelar/Mercury Pictures. (b) Jose Crespo. **488** From the Collections of the St. Louis Mercantile Library at the University of Missouri-St. Louis. (bkgd) © PhotoDisc/ Getty Images. **489** (t) Smithsonian Institution/National Anthropological Archives (#83-15549). (b) Mr. and Mrs. Charles Diker Collection. **490** (t) Mr. and Mrs. Charles Diker Collection. (b) Missouri Historical Society, St. Louis. **491** (t) Collection National Cowboy Hall of Fame and Western Heritage Center, Oklahoma City, Oklahoma. (b) Thaw Collection, Fenimore Art Museum, Cooperstown, New York. Photo ©1998, John Bigelow Taylor, N.Y.C. **492** Bettmann/CORBIS. **494** Library of Congress. **496–7** Solomon D. Butcher Collection, Nebraska State Historical Society. **497** National Archives. **498–9** (bkgd) © Daryl Benson/ Masterfile. **498** Roy Inman/Mercury Pictures. **500** Nebraska State Historical Society. **501** Nebraska State Historical Society. **502–3** photo courtesy Andrea Warren and the McCance family **504** Nebraska State Historical Society. **505** Nebraska State Historical Society. **506** The Kansas State Historical Society, Topeka, Kansas. **508–9** The Kansas State Historical Society, Topeka, Kansas. **511–2** The Kansas State Historical Society, Topeka, Kansas **513** Courtesy Billie Thornburg. **515** (bkgd) © PhotoDisc/ Getty Images. **516–7** The Kansas State Historical Society, Topeka, Kansas. **516** Charlie Riedel. **517** National Archives. **518–9** Charlie Riedel. **520–1** Steve Kaufman/ CORBIS. **521** ©Hulton Getty/Liaison Agency. **522–3** (bkgd) © Peter M. Wilson/Corbis. **522** (t) Courtesy Julius Lester. (b) Miles Pinkney. **544–7** ©1998 David Nance. **548** Brown Brothers. **549** ©Bettmann/CORBIS. **550–1** (bkgd) © David Muench/Corbis. **563** (t) Courtesy Diane Stanley. (b) Courtesy Raúl Colón. **566** (t) Alan Ross/ Stone/Getty Images, (b) Hawaii State Archives **567** California History Section, California State Library. **566–7** (b) Alan Ross/Stone/Getty Images. **568** (t) Southern Pacific Photo, Union Pacific Museum Collection. (b) Union Pacific Museum Collection **569** Billy Hustace/ Stone Getty Images. **570–0A** (bkgd) © Ed Freeman/The Image Bank/Getty Images. **570** (b) © 2001 Werner Forman/Art Resource, NY. **570H–K** University of Alaska Fairbanks, Archives, Alaska & Polar Regions Department, C.S. Farnsworth Collection. **570L** (t) University of Alaska Fairbanks, Archives, Alaska & Polar Regions Department, C.S. Farnsworth Collection, (b) Fotosearch. **574** Courtesy HarperCollins Publishers. **575–8** from *Childtimes: A Three-Generation Memoir* by Eloise Greenfield and Lessie Jones

Little. Copyright © 1979 by Eloise Greenfield and Lessie Jones Little. Copyright © 1971 by Pattie Ridley Jones. Reprinted by permission of HarperCollins Publishers. **579** (t) Michael K. Nichols/National Geographic Image Collection. (b) Staffan Widstrand/CORBIS. **580** (l) Hugo Van Lawick/National Geographic Image Collection. (r) Michael K. Nichols/National Geographic Image Collection. **581** (t) Jonathan Blair/Corbis. (b) Gerry Ellis/ENP Images. **587** © The Walt Disney Company, courtesy The Kobal Collection. **588** (t) Bill Frakes/Life Magazine © Time Inc. (b) © PhotoDisc/Getty Images. **589** (t) Otto Greule/Allsport. (b) Bill Frakes/Life Magazine © Time Inc. **590** Al Bello/Allsport. **591** Doug Rensinger/Allsport. **592** © PhotoDisc/Getty Images. **594—5** (bkgd) © Frans Lanting/Minden Pictures. **595** (m) C Squared Studios/Photodisc Green/Getty Images. **596—7** (bkgd) Gavriel Jecan/Corbis. **596** Courtesy of George Ancona. **597** (mr) George Ancona, (b) George Ancona, 1993. **598—9** (bkgd) Gavriel Jecan/Corbis. **598** George Ancona. **600** Roy Corral/Allstock/PictureQuest. **600—1** (bkgd) ©Carol Havens/CORBIS. **601** (m) ©Galen Rowell/CORBIS. (b) ©Alissa Crandall/CORBIS. **602—3** (bkgd) © Royalty-Free/Corbis. **617** Courtesy Michio Hoshino. **618** © PhotoDisc/Getty Images. **619** © PhotoDisc/Getty Images. **624** CORBIS Royalty Free. **626** Claus Meyer/Black Star/PictureQuest. **627** (t) David Hiser/Stone/Getty Images. (b) ©Wolfgang Kaehler/CORBIS. **628—9** (bkgd) David Notton/Taxi/Getty Images. **628** (inset) Courtesy George Ancona. (frame) © PhotoDisc/Getty Images. **644** ©Amos Nachoum/CORBIS. **645** ©Raymond Gehman/CORBIS. **646** (bl) Ben Osborne/Stone/Getty Images. (br) Art Wolfe/Stone/Getty Images. **648** © PhotoDisc/Getty Images. **650** (icon) © PhotoDisc/Getty Images. (t) Courtesy Jean Craighead George. (b) Tom Iannuzzi/Mercury Pictures. **650—1** (bkgd) Alan Majchrowicz/The Image Bank/Getty Images. **666** © PhotoDisc/Getty Images. **668** Courtesy of Dr. Robin Schlocker. **669** (t) Courtesy of Dr. Robin Schlocker. (b) © PhotoDisc/Getty Images. **670** ©Lynn M. Stone/Animals Animals. **671** (t) Virginia Living Museum/Photo by Ron Godby. (b) **672—2A** (bkgd) © Stuart Westmorland/The Image Bank/Getty Images. **672** (b) C Squared Studios/Photodisc Green/Getty Images. **672C—F** Christopher G. Knight. **672G** (t) Christopher G. Knight, (b) Peter Johnson/Corbis. **675** © PhotoDisc/Getty Images. **676** © PhotoDisc/Getty Images. **677** © PhotoDisc/Getty Images. **678** Zeva Oelbaum/Envision. **679** G. Brad Lewis/Stone/Getty Images. **680** Corbis Royalty Free. **681** © PhotoDisc/Getty Images. **682** Eastcott/Momatiuk/Stone/Getty Images. **683** Solomon D. Butcher Collection, Nebraska State Historical Society. **684** CORBIS/Galen Rowell. **685** © PhotoDisc/Getty Images. **686** Comstock KLIPS. **688** © Carr Clifton/Minden Pictures.

Assignment Photography
138 (bkgd), **153**, **160—1**, **414—5**, **624—5** © HMCo./Joel Benjamin. **78**, **80—81** © HMCo./Morocco Flowers. **107**, **231**, **335**, **439**, **571**, **673** © HMCo./Michael Indresano Photography **283** Michelle Joyce. **47**, **225** (r), **305** (r) © HMCo./Allan Landau. **409** (r), **433** (r), **487** (r), **543** (r) © HMCo./Ken Karp.

694

Illustration
29—44, **115** Phil Boatwright. **102—105** Stefano Vitale. **106B—H** Mike Adams. **108—109** Tim Jessell. **121**, **123** Craig Spearing. **132—135** Roman Duners. **185** (inset) **186—201**, **203** Paul Lee. **230I—P** Stephen Fuller. **232—33** Fabian Negrin. **241**, **284** William Brinkley and Associates. **314—327**, **329** (r) Copyright © 2001 by Leonard Jenkins. **331—333**, Mike Reed. **334B—H** Joel Spector. **334I—L** C. B. Mordan. **338—341** Stephanie Langley. **347—357**, **359** ® Nneka Bennett. **394**(i) **396—406**, **407**(i) Kees de Kiefte. **418—430** Nancy Carpenter. **434—437** Copyright © 2001 by Vivienne Flesher. **438B—H** Melanie Mitchell. **440—457** Michael Chesworth. **464—466** Richard Garland. **549**, **600**, **627** XNR Productions, INC. **550**(l) **551—562**, Copyright © 2001 by Raúl Colón. **570B—D**, **570F—G** Nick Spender. **572** Ken Joudrey. **620—623** Michael Rothman. **647** David Ballard. **648—649** Robert Hynes. **652—664** Gary Aagaard.

Index

Boldface page references indicate formal strategy and skill instruction.

Expanding literacy. *See* Skills links.

Expository text, *26, 48–51, 54, 57–75, 78–81, 82, 84–98*

Extra Support/Intervention. *See* Reaching All Learners.

Fact and opinion. *See* Comprehension skills.

Fiction. *See* Literary genres; Selections in Anthology.

Figurative language. *See* Literary devices.

Fluency
assessing, *41, 67, 93, 113, M15, M23, M46*
modeling, *25G, 51O–51R, 53S, 81O–81R, 81CC, 105O–105R, 107K, 129O–129R*
practice for, *41, 51O–51R, 67, 81O–81R, 93, 105O–105R, 113, 129O–129R, M15, M23*
See also Creative dramatics.

Generalizations, making. *See* Comprehension skills.

Genre. *See* Literary genres.

Get Set to Read
Buildup to a Shakeup, 26
Photographing Wild Weather, 54
The World of Volcanoes, 82
See also Background building; Vocabulary, selection.

Glossary in Student Anthology, *G1–G6*

Grammar and usage
parts of a sentence
subjects and predicates, simple and complete, ***51J,*** *53E, 105L, M42, R20–R21*
sentence structure
compound sentences, ***81I–81J,*** *M43, R22–R23*
sentences, types of
declarative, ***51I,*** *51N,* ***129I,*** *M42, R20–R21*
exclamatory, ***51I,*** *51N,* ***129I,*** *M42, R20–R21*
imperative, ***51I,*** *51N,* ***129I,*** *M42, R20–R21*
interrogative, ***51I,*** *51N,* ***129I,*** *M42, R20–R21*
speech, parts of. *See* Speech, parts of.
spelling connection. *See* Lessons, specific, grammar.
usage
run-on sentences, ***81J,*** *R22–R23*
sentence fragment, ***105L***
sentence variety, ***129I–129J***

Graphic information, interpreting
calendars, *65*
charts, *81,* ***105H***

computer-generated weather maps, *79*
diagrams, *65*
globes, ***105H***
graphs, *81,* ***105H***
maps, *25G, 25H, 26, 50, 54, 77, 82,* ***105H***
satellite photos, *79*
tables, ***105H***
time lines, *87, R8*

Graphic organizers
category chart, *83C, 84, 85, 90, 98, 99, 105A*
charts, *31, 81A, 105A, 105M*
classification chart, *97*
clusters, *53B*
diagrams, *61*
event map, *28, 34, 44, 45*
folktale chart, *103, 105*
K-W-L charts, *48, 51*
log book, *71*
main ideas/details, *95*
schedules, *71*
selection map, *56, 57, 81A*
sequence charts, *95, M9, M16, M24*
story details, *37*
story map/story frames, *43*
summarize, *75*
tall tale chart, *107J*
timeline, *R8*
topic/main idea chart, *89*
word webs, *23J, 51J, 51M, R19*

Graphophonemic/graphophonic cues. *See* Phonics.

Handwriting, *53G*

Home-Community Connection. *See* Home/Community Connections book.

Home-School Connection. *See* Home/Community Connections book.

Homework. *See* Home/Community Connections book.

Illustrators of Anthology selections
Adams, Mike, *M10*
Boatwright, Phil, *45, 114*
Lorraine, Walter, *125*
Spearing, Craig, *119*
Van Allsburg, Chris, *110*

Independent and recreational reading
suggestions for, *23E–23F, 51B, 51O–51R, 81B, 81O–81R, 105B, 105O–105R, R2–R3, R4–R5, R6–R7*
See also Reading modes.

Independent writing
suggestions for, *51L, 81L, 105L*
See also Language Center; Teacher's Resource Blackline Masters.

Individual needs, meeting. *See* Reaching All Learners.

Inferences, making
about author's craft, *92, 98, 105, 116, 120*
about characters' actions and feelings, *31, 44, 60, 62, 70, 72, 74, 76, 88, 103, 105, M20*
by drawing conclusions, *38, 40, 51, 86, 94, 100, 105, 122, M14*
from text organization, *81, 89*
See also Comprehension skills, cause and effect; Comprehension skills, generalizations, making.

Inflected forms. *See* Structural analysis.

Information skills
atlas, using an, ***129H***
collecting data, *51, 81*
comparing different sources, *51, 51H, 105H*
graphic aids: maps, globes, charts, tables, and graphs, using, ***105H, 129H***
interview, conducting an, *M27*
presenting information, *51, 51H, 81, 81BB, 101*
print and electronic card catalogs, using, ***81H***
print and electronic reference sources, using, ***51H***
See also Reference and study skills.

Informational selection, structure of. *See* Comprehension skills, text organization.

Journal, *29, 47, 53A, 57, 77, 85, 101, 111*

Judgments, making. *See* Comprehension skills.

Knowledge, activating prior. *See* Background, building.

K-W-L strategy. *See* Graphic organizers.

Language and usage. *See* Grammar and usage.

Language Center, *51M–51N, 81M–81N, 105M–105N, 129M–129N*

Language concepts and skills
descriptive language, *62, 66*
figurative language. *See* Literary devices.
primary language activities. *See* English Language Learners.
sensory language, *52, 53, 53B,* ***53C***

Reaching All Learners

Challenge, *34, 44, 51, 51E, 74, 81, 81E, 84, 98, 105, 118, 124, 129E, M10, R9, M16, M32, R11, R13, R15, R17, R19, M24*

English Language Learners, *25H, 26, 35, 39, 46, 47, 50, 54, 59, 70, 76, 80, 82, 84, 100, 104, 108, 111, 113, 114, 116, 117, 121, 126, 129, 129G, M12, M14, R3, R5, R7*

Extra Support/Intervention, *29, 30, 31, 34, 38, 41, 44, 51E, 57, 64, 67, 68, 74, 79, 81E, 84, 85, 86, 89, 90, 91, 93, 98, 99, 101, 105E, 111, 113, 114, 115, 117, 120, 126, 129E, M11, M12, M17, M19, M25*

On Level Students, *44, 74, 84, 98*

See also Reaching All Learners.

Reading across the curriculum. *See* Content areas, reading in the; Links, content area.

Reading fluency. *See* Fluency.

Reading log. *See* Journal.

Reading modes

cooperative reading, *35, 69, 90*

echo reading, *105R*

guiding comprehension. *See* Critical thinking.

independent reading, *35, 69, 90, R2–R4, R4–R5, R6–R7*

oral reading, *23N, 26, 51, 51O–51R, 54, 67, 81O–81R, 93, 105, 105O–105R, 111*

paired reading, *53Q, 53R, 61, 67, 93*

teacher read aloud, *25G–25H, 53S–53T, 81CC–81DD, 107K–107L*

See also Rereading.

Reading strategies. See Strategies, reading.

Reading traits

Decoding Conventions, *81B, 129B*

Establishing Comprehension, *51B*

Integrating for Synthesis, *105B*

Reading-Writing Workshop (process writing)

conferencing, **53A, 53E**

evaluating, **53G–53H**

reading as a writer, **53**

steps of

drafting, **53C–53D**

prewriting, **53A–53B**

proofreading, **53E–53F**

publishing and sharing, **53G**

revising, **53E**

student model, **52–53**

subjects

description, **51S–51T, 52–53H**

See also Writing skills.

Reads on and rereads. *See* Strategies, reading, Monitor/Clarify.

Reference and study skills

book, parts of a

index, *51G*

table of contents, *R2*

electronic sources

atlas, *51H, 105,* **129H**

card catalog, *81H*

electronic encyclopedia, **51H**

Internet, *23I, 25E, 51, 51H, 53Q, 99, 107J, M1*

thesaurus, *51H, M38, R15*

graphic sources. *See* Graphic information, interpreting.

information, organization of

chart, *81, 101*

diagram, making a, *81AA, 81BB, M24*

glossary, making a, *81BB*

graph, *81*

map making, *53R, M7, M26*

See also Graphic information, interpreting.

information skills. *See* Information skills.

library

call number, *81H*

card and electronic catalog, **81H**

organization, **81H**

using, *51H*

reference resources

atlas, *51H, 51M, 81M, 105, M7*

books, *25F, 81H, 101, 105, M1*

charts, *80*

classified ads, *76*

computer models, *80*

dictionary, *51H, 51M, 81J*

encyclopedia, *25E, 25F, 51, 51H, 53Q, 81J, 105, 107I, 107J, M1*

globe, *82*

map, *23J, 25F, 53R, 81M, 82, R13*

newspaper, *23I, 81*

thesaurus, *51G, 51H*

videotapes, *81H*

study strategies

K-W-L strategy, *49*

notes, taking. *See* Notes, taking.

skimming and scanning, *48, 48, 81B, 73*

See also Research activities.

Rereading

cooperatively, *41, 67, 93*

for comprehension, *88, 95, 96*

independently, *41, 67, 93*

to support answer, *65, 68, 81*

with expression and intonation, *41, 51P, 51R, 67, 81R, 93, 105R, 129R, M15, M23*

Research activities, *23I, 25E, 25F, 51D, 53Q, 53R, 81AA, 81BB, 101, 105, 107I, 107J, M24*

Responding to literature, options for

art, *R3*

discussion, *34, 44, 46, 69, 74, 76, 81N, 81O, 81P, 81Q, 81R, 90, 98, 100, 105N, 128, 129N, R3, R5, R7*

listening and speaking, *47, 51N*

Internet, *47, 77, 101*

personal response, *47, 77, 101*

viewing, *77*

writing, *46, 76, 100, 128*

Reteaching, *R8, R10, R12, R14, R16, R18, R20–R25*

Retelling

information, *75*

story, *33, 45*

Revising. *See* Reading-Writing Workshop, steps of; Writing skills, revising.

Root words. *See* Structural analysis.

Science activities. *See* Cross-curricular activities.

Selecting books. *See* Independent and recreational reading.

Selections in Anthology

career article

"Storm Warning," *78–81*

fiction

Night of the Twisters by Ivy Ruckman, illustrated by Mike Adams, *102–105*

folktale

"Princess and the Warrior, The," *102–105*

nonfiction

Blizzard! by Jim Murphy, *M18–M24*

Volcanoes by Seymour Simon, *84–98*

realistic fiction

Earthquake Terror, by Peg Kehret, *28–44*

science articles and features

"El Niño," by Fred Pearce, *48–51*

tall tales

February by Sid Fleischman, *125–127*

John Henry Races the Steam Drill by Paul Robert Walker, *114–118*

Paul Bunyan, the Mightiest Logger of Them All by Mary Pope Osborne, *110–113*

Sally Ann Thunder Ann Whirlwind by Mary Pope Osborne, *119–124*

See also Leveled Readers; Leveled Theme Paperbacks; Teacher Read Aloud.

Self-assessment

reading, *41, 77, 93, 101*

writing project, *53G–53H*

Self-correcting reading strategy. *See* Strategies, reading, monitor/clarify.

Semantic cues. *See* Decoding skills, context clues; Vocabulary skills.

Sentences. *See* Grammar and usage.

Sequence of events. *See* Comprehension skills.

Setting. *See* Story elements.

Shared learning. *See* Cooperative learning activities.

Skills links
folktale, how to read a, **102–105**
science article, how to read a, **48–51**
sequence chart, how to read a, **78–81**

Skimming and scanning, 48, 73

Social studies activities. *See* Cross-curricular activities.

Sound-spelling patterns. *See* Phonics; Spelling.

Speaking
complete sentences, 51M
composing sentences, 51M
conversation, 105N
debate, holding a, M6
describing, 35, 38, 66, 75, 82, 97, R9
discussion, 25B, 26, 32, 33, 34, 35, 44, 45, 47, 48, 51I, 51N, 65, 69, 74, 75, 81B, 81N, 82, 90, 98, 99, 105J, 105N, 129N
dramatics. *See* Creative dramatics.
explanation, 26, 57, 81H, 97, 105N, R9
expressing opinions, 76, 99, 100, 105N
guidelines
for a literature discussion, 81N
for a newscast, 47, M27
for asking clarifying questions, 105N
for disagreeing politely, 105N
for holding a discussion, 51N, 81N
for planning order, 47
for respecting the opinions of others, 51N
for speaking clearly, 51N
for sticking to the topic, 51N, 81N
for taking turns, 81N, 105N
for using notes, 47
literature discussion. *See* Responding to Literature, options for, discussion.
oral presentation, 47
personal narrative, sharing a, R9
process, explaining a, R9
purpose for
analyzing literature. See Literature, analyzing.
contributing information, 25B, 26, 32, 33, 34, 35, 44, 45, 47, 48, 51I, 51N, 65, 69, 74, 75, 81B, 82, 90, 98, 99, 105J
to use new vocabulary or language, 26, 54, 81H, 105F, 129F
radio newscast, **M27**
retelling. *See* Retelling.
rephrase sentences, 105J
role-play. *See* Creative dramatics.
sharing, 35, 45, 47, 51D, 53R, 69, 72, 73, 75, 90, 99, 105P
summary. *See* Summarizing, oral summaries.
writing conferences. *See* Reading-Writing Workshop, conferencing.

See also Creative dramatics; Reading, modes; Rereading.

Speech, parts of
adjectives
superlatives, 114
conjunctions, **81I–81J**, 81M, M43, R22
nouns
appositives, **129J**
singular and plural, **105I–105J**, M43, R24–R25

Spelling
assessment, 51E, 51F, 81E, 81F, 105E, 105F, 129E, 129F, M40, M41
consonants, silent, M41
dictionary, using a, 51F
frequently misspelled words, 53F
games, 51F, 81F, 105F, 129F
integrating grammar and spelling, 51I–51J, 81I–81J, 105I–105J
patterns
a-consonant-*e*, 81E–81F
ai and *ay*, 81E–81F
ee and *ea*, 81E–81F
i-consonant-*e*, 81E–81F
i and *igh*, 81E–81F
consonant-*e*, *oa, ow, o*, 105E, 105F
yoo spelled *u*-consonant-*e, ue, oo, ui, ou*, 105E, 105F
proofreading, 51F, 53F, 81F, 105F, 129F
vowel(s)
/ā/, /ē/, /ī/ sounds, **81E–81F**, M40
/ō/, /o͞o/, /yo͞o/ sounds, **105E–105F**, 105M, M40
short vowels *a, e, i, o, u*, **51E–51F**
vowel changes, **129E**
See also Decoding skills.

Story elements
character, 43
plot
climax, 61
events, 43, 61, 88
problem/solution, 43, 44
rising action, 61
setting, 26, 37, 43
See also Comprehension skills; Graphic organizers, story map.

Storytelling. *See* Speaking.

Strategies, reading
Evaluate, BTS10–BTS11
Monitor/Clarify, BTS6–BTS7, 84, 85, 88, 89, 90, 93, 96, 99
Phonics/Decoding, BTS4–BTS5, **29,** 41, 51C, 51D, 51F, 57, 64, 81D, 85, 86, 105C, 105D
Predict/Infer, BTS2–BTS3, **27B,** 28, 29, 31, 32, 34, 38, 42, 45, M10, M20
Question, BTS8–BTS9, **56,** 57, 64, 67, 68, 72, 74, 75

Summarize, BTS12–BTS13, 81, **110,** 113, 117, 118, 124, 127

Strategies, writing. *See* Reading-Writing Workshop.

Structural analysis
base words and affixes, **51C,** 51M, M36, R14, R18
inflected forms
changing y *to* i, 105I, 105J
-*ed,* -*ing,* 51E, 51M
-*s* or -*es,* 105I, 105J
prefixes
con-, de-, dis-, e-, in-, inter, 105N
ex-, 85
out-, 121
re-, 99, 105N
un-, 35
suffixes
-*ion,* -*ive,* -*or,* -*ure,* 105N
-*sion,* 85
-*tion,* 64
-*ment,* 57
syllables, 64, **81C,** 81N, M36, R16
word roots
Greek word *phot,* 81J
struct and *rupt,* **105C,** 105N, M37, R18
vis and *vid,* **129C,** 129M
See also Decoding skills; Vocabulary, building.

Student self-assessment. *See* Assessment, planning for; Self-assessment.

Study skills. *See* Reference and study skills.

Study strategies. *See* Reference and study skills.

Suffixes. *See* Structural analysis.

Summarizing
oral summaries, 25B, 34, 35, 44, 45, 54, 68, 69, 74, 75, 91, 98, 99, R3, R5, R7

Syntactic cues. *See* Structural analysis.

Syntax. *See* Decoding, context clues.

Teacher-guided reading. *See* Critical thinking.

Teacher Read Aloud
fiction
The Pumpkin Box by Angela Johnson, BTS6–BTS19
narrative nonfiction
"The Wreck of the E.S. Newman" from *Cricket* by Ruth Ewers, 25G–25H
science articles and features
"Making Waves!" from *Contact Kids* by Gail Skroback Hennessey, 81CC–81DD
"Hurricanes: Weather at Its Wildest" by Fran